BRITANNIA ROMANA

ROMAN INSCRIPTIONS AND ROMAN BRITAIN

R S O TOMLIN

OXBOW | books
Oxford and Philadelphia

First published in 2018
Reprinted in paperback in 2020 and 2022 in the United Kingdom by
OXBOW BOOKS
The Old Music Hall, 106–108 Cowley Road, Oxford, OX4 1JE

and in the United States by
OXBOW BOOKS
1950 Lawrence Road, Havertown, PA 19083

Paperback Edition: ISBN 978-1-78925-548-5
Digital Edition: ISBN 978-1-78570-701-8 (epub)

A CIP record for this book is available from the British Library

Library of Congress Cataloging-in-Publication Data

Names: Tomlin, Roger, 1943- author.
Title: Britannia Romana : Roman inscriptions and Roman Britain / R.S.O. Tomlin.
Description: Oxford ; Philadelphia : Oxbow Books, 2018. | Includes bibliographical references and index.
Identifiers: LCCN 2017035745 (print) | LCCN 2017037981 (ebook) | ISBN 9781785707018 (epub) | ISBN 9781785707025 (mobi) | ISBN 9781785707032 (pdf) | ISBN 9781785707001 (hardback) | ISBN 9781785707018 (ebook)
Subjects: LCSH: Great Britain--History--Roman period, 55 B.C.-449 A.D. | Inscriptions, Latin--Great Britain. | Romans--Great Britain.
Classification: LCC DA145 (ebook) | LCC DA145 .T66 2017 (print) | DDC 936.2/04--dc23
LC record available at https://lccn.loc.gov/2017035745

Printed in the UK by CMP (UK) Limited
Typeset in the UK by Frabjous Books

For a complete list of Oxbow titles, please contact:

UNITED KINGDOM
Oxbow Books
Telephone (01865) 241249
Email: oxbow@oxbowbooks.com
www.oxbowbooks.com

UNITED STATES OF AMERICA
Oxbow Books
Telephone (610) 853-9131, Fax (610) 853-9146
Email: queries@casemateacademic.com
www.casemateacademic.com/oxbow

Oxbow Books is part of the Casemate Group

Front cover: BRITANNIA: portrait from a mosaic floor depicting the Roman provinces found in Zeugma (Belkis, in Turkey): Antikensammlung, Staatliche Museen zu Berlin (Preussischer Kulturbesitz)
Back cover: Above: To the god Jupiter Capitolinus: stone dedication plaque ornamented with eagle-headed peltae (Maryport 12.61). Below: Gold signet ring of Ti(berius) Julius Catuarus, the bezel incised with his name retrograde in the genitive case (Fishbourne 2.16)

antiquis amicis meis
et deae Romae sacrum

CONTENTS

PREFACE

This book originates long ago, when I asked Robin Burn (who died in 1991) if I might prepare a new edition of his *The Romans in Britain: An Anthology of Inscriptions* (2nd edition, 1969). He notably inspired Lawrence Keppie, who dedicated his own *Understanding Roman Inscriptions* (1991) to Burn, having been taught by him from 'that massive, then newly available tome *The Roman Inscriptions of Britain* (vol. I), which we seemed to devour almost from cover to cover as the weeks progressed'. Burn, who was able to 'make even the apparently most uninspiring text seem interesting, and to draw out its unique contribution to our understanding of the ancient world', kindly agreed to my request, and even gave me his own annotated copy. But when I set to work, I quickly found it was impossible to rewrite someone else's book, and I laid the project aside. I returned to it about five years ago, but deliberately did not consult *The Romans in Britain* again, only retaining its format of inscriptions linked by narrative and commentary, which I found more difficult to sustain than I had expected.

Whatever its original inspiration, therefore, *Britannia Romana* is a new book. It owes more to my experience since 1975 of editing the annual 'Roman Britain (Inscriptions)' survey in *Britannia* with Richard Wright and Mark Hassall, of compiling the Addenda and Corrigenda (1995) to Collingwood and Wright's *RIB* I, of editing their *RIB* II (1990–95) with Sheppard Frere, and of writing up *RIB* III (2009) from my own work and that of Wright and Hassall. If there is any credit, it belongs also to these scholars, and to Eric Birley, John Mann and Ian Richmond, who in various ways introduced me to the epigraphy of Roman Britain.[1]

The title is chosen in tribute to another book which also introduced students of Roman Britain to Roman inscriptions, John Horsley's *Britannia Romana* (1732). This large folio appropriated the title of a recent booklet by John Pointer (1724), but Horsley may not have known this. His would-be successor collects inscriptions from Britain and

[1] The notes and bibliography briefly acknowledge my debt to many other scholars. For bibliography, parallels and cross-checking, the Epigraphik-Datenbank Clauss-Slaby (EDCS) has been invaluable. Some chapters were read by Scott Vanderbilt, who also made a photographic safari, and a full draft was closely scrutinised by Lawrence Keppie, whose well-informed comments have reduced the number of errors and omissions, but I admit sole responsibility for the survivors.

elsewhere[2] by period or theme, so as to illustrate the Romans in Britain. The first eight chapters take the narrative from Claudius' invasion (AD 43) to the death of the last emperor to attempt the conquest of Britain, Septimius Severus (AD 211). The next four chapters cover the general themes of soldier and civilian, economy and society, government, religion. The last two chapters continue the narrative to the death of the last emperor to rule Roman Britain, Constantine III (AD 411). The supporting inscriptions are located by narrative and commentary within this wider context, showing how they may be read and interpreted – translation being an essential part of this process[3] – and how they are the raw material of history. Since this is an illustrative guide, not an exhaustive corpus, I have not attached a full bibliography to each inscription, and I have preferred texts which are more or less complete and do not require minute discussion and restoration. In self-defence I must echo Oxford's greatest historian of the Roman Empire: 'A full catalogue would be instructive, and tedious.'[4]

To Keppie's illuminating introduction let me add Arthur Gordon's *Illustrated Introduction to Latin Epigraphy*. Sandys' *Latin Epigraphy*, despite its age, still gives succinct answers to many questions. Written from an Italian perspective, but very informative and richly illustrated with case studies, is Alison Cooley's *Cambridge Manual of Latin Epigraphy*. The older University has just responded with the *Oxford Handbook of Roman Epigraphy*, edited by Christer Bruun and Jonathan Edmondson. For Britain itself, but within the wider Roman context, there is Tony Birley's *People of Roman Britain* and his incomparable *Roman Government of Britain*.[5] Also outstanding for clarity of comment and its careful selection of 290 items is Val Maxfield and Brian Dobson's *Inscriptions of Roman Britain*.[6]

Roger Tomlin

Wolfson College, Oxford

---

[2] Each item is located by the modern place-name (with the ancient in brackets, unless it is almost identical), except when the ancient place-name is more familiar or has no modern equivalent. For British place-names see Rivet and Smith 1979. Present location (in museums, etc.) has not been added, but for Britain will be found in *RIB* and the *RIB* website. For inscriptions which are illustrated, see also the Photo Credits.

[3] Editors who translate a text are not condescending to readers who know less Latin than they do, but providing 'the best (as it is the briefest) possible commentary' (Turner 1968, 70).

[4] Syme 1958, 87.

[5] 'Incomparable' is justly accorded to Frere 1987 by Birley 2005, and extended to the latter by a review in *Gnomon* 85 (2013), 237–41.

[6] Now fully revised by Grocock (2017).

INTRODUCTION

Lettering

Roman cursive handwriting is difficult, even for specialists. It varies according to the medium, whether it is 'soft' (pen and ink) or 'hard' (incised with a stylus).[1] It changes over time, especially in the later third century AD when 'New Roman Cursive', the ultimate ancestor of our own handwriting, begins to displace 'Old Roman Cursive'. Close examination of the original is ideal, but tabulations of letter-form provide a starting-point.[2] It is easy, though, to sympathise with the comic slave Pseudolus when his master asks him to read a worrying communication: 'These letters are trying to breed; they're climbing over each other ... What sort of hands do chickens have? It was a chicken wrote these tablets.'[3] By contrast, the capital letters used to cut 'monumental' stone inscriptions are straightforward. Another fictional character, a self-educated businessman with a chip on his shoulder, says that he can at least read 'the letters in stone inscriptions'.[4] And so can we, given a fair chance.

We have inherited the Roman alphabet, which is why its capital-letter forms are familiar. Stone-cutters were sometimes influenced by the brush-drawn letters which guided them; they might save space and effort by combining two or more letters by means of ligature, a tendency that increases from the later second century AD, but their letter-forms do not look very strange. Sometimes they cut an 'open' A (without cross-bar), and there are more subtle differences, which fortunately are overlooked by at least some forgers of Roman inscriptions. The most important difference is that the Romans had no U or W, since V did duty for both the vowel *u* and the consonant *v*. They also had no J, since they did not distinguish between the vowel *i* and consonantal *i*, as we do in transliterating *Iulius* (for example) as 'Julius'. They seldom used K since C largely took its place; and seldom Y and Z, since they were only used to transliterate Greek words.

1 Bowman and Thomas 1983, 32. The Latin spelling of *stilus* with an *i* (which survives in 'stiletto') has become 'stylus' in modern English.

2 Bowman and Thomas 1983, 53–68. Tomlin 1988, 84–94. Tomlin 2016, 19–22 ('Letterforms').

3 Plautus, *Pseudolus* i.1.23–8, *quaerunt litterae hae sibi liberos; alia aliam scandit. ... habent quas gallinae manus? nam has gallina scripsit.*

4 Petronius, *Satyricon* 58.7, *lapidarias litteras scio.*

Punctuation

The 'massing' of letters in inscriptions can be intimidating, since the Romans often ranwordstogether and used almost no punctuation. Only handwritten documents are 'paragraphed' by the convention of beginning a new sentence to the left, and too often they do not separate words. In 'monumental' stone inscriptions, words are sometimes separated by a space, but a frequent convention is to insert a medial point; it may be round, triangular, or even a 'leaf-stop', a stylised ivy leaf (*hedera*) as in **6.27**, **10.04**, **11.33** and **12.21**. It is also used to mark abbreviation. To save space, words are often divided between lines, but there is no hyphen or other indication.

Abbreviations and symbols

The Romans abbreviated 'by suspension', by omitting the end of a word, and even reducing it to its initial letter. A special instance is C for *G(aius)*, since G was originally not distinguished from C.[5] Number was indicated by repeating the final letter, for example AVGG for two *Aug(usti)* and even AVGGG for three *Aug(usti)* in **8.15**, **13.01** and **13.21**. Many abbreviations are still obvious, for example IMP for *imp(erator)* and CAES for *Caes(ar)* at the heading of many building-inscriptions, and some must have been so familiar that they virtually became symbols, for example the tombstone-heading D M for *D(is) M(anibus)*, 'to the Shades of the Dead'. But a minority would have been understood only by the dedicator and his immediate circle. Later we will see an altar (**12.51**) with the dedication D R S, three initials brilliantly solved by John Horsley but not by Thomas Surridge a century later, but here is an extreme example:

<**0.01**> *Old Carlisle (?Maglona)*

T ◦ B ◦ A ◦ T ◦ A
VR ◦ ATE
CO ◦ C ◦ AV
G ◦ VOT
S ◦ L ◦ A ◦ FE

RIB 902+*add.*

Not many inscriptions are as difficult as this altar. Every single word has been abbreviated, except

[5] **9.05** and **9.42** are rare exceptions of G for *Gaius*, as is the potter's signature **11.15**. Abbreviation by contraction, such as NVB for *numinibus* (**11.17**), is rare.

for the dedicator's cognomen.[6] The stone-cutter helpfully marked each abbreviation with a medial point, unless it coincided with a line-ending; but here, since the hyphen was not yet invented, he could not indicate whether one line continued into the next. However, since it is an altar, we may expect to find the predictable sequence of deity – dedicator – description of dedicator – concluding formula. And less predictably, it is easier to start at the end and work backwards, a reversal which often helps in deciphering a cursive (handwritten) document.

VOT is inevitably *vot(um)* ('vow'), and FE *fe(cit)* ('has made'). They are separated by three initials familiar from variants of the very common V S L M formula, itself almost a symbol, which can be taken with *vot(um)* as *s(olvit) l(ibens) a(nimo)*, 'has paid his vow willing in heart' (compare **13.12**). *fe(cit)* is thus redundant, but reinforces *s(olvit)* or carries the sense 'has made (this altar)'. Next the dedicator. The sequences A | VR for *Aur(elius)* and AV | G for *Aug(ustus)* (etc.) are so common that the dedicator must be a *T(itus) Aur(elius)* who describes himself as C AV | G, the intervening letters being his cognomen *Ateco*. This is unique, but is an acceptable Celtic name formed by combining the intensive prefix *Ate-* with the suffix *-co*; the derived *Atecorius* has been found.[7] C AV | G is more difficult, but the *ala Augusta* is so well attested at Old Carlisle[8] that the dedicator was most likely a junior officer in this cavalry regiment, *c(urator) (alae) Aug(ustae)* like Insus at Lancaster (**4.01**), even though the abbreviation would be extreme. Otherwise he may have originated *c(ivitate) Aug(...)*, from a 'city' with *Augusta* in its name. Lastly his dedication. In default of parallels, this can only be guessed; the best guess so far, but by no means certain, is that it was the local personification, Brigantia (**12.17**), treated as a protective goddess. With some reservation, therefore, we may transcribe and translate:

> ?T(utelae) B(rigantiae) A(ugustae) T(itus) A-
> ur(elius) Ate-
> co ?c(urator alae) Au-
> g(ustae) vot(um)
> s(olvit) l(ibens) a(nimo) fe(cit)

> 'To the Protecting Goddess, August Brigantia, Titus Aurelius Ateco, *curator* of the Cavalry Regiment Augusta, paid his vow willing in heart (and) made (this).'

This inscription, although it is so abbreviated, contains no symbols. Pure symbols are relatively uncommon, except for numerals, which originated as symbols and were assimilated to letters. See, for example, the '1,000' in the title of a 'millliary' cohort at High Rochester (**13.03**). Since many of our inscriptions like this are military, the

---

6 A Roman citizen bore three names, praenomen (for example *Gaius*), nomen (*Iulius*) and cognomen (*Caesar*).

7 *Tyche* 24 (2009), 163–214 No. 40 (Carnuntum).

8 **9.09**, **13.15**, *RIB* 893, 894, 895, 905 and 907.

most common symbol is *(centuria)* or *(centurio)* for 'century' or 'centurion', inscribed as C reversed or as an acute-angled double-stroke like modern '7', by which it is conveniently transcribed (in **9.19**, for example).

Dating

A few inscriptions are dated by the pair of 'ordinary' consuls[9] annually elected at Rome, and many more by the titles of the emperor named, for example his number of consulships and acclamations as *imperator* on his accession and after a victory, and especially by the year of his tribunician power, which he received on accession and renewed annually on 10 December. But the majority of inscriptions are not dated in these ways, and an approximate date must be deduced from the archaeological and historical context including 'order of battle' (in which Eric Birley excelled), from the lettering (at the risk of being over-subjective), and from the formulation. The splendid epitaph of the procurator Classicianus (**2.19**), for example, is an early instance (*c.* AD 65 from its historical context) of the use of *Dis Manibus* unabbreviated, a practice which continues until about the reign of Trajan (AD 98–117), when it is replaced by the abbreviation D M. This is a useful rule, but it must be remembered that *Dis Manibus* persists in two inscriptions which are at least Hadrianic (AD 117–38), the epitaphs of a veteran of the newly-arrived Sixth Legion Victrix, and of a man who married an *Aelia*, the daughter probably of an auxiliary soldier enfranchised by Hadrian.[10]

Damage to inscriptions

These conventions soon become familiar. The real difficulty in transcribing new inscriptions is their state of preservation. It is easy to think of them as timeless evidence, not as the survivors of seventeen, eighteen, nineteen centuries of neglect and mistreatment. Perspectives change. Richard Grasby, the very experienced author of *Lettercutting in Stone* (1989), was once asked how long his building-inscription could be expected to last; he had just cut it in Indiana limestone, and the architects were worried that storms might wash away the lettering. 'Two or three hundred years' for the 9-inch letters, he thought, but the smaller letters would need to be 'refreshed' after 75–100 years. The architects were much amused: 'Mr Grasby, this piece of real estate won't be there in 25 years' time.'

Later we will see a Chester tombstone (**9.21**) in which the space left for the widow was never filled, and **6.85** from York which became someone else's coffin-lid. At Vindolanda a mausoleum (**5.01**) was quarried to rebuild the commandant's

---

9 'Ordinary' because they gave their name to the year, like the former governor of Britain, Suetonius Paulinus, when he became consul for the second time in AD 66 (**1.04**). But later in the year they were replaced by 'suffects', who would thus rank as ex-consuls for promotion to provincial governorships.

10 *RIB* 252 (Lincoln), 2029 (Stanwix).

house, and tombstones were used to repair the walls and east gate.[11] A dedication there to the goddess Gallia (**12.16**), in which Gallic recruits emphasise their solidarity, became a Roman drain-cover. Valerius Geminus' tombstone at Alchester (**2.03**) was broken into twenty pieces to build the Roman town wall, and at London the great altar-tombstone of Classicianus (**2.19**) went into a Roman bastion. The legionary cemetery at Chester was deliberately quarried to rebuild the Roman north wall (**3.15**). This may have been an act of spite, just as the names and titles of deposed emperors were erased when their 'memory' was condemned, and a milestone of Carausius (**14.03**) was turned round and re-used for Constantine (**14.10**). The altar which Lunaris painstakingly shipped from York to Bordeaux for dedication to the local goddess (**11.39**) became a building-block in the Roman city wall. Oddest of all, perhaps, is this building-record:

<**0.02**> *Corbridge (Coria)*

leg(ionis) XXX VV
coh(ors) VII

RIB 1166+*add.*

'Of the Thirtieth Legion Ulpia Victrix, the Seventh Cohort (made this).'

This 'centurial stone' was found in 1912, and *RIB* follows Haverfield in concluding that the first X is a later insertion in Roman times, thus making the Twentieth Legion into the Thirtieth; LEG XXVV has become LEG XXXVV.[12] X is obviously an insertion, but when it was found, the insertion had weathered. Trajan's Thirtieth Legion was based on the lower Rhine for most of its history, and is never attested in Britain. Is this now evidence that it once sent a detachment to Hadrian's Wall – or is it more significant that Kipling published *Puck of Pook's Hill* in 1906? The narrator of its three Roman chapters is an officer serving on Hadrian's Wall in the AD 380s called Parnesius (a name otherwise unattested), who describes himself as 'a Centurion of the Seventh Cohort of the Thirtieth Legion – the Ulpia Victrix'. When this stone was found, Kipling at first suspected a 'leg-pull', but when he was assured it was perfectly genuine, took it as confirmation of his own 'honest research'. The mystery remains.[13]

In the post-Roman period, any sense of continuity was lost. Hexham Abbey, like other churches near Hadrian's Wall, was built of Roman stone: its atmospheric Saxon crypt incorporates two Roman altars and a large building-stone of Septimius

---

11 *RIB* 1713; III, 3365 and 3366.

12 *V(aleria) V(ictrix)* becomes *U(lpia) V(ictrix)*, since V serves both as consonantal *v* and the vowel *u*.

13 Kipling 1937, 189–90. Rivet 1976, 7–8.

Severus in the ceiling, where the erasure of his son Geta's name can still be seen.[14] At Carlisle a richly carved altar became a Norman lintel in the Castle (**13.04**). A stone coffin from York became a horse trough in Hull (**9.52**). When Christopher Hunter of Durham visited the site of the Roman fort of Ebchester in 1702, he 'enquired of the most understanding inhabitants concerning what has been found there whilst they digged up the Ruins of this place; all confess they have dug up many Inscriptions, but (because no body there understood them) they always broke them.'[15] At the nearby fort of Binchester there was a persistent legend that coalminers when they went down in the lift-cage saw 'lettered stones' through the grill, Roman inscriptions used to revet the shaft. The Vinovia Colliery is now abandoned, and its shaft is full of water. Those stones are drowned beyond recovery, unlike five altars from Hadrian's Wall which were rediscovered in 1973 in a lake at Godalming.[16]

Many such vicissitudes are reported by *RIB* and *RIB* III, but they do not include one which is celebrated in literature, since the stone is strictly not epigraphic despite incorporating a panel which however was not inscribed. Near the Borders fort of Risingham was a rock-cut standing figure, probably that of the god Cocidius, which even in the early nineteenth century attracted visitors. The landowner, a Mr Shanks, saved it from being quarried, but later his son resented the trespassing on his land, and broke it up. His vandalism was denounced in 1817 by no less a writer than Walter Scott, in language which unconsciously echoes Basilia's curse tablet at Bath (**14.01**): 'a sulky churlish boor has destroyed the ancient statue, or rather bas-relief, popularly called Robin of Redesdale. It seems Robin's fame attracted more visitants than was consistent with the growth of the heather, upon a moor worth a shilling an acre. ... pray with me that he may be visited with such a fit of the stone, as if he had all the fragments of poor Robin in that region of his viscera where the disease holds its seat.'[17]

At Ravenglass during excavation in 1881, an inscription was found, but it was 'thrown into the sea before it had been recorded'.[18] As late as 1971, a small inscribed stone was discovered during a rescue dig in Kent, but it was not removed in time, and is now underneath the Dover bypass.[19] Also in Kent, at Chevening House, was the great career-inscription of Tiberius Claudius Candidus.[20] This came from Tarragona (Tarraco), where it was presented to the first Earl of Stanhope, a British general during the War of the Spanish Succession (1701–14). Candidus, a general of Septimius Severus, was himself remotely associated with Britain, since early in his career he had been an equestrian officer in the Second Legion Augusta. After

14 *RIB* 1122, **7.06** (now lost), *RIB* 1151.

15 Letter of 12 April 1702, published in *Philosophical Transactions* 278 (1702), 1129.

16 *RIB* 1977+*add.*, 1992+*add.*, 1994+*add.*, III, 3439, and another which is not inscribed. See Bird 1974.

17 Dedicatory epistle to *Ivanhoe*. Birley 1961, 239–40.

18 *RIB* 795.

19 *RIB* III, 3033.

20 *ILS* 1140, now British Museum 1994, 0122.2.

almost three centuries, his statue-base was removed from Chevening House by the Trustees who did not offer it to a museum, despite one of them being the Director of the Victoria and Albert Museum: they sold it on the open market, from which it was retrieved by the British Museum in 1994, after an export ban had been successfully imposed.

Editorial conventions

No wonder that many inscriptions are now 'lost' – an altar from Bar Hill,[21] last reported in the early seventeenth century, was only rediscovered in 1976 – so that readings depend on old and incomplete transcripts. Somewhere near the fort of Borrow Bridge beside the M6 in Lunedale is a sculptured tombstone now covering a culvert; one of the workmen who buried it remembered seeing the letters XX, part of a numeral.[22] No wonder too that many inscriptions have been broken up and re-used as building-stones, which means that damaged letters must be reconstructed, and missing ones restored. To qualify their readings, epigraphists have evolved a bewildering variety of brackets, but they are essential: 'it is crucial not to mislead the reader into thinking that letters in a text are more legible than they really are.'[23]

Since this book presents texts which have already been well edited, it can afford to simplify editorial conventions. Its transcripts, unlike that of **0.01** (Old Carlisle) just quoted, are not 'diplomatic' (letter-by-letter). They retain the Roman line-division except in long texts such as military diplomas, so (modern) punctuation is often unnecessary, but they do hyphenate words divided between lines, separate words and capitalise proper names and titles, but otherwise use lower-case and do not mark ligatures. Abbreviations have been resolved, lost letters restored if possible. Consonantal *u* has been transcribed as *v*. Full punctuation has not been attempted, since it is absent in the original and can be deduced from the translation; in general it follows that of the first editor, or is intended to make the syntax and structure of longer texts more evident. Readings and translations are based on the publications cited, especially *RIB* for texts from Britain, but they may occasionally diverge. Technical terms are translated if possible, or at least explained. The eight Greek inscriptions have been modernised by adding accents and breathings, which were not there in the original.

The most important distinction is that between round brackets, which are used to resolve (abbreviations), and square brackets, which restore [letters which have been lost]. Editors often underdot letters which are damaged or of uncertain reading, a useful convention which may nonetheless betray an 'uneasy conscience'.[24] But for

21 *RIB* 2187+*add.*
22 *RIB* 756.
23 Cooley 2012, 351.
24 Turner 1968, 70.

the sake of simplicity, it has not been adopted here. The simplified conventions may now be tabulated.

In the transcripts:

(abc) letter(s) omitted in the original by abbreviation
[abc] letter(s) missing through weathering or damage but restorable with certainty
[[abc]] letters deleted on the stone, but restorable with certainty
[...] letter(s) missing in the original through weathering or damage
... trace of letters, not deciphered
. . . inscription or document broken here
| division between lines in military diplomas; in metrical texts, between verses
ABC word or passage which cannot be interpreted
(!) divergent spelling or mis-spelling[25]
? reading or restoration not certain
{a} letter erroneously included[26]
<a> letter omitted by mistake[27]

In the commentary:

[a] letter pronounced
| line division; in metrical texts, division between verses
★ conjectural or reconstructed form

[25] Often no more than a 'Vulgarism', a spelling influenced by the pronunciation.

[26] Sometimes by mistake, but often with the intention of bringing the spelling closer to the pronunciation, for example *exs* for *ex* (**2.14**) and *sexs* for *sex* (**12.01**).

[27] Again, this often reflects the pronunciation, notably *e* for *ae*. It can be difficult to decide whether an omission is really a mistake rather than due to abbreviation, and *RIB* avoids the distinction by transcribing both as (abc).

1

THE INVASION OF BRITAIN

Julius Caesar and Augustus

The first invasion was led by Julius Caesar, who on 25 September 54 BC wrote 'from the shores of Nearest Britain' to the orator Cicero in Rome.[1] His letter would have been our first written document, had it survived, but Caesar withdrew from Britain, and for almost another century the island remained inviolate and illiterate. When the Roman army returned in AD 43, one of its officers, according to the historian Tacitus – in his treatise on oratory, it must be said – met a native Briton, an old man, a *very* old man, who admitted to having fought against Caesar the last time.[2] He was living proof of the Greek thesis that Britons lived much longer than Africans because of the cold, living as long as 120 years.[3] Throughout his long life, another invasion had been on the imperial agenda.[4] The opportunity had been offered to Caesar's adoptive son Augustus, the first Emperor:

<1.01> *Ankara (Ancyra)*

ad me supplices confugerunt [r]eges ... Britann[o]rum Dumnobellaunus et Tin[comarus]

Augustus, *Res Gestae* 32.1 (Cooley 2009)

'Kings sought refuge with me as suppliants ... (including) Dumnobellaunus and Tincomarus of the Britons.'

The words are taken from Augustus' own account of his achievements (*res gestae*) which was inscribed on two bronze pillars in front of his tomb at Rome.[5] These were melted down long ago, but a contemporary copy was inscribed on the stone

---

[1] Cicero notes its receipt a month later, on 24 October (*ad Atticum* 4.18, 5), *litteras datas a litoribus Britanniae proximae a(nte) d(iem) VI Kal(endas) Oct(obres)* (with Shackleton Bailey's emendation of *proximo* to *proximae*). It may have been a joint letter with Cicero's brother Quintus, who was also in Britain.

[2] Tacitus, *Dialogus* 17.4.

[3] ps.Plutarch, *De placitis philosophorum* 911 B–C, quoting the doctor Asclepiades of Bithynia who was patronised by the Roman aristocracy at the end of the second century BC (Cicero, *de oratore* i 14.62). He prescribed wine and lived to a great age (Pliny, *Hist. Nat.* vii 124).

[4] Analysed in detail by Birley 2008(b), 179–86.

[5] Preamble to the *Res Gestae* with Suetonius, *Divus Augustus* 101.4. *Tin[comarus]* is restored by Cheesman 1998.

walls of the surviving temple of Rome and Augustus at Ancyra (Ankara). This was called 'the Queen of Inscriptions' by Mommsen, but nonetheless it is only a copy of a copy of Augustus' original text, which itself shows internal signs of revision. It is also a masterpiece of self-presentation by a political genius. Therefore, when we study 'monumental' inscriptions, however important they may be, we must bear in mind that they are copies of a written draft now lost; and also ask ourselves why they were inscribed in the first place.

Augustus names other 'suppliant' kings, from Germany and Parthia, who by taking refuge with him admitted Roman suzerainty and provided an excuse for intervention. But the conquest of mainland Europe diverted him from Britain, and his immediate successor Tiberius was 'not interested in expanding the Empire'.[6] The successful invasion was achieved by an unlikely successor, Tiberius' nephew Claudius, the grandson of Augustus' second wife Livia, who was descended on the other side from Caesar's sister.

Claudius invades Britain: officers and men

We can guess the ultimate time and place of Claudius' decision to invade Britain: it was the afternoon of 24 January AD 41, behind a curtain in the imperial Palace.[7] Tiberius' immediate successor Gaius (Caligula), great-grandson of Augustus and Claudius' own eccentric and dangerous nephew, had just been murdered by officers of the Praetorian Guard; among the courtiers who fled for their lives was Claudius. A marauding guardsman found him hiding behind the curtain, pulled him out, and persuaded his comrades to proclaim him Emperor: if there were no emperor, the Guard would be redundant. Claudius, long since rejected by Augustus as incompetent and driven into the ignoble company of women and historians, nonetheless belonged to a family which had produced statesmen and generals for many generations; his own father Drusus had led a Roman army to the Elbe, and his late brother Germanicus, whose name he shared, had been wildly popular despite his costly and inconclusive German campaigns. Caligula, the son of Germanicus, had actually planned an invasion of Britain. For personal and political reasons, therefore, Claudius needed military glory. By conquering Britain, where Julius Caesar and Caligula had failed, he would equal his ancestors and justify his accession.

Two years later, in the summer of AD 43, a powerful army had been concentrated under the command of Aulus Plautius, a kinsman of Claudius' first wife. Inscriptions will in due course name many of its non-Roman, 'auxiliary' units, but the nucleus was four Roman legions, about 20,000 heavy infantry and military engineers. They were the Second Legion Augusta, the Fourteenth Gemina (later Martia Victrix) and the Twentieth (later Valeria Victrix) from the two Rhine armies, and the Ninth

[6] Tacitus, *Annals* iv 32, *princeps proferendi imperii incuriosus erat.*

[7] Suetonius, *Divus Claudius* 10. See further Wiseman 1991.

Legion Hispana which Plautius brought with him from the Pannonian army on the middle Danube. They were probably supported by detachments from other legions.[8] With the addition of the Sixth Legion Victrix, which replaced the Ninth in AD 122, they will be responsible for many of our inscriptions. The Second Legion was commanded by a future emperor, Vespasian, and his ancient biographer says that he owed his appointment to Claudius' secretary Narcissus: Narcissus and Vespasian's mistress, Caenis, had both once been slaves owned by Claudius' mother; the epitaph of Caenis even survives, but naturally omits such details.[9] This again illustrates the limitations of epigraphic evidence: 'monumental' inscriptions are self-conscious public documents which do not retail gossip. But they do name officers and men who accompanied Claudius to Britain, not necessarily Romans from Rome, but Italians and even provincials, including this high-flying man of (Greek) letters:

<**1.02**> *Ephesus*

[Ti(berio) Claud]io Ti(berii) Claudi
[...]i f(ilio) Quir(ina tribu)
[Ba]lbillo
[... a]edium divi Aug(usti) et
[... e]t lucorum sacro-
[rumque omnium qu]ae sunt Alexan-
[driae et in tota Aegypt]o et supra mu-
[s]eum et a[b Alexandri]na bybliothece(!)
et archi[erei et ad Herm]en Alexan-
dreon pe[r annos ...] et ad legati-
ones et res[ponsa ?Graeca Ca]esaris Aug(usti)
divi Claud[i] e[t trib(uno) milit(um) le]g(ionis) XX et prae[f(ecto)]
fabr(um) divi Cla[udi et d(onis) d(onato) in tri]um[pho a divo]
Claudio [corona ... et hasta]
pura [...]
[...]

Inschriften von Ephesos, VII.1, 3042

'To Tiberius Claudius Balbillus, son of Tiberius Claudius [...]us, of the *Quirina* voting-tribe, supervisor of [...] and the temples of the deified Augustus and [...] and all the sacred groves in Alexandria and the whole of Egypt, and the Museum, the Library at Alexandria, High Priest ... for Hermes of Alexandria, for [...] years; Secretary for delegations and answers in Greek of the deified Caesar Augustus Claudius; military

8 As Keppie notes (2000(b), 84), only the Second and the Twentieth are 'firmly documented' in AD 43, but the Twentieth and the Ninth can safely be inferred. For likely detachments of Fourth Macedonica (Upper Germany), Fourth Scythica (Moesia) and Eighth Augusta (Pannonia), see the careers of Julius Camillus (**1.06**), Vicirius Proculus (**1.08**) and Claudius' doctor Stertinius Xenophon (*PIR*[2] S 913) respectively.

9 Suetonius, *Divus Vespasianus* 3–4.1. Her epitaph is *CIL* vi 12037; compare Dio 66. 14, 1–3.

tribune of the Twentieth Legion; aide-de-camp to the deified Claudius, and decorated by him in his triumph with a Crown and Untipped Spear [...]'

Since Claudius is now a god, the inscription is later than his death (13 October AD 54), and too fragmentary for it to be clear what Balbillus' duties really were, but the accumulation of Egyptian 'cultural' posts is striking, in view of his speedy promotion by Nero to govern the whole of Egypt as prefect (AD 55–59).[10] Tacitus implies that this was due to the influence of another literary figure, Nero's former tutor Seneca; certainly Seneca cites Balbillus as 'a most rare master of every literary form, and author of *The Battle of the Dolphins and Crocodiles*'.[11] This epic poem does not survive, but from the perspective of Britain it is the outset of his career which is more interesting. The post of *praefectus fabrum*, despite its title (literally 'prefect of engineers'), was by now an honorary appointment on the staff of a senatorial magistrate, either a consul or praetor at Rome or a proconsul in the provinces, which was sought by young equestrians embarking on a public career. But for Balbillus his chief was the Emperor himself, and his prefecture led to a staff appointment in one of the invading legions. Since he was then promoted to a post at court for which the requisite was a good Greek style, it is difficult to imagine, in spite of his being decorated, that he saw much actual fighting.

Details of this fighting elude us also, for Tacitus narrated it in a book of the *Annals* now lost. Even the army's landing-place is uncertain, although it is likely to be Richborough, where many disconnected fragments survive of the inscribed marble cladding of a monument.[12] We know from Dio Cassius that Aulus Plautius forced a river-crossing and advanced as far as the Thames, his objective being Camulodunum (Colchester), the capital of the dominant tribe of the south-east, the Catuvellauni. Claudius meanwhile had left Rome in the hands of his friend Lucius Vitellius and travelled north with a large entourage; a dozen of his senior staff officers or *comites* ('companions') are known,[13] including this kinsman of Aulus Plautius:

---

[10] This Balbillus can be identified with the prefect of Egypt, but probably not with the 'astrologer' Balbillus whom Nero consulted about a comet in AD 60 or 64 (Suetonius, *Nero* 36.1, *Balbillo astrologo*), since the prefect would then have only just returned to Rome from his important governorship, and Suetonius would surely have identified him as such. But the astrologer Balbillus may have been the unnamed son of the famous astrologer Thrasyllus who predicted Nero's accession (Tacitus, *Annals* vi 22).

[11] Tacitus, *Annals* xiii 22; Seneca, *Quaest. Nat.* 4.2, 13, *perfectus in omni litterarum genere rarissime auctor de proelio delphinorum cum cocodrillis commisso adfertur.*

[12] *RIB* 46–65. Frere and Fulford 2001 reassert the Richborough narrative against Hind 1989.

[13] Assembled with full commentary by Birley 2005, 214–23; Birley 2008(b), 191–5.

<1.03> *Tivoli (Tibur)*

Ti(berio) Plautio M(arci) f(ilio) Ani(ensi tribu)
Silvano Aeliano
pontif(ici), sodali Aug(ustali),
IIIvir(o) a(ere) a(rgento) a(uro) f(lando) f(eriundo), q(uaestori) Ti(beri) Caesaris,
legat(o) leg(ionis) V in Germania,
pr(aetori) urb(ano), legat(o) et comiti Claud(i)
Caesaris in Brittannia, consuli,
proco(n)s(uli) Asiae, legat(o) pro praet(ore) Moesiae
...

ILS 986; *Inscriptiones Italiae* iv.1, No. 125

'To Tiberius Plautius Silvanus Aelianus, son of Marcus, of the *Aniensis* voting-tribe; pontifex, priest of Augustus, member of the Board of Three for minting bronze, silver and gold; quaestor of Tiberius Caesar; legate of the Fifth Legion in Germany; urban praetor; legate and companion of Claudius Caesar in Britain; consul; proconsul of Asia; propraetorian legate of Moesia ...'

This is the beginning of an unusually long epitaph inscribed on marble in front of the tower-like mausoleum of the Plautius family outside Tibur, still standing in the suburbs of modern Tivoli; it gives a detailed account of Aelianus' later achievements on the lower Danube – the resettlement of 100,000 refugees from across the river, diplomatic dealings with potentially hostile chieftains, even the export of wheat to Rome – when he governed Moesia in Nero's reign. The epitaph concludes:

hunc legatum in
{in} Hispaniam ad praefectur(am) urbis remissum
senatus in praefectura triumphalibus
ornamentis honoravit, auctore imp(eratore)
Caesare Augusto Vespasiano, verbis ex
oratione eius q(uae) i(nfra) s(cripta) s(unt):
Moesiae ita praefuit, ut non debuerit in
me differri honor triumphalium eius
ornamentorum, nisi quod latior ei
contigit mora titulus praefecto urbis.
hunc in eadem praefectura urbis imp(erator) Caesar
Aug(ustus) Vespasianus iterum co(n)s(ulem) fecit

'When he had been recalled from being legate in Spain to become prefect of the City, and was holding the prefecture, the Senate honoured him with the decorations of a triumph on the motion of the Emperor Caesar Augustus Vespasian, whose speech included the following words:

'"His governorship of Moesia was such that the award of his triumphal decorations ought not to have been left to me; however, his claim is the greater after this delay, since he is now prefect of the City."

'The Emperor Caesar Augustus Vespasian made him consul for the second time (AD 74) while he was still prefect of the City.'

Aelianus, as prefect of the City, was responsible for law and order at Rome: it was a senior post of great prestige, recently held by Vespasian's elder brother Sabinus. In the second century it crowned the careers of two governors of Britain, Lollius Urbicus (**6.02**) who built the Antonine Wall, and the future emperor Pertinax (**7.02**). Aelianus was also honoured retrospectively for his governorship of Moesia: no doubt Nero had treated him shabbily, but Aelianus in Britain, as the former commander of a legion who enjoyed the confidence both of Claudius and the commander-in-chief, would have been senior to Vespasian; it is likely that Vespasian was now repaying a past favour. Tacitus omits Aelianus' Danubian governorship from the *Annals*, but it is a striking instance of the Early Empire's ability to absorb non-Roman peoples en masse. Later renewed trouble on the Danube forced Domitian to withdraw a legion from Britain (**4.03**), and thus to bring its conquest to a halt. Indeed, to anticipate three centuries, the 'decline and fall' of the Roman Empire in the West was accelerated by its failure to control another mass of refugees from across the Danube. These were the Goths, whose shattering defeat of the Roman army at Adrianople (Edirne) in AD 378 set in train the progressive loss of outlying provinces, including Britain.

But this is to finish the story before it has begun. Aelianus like the rest of Claudius' entourage arrived in Britain, and the advancing army, which had paused tactfully at the Thames, was now impelled to cross; Claudius entered Camulodunum in triumph. He had reinforced the army with more than elephants and his *comites* in purple-banded clothes, the Roman equivalent of red tabs and gold braid; he was escorted by a detachment of the guardsmen who had made him emperor:

<**1.04**> *Rimini (Ariminum)*

M(arco) Vettio M(arci) f(ilio) Ani(ensi tribu) Valenti
mil(iti) coh(ortis) VIII pr(aetoriae), benef(iciario) praef(ecti) pr(aetorio),
donis donato bello Britan(nico)
torquibus armillis phaleris,
evoc(ato) Aug(usti) corona aurea donat(o),
(centurioni) coh(ortis) VI vig(ilum), (centurioni) stat(orum), (centurioni) coh(ortis) XVI
urb(anae), (centurioni) c(o)ho(rtis)
II pr(aetoriae), exercitatori equit(um) speculatorum, princip(i)
praetori leg(ionis) XIII Gem(inae) ex trec(enario), [p(rimo) p(ilo)] leg(ionis) VI
Victr(icis), donis donato ob res prosper(e)
gest(as) contra Astures torq(uibus) phaler(is) arm(illis),

trib(uno) coh(ortis) V vig(ilum), trib(uno) coh(ortis) XII urb(anae), trib(uno) coh(ortis) III pr(aetoriae), [p(rimo) p(ilo) II] leg(ionis) XIIII Gem(inae) Mart(iae) Victr(icis), proc(uratori) imp(eratoris) [Neron(is)] Caes(aris) Aug(usti) prov(inciae) Lusitan(iae), patron(o) coloniae, speculator(es) X h(onoris) c(ausa),
G(aio) Luccio Telesino G(aio) Suetonio Paulino co(n)s(ulibus)

ILS 2648; Dobson 1978, 298, No. 69

'To Marcus Vettius Valens, son of Marcus, of the *Aniensis* voting-tribe, soldier of the Eighth Cohort of the Guard, attached to the staff (*beneficiarius*) of the Prefect of the Guard, decorated in the British War with Torques, Bracelets and Medallions, decorated with the Gold Crown as an imperial re-enlisted veteran (*evocatus Augusti*), centurion in the Sixth Cohort of the Watch, centurion of couriers, centurion in the Sixteenth Urban cohort, centurion in the Second Cohort of the Guard, instructor of the mounted police (*speculatores*), centurion chief of staff of the Thirteenth Legion Gemina and former *trecenarius*, first-ranking centurion of the Sixth Legion Victrix, decorated with Torques, Medallions and Bracelets for successes against the Asturians, tribune of the Fifth Cohort of the Watch, tribune of the Twelfth Urban cohort, tribune of the Third Cohort of the Guard, first-ranking centurion for the second time of the Fourteenth Legion Gemina Martia Victrix, procurator of the Emperor Nero Caesar Augustus of the province of Lusitania, patron of this Colony, the ten *speculatores* (erected this) in his honour, in the consulship of Gaius Luccius Telesinus and Gaius Suetonius Paulinus (AD 66).'

Vettius Valens was in his mid-50s when this inscription was erected. In AD 43 when he was decorated for his part in the invasion, he was already quite a senior guardsman, since he was attached to the staff of the commander of the Guard before completing his 16 years' service and being retained as an *evocatus*. Since this was accompanied by a second decoration, the Gold Crown, it looks as if it coincided with Claudius' triumph. Valens then proceeded to the usual three centurionates of increasing importance at Rome, in the Watch or fire brigade, then the Urban Cohorts or 'police' commanded by the Prefect of the City, and finally the Guard, in which he also became the trainer and of its mounted element, a corps d'élite of 300 troopers (compare **8.19**). The title *trecenarius* seems to have been applied to officers who had held all three centurionates at Rome, the Watch, the Urban Cohorts and the Guard.[14] Then he went to north-west Spain as the first-ranking centurion of the Sixth Legion Victrix ('Victorious'), in which he was decorated once more in a 'colonial' war against the Astures, a powerful tribe in the north-west which had bitterly resisted conquest by Augustus but now contributed units to the army, including the two cavalry regiments (*alae*) and the two part-mounted cohorts which served in Britain. Valens then returned to Rome, this time as a battalion commander, culminating in the Guard by AD 65. This date can be deduced from his next post, which would have lasted a year: he went back to Britain as the first-

[14] Mann 1983.

ranking centurion of the Fourteenth Legion, originally Gemina ('Twin', because it had been formed by amalgamating two legions), but now 'Martial and Victorious' as well for its defeat of Boudica 4 or 5 years before.[15] This inscription, which honours him in his home town, was commissioned by the legion's ten *speculatores* (legionaries seconded to the governor's staff as couriers and policemen) when news came of his promotion to Lusitania.

As procurator of Lusitania (modern Portugal), the equestrian official in charge of the province's finances, Valens was second in importance to the senatorial governor himself. The latter, as it happens, was Otho, the discarded husband of Nero's empress Poppaea, now eking out a gilded exile like the Duke of Windsor in the Bahamas, but destined to be briefly emperor in AD 69. Unfortunately we do not know whether Valens joined Otho's coup, only that he raised his family to the equestrian equivalent of nobility: this is the term that Tacitus applies to the grandfathers of his hero Agricola, who both became procurators.[16] Valens' own grandson entered the Senate and was even honoured by the province of Britain as its patron (**10.24**). The family evidently survived and kept its connection with Britain, perhaps because Valens escaped involvement in AD 69; if so, he was a wiser man or more fortunate than a fellow-tribune in the Guard, who may indeed have also been a fellow-guardsman in AD 43:

<**1.05**> *Turin (Augusta Taurinorum)*

G(aio) Gavio L(uci) f(ilio)
[S]tel(latina tribu) Silvano
[p]rimipilari leg(ionis) VIII Aug(ustae),
[t]ribuno coh(ortis) II vigilum,
[t]ribuno coh(ortis) XIII urban(ae),
[tr]ibuno coh(ortis) XII praetor(iae),
[d]onis donato a divo Claud(io)
bello Britannico
[to]rquibus armillis phaleris
corona aurea,
[p]atrono colon(iae) d(ecreto) [d(ecurionum)]

ILS 2701

'To Gaius Gavius Silvanus, son of Lucius, of the *Stellatina* voting-tribe, first-ranking centurion of the Eighth Legion Augusta, tribune of the Second Cohort of the Watch, tribune of the Thirteenth Urban Cohort, tribune of the Twelfth Cohort of the Guard, decorated by the deified Claudius in the British War with Torques, Bracelets and Medallions, and the Golden Crown; patron of the Colony, by decree of the councillors.'

15 Only *Gemina* in **2.11**, but subsequently famous for defeating Boudica (Tacitus, *Histories* ii 11).

16 *Agricola* 4.1, *utrumque avum procuratorem … quae equestris nobilitas est.*

This dedication can also be closely dated, since – unknown to the councillors of Turin – their patron's career was about to end. As tribune of the Guard in AD 65, Silvanus joined the great conspiracy against the emperor Nero in which he played an ambiguous part: after bringing Nero's order to Seneca that he kill himself, he was denounced in his turn; despite being acquitted, he chose to follow Seneca into suicide.[17] Like Vettius Valens (**1.04**), he qualified for the three tribunates at Rome by having been the first-ranking centurion of a legion, but these tribunates cannot have lasted long enough for him to have been *primus pilus* more than 20 years before: the councillors have recorded only the highlights of his career, without specifying what his post was in AD 43. He may have been a centurion[18] already, but it seems more like that he was a guardsman like Valens, if not yet an *evocatus*.

This term *evocatus* is used of legionaries 'recalled' to the Colours, but especially of guardsmen, when it is usually qualified as 'imperial' (*evocatus Augusti*). But its use has caused difficulty in this third inscription:

<**1.06**> *Avenches (Aventicum)*

[G(aio)] Iul(io) G(ai) f(ilio) Fab(ia tribu) Camillo
[s]ac(erdoti) Aug(usti) mag(ni?), trib(uno) mil(itum)
[l]eg(ionis) IIII Maced(onicae), hast(a) pura
[e]t corona aurea donato
[a] Ti(berio) Claudio Caesare Aug(usto)
[G]er(manico) cum ab eo evocatus
[i]n Britannia militasset,
[c]ol(onia) Pia Flavia Constans
Emerita Helvetior(um)
ex d(ecreto) d(ecurionum)

CIL xiii 5093 = *ILS* 2697+*add.*

'To Gaius Julius Camillus, son of Gaius, of the *Fabia* voting-tribe, priest of the great Augustus, military tribune of the Fourth Legion Macedonica, decorated with the Untipped Spear and the Gold Crown by Tiberius Claudius Caesar Augustus Germanicus when he was recalled (*evocatus*) by him and served in Britain. The *colonia* of the Helvetii, Dutiful, Flavian, Constant, Veteran, by decree of the city-councillors.'

The titles of Aventicum refer to its re-foundation by Vespasian (whence *Flavia*) as a 'colony' (*colonia*), a new Roman city settled by legionary veterans (*emeriti*), which

[17] Tacitus, *Annals* xv 50, 60–1, 71.

[18] Not necessarily in the Eighth Legion, although Claudius' doctor Stertinius Xenophon, a tribune in that legion, was decorated in Claudius' British triumph (*PIR*² S 913, inscriptions quoted by Birley 2008, 197).

means that more than 25 years have elapsed since Camillus was decorated for his part in the invasion of Britain. He probably owed this belated recognition to his daughter Julia Festilla, who provided in her will for a duplicate of this inscription.[19] The use of *evocatus* may only mean that Camillus, like Vettius Valens (**1.04**), was serving in the Guard when he was decorated; but since the decorations he received are typical of equestrian officers in the pre-Flavian period,[20] it is more likely that he was actually tribune of the Fourth Legion Macedonica when Claudius 'recalled' him, a rare instance of this verb being used in its general sense. This would indicate that his legion contributed a detachment to the legionary component of the invading army.

There is less uncertainty about another legionary officer, the camp commandant of the Second Legion Augusta. Anicius Maximus was promoted for his part in the invasion, as we know from the inscription erected in his honour by the capital of Roman Egypt, Alexandria, at his home town of Pisidian Antioch in southern Asia Minor. His origins and career are eloquent of the 'colonial élites' from which many officers were drawn:

<**1.07**> *Pisidian Antioch (western Turkey)*

P(ublio) Anicio
P(ubli) f(ilio) Ser(gia tribu) Maxi-
mo praefecto
Gn(aei) Domiti Ahenobar-
bi, p(rimo) p(ilo) leg(ionis) XII Fulm(inatae), praef(ecto)
castror(um) leg(ionis) II Aug(ustae) in
Britannia, praef(ecto) ex[er]citu(s) qui est in Aegypto,
donato ab imp(eratore) donis
militaribus ob expeditionem, honorato
coron(a) murali et
hasta pura ob bellum
Britannic(um), civitas Alexandr(iae) quae est
in Aegypto, h(onoris) c(ausa)

ILS 2696

'To Publius Anicius Maximus, son of Publius, of the *Sergia* voting-tribe, prefect of Gnaeus Domitius Ahenobarbus, first-ranking centurion of the Twelfth Legion Fulminata, camp commandant of the Second Legion Augusta in Britain, commandant of the army which is in Egypt, decorated by the Emperor for the expedition, honoured with Mural Crown and Untipped Spear for the British War, (from) the city of Alexandria in Egypt, to do him honour.'

---

[19] *CIL* xiii 5094 (Avenches), the same text (as far as ... *militasset*), but ending with *Iul(ia) Camili(!) fil(ia) Festilla ex testamento*.

[20] Maxfield 1981, 161.

Pisidian Antioch was a *colonia* founded by Augustus for his legionary veterans. It was a little Rome built on seven hills, a Latin-speaking enclave in the Greek east which even displayed its own copy of the founder's *Res Gestae* (**1.01**). Anicius Maximus, like Caristanius Fronto (**1.11**), belonged to the local nobility of Antioch: he received the honour of deputising as 'prefect' (acting-mayor) for Domitius Ahenobarbus when the latter was formally elected to the city's annual magistracy. Ahenobarbus was the head of an ancient noble family which had become entangled with the imperial house (he was in fact Claudius' first cousin), and by marrying Claudius' niece he fathered the future emperor Nero; this mésalliance ensured that he was remembered as 'detestable in every part of life'.[21] His titular deputy, Anicius Maximus, was probably commissioned directly as a centurion because of his high social standing, and rose to be the first-ranking centurion of one of the four Syrian legions; from this he was posted to the other end of the Empire, to be the senior professional soldier of the Second Legion Augusta, where he ranked third after the legate (Vespasian) and the senior 'senatorial' tribune (*tribunus laticlavius*), a young man usually of senatorial family who aspired to a senatorial career. He received the decorations appropriate to his rank for his part in the conquest of Britain, and rose higher still, in the East once more, as camp commandant to both the Egyptian legions combined. He and Balbillus are the first of more than a dozen officers and administrators whose careers are known to have taken them from Britain to Egypt.[22]

The victory celebrated

Claudius, although he was guarded in Britain by loyal careerists in the Guard that proclaimed him, and only spent sixteen days on the island, was absent from Rome for six months, where anxiety and pride were felt, or at least advertised.[23] These feelings extended to Italy and 'Roman' towns elsewhere. Claudius in his days of academic obscurity had learnt the Etruscan language to write their history, and now in AD 45 a dignitary in the Etruscan town of Rusellae dedicated a statue of the 'British Victory'. On the plinth was inscribed:

---

[21] Suetonius, *Nero* 5.1, *omni parte vitae detestabilem*.

[22] Drexhage 1998 (summarising their careers at 185–7). Bowman 2006.

[23] *CIL* vi 3751 = 31282 = 36894. *CIL* vi 917. Dedications are collected with commentary by Bérard, Cogitore and Tarpin 1998, 385–6; Christol, Drew-Bear and Taşlialan 2001, 15; Standing 2003; Birley 2008(b), 198–201.

<**1.08**> *Rusellae (near Roselle in Tuscany)*

voto [s]uscepto
[p]ro salute et reditu et
victoria Britanni-
ca Ti(berii) Claudi Caesa-
ris Aug(usti) Germanici
pont(ificis) max(imi), tr(ibunicia) pot(estate) V, imp(eratoris)
X, p(atris) p(atriae), co(n)s(ulis) des(ignati) IIII,
A(ulus) Vicirius Proculus
flamen Aug(ustalis), tr(ibunus) mil(itum),
victoriae Britanni-
cae votum solvit

AE 1980, 457

'Vow made for the safe return and the British Victory of Tiberius Claudius Caesar Augustus Germanicus, pontifex maximus, in the fifth year of his tribunician power (AD 45), acclaimed emperor ten times, Father of his Country, consul designate for the fourth time (for AD 47). Aulus Vicirius Proculus, priest of Augustus, military tribune, has paid his vow to the British Victory.'

Claudius bears the usual imperial titles: *Caesar* and *Augustus* to symbolise his descent from the founders of the Empire; *pontifex maximus* as the elected head of the Roman state religion; and the powers, but not the actual office, of tribune of the plebs, which Augustus regarded as his 'title of supreme power' since it symbolised his protection of the People.[24] It was renewed annually on 10 December, the day on which the tribunes entered office, so it marked the number of regnal years. In AD 43 Proculus had promised to dedicate a statue if Claudius returned safely, and now he 'paid' his vow. (Roman religion, like Roman social life, was a contract which imposed reciprocal obligations upon inferiors and superiors alike.) Unfortunately he does not specify the legion in which he was tribune, but it is tempting to see it as one of the four which invaded Britain; if so, he would have subtly advertised his own contribution to the victory, as well as his loyalty to the new Emperor as a priest of the Imperial Cult. There would also be the intriguing coincidence that another Aulus Vicirius Proculus, presumably his grandson, was governor of Britain in AD 93.[25]

The question is complicated by the tombstone of one Aulus Vicirius (cognomen

[24] Tacitus, *Annals* iii 56, *summi fastigii vocabulum*; i 2, *ad tuendam plebem. tribunicia potestas* is usually abbreviated in inscriptions and may be resolved either as genitive or as ablative, since both cases are found when it is not abbreviated. The ablative has been adopted here, except in **4.13**. where the genitive is explicit.

[25] Aulus Vicirius Proculus (cos. suff. AD 89), now attested in a diploma fragment (*AE* 2008, 1754, with Eck and Pangerl 2008). Aulus Vicirius Martialis (cos. suff. AD 98) is probably his younger brother.

now lost), who received a public funeral at Siena; he too was a military tribune, but tribune of the Fourth Legion Scythica. If he were the same man, and were indeed celebrating his own contribution to the victory, it would mean that this legion sent a detachment from Moesia to Britain.[26] But he may only have been a kinsman. There was no need actually to serve in Britain to celebrate victory in Britain:

<**1.09**> *Corinth*

Ti(berio) Claudio P(ublii) f(ilio) Fab(ia tribu) Dinippo
IIvir(o), IIvir(o) quinq(uennali), augur(i),
sacerdoti Victoriae
Britann(icae), trib(uno) mil(itum) leg(ionis) VI,
annonae curatori,
agonothete Neroneon
Caesareon et Isthmion
et Caesareon, tribules
tribus Atiae

AE 1917/18, 1 (West 1931, No. 86)

'To Tiberius Claudius Dinippus, son of Publius, of the *Fabia* voting-tribe, joint-mayor, quinquennial joint-mayor, priest of the British Victory, military tribune of the Sixth Legion, curator of the corn-supply, games-giver of the Neronian and Caesarian Games, the Isthmian Games and the Caesarian Games, (from) the tribesmen of the *Atia* voting-tribe.'

Corinth, which had been refounded by Julius Caesar as a Roman *colonia*, was the capital of Achaia, the Roman province of Greece, and in the first century it used Latin as its official language. This is the best preserved of at least ten inscriptions in which the council and the individual voting-tribes honour Dinippus in almost identical terms.[27] Like Vicirius Proculus, he too had been a military tribune, and some of the inscriptions call the Sixth Legion *Hispaniensis* because it was in Spain until AD 70 (compare **1.04**). Oversight of the corn supply at Corinth seems to have been a special post there in times of shortage. The old Isthmian Games at Corinth had been supplemented by emperors who added their own names; Nero's in due course was replaced by that of Trajan. All of this means that Dinippus was rich and influential in the AD 40s and 50s, a local magnate with no direct involvement in

[26] *CIL* xi 1806. Devijver identified them at first (*PME* V 111), but later distinguished them (Suppl. I and II, V 111 and V 111 bis) on the grounds that *CIL* xi 1806, by abbreviating *Dis Manibus* to *D M*, must be considerably later. But the stone is broken here, and it is unclear whether it was abbreviated or not. Eck (2000, 486) identifies them, with the implication suggested. An unknown senator from Rusellae served as legionary tribune in the 'British army' (*exercitus Britannicus*), but this need not mean the actual expeditionary force: *AE* 1980, 445, with Birley 2005, 277–8.

[27] West 1931, Nos. 86, 87, 88, 89, and (very fragmentary) 90, 91, 92. Kent 1966, Nos. 158, 159, 160, 161, 162, 163. Standage 2003, 284–6 (illustrating Kent No. 160).

the Victory whose priest he was; the cult seems to have died with him, since he is the only known incumbent. Also from Corinth is this inscribed statue-base:

<**1.10**> *Corinth*

Victoriai
sacrum

West 1931, No. 11

'Dedicated to Victory.'

But not just any victory. The spelling of AI for AE is not a Graecism, but an archaising affectation also found on Claudius' Arch at Rome (**1.13**). This is a victory of Claudius, therefore, and probably a dedication to the British Victory by its priest Dinippus. It is celebrated more elaborately by another Roman 'colonial' magnate in the Greek-speaking East:

<**1.11**> *Pisidian Antioch (western Turkey)*

Ti(berio) Claudio
Caisari Aug(usto)
Germanico
pont(ifici) max(imo), co(n)s(uli) III,
trib(unicia) pot(estate) V, p(atri) p(atriae),
pro incolumitate
eius et victoria
Britannica ex
voto quod susce-
perat cum liberis
suis, statuam, ludos
iuvenales, hostias,
venationem dedit
G(aius) Carista{t}n-
ius Fronto
Caisianus Iullus
duumviralis III,
pontifex, trib(unus)
leg(ionis) XII Fulmin(atae),
praif(ectus) cohort(is)
Bospor(anorum), praif(ectus)
fabrum VI

Tyche 16 (2001), 1–20 (*AE* 2001, 1918)

> 'To Tiberius Claudius Caisar Augustus Germanicus, pontifex maximus, consul three times, in the fifth year of his tribunician power (AD 45), Father of his Country; for his safety and the British Victory, according to the vow he undertook with his children, this statue, Youth Games, animal sacrifices, a wild-beast show, was given by Gaius Caristanius Fronto Caisianus Iullus, duumvir three times, pontifex, tribune of the Twelfth Legion Fulminata, prefect of the Cohort of Bosporani, aide-de-camp six times.'

Like the Corinthian dedication to Victory, this long text pays tribute to Claudius by adopting the 'archaic' spelling of AI for AE in the words *Caisari*, *Caisianus* and *praif(ectus)*. It is inscribed on the front of a square pillar, which (with its now missing capital) would have supported a statue of the Emperor some three metres above the ground. Its dedicator was not only rich, as the catalogue of his local benefactions was intended to show, but also influential; not just at Antioch, where he was joint-mayor (*duumvir*) but in the wider Empire: six times aide-de-camp like Balbillus (**1.02**), like Anicius Maximus (**1.07**) he twice received the honour of deputising as 'prefect' (acting-mayor) for visiting army-commanders when they were formally elected to the annual magistracy. This detail comes from two other inscriptions, one of them the plinth of his public statue, 'the first ever voted by the Council'; the date of one appointment, it can be deduced, was in AD 4, and the other perhaps even earlier.[28] It follows that in AD 45 Caristanius was aged about seventy, an elder statesman, whose equestrian military service was many years ago. Moreover, it was entirely eastern; his legion and cohort were probably then in Syria. Like Claudius Dinippus (**1.09**), if not Vicirius Proculus (**1.08**), he had no direct connection with the invasion of Britain, but used it to demonstrate his own loyalty and influence. Coincidentally and unknown to him, however, like Vicirius Proculus he would acquire a British connection many years later: another Gaius Caristanius Fronto of Antioch, probably his great-grandson, achieved senatorial rank and commanded one of the legions with which Agricola conquered the north (**3.17**).[29]

Claudius was voted the title *Britannicus* for his conquest of Britain, but modestly passed it to his infant son, who thus became known as 'Britannicus'. Vicirius Proculus prayed for *his* welfare too.[30] But the title died with Britannicus in AD 55, soon after the accession of his rival Nero, who was plausibly thought to have poisoned him.[31] We know from inscriptions that the title was not resumed by Domitian, Hadrian or Antoninus Pius for their own successes in Britain, although Pius struck coins in AD 143 to celebrate Victory in Britain. This was his own victory, but

---

[28] *ILS* 9502 (*huic primo omnium publice d(ecreto) d(ecurionum) statua posita est*) and 9503, now *AE* 2001, 1919 and 1920, with correction of his cognomen to *Iullus*; full commentary by Christol, Drew-Bear and Taşlialan 2001.

[29] Another branch of the family remained equestrian, producing the prefect Caristanius Justianus (**6.24**).

[30] *AE* 1980, 458, *[p]ro salute Ti(berii) Claudi(i) Caesaris Aug(usti) f(ilii) Brittannici.*

[31] Tacitus, *Annals* xiii 15–17.

coincidentally it was the centenary of the Claudian invasion.[32] The title was only resumed by Commodus, and later by Septimius Severus and Caracalla, Carinus and Numerian, Diocletian and his colleagues, and then finally by Constantine. But Claudius' achievement was unparalleled in AD 48, when he rhetorically refused to mention it. We have his very words to the Senate, during the debate on whether senators should be admitted from Gaul, which is why his speech was inscribed verbatim on bronze at Lugdunum (Lyon), the Roman capital of Gaul and Claudius' own birthplace; it also saw a dedication for Claudius' safe return from Britain.[33] In this speech Claudius the historian digresses from his main theme, the widening recruitment of the Empire's ruling class, to the early history of Rome:

<1.12> *Lyon (Lugdunum)*

iam si narrem bella a quibus
coeperint maiores nostri et quo processerimus, vereor ne nimio
insolentior esse videar et quaesisse iactationem gloriae pro-
lati imperi ultra oceanum

ILS 212

'But now, were I to describe the wars from which our ancestors began, and how far we have advanced, I am afraid of giving the impression of being arrogant and of seeking an opportunity to congratulate myself on extending Roman rule beyond the Ocean.'

The Senate, by dutifully voting Claudius a triumph and a triumphal arch for his conquest of Britain, had not allowed this modesty to be an obstacle. Here is the inscription on the Arch when its was erected on the northern approaches to Rome, where the Aqua Virgo aqueduct (newly rebuilt by Claudius) crossed a major road:

<1.13> *Rome*

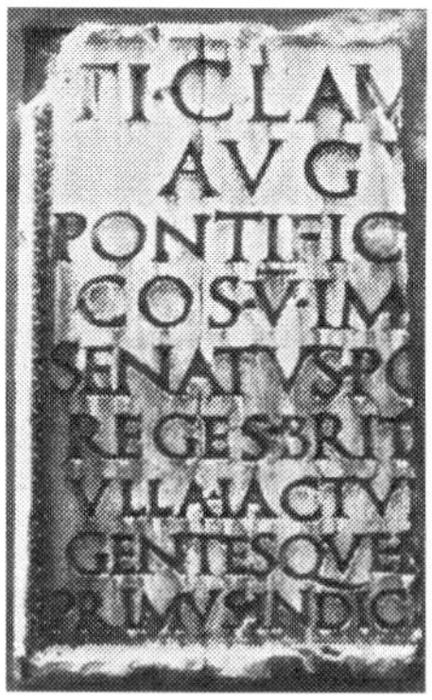

Ti(berio) Clau[dio Drusi f(ilio) Cai]sari
Augu[sto Germani]co
pontific[i maxim(o), trib(unicia) potes]tat(e) XI,
co(n)s(uli) V, im[p(eratori) XXII, cens(ori), patri pa]triai,
Senatus Po[pulusque] Ro[manus, quod]
reges Brit[annorum] XI d[evictos sine]
ulla iactur[a in deditionem acceperit]
gentesque b[arbaras trans Oceanum]
primus in dici[onem populi Romani redegerit]

---

[32] *BMCRE* IV, No. 1613, *sestertius* with the figure of *Victoria* captioned BRI TAN. The caption IMPERATOR II refers it to the only imperatorial salutation taken by Pius after his accession.

[33] *AE* 1998, 944, to Jupiter and Victory (with the dedicator's name now lost), *pro salute et reditus*(!) *Ti(berii) Claudi Caesaris Aug(usti) Ger(manici).*

ILS 216, with Barrett 1991

> 'To Tiberius Claudius Caesar Augustus Germanicus, son of Drusus, pontifex maximus, in the eleventh year of his tribunician power (AD 52), consul five times, *imperator* 22 times, censor, Father of his Country, from the Roman Senate and People, because he received in surrender eleven kings of the Britons conquered without loss and first brought the barbarian peoples across the Ocean under the authority of the Roman people.'

The Arch has disappeared, but extensive remains were found in 1562 and 1641. Subsidiary inscriptions evidently named members of Claudius' immediate family like his mother and father, and his brother Germanicus. Quoted here is the main inscription, of which only the left-hand quarter survives intact; the rest has to be reconstructed from a few fragments and another Arch at Cyzicus (see below). Some details of Claudius' achievement remain uncertain: we are not sure how many British kings there were, and whether they were 'defeated' or 'surrendered'. AI for AE in *patriai* and *[Cai]sari* is the archaising affectation already seen at Corinth (**1.09**) and Pisidian Antioch (**1.11**); it was a subtle compliment to the imperial antiquary, but politically more important was the compliment to his generalship. A victorious general during the Republic, including even the unwarlike Cicero in Cilicia, was acclaimed by his army as *imperator* (literally 'commander-in-chief', but hence 'emperor'), and thereby claimed the right to enter Rome in triumph. But the first Emperor, Augustus, the *imperator* par excellence, soon monopolised this distinction for himself and his family; his generals served only as his deputies or 'legates' (*legati*), lieutenant-generals with delegated powers, and like Aelianus (**1.03**) received no more than 'triumphal decorations', the outward insignia of a triumph. In a career lasting more than 50 years, Augustus was acclaimed 'Emperor' 21 times, a total already surpassed by Claudius in 11 years, sure sign of his insecurity and his need for military recognition.

In Asia Minor on the Sea of Marmara, the expatriate community of Romans at Cyzicus erected an arch of their own with an inscription[34] commemorating Claudius' conquest of Britain; and in the south-west, at Aphrodisias in Caria, a city which prospered from the local cult of Julius Caesar's divine ancestress Aphrodite (identified with Roman Venus), a marble panel was added to the two-storey colonnade which led to her temple. Claudius, heroically nude, bestrides an Amazon-like figure which wears a short tunic and boots; with one hand he draws back her head, with the other he is about to plunge a spear into her bare breast. Underneath is a double caption:

[34] *ILS* 217.

<1.14> *Aphrodisias (western Turkey)*

Τιβέριος Κλαύδιος Καῖσαρ Βρεταννία

Smith 2013, 145–7, C10 and C-base 12

'Tiberius Claudius Caesar' *and* 'Britannia'

The spectator is left in suspense as to whether Claudius is going to strike the death-blow, or will relent and raise a fainting Britannia to her place among the provinces of Rome.

2

THE CONQUEST OF LOWLAND BRITAIN

Officers and men

The Aphrodisias panel of Claudius bestriding Britain is a classical portrait of Roman imperialism which celebrates the triumph of civilisation over barbarism; or at least the supremacy of brute force when it is better organised and better armed than the opposition. It will be another century before the peaceable figure of Britannia hands a wreath to the eagle of the Twentieth (**6.13**). This legion's earliest known tombstone in Britain echoes the triumphalism of Aphrodisias:

<2.01> *Colchester (Camulodunum)*

M(arci) Favoni M(arci) f(ili) Pol(lia tribu) Faci-
lis (centurionis) leg(ionis) XX, Verecund-
us et Novicius lib(erti) posu-
erunt, h(ic) s(itus) e(st)

RIB 200

'(The monument) of Marcus Favonius Facilis, son of Marcus, of the *Pollia* voting-tribe, centurion of the Twentieth Legion. Verecundus and Novicius his freedmen set it up. He is buried here.'

Such an early epitaph is probably in the genitive case as translated, like that of Cornelius at Lincoln (**2.13**), but the diagnostic words are abbreviated or ambiguous. Camulodunum became the capital of the new province, and a legion was based there; this inscription shows that it was the Twentieth. Facilis was cremated and his ashes were buried in a lead urn marked by a tombstone which was carved by a legionary craftsman, not from

British limestone like the contemporary tombstone of Longinus (**2.02**), but from the Lothringer Freestone which the legion had been using for monuments at Neuss, its previous base on the Rhine.[1] The centurion's jug ears and forward-combed hair recall contemporary portraits of Claudius himself. He is wearing uniform, a cuirass and broad military belt girt with dagger; one hand rests on the pommel of his sword, the other on his vine-branch (*vitis*), the 'swagger-stick' which symbolised his power to flog defaulters. He surveys the newly-conquered province with the self-assurance of a Panzer general confronting sub-humans: ironically, the fine state of preservation of his monument is due to its having been pushed over soon after it was erected, no doubt when Boudica sacked Camulodunum.

Nearby stood one of the grandest cavalry tombstones in Britain, rivalled only at Lancaster (**4.01**) and Corbridge (**4.09**), but it too was toppled by Boudica. Under a niche dominated by a funerary Sphinx and two lions, each with a snake in its paws, Longinus Sdapeze placidly sits his caparisoned horse. Tucked beneath its hooves in a foetal crouch lies a naked unbarbered barbarian. The stone itself was found in 1928, but the detached face of Longinus' effigy was recovered only in 1996; the metal lance he once held has vanished into rust, accentuating his unwarlike appearance; in the pleasant words of Jocelyn Toynbee, 'both the mount and the rider have the air of consciously posing for their picture after the fight is over.'[2]

<2.02> *Colchester (Camulodunum)*

Longinus Sdapeze
Matyci f(ilius) duplicarius
ala prima Tracum pago
Sardi(ca), anno(rum) XL, aeror(um) XV,
heredes ex{s} testam(ento) [f(aciendum)] c(uraverunt),
h(ic) s(itus) e(st)

RIB 201+*add.*

'Longinus Sdapeze, son of Matycus, duplicarius in the First Cavalry Regiment of Thracians, from the district of Sardica, aged 40, of 15 years' service, lies buried here; his heirs under his will had this set up.'

The aspirated [th] of 'Thracians', theta in Greek, is often reduced to 't' in Latin inscriptions. Longinus like Rufus Sita (**2.05**) was a Thracian with a double name, no doubt because he assumed a Latin name when he joined the Roman army. He came from what is now

[1] Hayward 2006.

[2] Toynbee 1962, 158. *Britannia* 28 (1997), 432.

Bulgaria (its capital Sofia is the ancient Sardica), and his military service afforded him a lavish tombstone. The rank of *duplicarius* meant that he received double pay as the second-in-command of a troop (*turma*) of thirty men. *exs* is often written for *ex* as in **2.14** (with note), so as to reinforce the 'correct' pronunciation against a tendency to reduce the [ks] sound to [s].[3]

This powerful combination of a legion and a cavalry regiment, which pointedly occupied the late capital of the Catuvellauni, formed a strategic reserve at the governor's immediate disposal, but the other military formations and units which now fanned out across the new province could themselves be rapidly assembled into a field army. Some of their semi-permanent bases have been identified by aerial photography and archaeological excavation, and even by the chance survival of tombstones, but many uncertainties remain. Quite a recent discovery is the tombstone of a legionary veteran which was broken up for re-use in the walls of a small Roman town just north of Oxford:

<**2.03**> *Alchester*

Dis Manibus
L(ucius) Val(erius) L(uci filius) Pol(lia tribu) Gemi-
nus For(o) Germ(anorum)
vet(eranus) leg(ionis) [I]I Aug(ustae),
an(norum) L h(ic) s(itus) e(st),
h(eres) f(aciundum) c(uravit)
e(x) t(estamento)

RIB III, 3121

'To the Shades of the Dead. Lucius Valerius Geminus, son of Lucius, of the *Pollia* voting-tribe, from Forum Germanorum, veteran of the Second Legion Augusta, aged 50, lies buried here. His heir saw to making this in accordance with his will.'

Ancient references to Geminus' place of origin (in line 3) always abbreviate the second word to GERM, so we do not know whether this stood for 'Germans' or for 'Germanicus', but it was in the Alpine foothills south of Turin. Line 6 actually reads H E C, which *RIB* takes to be an unusual abbreviation for *he(res) c(uravit)*, but Tony Birley has seen is probably a stone-cutter's error for the common formula H F C, *h(eres) f(aciundum) c(uravit)*, 'his heir saw to making this'.[4] The 20 fragments of this important epitaph were painstakingly recovered by Eberhart Sauer, the excavator of the legion's first base at Alchester, who has discussed in detail its bearing on the

[3] Thus *visit* for *vixit* in **14.13**.

[4] Birley 2011, 684. For HE as *he(res)*, compare **4.04**.

legion's early movements.[5] Geminus was a veteran, not a serving legionary, but like other veterans he probably retired to where his legion had once been stationed; by the time of his death, which can only be dated to the AD 60s or later by the use of the formula *Dis Manibus*, the Second had long since moved on, to Exeter or even to Caerleon. The difficulty is that the list of its early conquests under Vespasian as legate, 'two powerful tribes, more than twenty towns, and the Isle of Wight', implies that it was operating much further south and to the south-west.[6] We would have expected to find the Fourteenth Legion at Alchester, not the Second.

Geminus' age at death is obviously an estimate, 'age-rounding' as it is called: the date of his enlistment would have been on record, but not his date of birth, and even if he had known it himself, it is unlikely that his heir would have done. But if he was now '50', it implies that at least thirty years had passed since his enlistment. Despite the uncertain date of his tombstone, therefore, it is quite likely that he joined the legion before AD 43. The same can be said of another early legionary, this time from the Ninth:

<2.04> *Lincoln (Lindum)*

G(aio) Saufeio
G(ai) f(ilio) Fab(ia tribu) Her(aclea)
militi legio(nis)
VIIII,
annor(um) XXXX,
stip(endiorum) XXII
h(ic) s(itus) e(st)

RIB 255

'To Gaius Saufeius, son of Gaius, of the *Fabia* voting-tribe, from Heraclea, soldier of the Ninth Legion, aged 40, of 22 years' service; he lies here.'

The legion left Lincoln (Lindum) for York in *c.* AD 71, which means that Saufeius must have joined it before AD 50; and his place of origin, Heraclea in Macedonia, suggests that he did so before it left Pannonia in AD 43.[7]

Another Roman spearhead reached Gloucester (Glevum), the lowest point at which the Severn could be bridged. Here at Kingsholm there was another Thracian unit. A tombstone evokes with more vigour, but less skill, the same motif of the Triumphant Horseman:

---

5 Sauer 2005.

6 Suetonius, *Divus Vespasianus* 4.1, *duas validissimas gentes superque viginti oppida et insulam Vectem.*

7 *ILS* 928 with *AE* 1919, 1, implies that the Ninth once had the title *Macedonica*, implying service there, but this is likely to have been in the reign of Augustus, too early for Saufeius.

<2.05> *Gloucester (Glevum)*

Rufus Sita eques c(o)ho(rtis) VI
Tracum, ann(orum) XL, stip(endiorum) XXII,
heredes ex{s} test(amento) f(aciendum) curave(runt),
h(ic) s(itus) e(st)

RIB 121

'Rufus Sita, trooper of the Sixth Cohort of Thracians, aged 40, of 22 years' service, lies buried here. His heirs had this erected according to the terms of his will.'

exs is written for *ex*, as it is for Longinus (**2.02**). Like him, Rufus Sita was a Thracian who took an extra Latin name (*Rufus*) when he joined the Roman army. This may have been in AD 26, when Roman recruiting provoked an uprising in Thrace which legionaries crushed with the aid of loyal Thracian auxiliaries; if Rufus had been involved, he cannot have died later than AD 48. Longinus by contrast, with his 15 years' service, cannot have joined the army before *c.* AD 30. Both men like Saufeius (**2.04**) were 'aged 40' at death, an obvious estimate. Longinus, it may be noted, was being paid more than twice as much as Rufus. Rufus, as a trooper in a part-mounted cohort, probably got the same as a legionary foot-soldier. Troopers in a cavalry regiment, however, were paid more than this, and Longinus was receiving double that; how much this was exactly, we do not know, only that it was better than the pay of a flag-bearer (*vexillarius*) in the legionary cavalry.[8]

Upstream from Gloucester, at the other other major crossing of the Severn, was a second Thracian part-mounted cohort. This was at Wroxeter (Viroconium), the Roman forerunner of medieval Shrewsbury, and like it the nodal point of the middle Marches. Its early history is complex, with several forts known in the area, but as at Gloucester, an auxiliary unit may have preceded the legion:

<2.06> *Wroxeter (Viroconium)*

Tib(erius) Claud(ius) Tiri-
ntius eq(ues) coh(ortis) [..]
Thracum an[n]-
orum LVII sti[p]-
endior(um) XX[...]
h(ic) s(itus) [e(st)]

RIB 291+*add.*

'Tiberius Claudius Tirintius, trooper of the [...] Cohort of Thracians, aged 57, of [...] years' service, is buried here.'

[8] It was a promotion for Tiberius Claudius Maximus, *vexillarius equitum* in a legion, to become *duplicarius* in an *ala* (*AE* 1969/70, 583).

Tirintius' name is Greek, *Tirynthius* spelt in a Latin way, probably because he too came from Thrace, where Greek was spoken. The numeral of his cohort is now lost, but it was probably 'I', not 'VI' like that of Rufus Sita (**2.05**). The numeral of his years of service is unfortunately incomplete but, judging by his age, it was 37 or so. If his unit was raised at the same time as that of Rufus Sita, he would then have died in *c.* AD 63. By then, however, Wroxeter was a legionary base (**2.11** and **2.12**): either the Thracians were 'brigaded' with the legion or, more likely, they already existed as a unit in AD 26 (Tirintius being one of the loyalists in that uprising) and thus reached Wroxeter before the legion did. The other evidence of date is Tirintius' full name, which indicates a grant of Roman citizenship from Claudius or Nero, probably for completing 25 years' service, this being an economical way of rewarding auxiliary soldiers. (Legionaries by contrast received a land grant, or a bounty in cash equal to more than ten years' pay. It was only in the reign of Trajan that auxiliary soldiers were then automatically discharged.) Tirintius was thus a very old soldier, who may have been already approaching his jubilee of 25 years at the time of the invasion, and who served at least another ten years as a Roman citizen before he died, still in the saddle.

Meanwhile the Roman high command had soon decided to evacuate Camulodunum (Colchester), which in AD 49 was converted into a *colonia* settled by legionary veterans. The Twentieth was moved to Kingsholm, Gloucester, to judge by the fragment of an early tombstone[9] found there with that of Rufus Sita (**2.05**), while its former companion the *ala Thracum* held a key point en route. This was Corinium (Cirencester), where major routes from the east (Akeman Street) and the south (Ermin Street) joined the Fosse Way, the road linking the Midland garrisons with the south-west. At Cirencester appears a comrade of Longinus (**2.02**) in the cavalryman's favourite pose, firmly in the saddle, driving his lance into a fallen enemy:

<2.07> *Cirencester (Corinium Dobunnorum)*

Sextus Vale-
rius Genialis
eq(u)es alae Trhaec(um)
civis Frisia(v)us, tur(ma)
Genialis, an(norum) XXXX st(ipendiorum) XX
h(ic) s(itus) e(st) (h)e(res) f(aciendum) c(uravit)

RIB 109+*add.*

'Sextus Valerius Genialis, trooper of the Cavalry Regiment of Thracians, a tribesman of the Frisiavi, from the troop of Genialis, aged 40, of 20 years' service, is buried here. His heir set this up.'

[9] *RIB* 122.

Yet another soldier 'aged 40' at death. The Frisiavones (as the correct form seems to have been) were a tribe of northern Belgica, a major recruiting-ground of Roman auxiliary cavalry ever since the Gallic campaigns of Julius Caesar. It therefore looks as if the regiment was serving on the lower Rhine, like the Twentieth Legion, when it joined the army of invasion. The spelling of 'Thracian' is odd: [th] is not native to Latin, as already noted (**2.02**), but the stone-cutter knew there ought to be an *h* somewhere; only he guessed wrong. The same confusion arises at Carlisle (**13.04**), 150 years later. Genialis by coincidence has the same name as his troop-commander; it was popular with soldiers, and at Carlisle was even borne by two troop-commanders at the same time (out of sixteen).[10] It is more noteworthy that Valerius Genialis was already a Roman citizen when he joined the regiment.

Corinium, the new capital of the Dobunni, with its excellent communications and rich farmland, flourished after the soldiers left in the Flavian period. It became one of the greatest cities of Roman Britain, a provincial capital in fact (**14.07**). Another early fort with a glittering future was at Bath, or rather just outside it, at Walcot, where the London road met the Fosse Way. A Spanish cavalryman was buried here, his epitaph inscribed below a crude two-dimensional relief of a horse, one hoof daintily raised, trampling a prostrate barbarian:

<2.08> *Bath (Aquae Sulis)*
L(ucius) Vitellius Ma-
ntai f(ilius) Tancinus
cives(!) Hisp(anus) Caurie<n>sis
eq(ues) alae Vettonum c(ivium) R(omanorum)
ann(orum) XXXXVI stip(endiorum) XXVI
h(ic) s(itus) e(st)

RIB 159+*add.*

'Lucius Vitellius Tancinus, son of Mantaus, a Spanish tribesman from Caurium, trooper of the Cavalry Regiment of Vettones, Roman Citizens, aged 46, of 26 years' service, lies buried here'

Cives is written for *civis*, a common instance[11] of the confusion in spoken Latin between [e] and [i] if unstressed; *Cauriesis* for *Cauriensis* also echoes this 'Vulgar' Latin, which often reduced [ns] to [s], as in *Vindolandesses* (**12.73**). Tancinus came from Lusitania, modern Portugal, although Caurium (now Corio) is actually in Spain; it was in the territory of the Vettones, the tribe from which this cavalry regiment was raised. The name *Tancinus* is attested there, and our Tancinus was

[10] *Tab. Luguval.* 1.4 and 46; 16.i.10 (identified as *senior*) and ii.34.

[11] Also found in **2.20**, **9.52**, **11.09** and **11.36**.

evidently a founder member of the regiment. His full name suggests that he was a new citizen who took his patron's name, Lucius Vitellius, the courtier who shared the censorship with Claudius in AD 46–7. Tancinus was not being rewarded for 25 years' undetected crime like Tirintius (**2.06**): his regiment bears the title 'Roman Citizens', which was a battle honour recording the grant of citizenship to all its members at the same time, and a neat explanation is that the *ala* after distinguishing itself in the invasion was enfranchised by the censors.[12] (Claudius must have allowed his colleague to share the honour of naming new citizens, a constitutional pedantry typical of him.) Tancinus' tombstone in style and lettering is early, and can easily be dated to the reign of Claudius or Nero. The absence of *Dis Manibus* in the formulation supports this conclusion.

The question is unfortunately not quite so simple. Roman citizenship had once been granted en masse to a Spanish cavalry unit in 89 BC, but this battle honour is not attested again until the reign of Vespasian. Arguments from silence are risky, but at the moment no other regiment is known to have been thus honoured by the Julio-Claudian emperors. Moreover second-generation Roman citizens in Iberia sometimes used their father's cognomen in their filiation, rather than his praenomen (for example *Luci filius*), and the nomen *Vitellius* (borne by a woman) is also found at Caurium. Paul Holder has therefore argued that the regiment was decorated by Vespasian or his sons, so that Tancinus was not stationed at Bath, but only an unsuccessful visitor to the spa.[13]

Tancinus, or rather his executors, did not know the problem they were posing to modern scholars by their Roman habit of not dating tombstones.[14] Before reaching a conclusion, we may turn to another tombstone, a superbly carved altar of white marble which now stands behind railings in a reeking patch of weeds inside the Porta di San Paolo at Rome; once it stood beside the road to Ostia and named an officer who may – the odds are 50/50 – may have commanded Tancinus' regiment.

<2.09> *Rome, Via Ostiensis*

M(arcus) Stlaccius G(ai) f(ilius) Col(lina tribu)
Coranus
praef(ectus) fabrum, equo
publico ex quinque
decuriis, praef(ectus) coh(ortis) V
Bracar(um) Augustanorum
in Germania, trib(unus) mil(itum) leg(ionis) II
Aug(ustae), praef(ectus) equitum alae

[12] Maxfield 1981, 230–1.

[13] Holder 1980, 31.

[14] Dated tombstones tend to be 'late', the only British examples being *RIB* 1255 (perhaps AD 278) and III, 3045 (AD 258).

Hispanorum in Britannia,
donis militaribus donatus
corona murali hasta pura
sibi et
G(aio) Stlaccio Capitoni patri
G(aio) Stlaccio G(ai) f(ilio) Col(lina tribu) Capitoni fratri
L(ucio) Stlaccio G(ai) f(ilio) Col(lina tribu) Frontoni fratri
Claudiae Secundae uxori

ILS 2730

'Marcus Stlaccius Coranus, son of Gaius, of the *Collina* voting-tribe, aide-de-camp, equestrian (allotted) a public horse and a member of the five boards of jurors, prefect of the Fifth Cohort of Bracares Augustani in Germany, military tribune of the Second Legion Augusta and cavalry prefect of the Cavalry Regiment of Spaniards in Britain, decorated with Mural Crown and Untipped Spear, (built this tomb) for himself and Gaius Stlaccius Capito his father; Gaius Stlaccius Capito, son of Gaius, of the *Collina* voting-tribe, his brother; Lucius Stlaccius Capito, son of Gaius, of the *Collina* voting-tribe, his brother; and Claudia Secunda his wife.'

Coranus, like Julius Quadratus (**5.11**) and Maenius Agrippa (**5.12**), belonged to the equestrian élite which received a (notional) horse to serve in the cavalry of archaic Rome, an honour which in military terms was about as real as a modern British knighthood.[15] He does not explicitly say that his legionary tribunate was held in Britain (he might, for example, have been promoted to a cavalry command in the army of invasion), nor does he explicitly say where and when he was decorated. However, since he received the same decorations as another equestrian officer in the Second Legion Augusta, Anicius Maximus (**1.07**), it is quite likely that he too was decorated for his part in the invasion, perhaps while he was still a legionary tribune. He was certainly a prefect of cavalry in Britain, but he does not identify his *ala* explicitly, and we have two candidates: Tancinus' *ala Hispanorum Vettonum* (**2.08**) and the *ala I Hispanorum Asturum* (**3.05** and **9.35**). Perhaps there was only one 'Spanish' regiment in Britain at the time; but more likely, from the perspective of the Via Ostiensis, its full title was unknown or did not really matter.

Coranus' career strengthens the case for supposing that Tancinus' regiment distinguished itself, but does not confirm it. Many epigraphic questions can only be answered by balancing probabilities, but on balance it looks as if Tancinus did come to Britain in AD 43; the formulation of his tombstone suits this early date.[16] The legions meanwhile, like the cavalry, undoubtedly saw much fighting. In the Second Legion, the fates marked out Vespasian, to use Tacitus' phrase, and his senior officers like Anicius Maximus and possibly Coranus were decorated.[17]

[15] Other examples are Pertinax (**7.02**) and Antonius Gargilianus (**10.20**).
[16] Maxfield 1981, 231.
[17] Tacitus, *Agricola* 13.3, *monstratus fatis Vespasianus*. **1.07** (Maximus). **2.09** (Coranus).

The military emphasis soon shifted from the south to the Welsh Marches, where last-ditch resistance was led by Cunobelinus' son Caratacus. Even after he succumbed to the Roman armoured advance in AD 51, the Welsh tribes fought on. In AD 57, Nero appointed a new governor, Quintus Veranius, who had distinguished himself as the first governor of Lycia (in south-west Turkey) when it was annexed by Claudius. This entailed mountain warfare, which is why Veranius was chosen to complete the conquest of Wales, so Eric Birley argued, and further support was then provided by Arthur Gordon's identification of a large fragment of Veranius' own epitaph.[18] Its beginning is lost, and the detailed account of his five years in Lycia is fragmentary, but it concludes with his subsequent honours:

<2.10> *Pratolungo*

... propter quae auctore
[Ti(berio) Claudio Caesare Augusto Germanico] consul designatus in consulatu
nominatione
[eiusdem in locum ...]ni augur creatus in numerum patriciorum adlectus est
[curatori iudicio Neronis Augusti Germ]anici aedium sacrarum et operum locorumque
[publicorum statuam posuit equester] ordo et populus Romanus consentiente senatu ludis
[... ?factus est cum non p]etierit ab Augusto principe cuius liberalitatis erat minister
[legatus Neronis Augusti German]ici provinciae Britanniae in qua decessit

[Verania f(ilia) Q(uinti) Ve]rani vixit annis VI et mensibus X

Gordon 1952 (*AE* 1953, 251)

'... Therefore he was designated consul on the proposal of Tiberius Claudius Caesar Augustus Germanicus, and in his consulship (AD 49) by nomination of the same was created augur in place of [...]nus (*or* [...]nius) and adlected among the patricians. As Curator of sacred buildings and public works by decision of Nero Augustus Germanicus, a statue was erected in his honour by the equestrian order and the Roman people with the Senate's consent. ... games ... he was made, although he did not seek it from the august Emperor whose generosity he administered, the legate of Nero Augustus Germanicus of the province of Britain, in which he died. Verania, the daughter of Quintus Veranius, lived six years and ten months.'

Veranius' father had been a close friend of Germanicus, Nero's grandfather, the brother of Claudius, so this imperial favour is not surprising, but he justified it in Lycia. The augurship and patriciate were high social distinctions in the Emperor's gift, the patrician families being the oldest Roman aristocracy, and the augurs one

[18] Birley 1952. Gordon 1953 (reviewed by Oliver in *AJP* 75 (1954), 206–10).

of the four senior priesthoods. Cicero and Pliny (the Younger) were both proud of becoming augurs, and when Vespasian sent Julius Agricola to govern Britain, he likewise made him a patrician and a pontifex.[19] After his consulship, Veranius was prominent in Roman public life, but the detail depends on how the text is restored; the reference is probably to Nero's new amphitheatre and issue of public largesse (*congiarium*) in AD 57, which Tacitus dismisses as unworthy of historical record.[20] In this very full catalogue of achievement and honours, the mission to Britain is noted briefly at the very end. The reason is that it was an anticlimax: Veranius, who was now in his mid-40s, died within a year, after only a minor campaign against the Silures. In his will he claimed he would have 'conquered the province' had he lived two years more, but Tacitus is sceptical.[21]

Like Gloucester already, Wroxeter now became a legionary base. Two or three tombstones record the early presence of the Fourteenth Legion, since they antedate the Boudican revolt (in AD 60 or 61), when the legion received the further titles of 'Martial and Victorious' for defeating her (**1.04**). Here is the sobering epitaph of its Eagle-bearer:

<**2.11**> *Wroxeter (Viroconium)*

[T(itus) F]laminius T(iti filius) Pol(lia tribu) Fa[v(entia)]
[an]norum XXXXV stip(endiorum) XXII mil(es) leg(ionis)
[XII]II Gem(inae) militavi aq(uilifer), nunc hic s[u]m.
[Hoc] legite et felices vita plus min[us] e[ste:]
[d]i uva vini et aqua prohibent ubi
Ta[r]tar(a) aditis; vivite dum si[dus]
vitae dat tempus honeste

RIB 292+*add.*

'Titus Flaminius, son of Titus, of the *Pollia* voting-tribe, from Faventia, aged 45, of 22 years' service, a soldier of the Fourteenth Legion Gemina. I served as the Eagle-bearer, now here I am. Read this and be happy, whether more or less, in your lifetime. The gods prohibit you from the wine-grape and water when you enter Tartarus. Live honourably while your star gives you time for life.'

Like Saufeius (**2.04**), and even aristocrats like Lucius Vitellius, Aulus Plautius and Quintus Veranius, Flaminius has no distinguishing cognomen, but this is rare after the mid-first century. He comes from Cisalpine Gaul (Lombardy), the prime recruiting-ground of the western legions since the late Republic. His epitaph, somewhat damaged, is cut into the base which once carried his figure in high relief, but now

[19] Tacitus, *Agricola* 9.1 and 6.

[20] *Annals* xiii 31. Veranius' career is fully discussed by Birley 2005, 37–43.

[21] *Annals* xiv 29.

only his booted feet and the base of the eagle-standard remain. When it was found in 1861, the Canadian scholar John McCaul correctly understood AQ as *aq(uilifer)*, but his insight found no favour; even *RIB* understands AQ as *a(t)q(ue)*, but this contraction is unparalleled and linguistically unlikely; besides, why not write AC or ET instead? However, AQ is a standard abbreviation in lists of legionaries' names where space was limited, and it occurs in the epitaph[22] of another Eagle-bearer; its meaning would have been self-evident when Flaminius' figure was intact with its Eagle. His tombstone would have resembled that of a previous Eagle-bearer, Gnaeus Musius, when the legion was still at Mainz.[23] The author of his metrical epitaph intended it to be poignant: even the Regimental Sergeant-Major, so to speak, is now dust and dry ashes. There is nothing to drink in Hades.

Flaminius died before *c.* AD 61. With his 22 years' service, therefore, he must have waded ashore on D Day in AD 43, like this comrade also from north-east Italy:

<2.12> *Wroxeter (Viroconium)*

M(arcus) Petronius
L(uci) f(ilius) Men(enia tribu)
Vic(etia), ann(orum)
XXXVIII,
mil(es) leg(ionis)
XIIII Gem(inae)
militavit
ann(os) XVIII
sign(ifer) fuit
h(ic) s(itus) e(st)

RIB 294

'Marcus Petronius, son of Lucius, of the *Menenia* voting-tribe, from Vicetia (Vicenza), soldier of the Fourteenth Legion Gemina, served 18 years, was a standard-bearer, is buried here.'

This tombstone too is earlier than AD 61, which places Petronius' enlistment before AD 43. Like Saufeius (**2.04**) and Flaminius (**2.12**), he has no cognomen. Another sign of early date is the absence of *Dis Manibus*. The Twentieth Legion meanwhile, as we have seen, was probably at Kingsholm, Gloucester, and the Second by elimination (there are no inscriptions yet to prove it) had left Alchester for Exeter by *c.* AD 55. The remaining legion, the Ninth, was at Lincoln, where it has left five early tombstones; only one soldier has a cognomen, and there is no instance

[22] *CIL* viii 2782 (the Third Legion Augusta at Lambaesis).
[23] *ILS* 2341, illustrated as Éspérandieu 1907–66, No. 5790.

of *Dis Manibus*.[24] **2.04** has been quoted already; here is another, which was found in 1800 but subsequently lost:

<**2.13**> *Lincoln (Lindum)*

Q(uinti) Corneli
Q(uinti) f(ili) Cla(udia tribu) eq(uitis)
le(gionis) VIIII [(centuria)] Cassi
Martialis, an(norum)
XL stip(endiorum) XIX
h(ic) s(itus) e(st)

RIB 254

'(The monument) of Quintus Cornelius, son of Quintus, of the *Claudia* voting-tribe, trooper of the Ninth Legion, century of Cassius Martialis, aged 40, of 19 years' service, (who) is buried here.'

Cornelius' origin is not recorded, and his name is not distinctive. Like Saufeius, Flaminius and Petronius, he did not have a cognomen. He belonged to the legion's small cavalry detachment, only 120 men, one-quarter the size of an *ala*, whose names were carried on the books of their centuries (compare **5.35**). We may suspect that he survived his legion's defeat by Boudica by being on horseback. To understand this suspicion, and why those Colchester tombstones were toppled, we must turn to the internal politics and economy of the new province.

Businessmen and other civilians

London was founded by the Romans soon after the invasion, and prospered from its strategic location; on the eve of its destruction by Boudica in AD 60 or 61, Tacitus describes it as being, not a Roman *colonia* like Colchester, but 'very full of businessmen and commerce'.[25] Detail has been added to his vignette by the recent trove of writing-tablet fragments excavated in the Walbrook mud and silt beneath the Bloomberg site in the City. Roman London's first voices, as they have been called[26] since they were inscribed during the first half-century of Londinium, are waxed stylus writing-tablets of the usual type, thin rectangles of wood, usually silver fir (*abies alba*), recessed to take a smooth layer of black wax. The text was written into this with a needle-like stylus which exposed the pale wood underneath, fortunately for us, since the wax itself has now perished and only the cuts and bruises left in the wood can still be read. Among them is this fragment, the earliest dated document ever found in Britain:

---

[24] **2.04**, **2.13**, *RIB* 256 (Lucius Sempronius Flavinus), 257 and 260.

[25] *Annals* xiv 33, *copia negotiatorum et commeatuum maxime celebre*.

[26] Tomlin 2016.

<2.14> *London (Londinium)*

Nerone Claudio Caesare Augusto
 Germanico II L(ucio) Calpurnio Pisone
 co(n)s(ulibus) VI Idus Ianuarias
Tibullus Venusti l(ibertus) scripsi et dico me
 debere Grato <S>puri l(iberto) (denarios) CV ex{s} pretio
 mercis quae vendita et tradita <est>
 quam pecuniam ei reddere debeo
 eiue ad quem ea res pertinebit
 . . .

Tab. Lond. Bloomberg 44

'In the consulship of Nero Claudius Caesar Augustus Germanicus for the second time and of Lucius Calpurnius Piso, on the sixth day before the Ides of January (8 January AD 57). I, Tibullus the freedman of Venustus, have written and say that I owe Gratus the freedman of Spurius 105 *denarii* from the price of the merchandise which has been sold and delivered. This money I am due to repay him or the person whom the matter will concern ...'

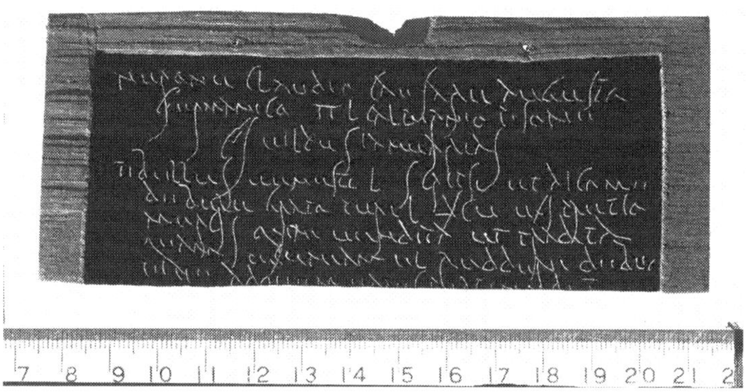

The date is neatly matched by the archaeological context, which is pre-Boudican (AD 53–60). One freedman writes to another to acknowledge a debt; they were probably acting as the agents or partners of their sometime owners, now their 'patrons', just as Florentinus, the slave of Sextus Cassius [...]tus, writes by order of his master that the latter has received two payments in respect of a farm.[27] In writing *exs* for *ex* ('from'), Tibullus is intruding *s* after *x* to reinforce the [ks] sound, something often found in British Latin.[28] The fragment breaks off with a formula found in other financial documents such as the Carlisle loan-note (**3.21**) and the London deed of

[27] *Tab. Lond. Bloomberg* 50, dated by the consuls of AD 85: *Florentinus Sex(ti) Cassi [...]ti seru[u]s scrips[i] iussu domini mei eum accepisse pensiones duas ex fundo ...*
[28] Smith 1983, 919–20. Other examples are **2.02**, **2.05** and **12.01**.

sale of a slave-girl (**10.38**). Tibullus in fact is writing the City's first-ever financial document, a distinction now greater than that of bearing the name of a famous Roman poet. Oddly enough, the two of them seem to be the only instances of the cognomen *Tibullus*: slaves often received a fanciful name which they retained as freedmen, and perhaps Venustus had literary tastes. Since he is identified by his cognomen, *Venustus*, not by his praenomen like Spurius, the patron of Gratus, he was probably not a Roman citizen; and if not, he cannot be the London contractor Marcus Rennius Venustus (**2.21**).

Within a few years of the conquest, London had become the business centre of the province, even if it was not yet the formal capital nor the only centre of power. The Arch of Claudius (**1.13**) recorded the conquest or surrender of at least eleven 'kings of Britain'. The Romans did not necessarily dispossess native rulers, if they were willing to submit without a struggle. Like other intelligent imperialists, they used 'indirect rule', since it was cheaper to make native authorities responsible for local law and order than to use expensive fighting troops as police. Kingdoms which had welcomed Roman intervention against the overbearing Catuvellauni were allowed to linger for a while like Red Indians on their reservations, notably the Iceni in East Anglia, the Brigantes in the north, and the Regini in Sussex and Hampshire. These latter were ruled by a 'client king', to use the modern term, whose capital was probably Noviomagus (Chichester). Here a guild of 'craftsmen', shipwrights perhaps, since they were honouring the god of water and the goddess of technology, erected a loyal dedication:

<**2.15**> *Chichester (Noviomagus)*

[N]eptuno et Minervae
templum
[pr]o salute do[mu]s divina[e]
[ex] auctoritat[e Ti(beri)] Claud(i)
[To]gidubni re[g(is) ?m]agni Brit(annorum)
[colle]gium fabror(um) et qui in eo
[sun]t d(e) s(uo) d(ederunt) donante aream
[?Pud]ente Pudentini fil(io)

RIB 91+*add.*

'To Neptune and Minerva a temple, for the welfare of the imperial house, by authority of Tiberius Claudius Togidubnus, great king of the Britons; given by the guild of craftsmen and those who are in it, from their own resources; the site given by Pudens son of Pudentinus'

This famous inscription is damaged in two crucial places. The king's first two names tell us that like Tirintius (**2.06**) he received Roman citizenship from Claudius, and

Tacitus comments in AD 98 that Cogidumnus (as he calls him) 'remained utterly loyal within living memory'. This at least is the reading of the single independent manuscript (*E*) of the *Agricola*, but a contemporary, ninth-century, editor (E^2) notes that *another* manuscript (now lost) read 'Togidumnus'. This, or rather 'Togidubnus', is a much more plausible Celtic name. It is eloquent of the internationalism of scholarship that this point was made by Charles Murgia, an American philologist of Italian descent working in California, and that we owe a still more important point to the Dutch archaeologist Jules Bogaers.[29] The Chichester inscription was always thought to give Togidubnus (let us now call him) the anomalous title of *rex et legatus Augusti*, client king and lieutenant of the Emperor, until Bogaers demonstrated that this reading is unfounded; instead, Togidubnus apparently received the very rare title of 'great king' (*rex magnus*), meaning only that he ruled over several tribes. Tacitus notes his loyalty to Rome, but sourly adds that it is 'ancient Roman practice for kings even to be agents of Roman rule'.[30] The Romans, like the Hanoverian kings in Scotland, were turning tribal chieftains into landowners loyal to the central government: the great Flavian villa built at Fishbourne, on the site of an early military base, has been attractively identified as a palace for Togidubnus in his old age. Nothing is known of his previous career – like the Jewish prince Herod Agrippa, had he been sent to Rome by a royal grandfather to be educated? – but he was evidently chosen by Claudius to succeed Verica, the king whose expulsion had given him the excuse of intervening in Britain.[31]

A rare discovery at Fishbourne reveals that Togidubnus was not the only quisling. A plain gold ring of mid first-century date carries its owner's name cut neatly in reverse within the flat oval bezel:

<2.16> *Fishbourne*

Ti(beri) Claudi Catuari

Britannia 27 (1996), 455, No. 48, with Tomlin 1997(b)

'(The seal) of Tiberius Claudius Catuarus.'

The name *Catuarus* is Celtic, but his full name proclaims that he was a Roman citizen. But more than this: at this date a gold ring would have been rightfully worn only by a Roman *eques*, a gentleman who possessed a minimum capital of 100,000

29 Murgia 1977, 339. Bogaers 1979.

30 Tacitus, *Agricola* 14.1, *quaedam civitates Cogidumno regi donatae (is ad nostram usque memoriam fidissimus mansit), vetere ac iam pridem recepta populi Romani consuetudine, ut haberet instrumenta servitutis et reges.*

31 He may even have been the Catuvellaunian prince Togodumnus who at first resisted the invasion (Hind 2007, 98–100).

denarii, more than a legionary soldier would have earned in four hundred years. So Catuarus cannot be just an enfranchised auxiliary like Tirintius (**2.06**); he was a very rich man, almost certainly a local magnate who sided with the Romans like Togidubnus, and was rewarded with citizenship by Claudius. We might call him a quisling, but a kinder comparison would be with an amenable Indian maharajah, honoured by the Queen Empress with a knighthood.

The Romans like other imperialists prided themselves on their loyalty to submissive allies: for centuries such alliances had duly entangled them with new enemies who could be subdued in their turn. But this policy, so successful in the south of Britain, received a severe check in the east, in the kingdom of the Iceni, because of another imperial tradition, rapacity: in the words attributed to a Caledonian chieftain by Tacitus, 'they plunder, they butcher, they ravish, and call it by the lying name of empire.'[32] Caesar, although he does not say so, was thought to have invaded Britain for the sake of its pearls, silver and gold, even if one of his officers told Cicero that they had not found a grain of silver in the island.[33] Claudius, by committing one-seventh of the entire Roman army to the invasion, was making an enormous investment, and it is not surprising that he sought immediate dividends. Britain was undoubtedly rich in minerals, the 'reward of victory', Tacitus calls them.[34] Its abundant lead was a by-product of silver refining, which is why the lead mines are called 'silver works' (**2.17**), and an idea of the scale involved can be gained from looking at the Great Bath at Bath: it is lined with 42 sheets of lead, weighing 8½ tons. Many lead ingots or 'pigs' have also been found, which can be dated by their moulded inscriptions:

<**2.17**> *Mendip Hills, Somerset*

Ti(berius) Claud(ius) Caesar Aug(ustus) p(ontifex) m(aximus) tr(ibunicia) p(otestate) VIIII imp(erator) XVI de Britan(nicis)

RIB II.1, 2404.1

'Tiberius Claudius Caesar Augustus, pontifex maximus, in the ninth year of his tribunician power (AD 49), acclaimed Emperor 16 times. (Lead) from the British (mines).'

This ingot is now lost, and the reading depends on Leland (1544). It is conventionally expanded in the nominative case (explicit only in *Caesar*), but might have been genitive like the next:

32 Tacitus, *Agricola* 30, *auferre trucidare rapere falsis nominibus imperium … appellant* (trans. Birley).

33 Suetonius, *Divus Iulius* 47; Cicero, *ad fam.* vii 7.1, with *ad. Att.* iv 16.7 (not one *scripulum*, 1/24th of an ounce).

34 Tacitus, *Agricola* 12, *fert Britannia aurum et argentum et alia metalla, pretium victoriae.* Ogilvie and Richmond 1967, Appendix 4.

<**2.18**> *near Stockbridge, Hants*

(i) *moulded on top*: Neronis Aug(usti) ex K(alendis) Ian(uariis) IIII co(n)s(ulis) Brit(annicum)
(ii) *moulded on front*: [e]x K(alendis) Iul(iis) p(ontificis) m(aximi) co(n)s(ulis)
(iii) *stamped on the back*: ex argent(ariis) G(ai) N[i]pi Asca[ni] + + +

RIB II.1, 2404.3

'British (lead) of Nero Augustus, consul for the fourth time (AD 60), from 1 January.' (ii) 'pontifex maximus and consul, from 1 July' (iii) 'From the silver works, (by agency) of Gaius Nipius Ascanius.'

These are both ingots of Mendips lead, which will appear later at Bath as a writing-material (**11.06**); the second ingot was lost perhaps on its way to the south-coast ports. The inscriptions are little more than dates, that of **2.17** apparently up-dated half-way through the year, but these dates are significant: the mines were producing raw silver – and lead, of course – within six years of the army landing. The name of the lessee Gaius Nipius Ascanius also occurs on a later ingot (**3.12**), this time from the Flintshire (Clwyd) mines, and he was evidently working the mines under concession. But if Seneca's enemies are to be believed, Ascanius was not the only vulture flapping close behind the eagles of Rome.

The philosopher and essayist Seneca, whose political influence and suicide have been mentioned already, was a brilliant Latin stylist. A wayward critic called his style incoherent, 'sand without lime', but the critic was the emperor Caligula, whose own sister Agrippina nonetheless chose Seneca to tutor her son Nero.[35] Caligula's criticism is misattributed to Nero by John Aubrey in his *Brief Life* of the Oxford don Ralph Kettell (1563–1643), who 'was wont to say that Seneca writes as a Boare does pisse, *scilicet* by jirkes.' When Nero succeeded Claudius, his tutor graduated from coining epigrams and antithesis to writing the Emperor's speeches (his pupil preferred poetry) and even to deciding their content. In the process Seneca became a multi-millionaire, despite being a Stoic moralist of austere personal habits. According to his enemies, he had ten million *denarii* invested in Britain: this would have been more than thirty tons of silver coin, enough money to have fed, clothed and paid the army of occupation for a year. It was Seneca's decision to call in his loans which contributed to the disaster of Boudica's revolt, again according to his enemies, but the true cause was the harsh, arbitrary nature of Roman rule, of which this would have been a symptom. 'The British readily endure taxation', Tacitus famously comments, 'provided it is fair.'[36]

[35] Suetonius, *Gaius 53.2, harenam sine calce.*

[36] *Agricola*, 13.1, *Britanni dilectum ac tributa et iniuncta imperii munia impigre obeunt, si iniuriae absint.* What Dio (62.2.1) states as fact, Tacitus (*Annals* xiii 42) puts into the mouth of an enemy of Seneca, but if true, it may reflect the idea attributed to Nero of abandoning Britain (Suetonius, *Nero* 18).

The great revolt

The story also is well known. Prasutagus, client king of the Iceni, died and the imperial procurator Decianus Catus annexed his kingdom brutally. This triggered the great revolt led by his widow Boudica (the 'Boadicea' of modern legend), whose name is the Celtic equivalent of Victoria, and it shook Roman rule to its foundations. The Roman veterans at Colchester were massacred and the Ninth Legion intervened disastrously, its legate Petillius Cerialis fleeing for his life with the cavalry contingent, which probably included Cornelius (**2.13**). Meanwhile the governor Suetonius Paulinus was campaigning in North Wales and was forced to abandon London and Verulamium (St Albans) to their fate, before he could give battle successfully with a diminished field army.[37] This was largely the Fourteenth Legion, and although there is no direct epigraphic evidence of these events, it can be seen by comparing Vettius Valens' inscription (**1.04**) with Flaminius' tombstone (**2.12**) that the legion now acquired the extra titles 'Martial' and 'Victorious'. It was 'famous for suppressing the revolt in Britain', says Tacitus.[38] His narrative of the revolt and its aftermath, which must incorporate the memories and prejudices of his father-in-law Agricola, a legionary tribune at the time and favoured by Suetonius Paulinus, can be checked against an extraordinary survival. This is the tombstone of the next procurator of Britain, Julius Classicianus, the official expected to reform the abuses which had prompted the revolt, whose report prompted the recall of Suetonius Paulinus. Classicianus evidently died in post, since he was buried in London, which by implication had now become the provincial capital. Two fragments of his epitaph survive because centuries later his large handsome tombstone, altar-shaped, was cannibalised for the Roman walls of London:

<2.19> *London (Londinium)*

Dis
[M]anibus
[G(ai) Iul(i) G(ai) f(ili) F]ab(ia tribu) Alpini Classiciani
[...]
proc(uratoris) provinc(iae) Brit[anniae]
Iulia Indi f(ilia) Pacata I[nduta?]
uxor

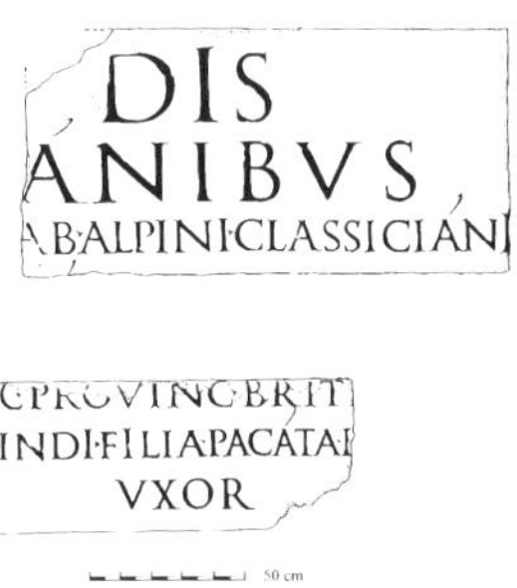

RIB 12+*add.*, with Grasby and Tomlin 2002

'To the Shades of the Dead (and) of Gaius Julius Alpinus (*or* Alpinius) Classicianus, son of Gaius, of the *Fabia* voting-tribe [...] Procurator of the Province of Britain. Iulia Pacata Induta(?), daughter of Indus, his wife, (set this up).'

---

[37] Tacitus, *Annals* xiv 31–9.

[38] *Histories* ii 11, *praecipui fama quartadecumani, rebellione Britanniae compressa.* It is uncertain whether the detachment of the Twentieth, which also took part, now gained the titles *Valeria Victrix* for the whole legion.

The upper piece was found in 1852. The contemporary antiquary Charles Roach Smith thought that 'Classicianus' might actually be the procurator, a view that Hübner, when he published the stone in 1873, said 'needs no refutation'; and according to R G Collingwood in 1928, was 'obviously wrong'.[39] Collingwood was forced to recant when the lower piece was found in 1935, an object lesson against the well-balanced judgement – or is it the professional caution and pessimism? – of epigraphists.

The lettering and layout, which are superb, lay emphasis on the *Dis Manibus* formula, which has been significantly absent from the tombstones quoted so far; this is an early instance, but it soon became standard, so that after the early second century it was abbreviated to D M. That the *a* of *Manibus* was 'long' is indicated by an *apex*, an acute accent, a feature found in the Vindolanda Tablets but almost unique in the stone inscriptions of Roman Britain.

The names *Gaius Iulius* suggest that an ancestor was enfranchised by Julius Caesar, probably in Gaul, since the names *Alpinus* and *Alpinius* are found there. In AD 69, a Julius Alpinus was a leader of the Helvetii, and the Alpinius brothers were among the leading Treveri. Another Treveran is Julius Classicus, who in AD 69 was prefect of an *ala* when he rebelled against Rome; he was of 'royal' descent, and may have been a kinsman of Classicianus. This likelihood has been enhanced by one of the Bloomberg London writing-tablets, which shows that he was prefect of the Sixth Cohort of Nervii in the early AD 60s, perhaps by the recommendation of Classicianus. It was surely one of the eight auxiliary cohorts drafted in from Germany after Boudica was defeated.[40] Classicianus also would have commanded Roman auxiliary units in his earlier career, details of which were recorded on the missing middle block; all that survives of the text here is another *apex*. The most illuminating detail is the name of his wife, the daughter of Indus (without qualification) who must be the Treveran grandee who raised his own cavalry regiment in AD 21 at Trier to suppress a Gallic uprising.[41] This became the *ala Indiana* (**2.20**). It follows that Classicianus was of aristocratic but provincial origin, and married into a provincial family which supported Roman rule. His different perspective may have made him more sympathetic than Suetonius Paulinus was to the recently conquered Britons, but then Paulinus was an Italian who had been fighting far from home with his back to the wall.

---

39 *CIL* vii 30, *quod non eget refutatione*. (Hübner's *CIL* vii is the forerunner of *RIB*.) Collingwood 1928, 171, No. 6 (taking [F]AB to be an abbreviated nomen).

40 *Tab. Lond. Bloomberg* 33, noting Tacitus, *Ann.* xiv 38 (the eight cohorts); a connection between Classicus and Classicianus had already been suggested by Wightman (1985, 68) and Birley (2005, 304).

41 Tacitus, *Annals* iii 42.

Recovery

The army's losses in Britain were made good by a transfusion of legionaries and auxiliary infantry from the Rhineland; three cohorts, including the Nervii commanded by Classicus, are named in the Bloomberg London tablets.[42] The transfusion included one thousand cavalry, which would probably have been two cavalry regiments (*alae*). One of these may have replaced the Thracians at Cirencester:

<2.20> *Cirencester (Corinium Dobunnorum)*

Dannicus eq<u>es alae
Indian(ae), tur(ma) Albani,
stip(endiorum) XVI, cives(!) Raur(icus)
cur(averunt) Fulvius Natalis it(!)
Fl[av]ius Bitucus ex testame(nto)
h(ic) s(itus) e(st)

RIB 108

'Dannicus, trooper of the *ala Indiana*, troop of Albanus, of 16 years' service, a tribesman of the Raurici, lies buried here. Fulvius Natalis and Flavius Bitucus had this erected under his will.'

Here is another instance of the Vulgarism *cives* as in **2.08**, but *it* for *et* is only a stone-cutter's mistake. Dannicus' regiment had nothing to do with India; like the *ala Sebosiana* (**3.14**), the *ala Petriana* (**4.09**) and the *ala Tampiana* (**4.05**), or indeed Skinner's Horse in British India, it was named after its first commander, the Julius Indus just mentioned.[43] After quelling the Gallic revolt, this crack unit served in Upper Germany, which is where it recruited Dannicus, since he came from the territory of Augusta Rauricorum, Augst in Switzerland; it was beginning to lose its original ethnic character by recruiting locally. Since one of the executors is *Fl[av]ius*, not *Fu[lvius]* (the second letter, although damaged, begins with a vertical stroke), the tombstone must be Flavian; he was probably a veteran discharged after Vespasian's accession (AD 69).

The army licked its wounds, and Suetonius Paulinus was replaced by the peaceable Petronius Turpilianus, a pledge of continuity perhaps, since he was a nephew of the first governor, Aulus Plautius. Life soon returned to London and Verulamium, to judge by another Bloomberg London tablet, this well-dated contract:

---

42 *Tab. Lond. Bloomberg* 48 (Vangiones) and 55 (Lingones).

43 For *alae* named after their commanders, see E Birley 1988, 368–84.

<2.21> *London (Londinium)*

P(ublio) Mario Ce(lso) L(ucio) Afinio Gallo co(n)s(ulibus) XII Kal(endas) Novembr(es)
M(arcus) Renn[iu]s Venustus me condux{s}isse
a G(aio) Valerio Proculo ut intra
Idus Novembres perferret a [[Londi]]
Verulamio penoris onera viginti
in singula (denarii) quadrans vecturae
ea condicione ut per me mora
(asses) I Londinium quod si ulnam
om[n]e[m] ...
. . .

Tab. Lond. Bloomberg 45

'In the consulship of Publius Marius Celsus and Lucius Afinius Gallus, on the twelfth day before the Kalends of November (21 October AD 62). I, Marcus Rennius Venustus, (have written and say that) I have contracted with Gaius Valerius Proculus that he bring from Verulamium by the Ides of November (13 November) twenty loads of provisions at a transport-charge of one-quarter *denarius* for each, on condition that … one *as* … to London; but if … the whole …'

The writer accidentally omitted the verb(s) that governed the infinitive (*conduxsisse*) in line 2, and in line 4 he began to write 'London' by mistake for 'Verulamium'. He does not specify the size of a 'load', but there were 16 *asses* to the *denarius*, so the charge would have been four *asses* per load; to put this into context, remember that a legionary was paid ten *asses* a day before stoppages.[44] The word for 'provisions', *penus* (genitive *penoris*), is that used to describe a quality of fish sauce (**11.27**). The remaining lines are badly preserved, but the 'condition' seems to have been that one *as*, one-quarter of the fee per load, would be retained until the whole delivery had been made. The most striking detail is the date. Tacitus refers the destruction of Verulamium and London, with the loss of 70,000 lives, to the year AD 61, but most modern scholars have preferred the earlier date of AD 60.[45] This document supports their conclusion; but even so, since it was written in October AD 62, it suggests that both cities made a rapid recovery.

By about AD 66 Nero felt confident enough to withdraw the pugnacious Fourteenth Legion for service in the east, and when the great Jewish revolt broke out in the same year, he sent Vespasian to suppress it: the former legate of the Second Legion Augusta possessed the necessary combination of military competence and social obscurity. He could be trusted to suppress the revolt (which he did), but not to be the rival of Nero. His chance came in AD 69 when Nero was dead, in

[44] Tacitus, *Annals* i 17.
[45] Birley 2005, 43–52.

the famous Year of the Four Emperors, when the others were Galba (a sometime member of Claudius' staff in Britain), Otho (Vettius Valens' governor of Lusitania), and Vitellius (a son of Claudius' vicegerent). Vespasian was the candidate of the eastern and Danubian legions, and when they had installed him, Rome was ruled by another successful usurper who needed military glory. This was still available in Britain with its open frontiers where, in Tacitus' words, there was now 'a succession of great generals and splendid armies, and the hopes of our enemies dwindled'.[46]

[46] *Agricola*, 17.1, *magni duces, egregii exercitus, minuta hostium spes.*

3

THE CONQUEST OF UPLAND BRITAIN

The legions

Britain had played little part in the Year of the Four Emperors. The Fourteenth Legion arrived too late to fight for Otho at the first battle of Cremona, and was sent back to Britain by Vitellius, where it nursed a grudge against him. An inscription from Spain, too fragmentary to be quoted here, details the remarkable career of one of its tribunes, Marcus Cornelius Nigrinus Curiatius Maternus, whom Vespasian made a Senator in AD 73/4, no doubt as a reward for his support in AD 69.[1] Detachments of the other three legions fought unsuccessfully for Vitellius against the Flavians at the second battle of Cremona, but after his defeat the army in Britain swung round towards Vespasian because of his distinguished command of the Second Legion under Claudius.[2] In reporting this, Tacitus implies that the lead was taken by the Second Legion Augusta; whether or not it really remembered Vespasian a quarter-century later, the career of its second-in-command is suggestive:

<3.01> *Pisidian Antioch (western Turkey)*

[L(ucio) Antistio L(uci) f(ilio)]
Gal(eria tribu) Rustico co(n)s(uli),
leg(ato) imp(eratoris) Caesaris [[Domi-]]
[[tiani]] Aug(usti)
pro pr(aetore) provinciarum
Capp(adociae) Galat(iae) Ponti Pisid(iae)
Paphl(agoniae) Arm(eniae) Min(oris) Lyca(oniae), praef(ecto)
aer(arii) Sat(urni), proco(n)s(uli) provinc(iae) Hisp(aniae)
[ul]t(erioris) Baetic(ae), leg(ato) divi Vesp(asiani) et divi Titi
et imp(eratoris) Caesaris [[Domitiani]] Aug(usti)
[[Germanici]] leg(ionis) VIII Aug(ustae), cura-
tori viarum Aureliae et Corne-

---

[1] *AE* 1973, 283 = Alföldy and Halfmann 1973, who identify him with the menacing legate of Syria in AD 97 (Pliny, *ep.* ix 13.11).

[2] Tacitus, *Histories* iii 22; 44.

liae, adlecto inter praetorios
a divo Vespasiano et divo Tito,
donis militaribus donato ab iisdem
corona murali cor(ona) vallari
corona aurea vexillis III
hastis puris III, trib(uno) mil(itum) leg(ionis) II
[A]ug(ustae), X vir stlitibus iudicand(is),
[p]atrono coloniae quod
[ind]ustrie prospexit annon(ae)

AE 1925, 126

'To Lucius Antistius Rusticus, son of Lucius, of the *Galeria* voting-tribe: consul, praetorian legate of the Emperor Caesar Domitian (*erased*) Augustus of the provinces of Cappadocia, Galatia, Pontus, Pisidia, Paphlagonia, Armenia Minor and Lycaonia; prefect of the Public Treasury, proconsul of the province of Further Spain (Baetica), legate of the deified Vespasian and the deified Titus and the Emperor Caesar Domitian (*erased*) Augustus Germanicus (*erased*) of the Eighth Legion Augusta, curator of the Aurelian and Cornelian Roads, enrolled among senators of praetorian rank by the deified Vespasian and the deified Titus; awarded military decorations by them, the Mural Crown, the Rampart Crown, the Golden Crown, three Banners and three Untipped Spears, military tribune of the Second Legion Augusta, member of the Board of Ten for judging lawsuits, patron of the Colony, (in honour of) his attention to the corn supply.'

This is the beginning of a long inscription from the home town of Anicius Maximus (**1.07**) and Caristanius Fronto (**1.11**), which honours the provincial governor for his decisive action in a food-shortage under Domitian whose name and title of *Germanicus* have been erased because his 'memory' was formally condemned after his death, a fate later shared by Commodus and some third-century emperors. The inscription also quotes the letter in which Antistius Rusticus forbade profiteering and imposed a price of one *denarius* to the *modius* (bushel) of corn: the famine price of *Revelations* 6.6, 'a measure of wheat for a penny', and perhaps the same famine. His career is given in reverse order, beginning with the minor magistracy at Rome of chairing a jury. Other inscriptions date his governorship of Baetica (Andalusia), his native province, to AD 84 and his consulship to AD 90.[3] The inscription from Pisidian Antioch honours him as the most important governor in Roman Asia Minor, general of a two-legion army on the upper Euphrates, but from a British perspective the start of his career is of greater interest, when he was the 'senatorial' tribune of the Second Legion Augusta and thus its second-in-command. This would have been in AD 69, since he was promoted in the censorship of AD 73–4 like Maternus of the Fourteenth, and also received decorations appropriate to the legate of a legion, above his rank, no doubt for 'political and public services', the part he

[3] Birley 2005, 280.

played in the British army's change of loyalties. Both Rusticus and Maternus enjoyed splendid careers under Vespasian and his sons which ended abruptly: Rusticus died in the office just mentioned, and his widow carried home the urn containing his ashes; while Maternus was governor of Syria when Domitian died, and after an ambiguous interval was out of office so quickly (whether by death or dismissal, we know not) that his successor had not even arrived.[4]

Also in AD 69, when the Danubian legions invaded Italy to make Vespasian emperor, two veterans of the Boudican revolt declared their support; they were Agricola and Petillius Cerialis. The cavalry of the Ninth had saved Cerialis' life in AD 60 or 61; he now commanded a cavalry column in the final advance on Rome and displayed 'the lack of caution which was his hallmark', to quote his modern biographer. A more charitable judgement is that he was energetic and 'had (like Caesar) a capacity for extricating himself from the difficult situations into which lack of caution and foresight might lead him'. Perhaps he embodied the self-confidence and aggressiveness typical of Roman expansion which so often brought success.[5] On this occasion, however, a mishap ensued, but Cerialis' close connection with Vespasian (he was probably his son-in-law) brought him two plum appointments, first to crush the Batavian Revolt on the lower Rhine, and then to renew the offensive in Britain. Agricola, who had meanwhile been recruiting legionaries in North Italy, now returned to Britain as one of Cerialis' four lieutenants, the legate of the Twentieth Legion. This legion had replaced the Fourteenth at Wroxeter, as we can deduce from its only gravestone there:

<3.02> *Wroxeter (Viroconium)*

G(aius) Mannius
G(ai) f(ilius) Pol(lia tribu) Secu-
ndus Pollen(tia)
mil(es) leg(ionis) XX
an<n>oru<m> LII
stip(endiorum) XXXI
ben(eficiarius) leg(ati) pr(aetorii)
h(ic) s(itus) e(st)

RIB 293+*add.*

'Gaius Mannius Secundus, son of Gaius, of the *Pollia* voting-tribe, from Pollentia, soldier of the Twentieth Legion, aged 52, with 31 years of service; seconded to the staff of the legionary legate. He is buried here.'

[4] Martial, *ep.* 9.30 (the return of Rusticus' urn). Alföldy and Halfmann 1973 (Maternus).

[5] Respectively Birley 1973, 183, amplified in Birley 2005, 66; Wightman 1970, 45; Goldsworthy 2003, 164–73 ('On Campaign').

Like the tombstone of Longinus (**2.02**), this is surmounted by a pair of lions. The odd-looking ANORV (for *annorum*) is phonetic: *-nn-* and *-n-* would sound almost the same, and the final *-m* was so lightly sounded as to be virtually omitted. Secundus, who came from north Italy, had served longer than the usual 25 or 26 years after which a legionary was discharged, no doubt because he had been promoted to the staff; his title of *beneficiarius* means that he owed this promotion to the favour (*beneficium*) of the officer concerned. This was the *legatus praetorius*, a rare synonym for the 'legionary legate', so called since he was always an ex-praetor. He may even have been Agricola himself, but it is also possible that Secundus, as an administrator in his 50s, did not actually accompany the legion on active service in the north (**3.21**).

Vespasian's 'forward policy' in Britain entailed his decision to restore the garrison to four legions. The Second Legion Adiutrix had been formed in AD 69 or 70 from the Adriatic fleet based at Ravenna which had deserted Vitellius for Vespasian; hence the legion's Civil War title of *Pia Fidelis* ('dutiful and loyal'). Its other title, *Adiutrix* ('auxiliary'), tactfully recalls its non-legionary origins. This legion spent only fifteen years in Britain, during the flood-tide of the Flavian advance and its first ebb, but it has left more than a dozen tombstones at its two successive bases. The first was Lincoln, where it replaced the Ninth:

<3.03> *Lincoln (Lindum)*

T(itus) Valerius T(iti) f(ilius)
Cla(udia tribu) Pudens Sav(aria)
mil(es) leg(ionis) II A(diutricis) p(iae) f(idelis)
(centuria) Dossenni
Proculi, a(nnorum) XXX
aera [V]I, h(eres) d(e) s(uo) p(osuit)
h(ic) s(itus) e(st)

RIB 258

'Titus Valerius Pudens, son of Titus, of the *Claudia* voting-tribe, from Savaria, soldier of the Second Legion Adiutrix Dutiful and Loyal in the century of Dossennius Proculus, aged 30, of six years' service; his heir set this up at his own expense; he lies here.'

The tool carved at the base of the tombstone is a *dolabra*, the pioneer's axe used for clearing ground and entrenching, but in the gable above is the trident of Neptune between two dolphins (compare **5.07**), an allusion to the legion's naval origin. Pudens came from Savaria, now Szombathely in Hungary, where Claudius founded a veteran *colonia* which shared his own voting-tribe of *Claudia*; the Ravenna fleet was recruited from the Danubian provinces, a foretaste of their military potential which reached its climax in the third century (compare **13.04**), when they provided whole legions, the Praetorian Guard, and even emperors.

The Ninth Legion was advanced to a new fortress at Eboracum (York), Cerialis' compliment to his old legion, which must have played a major role in the conquest of the largest tribe in northern Britain, the Brigantes. York remained a legionary fortress throughout the Roman period, and in the third century it also became the capital of the new northern province, Lower Britain; two emperors even died here on campaign, Septimius Severus in AD 211, and Constantius I in AD 306. Here is a much earlier tombstone:

<3.04> *York (Eboracum)*

L(ucius) Duccius
L(uci filius) Volt(inia tribu) Rufi-
nus Vien(na)
signif(er) leg(ionis) VIIII
an(norum) XXIIX
h(ic) s(itus) e(st)

RIB 673

'Lucius Duccius Rufinus, son of Lucius, of the *Voltinia* voting-tribe, from Vienne; a standard-bearer of the Ninth Legion, aged 28. He is buried here.'

This is a first-century inscription, erected soon after the legion arrived in *c.* AD 71, to judge by the absence of *Dis Manibus* and the use of the H S E formula. Rufinus holds the battle standard of his century or 'company', and carries what looks like a briefcase; it is probably a block of writing-tablets, whether his last will and testament or the company accounts which he kept. Like many legionaries in Britain, he came from southern Gaul; like Cominius Severus (**4.03**), Valerius Iullus (**5.44**) and Maximius Gaetulicus (**6.37**), specifically from Vienne in the Rhône valley (not Vienna, whose Roman name was *Vindobona*).[6]

A legion at Caerleon

Cerialis advanced as far as Carlisle (Luguvalium), since trees felled in the winter of AD 72/73 were used to build the earliest fort there. He then returned to Rome for a second consulship in AD 74, while his successor, Sextus Iulius Frontinus, secured the western flank. In South Wales the tribe of the Silures, having successfully resisted earlier attempts at conquest, now succumbed; a tribal capital was organised at Venta

[6] Another legionary of the Twentieth also came from Vienne (*RIB* 525). According to Forni 1953 (164, 174, 181, 189), it is the single most frequent origin in Gallia Narbonensis, with 30 legionaries in all.

(Caerwent) east of the new legionary base at Isca (Caerleon) on the River Usk. One of the tribunes' houses in the centre of the fortress underlies the Roman Legionary Museum, and it is just possible that we know the career, but not the name, of its first occupant. He would have distinguished himself during the Flavian advance:

<**3.05**> *Ilipa (Alcala del Rio, just north of Seville)*

[*two lines lost*]
in Britan[nia praef(ecto) coh(ortis)]
II Vasconum equit(atae), [trib(uno) mi]-
litum legionis II Aug(ustae), praef(ecto)
alae I Asturum, donis donato
corona murali et coronis
aureis IIII item vexillo et hastis
puris V, honorato ab exerci-
tibus in quibus militavit bigis
auratis et statuis equestribus, Q(uintus) Fulvius Euchir
IIIIIIvir Aug(ustalis)
amico bene merenti

ILS 2712

'To [... and] in Britain prefect of the Second Cohort of Vascones part-mounted, military tribune of the Second Legion Augusta, prefect of the First Cavalry Regiment of Asturians; decorated with Wall Crown, four Gold Crowns, also with Banner and five Untipped Spears; honoured by the armies in which he served with a gilded chariot and equestrian statues. Quintus Fulvius Euchir, *sevir Augustalis*, to his well-deserving friend.'

This inscription (now lost) comes from the heart of Baetica, the home-province of Antistius Rusticus (**3.01**). It was the richest and most romanised province of Roman Spain, and it was oil-rich: the fired clay of Baetica is a common site-find in Britain, in thick sherds of the globular Dressel 20 amphora, in which Andalusian olive oil was exported. It was also the home-province of Trajan and his cousin Hadrian, the first emperors who were not Italians by birth, although of Italian descent. The career of this nameless officer is not explicitly dated, and widely divergent dates have been suggested, but there is circumstantial evidence. His military decorations are so lavish compared with those of Anicius Maximus (**1.07**), a more senior officer in the same legion, that they must have been accumulated on three or four occasions. Since he was honoured by two armies, but all three of his equestrian commands were held in Britain, it follows that he must have come here with the Second Cohort of Vascones from another army. This was evidently in Germany. The Vascones were the Basques of north-eastern Spain. Galba, when he usurped the throne in AD 68, raised auxiliary cohorts of Vascones; their prefects, like most of his appointments at this time, would have been local gentry. These cohorts distinguished themselves in the Rhineland soon after, at the end of AD 69, when German rebels surprised and nearly destroyed a force of legionaries trying to raise the siege of Vetera; it was only saved by the opportune arrival of the Vascones.[7] The Second Cohort subsequently belonged to the British army, since it is listed here in AD 105 by the Sydenham diploma[8] and in AD 122 by the Brigetio diploma (**5.04**). It bears the battle honour *civium Romanorum*, which was surely awarded for its feat of arms in the Rhineland, when its prefect would have been decorated. The cohort would then have helped Cerialis crush the Batavian Revolt, and would have been one of the units which accompanied him to Britain in AD 71. In the continuous campaigning of the AD 70s, its anonymous prefect was promoted twice within the same army, no doubt because it wanted to retain him; his further decorations indicate as much. Yet his previous (Rhineland) army still remembered him; by implication his services had been extraordinary, and if he had indeed saved a legion, this is not surprising.

It was an unusual career, so unusual that the authenticity of this inscription has been doubted. The scale of decorations is unparalleled for the recipient's equestrian rank, and (still more disturbing) a chariot-statue (*biga*) is not attested otherwise as a military decoration: it was a civic honour granted to local benefactors in Italy and Africa, most often for their generosity in giving gladiatorial games.[9] But if this is an eighteenth-century forgery (it was found in 1767, and an impression made from it was available to the nineteenth-century editor), it displays astonishing command of detail, not to say successful guesswork: evidence that the Vascones and the Asturians served in Britain would not have been available at the time. So the inscription is worth including, but with a question mark.

In the courtyard of that tribune's house at Caerleon was a well, in which was found an ink writing-tablet like those from Carlisle (**3.14**) and Vindolanda (**4.17**), which is the earliest of all manuscripts from Wales. It is a Roman military memorandum written across the grain of a stiff wood shaving used like paper. Unfortunately it is too fragmentary to be transcribed here; it is only the right-hand portion of a note of military assignments, the ends of lines apparently referring to detachments being sent to get pay and timber.[10] This scrap of 'paper' survived in the waterlogged depths of the well, which also preserved a bronze pan with handle (*trulla*), part of a soldier's mess-kit. It carried an unusual range of stamps and graffiti:

<3.06> *Caerleon (Isca)*

First the maker's stamp: Maturus f(ecit)

'Maturus made (this)'.

---

[7] Tacitus, *Histories* iv 33–4.

[8] *RIB* II.1, 2401.2.

[9] Zelazowski 1997. Maxfield 1981, 271, segregates it as a forgery.

[10] *Britannia* 17 (1986), 450, No. 84, *[... ad opin]ionem peten(dam) ... [... ma]teriarum.*

Then a second stamp: Ala I Th(racum)

'The First Cavalry Regiment of Thracians'.

RIB II.2, 2415.39

This is the unit already seen at Colchester (**2.02**) and Cirencester (**2.07**), where it was replaced by the *ala Indiana* (**2.20**). What was it now doing at Caerleon? There are various explanations, including the possibility that it was not there at all, the pan having been 'borrowed' by a legionary. But Thracian cavalry is also found at the legionary bases of Gloucester (**2.05**) and Wroxeter (**2.06**), and the First Cavalry Regiment had previously been associated with the Twentieth Legion at Colchester (**2.02**), so it is likely that it was now associated with the Second at Caerleon in the initial conquest of South Wales.

The owner's name is scratched in wavering cursive letters: *Lucca*. This is a Celtic name, not Thracian, but by now the regiment had lost its founder-members. However, to complicate matters, this is a woman's name, for we know another Lucca, the daughter of Lucco the Dobunnian (**4.11**). Underneath the handle, there is a crudely punched numeral: LI, '51'. An *ala* numbered about 500 men, and the army may have ordered a large consignment from Maturus (two other pans by him are known); if so, this is the only survivor of the Thracians' allotment.

Whether the regiment was actually based at Caerleon remains an open question. The fortress was undoubtedly built for the Second Legion Augusta, whose presence here until at least the later third century is attested by many inscriptions and stamped tiles. Its surviving tombstones are all headed by the abbreviated formula *D(is) M(anibus)*, and are thus later than those we have seen from earlier legionary bases. Here is one of its earliest:

<3.07> *Caerleon (Isca)*

D(is) M(anibus)
G(aius) Valerius G(ai) f(ilius)
Galeria (tribu) Victor
Lugduni, sig(nifer) leg(ionis) II Aug(ustae),
stip(endiorum) XVII annor(um) XLV, cu-
ra(m) agent(e) Annio Perpetuo h(erede)

RIB 365+*add.*

'To the Shades of the Dead; Gaius Valerius Victor, son of Gaius, of the *Galeria* voting-tribe, from Lugdunum (Lyon), standard-bearer of the Second Legion Augusta, of 17 years' service, aged 45; (erected) under the supervision of Annius Perpetuus his heir.'

Another legionary standard-bearer from southern Gaul, but unlike Duccius Rufinus (**3.04**), he came from Lyon, twenty miles up-river from Vienne and its bitter rival; this old rivalry made them chose different sides in the civil wars of AD 68/9. Like the veteran Valerius Verecundus (**9.43**), Valerius Victor has the colourless name typical of legionaries whose ancestors have been enfranchised by late-Republican proconsuls. His epitaph looks second-century, but cannot be closely dated.

The legion was the muscle behind the auxiliary units which probed like fingers up the Welsh valleys, patrolling the new network of roads which isolated the mountain massifs. The epigraphic evidence is slight, since the military occupation of Wales was much reduced when the army moved north under Hadrian and the Antonines, but here is some more first-century evidence of cavalry, at the fort of Y Gaer outside Brecon:

<**3.08**> *Brecon Gaer (?Cicucium)*

Diis M[anibus]
Cand[idi ...]
ni fili [eq(uitis) alae]
Hisp(anorum) Vett(onum) [c(ivium) R(omanorum), tur(ma)]
Clem(entis), dom[o ...]
an(norum) XX stip(endiorum) III, h(eres) [ex t(estamento) f(aciendum) c(uravit)]

RIB 403

'To the Shades of the Dead (and) of Candidus, son of [...]nus, trooper of the Cavalry Regiment of Spanish Vettones, Roman citizens, of the troop of Clemens, from [...] aged 20, of 3 years' service. His heir saw to the making of this according to his will.'

Only the left-hand half of this handsome slab survives, but much of the text can be reconstructed; but not the name of Candidus' father or his place of origin. The upward extension of the first I and of H show that I is ligatured to them, II and HI respectively. The use of *Diis Manibus* unabbreviated (with *Diis* not even contracted to *Dis*) is no later than the early second century. Candidus' regiment was last seen at Bath (**2.08**), from which it has evidently advanced to the conquest of Wales. It now occupies an ideal cavalry base, at the focal point of radiating valleys.

Also from Y Gaer is a sherd from a samian platter which can be dated by its form (Drag. 18) and the maker's stamp to the period AD 65/90. Underneath in capital letters is the autograph of one of Candidus' comrades:

<**3.09**> *Brecon Gaer (?Cicucium)*

GIINIAL, *Genial(is)*.

RIB II.7, 2501.209

'(Property) of Genialis.'

Perhaps we can even put a face to the name. Also from Y Gaer is this quarry-face graffito:

<**3.10**> *Brecon Gaer (?Cicucium)*

head in profile GENI

RIB III, 3113

The reading of these 'pecked' letters is not quite certain: they were first published as CENT, and the profile seen as a caricature of 'the cent(urion)', but the graffito is more easily understood as the self-portrait of *Geni(alis)*. 'Genial', like 'Candid', is a typical soldier's name; we have already seen two troopers called *Genialis* (**2.07** and **3.09**), and at Corbridge and Carlisle, which were also cavalry forts at this time, there were troop-commanders (decurions) called *Candidus* (**4.09**) and *Genialis*.[11]

And further north

Like the Normans, the Romans seem to have secured South Wales before the North. In AD 77 Frontinus was succeeded by Tacitus' hero Agricola, who was immediately confronted by a crisis in Snowdonia, where the Ordovices had almost annihilated a cavalry regiment. He responded by virtually wiping out the tribe, an act of genocide admired by Tacitus although it was worthy of his villain, Domitian, who reported the destruction of an African tribe to the Senate: 'I have forbidden the Nasamones to exist'.[12] It cleared the way to the last Welsh fastness, the island of Mona (Anglesey), from which Suetonius Paulinus and the young Agricola had been recalled by the revolt of Boudica.

Agricola's first campaign, which culminated in the conquest of Anglesey and its copper mines, was only what is cold-bloodedly called 'mopping-up'. The Flintshire (Clwyd) lead mines in the territory of the Deceangli were already in production: two ingots from the same mould, and thus probably the load of a single pack-animal, were found in *c.* 1830 near Tamworth, famous for its other pigs:

[11] *Tab. Luguval.* 1.4 and 46; 16.i.10 (qualified as *senior*) and ii.34.
[12] Dio 67.4.6.

<3.11> *Hints Common, Staffs.*

imp(eratore) Vesp(asiano) VII T(ito) imp(eratore) V co(n)s(ulibus)
(*moulded on the side of the first*): Deceang[l(icum)]

RIB II.1, 2404.34 and 35

'(Cast) while the Emperor Vespasian was consul for the seventh time, and Titus *imperator*, for the fifth time (AD 76). Deceanglic (lead).'

There is a point of constitutional propriety here: Vespasian as the Emperor is using *imperator* as part of his name; his son Titus, although in fact he shared his father's imperial powers, placed *imperator* after his name as a title. These lead pigs are evidence like **2.17** and **2.18** of the rapid exploitation of Britain's mineral resources after conquest. Another ingot from the Flintshire field even bears a familiar name:

<3.12> *Carmel, Clwyd*

G(ai) Nipi Ascani

RIB II.1, 2404.38

'(Product) of Gaius Nipius Ascanius.'

The rarity of the name guarantees the identification: Ascanius' tentacles now stretched from the Mendips (**2.18**) to North Wales. Some of the lead went into providing a water-supply for the new fortress at Chester (Deva); three lead pipes found there have identical moulded inscriptions:

<3.13> *Chester (Deva)*

imp(eratore) Vesp(asiano) VIIII T(ito) imp(eratore) VII co(n)s(ulibus) Gn(aeo) Iulio Agricola leg(ato) Aug(usti) pr(o) pr(aetore)

RIB II.3, 2434.1

'(Made) when the Emperor Vespasian was consul for the ninth time, and Titus *imperator*, for the seventh time (AD 79), in the governorship of Gnaeus Iulius Agricola.'

Agricola is such a familiar figure – thanks to his foresight in marrying his daughter to the great historian who wrote his biography – that it comes as a shock to realise, not only that this is the earliest inscription from Britain to name a governor, but that if Tacitus' *Agricola* had perished like some of the books of his *Annals*, this inscription would be almost our only evidence of Agricola's existence. Otherwise there is only an inaccurate paragraph in the Byzantine epitome of Dio Cassius, the marble fragments from the forum at Verulamium (**10.10**), and this shaving from Carlisle:

<**3.14**> *Carlisle (Luguvalium)*

[...]
[eq(uiti) al]ae Sebosianae sing(ulari)
Agricolae

Tab. Luguval. 44

'To [...], trooper of the Cavalry Regiment Sebosiana, bodyguard of Agricola.'

This is the end of the address of a letter, written in ink on a wooden tablet like those from Caerleon[13] and Vindolanda (**4.17**). The recipient's unit, like the *ala Indiana* (**2.20**), was a Gallic cavalry regiment named from its first commander. It belonged to the Upper German army when it fought for Vitellius in AD 69, and was evidently taken to Britain by Cerialis in AD 71; later we will see it at Inveresk (**6.16**), perhaps Binchester (**12.39**), and at Lancaster (**13.28**). Provincial governors were escorted by guards (*singulares*) mounted or infantry, auxiliary soldiers seconded from their existing units. They are usually called *singulares consularis*, 'bodyguards of the governor' (since he was an ex-consul), but in the first century, like this guardsman, they took title from the governor's name.[14] Precious though the reference is to Agricola, it is a pity that the man's own name has perished. Other scraps of tablets have been found at Carlisle which relate to its occupation by the *ala Sebosiana* (**3.14**), posing the question of whether the recipient of this letter was actually there in Agricola's entourage, or only because he had returned temporarily to his unit. The same question will be

[13] *Britannia* 17 (1986), 450, No. 84 (cited before **3.06**).
[14] Speidel 1978(a).

posed by the gravestone of a later member of this regiment, another *eques singularis*, who was buried at Inveresk (**6.16**). The most likely answer is that his regiment was specified only to identify him, and that he received this letter somewhere else, but took it with him back to Carlisle. There is an exact parallel from Vindolanda, where a letter has been found addressed to another auxiliary cavalryman in the governor's entourage, Veldeius his equerry (*equisio consularis*), who was at London.[15]

A legion at Chester

The Second Legion Adiutrix now moved from Lincoln to Chester. Considering that it was only there for about ten years, an extraordinary number of its tombstones have survived; at least eleven, and probably thirteen. The reason is that they were subsequently used by the Romans themselves to rebuild the north wall of the fortress. Here is an example:

<**3.15**> *Chester (Deva)*

[... ?Voltim]-
esis Pudens G(ai) fil(ius)
Ser(gia tribu) Augusta, eq-
ues leg(ionis) II Ad(iutricis) p(iae) f(idelis),
annorum XXXII
stipendiorum
XIII, h(ic) s(itus) es[t]

RIB 482+*add.*

'... Voltimesis Pudens, son of Gaius, of the *Sergia* voting-tribe, from Augusta, trooper of Second Legion Adiutrix Dutiful and Loyal, aged 32, of 13 years' service, is buried here.'

This is one of the stones extracted in 1891 by a young Cambridge archaeologist whose father had been appointed Archbishop of Canterbury in 1883 by W E Gladstone. Thirty years later, by now the popular novelist E F Benson, who would soon be creating the immortal Mapp and Lucia, he published a sprightly account of taking his drawings to Gladstone at Hawarden. Gladstone, who was then over 80 and about to become Prime Minister for the fourth time, had given him a lecture 'full of fire and gesticulation' on how to make a squeeze, the papier-mâché impression used by epigraphists to record inscriptions. 'He instantly plunged into the subject of Roman legionaries in Britain as if nothing else really mattered or ever had mattered to him.'[16]

---

15 *Londini* (locative): see *Tab. Vindol.* II, 310, with commentary; but Birley 2002, 36–40, argues that such place-names record the place of writing. For the *ala Sebosiana* at Carlisle, see Tomlin 1998.

16 Benson 1920, 277.

A politician with a proper sense of priorities. This particular legionary came from Augusta Praetoria, Aosta in North Italy, as we know because it was enrolled in the *Sergia* tribe. His nomen is largely lost, but the termination *esis* is most unusual and the only candidate seems to be the north-Italian nomen *Voltimesis*. At all events, he was already a Roman citizen when he joined the legion, which implies that he was not a marine from Ravenna, but a civilian recruited by Agricola himself in AD 70.[17] This brings us to AD 83 for his death, the year of Agricola's last campaign and final victory. Six of these tombstones record the deceased's years of service, three of them '13 years': perhaps they were all casualties of the Mons Graupius campaign, who came home as invalids or even as a jar of ashes like Antistius Rusticus (**3.01**) and the Emperor Septimius Severus. Here is the tombstone of another trooper of the legion, who also died during Agricola's campaigns, although the exact date is ambiguous:

<**3.16**> *Chester (Deva)*

[...]inus eque[s leg(ionis]
II Ad(iutricis) p(iae) f(idelis) (centuria) Petroni
Fidi stipendio-
rum IXI anno-
rum XXV
hic sepul<tu>s est

RIB 481+*add*.

'[...]inus, trooper of the Second Legion Adiutrix Dutiful and Loyal, in the century of Petronius Fidus, of eight years' service, aged 25, is buried here.'

The incised lettering, notably the 'cursive' M and R, reflects the painted text (or perhaps the handwritten draft) which preceded it. The stone-cutter made a mistake over the first numeral; the editors of *RIB* think he intended XI ('11'), which would imply an age at enlistment of only 14. Other instances of this are known, even at Chester, but from 18 to 20 was usual. Alternatively the stone-cutter intended IIX, an unusual form of '8' which however is found on another Chester tombstone.[18] This seems more likely. If so, the deceased would have died in AD 78, when Agricola advanced from Chester into north-west Britain.

The north again

While Frontinus and then Agricola were still conquering Wales, the Ninth Legion at York guarded their northern flank. When Agricola resumed the northern offensive, this legion formed his right wing. Thanks to the survival of yet another inscription

[17] Birley 1988, 334.
[18] *RIB* 501.

at Pisidian Antioch, we know who the legate was:

<**3.17**> *Pisidian Antioch (western Turkey)*

G(aio) Caris[ta]-
nio G(ai) f(ilio) Ser(gia tribu) F[ron]-
toni trib(uno) mil(itum), p[raef(ecto)]
eq(uitum) al(ae) Bosp(oranorum), adl[e]-
cto in senatu(m) inte[r]
tribunic(ios), promoto in-
ter praetorios, leg(ato) pr(o)
pr(aetore) Ponti et Bithyn(iae), leg(ato) imp(eratoris)
divi Vespasian(i) Aug(usti) leg(ionis)
IX Hispanae in Britann(ia),
leg(ato) pro pr(aetore) divi Titi
Caes(aris) Aug(usti) et imp(eratoris) Domitian(i)
Caes(aris) Aug(usti) provinc(iae) Pam-
phyliae et Lyciae, patro-
no col(oniae)

T(itus) Caristanius Cal-
purnianus Rufus
ob merita eius h(onoris) c(ausa)

ILS 9485

'To Gaius Caristanius Fronto, son of Gaius, of the *Sergia* voting-tribe, military tribune, cavalry prefect of the Cavalry Regiment of Bosporani, enrolled in the Senate among the ex-tribunes, promoted to the ex-praetors, assistant governor of Pontus and Bithynia, legate of the deified emperor Vespasian Augustus of the Ninth Legion Hispana in Britain, imperial governor of the deified emperor Titus Caesar Augustus and of the emperor Domitian Caesar Augustus of the province of Pamphylia and Lycia, patron of the Colony. Titus Caristanius Calpurnianus Rufus (erected this) in his honour and for his merits.'

Caristanius Fronto and a brother (or cousin) called Caristanius Julianus were probably great-grandsons of the Caristanius Fronto (**1.11**) who celebrated Claudius' British Victory. In AD 69 they were of equestrian rank and commanded cavalry regiments in the eastern armies which proclaimed Vespasian; as a result they were promoted to the Senate like Curiatius Maternus[19] and Antistius Rusticus (**3.01**) in the censorship of AD 73–4. Thus they caught up with their senatorial contemporaries in the west, without the necessity of holding the qualifying magistracies at Rome.[20] Fronto now

---

[19] Mentioned at the beginning of this chapter (*AE* 1973, 283).

[20] For Julianus see *AE* 1932, 87. Birley 2005, 241, reads a third *Caristanius* of senatorial rank in *Tab. Vindol.* II, 326, but the traces are insufficient. Another branch of the family remained equestrian, to judge by Caristanius Justianus (**6.24**), prefect at Bar Hill.

served as assistant governor to the senatorial proconsul of Pontus and Bithynia (in north-western Turkey), and then was sent to Britain to command the Ninth Legion. The date of this appointment can be calculated quite closely since only Vespasian (who died in AD 79) is named, whereas the next post was held under his sons Titus (who died in AD 81) and Titus' successor Domitian. Since legionary commands probably averaged three or four years, Fronto was in Britain during *c.* AD 76–79.

Agricola enjoyed a longer governorship of Britain than any other governor known to us, except possibly Ulpius Marcellus (**7.09**), seven years against the usual three or four. Tacitus did not burden his first readers with the details of geography and chronology that we would have welcomed, but by carefully plotting his narrative against other scraps of evidence, we can reckon that by the end of AD 81, the year of Titus' death, Agricola had overrun the whole of Scotland south of the Clyde-Forth isthmus. Meanwhile Brigantia, like other new conquests, was being made to pay its way; here is a lead pig from Yorkshire:

<**3.18**> *Heyshaw Moor*

imp(eratore) Caes(are) Domitiano Aug(usto) co(n)s(ule) VII

and in front:

Brig(anticum)

RIB II.1, 2404.62, with *Britannia* 38 (2007), 365 (a)

'When the Emperor Caesar Domitian Augustus was consul for the seventh time (AD 81).' 'Brigantian (lead).'

The letters stand proud, having been cut into the mould in reverse. This is the better-preserved of two identical ingots found together in 1735. They can be dated very closely, for Domitian did not become Emperor until 13 September AD 81, and became consul for the eighth time on 1 January AD 82. It is a sad commentary on the vicissitudes of epigraphic documents that this ingot was sold at auction in 2007, when the Yorkshire Museum was unable to buy it, while the other ingot, its twin, was given to the British Museum in 1772.[21]

Agricola next year, in AD 82, advanced north of the Clyde-Forth isthmus, in what looks like an extension of his command, a renewed mandate of conquest which can only have come from the new emperor Domitian. Tacitus, who hated Domitian, is silent on the subject. Success at first eluded Agricola because the Ninth Legion – unlucky as usual – suffered a surprise attack by night.[22] It was the

---

21 Bonhams (London) sale of Antiquities, 26 April 2007, lot 303. Its twin is *RIB* II.1, 2404. 61.

22 Tacitus, *Agricola* 26, *nonam legionem ut maxime invalidam.*

'weakest' of the legions, a comment that can be explained with the help of another career-inscription:

<**3.19**> *Tivoli (Tibur)*

L(ucio) Roscio M(arci) f(ilio) Qui(rina tribu)
Aeliano Maecio
Celeri
co(n)s(uli), proco(n)s(uli) provinc(iae)
Africae, pr(aetori), tr(ibuno) pl(ebis), quaest(ori)
Aug(usti), Xvir stlitib(us) iudic(andis),
trib(uno) mil(itum) leg(ionis) IX Hispan(ae)
vexillarior(um) eiusdem
in expeditione Germanica,
donato ab imp(eratore) Aug(usto)
militarib(us) donis corona
vallari et murali vexillis
argenteis II hastis puris II,
salio
G(aius) Vecilius G(ai) f(ilius) Pal(atina tribu) Probus
amico optimo
l(oco) d(ato) s(enatus) c(onsulto)

ILS 1025

'To Lucius Roscius Aelianus Maecius Celer, son of Marcus, of the *Quirina* voting-tribe; consul, proconsul of the province of Africa, praetor, tribune of the people, quaestor of the Emperor, chairman of juries, military tribune of the Ninth Legion Hispana (commanding) a detachment of the same in the German campaign, decorated by the Emperor with military decorations, Rampart Crown and Mural Crown, two Silver Banners, two Untipped Spears, *salius* priest. (From) Gaius Vecilius Probus, son of Gaius, of the *Palatina* voting-tribe, to his excellent friend; site given by decree of the town council.'

This is the career, perhaps incomplete, of a grandee of Tibur (he was a member of its ancient college of *salii* which celebrated the worship of Hercules) who achieved the consulship in AD 100. His father is likely to have been Marcus Roscius Coelius who commanded the Twentieth Legion in AD 69, which in that crisis-year he was unable to control; he was replaced by Agricola.[23] But he achieved the consulship in AD 81, and two years later his likely son was an aspirant senator; in AD 83 he was 'senatorial' tribune of the Ninth Legion, the date being implied by the reference to 'the German campaign' in which he was decorated. Domitian is 'the Emperor' tactfully not named, since by the time this inscription was erected his 'memory' had been condemned. The campaign is his war against the Chatti for which he celebrated

[23] Tacitus, *Agricola* 7.3 (unnamed) with *Hist.* i 60. Birley 2005, 237–8.

a triumph which, according to Tacitus, coincided embarrassingly with Agricola's real victory at Mons Graupius. From this inscription we can see that the Ninth Legion had been weakened by sending a powerful detachment to the Rhine under its second-in-command, who later received the decorations appropriate to his rank.

By contrast an equestrian officer in the British army, very much his junior, received decorations on an unprecedented scale. The occasion is not specified, but arguably it was Mons Graupius. The evidence is his tombstone in eastern Libya, where he died on active service:

<**3.20**> *Cyrene*

G(aio) Iulio G(ai) f(ilio) Vo[l(tinia tribu)]
Karo ex provincia Narbo-
nensi trib(uno) mil(itum) leg(ionis) III Cy[r(enaicae)]
praef(ecto) coh(ortis) II Astyrum(!) eq(uitatae)
donato bello Brittanico c[or(ona)]
murali corona vallari cor(ona)
aurea hasta pura
[c]entyriones(!) et
milites leg(ionis) III Cyr(enaicae) et leg(ionis)
[X]XII missi in provinciam
[C]yrenensium dilectus caus{s}a

AE 1951, 88

'To Gaius Julius Karus, son of Gaius, of the *Voltinia* voting-tribe, from the province of Narbonensis, military tribune of the Third Legion Cyrenaica, prefect of the Second Cohort of Asturians part-mounted, decorated in the British War with Wall Crown, Rampart Crown, and Untipped Spear, (from) the centurions and soldiers of the Third Legion Cyrenaica and the Twenty-Second Legion sent to the province of Cyrene for recruiting purposes.'

The province was Greek-speaking, and there is a hint of Greek in *Astyrum* and *centyriones*: Latin used the letter Y only for transcribing the Greek vowel *u*, here of course erroneously. Karus' mission is earlier than the AD 120s, when the Second Legion Traiana replaced the two Egyptian legions, and has been dated by the two milestones of AD 100 which record a road built from Cyrene 'by means of recruits raised from the province of Cyrene'.[24] But no 'British War' is known from the late AD 90s, whereas two are attested in which Karus might well have distinguished himself, the campaigns of Agricola, and the trouble at Hadrian's accession (**5.01**). The unparalleled scale of his decorations, however, suits Domitian much better than Hadrian, who was parsimonious with such awards.[25]

---

24 *AE* 1951, 210 and 1957, 133 (Cyrene), *viam … per tirones lectos ex provincia Cyrenensi*.

25 Maxfield 1981, 164–5. The chronology is fully discussed by Birley 1961, 23–4, before Roxan (1976,

One of Agricola's bases was Carlisle, where he is named on the letter (**3.14**) addressed to one of his bodyguards (*singulares*). He was not necessarily there himself, but one of his legions certainly was, as another Carlisle writing-tablet reveals. This is not an ink text like the letter, but a stylus tablet; the wax has been lost as usual, but the scratches are legible. They belong to the top half of the first 'page':

<**3.21**> *Carlisle (Luguvalium)*

imp(eratore) Domitiano VIIII co(n)s(ule)
VII Idus Novembres. Q(uintus) Cassius
Secundus miles leg(ionis) XX (centuria) Calvi
Prisci scribsi(!) me debere
G(aio) Geminio Mansueto militi
leg(ionis) eiusdem (centuria) Vetti Proculi denarios centum quos [tibi?]
. . .

Tomlin 1992

'In the ninth consulship of the Emperor Domitian, on the seventh day before the Ides of November (7 November AD 83). I, Quintus Cassius Secundus, soldier of the Twentieth Legion, century of Calvius Priscus, have written that I owe Gaius Geminius Mansuetus, soldier of the same legion, century ofVettius Proculus, one hundred *denarii* which [I will repay you . . . *date due and interest*]'

This was found underneath Tullie House Museum in Carlisle, when by digging through the cellar floor archaeologists struck a cobbled Roman road. In a pothole were first-century samian sherds and this tablet. It carries a standard soldier's loan-note in which the scribe wrote *scribsi* for *scripsi*, as in a contemporary loan-note[26] from London; perhaps an echo of the present tense *scribo*, or because this was how he pronounced it. The two legionaries are identified in the usual way by their centuries. Neither Geminius Mansuetus nor the centurions are otherwise known, but the tombstone of Cassius Secundus has probably survived (**9.36**). The date is that of the army's first pay-rise for more than a century: Domitian in AD 83 increased legionary pay before stoppages from 225 to 300 *denarii* a year, paid probably in three annual instalments, so it looks as if Secundus is anticipating his first instalment. November AD 83 is also just after Agricola's crowning victory at Mons Graupius (in the late summer of AD 83), when the legions watched the auxiliaries rout the Caledonians. Now they have returned to base and a less demanding duty, that (in Saki's phrase) of beating their swords into Bank Shares.

63–4) showed that Karus' cohort need not be identified with another of that name in Germany in AD 89; and also by Jarrett 1994, 53–4, and Birley 2005, 93–4, who is convinced by Jarrett's argument for Mons Graupius.

[26] *Tab. Lond. Bloomberg* 53 (dated 15 March AD 82).

4

RETREAT AND CONSOLIDATION

The pitiless élan of Agricola's conquests is celebrated by a masterpiece of sculpture at one of his forts, Lancaster. This tombstone shows a mounted cavalryman, his face turned towards the spectator, who wears a plumed helmet like Flavinus the standard-bearer (**4.09**) or the god Victorious Mars (**6.12**), a cloak pinned with a rosette-brooch, a baldric and jerkin, breeches and short boots. He holds a shield in his left hand; in his right, a short sword instead of the usual lance. This is to emphasise the other object he is holding by its hair, a detached human head which has been taken as a trophy from the naked warrior crouching under his stallion's hoofs. This macabre detail recalls the supreme achievement of his contemporary, the cavalryman Tiberius Claudius Maximus, who was promoted by Trajan in person 'for capturing Decebalus and bringing his head to him.' Maximus was serving as an advanced scout (*explorator*), and his tombstone shows him arriving on horseback just as the Dacian king stabbed himself.[1]

The Lancaster headhunter's epitaph is inscribed below, in stylish letters which followed a brush-painted text and were originally coloured red:

<4.01> *Lancaster*

Dis
Manibus Insus Vodulli
[fil]ius cive(s)(!) Trever eques alae Aug(ustae)
[t(urma)] Victoris curator, Domitia [?h(eres) f(aciundum) c(uravit)]

RIB III, 3185

'To the Shades of the Dead. Insus son of Vodullus, a citizen of the Treveri, trooper of the Cavalry Regiment Augusta, [troop] of Victor, *curator*. Domitia [his heir had this set up].'

cive(s) is the alternative form of *civis* already seen in the epitaphs of two other cavalrymen, Tancinus (**2.08**) and Dannicus (**2.20**). Like Dannicus' *ala Indiana*, Insus

[1] Speidel 1970 (*AE* 1969/70, 583), *quod cepisset Decebalu(m) et caput eius pertulisset ei.* Connolly 1988.

originated from Trier; and since his regiment, the *ala Augusta*, is already attested at Lancaster by the epitaph of Julius Apollinaris who also came from Trier[2], it is likely that they both entered the regiment when it was in the Rhineland, before Petillius Cerialis brought it to Britain. Its identity is not certain, since three or four *alae* in Britain bear the title *Augusta*, but it may well be the *ala Augusta ob virtutem appellata* ('styled Augusta for its valour') which becomes the first (Hadrianic) garrison of Chesters (**5.03**).[3] Despite his splendid tombstone, Insus as *curator* was quite a junior under-officer in his cavalry troop of thirty men. Domitia does not state her relationship to him, but she was probably his informal 'wife'. Nor does she state his age and length of service, but his comrade Apollinaris was aged 30; both men are likely to have fought for Agricola.

Agricola left Britain in AD 84, aged only 43, a year older than Julius Caesar when he embarked on the nine-year conquest of Gaul; but the last nine years of Agricola's life were spent in forced retirement, and it is likely that his frustration inspired Tacitus' comment that Britain was now 'entirely conquered and immediately let go'.[4] This was an exaggeration. Agricola never penetrated the Highlands, and after his crowning mercy of Mons Graupius the surviving Caledonians were sealed off in their mountains by forts in the intervening valleys, like cockroaches behind the wallpaper. Southern Scotland was systematically occupied:

<**4.02**> *Ardoch*

Dis Manibus
Ammonius Da-
mionis (filius) (centurio) coh(ortis)
I Hispanorum
stipendiorum
XXVII, heredes
f(aciendum) c(uraverunt)

RIB 2213; Keppie 1998, No. 47

'To the Shades of the Dead. Ammonius son of Damio, centurion of the First Cohort of Spaniards, of 27 years' service. His heirs had this made.'

The unabbreviated formulas *Dis Manibus* and *stipendiorum* date this epitaph to the first century, and thus to the first, Flavian (not Antonine, second) occupation of Ardoch. Ammonius was not a Roman citizen despite his long service (another sign of early date), and his name is eastern, one found particularly in Egypt, where there was a famous shrine of Zeus Ammon. If Ardoch was evacuated in AD 86 or

2 *RIB* 606+*add.*

3 Jarrett 1994, 40.

4 *Histories* i 2, *perdomita Britannia et statim omissa.*

early 87, Ammonius must have enlisted in the late AD 50s, when the cohort was still in the east, so his career took him from one end of the Empire to the other.[5] This is the Empire's most northerly epitaph, if we exclude Tacitus' obituary notice of Aulus Atticus, the prefect of a cohort whose 'youthful ardour and mettlesome horse' carried him into the enemy lines at Mons Graupius.[6]

One of the four legions was committed to the new frontier, which it supervised from the new fortress of Inchtuthil on the river Tay. The only inscription found here, apart from stamped samian ware, is a piece of tile with the paw-marks of a small dog 'moving fast', so the chronology depends on numismatic evidence.[7] In AD 86 or early 87 it was systematically demolished before it had even been completed. The building timbers were salvaged, but almost ten tons of nails were carefully buried to deny them to the enemy. The legionary garrison, which was probably the Twentieth, was withdrawn; and from the way the demolition parties dealt with the surplus samian ware in store – smashing it up to block the drains they had just dug – the Legion was very angry indeed.[8]

Soldiers can hardly be expected to understand or forgive military cutbacks. The reason lay out of sight, on the Danube, where in AD 85 Decebalus and the Dacians invaded Moesia from Transylvania and in AD 86 or 87 defeated a Roman counter-attack. Reinforcements were urgently needed, and Domitian decided to withdraw the Second Legion Adiutrix from Britain, the formation whose investment there had made his father's forward policy possible. Soon it is found on the middle Danube:

<4.03> *Sirmium (Sremska Mitrovica, near Belgrade)*

T(itus) Cominius
T(iti) f(ilius) Volt(inia tribu) Seve-
rus Vienna (centurio)
leg(ionis) II Adiutric(is)
donis donat(us)
ab imp(eratore) Caesare
Aug(usto) bello Dacico
torquibus armill[i]s
phaleris corona val-
lari, vixit ann(os) XXXXV
T(itus) Caesernius Macedo
proc(urator) Aug(usti) her(es) ex test(amento) p(osuit)

ILS 9193

[5] The cohort is attested in Galatia in *c.* AD 70 by *ILS* 9499 (Ephesus).
[6] *Agricola* 37.6, *iuvenili ardore et ferocia equi hostibus inlatus.*
[7] Pitts and St Joseph 1985, 340.
[8] Burn 1969, 74.

> 'Titus Cominius Severus, son of Titus, of the *Voltinia* voting-tribe, from Vienne; centurion of the Second Legion Adiutrix, decorated by the Emperor Caesar Augustus with Torques, Bracelets, Medallions and the Mural Crown in the Dacian War; lived 45 years. Titus Caesernius Macedo, imperial Procurator, his heir, set up (this monument) under his will.'

This richly decorated slab commemorates another legionary like Duccius Rufinus (**3.04**) who came from Vienne. He was buried at Sirmium, which for centuries was the focal point of the middle Danube frontier (**13.23**). The anonymous emperor is Domitian, this tombstone having been erected after AD 96, when his 'memory' was condemned. The Dacian War is probably that of AD 89, in which he took personal command. Cominius Severus must have accompanied the legion from Britain, perhaps as an officer in a forward detachment: there is a long inscription from Baalbek which details the career of Gaius Velius Rufus, who once commanded a field force drawn from eight legions including the Second Legion Adiutrix and the three British legions. Its chronology is difficult, but David Kennedy has suggested that Rufus' expedition was part of the Danubian operations in AD 89.[9] Certainly the whole legion was there by AD 92, when we know that its senior tribune was decorated 'by vote of the (other) five tribunes of the legion'.[10] By now it was based at Aquincum (Budapest), where this tall tombstone depicts a legionary who must have followed Agricola into battle:

<4.04> *Budapest (Aquincum)*

G(aius) Castriciu-
s G(ai filius) Off(entina tribu) Vict-
or (domo) Como mil(es)
leg(ionis) II Ad(iutricis) (centuria) M(arcii)
Turbonis, ann(orum)
XXXVIII stip(endiorum) XIIII
h(ic) s(itus) e(st). L(ucius) Lucilius fr(ater)
et he(res) posuit p(ro) p(ietate)

CIL xiii 14349.2 = *Tituli Aquincenses* II, 588

> 'Gaius Castricius Victor, son of Gaius, of the *Offentina* voting-tribe, his home Comum (Como), soldier of the Second Legion Adiutrix, century of Marcius Turbo, aged 38, after 14 years' service, is buried here. Lucius Lucilius, his brother and heir, erected (this) out of respect.'

Like the Lancaster tombstone (**4.01**), this is a daunting image of Agricola's army. Victor radiates murderous self-confidence as he stands there with his broadened

---

[9] *ILS* 9200 (Baalbek), with Kennedy 1983. Strobel 1986.

[10] *ILS* 2719, *optioni(!) tribun[or(um) | le]gionum(!) quinq(ue)*, corrected by Strobel 1988.

torso and enlarged left hand. On his head a horned helmet, he wears a mail shirt and 'apron', the studded straps hanging from his belt. His sword hangs from a baldric on his right hip, there is a dagger on his left. His right hand holds two *pila*, the close-range armour-piercing missile typical of the legions; his left hand supports an oval shield bearing a Gorgon's head amidst thunderbolts.

Victor came from Comum (Como) on the Alpine edge of northern Italy; it was enrolled in the *Oufentina* voting-tribe (**12.68**), of which *Offentina* is a variant spelling. His nomen *Castricius* is widely attested in Italy and the western provinces. The lettering and the use of H S E without *Dis Manibus* accord with the date in the mid- AD 90s given to this stone, ever since Ritterling noticed the centurion's unusual name: he is Quintus Marcius Turbo, one of the future Emperor Hadrian's oldest friends, whose praetorian prefect he was for most of the reign. Their friendship can be dated to AD 95, when Hadrian was the senatorial tribune (*tribunus laticlavius*) of the very legion in which Turbo was a centurion, the Second Legion Adiutrix.[11] From the British point of view, therefore, it follows that Victor must have joined the legion in about AD 80, and would have served with it in Scotland.

It is likely that the British army also had to part with some cavalry, at least for a time, but this loss cannot be dated so closely:

<**4.05**> *Carnuntum (Petronell, east of Vienna)*

T(itus) Flavius
Crensces(!)
equ(es) al(a)e Tam(pianae) ve-
x(illationis) Brit(annicae), an(norum) XXX st(ipendiorum) XV
dom(o) Durocor(toro) Rem(orum)
h(ic) s(itus) e(st). Flavius Silvan-
us dec(urio) a[l(a)e ei]usd(em)
h(eres) [e(ius)] f(ecit)

ILS 2515

'Titus Flavius Crescens, trooper of the Cavalry Regiment Tampiana in the detachment from Britain, aged 30, of 15 years' service, his home Reims, is buried here. Flavius Silvanus, decurion of the same regiment, his heir, made (this monument).'

The early history of the *ala I Pannoniorum Tampiana*, to give the regiment its full name, is not known, but it was explicitly raised in Pannonia, and probably by Augustus or Tiberius since it bears the name of an early prefect like the *ala Indiana* (**2.20**). In AD 103 and 122 it is listed in the British army, but was transferred to Noricum soon after.[12] The tombstone of Crescens, and thus its service in Pannonia, cannot

[11] Birley 1997, 31.
[12] Spaul 1994, 215–16. E Birley 1988, 382 and 299.

be certainly dated, but the late first century is suggested by the use of the H S E formula without *Dis Manibus*, and the nomen *Flavius* borne by both soldiers, the sons perhaps of Flavian veterans.

Apart from this tombstone, the first document to name the *ala Tampiana* is the Malpas diploma of AD 103. A 'military diploma' (the term is modern) consisted of two bronze plates hinged together, on which was inscribed the text of an imperial grant of citizenship to auxiliary veterans discharged at any one time from a provincial army, listing all their units. The original was posted at Rome on a bronze tablet, all of which like the *Res Gestae* (**1.01**) have been been melted down long ago, but the diploma remains as a certified copy in miniature, issued to the individual veteran whose name and unit are specified: no doubt he had applied for this durable certificate of his new status, and was duly charged for it. At least 800 have now been found, often by metal detectorists, and although many are only fragments, they provide much of our knowledge of the Roman 'order of battle'. Each was inscribed in duplicate, the 'inner' copy being sealed by seven witnesses, the usual precaution against illicit alteration of a legal document; the 'outer' text remained available for consultation. This particular example is addressed by Trajan to veterans discharged from auxiliary units in the British army:

<**4.06**> *Malpas, Cheshire*

... [e]quitibus et peditibus, qui militant in alis quattuor et cohortibus decem et una, quae appellantur I Thracum et I Pannoniorum Tampiana et Gallorum Sebosiana et Hispanorum Vettonum c(ivium) R(omanorum) ... et sunt in Britannia sub L(ucio) Neratio Marcello, qui quina et vicena plurave stipendia meruerunt, quorum nomina subscripta sunt, ipsis liberis posterisque civitatem dedit et conubium cum uxoribus, quas tunc habuissent cum est civitas iis data, aut, siqui caelibes essent, cum iis quas postea duxissent dumtaxat singuli singulas.

RIB II.1, 2401.1 (conflated text)

'(The Emperor Trajan) has granted to the cavalrymen and infantrymen who are serving in four alae and eleven cohorts called: (1) I Thracum and (2) I Pannoniorum Tampiana and (3) Gallorum Sebosiana and (4) Hispanorum Vettonum, Roman citizens, (*the names of the eleven cohorts follow*), and are stationed in Britain under Lucius Neratius Marcellus, who have served twenty-five or more years, whose names are written below, citizenship for themselves, their children and descendants, and the right of legal marriage with the wives they had when citizenship was granted to them, or, if any were unmarried, with those they later marry, but only a single one each.'

The date follows (19 January AD 103), and the witnesses' names. The recipient is a troop-commander:

alae Pannoniorum Tampianae, cui praeest G(aius) Valerius Celsus, decurioni Reburro Severi f(ilio), Hispano.

'To Reburrus, son of Severus, from Spain, decurion of ala I Pannoniorum Tampiana, commanded by Gaius Valerius Celsus.'

The translation is by Margaret Roxan, who published this and many other diplomas with awesome erudition and command of detail. Her work has been ably continued by Paul Holder.[13] We have already seen these four *alae* elsewhere; they and the eleven cohorts comprise only part of the British garrison, but the great Brigetio diploma (**5.04**), by coincidence also issued to a veteran of the *ala Tampiana*, gives what must be almost the complete list in AD 122.

After AD 86/7 the army in Britain was no longer large enough to hold the whole of Agricola's conquests, but Tacitus' epigram is unfair to Domitian, who had been forced to choose between the vital Danubian frontier and the northern periphery, where in fact he withdrew only to the Cheviots. The fort of Trimontium (Newstead), where Dere Street crossed the river Tweed, was even enlarged, and was now strongly held by infantry and cavalry in separate compounds.[14] A commanding officer's name is painted on the neck of a wine amphora from southern Gaul (Peacock and Williams 27), found in a Flavian rubbish pit:

<**4.07**> *Newstead (Trimontium)*

Atti Secundi tr(ibuni)
lagunu(m) m(odiorum) III

'(Property) of Attius Secundus the tribune, a jar of three *modii*'

RIB II.6, 2492.7

Lagunum is a variant of *lagena*, the final *m* being omitted as in *an(n)oru(m)* (**3.02**) because it was hardly sounded. Attius Secundus as a military tribune may have been a legionary officer in command of a powerful detachment, but he was more likely the commander of a double-strength milliary (1000-strong) auxiliary cohort. His jar is also of commanding capacity: three *modii* (26.3 litres) are almost six gallons, the equivalent of three dozen bottles of wine.

Compare this with another letter from Carlisle, this time a Flavian waxed stylus tablet on the back of which the address has been scratched:

---

13 In the long series of *Roman Military Diplomas*. For Margaret Roxan, see Wilkes 2003. The largest collection is in Mainz, and has been well photographed (Pferdehirt 2004)..

14 Despite Richmond 1950 and the letter to Martialis (**4.08**), it is far from certain that the infantry component was legionary.

<**4.08**> *Carlisle (Luguvalium)*

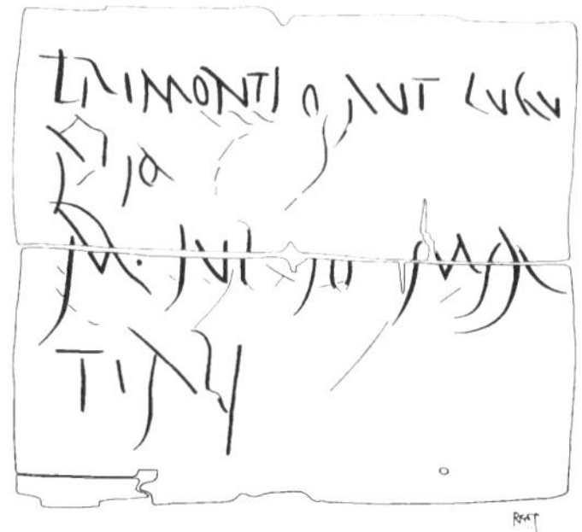

Trimontio aut Lugu-
(v)a[l]io
M(arco) Iulio Mar-
tiali

Britannia 19 (1988), 496, No. 31

'To Marcus Iulius Martialis, at Newstead or Carlisle.'

These two locatival ablatives are the choice of places to which the letter was to be sent, not the place of writing; this at least the writer would have known. His letter was subsequently re-used by breaking one of its tablets in half, and cutting two more notches for the new binding-cord. This may have been done by the recipient, Julius Martialis, whose name is typical of legionaries, even if he is not identified as such: perhaps his legion had detachments at both places. We have already seen (**3.21**) there were soldiers of the Twentieth at Carlisle (*Luguvalium*) in AD 83, which is where this letter was found. The alternative *Trimontium* ('the Triple Mountain') is for once a British place-name that is obvious: the far-visible three peaks of the Eildon Hills above Newstead.

The garrison of Newstead thus mitigated its northern exile by receiving letters and importing wine. Some distance to the south, where Dere Street crossed the river Tyne, was Coria (Corbridge), at this time occupied by another pair of units; there seems to have been infantry from Vindolanda[15] and certainly a cavalry regiment:

<**4.09**> *Corbridge (Coria)*

Dis Manibus Flavinus
eq(ues) alae Petr(ianae) signifer
tur(ma) Candidi an(norum) XXV
stip(endiorum) VII h(ic) s(itus) e(st)

RIB 1172+*add.*

'To the Shades of the Dead. Flavinus, trooper of the *ala Petriana*, standard-bearer, from the troop of Candidus, aged 25, of seven years' service, is buried here.'

Flavinus' tombstone, with its triumphant horseman and the cramped but entire barbarian doubled up beneath the horse's hoofs, has almost the impact of Insus' tombstone at Lancaster (**4.01**); it survives because it was carted to Hexham Abbey as

---

[15] *Tab. Vindol.* II, 154.7, recording 337 men outposted to Corbridge (*Coris*).

building material, where it now stands in the transept. Flavinus is wearing a plumed helmet, probably a parade helmet like those found at Ribchester, Newstead and Crosby Garrett, which have a metal face-mask visor; he has a torque round his neck, and as the standard-bearer of his troop he carries a lance tipped with an imperial bust set in a crown of rays. The use of *Dis Manibus* unabbreviated, and H S E, date the stone to the first century; and probably before AD 98, when a diploma gives the regiment the collective title of *c(ives) R(omani)*. Like the *ala Indiana* (**2.20**), it was named after its first commander.[16]

The Scottish Borders were thus firmly held, but by withdrawing that legion from within sight of the Highlands, Domitian insensibly lost the initiative in Britain. The Twentieth Legion was now withdrawn to Chester, where it filled the gap left by the Second Legion Adiutrix. Even Chester was a long way from Italy:

<**4.10**> *Chester (Deva)*

Fortunae Reduci
[A]esculap(io) et saluti eius
libert(i) et familia
T(iti) P[o]mponi T(iti) f(ili) Gal(eria tribu) Mamilian[i]
Rufi Antistiani Funisulan[i]
Vetton[i]ani leg(ati) Aug(usti)
d(ederunt) d(edicaverunt)

RIB 445

'To Fortune the Home-Bringer, to Aesculapius and his welfare, the freedmen and slave-household of Titus Pomponius Mamilianus Rufus Antistianus Funisulanus Vettonianus, son of Titus, of the *Galeria* voting-tribe, imperial legate, gave and dedicated (this).'

Aesculapius was the god of medicine, protector of homesick servants afraid of catching the diseases endemic in them foreign parts. The insertion of the possessive pronoun *eius* ('his') implies that the 'welfare' (*salus*) is that of their master, although *RIB* understands it to be the divinity Salus ('Health') as in **12.85**. Titus Pomponius Mamilianus (his other names advertise family connections or adoption) became consul in AD 100, so we can date his legionary command to the early AD 90s. Later (in *c.* AD 107) he received two letters from Pliny, who sent him poems for comment, likening them to sparrows and doves among the eagles: by this time, Mamilianus was evidently governing a province with a legionary garrison. Tony Birley notes that Pliny calls him 'very learned and serious, and above all very sincere (he had praised Pliny's verses)'.[17] His other names suggest a connection with Funisulanus

---

[16] *CIL* xvi 43, with E Birley 1988, 249–50. Unless this title was omitted by accident, the tombstone may antedate the Mons Graupius campaign (AD 83), the likeliest occasion for the award.

[17] Birley 2005, 241; Pliny *epp.* 9.16, 9.25.

Vettonianus, Domitian's choice in AD 85/6 for the key Danubian command of Upper Moesia, the sort of post that Tacitus and Agricola thought should have gone to Agricola. The name *Funisulanus Vettonianus* is still borne in the third century by a tribune at Birdoswald, who may have owed it to a freedman ancestor manumitted by this man.[18]

Archaeologically there is evidence that Agricola's remaining conquests north of the Tyne-Solway isthmus were lost or at least abandoned, not by Domitian, but by Trajan *optimus princeps*, 'the Best of Emperors', fairly soon after his accession in AD 98 which Agricola is said to have predicted. Trajan's withdrawal in Britain to the Stanegate 'frontier', to the forts and fortlets of the road which ran east from Carlisle to Corbridge and beyond, is in contrast with his aggressiveness on the Danube. The inhabitants of Britain contributed to his success there, as we know from three diplomas (compare **4.06**) issued to veterans of his Dacian wars, the first of which was found at the site of the legionary fortress of Brigetio in modern Hungary. Only the second leaf survives, consisting of the second 'page' of the inside text and (overleaf, not quoted) the names of the seven witnesses. Trajan is addressing veterans of the army of Upper Moesia:

<**4.11**> *Brigetio (Szőny)*

[... conubi]-
um cum uxoribus quas tunc habuissent cum est
{est} civitas iis data aut siqui caelibes essent cum
iis quas postea duxissent dumtaxat singuli sin-
gulas pr(idie) Idus Ian(uarias)
Ti(berio) Iulio Candido Mario Celso II
G(aio) Antio Iulio Quadrato II co(n)s(ulibus)

cohort(is) I Britannicae (milliariae) c(ivium) R(omanorum) cui prae(e)st
Q(uintus) Caecilius Redditus
pediti
Lucconi Treni f(ilio) Dobunn(o)
et Tutulae Breuci filiae uxori eius Azal(ae)
et Simili f(ilio) eius
et Luccae filiae eius
et Pacatae filiae eius.

descriptum et recognitum ex tabula aenea quae
fixa est Romae

CIL xvi 49

'... the right of legal marriage with the wives they had when citizenship was granted to

[18] *RIB* 1879.

them or, if any were unmarried, with those they later marry, but only a single one each. On the day before the Ides of January in the consulship of Tiberius Iulius Candidus Marius Celsus for the second time and Gaius Antius Iulius Quadratus for the second time (12 January AD 105).

'To Lucco son of Trenus, a Dobunnian, infantryman of the First Cohort Britannica, one thousand strong, Roman Citizens, commanded by Quintus Caecilius Redditus; and to Tutula daughter of Breucus, his wife, an Azalian; and to Similis his son; and to Lucca his daughter; and to Pacata his daughter.

'Copied and checked from the bronze tablet set up at Rome.'

The first 'page' would have carried Trajan's name and titles, followed by a list of the auxiliary units concerned. This copy was issued to Lucco, who in January AD 105 would have served 25 years: he must have enlisted in *c.* AD 79, and would have been born in *c.* AD 60, in what is now Gloucestershire/Avon. The tribal capital was at Corinium (Cirencester), and the derived name *Luccianus* is known at Bath.[19] Other diplomas show that his cohort was already in Pannonia by AD 80, but that in AD 103/7 it had been transferred to Upper Moesia and had gained the title of 'Roman Citizens'. This would have been awarded by Domitian or Trajan, and it is odd that Lucco is not explicitly called 'Titus Flavius' or 'Marcus Ulpius' (compare **4.12** and **4.13**). The cohort's title associates it with Britain, either because it was formed there, or possibly because it served there. At all events, it must have left Britain soon after Lucco joined it (possibly he was a founder-member) and it arrived in Pannonia. There he married a woman of the Azali, significantly a tribe of northern Pannonia in the area of Brigetio where this diploma was found. Her father was called Breucus, which however is the name of a tribe in the Sava valley, and is a personal name typical of southern Pannonia. (There is other evidence which suggests that the Azali were originally a south-Pannonian tribe uprooted by Tiberius and transferred to the Danube.) Lucco's marriage was not valid in Roman law, since as a serving soldier he was not allowed to marry, but it was treated as an informal union which this diploma recognises retrospectively. The children thus became legitimate, and Roman citizens like their mother and father. The son was called Similis, 'Like' (his father); quite a common name, and a delicate compliment to his mother's fidelity.[20] The elder daughter was named after her father, the younger one was called 'Pacified'; perhaps an allusion to the peace-treaty (AD 103) after Trajan's first Dacian War. This peace did not last, but by then Lucco had retired. Trajan was at Rome in January AD 105 (he did not leave for his second Dacian War until June), but we do not know whether he was then discharging Danubian veterans as a matter of routine, or to spare them an arduous campaign, or simply to comb out the elderly. (Trajan, who may have been born as early as AD 53, was

---

19 *Tab. Sulis* 30.6. It is often found in 'Roman' guise as *Lucius*, *Lucillus*, *Lucianus*, etc.

20 Burn 1969, 35.

in fact older than Lucco.) Lucco had not seen Britain for a quarter-century, and would in any case have had to pay for the five passages 'home', so instead he and his family returned from Upper Moesia to the north-Pannonian homeland of his wife. Sentiment apart (it had been his military station), he probably owned land there through his wife, by dowry or inheritance.

Quite a biography can be extracted from this formulaic document. The other two diplomas were found together in 1939 at a major frontier-fort of the new province of Dacia, in what is now northern Romania. Both were issued to British veterans of a much-decorated unit, the first being dated 2 July AD 110; here is the recipient:

<**4.12**> *Porolissum*

coh(ortis) I Britton(um) (milliariae) Ulpiae torquat(ae) c(ivium) R(omanorum) cui prae(e)
st M(arcus) Aemilius Bassus
ex pedite
M(arco) Ulpio Sacci f(ilio) Longino Bel[go]
et Vitali f(ilio)

CIL xvi 163

'Of the First Cohort of Britons one thousand strong, Trajan's Own, Awarded Torques, Roman Citizens: ex-infantryman Marcus Ulpius Longinus, son of Saccus, a *Belgus*; and to his son Vitalis.'

Longinus came from the Belgae, a British tribe whose capital was Venta (Winchester). His father bore the rare Celtic name *Saccus*, but gave his son a colourless 'Roman' name, the same as that assumed by the Thracian Sdapeze (**2.02**). Longinus chose an equally colourless 'Roman' name for his son. He was already a Roman citizen when he received his diploma, for reasons which appear from the other diploma:

<**4.13**> *Porolissum*

imp(erator) Caesar divi Nervae f(ilius) Nerva Traia-
nus Augustus Germanic(us) Dacicus pontifex
maximus tribunic(iae) potestatis XIIII
imp(erator) VI co(n)s(ul) V p(ater) p(atriae)

peditibus et equitibus qui militant
in cohorte I Brittonum milliaria
Ulpia Torquata p(ia) f(ideli) civium Romano-
rum quae est in Dacia sub D(ecimo) Terentio
Scauriano, quorum nomina sub-
scripta sunt, pie et fideliter ex-
peditione Dacica functis ante

emerita stipendia civi-
tatem Romanam dedit

a(nte) d(iem) III Idus Aug(ustas)
Darnithithi
L(ucio) Minicio Natale
Q(uinto) Silvano Graniano co(n)s(ulibus)
pediti
M(arco) Ulpio Adcobrovati f(ilio) Novanticoni Ratis

descriptum et recognitum ex ta-
bula aenea quae fixa est Ro-
mae in muro post templum
divi Aug(usti) ad Minervam

CIL xvi 160 (outer text)

'The Emperor Caesar Nerva Trajan Augustus, son of the deified Nerva, Conqueror of Germany, Conqueror of Dacia, pontifex maximus, in his fourteenth year of tribunician power (AD 110), acclaimed *imperator* six times, consul five times, Father of his Country, has granted Roman citizenship before the expiry of their service to the infantry and cavalry who are serving in the First Cohort of Brittones, a thousand strong, Trajan's Own, Awarded Torques, Dutiful and Loyal, Roman Citizens, which is in Dacia under Decimus Terentius Scaurianus; to those whose names are written below, who served dutifully and loyally in the Dacian Campaign.

'On the third day before the Ides of August at Darnithithum, in the consulship of Lucius Minicius Natalis and Quintus Silvanus Granianus (11 August AD 106).

'To infantryman Marcus Ulpius Novantico, son of Adcobrovatus, from Ratae.

'Copied and checked from the bronze tablet set up at Rome on the wall behind the temple of the deified Augustus near (the statue of) Minerva.'

This diploma was issued in AD 110, but confirmed the block grant of citizenship to the cohort in AD 106 for gallantry in the field during the second Dacian War. (It received other battle honours too.) Darnithithum is an unknown place in Dacia, the site of Trajan's headquarters that day. Novantico was thus already a Roman citizen in AD 110, unlike Reburrus (**4.06**) and Lucco (**4.11**), when his status was confirmed on discharge as a veteran. He came from Ratae, modern Leicester, which was the tribal capital of the Corieltauui.[21] His outlandish names caused the engraver trouble: the inside text (which no one would have seen) mis-spells it as *M(arco) Ulpio Adcoprovati f(ilio) Novantico*(!) as if this were a dative; in the outer text, it was awkwardly corrected by adding NI between the lines.

---

21 *RIB* II.5, 2491.150 with *Britannia* 34 (2003), 382, add. (c).

Lucco, Longinus and Novantico were British Celts who became Roman citizens, fought and grew old far from their native land. Evidently they never returned, and the same is true of this Briton:

<**4.14**> *Rome*

D(is) M(anibus)
M(arco) Ulpio Iusto
eq(uiti) sing(ulari) Aug(usti)
militavit an(nos) XXV
vix(it) ann(os) XLV natione
Britto, fec(it) M(arcus) Ulpius
Respectus vet(eranus) Aug(usti)
amico optimo de se
bene merenti

CIL vi 3301 = Speidel 1994, No. 343

'To the Shades of the Dead (and) to Marcus Ulpius Justus, cavalryman of the Imperial Horseguards, (who) served 25 years, lived 45 years; by nationality a Briton. Marcus Ulpius Respectus, Imperial veteran, did (this) for an excellent friend who deserved well of him.'

The Imperial Horseguards were based at Rome, and recruited from the cavalry (*alae* and part-mounted cohorts) of the provincial armies.[22] Both men are *Marcus Ulpius* and would have received citizenship from Trajan on discharge, unless they had already earned it like Longinus and Novantico. Justus is not explicitly a veteran like his executor Respectus, but this is almost certainly the case, since he had served 25 years and there is no mention of his troop (*turma*), which would have implied he was still in service.

Britain was now remote from what Trajan (like Domitian) saw to be the Empire's more pressing needs. The British legions meanwhile flung away ambition and turned to rebuilding their fortresses. We have two important texts of this consolidation, from Caerleon and York, contemporary with the most 'classic' of Roman inscriptions, that from the base of Trajan's Column in Rome. The latter is familiar, at least at second-hand, since it has become the basis of twentieth-century public lettering styles.[23] First Caerleon:

---

22 Speidel 1994.

23 *CIL* vi 960, with Evetts 1979 and Grasby 2013, Study 1. Two well-cut fragments from Chester (*RIB* 464+*add.*, III, 3153) may belong to Trajanic rebuilding there.

<4.15> *Caerleon (Isca)*

imp(eratori) Caes(ari) div[i Nervae f(ilio)]
Nervae Traia[no Aug(usto)]
Ger(manico) pontif(ici) maxim[o trib(unicia)]
potest(ate) p(atri) p(atriae)
co(n)s(uli) III
leg(io) II Aug(usta)

RIB 330+*add.*

'For the Emperor Caesar Nerva Trajan Augustus, son of Nerva, Conqueror of Germany, pontifex maximus, with tribunician power, Father of his Country, consul for the third time (AD 100), the Second Legion Augusta (erected this).'

Trajan took the name of his predecessor, the ephemeral emperor Nerva (AD 96–8), who adopted him. He has the usual imperial powers and titles, including the honorific 'Father of his Country'. This was treated by the first emperor, Augustus, as the climax of all his honours, and he assumed it only after some thirty years of absolute power; whence the convention that emperors waited a while to deserve it, but this inscription shows that they no longer waited very long.

In form it is an inscription in Trajan's honour, and the building to which it belongs is not specified; when it was in situ, this would have been obvious, but now we can only guess, since this handsome slab of white Italian marble was re-used by the Romans themselves as a paving-stone. The letters were painted with red oxide or vermilion, making a brave contrast against the white. A faithful replica was drawn and cut by Richard Grasby, and is now displayed at the Centre for the Study of Ancient Documents in Oxford.[24] He was impressed by the meticulous design, and how the carver followed every shaped brush stroke of the signwriter. Yet the roots of the V-cut strokes were seldom cleaned out, rough striations and uncut stone remaining in the letters, which suggests that the stone-cutter was only interested in the outline of each letter, the V-cut being no more than a device for holding the paint. The Romans seem to have been concerned more with colour contrast and the two-dimensional graphic effect than with the inscription's sculptural qualities, the interplay of light and shade within the letters themselves.

The somewhat laboured symmetry of this grand inscription, its first three crowded lines followed by three lines of words in splendid isolation, prompted Richard Grasby and David Zienkiewicz to examine its design more closely. Their measurements have revealed a relentless grid structure underlying not only the setting-out of lines and spaces, but the letters also.[25] Yet the mathematical symmetry of each centred

[24] Grasby in his retirement from professional letter-cutting was Research Associate at the Centre (CSAD), which has published his *Studies* (Grasby 2013). **2.19** is drawn by him.

[25] Grasby 2013, Study 2.

line was spoilt at the last moment when a third stroke was added to the numeral after COS. This changed the date from Trajan's second consulship (AD 99) to his third (AD 100): the project evidently took longer than expected and, to judge by the disharmony of the third stroke, by now someone was in a hurry.

The other inscription is from York. Its letters compared with those at Caerleon are of slightly greater weight, there is a greater contrast between the thick and thin elements of the strokes, and the serifs are more pronounced. The carving is cleaner and more consistent, and the words are 'massed' to fill the available space:

<4.16> *York (Eboracum)*

[i]mp(erator) Caesar
[divi N]ervae fil(ius) Ne[rva]
[Trai]anus Aug(ustus) Ger[m(anicus) Dac]-
[icus po]ntifex maximu[s tribun]-
[iciae po]estatis XII imp(erator) V[I co(n)s(ul) V p(ater) p(atriae)]
per leg(ionem) VIIII Hi[sp(anam)]

RIB 665+*add.*

'The Emperor Caesar Nerva Trajan Augustus, son of the deified Nerva, Conqueror of Germany, Conqueror of Dacia, pontifex maximus, in the twelfth year of his tribunician power (AD 108), acclaimed *imperator* six times, consul five times, Father of his Country, by the agency of the Ninth Legion Hispana.'

The surviving text does not specify the building, but since it was found near the south-east gate *RIB* has restored the redundant noun (*portam*) and verb (*fecit*). They are not needed. Epigraphically speaking, the Legion was going out in style, for this majestic stone is its last. It is missing from the inscribed list of Marcus Aurelius' legions[26], but we do not know where and when it disappeared. The favoured candidate used to be the crisis at Hadrian's accession (AD 117), when his ancient biographer says that 'the Britons could not be held under Roman control' and the orator Fronto implies there were heavy casualties; this is the basis of the modern myth that the Legion and its Eagle marched into the northern mist and were never seen again.[27] But Eric Birley and Lawrence Keppie have developed Ritterling's shrewd insight that the careers of at least five of the Legion's officers require that it still existed in the AD 120s, and even as late as *c.* AD 140. A stamped tile and a stamped *mortarium* of the Legion have also been found in a Hadrianic context at the lower-Rhine fortress of Nijmegen. This evidence is not conclusive (it may

[26] *ILS* 2288.

[27] Hist. Aug. *Hadrianus* 5.2, *Britanni teneri sub Romana dicione non poterant.* Fronto (writing to Marcus Aurelius *de bello Parthico*, 2), *avo vestro Hadriano imperium obtinente quantum militum ab Iudaeis, quantum ab Britannis caesum*. The resulting myth was brilliantly developed by Rosemary Sutcliffe (1970).

only mean that a detachment survived), but it strongly suggests that Trajan sent the legion to the Rhine as part of a 'musical chairs' progression of legions to his Parthian War; despite what happened to Britain after his death, he must have reckoned that two legions were sufficient to hold the reduced province. The Ninth would then have left Germany for the east, where we know that an unidentified legion was destroyed in the Jewish revolt (AD 132–5), and another in the Parthian invasion of Armenia (AD 161). One day perhaps, anywhere from the Rhine to the Tigris, the inscription will be found that will answer these questions.[28]

Vindolanda

Before leaving Trajan's Britain, it is a relief to turn from these uncertainties to the discovery and publication of the Vindolanda tablets. For epigraphists and students of the Roman army this achievement matches the Bletchley Park decipherment of the German wartime Enigma traffic, a stream of unguarded if allusive and fragmentary texts miraculously revealed. The tablets are written in ink on paper-like strips of wood, the same as those from Caerleon[29] and Carlisle (**3.14**), but found in far greater numbers. They survive with other wooden objects and organic material like leather in the waterlogged, anaerobic, levels of the earliest forts at Vindolanda which underlie the visible stone fort and other buildings to the west. The first tablets were found by Robin Birley in 1973, and his excavations have yielded hundreds more; their publication is due to experienced conservation at Vindolanda, to Alison Rutherford's innovative infra-red photography, and to years of painstaking decipherment and brilliant elucidation by two great papyrologists, Alan Bowman and David Thomas.[30] These fascinating documents are the British equivalent of the military papyri found in Egypt and on the Euphrates at Dura Europos, and they illuminate the northern frontier in the first years of the second century. We have just seen two records on stone of legionary building-work; here are two glimpses in manuscript of the organisation required, the first a military work-sheet:

<**4.17**> *Vindolanda*

Nonis Martii[s]
missi ad hospiti[u]m cum Marco medico
faciendum structores n(umero) XXX
[a]d lapidem flammandum n(umero) XVIIII
[a]d lutum vim[ini]bus castrorum facien-
[dum] ...

---

28 E Birley 1988, 316–25, 'The fate of the Ninth Legion'. Keppie 2000(b), 92–4.

29 *Britannia* 17 (1986), 450, No. 84 (cited before **3.06**).

30 *Tabulae Vindolandenses* I, II and III, supplemented by *Britannia* 41 (2010), 187–224, and 42 (2011), 113–44, with contributions by other scholars including Jim Adams and Tony Birley. See further, Bowman 1994 and Birley 2002.

Tab. Vindol. II, 156

'On the Nones of March (7 March)
sent with Marcus, the medical orderly, to build
the residence, builders, in number 30.
to burn stone, in number 19.
to produce clay for the wattle fences of the fort
...'

The 'residence' is someone's living quarters, but like so much in these texts, only the writer and his contemporaries knew what it was. Despite the reference to a 'medical orderly', this *hospitium* is unlikely to have been the 'hospital', which was called the *valetudinarium*.[31] The 'stone-burning' means lime-burning for mortar, the clay would be used for wattle-and-daub walls. The other text is a letter from an anxious underling to his chief:

<**4.18**> *Vindolanda*

[...]
quem modum carrulorum
missurus sis domine
deliberare tecum debes
ad lapidem portandum.
Voconti enim centu[ria]
carrulis uno die la[pidem]
[...]

nisi rogas Voconti[um]
ut lepidem(!) exp[licet]
non explicabi[tur]
rogo ut rescri[bas ?mihi]
quid velis me [facere]
opto bene [valeas]

Tab. Vindol. II, 316

'... you ought to consider, my lord, what quantity of wagons you are going to send to carry stone, for the century of Vocontius ... in one day with wagons ... (*2nd hand*) Unless you ask Vocontius to sort out the stone, it will not be sorted out. I ask you to write back what you want me to do. I hope you are in good health.'

This stone was perhaps intended for road-making rather than building-work. The editors recall a contemporary papyrus letter of AD 107 from the new province of Arabia (modern Jordan), in which an Egyptian legionary writes to his father that 'while others ... were breaking stones all day, I had none of this.' The reason is that

---

31 *Tab. Vindol.* II, 155.6. For this question, see the editors' commentary on both tablets.

he has wangled a clerical job instead.[32] What ever would they have thought, these two clerks, could they have seen the quarrying and the carting that were soon going to be needed for Hadrian's Wall? The Emperor himself would be keeping Vocontius up to the mark.

There is no space to do justice to this wealth of documentation; we can only thank Vindolanda and its excavators, and conclude with one of Roman Britain's most engaging texts, a letter sent to the commandant's wife by the wife of another prefect, inviting her to a birthday party. The body of the letter is in the elegant hand of a secretary, but the four-line signature (which in a Roman letter was a closing greetings) is written by the lady herself, 'almost certainly the earliest known example of writing in Latin by a woman':

<**4.19**> *Vindolanda*

Cl(audia) Severa Lepidinae [suae
[sa]l[u]tem
III Idus Septembr[e]s soror ad diem
sollemnem natalem meum rogo
libenter facias ut venias
ad nos iucundiorem mihi
[diem] interventu tuo factura si
[...] (*space*)
Cerial[em t]uum saluta Aelius meus [...]
et filiolus salutant

(*2nd hand*)
sperabo te soror
vale soror anima
mea ita valeam
karissima et {h}ave

(*On the back, 1st hand*)
Sulpiciae Lepidinae
Cerialis
a S[e]vera

Tab. Vindol. II, 291

'Claudia Severa to her Lepidina greetings. On the third day before the Ides of September (11 September), sister, for the day of the celebration of my birthday, I give you a warm invitation to make sure that you come to us, to make the day more enjoyable for me by your arrival, if you are present (?). Give my greetings to your Cerialis. My Aelius and my little son send their greetings. (*Signature*) I shall expect you, sister. Farewell, sister, my dearest soul, as I hope to prosper, and hail. (*Address*) To Sulpicia Lepidina, wife of Cerialis, from Severa.'

---

32 *P. Mich.* VIII 466.

'My dearest soul'. By happy coincidence a gold ring of much later date has been found at Vindolanda; its gemstone reads:

<**4.20**> *Vindolanda*

anima mea

RIB II.3, 2423.4

'My (dearest) soul.'

5

HADRIAN AND HADRIAN'S WALL

Hadrian turns to Britain

The writing-tablets have made Vindolanda famous, but its fine museum is also rich in stone inscriptions and other inscribed objects such as the 'Dearest Soul' ring (**4.20**).[1] One of the most important is this tombstone, since it probably alludes to warfare which drew the new Emperor's eye to Britain:

<5.01> *Vindolanda*

D(is) [M(anibus)]
T(itus) Ann[ius? ...]
centur[io cohortis I]
Tungr[orum stipen]-
diorum [... annorum ...]
T in bell[o ... inter]-
fectus [...]
fil(ius) et *ARC*[...]
h(eredes) e[x test(amento) f(aciundum) c(uraverunt) ...]

RIB III, 3364

'To the Shades of the Dead. Titus ?Annius [...], centurion of the First Cohort of Tungrians, [after ...] years of service, aged [...], killed in the war [...]. [...] his son and [...], his heirs under his will, had (this) made.'

This is the left-hand portion of a massive slab from a mausoleum which the Romans cannibalised when they built the fourth-century commandant's house (*praetorium*), but we do not know how wide the original was. It is not really possible to restore the text, different solutions being offered by Tony Birley and by *RIB*, which depend on

[1] Tomlin 2012(b).

whether the deceased was a centurion of the Tungrians who garrisoned Vindolanda, or was in fact a legionary centurion who was their acting-commander (*praepositus*).[2] However, they agree on a Hadrianic date: the abbreviation of *Dis Manibus* to its initials is second-century, but to write *stipendiorum* in full is unusual after the first century. The 'war' in which this centurion was killed is therefore likely to be the trouble at Hadrian's accession, in which it was once thought the Ninth Legion disappeared. A peculiarity of the text is the large and emphatic letter T which begins line 6, as if it were an important abbreviation: it is tempting to understand it as *t(itulum)*, an 'epitaph' or 'monument', which introduces a clause like *t(itulum) in bell[o amisit inter]fectus*, 'he lost due burial in war by being killed'. This would make the mausoleum a cenotaph, like **11.24** and the memorial to a centurion killed in the Varus disaster in Germany, whose ashes would be buried 'when possible'. It would articulate the ancient dread of becoming 'ashes without an epitaph', the phrase of the younger Pliny, who tells the story of a house terrorised by a ghost until it was laid to rest when human remains were located in the courtyard and given proper burial.[3]

Nothing more is known of this war in Britain, and the London writing-tablet (**10.22**) dated 14 March AD 118, which details the hearing of a property dispute in Kent, would suggest that the trouble was located in the north, as might be expected. Hadrian responded by appointing an experienced general as governor, who is not named by any British inscription, but is well recorded elsewhere.[4] Here is the fullest record of his name, his many names, and of his long career:

<**5.02**> *Terracina (Tarracina)*

Q(uinto) Roscio Sex(ti) f(ilio)
Quir(ina tribu) Coelio Murenae
Silio Deciano Vibull<i>o
Pio Iulio Eurycli Herclano
Pompeio Falconi, co(n)s(uli),
XVvir(o) s(acris) f(aciundis) proco(n)s(uli) provinc(iae) Asiae leg(ato) pr(o) pr(aetore)
imp(eratoris) Caes(aris) Traiani Hadriani Aug(usti) provinc(iae)
Brittanniae, leg(ato) pr(o) pr(aetore) imp(eratoris) Caes(aris) Nervae
Traiani Aug(usti) Germanici Dacici
[pr]ovinc(iae) Moesiae inferior(is), curatori
[via]e Traianae et leg(ato) Aug(usti) pr(o) pr(aetore) provinc(iae)

---

2 The Vindolanda diploma of AD 146 (*RIB* II.1, 2401.9), since it was issued to a veteran of the cohort, implies that it was still there in *c.* AD 122 when he enlisted. But by AD 128 it had evacuated Vindolanda in favour of a Wall fort, and thence to the Antonine Wall (**6.21**).

3 *ILS* 2244 (Xanten), *[ce]cidit bello Variano, ossa [i]nferre licebit*. Pliny, *ep.* vi 10.3, *cinerem sine titulo*. The ghost story is in *ep.* vii 27.

4 Sherwin-White 1966, 138–9. Birley 2005, 114–19, with full commentary.

[Iudaeae e]t leg(ionis) X Fret(ensis), leg(ato) pr(o) pr(aetore) prov(inciae) Lyciae
[et Pamphyl]iae leg(ato) leg(ionis) V Macedonic(ae)
[bello Dacico donis militari]bus donato
. . .

ILS 1035

'To Quintus Roscius Coelius Murena Silius Decianus Vibullius Pius Julius Eurycles Herclanus Pompeius Falco, son of Sextus, of the *Quirina* voting-tribe, consul, member of the Board of Fifteen for conducting sacrifices, proconsul of the province of Asia, propraetorian legate of the Emperor Caesar Trajan Hadrian Augustus of the province of Britannia, propraetorian legate of the Emperor Caesar Nerva Trajan Augustus Conqueror of Germany Conqueror of Dacia of the province of Lower Moesia, Curator of the Via Traiana, and imperial propraetorian legate of the province of Judaea and the Tenth Legion Fretensis, propraetorian legate of the province of Lycia and Pamphylia, legate of the Fifth Legion Macedonica in the Dacian War, decorated ...'

Pompeius Falco as legate of Lower Moesia was already commanding three legions on the lower Danube when he was transferred to Britain. Previously he had commanded a legion in Trajan's first Dacian War (AD 101–02), and then a second legion as governor of Judaea, before becoming consul in AD 108 and thus qualifying for a major army command. To be *quindecimvir sacris faciundis* was a social rather than religious distinction: he was appointed to one of the four great priestly colleges, custodian of the Sibylline oracles and overseer of imported cults new and old; the historian Tacitus would have been a colleague.[5] Falco's many names advertise his connection, by adoption or inheritance, with distinguished families, for example those of Julius Eurycles Herculanus, whom Augustus recognised (and later deposed) as ruler of Sparta, and of Marcus Roscius Coelius, legate of the Twentieth Legion in AD 69 (**3.19** with note). By marrying the daughter of Quintus Sosius Senecio,

[5] Syme 1958, 65; 664.

twice appointed consul by Trajan, he gained another British connection: Sosia Polla was the granddaughter of Julius Frontinus, the conqueror of Wales. When Falco subsequently became proconsul of Asia, she died on the offshore island of Samos, so she probably accompanied him also to Britain.[6]

The open frontier in the north was one of the problems which drew Hadrian to Britain in AD 122, the first reigning Emperor to visit the island since Claudius. His enterprise evoked amused admiration from a courtier named Florus, who wrote a poem beginning: '*I* don't want to be Emperor and go walkabout among the Britons'.[7] Hadrian responded with the prim parody: '*I* don't want to be Florus and go walkabout among the wine-bars (*tabernas*)'. In Britain, according to his ancient biographer who reports the badinage, Hadrian reformed many things 'and was the first to build a wall eighty miles long to separate barbarians from Romans'. This is the only literary source to credit Hadrian with his wall, and incidentally the only statement of its purpose.[8] The Brigantes in the north were only 'Romans' in the sense of being ruled by Rome, but we shall soon see one serving in the Roman army (**6.18**). Tacitus obscurely remarks that Agricola, if defensive-minded, might have stopped at the Clyde-Forth isthmus: 'if the army's valour and the glory of Rome allowed it, a boundary-line was available inside Britain itself'. With the occupation of this isthmus, 'the enemy had been pushed into what was virtually another island'.[9] Agricola went even further, of course, but Hadrian was not minded to emulate him, nor even to re-occupy the northern isthmus. But his solution was somewhat similar, even if it was of megalomaniac simplicity: the building of a wall from sea to sea across the waist of the largest island known to the Romans.[10] The scale and subsequent elaboration of this idea have been recognised by John Mann, tongue in cheek perhaps, as what psychologists would call 'displacement activity' to compensate for not conquering the other half of Britain. Hadrian's Wall, justly described by Sir Ian Richmond as 'the most august Roman monument in Britain', may also be an admission of defeat.[11]

---

[6] *ILS* 1037 (Samos), dedicated by Falco to his 'most saintly' wife, is surely her gravestone: *Sossiae Pollae Pompeius | Falco proco(n)s(ul) Asiae | sanctissimae uxori.*

[7] Hist. Aug. *Hadrianus* 16.3, *Ego nolo Caesar esse | ambulare per Britannos.*

[8] Hist. Aug. *Hadrianus*, 11.2, *murumque per octaginta milia passuum primus duxit, qui barbaros Romanosque divideret.* The two fragments of *RIB* 1051 (Jarrow) refer to a 'need' (*necessitas*), perhaps that of building the Wall, but despite Richmond's speculative reconstruction, it is uncertain whether there was one inscription or two, and whether they are Hadrianic or ?Severan, let alone what the content was.

[9] *Agricola*, 23, *si virtus exercitus et Romani nominis gloria pateretus, inventus in ipsa Britannia terminus ... summotis velut in aliam insulam hostibus.* It was AD 81, the year of Domitian's accession, who undoubtedly authorised the further advance. Tacitus, who hated Domitian, would not give him the credit.

[10] The traditional view that Hadrian himself designed the Wall is reasserted by Breeze 2009.

[11] Mann 1974, 532 (Mann 1996, 82). Richmond's phrase in his editions of Bruce 1863 was retained by C M Daniels in the 13th edition (1978), 175, but not by Breeze 2006.

The Empire's shift from the offensive to the defensive was a long process, lasting for two centuries between Augustus' loss of three legions in Germany (AD 9) and the death of Septimius Severus at York (AD 211), but if one sought a turning-point it might be the reign of Hadrian, that most intelligent and conscientious of Emperors who rejected the risky aggressions of Trajan in the East. Instead of using his thirty legions to make fresh conquests, 'fishing with a golden hook' in Augustus' phrase[12], Hadrian preferred to keep them on standby. This potential surrender of the initiative was masked by a new cult, that of Discipline personified. *Discipulina* meant much more than 'military obedience'; it meant 'learning' (from the verb *discere*), the training and technology, communications, logistics and organisation, that contributed so much to Roman military superiority:

<**5.03**> *Chesters (Cilurnum)*

[D]iscipulinae
imp(eratoris) Had(riani) Aug(usti)
ala Aug(usta)
[o]b virt(utem) appel(lata)
[...]

RIB III, 3298

'To the Discipline of the Emperor Hadrian Augustus, (dedicated by) the Cavalry Regiment styled Augusta for its valour [...]'

This fragmentary altar was found in the bank of the North Tyne outside a Wall fort, unearthed apparently by cows drinking from the river. Their amateur fieldwork has given us the earliest dedication to Discipline found anywhere in the Empire, one which confirms the evidence of coins that the cult was introduced by Hadrian. The text also names the first garrison of Chesters, confirming that the fort is Hadrianic and was built for a cavalry regiment. This may be the *ala Augusta* already seen at Lancaster (**4.01**), but although the *ala Augusta ob virtutem appellata* retained its full name until the mid-third century, it is not listed by any diploma, unless it is the *ala Augusta Gallorum* of the great Brigetio diploma.[13] This provides a panorama of the British army as seen by Hadrian, and is unique in naming so many British auxiliary units, 50 in all:

<**5.04**> *Brigetio (Szőny)*

imp(erator) Caesar divi Traiani Parthici f(ilius) divi Nervae nepos Tra|ianus Hadrianus

[12] Suetonius, *Divus Aug.* 25.4, *aureo hamo piscantibus* (making war against the odds).

[13] **13.15** (Old Carlisle, AD 242). *RIB* II.1, 2401, with Table 1. Jarrett 1994, 40–1, prefers to identify the *ala Augusta Gallorum* with the *ala Augusta Gallorum Proculeiana*.

Augustus pontifex maximus tribu|nic(ia) potestat(e) VI co(n)sul III proco(n)s(ul) | equitib(us) et peditib(us) qui militaverunt in alis decem et trib(us) et coh<or>||tib(us) triginta et septem, quae appellantur (1) I Pannonior(um) Sabinian(a) | et (2) I Pannon(iorum) Tampian(a) et (3) I Hispan(orum) Astur(um) et (4) I Tungror(um) et (5) II Astur(um) | et (6) Gallor(um) Picentiana et (7) Gallor(um) et Thrac(um) Classiana c(ivium) R(omanorum) et (8) Gallor(um) | Petriana (milliaria) c(ivium) R(omanorum) et (9) <G>allor(um) Sebosiana et (10) Vetton(um) Hispan(orum) c(ivium) R(omanorum) et | (11) Agrippiana Miniata et (12) Aug(usta) Gallor(um) et (13) Aug(usta) Vocontior(um) c(ivium) R(omanorum); et (1) I || Nervia German(orum) (milliaria) et (2) I Celtiberor(um) et (3) I Thrac(um) et (4) I Afror(um) c(ivium) R(omanorum) et (5) I | Lingon(um) et (6) I fida Vardullor(um) (milliaria) c(ivium) R(omanorum) et (7) I Frisiavon(um) et (8) I Vangion(um) | (milliaria) et (9) I Hamior(um) sagitt(ariorum) et (10) I Delmat(arum) et (11) I Aquitan(orum) et (12) I Ulpia Traia|na Cugern(orum) c(ivium) R(omanorum) et (13) I Morin(orum) et (14) I Menapior(um) et (15) I Sunucor(um) et (16) I B<a>etas|ior(um) et (17) I Batavor(um) et (18) I Tungror(um) et (19) I Hispan(orum) et (20) II Gallor(um) et (21) II || Vascon(um) c(ivium) R(omanorum) et (22) II Thrac(um) et (23) II Lingon(um) et (24) II Astur(um) et (25) II Delmatar(um) | et (26) II Nervior(um) et (27) III Nervior(um) et (28) III Bracar(augustan)or(um) et (29) III Lingon(um) | et (30) IIII Gallor(um) et <(31) IV Lingonum et> (32) IIII Breucor(um) et (33) IIII Delmatar(um) et (34) V Raetor(um) | et (35) V Gallor(um) et (36) VI Nervior(um) et (37) VII Thrac(um), quae sunt in Britan|nia sub A(ulo) Platorio Nepote, quinque et viginti stipendis || emeritis dimissis honesta missione per Pompeium | Falconem, quorum nomina subscripta sunt, ipsis libe|ris posterisq(ue) eorum civitatem dedit et conub(ium) cum uxo|rib(us) quas tunc habuissent, cum est civitas iis data, | aut, siqui caelibes essent, cum iis quas postea duxis||sent, dumtaxat singuli singulas.
A(nte) d(iem) XVI K(alendas) Aug(ustas), | Ti(berio) Iulio Capitone, L(ucio) Vitrasio Flaminino co(n)s(ulibus).
| Alae I Pannonior(um) Tampianae qui prae<e>st | Fabius Sabinus, | ex sesquiplicario || Gemello Breuci f(ilio), Pannon(io).
| Descriptum et recognitum ex tabula aenea quae fixa est | Romae in muro post templum divi Aug(usti) ad Minervam.
| Ti(beri) Claudi Menandri | A(uli) Fulvi Iusti | Ti(beri) Iuli Urbani | L(uci) Pulli Daphni | L(uci) Noni Victoris | Q(uinti) Lolli Festi | L(uci) Pulli Anthi.

CIL xvi 69 (outer text with corrections from the inner)

'The Emperor Caesar Trajan Hadrian Augustus, son of the deified Trajan, grandson of the deified Nerva, pontifex maximus, in his sixth year of tribunician power, three times consul, proconsul, has granted to the cavalrymen and infantrymen who served in 13 alae and 37 cohorts called (*50 names*) which are in Britain under Aulus Platorius Nepos, who have served 25 years and have been honourably discharged by agency of Pompeius Falco, whose names are written below, citizenship for themselves, their children and descendants, and the right of legal marriage with the wives they had when citizenship was granted to them, or, if any were unmarried, with those they later marry, but only a single one each.

'On the sixteenth day before the Kalends of August in the consulship of Tiberius Iulius

Capito and Lucius Vitrasius Flamininus (17 July AD 122).

'To Gemellus son of Breucus, a Pannonian, retired *sesquiplicarius* of the First Cavalry Regiment of Pannonians Tampiana, commanded by Fabius Sabinus.

'Copied and checked from the bronze tablet set up at Rome on the wall behind the temple of the deified Augustus near (the statue of) Minerva.'

(*Sealed by seven named witnesses*)

These 50 auxiliary units are not quite a complete list, since (like other diplomas) the Brigetio diploma lists only those which were discharging veterans, but Paul Holder has estimated that in AD 122 there were 14 alae and about 47 cohorts (seven double-strength or 'milliary'), about 35,000 men in all. David Breeze estimates as many as 63 or 64 units.[14] This well-preserved diploma was found like Lucco's (**4.11**) in modern Hungary, on the site of the Danubian fortress of the First Legion Adiutrix. It was found in 1930, and was bought by the British Museum because of its relevance to Roman Britain. Holder estimates that 'some 550 copies' might have been required of this issue, and fragments of another four have been found since.[15] This incidentally is a high survival-rate. The papyrologist Robert Fink reckoned that the imperial Roman army, with three pay-records annually for each man, must have produced in the three centuries from Augustus to Diocletian, 'at the very least 225,000,000 individual pay-records'. It is difficult to estimate how many have actually survived, since possible documents are fragmentary and of uncertain reference, but they are certainly few and far between; only three legionaries, for example, pay-sheets and all, are named in full.[16]

Gemellus, the auxiliary who received the Brigetio diploma, was a *sesquiplicarius*, so-called because he received 'one and a half times' the basic rate of pay; he was third-in-command of a cavalry troop of 30 men in a regiment we have already seen at Carnuntum (**4.05**). Its commander, Fabius Sabinus, is presumably the man of that name later prefect of the Ravenna fleet in AD 139.[17] Gemellus was a Pannonian, his father's name being the same as that of Lucco's father-in-law (**4.11**); since both diplomas were found at Brigetio, he may even have been Lucco's brother-in-law. At all events, he returned home (at his own expense) after 25 years' service, so he must have enlisted in AD 97, when the regiment or part of it was probably in Pannonia (**4.05**).

[14] Holder 1982, 17. Breeze 2006, 43.

[15] Holder in *RMD* V (2006), note 3 to No. 361, citing another two; the fifth is *Britannia* 39 (2008), 381, No. 18, found in 2007.

[16] Fink 1971, 242. The legionaries are all from Syria or the Lebanon: Gaius Messius of Beirut (Cotton and Geiger 1989, 35–56, No. 722), Julius Proculus of Damascus (*RMR* 68) and Valerius Germanus of Tyre (*RMR* 68 again). A fourth is partly named in *RMR* 69, and auxiliaries are listed in the fragmentary *RMR* 70. Other possible pay-records are Cotton and Geiger, 77, No. 733 (a single word), *RMR* 71, 72, and Addenda 129, 130, 131, 132.

[17] Diploma dated 22 August 139 (*AE* 2007, 1786).

Since the veterans have been discharged by Pompeius Falco (**5.02**), but Platorius Nepos is said to be the governor, the latter can have only just arrived. Subsequently he is named by seven inscriptions from Hadrian's Wall, and his career is tabulated by this inscription from north-east Italy:

<**5.05**> *Aquileia*

A(ulo) Platorio A(uli) f(ilio)
Serg(ia tribu) Nepoti
Aponio Italico
Maniliano
G(aio) Licinio Pollioni
co(n)s(uli), auguri, legat(o) Aug(usti)
pro praet(ore) provinc(iae) Bri-
tanniae, leg(ato) pro pr(aetore) pro-
vinc(iae) German(iae) inferior(is),
leg(ato) pro pr(aetore) provinc(iae) Thrac(iae),
leg(ato) legion(is) I Adiutricis,
quaest(ori) provinc(iae) Maced(oniae),
curat(ori) viarum Cassiae Clodiae Ciminiae novae
Traianae, candidato divi
Traiani, trib(uno) mil(itum) leg(ionis) XXII
Primigen(iae) p(iae) f(idelis), praet(ori), trib(uno)
pleb(is), IIIvir capitali
patrono
d(ecreto) d(ecurionum)

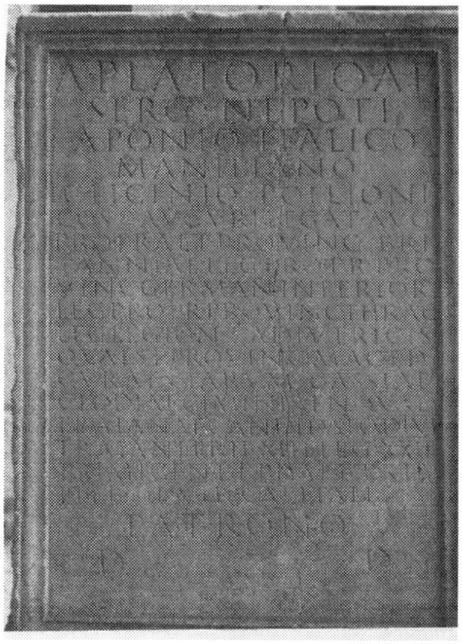

ILS 1052

'To Aulus Platorius Nepos Aponius Italicus Manilianus Gaius Licinius Pollio, son of Aulus, of the *Sergia* voting-tribe, consul (AD 119), augur, imperial propraetorian legate of the province of Britain, propraetorian legate of the province of Lower Germany, propraetorian legate of the province of Thrace, legate of the First Legion Adiutrix, quaestor of the province of Macedonia, commissioner of the *Cassia, Clodia, Ciminia* and *nova Traiana* roads, candidate of the Deified Trajan, military tribune of the Twenty-Second Legion Primigenia Dutiful and Loyal, praetor, tribune of the plebs, member of the Board of Three for Prisons, patron (of this city), by decree of the city councillors.'

Like Pomponius Mamilianus (**4.10**) and Pompeius Falco (**5.02**), Nepos displays 'polyonomy', his many extra names indicating family connections or adoptions. His career is given in reverse order, though there is some confusion in his earliest posts. He was a close friend of Hadrian before his accession, and since he belongs to the same voting-tribe, he may have come like him from Baetica (Andalusia).[18] He

[18] Hist. Aug., *Hadrianus* 4.2 and 23.4.

commanded a legion in Trajan's Parthian War, and with the accession of Hadrian (AD 117) his rise was rapid: governor of Thrace, consul (AD 119), and then governor of Lower Germany with its two legions; here he survived an imperial tour of inspection and accompanied Hadrian to Britain, a promotion, since it was a province of three legions. One of these was the Sixth Legion Victrix, previously part of the garrison of Lower Germany, which was now transferred to Britain; Aulus Plautius and Petillius Cerialis had likewise both brought legions with them from their previous commands. This legion, however, since it filled the gap left by the Ninth, was an agent of consolidation, not of conquest. More than half a century later, its transfer was remembered as an early episode in the career of an elder statesman:

<5.06> *Rome, Forum of Trajan*

M(arco) Pontio M(arci) f(ilio) Pup(iena tribu)
Laeliano Larcio Sabino, co(n)s(uli), pon-
tifici, sodali Antoniniano Veriano,
fetiali, leg(ato) Aug(usti) pr(o) pr(aetore) prov(inciae) Syriae, leg(ato) Aug(usti)
pr(o) pr(aetore) prov(inciae) Pannon(iae) super(ioris), leg(ato) Aug(usti) pr(o) pr(aetore) Pan-
non(iae) infer(ioris), comiti divi Veri Aug(usti), donato donis
militarib(us) bello Armeniaco et Parthico
ab imp(eratore) Antonino Aug(usto) et a divo Vero Aug(usto)
[coron(is)] mu[rali vallari clas]sica aur[ea]
[hast(is) puris IIII vexill(is) IIII, comiti imp(eratoris) Anto]-
[n]ini Aug(usti) et divi Veri bello Germanic(o)
item comiti imp(eratoris) Antonini Aug(usti) Germanici Sar-
matici, leg(ato) leg(ionis) I Miner(viae), curatori civit(atis) Araus(ionis)
prov(inciae) Galliae Narb(onensis), praetori, trib(uno) pleb(is) candidato
imp(eratoris) divi Hadriani, ab act(is) senat(us), quaestor(i) prov(inciae)
Narb(onensis), trib(uno) mil(itum) leg(ionis) VI Victr(icis) cum qua ex Germ(ania) in
Brittan(iam) transiit, IIIIvir(o) viar(um) curandar(um).
huic senatus auctore M(arco) Aurelio Antonino Aug(usto)
Armeniac(o) Medic(o) Parthic(o) maximo Germ(anico) Sarmat(ico)
statuam poni habitu civili in foro divi Traiani
pecunia publica censuit

ILS 1094 and 1100

'To Marcus Pontius Laelianus Larcius Sabinus, son of Marcus, of the *Pupiena* voting-tribe, consul (AD 145), pontifex, priest of the cult of Antoninus and Verus, *fetialis* priest, imperial propraetorian legate of the province of Syria, imperial propraetorian legate of the province of Upper Pannonia, imperial propraetorian legate of the province of Lower Pannonia, companion of the deified Verus Augustus, given military decorations for the Armenian and Parthian War by the Emperor Antoninus (Marcus Aurelius) and the deified Verus Augustus, (consisting of) Mural, Rampart, Fleet and Golden Crowns, four Untipped

> Spears, four Banners; companion of the Emperor Antoninus Augustus and the deified Verus in the German War; likewise companion of the Emperor Antoninus Augustus Conqueror of Germany and Sarmatia; legate of the First Legion Minervia, Curator of the city of Arausio (Orange) in the province of Gallia Narbonensis, praetor, tribune of the plebs, candidate of the deified Emperor Hadrian, record-keeper of the Senate, quaestor of the province of Narbonensis, military tribune of the Sixth Legion Victrix with which he crossed from Germany to Britain, one of the Four Commissioners for Roads. The Senate decided on the proposal of Marcus Aurelius Antoninus Augustus, Conqueror of Armenia and Media, Greatest Conqueror of Parthia, Conqueror of Germany and Sarmatia, that a statue of him in civilian dress should be set up in the Forum of Trajan at public expense.'

Pontius Laelianus as a young man in AD 122 was second-in-command of the Sixth Legion Victrix 'with which he crossed from Germany to Britain', which would have brought him to Hadrian's notice again, after Hadrian had already sponsored his early senatorial career. A *pontifex* was a member of the most senior priestly college headed by the Emperor as *pontifex maximus*, while the *fetiales* were an ancient priesthood revived by Augustus, responsible for the formal declaration of war and making treaties; little expertise was required for either appointment, they were social distinctions. In the pacific reign of Antoninus Pius (AD 138–61), Laelianus commanded two major armies, first in Upper Pannonia and then Syria. When Marcus Aurelius at his accession was faced by the threat of war on two fronts, he sent his inexperienced colleague Lucius Verus to the east, with Laelianus as a senior adviser. Here he is said to have been a strict disciplinarian, but this may be no more than a cliché: the city-based Syrian army was regularly 'disciplined' before campaigning, and Laelianus after all had commanded it only 10 years before. However, he was lavishly decorated and, with his Danubian experience, he was chosen by Marcus for the bitter fighting of the early AD 170s in central Europe. He would then have been aged about 70, so this inscription is probably his obituary.[19]

We may even know the commander of the Sixth Legion in AD 122, Publius Tullius Varro, who was certainly its legate now or a little earlier, after being legate of another legion; such a repetition is most unusual, and it may mean that an experienced general was specially chosen for the mission.[20] The legion marked its arrival in northern Britain by dedicating two handsome altars at Newcastle where a new bridge crossed the Tyne, 'Hadrian's Bridge' (*pons Aelius*), named after Publius Aelius Hadrianus:

---

[19] Birley 2005, 284–5, his consulship dated by *RMD* V 397, n. 4.

[20] Birley 2005, 246, commenting on *ILS* 1047, which takes Varro's career to the governorship of Upper Moesia and the proconsulate of Africa. Compare Aurelius Polus Terentianus (**7.13**).

<**5.07**> *Newcastle upon Tyne (Pons Aelius)*

Neptuno le(gio)

VI Vi(ctrix)

p(ia) f(idelis)

RIB 1319+*add.*

'To Neptune, the Legion VI Victrix Dutiful and Loyal (set this up)'

<**5.08**> *Newcastle upon Tyne (Pons Aelius)*

Ociano(!) leg(io)
VI Vi(ctrix)
p(ia) f(idelis)

RIB 1320+*add.*

'To Ocean, the Legion VI Victrix Dutiful and Loyal (set this up)'

These altars were found in the river bed, at the presumed site of the Roman bridge. Neptune receives the attributes of a sea god, a dolphin and trident (compare **3.03**), but he is really the Roman god of water who is appropriately worshipped with Ocean where the estuary meets the open sea; lead tablets addressed to him have been found in the Hamble estuary (**12.75**), and in the Thames estuary at the site of London Bridge.[21] *Ociano* (*i* for *e*) is a 'Vulgar' spelling, but the pronunciation would have been the same. Ocean is specifically the North Sea, the ship's anchor implying that the Legion was grateful to have been allowed to cross it safely. Claudius had congratulated himself on crossing Ocean (**1.12**), and three centuries later, so did the emperor Constans (**14.14**).

[21] *Britannia* 18 (1987), 360, No. 1 (as *Metunus*).

It is unusual for a legion to dedicate an altar collectively: in Britain the only other instances are by the Twentieth at Chester (**12.27**, to the Nymphs and Springs) and by the Second at Corbridge (to the Discipline of the Emperors).[22] It is also unusual for the name of the deity to be inscribed on the capital of an altar before the reign of Septimius Severus; the only other instances occur at Antonine forts in Scotland.[23] For this reason, therefore, the Hadrianic dating has been questioned.[24] But the imagery strongly implies that the legion had just arrived in the Tyne estuary by sea, and the unusual layout may have been meant to emphasise the legion's name and the maritime symbols by reserving the whole of the die for them. The layout is comparable with that of Cocceius Firmus' four altars at Auchendavy: two capitals are inscribed with the deity's name, the other two are not, and the criterion is obviously not one of date, but whether the whole text would fit within the die.[25]

The Sixth Legion now replaced the Ninth at York, and remained there until the end of the Roman period, but for the moment it was busy with the new Wall; so many skilled masons and engineers were needed, that the three British legions were temporarily reinforced by yet another 3000 legionaries:

<**5.09**> Ferentinum

T(itus) Pontius T(iti) f(ilius) Pal(atina tribu) Sabinus
praef(ectus) coh(ortis) I Pann(oniorum) et Dalmat(arum)
eq(uitatae) c(ivium) R(omanorum), trib(unus) mil(itum) leg(ionis) VI Ferrat(ae),
donis donatus expeditione Par-
thica a divo Traiano hasta pura
vexillo corona murali, (centurio) leg(ionis) XXII
Primig(eniae), (centurio) leg(ionis) XIII Gemin(ae), primus pi-
lus leg(ionis) III Aug(ustae), praepositus vexilla-
tionibus milliaris tribus expedi-
tione Brittannica leg(ionis) VII Gemin(ae)
VIII Aug(ustae) XXII Primig(eniae), trib(unus) coh(ortis) III
vigilum, coh(ortis) XIIII urb(anae), coh(ortis) II praet(oriae),
p(rimus) p(ilus) II, proc(urator) provinc(iae) Narbonens(is),
IIIIvir i(uri) d(icundo) quinq(ennalis), flamen, patron(us)
municipi

ILS 2726 (back)

---

22 *RIB* 1127.

23 Kewley 1973, citing **12.58** and **12.60** (Auchendavy), **8.15** (Cramond), *RIB* 2160 (Croy Hill) and **6.26** (Old Kilpatrick). 29 such altars cannot be dated, but of 28 which can be, 'only seven may be assigned to the second century'.

24 Breeze 2006, 144–5.

25 **12.58** and **12.60** (with inscribed capitals); **12.18** and **12.59** (without).

> 'Titus Pontius Sabinus, son of Titus, of the *Palatina* voting-tribe, prefect of the First Cohort of Pannonians and Dalmatians part-mounted, Roman Citizens, military tribune of the Sixth Legion Ferrata (and) decorated by the deified Trajan in the Parthian Campaign with untipped spear, banner and mural crown, centurion of the Twenty-Second Legion Primigenia, centurion of the Thirteenth Legion Gemina, first-ranking centurion of the Third Legion Augusta, officer commanding the three detachments 1000-strong of the Seventh Legion Gemina, the Eighth Legion Augusta and the Twenty-Second Legion Primigenia in the British Campaign, tribune of the Third Cohort of the Vigiles, the Thirteenth Urban Cohort, the Second Cohort of the Praetorian Guard; first-ranking centurion for the second time, procurator of the province of Narbonensis, city magistrate in the fifth year, priest of the imperial cult, patron of the town.'

This is a statue-base, the face of which carries a summary dedication to Sabinus by his wife. The text here is that on the back, which details his whole career. Despite the names they have in common, he is not related to Pontius Laelianus (**5.06**), since they belong to different voting-tribes. Like many career-inscriptions, this honours a local magnate: the fifth-year magistrates were equivalent to the old Censors at Rome, revising the membership roll of the local senate. But Sabinus' career is very unusual in that, instead of proceeding from his successful tribunate in the legion to the command of an *ala*, he became a centurion instead; it has been suggested[26] that he was demoted for not accepting Hadrian's renunication of Trajan's conquests, but this is not borne out by his important part in Hadrian's British campaign. The length of his military career suggests instead that this is what he preferred. Centurions, unlike equestrian officers, were not restricted to short-term commissions, and some equestrians by birth preferred to be directly commissioned as a legionary centurion rather than to become the prefect of an auxiliary cohort. Two British examples are the African *eques* Octavius Honoratus, who was directly commissioned into the Second Legion Augusta by Antoninus Pius, and the future procurator of Britain, Valerius Pansa, who was twice first-ranking centurion (*primus pilus*).[27] Yet another is the future Emperor Pertinax (**7.02**), who is expressly said to have sought a centurion's commission, but to have settled for an equestrian prefecture.[28] Sabinus did not make this choice at the outset, but it was justified by his rapid promotion thereafter: after being tribune shortly before AD 117 (when Trajan died), he became the first-ranking centurion of the African legion within 5 years, that is, if he came to Britain in AD 122. To allow more time for his previous service in three legions, Eric Birley suggested that the reference was to a second (and later) 'British campaign',

[26] Letta 2007.

[27] Respectively *ILS* 2655, *(centurioni) adlecto ex eq(uite) R(omano) a divo Pio in leg(ionem) II Aug(ustam)* and *CIL* v 6513 (with Birley 2005, 311).

[28] Hist. Aug. *Pertinax* 1.5.

but there is no direct evidence of one; and the term *expeditio* usually implies that the Emperor was there in person.[29] At all events, Sabinus' responsibilities in Britain were far greater than those of a short-term equestrian officer: his 'task-force' was equivalent to half a legion at full strength, and even the logistics would have been demanding, for the Seventh Legion Gemina was based in north-west Spain, its only legion, but the Eighth Legion Augusta (at Strasbourg) and the Twenty-Second Primigenia (at Mainz) were the garrison of Upper Germany.

Both German armies, then, contributed to the British campaign. Lower Germany contributed the Sixth Legion, and like it, Sabinus' task-force arrived in northern Britain by ship, judging by a sad souvenir found in the bed of the Tyne at Newcastle: it is the decorative bronze plate which formed the centrepiece of a rectangular legionary shield, consisting of eight incised panels grouped round a central boss with the figure of an eagle. There is a legionary standard on either side, Mars above, and a bull with the constellation of Taurus below, the emblem of the the Eighth Legion Augusta; in the corners are the Four Seasons. Two revealing inscriptions have been punched in dots:

<**5.10**> *Tyne estuary*

(i) leg(io) VIII Aug(usta)

(ii) (centuria) Iuli Magni Iuni Dubitati

RIB II.3, 2426.1

'The Eighth Legion Augusta. Century of Julius Magnus, (the property) of Junius Dubitatus.'

Dubitatus may only have dropped his shield while disembarking, the cost of replacement being stopped from his pay, but perhaps he was drowned with it, like the junior officer from Chester who was shipwrecked (**11.24**). His commanding officer, Pontius Sabinus (**5.09**), fared much better in Britain, since his subsequent career was orthodox and successful, culminating in the charge of the public finances of Gallia Narbonensis (now Provence). But another centurion, Julius Quadratus, who may have accompanied Sabinus from Africa to Britain, did not have a good war:

<**5.11**> *Castellum Arsacalitanum, Numidia*

D(is) M(anibus)
M(arcus) Iulius G(ai) f(ilius) Quir(ina tribu)
Quadratus

[29] As in **1.07**, **3.19**, **6.02**, **9.19** and probably **9.28**. But **6.14** is an exception. The question is discussed by Breeze, Dobson and Maxfield 2012, who prefer the shorter chronology.

eq(uo) pub(lico) in V
dec(urias) allecto,
(centurio) leg(ionis) XIII Gem(inae)
in Dacia,
(centurio) leg(ionis) III Aug(ustae) in Afr(ica),
(centurio) leg(ionis) II Aug(ustae) Britta(niae),
def(unctus) Brittaniae
in procinctu.
v(ixit) a(nnos) XXXVIII
h(ic) s(itus) e(st)

AE 1957, 249

'To the Shades of the Dead. Marcus Julius Quadratus, son of Gaius, of the *Quirina* voting-tribe, (allotted) a public horse and enrolled in the five squadrons, centurion of the the Thirteenth Legion Gemina in Dacia, centurion of the the Third Legion Augusta in Africa, centurion of the Second Legion Augusta in Britain, died in Britain on active service. He lived 38 years (and) is buried here.'

Julius Quadratus did not rise from the ranks like most centurions; like Honoratus and Pansa, he was an equestrian, indeed one of the élite who received a 'public horse' like Stlaccius Coranus (**2.09**) and Maenius Agrippa (**5.12**).[30] The combination of the formulaic abbreviations D M and H S E suits the second quarter of the second century, and Eric Birley has noticed that Quadratus, who was directly commissioned into the centurionate like Pontius Sabinus (**5.09**), also shared the same sequence of the Thirteenth Legion Gemina and the Third Legion Augusta followed by a British posting; so it is possible they served on the same expedition.[31] If H S E is to be taken literally, it means that Quadratus' body was cremated in Britain, like the bodies of the Emperor Septimius Severus and the riding-master of the praetorian guard (**8.19**) a century later, and his ashes were shipped home to Africa.

For another young careerist the British campaign was a turning-point; like Sabinus (**5.09**) he too became a procurator, but like Agricola he is almost unique in his accumulation of posts in Britain:

<**5.12**> *Camerinum*

M(arco) Maenio G(ai) f(ilio) Cor(nelia tribu) Agrip-
pae L(ucio) Tusidio Campestri
hospiti divi Hadriani, patri
senatoris, praef(ecto) coh(ortis) II Fl(aviae)

[30] Other examples are Pertinax (**7.02**) and Antonius Gargilianus (**10.20**).

[31] E Birley 1988, 215.

Britton(um) equitat(ae), electo
a divo Hadriano et misso
in expeditionem Britan-
nicam, trib(uno) coh(ortis) I Hispanor(um)
equitat(ae), praef(ecto) alae
Gallor(um) et Pannonior(um) catafracta-
tae, proc(uratori) Aug(usti), praef(ecto) classis
Brittannicae, proc(uratori) provin-
ciae Brittanniae, equo pu-
blico patrono, municipi
vicani Censorglacenses
consecuti ab indulgentia
optimi maximique imp(eratoris) Anto-
nini Aug(usti) Pii beneficio inter-
pretationis eius privilegia quibus in p[e]rpetuum aucti
confirmatique sunt
l(oco) d(ato) d(ecreto) d(ecurionum)

ILS 2735

'To Marcus Maenius Agrippa Lucius Tusidius Campester, son of Gaius, of the *Cornelia* voting-tribe, host of the deified Hadrian, father of a Senator, prefect of the Second Flavian Cohort of Britons part-mounted, singled out by the deified Hadrian and sent on the British campaign, tribune of the First Cohort of Spaniards part-mounted, prefect of the armoured Cavalry Regiment of Gauls and Pannonians, imperial procurator, prefect of the British fleet, procurator of the province of Britain, equestrian (allotted) a public horse, patron of (this) town; (from) the Villagers of Censorglacium, thanks to his mediation having gained by the kindness of the best and greatest Emperor Antoninus Augustus Pius the privileges by which they are forever increased and strengthened. Site given by decision of the town-councillors.'

Yet another local magnate, but like Quadratus (**5.11**) he belonged to the equestrian élite, and his influence extended far beyond his home town. Maenius Agrippa was personally acquainted with Hadrian, whom he probably accompanied to Britain in AD 122.[32] He would have met a few Britons already in his first command, a 'British' cohort on the lower Danube, if any survived from its enrolment. In Britain he was promoted to command the cohort at Maryport on the Cumbrian coast, as we know from an altar found there before 1725, when it was being used as a sun-dial:

[32] For what follows, see Birley 2005, 307–9, and Breeze, Dobson and Maxfield 2012. Agrippa may even have entertained Hadrian at Maryport, but the most likely occasion is Camerinum in 117, when Hadrian is known to have toured Picenum (Birley, 308).

<5.13> *Maryport (Alauna)*

I(ovi) O(ptimo) M(aximo)
coh(ors) I His(panorum)
cui prae(est)
M(arcus) Maeni-
us Agrip(pa)
tribu(nus)
pos(uit)

RIB 823+*add.*, with *Britannia* 44 (2013), 395, add. (c)

'To Jupiter, Best and Greatest, the First Cohort of Spaniards, which is commanded by the tribune Marcus Maenius Agrippa, set (this) up.'

The missing top-left corner was only found in 2012, when the pit in which the altar had been buried was re-excavated. This excavation showed that many altars from Maryport were ruthlessly re-used as packing for the upright timbers of a late-Roman building, including Agrippa's three other dedications to Jupiter, already found in 1870.[33] The rank of tribune implies that his cohort was 'milliary' (double-strength), but this presents a problem, since military diplomas do not give it this status, and at least three of its other commanders at Maryport are only prefects.[34] Like the prefect Donatianus at Carvoran (**12.86**), Agrippa may have owed his tribunate to imperial favour, but since Caballius Priscus, his likely successor, was also a tribune[35], it is more likely that the cohort was enlarged at the time (compare **6.22** with note) or that Maryport was of particular importance in the first years of the Hadrianic frontier. It is usually thought that Agrippa dedicated each of his altars on 3 January, when the cohort renewed its vows for the welfare of the Emperor, which would imply that he spent 4 years at Maryport, before being promoted to command an *ala* on the lower Danube in Lower Moesia.[36] Tony Birley has pointed out that the governor of this province was Sextus Iulius Severus, who became governor of Britain in *c.* AD 130, which may account for Agrippa's return to Britain to command the fleet.[37] This had played its part in Agricola's conquests, and it is worth noting that the three legionary fortresses, like the two ends of the Wall, were sited on navigable estuaries; the fleet's importance was in logistics, not as a fighting force, and it contained engineers and masons (**5.37**). Agrippa's likely successor, Aufidius Pantera (**12.74**), was no sea-dog

33 *Britannia* 43 (2012), 294. Agrippa's other altars are *RIB* 824, 825 and 826.

34 *RIB* 821, 822, 827, 828 and 829; the status of 814 is uncertain.

35 *RIB* 817–20.

36 But Breeze, Dobson and Maxfield (2012) note that only *RIB* 823 is expressly dedicated by the cohort; 824 and 825 are dedicated by Agrippa alone, and since they link Jupiter with the *numen Augusti*, he may instead have been marking the anniversaries of his patron's accession.

37 Birley 2005, 307–9.

either. Meanwhile Agrippa, without leaving Britain, went from the fleet to the most senior equestrian appointment in Britain, the procuratorship, in which important financial post (by now towards the end of Hadrian's reign) he would have had the means, if not the inclination, to count the cost of building Hadrian's Wall.

Building Hadrian's Wall

This project by now had been much elaborated. Hadrian seems to have originally envisaged a northward-facing barrier across the waist of Britain, taking the high ground north of the Stanegate 'frontier' and its garrisons housed in forts in the more sheltered valleys of the rivers Tyne, Irthing and Eden. The work was divided among the legions, each of which divided its allotment between cohorts which laid the foundations ten (Roman) feet wide and built milecastles and turrets, and other cohorts which built the Wall curtain, working westward in stone as far as the river Irthing at Wall Mile 49, and then in turf except for turrets in stone, a change of material not satisfactorily explained.[38] There was a ditch in front of the Wall, which was pierced at every mile by a double gate and guard post (the 'milecastles'), and overlooked by two integral towers or 'turrets' between each milecastle at one-third of a mile intervals. The many gates would make it permeable to traffic, whether civil or military, but this traffic would be supervised. It was not a fighting-platform, but 'an elevated sentry-walk, the sentries being supplied from the garrisons of the milecastles and having the turrets as their immediate quarters when on duty'.[39] It was still 'eight feet wide and twelve feet high, running in a straight line from east to west' when Bede saw it, but the wall-walk was lost centuries ago, even if its existence can be deduced.[40] A modern army would have erected a razor-wire fence.

If each gate had its own tower, as seems likely, there would have been a tower every third of a mile, for 80 miles (*c.* 129 km). 'East to West as far as the eye can turn … one long, low, rising and falling, and hiding and showing line of towers. And that is the Wall!' The words of Kipling's fourth-century centurion were echoed by Camden when he saw it for himself in 1599: 'Verily I have seene the tract of it over the high pitches and steepe descents of hills, wonderfully rising and falling …'[41] Two ancient 'souvenirs' are thought to embody this vision, enamelled bronze vessels decorated with a moulded rectangular pattern suggesting a masonry wall and crenellated towers, and above it a moulded inscription. The first was found in 1725, the 'Rudge cup':

---

[38] Breeze 2006, 58–9, questioning the usual explanation that limestone (for lime) was no longer available.

[39] Collingwood 1921, 9.

[40] Bede, *Hist.* i 12, *octo pedes latum et XII altum, recta ab oriente in occasum linea* (trans. Colgrave and Mynors). The wall-walk has been reasserted (against Breeze 2006, 109–10) by Bidwell 2008(b).

[41] Kipling 1906, 'On the Great Wall'. Camden (in Holland's translation) is quoted by Birley 1961, 6.

<5.14> *Rudge, Wilts.*

a Mais Aballava Uxelod(un)um Camboglan(na){s} Banna

RIB II.2, 2415.53, with Breeze 2012 (Allason-Jones)

'From Bowness-on-Solway: Burgh-by-Sands, Stanwix, Castlesteads, Birdoswald.'

These are the Wall forts in sequence from the western end, except that Drumburgh (*Congabata*) has been omitted after Bowness-on-Solway. This bronze pan has lost its handle, but otherwise closely resembles the 'Amiens patera' which was found in 1949 and carries the same sequence of names, but with one addition:

<5.15> *Amiens (Samarobriva Ambianorum)*

Mais Aballava Uxellodunum Cambog[lanis] Banna Esica

AE 1950, 56, with Breeze 2012 (Maheo)

'From Bowness-on-Solway: Burgh-by-Sands, Stanwix, Castlesteads, Birdoswald, Great Chesters.'

ESICA is a phonetic spelling also found in the Ravenna Cosmography, a list of place-names compiled in *c.* AD 700 from a map now lost, but the Notitia Dignitatum preserves the correct form *Aesica*. The latter is a 'list of high offices' compiled at about the end of the fourth century, which devotes a chapter each to the two generals who then commanded frontier-troops in Britain, the Count of the Saxon Shore and the Duke of the Britains. In detailing their responsibilities, it is our principal source for the names of forts.

The 'patera' may have been brought to Amiens by a discharged veteran of the British garrison: a first-ranking centurion (*primus pilus*) of the Sixth Legion was buried there, and it was a transit point for troops on their way to Britain.[42] In 2003 the 'cup' and 'patera' were joined by a third vessel of the same type, the Ilam (or Staffordshire Moorlands) pan, which has also lost its handle. But the decoration is different, 'dragonesque' roundels filled with enamel. This may mean that the 'crenellated' pattern did not really represent the Wall, but was only part of the design repertoire; certainly it is found on two similar vessels which are not expressly Wall 'souvenirs'.[43] Above these roundels is incised:

<5.16> *Ilam, Staffs.*

Draconis Mais Co(n)gabata Uxelodunum Cam(b)og(l)anna rigore val(l)i Aeli

Britannia 35 (2004), 344, No. 24; Breeze 2012 (Jackson)

---

42 *CIL* xiii 3497; **8.12**, *euntes [ad] expedi[t(ionem)] Britanicam.*

43 Breeze 2012, 4–6 (the Hildburgh Fragment and the Bath Pan).

'(Property) of Draco, from Bowness-on-Solway: Drumburgh, Stanwix, Castlesteads, on the line of the Aelian Wall.'

This inscription was not moulded, but incised, which suggests that it was personal to Draco. Unfortunately there is no punctuation, which means that AELI is ambiguous. It might be the (imperial) nomen of Draco, if he were an auxiliary veteran enfranchised in Hadrian's reign who paid for this souvenir of his service, but it is more likely to be the adjective of *vallum*, the 'Aelian Wall', literally Hadrian's Wall: the obvious analogy is *pons Aelius*, Hadrian's Bridge at Newcastle, but many other military and civil structures were named after emperors. *val(l)um* is the Latin for 'wall', by which the Romans meant *the* Wall par excellence.[44] The Ilam pan would be the first evidence that his Wall was actually named after Hadrian, even if the name did not maintain itself; presumably it lapsed when his Wall was abandoned for the Antonine Wall. When the biographer of Hadrian and Antoninus Pius distinguishes one Wall from the other, he refers only to 'another' wall (*murus*), 'made of turf'.[45] *rigor* is a technical term used in land-surveying, to mean the straightest line between two points. This list includes Drumburgh, and (as COGGABATA) preserves its original name which incorporated *gabata*, the Celtic word for 'plate', corrupted by the Notitia Dignitatum into Latin *concavata* ('hollowed out'). This form shows the 'Vulgar' confusion between [b] and [v] which is frequent in the transmission of manuscripts, although it has not been found in the Latin of Roman Britain.

These 'souvenirs' mark the most important elaboration of Hadrian's 'blueprint', the decision to advance the garrisons from the Stanegate and to build new forts for them on the Wall itself. Housesteads, for example, overlies Turret 36b; and Greatchesters Milecastle 43. A further elaboration was the addition of a ditch and double bank to the south, an entrenchment (*fossatum*) mis-named by antiquaries as the 'Vallum', which was probably intended to prevent unauthorised access to the military zone. The original wall ten (Roman) feet thick was now reduced to a 'Narrow Wall' of eight feet, and was extended four miles (6.4 km) eastward from Newcastle to Wallsend. The first five miles (8 km) of the Turf Wall were also rebuilt in stone to the Narrow gauge. This complex sequence has been elucidated by a hundred years of excavation in which epigraphy has played an important but subsidiary role. No building inscriptions survive from the ditch, only one from the Turf Wall, and about ten from the Vallum, but there are hundreds from the stone wall, its milecastles and forts.

These inscriptions, apart from formal texts like **5.17** and **5.18**, are loosely known as 'centurial stones', a convenient term coined by Horsley in 1732, who was the first

---

44 Only **5.35** records building *p(er) val(lum)*, but the cognate verb *vallavit* is used of building the rampart at Carvoran (*RIB* 1816, 1818 and **5.45**), and the work of building the Antonine Wall is *opus valli* (*RIB* 2205 and **6.12**). Later **7.05** records success 'beyond the Wall' (*ob res trans vallum prospere gestas*), which the Antonine Itinerary identifies with the 'frontier' (464, 1, *a limite, id est a vallo*; compare 466, 5, and 474, 1–2), the Notitia's 'line of the Wall' (*Occ.* 40.32, *per lineam valli*).

45 Hist. Aug. *Antoninus Pius* 5.4, *alio muro caespiticio*. Bede, *Hist.* i 5,

to realise the relevance of a passage in Vegetius. Vegetius is a late-Roman military theorist with access to earlier sources now lost, who says that when legionaries dug a ditch and raised a rampart, each century was allotted a length by the legion's officers. The centurion checked the work for negligence or mistakes, and it was then inspected by the tribunes.[46] The centurial stones belong to this system of quality control, and (as Horsley realised) they can be used to work out the division of labour among the legions, their cohorts and centuries. About 150 centurions are named, many of them more than once, Lousius Suavis (the most prolific) actually six times, and deductions can be made of the movement of legions and the progress of the work.[47] The evidence is incomplete and complex, and it can only be illustrated here by a few examples here, but first a fundamental question. Which of the walls *was* Hadrian's Wall?

The long history of this question is teased out by Eric Birley in his *Research on Hadrian's Wall* (1961). Scholars from the sixteenth century onward tried to apportion the two walls (our Hadrian's Wall and the Antonine Wall) among the three imperial candidates offered by the ancient sources, Hadrian, Antoninus Pius, and Septimius Severus. Confusion is added by Gildas, a sixth-century British historian and moralist – in whose protracted sermon *The Ruin of Britain* morality wins the race, historical truth also ran – who attributes both walls to the sub-Roman period. The Antonine Wall was correctly identified by Camden, but he and his successors evolved various theories to distinguish between the work of Hadrian and Severus in the south; despite their misgivings as to the effectiveness of the Vallum, by the eighteenth century it came to be regarded as the Hadrianic predecessor of Severus' stone wall. The crucial epigraphic evidence was not available to Horsley, for it came from Hotbank milecastle (38) in the mid-eighteenth century, today a grassy platform defined by stone-robbers' trenches with a spectacular view westward past wooded basalt cliffs and over the peaty waters of Crag Lough:

<5.17> *Hotbank milecastle (38)*

imp(eratoris) Caes(aris) Traian(i)
Hadriani Aug(usti)
leg(io) II Aug(usta)
A(ulo) Platorio Nepote leg(ato) pr(o) pr(aetore)

RIB 1637+*add.* and 1638+*add.*

'(The work) of the Emperor Caesar Trajan Hadrian Augustus (built by) the Second Legion Augusta when Aulus Platorius Nepos was propraetorian legate.'

---

[46] *Epit.* iii 8.

[47] Stevens 1960.

It is most unusual for a building-inscription to begin with the Emperor's name in the genitive case; the only other British example is one from Moresby, also Hadrianic, but a little later and inscribed by the Twentieth Legion.[48] The left-hand half of *RIB* 1637 was found in *c.* 1715, but its find-spot was not recorded. This was only revealed in 1829, when the missing half was found in the nearby farm-house. Meanwhile an identical inscription (*RIB* 1638) had been found there in 1751. This proved at last that the stone wall was Hadrianic, which Hodgson was the first to see, in his famous extended footnote on the Wall.[49] Hotbank is still the only milecastle to have produced a pair of such inscriptions: they were presumably set over the two gates. Ninety-six in all must have been made, or at least intended, for Milecastles 1–48, but these are the only two to survive entire; fragments have been found at Cawfields (42) and Chapel House (47).[50] The latter milecastle was built by the Twentieth Legion:

<5.18> *Chapel House milecastle (47)*

[imp(eratori) Caes(ari) divi Traiani]
[fil(io) divi] Nervae ne[p(oti)]
[Trai]ano Hadria[no]
Aug(usto)
leg(io) XX V(aleria) V(ictrix)

RIB 1852+*add.*

'For the Emperor Caesar Trajan Hadrian Augustus, son of the deified Trajan, grandson of the deified Nerva, the Twentieth Legion Valeria Victrix (built this).'

---

[48] *RIB* 801.

[49] Hodgson 1840, II.3.

[50] *RIB* 1666 and **5.18** respectively. *RIB* 1702 resembles one, but comes from Vindolanda (Bidwell 1985, 9–10).

Hadrian's name is in the dative case, as usual in imperial building inscriptions, although the Ninth Legion used the nominative in its very last inscription (**4.16**), as if Trajan himself were the builder. However, it is odd that the Twentieth Legion does not name Platorius Nepos. The omission looks deliberate, since the stone-cutter seems to have found he had space to fill unexpectedly: note the additional, otiose item of Hadrian's imperial ancestry, and still more, the isolated AVG in line 4. Had the stone-cutter just been told the governor's name was not to appear on *Hadrian's* Wall? (The distance slabs of the Antonine Wall never name the governor responsible.) Or had the governor been withdrawn so abruptly, 'for consultation' no doubt, that his successor had not yet arrived? Hadrian's biographer tells us that he broke with Nepos, but not the date of his fall from favour.[51]

This is the first instance we have seen of the Twentieth legion's full title, which it gained in Britain; it is first attested in the late-Flavian period, but is usually thought to have been awarded for the legion's minor part in the defeat of Boudica. *Valeria Victrix* means 'Valiant and Victorious', and it is always abbreviated in British texts, usually to V V, no doubt because it was so familiar.

Later, when the first 5 miles (8 km) of the Turf Wall were rebuilt in stone, a new line was taken at Birdoswald, with the result that the next milecastle, High House (50), is the only Turf Wall milecastle not to have been rebuilt in stone. Among the debris buried by the Roman demolition party was found this unique fragment of an inscription from the Turf Wall, a splinter from an inscribed oak board:

<**5.19**> *High House milecastle (TW 50)*

[imp(erator..) Caes(ar..) Traian..]
[Had]ria[n.. Aug(ust..)]
[leg(io) ...] A(ulo) Pl[atorio Nepote]
[leg(ato) Aug(usti) pr(o) pr(aetore)]

RIB 1935+*add.*

'... the Emperor Caesar Trajan Hadrian Augustus. The ... Legion ... (built this) when Aulus Platorius Nepos was imperial propraetorian legate.'

This is the only fragment of a monumental inscription in wood to survive from Britain, although an uninscribed ansate panel (no doubt once painted) has been found at Carlisle.[52] The High House splinter does not include Hadrian's name and titles, and we do not know whether they were in the genitive or dative case. Collingwood was the first to examine it, and he saw that the letter-combinations RIA and APL could only belong to a Hadrianic building-inscription of Platorius Nepos, but his restoration of LEG II AVG and thus the genitive case for 'Hadrian'

[51] HA, *Hadrian* 15.2 and 23.4 (with Birley 2005, 124).
[52] Caruana 1987.

(etc.) is questionable: the Second Legion's known milecastles are 'short-axis', whereas High House is 'long-axis'.[53] But since we do not know the line-width of the inscription, which probably varied, we cannot deduce which of the other legions cut it; it might have been the Sixth, or even the Twentieth despite its omission of Nepos at Chapel House (**5.18**), since this practice may have started later. And what about Pontius Sabinus (**5.09**) and his 3000 legionaries?

The inscriptions cited so far are not strictly 'centurial', but in the broad sense of this term the Wall, its forts and the Vallum, have produced about three hundred centurial stones which with a few exceptions are Hadrianic.[54] They range from moulded panels to ordinary facing stones with a roughly pecked inscription. 'Blanks' have occasionally been found, perhaps intended for a painted inscription.[55] Where the same century is attested more than once, the 'handwriting' is usually different on each of its stones (**5.25** and **5.26** for example): evidently a century included more than one literate soldier. Some centurions even moved from one cohort to another:

<**5.20**> *Black Carts near Turret 29a*

coh(ortis) VI
(centuria) G(elli) P(h)ilippi

RIB III, 3303

'Of the Sixth Cohort, the century of Gellius Philippus (built this).'

<**5.21**> *Willowford near Turret 48b*

c(o)ho(rtis) V
(centuria) G(elli) P(h)ilippi

RIB III, 3407

'Of the Fifth Cohort, the century of Gellius Philippus (built this).'

5.20 is still in place, at the foot of the south face of the Wall; **5.21** has been re-used in a local farm building. Both stones fail to aspirate the centurion's cognomen, no doubt because Greek [ph] was not a sound native to Latin; but his other two stones, which do not record the cohort, write his his name correctly.[56] Philippus must have

[53] In line 4, Collingwood restored LEG PR PR in keeping with **5.17**, but the legion seems to have omitted AVG for reasons of space, which would not be the case here.

[54] **6.29** is explicitly later (AD 158), and a later date can also be argued (Mann 1990) on grounds of style or content for a few other stones such as **6.30**.

[55] For example near Milecastle 44: *Britannia* 8 (1977), 446, No. 112 with note.

[56] *RIB* 1572 and 1668.

transferred from the sixth cohort to the fifth, which was perhaps a promotion. There were ten cohorts in a legion, and six centurions within each, with the exception of the first, which seems to have had only five. The centurions of this first cohort, the *primi ordines* ('the first ranks'), enjoyed primacy, headed by the *primus pilus*; but what determined the movement of centurions within the lower cohorts is unclear. They were not simply promoted from the higher-numbered to the lower. A centurion of the Fifteenth Legion Apollinaris was *hastatus prior* of the sixth cohort when he died, but his previous posting had been PRinceps POSterior of the fifth cohort in the Fourth Legion Flavia[57]; and Flavius Virilis (**9.18**) was centurion in the ninth cohort after six previous centurionates.

Philippus' legion was probably the Twentieth, like that of other centurions just east of Willowford Bridge. This happens to be the best-represented legion, and it has left one of the few stones which seem to mark one end of a legionary 'length':

<**5.22**> *near Turret 41b*

l(egio) XX
V(aleria) V(ictrix)

RIB 1645

'The Twentieth Legion Valeria Victrix (built this)'

The feline head must be a wild boar's mask, the animal which symbolised the Twentieth. This is almost the only stone to name a legion without cohort or century, except for a distinctive group of stones just west of Birdoswald:

<**5.23**> *High House milecastle (50, Stone Wall)*

[l]eg(io) VI Vic(trix)
[p(ia)] fidelis
f(ecit)

RIB 1934

<**5.24**> *High House turret (50a, Stone Wall)*

leg(io) VI Vic(trix)
p(ia) fidelis
f(ecit)

RIB 1938+*add.*

'The Sixth Legion Victrix, Dutiful and Loyal, built (this).'

---

57 *ZPE* 71 (1988), 171, No. 2.

The identity of style is obvious, and is found in four other stones from the area, which have almost identical wording. They must belong to the rebuilding in stone of the first 5 miles (8 km) of the Turf Wall, clearly the work of the Sixth Legion.[58] One of the centurions was Sollius Julianus (**5.33**).

Most centurial stones name the century alone, but the legion can often be deduced from nearby stones naming legion and cohort:

<**5.25**> *west of Housesteads (Vercovicium)*

(centuria) Iuli
Candid(i)
f(ecit)

RIB 1632

'The century of Julius Candidus (built this).'

This stone was found in place, in the south face of the Wall. The roughly-incised letters are close to their handwritten forms, with an 'U'-like V, a sinuous L, and an open (unbarred) A.

<**5.26**> *Housesteads – Cawfields sector*

coh(ortis) I (centuria) Iu-
li Candid(i)

RIB 1646

'Of the First Cohort, the century of Julius Candidus (built this).'

This is the same century, with the lettering more formal, but the sloping tail of L still 'handwritten'. This time it is identified by cohort, as in *RIB* 1674, an almost identical text cut by a third hand. Other centurial stones in the sector identify the legion as the Twentieth, a conclusion which may be supported by this bronze disc found at Chester:

<**5.27**> *Chester (Deva)*

leg(ionis) XX
Iuli Ca-
ndidi

RIB II.3, 2427.14

'(Property) of Julius Candidus of the Twentieth Legion.'

---

[58] Mann 1990.

The disc has holes in the circumference, for stitching it to something as a name-tag. Unfortunately this man is not necessarily a centurion, and 'Julius Candidus' is a common name: one is buried at Corbridge, and another (an auxiliary soldier) at Benwell; there is even a centurion of this name at Old Kilpatrick. Since the latter is Antonine, he is unlikely to be the same as the Hadrianic centurion, who is in the First Cohort and thus already quite senior.[59]

Two other links between Chester and the Wall are much more certain. The first is deduced from a lead stamp or 'die' with mirror-image letters:

<**5.28**> *Chester (Deva)*

(centuria) Cl(audi) Aug(ustani)
Vic(toris)

RIB II.1, 2409.4

'Century of Claudius Augustanus, (product) of Victor.'

This die might have been used for stamping loaves of bread baked in a communal oven. The centurion's name is not unique (one Tiberius Claudius Augustanus was even procurator of Britain in the later first century), but he is probably the same as one who helped build the Wall:

<**5.29**> *near Turret 47b*

coh(ortis) III
(centuria) Cl(audi) Augu[s(tani)]

RIB 1855

'Of the Third Cohort, the century of Claudius Augustanus (built this).'

This century is found on two other stones.[60] The other link between Chester and the Wall is quite beyond doubt:

<**5.30**> *Walltown Crags*

coh(ortis) III
(centuria) Ferroni
Vegeti

RIB 1769

'Of the Third Cohort, the century of Ferronius Vegetus (built this).'

---

[59] *RIB* 1173, 1350 and **6.26**, with Birley 1983 (who notes still more centurions called 'Julius Candidus').

[60] *RIB* 1770 (without cohort) and 1811.

<**5.31**> *Willowford Bridge*

(centuria) Ferron[i]
Vegeti
coh(ortis) III

RIB 1867+*add.*

'The century of Ferronius Vegetus, of the Third Cohort, (built this).'

The word-order differs slightly, but the 'handwriting' looks the same. The same century is found at Chester:

<**5.32**> *Chester (Deva)*

c(o)hort(is) III
(centuria) Ferro(ni)

RIB 468

'Of the Third Cohort, the century of Ferronius (built this).'

The centurion's name is Italian (probably Etruscan) and most unusual; even the cohort number is the same. A similar link can be deduced between York and the Wall, at the western end of the 5-mile (8-km) stretch of Turf Wall rebuilt by the Sixth Legion:

<**5.33**> *Hare Hill*

coh(ortis) III (centuria)
M(arci) Solli Iuliani

RIB III, 3454

'Of the Third Cohort, the century of Marcus Sollius Julianus (built this).'

The name *Sollius* is well attested in Gallia Narbonensis (Provence), which is a likely origin for this officer. His name is also incised on a piece of leather found at the legion's headquarters:

<**5.34**> *York (Eboracum)*

(centuria) Solli Iuliani

RIB II.4, 2445.16

'The century of Sollius Julianus.'

The leather had previously been stamped three times, to identify it during the tanning process. It was then cut to shape and stitched, probably for a tent, as used by the army for operating in the field; thus the Latin phrase for 'under canvas' is *sub pellibus*, 'under skins'. The tent would have held a *contubernium*, a 'section' of eight men from the century commanded by Julianus.

These have all been legionary centurial stones, but here is a puzzle, a stone which is almost unique in being inscribed on two faces, and in recording building-work by cavalry:

<**5.35**> *near Brunton Turret (26b)*

(i) t(urma) L(uci) A(...) F(ani)
p(er) val(lum)
p(edes) CXIII
(ii) turm(a)
L(uci) A(...) Fani

RIB 1445+*add.*

'The troop of Lucius A(...) Fanus (built) along the Wall 113 feet; the troop of Lucius A(...) Fanus.'

This was a corner-stone, and fortunately the exact find-spot is known: 'lying loose in front of the Wall about 50 yds. west of Brunton turret'. It shows once again (see **5.16** and **7.05**) that *vallum* is the Roman name for the Wall, but where was the corner? The turret was 50 yards away (50.2 m), and the nearest gateway still further, so the answer must be a merlon in the battlements. This would support the idea that they were depicted by the Rudge Cup (**5.14**) and Amiens Patera (**5.15**), and certainly explain why a troop of 30 men could have built as much as 113 feet (34.4 m). Fanus is the decurion in charge: he is a Roman citizen who abbreviates his three names to their initials (quite a common form of abbreviation), but he was not necessarily a legionary. The legions had a small cavalry contingent (*equites legionis*), but there is no direct evidence that it was ordered by troops (*turmae*) commanded by decurions. Individual *equites* were identified by their century.[61] Without evidence for legionary *turmae*, therefore, we must assume that Fanus' men were auxiliaries, but direct evidence of building-work by cavalry is unusual:

[61] Breeze 1969, 53–4.

<5.36> *Binchester (Vinovia)*

Fortun(a)e
Reduci
Eltaominus
emeritus
ex arc(h)itec(to)
alae Vetto(num)
v(otum) s(oluit) l(aetus) l(ibens) m(erito)

Britannia 45 (2014), 434, No. 4

'To Fortune the Home-Bringer, Eltaominus, veteran and former engineer of the Cavalry Regiment ofVettones, has paid his vow gladly, willingly, deservedly.'

This altar was recently found in its original position in the well-preserved bath-house at Binchester: altars to Fortune are often found in bath-houses, perhaps because this was where naked soldiers felt most vulnerable.[62] Eltaominus, whose name is unique, had probably just been discharged and was about to return 'home' (compare **9.06**). His altar is the first record of an *architectus* in an *ala*, a military engineer in a cavalry regiment who might design and direct its building-work. But they are already attested in the *equites singulares Augusti* in Rome, the imperial cavalry guardsmen seconded from provincial cavalry units.[63]

Half a mile (0.8 km) to the west of Brunton Turret, at Chesters across the river, is a cavalry fort dated by an altar (**5.03**) to the reign of Hadrian, which has produced another corner-stone inscribed by a cavalry troop, the *turma Paterni*.[64] Since Chesters was built over the ditch and the Broad Wall foundations of the original Wall, as already noted for Housesteads and Great Chesters, the decision to add forts to the Wall was evidently an afterthought; but an early afterthought, since Platorius Nepos was still governor:

<5.37> *Benwell (Condercum), granaries*

imp(eratori) Caes(ari) Traiano
Hadr[ia]n(o) Aug(usto)
A(ulo) Platorio N[epote l]eg(ato) Aug(usti) pr(o) p[r(aetore)]
vexillatio c[lassis] Britan(nicae)

RIB 1340

[62] **12.55** with note.
[63] Speidel 1994, Nos. 9, 223, 321, ?580. In Britain other *architecti* are found at Carrawburgh (*RIB* 1542) and Birrens (**12.17** and *RIB* 2096), where auxiliary cohorts were stationed.
[64] *RIB* III, 3301.

'For the Emperor Caesar Trajan Hadrian Augustus, when Aulus Platorius Nepos was propraetorian legate, the detachment of the British fleet (built this).'

At first sight it is surprising to find the fleet engaged in building-work, but two stones record its work on the Wall-curtain:

<**5.38**> *probably near Birdoswald (Banna)*

ped(atura) cla(ssis)
Bri(tannicae)

RIB 1945

'The length in feet built by the British Fleet.'

RIB 1944, now lost, carried a similar text. The fleet also smelted iron and fired tiles in Kent and Sussex, and probably built its own bath-house at Beauport Park.[65] There is a long inscription from Numidia, a dedication appropriately to Patience, Valour and Hope, in which a legionary engineer tells the epic story of how he was called in to sort out the water-supply of Saldae.[66] En route he was attacked by brigands, and arrived naked and wounded, only to find the locals in despair: they had tunnelled their aqueduct through a hill from either end, but the two excavations had failed to meet. Our hero calculated the proper course and, to complete the work as fast as possible, allotted the different ends to auxiliaries and to soldiers from the fleet in competition.[67] So it is less surprising to find the fleet at Benwell engaged in legionary-type work; in fact its inscription, although sadly damaged, is quite as well-inscribed as this contemporary inscription cut by legionaries:

---

[65] *RIB* III, 3036.

[66] See the note to **9.06**.

[67] *ILS* 5795 (Lambaesis). The dedicator was a veteran of the Third Legion Augusta, based there.

<**5.39**> *Halton Chesters (Onnum)*

imp(eratori) Caes(ari) T[ra(iano) Hadriano]
Aug(usto) leg(io) VI V[ictrix p(ia) f(idelis)]
A(ulo) Platorio N[epote]
leg(ato) Aug(usti) pr(o) [pr(aetore)]

RIB 1427

'For the Emperor Caesar Trajan Hadrian Augustus, the Sixth Legion Victrix Dutiful and Loyal (built this), when Aulus Platorius Nepos was propraetorian legate.'

The missing text has to be restored, and the exact abbreviations are in doubt, but not the wording. As usual there was no need to specify the structure of which it formed part: it was evidently the west gate, for the stone, after exposure to the weather, fell onto the filled-up ditch of the Wall over which the gate was built.

Benwell and Halton Chesters belong to the governorship of Platorius Nepos, but other forts are somewhat later in Hadrian's reign:

<**5.40**> *Great Chesters (Aesica), east gate*

imp(eratori) Caes(ari) Trai(a)n(o) Had[ri]a-
no Aug(usto) p(atri) p(atriae)

RIB 1736+*add.*

'For the Emperor Caesar Trajan Hadrian Augustus, Father of his Country.'

This laconic inscription occupies less than half of the panel prepared for it; the top half is blank. Since it would have been set high above the gate, *RIB* charitably suggests that the stone-cutter intended his text to be more easily read from below, but this does not explain why he omitted both the unit responsible and the governor, in a mean and bottom-heavy text which incidentally reduced *Traiano* to TRAIN. However, there is a crumb of chronological comfort: Hadrian did not assume the title of *pater patriae* until AD 128, six years after the visit to Britain which initiated the Wall. In the same year, as it happens, we know the name of the general commanding the Twentieth Legion; he is now little more than a name, but it is a very long one:

<**5.41**> *Callenses in Baetica (Andalusia)*

imp(eratori) Caesari divi
Traiani Aug(usti) co(n)s(ulis) VI f(ilio) divi
Nervae co(n)s(ulis) III trib(unicia) p(otestate) II nepoti Traiano
Hadriano Aug(usto), pont(ifici) max(imo),

tribunic(ia) potest(ate) XII, p(atri) p(atriae), co(n)s(uli) III,
M(arcus) Messius Rusticus
Aemilius Papus Ar[r]ius Proculus
Iulius Celsus, sodal(is) Augustal(is), IIIIvir
viarum curandarum, tr(ibunus) mil(itum) leg(ionis) {V}III Aug(ustae),
[q(uaestor] pr(o) pr(aetore) provinc(iae) Africae, trib(unus) pleb(is),
pr(aetor) peregrinus, curator viae Aureliae,
leg(atus) Aug(usti) leg(ionis) XX V(aleriae) V(ictricis)
optimo principi

CIL ii 1371

'To the Emperor Caesar Hadrian Augustus, pontifex maximus, in the twelfth year of his tribunician power (AD 128), Father of his Country, consul three times; son of the deified Trajan Augustus, consul six times, and grandson of the deified Nerva, consul three times, and with tribunician power for two years; (dedicated by) Marcus Messius Rusticus Aemilius Papus Arrius Proculus Julius Celsus, *sodalis Augustalis*, Board of Four for the care of roads, military tribune of the the Third Legion Augusta, quaestor and acting-praetor of the province of Africa, tribune of the plebs, *praetor peregrinus*, supervisor of the via Aurelia, imperial legate of the Twentieth Legion Valeria Victrix; to the Best of Emperors.'

His principal name was Aemilius Papus, and his like-named father is mentioned (with Platorius Nepos) as one of Hadrian's friends. At Rome he belonged to a college responsible for the worship of the deified Augustus, and was the annually elected law officer (*praetor*) responsible for cases involving non-citizens (*peregrini*). The catalogue of his career concludes with the British command, which may well have prompted the dedication.[68] In Britain he would have found his legion fully engaged in building the Wall; and, as if the ditch and forts were not enough, it was also decided to dig the Vallum:

<5.42> *the Vallum west of Benwell (Condercum)*

coh(ortis) I
Dacor(um)
(centuria) Ael(i) Did-
a(e)

RIB 1365

'Of the First Cohort of Dacians, the century of Aelius Dida (built this).'

This is the most informative stone of a group of five found still in position in the Vallum mounds near Benwell, which marked the building-lengths of two centuries

[68] Birley 2005, 248.

north and south of the ditch.[69] Like other stones intended for insertion into turf-work, they are thin slabs, not masonry ashlars. It follows from this stone in particular that the Vallum, unlike the Wall proper, was the work of auxiliaries. None of the Vallum stones is explicitly dated, but a Hadrianic date at least is required by the centurion's nomen *Aelius*. His cognomen *Dida*, obviously his native name, may be Thracian; the Dacians were related to them, and Aelius Dida may thus have been a founder-member of the cohort. The lettering, which was inscribed with a mason's pick, is shallow and informal. II for E would not be used formally, but sometimes occurs on centurial stones; it is the regular form in handwritten stylus tablet texts, and is often used in the capital-letter 'signatures' scratched by owners on their crockery.

The Vallum is later than the forts, since undug causeways were left across it to allow access to them. There is one of these at Great Chesters, for example, but Carrawburgh, which is dated to *c.* AD 130 by a fragmentary inscription of the governor Julius Severus, was actually built over the Vallum.[70] Thus it was an even later afterthought, like the decision to recommission the fort at Carvoran, where the Maiden Way met the Stanegate. This fort awaits modern excavation, but two inscriptions suggest that, like Vindolanda, it was originally Flavian. The first is an object unique in Britain, a bronze grain measure of *modius* form shaped like an inverted bucket, which is inscribed with its capacity and the date:

<5.43> *Carvoran (Magnis)*

imp(eratore) [[Domitiano]] Caesare
Aug(usto) Germanico XV co(n)s(ule)
exactus ad (sextarios) XVII s(emis)
habet p(ondus) XXXIIX

RIB II.2, 2415.56

'In the fifteenth consulship (AD 90) of the Emperor Domitian Caesar Augustus, Conqueror of Germany; tested to the capacity of $17^{1}/_{2}$ pints; weight 38 (pounds).'

Roman epigraphists divide inscriptions into 'monumental' (in Britain, *RIB* I and III) and what they quaintly call 'instrumentum domesticum' (personal belongings, collected in *RIB* II). Thus a sub-literate centurial stone is classed as 'monumental', but the Carvoran *modius*, for all its superb lettering and official character, as 'instrumentum'. The *sextarius* symbol is S cut by a horizontal line: 546 cc, almost the same as a modern (Imperial) pint. The vessel actually holds 11.34 litres, just over 20 *sextarii*, and various solutions to this discrepancy have been suggested; perhaps there was a false bottom, now lost. The *modius* as a measure of capacity

[69] *RIB* 1361–4.
[70] *RIB* 1550.

was 16 *sextarii*, and this 17½ pints (*c*. 10 litres) measure, if it is not simply a *modius* enlarged by one-tenth for some unknown purpose, is puzzling. The most attractive suggestion is that it represents a soldier's grain ration for 7 days.[71] Domitian took the title *Germanicus* in AD 83, and his name has been erased after his 'memory' was condemned in AD 96. So the *modius*, although Domitianic, was still being used thereafter, and for dating-purposes it must be taken with the second item from Carvoran, a legionary gravestone:

<**5.44**> *Carvoran (Magnis)*

G(aius) Valerius G(ai filius) Vol(tinia tribu)
Iullus Vian(na) mil(es)
leg(ionis) XX V(aleriae) V(ictricis)

RIB 1826+*add*.

'Gaius Valerius Iullus, son of Gaius, of the *Voltinia* voting-tribe, from Vienne; soldier of the Twentieth Legion Valeria Victrix.'

Like Duccius Rufinus (**3.04**) and Cominius Severus (**4.03**), Iullus came from Vienne in Gallia Narbonensis; the city belonged to the *Voltinia* tribe, and is often written as 'Vianna' on legionary gravestones at Mainz. The simple style of this gabled tombstone, and in particular the absence of *Dis Manibus*, suggests a first-century date, certainly before Hadrian's Wall was built. Carvoran like Vindolanda belonged to the Stanegate 'frontier', and for a time it seems to have been derelict, since the Vallum here takes a northward diversion as if to separate the fort deliberately from the Wall. But almost immediately, still in Hadrian's reign, the decision was taken to rebuild it:

<**5.45**> *Carvoran (Magnis)*

(centuria) Silvani
vallavit
p(edes) CXII sub
Fla(vio) Secundo
[pr]aef(ecto)

RIB 1820

'The century of Silvanus built 112 feet of rampart under (the command of) Flavius Secundus the prefect.'

The verb *vallare* (to build a *vallum*) occurs in Britain only at Carvoran, in this and two other inscriptions from the same project.[72] It was evidently the revetment in

[71] Mann 1984.
[72] *RIB* 1816, 1818.

stone of the old turf rampart, which can be dated to AD 136/8 by a remarkable altar found in the bath-house of the fort:

<**5.46**> *Carvoran (Magnis)*

Fortunae Aug(ustae)
pro salute L(uci) Aeli
Caesaris ex visu
T(itus) Fla(vius) Secundus
praef(ectus) coh(ortis) I Ham-
iorum sagittar(iorum)
v(otum) s(olvit) l(ibens) m(erito)

RIB 1778

'To the Imperial Fortune, for the welfare of Lucius Aelius Caesar, because of a vision. Titus Flavius Secundus, prefect of the First cohort of Hamian Archers, willingly and deservedly paid his vow.'

The Hamian Archers were specialists originally recruited in Syria, at Hama, the only full-time archers in the British army.[73] There are dedications at Carvoran[74] to Syrian deities, and when Carvoran is fully excavated it will be interesting to see whether evidence is found of Syrian archers there. The only recorded veteran, discharged in AD 132 after 25 years' service, would not have seen Carvoran; surprisingly, he comes from the Lower Danube, from MOMS, perhaps an error for *Montanis*.[75] Aelius Caesar is Lucius Ceionius Commodus, whom Hadrian adopted in AD 136 as his son and successor; but perhaps Secundus indeed 'saw' something for, on 1 January AD 138, Aelius Caesar's imperial fortune ran out and he died at Rome. Hadrian, in failing health himself, and disheartened by paying out donatives to celebrate this futile adoption, allegedly kept saying: 'I have leant against a collapsing wall'.[76]

[73] Birley 2012.
[74] *RIB* 1780 and 1783.
[75] Eck, Pangerl and Holder 2010.
[76] Hist. Aug. *Hadrianus* 23.14, *in caducum parietem nos inclinavimus.*

6

THE ANTONINE WALL

The reconquest of the North

The great work which had occupied the British army for some fifteen years proved to be like Aelius Caesar, a collapsing wall. Hadrian just before he died in AD 138 adopted a new successor, Antoninus Pius, one of whose first decisions as Emperor was to supersede Hadrian's Wall. Instead, he decided to reconquer southern Scotland and to fortify the 'boundary-line' of Tacitus, the narrower Clyde-Forth isthmus. The frontier would be halved in length, the Empire would be enlarged a little and, perhaps most important, the new regime would gain an old-fashioned victory.[1] Hadrian's Wall by contrast looks modern: a prestige project wilfully expensive, completed years behind schedule, and at once rendered obsolete by a change of government.

This renewed 'forward policy' would have entailed reinforcing the British legions once again (compare **5.09**). At Birrens the Hadrianic outpost was demolished and replaced by a larger fort whose 'beautifully finished masonry' the excavator, Anne Robertson, considered to be the work of legionaries.[2] Since she wrote, the handsome inscription which names them has been found; it can be dated by its *pelta* and rosette being stylistically akin to the distance-slabs of the Antonine Wall itself. The lower right-hand quarter survives:

<6.01> *Birrens (Blatobulgium)*

[...]
[... ?vex(illationes)]
[leg(ionis)] VIII Aug(ustae)
[leg(ionis)] XXII Pri(migeniae)
[...] f(ecerunt)

RIB III, 3486

[1] The fiction that the Emperor was commander-in-chief allowed Pius to claim the whole credit: according to his panegyrist Fronto (*Pan. Lat.* viii (v), 14.2), although he stayed in Rome and delegated command in the field, he was in overall command like the helmsman of a warship.

[2] Robertson 1984, 280 and 284.

'...detachments of the Eighth Legion Augusta and the Twenty-Second Legion Primigenia made (this).'

The first two lines probably contained an abbreviated form of the Emperor's name, and the word *vexillationes* either in full or abbreviated.[3] These were the two legions of Upper Germany, which evidently contributed to the reconquest. The man chosen for this mission had once been second-in-command of the Twenty-Second, but he was now the governor of Lower Germany, as we know from the inscription to the statue just erected by his home town in Numidia (eastern Algeria):

<6.02> *Tiddis*

Q(uinto) Lollio M(arci) fil(io)
Quir(ina tribu) Urbico co(n)s(uli)
leg(ato) Aug(usti) provinc(iae) Germ(aniae)
inferioris, fetiali, legato
imp(eratoris) Hadriani in expedition(e)
Iudaica qua donatus est
hasta pura corona aurea, leg(ato)
leg(ionis) X Geminae, praet(ori) candidat(o)
Caes(aris), trib(uno) pleb(is) candidat(o) Caes(aris), leg(ato)
proco(n)s(ulis) Asiae, quaest(ori) urbis, trib(uno)
laticlavio leg(ionis) XXII Primigeniae,
IIIIviro viarum curand(arum),
patrono
d(ecreto) d(ecurionum) p(ecunia) p(ublica)

ILS 1065

'To Quintus Lollius Urbicus, son of Marcus, of the *Quirina* voting-tribe, consul, imperial legate of the province of Lower Germany, *fetialis* priest, legate of the Emperor Hadrian in the Jewish campaign in which he was decorated with an Untipped Spear and a Gold Crown, legate of the Tenth Legion Gemina, praetor and candidate of the Emperor, tribune of the *plebs* and candidate of the Emperor, legate of the proconsul of Asia, quaestor at Rome, senatorial tribune of the Twenty-Second Legion Primigenia, member of the Commission of Four for the maintenance of roads, patron (of Tiddis), (this statue) by decree of the town-councillors at public expense.'

The inscription dates from the period AD 136/8, since Hadrian (not yet deified) is still Emperor, and the 'Jewish campaign' is the Bar-Kokhba revolt (AD 132–5). This was ruthlessly crushed by Hadrian's best general, Julius Severus, who had been recalled from Britain for the purpose. Lollius Urbicus was a senior member of his staff, perhaps even his second-in-command, and in moments of leisure between

[3] *vexillationes* is unabbreviated on the similar slab from Bar Hill (*RIB* 2171).

destroying Jewish villages they may have discussed Britain and Hadrian's Wall. Urbicus already had experience of other frontiers, the upper Danube (he commanded the legion at Vienna) and the middle Rhine (second-in-command at Mainz). He had gained the qualifying magistracies at Rome with Hadrian's direct support, vital for an able and ambitious man of no family. Like Pontius Laelianus (**5.06**) he became a *fetialis*. His African background is brilliantly evoked by Colin Wells. At Tiddis, an isolated hill-top occupied since the Neolithic period, 'everything is red, the colour of the rock'; it was now a small Roman provincial town living off the wheatfields that surrounded it. The mausoleum of the Lollii is still there today, outside the town, and one of its inscriptions confirms the evidence of other texts, that Lollius Urbicus like Plautius Silvanus (**1.03**), Pertinax (**7.02**) and Postumius Varus (**12.71**), subsequently became Prefect of Rome. His career is a remarkable tribute to the Antonine period: 'at no other period of history could the second or third son of a Berber landowner from a very small town in the interior enjoy a career which took him to Asia, Judaea, the Danube, the Rhine and Britain, culminating in a position of great power and honour in the capital of the Empire to which all these regions belonged.'[4]

Thus described it might almost be the career of a third-century 'Illyrian' soldier-emperor, but next to nothing is known of the campaign in which Lollius Urbicus led the Roman army once more to within sight of the Highlands, and in AD 142 gave Antoninus Pius the only acclamation as *imperator* he ever took after his accession. Preparations began at Corbridge, which tends to reflect activity not on Hadrian's Wall, but further north (compare **8.11**). Two large granaries were built to provision the new advance, as we know from their inscriptions now displayed in the adjoining museum:

<6.03> *Corbridge (Coria)*

[imp(eratori)] T(ito) Aelio Anionino(!)
[Au]g(usto) Pio II co(n)s(uli)
[sub] cura Q(uinti) Lolii(!) Urbic^i(!)
[leg(ati) A]ug(usti) pr(o) pr(aetore) leg(io) II Aug(usta) f(ecit)

RIB 1147

'For the Emperor Titus Aelius Antoninus Augustus Pius, consul for the second time, under the charge of Quintus Lollius Urbicus, imperial propraetorian legate; the Second Legion Augusta built (this).'

[4] Wells 1984, 245–7.

<6.04> *Corbridge (Coria)*

imp(eratori) Caes(ari) [T(ito)] Ael[io]
Antonino A[ug(usto)] Pi[o]
III co(n)[s(uli) p(atri) p(atriae)]
sub cura Q(uinti) [Lolli Urbici]
leg(ati) Au[g(usti) pr(o) pr(aetore)]
leg(io) II A[ug(usta) f(ecit)]

RIB 1148+*add.*

'For the Emperor Caesar Titus Aelius Antoninus Augustus Pius, consul for the third time, Father of his Country, under the charge of Quintus Lollius Urbicus, imperial propraetorian legate; the Second Legion Augusta built (this).'

Both inscriptions have the elaborate *pelta* (shield-like) terminals favoured by Antonine inscriptions. The texts, fragmentary as they are, well illustrate how the formulaic nature of imperial building-inscriptions makes restoration possible. But human error is unpredictable: the stone-cutter made three mistakes in **6.03** – ANIONINO for *Antonino*, LOLII for *Lolli* and VRBIC^{A}I for *Urbici* – which were apparently avoided in **6.04**, where the reversal of R after V in *cura* is only a neat way of saving space in a crowded line (compare **13.08**). This is another reminder that inscriptions, although treated as primary texts, are only copies, like the medieval manuscripts which transmit ancient authors such as Tacitus. Still worse: papyrologists are ruefully aware that ancient literary manuscripts, if particularly beautiful, may also be particularly full of mistakes.[5] Likewise, when cutting an inscription letter by letter, it is possible to lose the sense of the whole word. This will happen to another beautiful Antonine inscription (**6.28**), so badly as to leave the meaning in doubt.

Just as Hadrian took the name of Trajan (**10.04**), Antoninus Pius took Hadrian's name when adopted by him; here he is only *Aelius*, but he is *Hadrianus* as well at High Rochester (**6.05**) and on the Antonine Wall (**6.07**); however, he retained his own praenomen *Titus*. He passes from 'Consul II' (AD 139) to 'Consul III' (AD 140) between the two Corbridge inscriptions, indicating that the granaries were built in successive years. He has also assumed the title *pater patriae*, rightly restored in **6.04** since it is known from his coinage.

From Corbridge, Dere Street led north into Scotland, and Lollius Urbicus' advance is marked by the reconstruction of the Flavian fort at Bremenium (High Rochester):

<6.05> *High Rochester (Bremenium)*

imp(eratori) Caes(ari) T(ito) Aelio

[5] Turner 1968, 93.

H(a)d(riano) Antonino Aug(usto) Pio p(atri) p(atriae)
sub Q(uinto) Lol(lio) Urbico
leg(ato) Aug(usti) pro prae(tore)
coh(ors) I Ling(onum)
eq(uitata) f(ecit)

RIB 1276

'For the Emperor Caesar Titus Aelius Hadrian Antoninus Augustus Pius, Father of his Country, under Quintus Lollius Urbicus, imperial propraetorian legate; the First Cohort of Lingones, part-mounted, built (this).'

The inscription is well-cut and quite carefully composed, but the second line is so crowded that the stone-cutter has abbreviated HADRIANO to HD ligatured, omitting the A by mistake. The Lingones, a tribe of Upper Germany, contributed four cohorts '500-strong' (*quingenariae*) and part-mounted (*equitatae*) to the British army, which are listed in the Hadrianic Brigetio diploma (**5.04**). One of the Bloomberg London tablets names an individual 'Lingonian' (*Lingonus*), which would imply that the cohorts arrived as reinforcements after the defeat of Boudica (AD 61).[6] After the retreat from Scotland, we will see the First Cohort again at Lanchester (**12.23**).

Building the new Wall

The High Rochester inscription is the only mention of Lollius Urbicus between the two Walls, but he was also responsible for the new Wall:

<**6.06**> *Balmuildy*

[imp(eratori) C(aesari) T(ito) Ael(io) Hadr(iano)]
[Antonino Aug(usto) Pio]
[p(atri)] p(atriae) leg(io) II Au[g(usta) sub]
Q(uinto) Lollio Ur[bico]
leg(ato) Aug(usti) pr(o) pr(aetore) [fec(it)]

RIB 2191; Keppie 1998, No. 22

'For the Emperor Caesar Titus Aelius Hadrian Antoninus Augustus Pius, Father of his Country, the Second Legion Augusta under Quintus Lollius Urbicus, imperial propraetorian legate, made (this).'

6 *Tab. Lond. Bloomberg* 55; compare Tacitus, *Annals* xiv 38.

Small fragments also survive of a second, very large, inscribed slab from the north gate of the fort.[7] Despite their shattered state, the wording of both inscriptions can be restored with the help of **6.05**. Like the Augustan History, they connect Lollius Urbicus with the Antonine Wall as well as with the advance into Scotland, since the fort at Balmuildy, where the Wall crosses the River Kelvin, was integral to it. This, in the phrase already quoted, was 'another wall, but made of turf'.[8] Its builders seem to have applied the lessons learnt from Hadrian's Wall to construct a continuous barrier consisting of road, wall and ditch, whose garrison was housed in a dense chain of alternating forts, larger and smaller, which formed part of the Wall itself. The Wall curtain and, so far as we know, the rest of the work, was scrupulously divided among the three British legions: the whole of the Second Legion, and detachments of the Sixth and Twentieth Legions. Detachments of two German legions (**6.01**) were busy in the rear.

The first 37 miles (59.5 km) of the Wall, from the Firth of Forth to Castlehill, was divided into three successive blocs each sub-divided into three legionary allotments measured in 'paces' of 5 feet (1.5 m). (One thousand paces made a Roman mile, 94.5% of one English mile.) The remaining 4 miles (6.4 km), from Castlehill to the Firth of Clyde, was divided into two much shorter blocs each sub-divided into three allotments measured in feet. The reason for this change seems to be the decision at this point to add some thirteen smaller forts to the six 'primary' Wall forts like Balmuildy, entailing a diversion of labour. All this has been deduced from the results of archaeological survey and excavation, and especially from a set of inscriptions unique in the whole Empire, the 'distance slabs' which recorded the lengths built by each legion. Some 20 slabs are known, from a conjectured total of 40, a very high rate of survival due probably to being buried when the Wall was abandoned; 16 are preserved by the Hunterian Museum, Glasgow, where they are fully described by Lawrence Keppie and placed in context.[9]

Here we will note only some particularly fine examples. The texts of the slabs are not identical, but they are closely related, notably in being dedicated to Antoninus Pius without mentioning Lollius Urbicus at all. They were decorated according to the taste of the legion concerned and the skill of its craftsmen, before being inserted into the turfwork of the Wall. They are thus a much grander version of the small stone slabs found in the Vallum of Hadrian's Wall, and were obviously intended to be a permanent record, but their high survival-rate and their unweathered appearance both suggest that they were deliberately buried by the Romans themselves less than 20 years later, when the Wall was abandoned.

The largest and most elaborate slab was found in 1868 at Bridgeness on the

---

[7] *RIB* 2192.

[8] Hist. Aug. *Antoninus Pius* 5.4, *Britannos per Lollium Urbicum vicit legatum alio muro caespiticio summotis barbaris ducto.*

[9] Keppie 1998, esp. 50–6, 72–90.

Firth of Forth, where it is thought to have marked the eastern terminal of the Wall, although this may actually have been at the fort of Carriden just to the east. There is a central panel defined by two rosettes and a *pelta* on each side, the three horns of each *pelta* being elaborated into beaked griffin-heads; and inscribed upon this panel:

<**6.07**> *Bridgeness*

imp(eratori) Caes(ari) Tito Aelio
Hadri(ano) Antonino
Aug(usto) Pio p(atri) p(atriae) leg(io) II
Aug(usta) per m(ilia) p(assuum) IIIIDCLII
fec(it)

RIB 2139+*add.*

'For the Emperor Caesar Titus Aelius Hadrian Antoninus Augustus Pius, Father of his Country, the Second Legion Augusta made (the Wall) for 4,652 paces.'

To the left of the panel is a vignette of the fighting which preceded the Wall: not of the legion fighting, nor even of legionaries engaged in building-work, which is a favourite scene on Trajan's Column, but of a cavalryman riding down a rabble of natives. To the right is a celebration of the *suovetaurilia*, the ritual purification of the Legion by the sacrifice of a pig, sheep and bull. The legion is identified by a flag (*vexillum*) which reads *leg(io) II Aug(usta)*; this might have been expected to mark a detachment (*vexillatio*), but here it serves as a caption, since the whole legion was in Scotland.[10] The flag flies in front of a temple-like pediment which frames a group of officers or men in civilian dress. The three sacrificial animals are being led to the altar, their faces bright with patient anticipation, while a piper is playing a drone-note to drown any unlucky sound. The presiding figure, formally dressed in a toga, is pouring a preliminary offering onto the altar. He is almost certainly the legate himself. By happy chance, the discovery of this marble statue base in north-west Turkey, we can deduce who he was:

[10] But a legion's marching standards may have included *vexilla* (Breeze 1989).

<6.08> *Bergama (Pergamum)*

Πατρέων ἡ πόλιc
Ἀ(υλοc) Κλ(αυδιοc) Χάρακα
ὕπατον Ρωμαίων,
ηγεμόνα Κιλικίαc
Λυκαονίαc Ἰcαυρίαc,
ηγεμόνα λεγιῶνοc Β Αυγ(ουcτηc),
ἐπιμελητήν ὁδοῦ
Λατείνηc,
[cτ]ρατηγὸν Ρωμαίων
[δια]λεχθέντα ὑπὸ τῆc
[cυγ]κλήτου
είς τοὺc ἀγορανομικοὺc,
ταμίαν Σικελίαc,
τὸν cυνγραφέα.
εἰcηγηcαμένου
Ὀκταβίου Χρυcάνθου

AE 1961, 320

'The city of Patras (honours) Aulus Claudius Charax, consul of the Romans, legate of Cilicia, Lycaonia and Isauria, legate of the Second Legion Augusta, curator of the Via Latina, praetor of the Romans, adlected by the Senate among the ex-aediles, quaestor of Sicily; the historian. Erected by Octavius Chrysanthus.'

Charax was not the only legate of this legion to be promoted governor of Cilicia, in what is now south-eastern Turkey.[11] His career can be closely dated, since we know that he was consul in AD 147. If the governorship of Cilicia (etc.) and the legionary command both lasted 3 years – a reasonable guess – then he was legate of the Second Legion Augusta in Britain in *c.* AD 141–3. His posts are listed in descending order, evidently by a Greek unfamiliar with Roman institutions, and his admission to the Senate without the need to hold junior magistracies suggests that he was a late starter who enjoyed imperial favour. The emperor would have been Hadrian, whose enthusiasm for Greek culture was notorious.

Charax spent lavishly on his home-city Pergamum where his name can still be read on the remains of his portico at the sanctuary of Aesculapius (**12.02**), and he also dedicated a statue there of Antoninus Pius as his 'benefactor'. Significantly he is honoured by the Greek port-city of Patras in the inscription just quoted, and also by Sparta, not only as a Roman senator and careerist, but as a Greek historian. In fact we know that he wrote *Hellenica* in 40 books, now lost but often quoted by Byzantine encyclopaedias for mythological detail.[12] But the most surprising feature

[11] Compare *RIB* 335 (Caerleon), fragmentary and now lost, but evidently part of a dedication by the legionary legate on his promotion to Cilicia.
[12] *PIR*² II, 189, C 831. Birley 2005, 253–4.

of his career is not just that he was a famous Greek writer and philanthropist, but that he never served as an equestrian officer or legionary tribune; thus before his appointment to a key command in Lollius Urbicus' army, he had no military experience whatsoever. In the 'Indian Summer' of the Antonines the Roman army, with centurions like Maximius Gaetulicus (**6.37**) and generals like Lollius Urbicus (**6.02**), could afford to carry some distinguished passengers. The Emperor Claudius and Claudius Charax, antiquarians a century apart, possessed much the same qualifications for their successful generalship in Britain.

Perhaps Charax re-read the Iliad and pondered the Trojan War during those long summer evenings in the North. A group of five distance slabs illustrates how his legion and detachments of the other two divided the 10-mile (16 km) bloc among them east of Castlehill. First comes the Twentieth Legion:

<6.09> *Eastermains, Kirkintilloch*

leg(io) XX
V(aleria) V(ictrix) fec(it)
m(ilia) p(assuum) III p(edes)
IIICCCIV

RIB 2184; Keppie 1998, No. 3

'The Twentieth Legion Valeria Victrix made 3,000 paces and 3,304 feet.'

The boar of the Twentieth Legion emerges from what looks like the Wall itself and advances towards a tree, a motif repeated on the lost Hutcheson Hill slab[13] and other uninscribed stones from northern Britain; evidently it was part of the Legion's iconographic repertoire. Unlike the other distance slabs, this stone, although complete, does not name Antoninus Pius, nor does it specify that there was only a detachment of the Twentieth present. The numeral is complex: there is a bar above the second III, indicating that 'thousands' are meant, and one must understand the second P as 'feet' (*pedes*), not 'paces' (*passus*). 3304 feet are $660\frac{4}{5}$ paces, giving a total of $3{,}660\frac{4}{5}$ paces. This obsessively exact total is almost the same as that claimed by the other two legions in this bloc. Here is the Second Legion, one of two stones:

<6.10> *near Balmuildy*

imp(eratori) Caes(ari) Tito Aelio
Hadriano Antonino
Aug(usto) Pio p(atri) p(atriae) leg(io) II
Aug(usta) pep(!) m(ilia) p(assuum) IIIDC-
LXVI s(emis)

RIB 2193; Keppie 1998, No. 5

[13] *RIB* 2198, noted after **6.13**.

'For the Emperor Caesar Titus Aelius Hadrian Antoninus Augustus Pius, Father of his Country, the Second Legion Augusta (made the Wall) for 3,666½ paces.'

In the composite numeral, the D for '500' was not a letter originally, but the right-hand half of the Greek letter used for '1000' which resembled O divided by a vertical line. The mason has cut PEP by mistake instead of PER, but otherwise the text is identical with the legion's other stone.[14] However, it has been decorated as well, by an inferior craftsman who has seen the legion's Bridgeness slab (**6.07**). On the left, there is the same cavalryman, but he is being crowned by Victory, and one of his hapless barbarians has overflowed onto the right. Above this casualty is stuck the legion's Eagle, and a capricorn, Augustus' birth sign of the Zodiac which he gave to his legion. The naïve militaria disposed at random, without any sense of composition, give this slab like the Brough-by-Bainbridge stone (**8.04**) the artless charm of a south-Persian tribal rug. Contrast the severity of the Sixth Legion's two stones:

<**6.11**> *Castlehill*

imp(eratori) Caesar(i) T(ito) Aelio
Hadriano Antonino
Aug(usto) Pio p(atri) p(atriae) vexillatio
leg(ionis) VI Victr(icis) p(iae) f(idelis)
per m(ilia) p(assuum) III DCLXVI s(emis)

RIB 2196; Keppie 1998, No. 6

'For the Emperor Caesar Titus Aelius Hadrian Antoninus Augustus Pius, Father of his Country, a detachment of the the Legion VI Victrix Dutiful and Loyal (made the Wall) for 3,666½ paces.'

The panel is flanked by elaborate *peltae* without any figures at all. The two ligatures (TI and TR) must be decorative, for the stone-cutter had plenty of space. The numeral 'D' is barred to distinguish it from the letter. The other stone carries almost the same text, but the text is massed more skilfully between two much plainer *peltae*.[15]

Four of these slabs record distances of exactly 3⅔ (Roman) miles; the fifth distance (**6.09**) is too close to be a coincidence. By plotting them against their find-spots, it has been deduced that the 10 miles (16 km) from Eastermains to Castlehill were neatly divided into three. But in the 4-mile (6.4 m) stretch west of Castlehill, from which come more than half the surviving slabs, there was the change already noted: the legions built much shorter lengths, and they measured them in feet. The exact divisions are too complex to be discussed here, but still the legionary masons lavished their skill upon the stones. Here are the two most elaborate; first the Sixth Legion:

---

[14] *RIB* 2186 (Keppie 1998, No. 4).
[15] *RIB* 2194.

<**6.12**> *Duntocher*

imp(eratori) C(aesari) T(ito) Aelio Hadr-
iano Antonino Aug(usto)
p(atri) p(atriae) vex(illatio) leg(ionis) VI
Victric<i>s p(iae) f(idelis)
opus valli p(edum)
MMMCCXL f(ecit)

RIB 2200+*add*. Keppie 1998, No. 11

'For the Emperor Caesar Titus Aelius Hadrian Antoninus Augustus, Father of his Country, a detachment of the the Sixth Legion Victrix Dutiful and Loyal made the Wall-work (for a distance of) 3,240 feet.'

In this composite numeral, the repeated symbol IXI for '1000' is not really M for *mille*, but derives from the Greek letter already mentioned after **6.10**. Often it is more rounded and looks like a modern '8' on its side, for example in the titulature of the First Cohort of Vardulli at High Rochester (**13.03**), which was 'milliary' (1000-strong). 'Pius' is omitted here, probably by mistake, although it is also missing from the Legion's other slab in this 4-mile stretch.[16] They both call the Wall a *vallum* like Hadrian's Wall.[17] VICTRICS is only a stone-cutter's mistake. The text is inscribed on a smaller panel held up by two Victories, each with her right foot on the globe. To their left is the god Mars in full armour, with spear and shield, wearing a three-plumed helmet like Insus the triumphant headhunter (**4.01**). To the right is an Amazon-like figure with a sword, significantly in its scabbard since the fighting is over, resting in the crook of her arm. She holds a flag to identify herself as *Virt(us) Aug(usta)*, the Imperial Valour. These four delightful deities at Duntocher look for all the world like a quartet of actors taking their bow after a successful performance, as indeed it was. The Twentieth Legion makes the same point at Hutcheson Hill:

<**6.13**> *Hutcheson Hill*

imp(eratori) C(aesari)
T(ito) Ae(lio)
Hadri-
ano
Anto-
nino
Aug(usto)
Pio p(atri) p(atriae)
vex(illatio) leg(ionis)
XX V(aleriae) V(ictricis)
fec(it)
per p(edum) III (milia)

[16] *RIB* 2205.
[17] **5.16**, **5.35** and **7.05**.

RIB III, 3507; Keppie 1998, No. 9

'For the Emperor Caesar Titus Aelius Hadrian Antoninus Augustus Pius, Father of his Country, a detachment of the the Twentieth Legion Valeria Victrix made (the Wall) for 3,000 feet.'

This stone was ploughed up in 1969, and is the only distance slab to be found since the nineteenth century. Its discovery compensates for the fate of the legion's other slab at Hutcheson Hill, which was found in 1865, sold for £2 and bought by the American Consul in Newcastle; despite contemporary protest, he sent it to Chicago, where it perished in the great fire of 1871.[18] Fortunately Collingwood Bruce had casts made of it, from which can be seen that the letter A has a V-shaped cross-bar. This is a Greek form not usually found in Latin inscriptions, and it seems to have been an idiosyncrasy of the Twentieth Legion at this time.[19] The text of both slabs is identical, except that the ill-fated Chicago slab abbreviates *Aelio* correctly as AEL instead of AE. **6.13** is far more decorative than its lost companion, which was conventionally inscribed in an ansate panel. The text of **6.13** is ingeniously distributed in small packets around what looks like a triumphal arch, with the Legion's wild boar fiercely passant below. The weight of ANTO|NINO and AVG | PIO P P is carried by two round panels on the shoulders of submissive bound captives, who can only watch while a female figure hands what looks like a doughnut to the Eagle of the Twentieth. This is actually a small wreath of victory, but the lady herself is not Victory, since she lacks the attributes of wings, globe and palm branch; Jocelyn Toynbee identified her as Britannia.[20] In the century since she was depicted as a conquered Amazon (**1.14**), Britannia has become Civilisation itself, thanking the uniforms that guard it.

The new Wall was finished, and attention could be turned elsewhere. Here is an epitaph from a main road in Italy, the Via Cassia a few miles north of Rome:

<**6.14**> *near Rome*

D(is) M(anibus)
Sex(to) Flavio Sex(ti) f(ilio) Quir(ina tribu) Quieto
p(rimo) p(ilo) leg(ionis) XX V(aleriae) V(ictricis), misso cum
exer(citu) in exp(editionem) Maur(etanicam) ab imp(eratore)
Antonino Aug(usto), praef(ecto) classis
Brit(annicae), Varinia Crispinilla coni<u>g<i>
pientissimo et Fl(avii) Vindex et Qui-
etus fil(ii) piissimi

AE 1960, 28

[18] *RIB* 2198 (Keppie 1998, No. 8). Keppie 2012, 108, justly comments: 'The bizarre story is testimony to contemporary indifference and the absence of any legal protection.'

[19] As noted by *RIB* III, p. 452, since when it has also been found on **12.80** and **12.81** (Inveresk).

[20] *Britannia* 1 (1970), 310. For a statue-base of 'Holy Britannia', see **12.15** (York).

> 'To the Shades of the Dead (and) to Sextus Flavius Quietus, son of Sextus, of the *Quirina* voting-tribe, first-ranking centurion of the Twentieth Legion Valeria Victrix; sent with an army to the Mauretanian campaign by the Emperor Antoninus Augustus; prefect of the British Fleet, (from) Varinia Crispinilla to her most dutiful husband and (from) Flavius Vindex and Flavius Quietus his most dutiful sons.'

This text is inscribed on a white marble altar topped by a pediment and two pinnacles. Each pinnacle is carved in low relief with a legionary standard, and on the lunette between them rides Flavius Quietus as a bearded huntsman on a lively horse, about to spear a charging boar. Hunting, 'the image of war without its guilt, and only five-and-twenty per cent of its danger' according to the novelist Surtees, is a favourite Roman tombstone motif; it symbolises human life lived intensely. Here it may even recall the crown of Quietus' legionary career (his earlier service is omitted), since the wild boar also symbolised the Twentieth Legion (**6.13**). The 'Mauretanian campaign' was prompted by a Berber uprising in Morocco and western Algeria, and is usually dated to *c.* AD 145/7 by the evidence of other inscriptions. Reinforcements arrived from Spain and the Danube, and a rock-cut inscription of AD 145 records the building of a road through the Aurès mountains in Numidia, by a detachment of the Sixth Legion Ferrata from Judaea.[21] Quietus probably brought a legionary detachment from Britain, to which his own legion, the Twentieth, would have contributed. When he was promoted to command the British Fleet, this 'army' presumably returned to Britain with him.[22] That it could be spared is a sign that northern Britain had been pacified, that the building-work was finished; indeed it has been independently calculated that the Antonine Wall took three seasons to build, which brings us neatly to the end of AD 144.[23]

The garrison of the Wall

Inscriptions have been found at six forts naming auxiliary units which garrisoned them. As usual they are not closely dated, which makes the chronology difficult, especially since Mumrills, Castlecary and Bar Hill have each produced evidence of two different units, and one unit (the Baetasii) is found at two different forts, Bar Hill and Old Kilpatrick. The issue is complicated by epigraphic evidence of all three legions, notably the four altars dedicated at Auchendavy by Cocceius Firmus[24], centurion of the Second Legion Augusta, but these legionary inscriptions can be

21 *ILS* 2479.

22 This is the most economical interpretation, but Verus possibly returned to Rome as a *primipilaris* before being despatched on a new mission (Dobson 1978, No. 130); Birley 2005, 318–19. For the evidence of Africans in the British army, including the possibility that some came from the Mauretanian campaign, see Swan 1992 and 1999.

23 Hanson and Maxwell 1983, 134–6.

24 **12.18**, **12.58**, **12.59** and **12.60**.

attributed to building-parties rather than to garrisons. At Rough Castle, however, the legionary centurion Flavius Betto (**6.19**) is explicitly the acting-commander of an auxiliary unit; and so probably is Flavius Verecundus at Westerwood (**9.16**). This is not the place to reconstruct the order of battle on the Wall, let alone its history, nor is it necessary, since it has been done so well by Bill Hanson and Gordon Maxwell.[25] But here is some of the epigraphic evidence, seen from east to west.

The large fort and civil settlement at Inveresk was 20 miles (32 km) east of the first Wall-fort, Carriden, but without being part of the Wall it was essential to its communications, since it was from here on the Firth of Forth that two main routes headed south-west and south-east, to Carlisle and Corbridge respectively.[26] Until recent years, its importance was reflected by a single stone inscription found in the mid-sixteenth century, this altar:

<**6.15**> *Inveresk (?Coria)*

Apollini
Granno
Q(uintus) Lusius
Sabinia-
nus
proc(urator)
Aug(usti)
v(otum) s(olvit) {S} l(ibens) {V} m(erito)

RIB 2132+*add.*

'To Apollo Grannus, Quintus Lusius Sabinianus, imperial procurator, paid his vow willingly, deservedly.'

The Roman god Apollo is identified with an important Celtic god who is attested only here in Britain, but whose cult was popular in the Rhineland and extended to the middle Danube. The intrusive letters in the bottom line (the formulaic V S L M) have not been explained, but they may be due to an early mis-reading which cannot now be checked, since the stone has long been lost. In the next four centuries until *RIB* I was published in 1965, Inveresk produced nothing but a minor 'centurial' stone and two graffiti.[27] Then in 1976 part of another altar dedicated by Sabinianus was found in the same location, the churchyard, which is significant since there is only one other dedication by an imperial procurator in the whole of

[25] Hanson and Maxwell 1983, 152–72, tabulated at 154–55 (Table 8.1, 'The probable garrisons of forts on the Wall'). For the epigraphic evidence in particular, see Keppie 1998.

[26] Bishop 2002.

[27] *RIB* 2133 (*c(o)h(ors VIII)*; *RIB* II.7, 610 and 787.

Britain.[28] It surely means that Sabinianus was paying a special visit to the Wall – a visit long enough to dedicate *two* altars – perhaps only to pay its garrison, but more likely to oversee its construction.

Finally in 2010, excavation at Inveresk produced two of the finest altars ever found in Britain, dedications to Mithras by a legionary centurion (**12.80** and **12.81**). They were preceded in 2007 by a chance discovery due to ploughing, the first Roman tombstone to be found in Scotland since **6.18** in 1834. Its upper half is missing, but enough remains to show that it depicted a cavalryman trampling the usual barbarian; the epitaph is inscribed in the ansate panel below:

<**6.16**> *Carberry (near Inveresk)*

D(is) M(anibus)
Cresc[e]ntis eq(uitis)
alae Sebosia(nae)
ex n(umero) eq(uitum) sing(ularium)
s[t]ip(endiorum) XV
h(eres) f(aciundum) c(uravit)

Britannia 39 (2008), 372, No. 5

'To the Shades of the Dead (and) of Crescens, cavalryman of the Cavalry Regiment Sebosiana, from the unit of Equites Singulares, of 15 years' service; his heir had this set up.'

Crescens belonged to the élite unit of mounted guardsmen (*equites singulares*) which escorted the governor, its members being drawn from the province's auxiliary cavalry units. Individual *equites singulares* like Crescens, despite being seconded from another unit, usually an *ala*, continued to belong to it for administrative purposes, which is why they often specify it in their inscriptions. At Carlisle, for example, the *singularis* of Agricola, who like Crescens belonged to the *ala Sebosiana*, is addressed as a member of that *ala* (**3.14**). But since *equites singulares* escorted the governor, they are usually attested at the provincial capital, which raises the question of why that letter was found at Carlisle, and why Crescens was buried near Inveresk, both so far from London.[29] It is quite possible that Crescens was on a special mission, or that he was attending the governor, perhaps even the procurator, on a tour of inspection. But the simplest answer is that the *ala Sebosiana* – which is almost certainly the cavalry regiment based in late-Flavian Carlisle – had now become the garrison of Inveresk: this was an important centre of communications, and the fort

[28] *RIB* III, 3499. *RIB* 2066 (Brampton) was dedicated by the procurator Cocceius Nigrinus towards the western end of Hadrian's Wall, but *RIB* 752+*add.* (Watercrook) was almost certainly not dedicated by a procurator.

[29] The question is discussed more fully in *Britannia* 39 (2008), 372–4, n. See also the note to **3.14**.

was quite large (5.7 acres/2.3 ha), which would suggest that it was intended for an *ala*. If this were the *ala Sebosiana*, Crescens may have returned there on leave or it may have been chosen as the appropriate place to commemorate him, whether by himself or his heir, who was probably a comrade-in-arms.

Even larger than Inveresk, and much the largest of the Wall forts, is Mumrills (6.5 acres/2.7 ha), where it is not surprising to find another cavalry regiment:

<6.17> *Mumrills*

Herculi
Magusan(o)
sacrum
Val(erius) Nigri-
nus dupli(carius)
alae Tun-
grorum

RIB 2140

'Sacred to Hercules Magusanus: Valerius Nigrinus, *duplicarius* of the Cavalry Regiment of Tungrians, (set this up).'

This altar was dedicated by a junior officer 'paid double' like Longinus Sdapeze at Colchester (**2.02**), meaning that he was the second-in-command of a troop of 30 men. It is the only dedication in Britain to Hercules Magusanus, a Germanic deity worshipped in Lower Germany and Gallia Begica, whose votaries are almost all soldiers or veterans. Almost the only other exception to this geographic concentration is an altar from Rome which was dedicated in AD 219 by Batavians and Thracians in the imperial mounted guards (*equites singulares Augusti*) who had been 'seconded from the province of Lower Germany'.[30] Bracelets dedicated to the god are known from lower Germany, including one from the Tungrian tribal capital Atuatuca Tungrorum (Tongres, near Liège in Belgium).[31] Nigrinus undoubtedly came from Lower Germany or Belgica, and was quite likely a Tungrian, with the implication that his regiment still recruited from source, despite having belonged to the British army since at least AD 98.[32]

[30] Speidel 1994, 87–8, No. 62 (correcting *ILS* 2188), *cives Batavi sive Thraces adlecti ex provincia Germania inferiore*; perhaps from the *ala I Thracum* at Vechten.

[31] CIL xiii 10027, 212(a), *He(rculi) M(agusano)*; compare 212(b), *Hercu(li) Magu(sano)*.

[32] When it is listed in the earliest diploma for Britain (*CIL* xvi 43), which since it was found near Liège was probably issued to a Tungrian veteran of the *ala* or the First Cohort of Tungrians (also listed). His discharge after 25 years suggests that his unit was formed in AD 73 after the Batavian Revolt.

This practice contrasts with that of the cohort which seems to have succeeded the Tungrians at Mumrills:

<**6.18**> *Mumrills*

Dis M(anibus) Nectovelius f(ilius)
Vindicis an(norum) IXXX
stip(endiorum) VIIII nat-
ionis Brigans
militavit in
coh(orte) II Thr(acum)

RIB 2142+*add.*

'To the Shades of the Dead. Nectovelius son of Vindex, aged 29, of nine years' service, a Brigantian by nationality, served as a soldier in the Second Cohort of Thracians.'

This is the tombstone of a north-British tribesman, the only Brigantian explicitly recorded in the Roman army.[33] Nectovelius at first sight is the Celtic son of a Roman father, but although *Vindex* is a Roman cognomen ('avenger'), chosen for example by the centurion Flavius Quietus (**6.14**) for his son, it is one of a group of names like *Docilis*, *Senicianus* and *Verecundus* which were popular with Rome's Celtic-speaking subjects for 'concealing' a Celtic name-element; hence the German term *Deckname* ('cover name'). The element here is **uindo-s* ('white', 'bright', 'happy'), as in *Vindolanda* and Welsh *Gwyn*. A famous instance is Julius Vindex, the governor of Gallia Lugdunensis who rebelled against Nero; his ancestors had been kings of Aquitania.

When did Nectovelius' grandfather choose this 'Roman' name for his son? Nectovelius died at the age of 29, which means that his father must have been born about 50 years earlier. The epitaph has been attributed to the Agricolan fort at Mumrills, since Agricola in AD 83 reinforced his army with 'the bravest of the Britons and those whose loyalty had been tested in a long period of peace.'[34] But it was only ten years since Cerialis' conquest of the Brigantes – hardly 'a long period of peace' – and even if Nectovelius be regarded as one of the 'brave' rather than the 'loyal', and died in the late AD 80s, it is inconceivable that his Brigantian grandfather was already pro-Roman in the early AD 40s. But his tombstone, even if Antonine, is important evidence of local recruitment which increased until the third century, when the Vindolanda dedication to the goddess Gallia (**12.16**) implies that it had

[33] Another Brigantian may have been Veluotigernus son of Magiotigernus, who is only described as 'British' (BRIT) in the unpublished diploma found near Lanchester in 2016 which was issued to him in AD 150 as a veteran of the German Fleet (*classis Germanica*).

[34] Tacitus, *Agricola* 29, *ex Britannis fortissimos et longa pace exploratos*. E Birley 1988, 300.

become the norm.[35] Unfortunately we do not know whether young Nectovelius was a conscript, or voluntarily exchanged an upland shepherd's life for the life of a soldier, but his epitaph is an index of the 'romanisation' of Roman Britain, that within two generations its unruly northern tribes should be helping to guard the frontier.[36]

Nectovelius' cohort was part-mounted (*equitata*), but contained only four troops of cavalry against the 16 in the *ala Tungrorum*. It follows that the garrison of Mumrills had been down-graded, but the reason for this reduction is unknown. Changes of garrison are found at other forts, as we will see, but it is unclear whether they amount to a systematic revision of the Wall's whole garrison, or are only piecemeal manipulation of available resources. At Rough Castle, two inscriptions record another auxiliary cohort, but one without any cavalry at all:

<**6.19**> *Rough Castle*

Victoriae
coh(ors) VI Ner-
viorum c(uius) c(uram agit)
Fl(avius) Betto (centurio) leg(ionis)
XX V(aleriae) V(ictricis)
v(otum) s(olvit) l(aeta) l(ibens) m(erito)

RIB 2144

'To Victory the Sixth Cohort of Nervii, under the acting command of Flavius Betto, centurion of the Twentieth Legion Valeria Victrix, paid its vow gladly, willingly, deservedly.'

Was this the 'victory' that had won the Antonine Wall, was it a subsequent success, or only a general aspiration? We are not told. The cohort was one of six raised from a tribe in northern Belgica which claimed German origins, and was famous for having nearly defeated Julius Caesar.[37] The Sixth Cohort, which makes this dedication, has recently been found in London in the early AD 60s (see note to **2.19**). In the reign of Severus it was active at Brough-by-Bainbridge (**8.04**), where it remained until the end of the Roman period.[38] At Rough Castle it is commanded, not by an equestrian prefect, but by a centurion seconded from his own legion as *praepositus*. But as at Brough-by-Bainbridge later, it was active in building:

---

[35] The evidence, despite its 'paucity', is illuminated by Dobson and Mann 1973.

[36] Hanson and Maxwell 1983, 192.

[37] Caesar, *Gallic War* ii 15–28. According to Shakespeare (*Julius Caesar* iii.2), Caesar was assassinated in the mantle he first wore 'That day he overcame the Nervii'.

[38] *Tab. Lond. Bloomberg* 33, citing Tacitus, *Annals* xiv 38. **8.04**, *RIB* 722+*add.* and III, 3216 (Brough-by-Bainbridge). Not. Dig. *Occ.* 40.56.

<**6.20**> *Rough Castle*

[imp(eratori) Ca]esari Tito
[Aelio] Hadriano
[Anto]nino Aug(usto)
[Pio] p(atri) p(atriae) coh(ors) VI
[Ner]viorum pri-
[nci]pia fecit

RIB 2145

'For the Emperor Caesar Titus Aelius Hadrianus Augustus Pius, Father of his Country, the Sixth Cohort of Nervii built this Headquarters Building.'

The stone-cutter was so punctilious in using a medial point to mark an abbreviation or a word-ending, that he added one to the end of each line, even interrupting the word *principia* (4–5) with a redundant point after PRI. When this slab was found in 1903, it was the first British inscription to refer to the *principia* (headquarters building), which the Birdoswald inscription (**14.06**) later distinguished from the *praetorium* (commandant's house); references have since been found also at Reculver and perhaps Caerleon.[39]

At Castlecary the wealth of epigraphic evidence is embarrassing: at least two legions, as well as two different auxiliary cohorts.[40] Both these are milliary and part-mounted, even though the fort is too small (3.5 acres) to have housed either at full strength. First this building inscription:

<**6.21**> *Castlecary*

imp(eratori) Caes(ari) T(ito) Ael(io) Ant(onino)
Aug(usto) Pio p(atri) p(atriae)
coh(ors) I Tungro-
rum fecit (milliaria)

RIB 2155; Keppie 1998, No. 18

'For the Emperor Caesar Titus Aelius Antoninus Augustus Pius, Father of his Country; the First Cohort of Tungrians, a thousand strong, built (this).'

We have already seen this cohort at Vindolanda (**5.01**), and will soon see the Second Cohort at Birrens (**6.33**). Both cohorts fought for Agricola at the battle of Mons Graupius, and like the *ala Tungrorum* (**6.17**) they derived from the tribe in

[39] *RIB* III, 3027, *aedem p[rinci]piorum cu[m b]asilica*, and 3028 (Reculver); 3083 (Caerleon).

[40] *RIB* 2156 (legion not stated), **7.12** and *RIB* 2151 (Leg VI), **12.55** (vexillations of Leg II and Leg VI).

Gallia Belgica whose name survives in modern Tongres.[41] The First Cohort, unless it was a building party like the Dalmatae at Chesters,[42] was not the only garrison of Castlecary:

<**6.22**> *Castlecary*

deo
Neptuno
cohors I
fid(a) Vardul(lorum)
c(ivium) R(omanorum) eq(uitata) (milliaria)
cui prae(e)st
Trebius
Verus pr-
aef(ectus)

RIB 2149+*add.*

'To the god Neptune; the First Loyal Cohort of Vardulli, Roman Citizens, part-mounted, a thousand strong, commanded by the prefect Trebius Verus.'

The cohort which dedicated this altar was raised from a tribe in northern Spain, and is first attested in Britain by the diploma of AD 98; but since it already bears the title of *c(ives) R(omani)*, it must have seen previous service, whether in Britain or elsewhere. Castlecary is an inland fort, and might seem a surprising location for a dedication to Neptune; but an altar was also dedicated to him at Vindolanda, about as far from the sea as one could be, and it shows that he was the Roman god of water, not just of the sea, which is why the four surviving messages addressed to him were all thrown into rivers.[43]

A veteran of this cohort called Saturninus, who incidentally came from Gloucester, which is evidence like Nectovelius of 'local' recruitment, was issued with a diploma found at Colchester. Only one corner survives, but it can be attributed to Antoninus Pius.[44] The commanding officer's name is lost except for his cognomen, which was *Verus*; this is quite common, but Tony Birley is surely right to identify him as Trebius Verus.[45] Unusually he was a prefect, not a tribune, although he commanded

[41] Tacitus, *Agricola* 36.1 with Ogilvie and Richmond 1967, 78.

[42] *RIB* III, 3300.

[43] *RIB* 1694 (Vindolanda). **12.75** (the Hamble estuary); *Britannia* 13 (1982), 408, No. 9 (the Tas at Caister St Edmund); 18 (1987), 360, No. 1 (the Thames at London Bridge); 25 (1994), 293, No. 1 (the Little Ouse at Brandon). The cohort is next found at Lanchester (*RIB* 1083), an inland fort which does not support the suggestion that the cohort dedicated its altar to Neptune 'on the eve of their withdrawal by ship' (Birley 2005, 151).

[44] *RIB* II.1, 2401.12.

[45] Birley 2005, 151. The chronology is tight, requiring that he commanded the cohort when it was withdrawn from the Wall.

a milliary cohort; this was not a permanent arrangement, for when the cohort dedicated an altar a few years later at Lanchester, it was duly commanded by a tribune.[46] However, since the officer commanding the First and Second Cohort of Tungrians, which were both milliary, is always called a 'prefect' and not a 'tribune', it has been suggested that his title deliberately recalled the 'prefect' once appointed by the Romans from the aristocracy to be chieftain of his tribe. This would be inverted snobbery articulating an historical reminiscence – like consultant surgeons calling themselves 'Mr', not 'Dr', because barber-surgeons were not physicians – but the hypothesis becomes less compelling if also required to explain what was evidently a temporary expedient with the Vardulli; and an altar has just been found which shows yet another milliary unit, the First Cohort of Vangiones, being commanded by a prefect.[47] Roy Davies was surely right to argue that when a milliary cohort was divided between two stations, it was nominally commanded by a prefect because of its reduced size, but with one detachment actually in the charge of a centurion. Thus at Castlesteads on Hadrian's Wall, a fort almost as small (3.75 acres/1.5 ha) as Castlecary, the Second Cohort of Tungrians is always 'commanded' by a prefect, but in all three inscriptions a centurion is named as the acting-commander (*princeps*).[48]

Bar Hill is another fort where two cohorts are attested, one of which is drawn from yet another tribe of Lower Germany, the Baetasii. These are listed in the diplomas of AD 103, 122, 124 and 135, but unlike the Vardulli they are not credited there with the title of *c(ives) R(omani)*. But they stress it in this inscription:

<6.23> *Bar Hill*

i[mp(eratori) Cae]sari
T(ito) Ae[l(io) Had(riano) An]tonino
Au[g(usto) Pio p(atri) p(atriae) c]oh(ors)
I B[aetasior(um) c(ivium)] R(omanorum) ob
vir[tutem et fi]dem

RIB 2170+*add.*

'For the Emperor Caesar Titus Aelius Hadrianus Antoninus Augustus Pius, Father of his Country, the First Cohort of Baetasii, Roman citizens for their valour and loyalty, (set this up).'

The title was surely new and precious, as if the cohort had just won it during the advance into Scotland. Its language recalls the elaborate title of the *ala Augusta ob virtutem appellata* at Chesters (**5.03**), but the cohort did not maintain its full title,

[46] *RIB* 1083.
[47] *Britannia* 46 (2015), 388, No. 6 (Papcastle), with discussion of such prefects at 389–90, n. 15. Maryport (**5.13**) presents a similar problem.
[48] *RIB* 1981, 1982 and 1983. Davies 1967.

being content with the abbreviated letters C R at Old Kilpatrick (**6.26**) and later at Maryport.[49] The Bar Hill fragments were found in the well of the headquarters building, together with an altar[50] dedicated by the cohort, which is fortunate since only one corner of its initial letter survives here; but despite the loss of the middle portion of text, it was successfully restored by Haverfield. It was not the only cohort to have garrisoned Bar Hill:

<**6.24**> *Bar Hill*

[d]eo Silv[ano]
[C]aristan[ius]
[I]ustianu[s]
praef(ectus)
[c]oh(ortis) I Ham[ior(um)]
v(otum) s(olvit) l(aetus) l(ibens) m(erito)

RIB 2167; Keppie 1998, No. 32

'To the god Silvanus Caristanius Justianus, prefect of the First Cohort of Hamians, paid his vow gladly, willingly, deservedly.'

The Hamians had previously garrisoned Carvoran (**5.46**) on Hadrian's Wall, to which they returned (**12.87**) after the Antonine Wall was evacuated. They left one of their prefects behind at Bar Hill: Julius Marcellinus was buried there, but his name says nothing about him.[51] However, the nomen of the prefect who dedicates this altar is distinctive: *Caristanius* recalls the magnate who celebrated Claudius' invasion of Britain and his descendant the legionary legate of Agricola (**3.17**). Justianus undoubtedly belonged to this family at Pisidian Antioch, descendants of an original colonist, but to a branch which remained equestrian in rank.[52] Another quite rare nomen is found at Castlehill:

<**6.25**> *Castlehill*

Campes-
tribus et
Britanni(ae)
Q(uintus) Pisentius
Iustus pr(a)ef(ectus)
coh(ortis) IIII Gal(lorum)
v(otum) s(olvit) l(aetus) l(ibens) m(erito)

[49] *RIB* 830. Its abbreviated tile stamps at Reculver (*RIB* II.4, 2468) omit it altogether.
[50] *RIB* 2169.
[51] *RIB* 2172.
[52] Birley 1961, 163–4.

RIB 2195; Keppie 1998, No. 41

'To the Goddesses of the Parade Ground and to Britannia, Quintus Pisentius Justus, prefect of the Fourth Cohort of Gauls, paid his vow gladly, willingly, deservedly.'

This is the only instance of *Pisentius* not to be found in Italy, where it belongs to a group of names which are probably Etruscan in origin.[53] The Campestres were exclusively worshipped by cavalry units; the *ala I Asturum*, for example, restored a temple dedicated to them at Benwell.[54] The expansion of BRITANNI is uncertain: it is probably *Britanni(ae)* in the sense of '(the land of) Britain', rather like the altar (**12.18**) dedicated by Cocceius Firmus at Auchendavy to 'the land of Britain' (*terrae Brita | nnicae*), but it might be a divinity, like 'Holy Britannia' (*Britanniae | sanctae*) at York (**12.15**). The British 'Mothers' (*matres*) are even possible, since at Cramond[55] the Campestres are called 'Mothers', which would suggest a dedication was intended to 'The Mothers, Campestres and British' (*Matribus Campestribus et Britannicis*), but there was not enough space on the die.

The Baetasii whom we have just seen at Bar Hill (**6.23**) also dedicated an altar at Old Kilpatrick, the fort which marked the Wall's western end on the Firth of Clyde; its lettering is unusually elegant:

<**6.26**> *Old Kilpatrick*

I(ovi) O(ptimo) M(aximo)
coh(ors) I Bae-
tasiorum
c(ivium) R(omanorum) cui pr-
aeest Publicius
Maternus praef(ectus),
c(uram) a(gente) Iulio Can-
dido (centurione) leg(ionis) I Italicae,
v(otum) s(olvit) l(aeta) l(ibens) m(erito)

RIB III, 3509; Keppie 1998, No. 43

'To Jupiter Best and Greatest. The First Cohort of Baetasii, Roman Citizens, commanded by the prefect Publicius Maternus, with Julius Candidus, centurion of the First Legion Italica, as its acting-commander, paid its vow gladly, willingly and deservedly.'

The equestrian prefect is named as the formal commander, but he was not present since the actual commander is a legionary centurion as *praepositus*, which strongly

[53] Schulze 1933, 210.
[54] *RIB* 1334. Birley 1961, 98.
[55] *RIB* 2135.

suggests that the cohort was divided – between Old Kilpatrick and Bar Hill presumably – and that here we have only a detachment. The centurion's name is not distinctive, and several centurions called 'Julius Candidus' are known, including one of the builders of Hadrian's Wall (**5.25** and **5.26**), but it is strange that he should belong to a legion on the lower Danube. This prompted the suggestion that he belonged to one of the detachments with which Septimius Severus reinforced the British army, since the name of the deity (Jupiter, abbreviated to I O M) is inscribed on the capital in Severan fashion.[56] But inscribed capitals are found on some Antonine altars, notably two (but only two) of the four dedicated by Cocceius Firmus at Auchendavy, where the reason is clearly that space was lacking on the die.[57] This pressure was felt also at Old Kilpatrick, for after the first three lines on the die, which are amply drawn, the lettering grows ever more cramped. Technically the centurion did belong to a Danubian legion, but he was only advertising his impending transfer, like the acting-commander at Maryport who described himself as centurion of the Tenth Legion Fretensis (in Judaea), or indeed the poet Porcius Iasucthanus at Lambaesis, headquarters of the Third Legion Augusta, who described himself as centurion of the Twentieth Legion Valeria Victrix (in Britain).[58] The Antonine date is confirmed by the altar's very fine lettering and its use of the formula *cui praeest* unabbreviated to C P. Its excellent state of preservation suggests that it was deliberately buried quite soon after, no doubt when the Wall was evacuated.

The Wall's outposts extended as far north as modern Perth, to the fort of Bertha (a modern coinage from 'Perth') at the confluence of the Almond with the Tay, where this sandstone slab was found by two schoolboys in the river bed:

<6.27> *Bertha*

Discipul-
inae
Augusti

RIB III, 3515

'(Dedicated) to the Discipline of the Emperor.'

Sir Ian Richmond kept a photograph of this fine inscription on his mantelpiece. Its graceful, elongated letters with their gentle curves reflect the underlying brush-strokes. The cult of Discipline, the static counterpart of a victorious offensive, was a tribute to the army's training and preparation; but since the cult was introduced by

56 Birley 1983, citing Kewley 1973.

57 **12.58** and **12.60**, by contrast with **12.59** and **12.18**.

58 *RIB* 814 (Maryport) and **13.12** (Lambaesis). For Iasucthanus see also *AE* 1995, 164 (Bu Njem), cited before **13.12**.

Hadrian (**5.03**), this inscription cannot be Flavian and must belong to the second, Antonine occupation of Bertha. It is the Roman Empire's most northerly stone inscription, and expresses the army's determination to stay there this time.

Back to Hadrian's Wall

It was not to be. A military crisis is revealed by coins struck in AD 155, bearing a reverse type of Britannia variously seen as 'dejected' or 'vigilant', but its nature must be surmised, whether for example it was a Brigantian revolt behind the Wall, as Haverfield suggested and Sheppard Frere accepts, or increasing pressure from the north, which seems more likely.[59] Whatever the underlying cause, Bertha like the Wall itself was evacuated, even if the exact chronology is difficult. It was revolutionised by Brian Hartley's demonstration from the samian ware that the Antonine Wall was not occupied after the early AD 160s, nor occupied concurrently with Hadrian's Wall. Nick Hodgson has now gone further and shown, by carefully weighing the evidence of archaeology and inscriptions, that the Antonine Wall was not reoccupied after the crisis which brought Julius Verus to Britain; instead, he recommissioned Hadrian's Wall and its outposts.[60] His arrival from Lower Germany, where he had been legate, is marked by this troop-movement:

<6.28> *Newcastle (Pons Aelius)*

imp(eratori) Antoni-
no Aug(usto) Pio p(atri)
pat(riae) vexil<l>atio
leg(ionis) II Aug(ustae) et leg(ionis)
VI Vic(tricis) et leg(ionis)
XX V(aleriae) V(ictricis) con<t>r<i->
buti ex(ercitibus) Ger(manicis) du-
obus sub Iulio Ve-
ro leg(ato) Aug(usti) pr(o) p(raetore)

RIB 1322+*add.*

'For the Emperor Antoninus Augustus Pius, Father of his Country, a detachment of the Second Legion Augusta and of the Sixth Legion Victrix and of the Twentieth Legion Valeria Victrix, (men) contributed to the two German armies, under Julius Verus imperial propraetorian legate.'

This unusually handsome slab is unweathered, probably because it was sheltered by the same shrine as the two altars of the Sixth Legion (**5.07** and **5.08**), although it

[59] Frere 1987, 136. Hodgson 1995.

[60] Hartley 1972. Hodgson 1995 and 2011. For Julius Verus, see Birley 2005, 145–9.

has been suggested that it was so full of errors that it was immediately discarded. The stone-cutter misunderstood the text drawn for him on the stone. He made *vexillatio* into VEXILATIO, the spacing of the letters showing that he overlooked the first I, and made the first L into I; he made *contributi* into CONRBVTI by overlooking T and I, which were evidently each ligatured to the adjoining letter; and he omitted R from the final PR. These errors do not affect the sense, but unfortunately there are worse problems due to over-abbreviation. It is unclear whether the legionaries were – quite literally – coming or going.

Contributi is masculine plural but it must qualify *vexillatio* (feminine singular): perhaps it is in apposition, and it is thus translated here, but this is an awkward solution. The Roman army would normally speak of *vexillationes* (plural) of three legions, not *vexillatio* (singular), so the editors of *RIB* may be right in supposing that *vexillatio* is a mistake for *vexillarii* ('men detached'). Otherwise it might be a misleading abbreviation, *vexillatio(nes)*, but this would require *contributae* (feminine plural). Nor is this all. *RIB* understands EX GER DVOBVS as *ex Ger(maniis) duobus,* 'from the two Germanies', but *Germaniis* is feminine and *duobus* masculine: hence the illuminating suggestion by John Wilkes that EX is not the preposition *ex* ('from') but an extreme abbreviation of *ex(ercitibus)*, 'to the (two) armies'.[61] This must be understood as dative, not ablative, in the absence of the preposition *ab* ('from' or 'by'), and given the word-order and the language of other vexillation-inscriptions: thus 'detachments *of* the British legions contributed *to* the German armies'. But Julius Verus came to Britain from Lower Germany, his previous post, and his British governorship involved a military crisis. Why then is he sending soldiers to Germany just when he needs them in Britain? One would expect him to be bringing troops with him *from* Germany.

Jules Bogaers suggested that a second EX was omitted in error: *ex ex(ercitibus) Ger(manicis) duobus*, 'from the two German armies'. This would then be a logical troop-movement, the British legions reinforced from the German armies, but the syntax is difficult. Michael Speidel is surely right to refine Wilkes' solution, by seeing the dedicators as a detachment drawn from the three British legions which had previously been sent to two German armies, but now returned to Britain. It came to the Tyne estuary because legionaries were needed in the north. The 'two' German armies may be those of Upper and Lower Germany, but it is better to suppose there were temporarily *two* armies in Upper Germany, its regular garrison and reinforcements from elsewhere.[62]

This is a good example of the spider's web of conjecture in which epigraphists buzz and get stuck. The inscribed text, for all its beauty, is opaque because of over-

---

[61] Contrast EXER in Quietus' epitaph (**6.14**) and in **12.82** (Piercebridge), which would have been explicit; even EXX would have done, the repeated X indicating a plural.

[62] As implied by *ILS* 1071 and *AE* 1924, 74, which describe its legate as responsible for the province 'and the army operating there' (*exercitus in ea tendentis*).

abbreviation and copying-errors, but it can be resolved: Julius Verus was arriving in the Tyne from Germany to deal with the crisis, bringing British reinforcements with him which were more needed in Britain than in Germany. The prime evidence that he recommissioned Hadrian's Wall is disarmingly slight, considering that this decision would last for the next two and a half centuries. It is a 'centurial' stone, now lost, of which two drawings[63] survive:

<**6.29**> *Wall-mile 8 or 9*

leg(io) VI V(ictrix) p(ia)
f(idelis) ref(ecit) Te-
r(tullo) et Sac(erdote) co(n)s(ulibus)

RIB 1389, with Hodgson 2011

'The Sixth Legion Victrix, Dutiful and Loyal, rebuilt (this) in the consulship of Tertullus and Sacerdos (AD 158).'

The initials S F have been cut in the triangular *ansa* either side of the main text, and are likely to be those of the centurion responsible.[64] This is the only centurial stone from the Wall to carry a date, just 20 years after the death of Hadrian, and it refers explicitly to *re*building (*refecit*). In being a simple ansate panel, it looks rather like a second stone of the Sixth Legion, undated but found in much the same area:

<**6.30**> *Heddon-on-the-Wall* (?)

leg(ionis) VI [V]i-
ct(ricis) perf-
ecit coh(ors) X

RIB 1388, with Hodgson 2011, 67

'Of the Sixth Legion Victrix, the Tenth Cohort completed (this).'

This stone too is lost, and survives only as a drawing. Wright in *RIB* conjectured the verb *re[f]ecit* ('rebuilt'), which better suits the formulation of *RIB* 1389, but Hodgson's reading is more faithful to the drawing. 'Completion' may allude to work left unfinished by their Hadrianic predecessors (see below). Both stones are probably related to a much more elaborate stone, which was re-used with other Roman stones to build a pele tower at Newburn:

---

[63] The second drawing is published by Hodgson 2011, whose minute study of the provenance and historical significance of **6.29** is followed here.

[64] S F is not known as a military abbreviation. Hodgson (2011, 63, n. 9) cites *ILS* 2198 as warrant for *s(igni)f(er)*, but another piece has since been found and the reading is actually *b(ene)f(iciarius)* (Speidel 1994, No. 559).

<**6.31**> *taken to Newburn, south of Wall-mile 9–10*

leg(ionis) XX V(aleriae) V(ictricis)
c(o)ho(rtis) IIII
(centuria) Lib(urni) Fro(ntonis)
(centuria) Tere(nti) Mag(ni)

RIB 2077+*add.*

'Of the Twentieth Legion Valeria Victrix, the Fourth Cohort: the century of Liburnius Fronto (and) the century of Terentius Magnus (built this).'

This stone, like the other two, is not dated, but is surely not Hadrianic. It is decorated with figures in relief unlike the usual centurial stone, and it names two centuries, not one. The text is inscribed around the figure of an eagle with a wreath in its beak like the Legion's eagle on its Antonine Wall distance-slab (**6.13**), between a flag (*vexillum*) to the left inscribed LEG XX, and to the right a legionary standard (*signum*). Since two centuries are named, the *vexillum* is not just a caption like that in **6.07**, but should be taken literally, to indicate a legionary detachment or 'vexillation' (*vexillatio*). The centurions' names are abbreviated, but the first can be expanded from an altar which was found at Benwell, three miles to the east; conveniently, it also gives the date:

<**6.32**> *Benwell (Condercum)*

I(ovi) O(ptimo) [M(aximo) Dolic]he-
no et n[u]minibus
Aug(ustorum) pro salute imp(eratoris)
Caesaris T(iti) Aeli Hadr(iani)
Antonini Aug(usti) Pii p(atris) p(atriae)
et leg(ionis) II Aug(ustae)
M(arcus) Liburnius Fron-
to (centurio) leg(ionis) eiusdem
v(otum) s(olvit) l(ibens) m(erito)

RIB 1330+*add.*

'To Jupiter Dolichenus Best and Greatest, and to the Divinities of the Emperors, for the welfare of the Emperor Caesar Titus Aelius Hadrian Antoninus Pius, Father of his Country, and of the Second Legion Augusta; Marcus Liburnius Fronto, centurion of the same legion, willingly and deservedly paid his vow.'

Jupiter Dolichenus was a protective sky-god originally worshipped at Doliche in Commagene (now Dülük in south-eastern Turkey, where his hilltop temple-site has been usurped by a radar station), whose cult was carried westward by the Roman army.[65] Here at Benwell it is coupled with the imperial cult: by honouring the

[65] Speidel 1978(b). For other dedications to Jupiter Dolichenus, see **12.82**, **12.83** and **12.84**.

Emperor's *numen*, his god-like quality, the centurion could give Antoninus Pius divine honours without actually calling him a god. Since *numinibus* is plural but there was only one Emperor at the time, his *numen* is assimilated to the *numina* of his predecessors who have become gods (*divi*).[66] Liburnius Fronto derived his nomen ultimately from the name of a tribe at the head of the Adriatic, the Liburnians, famous for inventing a warship called the *liburna*. Other *Liburnii* are found in the Third Legion Augusta at Lambaesis, and even a legionary in Egypt who came from Ancyra, who would have been descended from a legionary veteran colonist.[67] Liburnius Fronto's name is distinctive enough to identify him with the centurion LIB FRO at Newburn, even though the latter was in the Twentieth Legion, not the Second. Fronto must have been transferred from one legion to the other – which came first we do not know – and this would have been easier if elements of both were active in the same area. Here there is other evidence of the Second Legion at the time, a group of small building-stones which again are not the usual 'centurial' stones, since they name the legion's cohorts, not individual centuries; and like **6.31** they are unusually decorated, in this case with elaborate finials (*peltae*) or the legion's symbols of capricorn and pegasus.[68]

Despite this accumulation of evidence for Antonine rebuilding, it remains a puzzle why it should be so localised. Had the original, Hadrianic working-parties left a gap? This would at least explain the use of the verb *perfecit* (**6.30**), if it was old work brought to completion. But it is worrying not to have a major inscription naming Julius Verus, like this from Birrens, the most western of the outpost-forts:

<6.33> *Birrens (Blatobulgium)*

imp(eratori) Caes(ari) T(ito) A[el(io)] Hadr(iano)
An[to]nino Aug(usto) [Pio po]nt(ifici)
max(imo) [tr]ib(unicia) pot(estate) XXI co(n)s(uli) IIII
coh(ors) II [Tung]r(orum) m[i]l(liaria) eq(uitata) ?c(ivium) ?L(atinorum)
sub Iu[lio Vero] leg(ato) Aug(usti) pr(o) pr(aetore)

RIB 2110

'For the Emperor Caesar Titus Aelius Hadrian Antoninus Augustus Pius, pontifex maximus, in the twenty-first year of tribunician power (AD 158), four times consul; the Second Cohort of Tungrians, a thousand strong, part-mounted, citizens with Latin rights, under Julius Verus imperial propraetorian legate.'

[66] Fishwick 1994. For another example, see **10.02**.

[67] *CIL* iii 6023 = 6606. For the 'province' of Liburnia, see **7.01**.

[68] *RIB* 1341, 1342, 1343, 1344, 1359, 1360 and 1358 (with Hodgson 2011, 67–8).

This is the same year as **6.29**, and they can both be reasonably attributed to the same programme. The letters are exceptionally well drawn and executed, a characteristic of this cohort's inscriptions at Birrens.[69] Although the drawing in *RIB* does not show it, the setting-out lines are still visible, and even the divider-points with which the round letters such as O were drawn.[70] The first Antonine fort was rebuilt with inferior workmanship which Anne Robertson attributed to auxiliaries, but this is not reflected in their epigraphy.

The Second Cohort here bears the unique title C L, which it always abbreviates.[71] *RIB* expands this to *c(ives) L(atini)* by analogy with the well-attested battle-honour *c(ives) R(omani)* which marked a block grant of Roman citizenship (compare **4.13**), but the difficulty of finding 'Latin Rights' borne by individuals prompted Wolff to suggest *c(oram) l(audata)*, the phrase applied to an officer who was 'publicly praised' by Marcus Aurelius for a feat of arms. This is an attractive idea, even if it is otherwise unparalleled, but Geza Alföldy reasserted *c(ives) L(atini)* by noting instances of individuals who professed this status, notably in a papyrus which abbreviates it to C L.[72] Denis Saddington reinforced his argument by suggesting that the Tungrian capital, the *municipium Tungrorum* (Tongres), had received Latin status which this title was intended to recall.[73] Still, it is strange that the Tungrians should have clung to this second-rate distinction as late as AD 241 at Castlesteads,[74] when almost everyone in the Empire was a Roman citizen, and Latin status was obsolete except for a few manumitted slaves who were 'Junian Latins'. Its very obscurity may be why they always abbreviated it – did they even remember what it meant? – but it was hardly memorable. To encourage further guessing, here is another guess: were the Tungrians proud of being *c(oronati) l(aurea)*, 'crowned with bay leaves' like a general at his triumph?[75]

It will be noticed that the Second Cohort duly decorates three of its altars at Birrens with leaves – but unfortunately for this suggestion they are not *bay* leaves. And it is

---

69 *RIB* 2092, 2100, 2104, 2107 and 2109. But some of their inscriptions are inferior (**9.17**, *RIB* 2094 and 2108).

70 Grasby 2013, Study 8 (*RIB* 2110).

71 Maxfield 1981, 232–3, noting this inscription and *RIB* 2092 and 2104 from Birrens (undated but Antonine), and *RIB* 1981, 1982 and 1983 from Castlesteads (only 1983 is dated, to AD 241). These are 'official' dedications: C L is omitted from a tombstone (*RIB* 2115) and altars dedicated by groups (*RIB* 2100, 2107 and 2108) or individuals (*RIB* 2094 and 2109) within the unit.

72 Wolff 1976 with *AE* 1956, 124; Alföldy 1986 (citing Sijpesteijn 1977, No. 50). Its relevance to the question of whether there were free-born provincial *Latini* in the Imperial period was denied by Millar (1977, 630–35).

73 Saddington 2004.

74 *RIB* 1982.

75 Livy 27.37.13, *decemviri coronati laurea praetextatique*; compare 10.7.9, *viros quos corona triumphali laureaque honoraritis*. Note also the initials of *Celer libertus*, who dedicated *RIB* 2094 at Birrens for the welfare of the cohort's prefect.

the *First* Cohort at Vindolanda which puts a dedication within a wreath.[76] Whatever the meaning of C L, rebuilding at Birrens finds its counterpart in the next outpost fort to the east:

<6.34> *Bewcastle (?Fanum Cocidi)*

leg(ionis) VI
V(ictricis) p(iae) f(idelis)
vexilla-
tio fec(it)

RIB III, 3480

'Of the Sixth Legion Victrix Dutiful and Loyal, a detachment built this.'

This stone is undated, but was re-used in a building of Period III (late-second / early-third century), so it can be attributed to Period II, the rebuilding of Bewcastle after the retreat from Scotland.[77] The builders may have been the detachment of the Sixth Legion active at Corbridge in the governorship of Julius Verus.[78] He is named again south of the Wall, at this Pennine fort:

<6.35> *Brough-on-Noe (Navio)*

imp(eratori) Caesari T(ito) [Ael(io) Hadr(iano)
[An]tonino Au[g(usto) Pio p(atri) p(atriae)]
coh(ors) I Aquitan[orum]
sub Iulio V[ero leg(ato)] Aug(usti)
pr(o) pr(aetore), inst[ant]e
[C]apitoni[o Pri]sco prae(fecto)

RIB 283+*add.*

'For the Emperor Caesar Titus Aelius Hadrian Antoninus Augustus Pius, Father of his Country; the First Cohort of Aquitanians under Julius Verus, imperial propraetorian legate, (built this) directed by Capitonius Priscus their prefect.'

When the four surviving pieces of this slab were found in 1903, the prefect's cognomen had been lost except for the last three letters, SCO. Evidently it ended in *-scus*, and in his drawing the excavator, John Garstang, restored it as *[Pri]scus*; but

[76] Respectively *CSIR* i.4, Nos. 7 (*RIB* 2100) and 9 (*RIB* 2104) (ivy leaves), No. 17 (uninscribed) (acanthus leaves). *Britannia* 44 (2013), 384, No. 5 (Vindolanda, wreath).
[77] Austen 1991, 42. The fort was built (Period I) by detachments of the other two legions (*RIB* 995).
[78] *RIB* 1132+*add.*

Haverfield at the time preferred *[Fu]scus* and Collingwood later *[Etru]scus*.[79] *Priscus* only came into its own in 1979, when the base of this altar was found at a fort on the lower Danube:

<6.36> *Sacidava (Musait-Dunareni, in the Dobrudja)*

[...]
[. Capitoni]-
[us] Prisc(us) p[r]-
aef(ectus) coh(ortis) I Aq-
ui(tanorum) et trib(unus) coh(ortis)
I Cil(icum)

AE 1981, 741 = 1982, 850

'[*dedication. praenomen* Capitonius] Priscus, prefect of the First Cohort of Aquitanians and tribune of the First Cohort of Cilicians.'

The dedicator's praenomen and nomen have been lost, but his cognomen is obviously *Priscus*. As tribune he now commanded a milliary cohort, but he mentions his previous command as prefect, COH I AQVI, which can be identified with the cohort at Brough-on-Noe.[80] Its prefect, whether his name is transmitted as *Capitonius [...]scus* or *[...] Prisc(us)*, is surely the same man. But his inscription at Brough-on-Noe, well dated though it is, illustrates the limitations of epigraphic evidence: motive and cause must be conjectured, and tempting though it is to fit every building-inscription into an historical context, we should not assume that the Roman army never built or repaired anything except as the result of enemy action. The 'Brigantian revolt' which was once deduced from this inscription is little more than a guess. On present evidence it is more likely that the Romans were shortening their lines of communications by returning to Hadrian's Wall and a system of frontier control which extended to its outposts and hinterland.

A very senior centurion

Fewer than 20 years separate the starting-points of Hadrian's Wall and the Antonine Wall, with only a short interval between the first being completed and the second begun, so that many legionaries must have worked on both. They probably included Maximius Gaetulicus, who many years later in AD 184, as the first-ranking centurion of a legion on the lower Danube, dedicated this statue-base in celebration of his long career:

79 Garstang 1904, Pl. IX.
80 Devijver 1982.

<6.37> *Novae (Svishtov), Bulgaria*

pro salute i[mp(eratoris)]
Victoriae Aug(ustae)
Pantheae sanctis-
simae L(ucius) Maximius
L(uci) f(ilius) Voltiniae (tribus) Gaetu-
licus Viennae, quod
tiro aput leg(ionem) XX V(aleriam) V(ictricem)
voveram nunc
p(rimus) p(ilus) leg(ionis) I Ital(icae) stip(endiorum)
LVII v(otum) s(olvi)
Marullo et Aeliano co(n)[s(ulibus)]

Kolendo and Bozilova 1997, 81, No. 46 (*AE* 1985, 735)

'For the welfare of the Emperor. To August Victory, most holy Universal Goddess. I, Lucius Maximius Gaetulicus, son of Lucius, of the *Voltinia* voting-tribe, from Vienne, as first-ranking centurion of the First Legion Italica with 57 years' service have now paid the vow I had promised as a recruit in the Twentieth Legion Valeria Victrix. In the consulship of Marullus and Aelianus (AD 184).'

The *primi pili* of the legion at Novae marked their elevation by dedications to various deities, but this is the most autobiographical. Gaetulicus chose Victory, to which he applied the Greek epithet *Panthea* ('universal goddess'), one that is also applied to the personifications Concordia and Fortuna, but this is the first instance of it being applied in Latin to Victory. Later we will see it applied in the masculine to Silvanus (**9.03**) at Risingham. At this supreme moment of his life Gaetulicus used his fullest and most formal nomenclature. Like Duccius Rufinus (**3.04**), Cominius Severus (**4.03**) and Valerius Iullus (**5.44**), he is yet another legionary from Vienne, who enlisted in AD 127, his legion being the Twentieth in Britain, which was then building Hadrian's Wall. He does not say when he was commissioned into the centurionate, but we know from other careers that for a legionary from enlistment this would normally take at least 13 years' service in the ranks and as a junior officer, so Gaetulicus was probably not yet a centurion when Hadrian died (AD 138) and the army advanced into Scotland.[81] But we do know that he was commissioned into the same legion, the Twentieth, thanks to the two altars he subsequently dedicated:

<6.38> *Great Chesters (Aesica)*

I(ovi) O(ptimo) M(aximo)
D[ol]ic(h)eno Lu-
cius Maxim-

81 Breeze 1974, 273 (after Baehr and Forni) = Breeze and Dobson 1993, 39.

ius Gaetulic-
us (centurio) leg(ionis) XX V(aleriae) V(ictricis)
v(otum) [s(olvit) l(ibens)] m(erito)

RIB 1725+*add.*

'To Jupiter, Best and Greatest, of Dolic(h)e, Lucius Maximius Gaetulicus, centurion of the Twentieth Legion Valeria Victrix, willingly and deservedly paid his vow.'

<**6.39**> *Newstead (Trimontium)*

deo
Apollini
L(ucius) Maximius
Gaetulicus (centurio)
leg(ionis)

RIB 2120+*add.*

'To the god Apollo, Lucius Maximius Gaetulicus, centurion of the Legion, (set this up).'

Neither of these altars is dated, and it is uncertain which was dedicated first; nor does Gaetulicus specify the nature of his commands. At Newstead indeed, like Cassius Fla(...) at Inveresk (**12.80** and **12.81**), he did not even think it was necessary to identify his legion. Perhaps he was acting-commander (*praepositus*) of an auxiliary unit at one fort or the other, Newstead or Great Chesters, but he would surely have named it. More likely he was commanding a legionary detachment which consisted of more than one century, whether it was only a building-party or an occupying force. Newstead may actually have been garrisoned by legionaries, to judge by barrack-blocks seen as legionary, and especially by the three altars dedicated by Arrius Domitianus, who like Gaetulicus was a centurion of the Twentieth.[82] The altar dedicated by Aelius Marcus, decurion of the *ala Vocontiorum*, suggests an important cavalry presence.[83] It remains uncertain whether Maximus and Domitianus commanded legionaries directly, or were the acting-commanders (*praepositi*) of a large force of auxiliaries at this major fort (14 acres/5.67 ha) where Dere Street crossed the river Tweed; it had been a key point in the Flavian frontier, and was

[82] *RIB* 2122 (Diana Regina); 2123 (Jupiter); 2124 (Silvanus).
[83] *RIB* 2121 (Campestres).

now reoccupied when the Antonine Wall was built, as being essential to the control of its hinterland, and was retained after the withdrawal from Scotland.[84]

Great Chesters by contrast was part of Hadrian's Wall, and it was surely built and first garrisoned before Gaetulicus became centurion; his altar there looks Antonine, with its chip-carved capital resembling those of the Tungrians at Birrens after the withdrawal from Scotland.[85] This event would better explain what legionaries were doing on Hadrian's Wall than the idea that they were simply caretakers while the Antonine Wall was the actual frontier: Gaetulicus presumably commanded the legionaries who refurbished Great Chesters when Hadrian's Wall was being recommissioned. But unless he was only a subordinate centurion at Newstead – and his imposing altar suggests that he was in overall command, like Arrius Domitianus – his command there must have been more important and thus later than at Great Chesters, which was a fort only about one-fifth the size (3 acres/1.2 ha). It would have been after the Antonine Wall had been abandoned, when Newstead was in the very front line.

Whatever the nature of his responsibilities in Britain, Gaetulicus must have left the province on being transferred to another legion, but he gives no more details of the career which ultimately brought him to Novae and the First Legion Italica; a generation later, Petronius Fortunatus (**9.19**), himself a recruit in that legion who rose from the ranks through a series of junior offices to the centurionate, served in 12 further legions during his 50 years' service. Gaetulicus, who served still longer, is not quite the longest-serving centurion known (that record is held by Aelius Silvanus with 61 years), but nonetheless, if he had enlisted like most legionaries between the ages of 18 and 21, he would now have been at least 75 years old.[86] This is later than the 'sixtieth year' at which Juvenal says that a centurion might achieve the rank of *primus pilus* after 'campaigning against Moors and Brigantes', but then he is thinking of an influential careerist who gained a direct commission.[87] Like the future Field Marshal Sir William Robertson, who enlisted in 1877 as a trooper in the 16th Lancers, Maximius Gaetulicus started at the very bottom as a *tiro*. His confidence that he would rise to the very top is a tribute to the upward mobility within the army of Hadrian and his successors; and 57 years later in AD 184, Gaetulicus must have been immensely experienced but, like the Roman Empire itself, perhaps getting a little stiff in the joints.

84 Hanson and Maxwell 1983, 151, 194; Hanson 2012.

85 *RIB* 2096, 2100, 2104.

86 Ages at enlistment are collected by Forni 1953, 135–41. E Birley 1988, 219–20, tabulates twenty centurions who served 40 years or more, including Aelius Silvanus (now *Tituli Aquincenses* II, 499) and Petronius Fortunatus (**9.19**).

87 Juvenal *Sat.* xiv 196–8, *dirue Maurorum attegias, castella Brigantum, | ut locupletem aquilam tibi sexagesimus annus | adferat.*

7

MARCUS AURELIUS AND COMMODUS

Two officers of the Sixth Legion

Fifty years almost to the day separate the deaths of Antoninus Pius (7 March AD 161) and Septimius Severus (4 February AD 211). In this half-century the tide of Roman rule in northern Britain continues to ebb and flow as on a darkling plain. In AD 161 the new emperor Marcus Aurelius – like Hadrian at his accession – is said by his ancient biographer to have been threatened by war in Britain.[1] His new governor was the formidable general Statius Priscus, but Marcus sent him to the East instead to cope with a much greater threat, the Parthian invasion of Syria.[2] He also reinforced the eastern armies with three legions[3] from the Danube, and it is likely that he told Priscus to take legionary reinforcements with him from Britain. The evidence is indirect, this tombstone from the eastern Adriatic coast:

<7.01> *Podstrana, Croatia (Epetium)*

D(is) M(anibus)
L(ucius) Artori[us Ca]stus (centurio) leg(ionis)
III Gallicae item [(centurio) le]g(ionis) VI Ferra-
tae item (centurio) leg(ionis) II Adi[utr(icis) i]tem (centurio) leg(ionis) V M[a]- c(edonicae)
item p(rimus) p(ilus) eiusdem [leg(ionis)], praeposito(!)
classis Misenatium, [pr]aef(ectus) leg(ionis) VI
Victricis, duci(!) leg(ionum) [triu]m Britanici-
{mi}arum(!) adversus Arm[enio]s, proc(urator) cente-
nario(!) provinciae Li[b(urniae) iure] glad(i)I, vi-
vus ipse sibi et suis [... ex] t(estamento)

ILS 2770, with Loriot 1997

---

[1] Hist. Aug. *Marcus* 8.8; compare *Hadrian* 5.2.

[2] Birley 2005, 151–5.

[3] First Minervia (*ILS* 1098, its legate Claudius Fronto brought it to 'the Parthian campaign' and was decorated by Marcus in 'the Armenian and Parthian War'); Second Adiutrix (*ILS* 8977, its legate Antistius Adventus was transferred to it from another legion for 'the Parthian campaign'); Fifth Macedonica (*ILS* 2311, a veteran who 'served in the Eastern expedition under Statius Priscus').

'To the Shades of the Dead. Lucius Artorius Castus, centurion of the Third Legion Gallica, also centurion of the Sixth Legion Ferrata, also centurion of the Second Legion Adiutrix, also centurion of the Fifth Legion Macedonica, also the first-ranking centurion of the same legion, acting-commander of the Fleet at Misenum, prefect of the Sixth Legion Victrix, general of (detachments of) the three British legions against the Armenians, procurator at a salary of 100,000 (sesterces) of Liburnia with capital jurisdiction, (provided for this tomb) by the terms of his will, for himself and his family in his own lifetime.'

The lettering is very fine, but the draughtsman or the stone-cutter made some mistakes. Although Artorius Castus (in the nominative) is clearly the subject, the case shifts to the dative in noting his posts of *praeposito*, *duci* and *centenario*, as if he had become his own dedicatee. *praef(ectus)* was cut as PRAEFF, although the repeated F should indicate a plural ('prefects'), and BRITANICIMIARVM is a blunder for *Britannicianarum*. It is incidentally an example of the 'continental' spelling *Britania* (see note to **8.12**). The inscription is undated, but the quality of the lettering and the well-executed band of lush ornament to left and right, twining scrolls inhabited by rosettes, would suggest it was Antonine (*c.* AD 140–90).

Artorius Castus was an equestrian, but virtually governor of Liburnia, the coast and islands of modern Croatia, the only one attested. His salary of 100,000 sesterces set him in the second grade of procurators, above those who earned 60,000 (see note to **8.13**), but he also exercised special authority: the 'right of the sword' (*ius gladii*) gave him jurisdiction in capital cases and the power of ordering executions. This would have infringed upon the powers of the senatorial legate of Dalmatia, of which Liburnia was part, and it is notable that his previous mission was also of a kind more often entrusted to senators.[4]

This handsome slab is now broken into two pieces, with an irregular band of letters lost in the gap between them, but the name of the deceased can be restored

[4] Wilkes 1969, 329, but reading *Arm[oricanos]* and attributing both appointments to Perennis (compare Hist. Aug. *Commodus* 6.2), which would be later than the dating suggested here. On balance, the 'Armenian' involvement seems preferable.

with the help of another inscription from Epetium which names Lucius Artorius Castus as first-ranking centurion (*primus pilus*) of the Fifth Legion Macedonica and prefect of the Sixth Legion Victrix.[5] This guarantees the restoration of ARTORI[VS CA]STVS across the gap in the first line (not counting D M, since it was cut outside the panel), and allows the gap to be measured: it narrows to two letters in the fifth line, the beginning of [PR]AEFF, before it widens again. In most lines some three or four letters have been lost, which means that the name of the province, LIBVRNIAE, must have been abbreviated; but, more importantly, that in the line above, only three or four letters have been lost from the name of Artorius Castus' opponents, the ARM[...O]S.[6] His post of *dux legionum* ('general of legions') means that he actually commanded, not whole legions, but elements of them, a 'task force' consisting of detachments drawn from the legions of a province. But who were his opponents?

At this crucial point the first editor, Carrara in 1850, read ARME[...], which (since he did not read the right-hand piece and then restore *Arme[nio]s*) rather suggests that he saw the remains of E in the broken edge; but if so, they have since been lost. Mommsen, who did not see the original, restored it in *CIL* as ARM[ORICANO]S, which would imply a campaign, not against the 'Armenians', but the 'Armoricans' of Brittany. Since there is no other reference to such a campaign, and the seven letters required cannot be fitted into the space available, Mommsen's restoration is difficult to accept, let alone the idea it has since inspired, the catalyst of much speculation, that Artorius Castus is the original 'King Arthur'. Loriot was surely right to dismiss this as a modern myth when he reasserted ARME[NIO]S, even though he worked from poor photographs and (to repeat) there was no longer evidence of a decisive E.[7] This campaign 'against the Armenians' has been attributed to the eastern wars of Caracalla or Severus Alexander, but the inscription looks earlier than the third century, and a more attractive attribution is to Statius Priscus' invasion of Armenia in AD 163. This was so successful that Marcus Aurelius and his colleague Lucius Verus, the nominal commander-in-chief, assumed the title of *Armeniacus* ('Conqueror of Armenia'). Statius Priscus, as already said, had just been transferred from governing Britain; that his army included British legionaries, under one of his own senior officers in Britain, Artorius Castus, is a brighter suggestion than to invoke the Celtic shades of 'Arthurian' legend.

This is the war against Parthia for which Pontius Laelianus (**5.06**) was decorated. Two future governors of Britain also distinguished themselves. Antistius Adventus, who came to Britain in *c.* AD 172, was decorated as commander of one of those

---

5 *CIL* iii 14224.

6 Birley 2005, 355, asserts Loriot's reading of ARME[NIO]S.

7 Loriot 1997. Much better photographs by Ortolf Harl are now available (ubi-erat-lupa.org/monument 24235), and guarantee that there is no trace of the letter lost after ARM. The extensive literature is collected by Christopher Gwinn (christophergwinn.com/celticstudies).

Danubian legions which reinforced the eastern army of Lucius Verus.[8] Helvius Pertinax, one of that army's equestrian officers, came to Britain as governor in AD 185, and like Julius Agricola and Clodius Albinus is the subject of an ancient biography. Agricola's was written by Tacitus, but Pertinax and Albinus fell victims to the so-called Augustan History. In view of its unreliability – the Life of Albinus is 'mostly fiction'[9] – it is surprising to find that for Pertinax it accords with this inscription which honours him in mid-career:

<7.02> *Brühl, near Cologne*

[P(ublio)] Helv[io Pertin]aci
[e]q(uo) p(ublico) p[raef(ecto) coh(ortis) VII G]al-
[l]or(um) e[q(uitatae), trib(uno) leg(ionis) VI Vi]ct(ricis),
[p]rae[f(ecto) ... pr]aef(ecto)
[a]lae ... [p]ro-
[c]ura[tori ad alime]nt(a),
[p]rae[f(ecto) class(is) Ger(manicae), pr]oc(uratori)
[A]ug(usti) a[d ducen(a) III Dac(iarum) i]d(em)
M[oesiae Super(ioris)]
Agr[ippinense]s

AE 1963, 52, with Devijver 1988

'To Publius Helvius Pertinax, (allotted) a public horse, prefect of the Seventh Cohort of Gauls part-mounted, tribune of the Sixth Legion Victrix, prefect of [...], prefect of the Cavalry Regiment [...], procurator of *alimenta*, prefect of the German Fleet, imperial procurator of the Three Dacian provinces and Upper Moesia at a salary of 200,000 (sesterces). (From) the People of Cologne.'

This statue-base was badly damaged when it was hollowed out to make a Roman sarcophagus, but it can be supplemented and restored in part with the help of the ancient biography.[10] It would have been erected when Pertinax was promoted from commanding the Rhine flotilla to a major financial post on the lower Danube, whose salary reflected its importance (see note to **8.13**). Here he played an increasingly important part in Marcus Aurelius' wars, with promotion to senatorial rank and the command of a legion, crowned by the consulship and a rapid series of provincial governorships which included Britain in AD 185. This is subsequent to the Cologne inscription, which likewise does not say that although equestrian he was only a freedman's son who made a false start as a *grammaticus* teaching the Latin language, rather like the future governor-general of Australia, Field-Marshal Viscount Slim,

[8] *ILS* 8977, with Birley 2005, 157–61. Attested in Britain only by *RIB* 1083 (Lanchesters).
[9] Birley 2005, 176.
[10] Hist. Aug. *Pertinax* 1–2 with Devijver 1988; Birley 2005, 172–4.

who began his own military career as an elementary schoolteacher in the slums of Birmingham. Pertinax escaped from school into an equestrian career by pulling strings to be appointed prefect of an auxiliary cohort in Syria; here he distinguished himself in the Parthian War, and was promoted to a tribunate in the Sixth Legion. It is tempting to see the choice of legion as confirmation that it had contributed to the invasion of Armenia, and also to suggest that Pertinax accompanied the vexillation when it returned to Britain. Here he was 'retained' (*retentus*), which may imply that he had already commanded British troops outside Britain, but certainly means that he was given a second appointment of equivalent rank, perhaps as 'prefect' (to quote the Cologne inscription, which no longer names the unit) of one of the auxiliary milliary cohorts like the Tungrians which were sometimes commanded by prefects (**6.22** with note) instead of tribunes. After Britain he achieved the third post in an equestrian career, the command of an *ala* on the Danube, before returning to his native north Italy to supervise *alimenta* (a system of child-maintenance derived from imperial funds invested in land), followed by the appointment at Cologne to the Rhine flotilla. Instead of Statius Priscus, Calpurnius Agricola the legate of Upper Germany was 'sent against the Britons' by Marcus Aurelius; but although he is named by seven British inscriptions, all from forts in the north-west or along Hadrian's Wall, none of them alludes directly to his mission. It is more significant that none comes from the Antonine Wall and its hinterland, since this is negative confirmation that Hadrian's Wall was now the frontier once more.[11] The date of AD 163 can be recovered at Corbridge from the few remaining fragments of a large slab dedicated by a detachment of the Twentieth Legion.[12] Also from Corbridge, but by another legion and much better preserved, comes this fine slab:

<**7.03**> *Corbridge (Coria)*

[[Soli Invicto]]
vexillatio
leg(ionis) VI Vic(tricis) p(iae) f(idelis) f(ecit)
sub cura Sex(ti)
Calpurni Agrico-
lae leg(ati) Aug(usti) pr(o) pr(aetore)

RIB 1137

'To the Unconquered Sun; a detachment of the Sixth Legion Victrix, Dutiful and Loyal, (built this) under the charge of Sextus Calpurnius Agricola, imperial propraetorian legate.'

---

[11] Hist. Aug. *Marcus* 8.8, *adversus Britannos quidem Calpurnius Agricola misus est*. The inscriptions are collected by Birley 2005, 155–7, who notes their distribution: *RIB* 589 (Ribchester), 793(?) (Hardknott), 1137 (**7.03**) and 1149 (Corbridge), 1703 (Vindolanda), 1792 (**12.87**) and 1809 (Carvoran).

[12] *RIB* 1149.

The dedication to *Sol Invictus* has been erased. Sixty years later, in AD 222, it may have been thought mistakenly to refer to the Syrian emperor Elagabalus, who identified himself with the Sun God of Emesa (Homs in Syria); when he was killed after 4 years of extravagant eccentricity, his 'memory' was condemned. The Corbridge garrison, when it heard the news, surely knew that its temple of the Sun was ancient and had been inscribed long before Elagabalus was born; but perhaps it was taking no chances.

Sarmatians with snow on their boots

When Marcus Aurelius was emperor, the army in Britain received more than divine reinforcement. In AD 175 the attempted coup of Avidius Cassius in Syria forced Marcus to make peace with the Sarmatians across the lower Danube; these nomadic horsemen now agreed to provide 8000 cavalry, 5500 of whom he sent to Britain, not only to reinforce the Roman north-west frontier but to remove them from the Danube frontier.[13] But since Syria would have been almost as far-flung, and Marcus was about to campaign there himself, he may have reckoned that Britain actually needed the cavalry. Unfortunately there is no record of what it did here, only some epigraphic echoes from Ribchester, where **9.31** and another tombstone[14] obscurely mention a Sarmatian cavalry regiment (*ala Sarmatarum*), which was apparently replaced by this smaller 'unit' (*numerus*) of Sarmatian cavalry:

<**7.04**> *Ribchester (Bremetennacum)*

deo san(cto)
[A]pollini Mapon(o)
[pr]o salute D(omini) N(ostri)
[et] n(umeri) eq(uitum) Sar-
[m(atarum)] Bremetenn(acensium)
[G]ordiani
[I]ul(ius) Antoni-
nus (centurio) leg(ionis) VI
Vic(tricis), domo
Melitenis,
praep(ositus) n(umeri) et r(egionis)
[v(otum)] s(olvit) l(aetus) l(ibens) m(erito).
[de]dic(atum) pr(idie) Kal(endas) Sep(tembres)
[im]p(eratore) d(omino) n(ostro) Gord[i]-
[ano A]ug(usto) II e[t] Pon-
[peia]no co(n)s(ulibus)

---

13 Dio 71.16.2, Antistius Adventus perhaps being responsible for 'absorbing' them (Birley 2005, 160).

14 *RIB* 595.

RIB 583+*add.*

'To the holy god Apollo Maponus for the welfare of Our Lord (the Emperor) and of the unit of Sarmatian cavalry of Bremetennacum, Gordian's Own. Julius Antoninus, centurion of the Sixth Legion Victrix, his home Melitene, acting-commander of the unit and the region, has paid his vow gladly, willingly, deservedly. Dedicated on the day before the Kalends of September in the consulship of Our Lord the Emperor Gordian Augustus for the second time with Pompeianus (31 August AD 241).'

This is not an altar, despite its wording, but a squared pedestal which probably supported a statue of the god. The left side has been cut away, but on the right is Apollo carved in high relief, standing with his lyre. He is identified with a god worshipped in northern Britain, to judge by three dedications to him at Corbridge by other officers of the Sixth Legion (**12.68** with note). On the back are two standing female figures, one of whom hands a casket to the other, who are identified by *RIB* as personifications of Lower Britain and the 'region' itself, the *regio Bremetennacensis*. The bold GORDIANI was not deleted when Gordian's 'memory' was condemned, but after *Mélitenis* in line 10, the inscription is now worn, and its reading was largely recovered by Geza Alföldy, except that he read Julius Antoninus as *praep(ositus) et pr(aefectus)* ('acting-commander and prefect'); but Antoninus surely held the same posts as his recent predecessor, Floridius Natalis, who rebuilt a temple at Ribchester.[15] Antoninus came from Melitene (now Malatya) on the middle Euphrates, the base of the Twelfth Legion Fulminata, in which he probably began his army career. As the region's acting-commander, he was now a 'district officer' equivalent to the *centurio regionarius* at Carlisle who appears in the Vindolanda correspondence.[16] This post he doubled with that of commanding the Sarmatians, who are now called a *n(umerus)* instead of an *ala*, a 'unit' instead of a 'regiment'. In the Notitia Dignitatum they have become a 'squadron' (*cuneus*), the title applied in the fourth century to cavalry units (*equites*) which had been reduced in size, which would suggest that the initial *ala* was already reduced in size and down-graded in consequence.[17] Like the contemporary *cuneus* at Lanchester, 'Gordian's Own' Suebi (**12.49**), they also take the name of their posting, *Bremetennacum*, a third-century practice which finds its full development in the army of the Late Empire.

Successful achievements beyond the Wall

The evidence of inscriptions for the army's operations in Britain during the reigns of Marcus Aurelius (AD 161–80) and Commodus (AD 180–92) is patchy because

[15] *RIB* 587, for the welfare of Severus Alexander by Floridius Natalis, *(centurio) leg(ionis) praep(ositus) n(umeri) et regi(onis)*.

[16] *Tab. Vindol.* II, 250.8–9.

[17] Hoffmann 1969, 211, 253. See also **12.50**.

they are allusive and of uncertain date. Geographically the most explicit is this altar from near the western end of Hadrian's Wall:

<**7.05**> *Kirksteads*

[...]
L(ucius) Iunius Vic-
torinus Fl[av(ius)]
Caelianus leg(atus)
Aug(usti) leg(ionis) VI Vic(tricis)
p(iae) f(idelis) ob res trans
vallum pro-
spere gestas

RIB 2034+*add*

'To [*deity*] Lucius Junius Victorinus Flavius Caelianus, imperial legate of the Sixth Legion Victrix Dutiful and Loyal, (set this up) because of successful achievements beyond the Wall.'

The deity may have been *Victoria Aug(usta)*, Imperial Victory, to whom other altars are dedicated.[18] The only indication of date is the reference to the 'Wall' (*vallum*), undoubtedly Hadrian's Wall in view of where the altar was found. It follows that the Antonine Wall was no longer occupied, which would suggest a late-Antonine or Severan date before the division of Britain, when the legate of the Sixth Legion would have been described as governor of Lower Britain. The dedicator might well be the Junius Victorinus who afterwards governed Upper Germany some time in the period AD 166–208.[19] On balance, therefore, the reign of Marcus or Commodus seems likely, the square lettering of the inscription and the comparative absence of ligatures (there are just two, in VIC and TRANS) supporting this date.

Even less specific is this altar from Corbridge:

<**7.06**> *Corbridge (Coria)*

. . .
Q(uintus) Calpurnius
Concessini-
us praef(ectus) eq(uitum)
caesa Cori-
onototar-
um manu pr-
aesentissimi
numinis dei(!) v(otum) s(olvit)

---

[18] **8.10** (another legionary legate); *RIB* 842, 843, 1731 and 2100 (auxiliary cohorts). VICTORIAE AVG is in fact ambiguous, since *Aug(usti)* is also possible, an expansion explicit in *CIL* xii 2389, *Victoriae Augusti*. This would be the Victory of a specific emperor. For Britain, compare **8.09** and *RIB* 844, *Victoriae (duorum) Aug(ustorum)*.

[19] Birley 2005, 263–4.

RIB 1142

'To [*deity*]. Quintus Calpurnius Concessinius, prefect of cavalry, after slaughtering a band of Corionototae, has paid his vow to a god of most immediate power.'

This was found in the crypt of Hexham Abbey, but is now lost, so we depend on Horsley's (1725) drawing. *RIB* suggests that the deity was Jupiter Dolichenus, to whom a similar phrase is applied at Rome.[20] The next word should have been *deo* (dative), grammatically speaking, but it has been attracted into the descriptive genitive which preceded it. The prefect Concessinius, like the war band he destroyed, is otherwise unknown. There is no indication of date at all, beyond what may be a tenuous echo of the dedication from Carlisle (**7.14**) in which another cavalry regiment celebrates a similar achievement towards the end of the reign of Commodus.

Commodus was the son of Marcus Aurelius, the first emperor ever born to a reigning emperor (in August AD 161), and he was inevitably the heir-apparent of his glum, conscientious father, despite his obvious inexperience and what proved to be a weak, corruptible nature. To ensure the succession, his father made him his nominal colleague at the end of AD 176, aged only 15. Ulpius Marcellus, the new governor of Britain, was thus the legate of *two* emperors:

<**7.07**> *Benwell (Condercum)*

deo Anocitico
iudiciis optimo-
rum maximorum-
que imp(eratorum) n(ostrorum) sub Ulp(io)
Marcello co(n)s(ulari) Tine-
ius Longus in p[re]-
fectura equitu[m]
lato clavo exorna-
tus et q(uaestor) d(esignatus)

RIB 1329+*add.*

'To the god Anociticus. (Dedicated by) Tineius Longus, having been decorated while prefect of cavalry under Ulpius Marcellus, consular governor, with the broad stripe and designated quaestor, by the decision of our best and greatest Emperors.'

This altar was found in 1862 outside the Wall fort of Benwell west of Newcastle, inside what proved to be the god's temple with two other altars, also dedicated by Roman officers, which call him *Antenociticus*. Nothing else is known of him except the stone head of his cult statue which was also found, a masterpiece of Celtic sculpture that excited Jocelyn Toynbee with its great diamond-shaped eyes and massive mop of wig-like hair: 'an art that contrives to be civilised without forfeiting

20 *ILS* 4316, *numini praestantiss(im)o* ('most efficacious power').

the power and appeal of its native genius'.[21] Longus does not name his regiment, but it was probably the *ala I Asturum*, which certainly garrisoned Benwell by AD 205/8 (**8.09**). His new 'broad stripe' was the purple edging which differentiated a senator's toga from an equestrian's with its 'narrow' purple stripe. He was advertising his promotion to senatorial rank, perhaps even thanking an obscure local deity for it, but he may already have had his eyes on the next magistracy at Rome, the praetorship, which would qualify him to command a legion; for Marcus Aurelius, in his pressing need of competent generals, was promoting other equestrian officers like Pertinax (**7.02**) into senatorial careers.

The Emperors praised by Longus for their discernment are Marcus Aurelius and Commodus, colleagues from AD 177 until the death of Marcus in AD 180, an identification which used to be contentious, in view of this inscription from Chesters which names Ulpius Marcellus as the legate of a single emperor:

<**7.08**> *Chesters (Cilurnum)*

aqua adducta
alae II Astur(um)
sub Ulp(io) Marcello
leg(ato) Aug(usti) pr(o) pr(aetore)

RIB 1463+*add.*

'Water brought (to the fort) for the Second Cavalry Regiment of Asturians under Ulpius Marcellus, propraetorian legate of the Emperor.'

The Emperor's name and titles which would have dated the work are missing; they were probably inscribed on a companion slab, as *RIB* suggests for the inscription of Elagabalus at Birdoswald which likewise omits him.[22] Since the 'memory' of Commodus was subsequently condemned like that of Elagabalus, it is probable that these companion slabs were deliberately destroyed. Chesters is attractively sited on the west bank of the North Tyne river, but the new aqueduct would have given it clean drinking-water, and a head of water for the riverside bath-house and to flush the drains and sewers. The fort was built for another cavalry regiment (**5.03**); but although there is a building inscription of the First Cohort of Dalmatae at Chesters, the decoration of which looks 'Antonine', we should not conclude that this infantry unit was actually its garrison.[23] It is well attested at Maryport in the reign of Antoninus Pius, and the Asturians are not said to have built their aqueduct for themselves; despite the recent discovery of an engineer (*architectus*) in another cavalry regiment at Binchester (**5.36**), there are other instances of building work

[21] *RIB* 1327 and 1328. Toynbee 1962, 146 with Frontispiece.
[22] *RIB* 1914.
[23] *RIB* III, 3300 with note.

being done 'for' cavalry regiments.[24] It is quite likely that the Dalmatae were, literally, a building-party, perhaps when Hadrian's Wall was recommissioned in *c.* AD 158. Maybe it was they who later built the aqueduct as well. At all events the *ala II Asturum*, now first attested at Chesters, remained there for the rest of the Roman period.

The single emperor implied by the Chesters inscription is undoubtedly Commodus, since Ulpius Marcellus is known to have governed Britain in his reign. This emerges from a difficult fragment of Cassius Dio's History, which for this period survives only in extracts and summaries made by Byzantine editors. The greatest war of Commodus' reign, we are told, was in Britain where 'the island tribes crossed the wall that separated them from the Roman legions, and did much damage, even killing an army-commander with his troops. Commodus in alarm sent Ulpius Marcellus after them.'[25] Taken out of context, this fragment raises questions without answering them. Which 'wall' did the tribes cross? Was the army commanded by the governor himself, or only by the legate of the Sixth Legion? (The Greek word *strategos* might refer to either.) Was Ulpius Marcellus 'sent' from another province, like Calpurnius Agricola from Upper Germany, or was he already governing Britain?

These questions have been much discussed, and are largely answered by three military diplomas of the same issue found in Bulgaria, which confirm a grant of citizenship by Marcus Aurelius and Commodus to veterans of the British army in AD 178.[26] This is the most complete:

<7.09> *Rhodope Mountains, Bulgaria*

imp(erator) Caesar divi Antonini filio(!), divi Veri Parthici
maxim(i) frater, divi Hadriani nepos, divi Traiani
Parthici pronepos, divi Nervae abnepos, M(arcus) Aurelius
Antoninus Aug(ustus) German[i]cus Sarmatic(us),
pontif(ex) max(imus), trib(unicia) potest(ate) XXXII,
imp(erator) VIIII, co(n)s(ul) III, p(ater) p(atriae) et

imp(erator) Caesar L(ucius) Aelius Aurelius Commodus Aug(ustus)
Antonin(i) Aug(usti) fil(ius), divi Pii nepos, divi Hadriani
pronepos, divi Traiani Parthici abnepos, divi Nervae
adnepos, Germanicus Sarmaticus tribunic(ia)
potest(ate) III, imp(erator) II co(n)s(ul) p(ater)
p(atriae)

equitibus et peditibus qui militaverunt in alis V quae
appellantur (1) Gallor(um) et Thrac(um) Classian(a) et

---

24 **13.28** (Lancaster) and **13.05** (Chesters), *instante ... prae[f(ecto) equitum]*, 'at the urging' of the cavalry commander.

25 Dio 72(73).8.1–6.

26 *RMD* III, 184 (with Roxan's note on p. 309, n. 15); *RMD* IV, 293 and 294. Birley 2005, 162–70.

(2) Aug(usta) Vocontior(um) et (3) I Pannonior(um) Sabinian(a) et (4) Sebosian(a) Gallor(um) et (5) Vetton(um) Hispanor(um); et cohortibus XVI (1) I Aug(usta) Nerv(iana) et (2) I Frisiavonum et (3) I Aelia Hispanor(um) et (4) I fida Vardul(l)or(um) et (5) I Celtiber(orum) et (6) III Lingonum et (7) II Hispanor(um) et (8) I Thrac(um) et (9) I Batavor(um) et (10) II Gallor(um) veter(ana) et (11) II Thrac(um) veter(ana) et (12) II Lingon(um) et (13) IIII Gallor(um) et (14) Vangion(um) et (15) VII Thrac(um) et (16) I Morinor(um) et sunt in Brittania sub Ulpio Marcello leg(ato), quinis et vicenis pluribusve stipendis emeritis dimissis honesta missione

quorum nomina subscripta sunt, civitatem Romanam, qui eorum non haberent, dederunt et conubium cum uxoribus, quas tunc habuissent, cum est civitas iis data, aut, cum iis quas postea duxissent dumtaxat singulis.

a(nte) d(iem) X kal(endas) April(es) Ser(vio) Scipione Orfito D(ecimo) Velio Rufo co(n) s(ulibus)

coh(ortis) II Gallor(um) veter(anae) cui praeest Domitius Hiero, ex equite Thiae Timarchi f(ilio) Daco.

descriptum et recognitum ex tabula aerea quae fixa est Romae in muro pos<t> templum divi Aug(usti) ad Minervam.

RMD IV, 293 (*conflated text*)

The seven official witnesses are listed overleaf. Here is a condensed translation:

'The emperor Caesar Marcus Aurelius Antoninus Augustus, son of the deified Antoninus, brother of the deified Verus, grandson of the deified Hadrian, great-grandson of the deified Trajan, great-great-grandson of the deified Nerva, Germanicus, Sarmaticus, in the 32nd year of his tribunician power (AD 178), acclaimed Emperor nine times, consul three times, Father of his Country; and the emperor Caesar Lucius Aelius Aurelius Commodus, the son of Antoninus Augustus (*with similar descent and titles*), to the cavalrymen and infantry who have soldiered in the five (*named*) cavalry regiments and seventeen (*named*) cohorts in Britain under the legate Ulpius Marcellus, having served 25 years or more and been honourably discharged, whose names are written below, have granted Roman citizenship for those who did not have it, and the legal right of marriage to the wives they had when citizenship was granted them or should marry thereafter, provided that they have only one wife. On the tenth day before the Kalends of April in the consulship of Servius Scipio Orfitus and Decimus Velius Rufus (23 March AD 178).

'To Thias son of Timarchus, a Dacian, ex-cavalryman of the Second Veteran Cohort of Gauls, which Domitius Hiero commands.

'Transcribed and checked from the bronze tablet at Rome fastened on the wall behind the temple of the deified Augustus, near (the statue of) Minerva.'

Marcus Aurelius Thias, as he now became, like his colleagues Thiodus of the Seventh Cohort of Thracians and Annius Victor of the First Cohort of Nervii, did not settle in Britain but returned home.[27] But thanks to him and his diploma, we can now date this British altar:

<**7.10**> *Old Penrith (Voreda)*

I(ovi) O(ptimo) M(aximo)
coh(ors)
II Gal(lorum) eq(uitata)
T(itus) Dom[i]ti-
us ?Heron
d(omo) Nicomedia
praef(ectus)

RIB 917

'To Jupiter Best and Greatest (from) the Second Cohort of Gauls part-mounted. Titus Domitius Heron, from Nicomedia, its prefect.'

This altar was drawn by Horsley, but is now lost. HERoN is what he saw, but he may have missed a ligatured I for *Hiero(n)*, the form in which the prefect's name appears in the diploma. The connection between cohort and prefect would have been explicit had they been linked by C P for *c(ui) p(raeest)* ('commanded by'), but perhaps this was accidentally omitted by the stone-cutter. The prefect, as his name suggests, came from the Greek East, from what is now the large Turkish port of Izmit.

These three diplomas prove that Ulpius Marcellus was already legate of Britain on 23 March AD 178, and indeed must have been there since AD 177, since no previous governor is named as having discharged the veterans. Since the British War ended in AD 184, when Commodus took the title of *Britannicus*, Marcellus must have been governor for about 7 years, as long as Julius Agricola himself, against the norm of 3 or 4 years; and just as Domitian extended Agricola's term when he succeeded Titus and decided to push beyond the Clyde-Forth isthmus, so Commodus must have retained Marcellus to cope with the crisis caused by the northern tribes crossing 'the wall', whether this was the remains of the Antonine Wall or Hadrian's Wall itself.

---

27 *RMD* III, 178, and IV, 294 respectively.

Unfortunately we know next to nothing of what Marcellus did about the incursion, except that he was ruthlessly successful and thus indirectly offended the jealous Commodus (another Agricolan echo, this), for Dio's Byzantine editor was interested only in Marcellus' eccentric showmanship: he advertised his vigilance and austerity by writing out his orders in advance on lime-wood tablets – the Latin term would have been *tilia*, the sort of ink-leaf tablets which were improvised at Vindolanda from alder wood – and arranging for them to be delivered hour by hour throughout the night; and he dieted ostentatiously on bread specially sent from Rome so that it would be stiff and stale. But despite this lack of real information, two inscriptions may reveal a renewed Roman presence in the far north, even if they cannot be dated with certainty and run counter to the current evidence of archaeology. The first is from the east gate of Carpow, a very large (25-acre/10-ha) fort on the Firth of Tay, whch has been firmly dated by excavation to the campaigns of Septimius Severus:

<7.11> *Carpow, Perths.*

[... I]MP E[T ...]
[...]S F[...]
[...]
[...]

Perhaps *[... i]mp(erator) e[t ...] | [...piu]s f]elix ...] | [...] | [...]*

RIB III, 3512

'... Emperor and ... Dutiful and Happy ... '

Except for three insignificant letter-fragments, one of which retains a straight edge (showing that there was more than one slab butted together), this is all that remains of the spacious, four-line text of a very grand building-inscription, to judge by the quality of the lettering and the large fragment of the left-hand *pelta* which is adorned by a figure of Victory standing on the globe, flanked by a capricorn, and above two winged horses (*pegasi*). These are the symbols of the Second Legion Augusta, which must have been responsible, perhaps in concert with another legion whose symbols would have appeared on the other *pelta*. The difficulty is that [I]MP E[T] is not necessarily the beginning of the inscription, and that this sequence is almost impossible to fit into known imperial titulature. The problem is discussed further by *RIB*, which notes that the inscription is much closer in style to the distance-slabs of the Antonine Wall than to the inscriptions which record Severus' reconstruction of the northern frontier, and conjectures that it is actually an inscription of Commodus, the first emperor to assume the titles *Pius Felix* (compare

7.13). Fragments of another inscription were found at the same gate, which were re-used by the Romans themselves, suggesting that Carpow has more than one building-period.[28]

A similar problem of date is posed by an altar from the old Antonine Wall, from a fort where the richness of epigraphic evidence is already an embarrassment,[29] one which is now heightened by the subtle insight of John Mann, an expert in legionary recruitment:

<**7.12**> *Castlecary*

deo
Mercurio
milites leg(ionis) VI
Victricis
pi(a)e f(idelis)
<a>ed(em) et sigillum
cives Italici
et Norici
v(otum) s(olverunt) l(aeti) l(ibentes) m(erito)

RIB 2148+*add.*

'To the god Mercury soldiers of the Sixth Legion Victrix Dutiful and Loyal, citizens of Italy and Noricum, (by erecting) this shrine and statuette, gladly, willingly, deservedly paid their vow.'

The crude lettering reflects the spoken language by reducing *ae* to *e* (the pronunciation would have been the same), and by eliding the final *-em* of *aedem* (which would have hardly sounded). It is surprising to find Italians in a British legion as late as the AD 140s, when Castlecary was built, but still more surprising to find 'Italians' combined with 'Noricans': the combination irresistibly suggests Marcus Aurelius' new Second Legion Italica, which was raised from Italians in *c.* AD 165 to defend the north-eastern approaches of Italy, and from *c.* AD 175 was based in Noricum (modern Austria), at Lauriacum on the upper Danube. The 'Italians' would have been founder-members of the legion (say until *c.* AD 190), the 'Noricans' local recruits who joined them. In combination they suggest a vexillation of the legion in *c.* AD 175–90, which was sent to Britain to reinforce the Sixth Legion but retained a sense of its identity. When did the British army need such a transfusion, and when could the army in Noricum best afford to give blood? Soon after the accession of Commodus (AD 180) is the likely answer, when there was peace on the Danube

[28] *RIB* III, 3513. A third inscription, *RIB* III, 3514, preserves part of a fine eagle-headed *pelta* which is surely 'Antonine'.

[29] At least two legions, as well as two different auxiliary cohorts, as noted before **6.21**.

but in Britain the Sixth Legion had just been mauled, and a counter-offensive was impending. It is disconcerting, though, to find the evidence at a fort of the Antonine Wall which had been disused for more than 20 years.

The heavy fighting in Britain caused indirect political repercussions at Rome, which must be pieced together from the unreliable biographies of Commodus and Pertinax, and the scraps of Dio Cassius which escaped his Byzantine editors. They are collected by Tony Birley, who has reconstructed the complicated series of events.[30] Soldiers in Britain were mutinous, we are told: they resented the replacement of senatorial officers by equestrians, which had been ordered by Commodus' chief minister Perennis, the prefect of the Guard and himself an equestrian; he may have been responding to their failed attempt to proclaim one of the legionary legates Emperor. The British army sent a powerful deputation to Rome, if that is really what it was, 1500 men whom Commodus pacified by surrendering Perennis to them. They lynched him, and his policies were reversed. Pertinax, whom Perennis had forced into retirement after his governorship of Syria, was sent to Britain to restore discipline as its governor, where he is said to have succeeded, despite almost being killed when a legion mutinied; but later he was relieved at his own request, 'because the legions resented being disciplined'.[31] So the choice of a legionary legate in these years would have been crucial:

<**7.13**> *Mainz (Mogontiacum)*

Libero et Apol-
lini pro salute
[[im[p(eratoris)] C[a]es(aris) M(arci) [Au]r(eli)]]
[[Commod[i] Pi[i] Fel(icis) Aug(usti) ...]]
[[...]]
[[...]]
[...] Q(uintus) Aurel(ius)
Polus Terentianus
cum Q(uinto) Aur(elio) Polo
Syriaco filio,
fetialis, leg(atus)
leg(ionis) XXII Pr(imigeniae) p(iae) f(idelis)
item leg(ionis) II Aug(ustae)

AE 1965, 240, with Birley 2005, 262

'To Bacchus and Apollo, for the welfare of the Emperor Caesar Marcus Aurelius Commodus, Dutiful and Happy Augustus [...] (dedicated by) Quintus Aurelius Polus Terentianus with his son Aurelius Polus; *fetialis*, legate of the Twenty-Second Legion Primigenia Dutiful and Loyal, and also of the Second Legion Augusta.'

---

30 Birley 2005, 168–70.

31 Hist. Aug. *Pertinax* 3.10, *dicens sibi ob defensam disciplinam infestas esse legiones*. Birley 2005, 172–4.

The name and titles of Commodus have been erased after his 'memory' was condemned, but they can still be partly read or at least reconstructed. The dedicator was a *fetialis* like Pontius Laelianus (**5.06**) and Lollius Urbicus (**6.02**) who is known to have been governor of the three Dacian provinces in AD 193, so he must have gained his consulship under Commodus. This would probably have followed a provincial appointment subsequent to his legionary commands, which can therefore be dated to the mid-AD 180s. Terentianus does not spell out which legion came first, but by putting the Second Legion emphatically at the end he implies that he was about to leave Mainz, the base of the Twenty-Second Legion, to take up a new command in Britain. A second legionary command was always exceptional, just as the Sixth Legion when it arrived in Britain was probably commanded by a legate who had already commanded another legion, so Birley is right to deduce that an experienced 'major general' was being found for a shaken army division in Britain.[32]

The officers of this army were living in interesting times. For the Sixth Legion to operate 'beyond the Wall', it would have first marched from York to Catterick, just south of Scotch Corner, where its road would divide, over the Stainmore Pass to Carlisle and the north-west, or straight on to Corbridge and the north. The importance of this junction is emphasised by an altar at Catterick which was dedicated to 'the god who invented roads and paths'; it was restored in AD 191 (**10.32**). Next year, probably, a successful massacre was celebrated by a cavalry officer at Carlisle. He dedicated an oddly-shaped inscription, a rectangular building-stone with a circular re-entrant in the bottom edge (it is more of a circle than the semicircle drawn by *RIB*), which formed the lintel of a lancet window shaped like a loophole. Only the left one-third survives:

<**7.14**> *Carlisle (Luguvalium)*

dei Herc[ulis Romani in]-
victi Con[ditoris virtu]-
tibus pro sa[lute ipsius et]
commiliton[um caesa manu]
barbaroru[m ab ala Augusta]
ob virtu[tem appellata]
P(ublius) Sextaniu[s ... civi]-
tat(e) Traia[nens(ium) v(otum) s(olvit) l(ibens) m(erito)]

RIB 946+*add.* with *Britannia* 30 (1999), 384, add. (d)

'To the virtues of the god Hercules, the Roman, Unconquered Founder; for the welfare of himself and his fellow-soldiers after the slaughter of a band of barbarians by the Cavalry Regiment styled Augusta for its valour; Publius Sextanius [...], from the City of the Traianenses, paid his vow willingly, deservedly.'

32 Birley 2005, 263; compare Publius Tullius Varro (ibid., 246).

This is the old regiment of the head-hunting Insus at Lancaster (**4.01**), the first garrison of Chesters (**5.03**); it was now based, not at Carlisle itself, but 11 miles (17.7 km) away at Old Carlisle.[33] The dedicator's cognomen and rank have been lost, but he is thought to be the prefect, gracefully condescending towards the men he commanded by calling them his 'fellow-soldiers', just like Julius Caesar and most of his successors as commander-in-chief (*imperator*) towards the army as a whole.[34] His place of origin was evidently named after Trajan, but it is uncertain whether it was *civitas Augusta Traiana* in Thrace or *colonia Ulpia Traiana* in lower Germany, the veteran 'colony' founded by Trajan near the legionary base of Vetera (Xanten). The use of *civitas* would suggest the former, but the latter would have been an origin shared with a veteran of the *ala Petriana* buried nearby at Old Penrith, not to mention legionaries at Caerleon and Chester. At Rome, three guardsmen who were Baetasii from lower Germany describe themselves simply as *Traianenses*.[35]

That cheerful phrase 'the slaughter of a band of barbarians' may echo the Corbridge altar (**7.06**), but since it is largely a restoration, however plausible, the parallel cannot be pressed. A better indication of date is the title of Hercules. The stone has broken just after CO in line 2, and it is difficult to decide whether the next letter, which is incomplete, was M or N. M is seductive, for it would prompt the restoration of *Com[modiani]*, as if Hercules were 'Commodus' Own'. In the very last days of his reign, an Italian town council which called itself 'Commodus' Own' advertised its devotion to him as the 'Unconquered Roman Hercules', and Dio quotes a letter of Commodus to the Roman Senate addressing it too as 'Commodus' Own', in which he assumes the very same title.[36] This incarnation would have been duly vouchsafed to the British army, but on balance it is better to read CON, which would give Hercules the title of *Con[ditoris]*. The coinage of Commodus gives the god this title in AD 192, which is the probable date of the inscription.[37]

When Commodus identified himself with the god Hercules, it scandalised contemporaries but did not protect him from his own courtiers. For fear that they would be executed next, they successfully plotted his assassination. Pertinax, by now the urban prefect of Rome like Lollius Urbicus before him (**6.02**), and thus an elder statesman in command of the Urban Cohorts, briefly became Emperor. But events soon showed that the Praetorian Guard was disaffected, and that the provincial armies had their own candidates.

---

33 *RIB* 893 (dated AD 188), 894 (AD 191), 895 (probably AD 197) and **13.15** (AD 242).

34 Campbell 1984, 32–9. But in **11.43**, the term is used by a decurion of the soldiers out-posted with him, and this is possibly Sextanius' rank too.

35 Devijver, *PME* S 47 (preferring Pflaum's suggestion of Thrace rather than Alföldy's Lower Germany). But compare *RIB* 935 (Old Penrith), 357 (Caerleon) and 506 (Chester). *CIL* vi 31140 (Rome) = Speidel 1994, No. 3 (dated AD 132).

36 *ILS* 400, dedicated by the *ordo decurionum Commodianor(um)* to Commodus as *invicto Romano Herculi*. Dio 72(73).15.5.

37 For a fuller discussion, see *Britannia* 30 (1999), 384–6.

8

SEPTIMIUS SEVERUS

The murder of Commodus on 31 December AD 192, like the suicide of Nero in AD 68, once more exposed what Tacitus called the Secret of Empire: an emperor could be made outside Rome.[1] Pertinax, the conspirators' choice, tragically recalled Galba: an elderly disciplinarian murdered by his own Guard. The real contenders proved to be the generals of the three most powerful armies, Clodius Albinus in Britain, Septimius Severus on the Danube, and Pescennius Niger in Syria. Severus, geographically the best placed, allied himself with Clodius Albinus and took the name *Pertinax* to justify his march on Rome, where he avenged Pertinax by disbanding the Praetorians and replacing them with a new élite Guard drawn from his own legions.[2] Then with Clodius Albinus at least neutral, Severus was free to move eastward. This crucial moment in the new regime, when the governor of Britain was briefly heir-presumptive, is caught by an altar at the port which served Rome:

<8.01> *Ostia*

Fortunae
Domesticae san-
ctae, ara(m) pro salute
et reditu L(uci) Septim(i)i
Severi Pertinacis
Aug(usti) [[et D(ecimi) Clodi]] Septi-
[[m(i)i Albini Caesaris]]
L(ucius) Valerius Frontinus
(centurio) coh(ortis) II vigil(um) sua pecunia
posuit cum suis
...

ILS 414

'To the holy Fortune of the Home, for the welfare and safe return of Lucius Septimius Severus Pertinax Augustus and of Decimus Clodius Septimius Albinus Caesar (*erased*);

[1] *Histories* i 4, *evulgato imperii arcano posse principem alibi quam Romae fieri.*

[2] Aurelius Syrio (**13.04**) for example.

Lucius Valerius Frontinus, centurion of the Second Cohort of the Watch, set up (this) altar at his own expense, with his family ...'

The text concludes with three more lines, consisting of unresolved abbreviations and the name of another centurion. The port of Ostia at the mouth of the Tiber was guarded by four centuries of the Watch, detached in turn from the main body at Rome, where it was responsible for night security and fire-fighting. This altar probably came from the courtyard of their barracks at Ostia, which still stand among the pine-trees. From its wording we can see that Severus bought off Clodius Albinus with the title of *Caesar*, which implied recognition as his junior colleague and heir presumptive, and the name *Septimius*, which implied adoption.

Severus returned from the East in AD 195 with Pescennius Niger dead, having by now fallen out with Clodius Albinus, who took the British army to Gaul to resist him. But it was defeated at the battle of Lyon (19 February AD 197), which removed Severus' last rival, and incidentally gave him Britain. Clodius Albinus' names and title except for the ambiguous *Septimius* were duly erased from the altar at Ostia. The effect of these events upon Britain is uncertain; archaeological evidence of destruction, difficult to date or attribute to hostile action, has been attributed to an uprising of the Brigantes or an incursion by northern tribes.[3] But inscriptions like this altar from the Pennines speak only of 'rebuilding':

<8.02> *Bowes (Lavatris)*

d<e>ae Fortunae
Virius Lupus
leg(atus) Aug(usti) pr(o) pr(aetore)
balineum vi
ignis exust-
um coh(orti) I Thr-
acum resti-
tuit, curan-
te Val(erio) Fron-
tone praef(ecto)
eq(uitum) alae Vetto(num)

RIB 730+*add.*

'To the goddess Fortune. Virius Lupus, imperial propraetorian legate, restored (this) bath-house burnt by the violence of fire, for the First Cohort of Thracians; (work) supervised by Valerius Fronto, prefect of the Cavalry Regiment of Vettones.'

[3] Frere 1987, 155–7.

DAE is for *deae*, since *-e-* and *-ae* were pronounced identically and were thus liable to be reduced to a single vowel: there are five other instances in *RIB*, and it also occurs in the Bath curse tablets.[4] The Vettones, formerly at Brecon (**3.08**), were now based at Binchester, the next fort to Bowes to the north-east; this may mean that their prefect was 'pulling rank' over the cohort-prefect at Bowes, but more likely that there was a temporary vacancy here. If LEG AVG, not AVGG (for two *Augusti*), is to be trusted, this altar must have been erected before 3 May AD 198, when Severus made his elder son *Augustus*; that is, within about a year of his gaining control of Britain. Virius Lupus was certainly his first governor of Britain, and we are told by Dio Cassius that he was forced to buy peace from the Maeatae of southern Scotland, but not that they had invaded the province.[5] This inscription is unfortunately not explicit. A bath-house with its furnace, its elaborate flues full of soot, its stock-pile of fuel, was peculiarly liable to catch fire. The fire could easily have been an accident, just as careful excavation of a timber building outside the nearby fort of Greta Bridge proved that the fire which destroyed it was started accidentally.[6] Fire ... and then water. The Bowes inscription suggests another from north Wales, which by no feat of the imagination can be attributed to enemy action; it was the routine repair of an essential amenity:

<8.03> *Caernarvon (Segontium)*

[imp(eratores) Caes(ares) L(ucius)] Sept(imius) Severus Pius Per-
[tinax et M(arcus) A]urel(ius) Antoninus
[Pius Aug(usti) et [[P(ublius) Sept(imius) Geta nob(ilissimus) Caes(ar)]]
[rivos] aquaeductium vetus-
[tate conla]bs(os)(!) coh(orti) I Sunic(orum) restit(uerunt)
...
[...]

RIB 430+*add.* with *Britannia* 44 (2013), 395, add. (b)

'The Emperors Caesars Lucius Septimius Severus Pius Pertinax Augustus and Marcus Aurelius Antoninus Pius Augustus and Publius Septimius Geta, the most noble Caesar (*erased*), have restored the channels of the aqueducts collapsed from age for the First Cohort of Sunici ...'

Severus' elder son Bassianus was renamed 'Marcus Aurelius Antoninus' in token of his father's fictive descent from Marcus Aurelius, and by proclaiming him *Augustus* in AD 198, Severus marked him as his titular colleague and heir apparent. Like the Emperor Gaius Caligula ('little military boot'), he is better known by his ancient

4 Compare **12.81**, *d{a}eo invicto My(thrae).*
5 Dio 75(76).5.4.
6 Casey and Hoffmann 1998, esp. 119.

nickname, 'Caracalla', which was the Celtic hooded cloak (**11.06**) he affected as Emperor. His younger brother Geta received the junior rank of *Caesar*, but his name and titles have been erased as usual, as they were from all inscriptions when he was murdered by Caracalla after their father's death.

The Emperors' names are in the nominative, marking them as the agents, not the dedicatees, just as Severus Alexander is said to have provided the aqueduct at South Shields 'for the use of the soldiers' (**13.11**). The tips of a few letters survive towards the end of the sixth line; they would have named the governor and probably the prefect who commanded the cohort. The Sunici (or Sunuci) were a tribe of Lower Germany, and the cohort is first listed in the Brigetio diploma (**5.04**); the Stannington diploma of AD 124 was actually issued to one of its veterans.[7] This is its only inscription on stone, but one of its soldiers wrote his name and that of the cohort in stylish capitals on a tile of the Twentieth Legion before it was fired (**11.13**).

A major inscription records rebuilding in the Pennines. The excavator is said to have turned it over and been so surprised to find it was inscribed that he dropped it and broke his foot. The text is inscribed on a panel within a rope-moulding, flanked to the left by a capricorn, a wingless Victory with palm-branch and wreath, standing on an orb, and an eagle perched on a thunderbolt holding a wreath; to the right by a military torque, a *genius* holding a cornucopia at an altar, and a sacrificial bull. These naïve militaria, like those on **6.10**, are symbols of victory and its celebration:

<**8.04**> *Brough-by-Bainbridge (?Virosidum)*

imp(eratori) Caesari Lucio Septimio
Severo Pio Pertinaci Aug(usto) et
imp(eratori) Caesari M(arco) Aurelio
Antonino Pio Felici Aug(usto) et
P(ublio) Septimio Getae no-
[[bilissimo Caes(ari) d(ominis)]]
n(ostris), imp(eratore) Antonino II et
Geta Caesare co(n)s(ulibus), centuriam
sub cura G(ai) Valeri Pudentis
amplissimi co(n)sularis coh(ors)
VI Nervior(um) fecit, cui praeest
L(ucius) Vinicius Pius praef(ectus) coh(ortis) eiusd(em)

RIB III, 3215

'For the Emperor Caesar Lucius Septimius Severus Pius Pertinax Augustus, and for the Emperor Caesar Marcus Aurelius Antoninus Pius Felix Augustus, and for Publius Septimius Geta, the most noble Caesar (*erased*), Our Lords, in the consulship of Antoninus for the

[7] *RIB* II.1, 2401.6.

second time and of Geta Caesar (AD 205), the Sixth Cohort of Nervii commanded by Lucius Vinicius Pius, prefect of the same cohort, built (this) barrack-block under the supervision of Gaius Valerius Pudens, senator and consular governor.'

Geta's name and titles were systematically erased from inscriptions, but in this instance line 5 which contained his name was apparently saved by the ambiguous *Septimio*, and only his titles disappeared from line 6. Valerius Pudens' title *(vir) amplissimus*, meaning 'senator', is a rare synonym for the usual *vir clarissimus*, which in Britain occurs only here and in Vinicius Pius' other two inscriptions from Brough-by-Bainbridge.[8] *Consularis* had long been an informal term for the imperial legate, since he was always an ex-consul. This bears upon an historical problem. Valerius Pudens' previous career is known from other inscriptions, notably one which records him as legate of Lower Germany before Caracalla became *Augustus*.[9] He was undoubtedly an ex-consul, yet the historian Herodian says that Severus divided Britain into two provinces in AD 197, and by *c.* AD 216 at least we know that 'Lower Britain' (northern Britain) had become a one-legion province governed by a praetorian legate. However, Severus' governors were active in the north, and they all seem to have been ex-consuls; there is no other evidence that he divided Britain, and various theories have been devised to reconcile these contradictions, not least Tony Birley's that Herodian was simply mistaken. Since Severus divided Syria in AD 194, immediately he gained control of it from Pescennius Niger, it would have been consistent for him to divide Britain in the same way, after disposing of Clodius Albinus. He may even have intended to do so – the basis of Herodian's statement, perhaps – but the immediate need for the whole British army in the north would have postponed the intention indefinitely. Birley is surely right in attributing the division to Caracalla in *c.* AD 216.[10]

Vinicius Pius was unusually energetic, architecturally and epigraphically speaking, since Camden in the late sixteenth century recorded two more of his inscriptions at Brough-by-Bainbridge which are now lost.[11] They belong to the governorship of Valerius Pudens' successor, Alfenus Senecio, a Numidian like Lollius Urbicus (**6.02**). We can see from Camden's drawing that *RIB* 722 was another large slab flanked by one, probably two, Victories; it recorded the construction of a rampart of uncoursed masonry with an outwork, *[vallum cum] bracchio caementicium*. These inscriptions are hardly evidence of enemy damage. They indicate extensive rebuilding, it is true, but would rampaging tribesmen have bothered to demolish a rampart; and if they had done so, would the Romans have given priority to rebuilding a barrack-block before the fort's defences? Alfenus Senecio is the most prolific in building-inscriptions of all the governors of Britain. There are at least ten, including this slab:

8 *RIB* 722+add. and 723+add. It has been restored in **13.05**, but is unspecific there.
9 *ILS* 9178.
10 Birley 2005, 333–6.
11 *RIB* 722+*add.* and 723+*add.*

<**8.05**> *Greta Bridge*

imp(eratoribus) Caes(aribus) L(ucio) Sep(timio) Severo
Pio Pertin(aci) et M(arco) Aur(elio) Antonini-
no Pio Aug(ustis) et [[P(ublio) Sep(timio) Getae]]
nob(ilissimo) Caes(ari) sub cura L(uci)
Alfeni Senecionis
leg(ati) eorum pr(o) pr(aetore)

RIB 746

'For the Emperors Caesars Lucius Septimius Severus Pius Pertinax, and Marcus Aurelius Antoninus Pius, Augusti, and for Publius Septimius Geta (*erased*), the most noble Caesar, under the supervision of Lucius Alfenus Senecio, their propraetorian legate.'

The inscribed text is bordered by a rope-moulding above and below, with a fussy, wreath-like *pelta* on either side, which is devolved from the much bolder *peltae* typical of Antonine inscriptions. By contrast with the Brough-by-Bainbridge inscription (**8.04**), Geta's name has been erased but his title was spared. The inscription was found near the north gate, of which it presumably formed part, so there was no need to specify what had been built. But at Birdoswald and Risingham, this is explicit:

<**8.06**> *Birdoswald (Banna)*

imp(eratoribus) Caes(aribus) L(ucio)
Sept(imio) Severo Pio
Pert(inaci) et M(arco) Aur(elio) A[nt]o-
nino Aug(ustis) [[et P(ublio) Sept(imio)
Getae nob(ilissimo) Caes(ari)]] hor-
reum fecer(unt) coh(ortes) I Ael(ia)
Dac(orum) et I T(h)racum c(ivium) R(omanorum) sub
Alfeno Senecione co(n)s(ulari)
per Aurel(ium) Iulianum tr(ibunum)

RIB 1909+*add.*

'For the Emperors Caesars Lucius Septimius Severus Pius Pertinax and Marcus Aurelius Antoninus, both Augusti, and for Publius Septimius Geta, the most noble Caesar (*erased*), the First Aelian Cohort of Dacians and the First Cohort of Thracians, Roman citizens, built (this) granary under Alfenus Senecio, the consular governor, by the agency of Aurelius Julianus, tribune.'

The inscription is badly worn from being re-used as a paving-stone (see **14.06**), but the absence of letters can be seen mid-way where Geta's full name and title were deleted. Aurelius Julianus, the tribune, was responsible for two cohorts; this is unusual, but perhaps they were below strength and together equivalent to a milliary cohort. They were represented by symbols on either side. To the left is a *falx*, the scythe-like sword attributed to the Dacians on Trajan's Column; but we do not know whether it was actually borne by the cohort here, or (as seems more likely) was retained as the 'regimental badge'.[12] To the right is a palm-branch for 'victory', that of the Thracians presumably, since they bear the title of 'Roman citizens' for bravery in some previous battle. This particular cohort is not otherwise known in Britain, but the Dacians, now attested at Birdoswald for the first time, remained its garrison until the end of the Roman period.

The other inscription implies a determination to retain the outpost forts:

<**8.07**> *Risingham (Habitancum)*

[imp(eratoribus) Caes(aribus) L(ucio)]
[Sept(imio) Severo Pio Pertin]-
[aci Arab(ico) Adi]ab(enico) Part(h)[i]co Maxi(mo)
co(n)s(uli) III et M(arco) Aurel(io) Antonino Pio
co(n)s(uli) II Aug(ustis) [[et P(ublio) Sept(imio) Getae nob(ilissimo) Caes(ari)]]
portam cum muris vetustate di-
lapsis iussu Alfeni Senecionis v(iri) c(larissimi)
co(n)s(ularis), curante Oclatinio Advento proc(uratore)
Aug(ustorum) n(ostrorum), coh(ors) I Vangion(um) (milliaria) eq(uitata)
cum Aem[i]l(io) Salviano trib(uno)
suo a solo restit(uit)

RIB 1234+*add.*

'For the Emperor Caesar Lucius Septimius Severus Pius Pertinax, Conqueror of Arabia, Conqueror of Adiabene, Greatest Conqueror of Parthia, consul three times, Augustus; and

[12] The *falx* also appears on *RIB* 1914 (Birdoswald). The Dacian name *Decibalus* occurs at Birdoswald (*RIB* 1920), which might be the find-spot of *RIB* II.7, 2501.156 (see note). Compare Aelius Dida (**5.42**), of the same cohort.

for the Emperor Caesar Marcus Aurelius Antoninus Pius, consul twice, Augustus; and for Publius Septimius Geta, the most noble Caesar (*erased*); the First Cohort of Vangiones, one thousand strong, part-mounted, together with its tribune, Aemilius Salvianus, restored (this) gate and its walls from ground-level after they had collapsed from age, by order of Alfenus Senecio, Senator and consular governor, under the supervision of Oclatinius Adventus the imperial Procurator.'

This long text was ingeniously crammed into a circle defined by a carved wreath, flanked by the standing figures of Mars and Victory. Geta has lost both his name and his title. The titles of his senior colleagues represent official history: *Pertinax* and *Marcus Aurelius Antoninus* have been mentioned already; *Arabicus* and *Adiabenicus* celebrate Severus' victory over Parthian dependencies in northern Mesopotamia; *Parthicus Maximus* his subsequent defeat of Parthia itself, Rome's eastern rival, the loose-knit empire that embraced modern Iran and Iraq. The Arch of Severus, which still dominates the route taken by triumphant generals from the Roman Forum to the Capitol, was erected 'because he restored constitutional government and extended the Empire of the Roman people'.[13] It remained only to add the title of *Britannicus Maximus*, Most Great Conqueror of Britain, by campaigning there in person.[14]

Inscriptions quite often refer to 'age' and dilapidation, but these references may be taken literally: we will find them applied to temples in London (**10.37** and **12.88**) and a government office outside Bath (**10.35**), where there is no question of damage due to enemy action. Barbarian invaders might loot and burn, but they had no cause to waste their time and energy in 'slighting' Roman defences like the Cromwellians at Corfe Castle. The Risingham inscription is long-winded in contrast to Greta Bridge, let alone York (**4.16**) a century before: it specifies what has been built, and why, but it is perversely mean with the lettering; it would have been easier to have saved space and letter-cutting by condensing the imperial titulature, but instead letters were combined and condensed by means of ligatures, until these became an end in themselves. TRIBVNO, for example, has been reduced to a monogram at the end of line 10. Since the slab was quite richly decorated, this was not done out of economy of effort; rather it implies a sense of decoration, and even a self-conscious literacy. The draughtsman is proudly raising the bar against the semi-literate, who might claim to be able to read capital letters, the plain letters of stone inscriptions.[15] These letters were no longer plain or self-evident.

The same tribune, Lucius Aemilius Salvianus, also dedicated an altar at Risingham to 'the unconquered god' Hercules.[16] He can be identified with a prominent citizen of Lambaesis in Numidia (eastern Algeria) where the African legion, Third Augusta, was based:

---

13 *ILS* 425, *ob rem publicam restitutam imperiumque populi Romani propagatum*.

14 *ILS* 432, 8917, both of AD 210. Also borne by Caracalla (**13.02** and **13.03**).

15 Petronius, *Satyricon* 58.7, *lapidarias litteras scio*, also quoted in the Introduction.

16 *RIB* 1215.

<8.08> *Lambaesis in Numidia (eastern Algeria)*

L(ucio) Aemilio Sal-
viano eg(regiae) m(emoriae) v(iro)
fratri L(ucius) Aemi-
lius Marcelli-
nus p(rimi) p(ilaris) secun-
dum verba tes-
tamenti eius
posuit,
curantibus
trib(us) Aemiliis Festo Cu-
rio et Chresto
libertis

CIL viii 2758

'To Lucius Aemilius Salvianus, a man of Distinguished Memory, his brother. Lucius Aemilius Marcellinus, retired first-ranking centurion (*primipilaris*), erected this in accordance with the words of his will, the work being supervised by the three Aemilii, Festus, Curius and Chrestus, his freedmen.'

The freedmen took their patron's nomen as usual, when they became Roman citizens on being manumitted. Salvianus' brother Marcellinus also erected a colonnaded temple at Lambaesis 'for love of his fellow-citizens', to which Salvianus posthumously contributed six columns in his will.[17] The brothers were thus local magnates, Marcellinus as the retired first-ranking centurion of the Legion, Salvianus as a former imperial procurator, which is what the title *vir egregius* means. This appointment would have followed the usual three equestrian military commands, the second of which, a tribunate in northern Britain rather than in the local legion, he may have owed to the governor of Britain, his fellow-Numidian Alfenus Senecio from nearby Cuicul.[18]

Salvianus' Risingham inscription, like a similar text from Chesters,[19] is exceptional in noticing the procurator of Britain, Oclatinius Adventus. Ten to twelve years later, in AD 217, this man nearly became Emperor: he was then joint praetorian prefect when Caracalla was murdered, but he conceded the throne to his younger colleague Macrinus, the first equestrian ever to be proclaimed Emperor. Adventus was compensated with two plums of the senatorial career, the consulship and the urban prefecture of Rome, in which he was remembered as an aged boor. His real fault was that he was no gentleman: unlike most equestrian procurators, Aemilius Salvianus for example, Adventus did not come from the landowning gentry, but

---

17 *AE* 1939, 37.
18 Birley 1979, 68.
19 *RIB* 1462.

had been a common soldier. He was not even a fighting soldier: to use another anachronism, he had a background in Intelligence, having first been a *speculator* and then centurion in the *frumentarii*, before becoming their commander at Rome as the *princeps peregrinorum*.[20] We do not really know what Adventus was doing in northern Britain, but Boris Rankov has made the attractive suggestion that, in view of his special qualifications, he was gathering operational intelligence for an impending imperial initiative.[21]

Another imperial visit to Britain

Septimius Severus had decided to visit Britain, the first Emperor to do so since Hadrian. By coincidence his brother, Septimius Geta, had first-hand experience of the island as the 'senatorial' tribune of the Second Legion Augusta.[22] But this was 40 years ago, and Geta died 4 years before Severus' arrival in AD 208, when he was responding ostensibly to an appeal from the governor of Britain, Alfenus Senecio; no doubt he also had political reasons of his own. The Emperor was commander-in-chief, and Severus' own career from usurper to the founder of a dynasty had convinced him that this command must be real. But there is a broad hint that Alfenus Senecio had already been involved in fighting as well as rebuilding:

<**8.09**> *Benwell (Condercum)*

Victoriae
[Au]g(ustorum) Alfe-
no Senecio-
n[e] co(n)s(ulari), felix
ala I Asto-
[ru]m *PRA*

RIB 1337+*add.*

'For the Victory of the Emperors while Alfenus Senecio was consular governor; happy is the First Cavalry Regiment of Asturians ...'

This large slab, an ansate panel supported by two Victories, was found in about 1669; it was taken to London, where Horsley drew it, but unfortunately it was destroyed in a fire soon afterwards, in 1737. The alternative spelling 'Astorian' is also found on a tombstone at Lincoln.[23] It is apparently followed by a regimental title, perhaps *pr(aetoria)* or *Br(itannica)*. Since Alfenus Senecio is the governor, this 'victory' must

[20] Austin and Rankov 1995, 194. For *speculatores* and *frumentarii* in the British army, see **10.29**, **10.30** (with note) and **10.17**.

[21] Rankov 1987.

[22] *IRT* 541; in the late AD 160s or early 170s, depending on whether he was older than Severus or not (A Birley 1988, 39).

[23] *RIB* 266, *alae II Astor(um)*.

have preceded Severus' arrival in Britain. There may be a further reference to it, on this altar also from Hadrian's Wall:

<**8.10**> *near Hexham*

Victoriae
Aug(ustae)
L(ucius) Iul(ius) Iuli[anus]
leg(atus) [leg(ionis) II Aug(ustae)?]
[...]

RIB 1138+*add.*

'For the imperial Victory. Lucius Julius Julianus, legate of the Second Legion Augusta ...'

This too has been lost, and again we depend on Horsley's drawing. The abbreviated dedication is ambiguous, since AVG might be *Aug(ustae)*, which has been adopted here, or *Aug(usti)* ('of the Emperor'), as if it referred to a specific victory. By contrast **8.09** is dedicated VICTORIAE AVGG, for the Victory of the *two* Emperors, who would be Severus and Caracalla. To restore the dedicator's command, he must be identified with the Lucius Julius Julianus who governed Achaia (Greece) in the period AD 198/209 and then became legate of the Second Legion Augusta.[24] This dating is not close enough to determine whether he was sharing in the 'victory' of Alfenus Senecio (**8.09**), or was making his dedication now that Severus had arrived (compare **8.10**), but the presence on the Wall of a legionary legate implies that his whole legion was there, not just a detachment. Since it was based at Caerleon in what became Upper Britain, this is more evidence that Britain had not yet been divided into two provinces, although if Severus was already there, any such division would not have applied. We move into certainty with an altar from Corbridge, which explicitly refers to the imperial expedition of AD 208–11. Perhaps it too was was dedicated to 'imperial Victory', but only the end of the text survives:

<**8.11**> *Corbridge (Coria), west granary*

. . .
[...]
[...]sit [...]
[...]norus
[... pr]aep(ositus) cu-
[ram] agens
horr(eorum) tempo-
[r]e expeditio-
nis felicissi(mae)

[24] *CIL* xi 4182 with Birley 2005, 266.

Brittannic(ae)
v(otum) s(olvit) l(ibens) m(erito)

RIB 1143

'... [...]norus, the officer in charge of the granaries at the time of the most successful British campaign, gladly and deservedly paid his vow.'

Once again (compare **6.03** and **6.04**), activity in the two great storehouses at Corbridge reflects interest in the road to Scotland, just as the fort at South Shields was now turned into a great supply-base. They were the logistic springboards that launched the largest Roman army the north of Britain ever saw, for Severus now added to the British garrison his own strategic reserve, notably his new Second Legion Parthica and the enlarged Praetorian Guard, as well as legionary detachments like those he mobilised for other campaigns. Field forces had been improvised from legionary detachments ever since the first century, for example Pontius Sabinus' three thousand men (**5.09**), but this expedient increased during the third century; many such detachments persisted into the fourth-century mobile army (*comitatenses*), by which time they had become independent of their parent formations and some had even acquired new names. A constituent of Severus' field army is revealed by this tombstone, later used to pave the road out of Amiens:

<8.12> *Amiens (Samarobriva Ambianorum)*

[D(is)] M(anibus)
[...]ius Se-
[...] miles
[leg(ionis) ?XXII Prim(igeniae)] p(iae) f(idelis), vex-
[ill(arii) l]eg(ionis) eiusdem
[m]onime[n]tum euntes
[ad] expedi[t(ionem)] Britanicam
[d(e)] s(uo) f(aciendum) c(uraverunt)

ILS 9123

'To the Shades of the Dead. [...]ius Se[...], soldier [of the Twenty-Second Legion Primigenia] Dutiful and Loyal. The men of the detachment of the same legion going on the British campaign saw to the making of his monument at their own expense.'

The extensive use of ligatures suggests a third-century date, and thus implies that the 'British campaign' was that of Severus. The spelling of 'British' (*Britanicus*) may be described as Continental, since no one in Roman Britain is known to have written 'Britain' with one T and one N in the modern manner; significantly the only instances from Britain are a fragmentary letter found in Carlisle addressed to someone 'in Britain' (*in Britania*), and an altar dedicated at Dover, the port of entry, to the goddess 'Britania'. Both writers, by implication, lived elsewhere.[25] The legion's name has been lost from this tombstone, but it was one which would have passed through Amiens on its way to Britain, most likely from Upper Germany or the Danube frontier, and also one which had *pia fidelis* in its titulature. On both counts the best candidate is the Twenty-Second Legion Primigenia from Mainz, which had already contributed to earlier campaigns in Britain.[26]

This tombstone shows that troops travelling between Britain and other frontiers passed through Amiens, as might be expected, since it is where major routes converge for Boulogne and the Channel crossing. It is also where a soldier lost his souvenir of Hadrian's Wall (**5.15**), and a first-ranking centurion of the Sixth Legion[27] was buried, but we do not know whether they were both in transit or living there as veterans. In AD 367 Amiens briefly housed the whole western field army on its way to the coast, when bad news from Britain drew the emperor Valentinian from his usual watch on the Rhine.[28]

Severus' entourage is likely to have included a new procurator of Britain, the successor of Oclatinius Adventus (**8.07**). Varius Marcellus was an equestrian careerist from Syrian Apamea, but he became a Roman senator and was buried south-east of Rome, just beyond the Alban Hills. His marble sacrophagus is inscribed in both Latin and Greek:

<**8.13**> *Velitrae (now in the Vatican)*

Sex(to) Vario Marcello
proc(uratori) aquar(um) (centenario), proc(uratori) prov(inciae) Brit(anniae) (ducenario),
proc(uratori) rationis privat(ae) (trecenario), vice praef(ectorum) pr(aetorio) et urbi functo
c(larissimo) v(iro), praef(ecto) aerari militaris, leg(ato) leg(ionis) III Aug(ustae)
praesidi provinc(iae) Numidiae,
Iulia Soaemias Bassiana c(larissima) f(emina) cum fil(i)is
marito et patri amantissimo
(*to the right, a Greek translation*)

ILS 478

'To Sextus Varius Marcellus, procurator of the aqueducts at a salary of 100,000 (sesterces), procurator of the province of Britain at a salary of 200,000 (sesterces), procurator of

[25] *RIB* II.4, 2443.5 (Carlisle) and **12.14** (Dover).
[26] **5.09** (Hadrianic), *RIB* 2216 and **6.01** (both Antonine). It also sent a detachment to Piercebridge under Caracalla (**12.82** with note).
[27] *CIL* xiii 3497 (name lost).
[28] Ammianus Marcellinus xxvii 8.1 with Tomlin 1974.

the Privy Account at a salary of 300,000 (sesterces), acting praetorian prefect and urban prefect, senator, prefect of the Military Treasury, legate of the Third Legion Augusta (and) governor of the province of Numidia: Julia Soaemias Bassiana, of senatorial rank, with her children to a most loving husband and father.'

Procuratorships were rated by salary according to their importance, the four grades being 60,000 sesterces a year (*sexagenarius*), 100,000 (*centenarius*), 200,000 (*ducenarius*) and 300,000 (*trecenarius*). To set these sums in context, note that in AD 220, when Sennius Sollemnis (**10.39**) was offered 25,000 sesterces for 6 months' service as a legionary tribune, this was probably 10 years' pay for a legionary in the ranks. We have already seen Artorius Castus (**7.01**) earning 100,000 in Liburnia, and Pertinax (**7.02**) 200,000 in Dacia and Moesia. Marcellus was even more successful: apparently he was appointed to the water-supply of Rome without first holding a lower-grade procuratorship at 60,000 sesterces, let alone the usual qualifying posts in the equestrian military career; and he served only once in each of the successively higher grades. The explanation lies in the name of his widow: she was the daughter of Julia Maesa, whose sister was the Empress Julia Domna (**8.17**). Marcellus, by marrying into the imperial family, gained the patronage of Severus and then of Caracalla. But the key moment of his career was when he temporarily replaced the two most powerful officials at Rome, who between them controlled the imperial Guard and the city's 'police', the Urban Cohorts. This must have been in December 211, when Caracalla deposed both prefects and murdered his brother and co-Emperor, the subsequently much-erased Geta.[29] Marcellus was rewarded for

---

[29] Halfmann 1982, esp. 226–34, endorsed by Birley 2005, 313–14. The gap in Marcellus' career between his charge of the aqueducts (independently attested in *c.* AD 198) and the mission to Britain in AD

his loyalty at this crucial moment by being promoted to the Senate, where he was first responsible for paying retirement bounties to legionaries, and then went to Africa to command its only legion. This would have led directly to the consulship and no doubt a major army command, had he not then died. The children who mourned his premature death included Bassianus, the future emperor 'Elagabalus' (**13.05**), whose accession in AD 218 he did not live to see.

Victory in Britain

Those dedications to Victory may have been anticipatory, like this altar which is dated to the year of Severus' arrival:

<**8.14**> *Greetland, near Halifax*

d(eae) Vict(oriae) Brig(antiae)
et num(inibus) Aug(ustorum)
T(itus) Aur(elius) Aurelian-
us d(edit) d(edicavit) pro se
et suis s(e) mag(istro) s(acrorum)

(*on the right side*)
Antonin[o]
III et Geta [II]
co(n)s(ulibus)

RIB 627+*add.*

'To the goddess Victoria Brigantia and to the Divinities of the (two) Emperors, Titus Aurelius Aurelianus gave and dedicated (this altar) for himself and his family, while he himself was Master of Rites, in the third consulship of Antoninus and the [second] of Geta (AD 208).'

The dedicator for once is not a 'Marcus' Aurelius, but a 'Titus', indicating that his ancestor had been enfranchised during the reign of Antoninus Pius (AD 138–61); but otherwise his name is as colourless as that of the lady Aurelia Aurelia(na) buried at Carlisle.[30] We do not know what he meant by SMAGS, but the expansion adopted here is an attractive guess by Richmond. This altar is one of eight dedications to Brigantia, all of them from Yorkshire and the Wall area, defining the tribal territory

208 is plausibly attributed to the hostility of the praetorian prefect Plautianus.

[30] *RIB* 959.

of the Brigantes whom she personified.[31] It is most unusual for an altar to be dated.[32] Fortunately this date did not form part of the main text, so it was overlooked when references to Geta were systematically erased 4 years later. Unless Aurelianus was in fact celebrating the tenth anniversary of Severus' defeat of Parthia, he was anticipating events in Britain. Only next year (AD 209) did Severus, like Agricola, Lollius Urbicus and Ulpius Marcellus before him, advance into the far north. The only explicit celebration of this achievement comes from his native Africa:

<**8.15**> *Gigthis*

Victoriae
Brittanicae
imp(eratorum trium) L(uci) Septimi Seve-
ri Pii Pertinacis et
M(arci) Aureli Antonini
[[et P(ubli) Septimi Getae]]
Aug(ustorum trium) Gigthens[es]
publice

ILS 436

'To the Victory in Britain of the (three) Emperors Lucius Septimius Severus Pius Pertinax, and Marcus Aurelius Antoninus, and Publius Septimius Geta (*erased*), (three) Augusti; the people of Gigthis (erected this) at public expense.'

Gigthis was a port which exported olive oil to Italy, situated on the border between Africa Proconsularis (Tunisia) and Tripolitania (western Libya) from which Severus came. This dedication probably belongs to the last months of his reign, after the promotion of his younger son Geta to *Augustus*, but some African inscriptions give him this rank earlier.[33] The imperial titles are abbreviated to IMPPP and AVGGG, to show that three emperors are meant, but when Geta's name was erased as usual, they were reduced to IMPP and AVGG, so as to remove any hint of his existence.

The loyal citizens of Gigthis may not have known any better than we do what Severus' victory amounted to, let alone how he intended to exploit it. Archaeological evidence of his activity in Scotland must be reconciled with his reconstruction of Hadrian's Wall to the south: at the River Gelt quarries south of Castlesteads in AD 207, the date was cut by a working-party.[34] The implication is that the Wall would

[31] *RIB* 628 (Castleford) also identifies her with Victory, but is not dated. At Birrens she is identified with Minerva (**12.17**) and at Corbridge with Caelestis (**12.85**).

[32] The only other British examples belong to AD 241/2: *RIB* 1983 (Castlesteads), 882 and 883 (Papcastle).

[33] A Birley 1988, 218.

[34] *RIB* 1009, *Apro et Maximo consulibus of(f)icina Mercati*. Literary sources credit Severus with building a wall 'from sea to sea' (A R Birley 1988, 255).

remain the frontier, and epigraphic evidence of Severus' activity further north is hard to find.[35]

A Severan date has been suggested for the Old Kilpatrick altar (**6.26**), but it is undoubtedly Antonine. Another altar does indeed come from a Severan fort in Scotland, but only in the sense that it was an Antonine fort on the Firth of Forth which was reconstructed because it guarded a useful harbour:

<**8.16**> *Cramond*

I(ovi) O(ptimo) M(aximo)
coh(ors) V Gall(orum
cui praeest
L(ucius) Minthonius
Tertullus
praef(ectus) v(otum) s(olvit) l(aeta)
l(ibens) m(erito)

RIB 2134

'To Jupiter Best and Greatest. The Fifth Cohort of Gauls, commanded by the prefect Lucius Minthonius Tertullus, paid its vow gladly, willingly and deservedly.'

The prefect's name is 'fabricated' from a Punic name, *Mintho*; a Marcus Minthonius Tertullus and three other Minthonii are recorded from Mactaris in Africa Proconsularis, which is surely his place of origin.[36] The family had adopted a 'Roman' name without concealing their origins: they would have been surprised to read the letter of a pagan professor of literature, Maximus of Madauros, who complained in AD 390 that the cult of Christian martyrs with un-Roman names was displacing the worship of Roman Jupiter; as an absurd example, he cited a martyr called *Miggo*.[37]

The deity's name is inscribed on the capital, not the die, but this does not make the altar Severan instead of Antonine.[38] The Fifth Cohort of Gauls is attested at South Shields in AD 213, and the apparent association of its lead sealings with those of the Emperor suggests that it was were already there during his campaigns.[39] The question of Cramond is complicated by the presence of another unit, the Second Cohort of Tungrians, but there is no indication of date, except that it did not bear the title of *c(ives) L(atini)*.[40] There is thus the suggestion of two periods at Cramond, but neither altar is obviously Severan. Another problem is posed by Carpow, as we

---

35 Hanson and Maxwell 1983, 207–10.

36 Birley 1961, 166, citing *CIL* viii 23420, 23401 (= *ILS* 4142) and 23437.

37 Augustine, *Letters* 16.2.

38 See the notes to **5.07** and **6.26**.

39 *RIB* III, 3272.

40 *RIB* 2135+*add*. For the title, see note to **6.33**.

have seen already (**7.11**), since the 'Antonine' epigraphy is at variance with the Severan date adduced by excavation.

The Emperor leaves Britain (and everything else)

It was expected that Severus, like Claudius in AD 43, would be returning safe and victorious from Britain:

<**8.17**> *Grosskrotzenburg*

pro salute victoria et
reditu imp(eratorum trium) Caesarum L(uci)
Septimi Severi Pertina-
cis et M(arci) Aureli Antonini
e[t] P(ubli) Septimi [[Getae]] Piorum
Aug(ustorum trium) et Iuliae Domnae
Augustae matris Aug(ustorum duorum) et
[ca]strorum, Q(uintus) Aiacius
[Mo]destus Crescentia-
[nus], leg(atus) G(ermaniae) s(uperioris), n(umini) [m(aiestatique) e(orum)] d(evotus)

ILS 433 = *CIL* xiii 7417

'For the welfare, the victory, and the return of the three Emperors Caesars Lucius Septimius Severus Pertinax, and Marcus Aurelius Antoninus, and Publius Septimius Geta (*erased*) Dutiful Augusti, and of Julia Domna Augusta the mother of the two Augusti and the Army; (from) Quintus Aiacius Modestus Crescentianus, legate of Upper Germany, devoted to their divinity and majesty.'

The name *Geta* has been erased as usual. Julia Domna was Severus' second wife and the mother of his two sons; she belonged to a quasi-royal Syrian family, hereditary priests of the sun god Elagabal at Emesa (Homs), the office inherited by her great-nephew Bassianus, the emperor 'Elagabalus' (**13.05**). Since her younger son Geta is now *Augustus*, this dedication must belong to the last months of Severus' life, when he had been in Britain for more than 2 years and his return might reasonably be expected to be imminent. But instead he died, at York, where he was cremated. His ashes were transported to Rome in a jar of 'purple stone': Egyptian porphyry perhaps, if this contingency had been anticipated when the expedition was mounted. He is said to have had a premonition at the time that he would not return, and later to have handled this urn with the words: 'You will hold a man whom the world did not hold'.[41]

[41] Dio 77.11.1 and 15.4. The urn was alabaster according to Herodian (3.15.7), but gold according to the Augustan History (*Severus* 24.2). Derbyshire 'Blue John' is Tony Birley's ingenious suggestion

The epitaphs also survive of two other casualties in the imperial party. The involvement of the first, a senior civil servant, is not quite certain:

<**8.18**> *Rome*

D(is) M(anibus)
G(ai) Iuli Iusti eq(uitis) R(omani)
scribae decur(iae)
aedilic(iae) mai(oris),
defuncti in prov(incia)
Britannia
Iul(ia) Calpurnia
Iusta
patri dulciss(imo)

ILS 1883

'To the Shades of the Dead (and of) Gaius Julius Justus, Roman *eques*, secretary in the major department of the aediles, died in the province of Britain. Julia Calpurnia Justa, for her dearest father.'

As an equestrian and a *scriba*, Justus was a permanent official of high rank in the secretariat attached to magistrates in the city of Rome, in his case the aediles who were responsible for the markets and other areas of civic administration. It is hard to imagine that these duties would bring him to Britain, but since some *scribae* proceeded to equestrian military commands, perhaps he was a trusted agent of the central government sent on a mission of inquiry; other examples are the imperial freedman Polyclitus after the Boudican revolt, and the imperial secretary (*notarius*) Paulus after the death of the usurper Magnentius in AD 353.[42] But since Severus was accompanied to Britain by imperial freedmen, and inscriptions show that he conducted routine imperial business there by responding to petitions, he must have taken senior civilian officials; economy of conjecture suggests that Justus was one of them.[43] If so, he shared the fate of an officer in the Guard, whose ashes were deposited in a richly carved marble chest now in Palermo:

(1988, 256, n. 1).

42 Tacitus, *Annals* xiv 39 and Ammianus Marcellinus xiv 5.6, respectively. For the duties of *scribae* see Purcell 1983 (noting Justus at 155, n. 182).

43 Dio 76(77).14.2 (*Caesariani* in Britain). *AE* 1971, 455 (Ephesus) honours a delegate who chased after Severus and Caracalla on diplomatic missions to Rome, Britain, Upper Germany, Sirmium, Nicomedia, Antioch, and 'as far as Mesopotamia'. *AE* 1986, 628 (Aenus in Thrace) once contained an extract from the imperial archives (*commentarii*) which recorded the response of Caracalla and Geta to a delegation at York on 12 September (*pr(idie) Idus Septemb(res) Ebora[ci]*) in a year which was probably AD 208.

<8.19> *Rome*

D(is) M(anibus)
G(aio) Cesennio Se-
necioni c(enturioni) c(o)hor(tis) II
pr(aetoriae) p(iae) v(indicis) exercitatori
equitum pr(aetorianorum) fecit G(aius) Ce-
sernius Zonysius(!) live-
rtus(!) et heres atfer-
ente(!) Zotico a Britt-
ania

ILS 2089; Bivona 1970, No. 219 (pl. CVI)

'To the Shades of the Dead (and) to Gaius Cesennius Senecio, centurion of the Second Praetorian Cohort, Dutiful and Avenging, trainer of the Praetorian cavalry; Gaius Cesernius Zonysius his freedman and heir made (this), with Zoticus bringing (his ashes) from Britain.'

This epitaph is carried by an ansate panel. A capital Greek sigma (S) has been used for Z, which was not a letter native to the Latin alphabet; like Y it was used only for transliterating Greek words. Both the freedmen have Greek names, but *Zonysius* is properly 'Dionysius', since the [dy] sound in Latin tended to be pronounced as [z]. *Livertus* for *libertus* is an example of the *b/v* interchange found in Italy and provinces with a significant Greek-speaking population, but not in Britain. The epitaph cannot be earlier than the reign of Septimius Severus, since it was he who gave the titles *Pia Vindex* to the Praetorian Cohorts. It can therefore be dated to AD 208/11, since an imperial visit to Britain was the only opportunity a Guards officer would get of dying there. He can reasonably be identified with Caesernius Senecio, a centurion of the Watch at Rome in *c.* AD 205, since they were regularly promoted into the Urban Cohorts and then the Praetorian Guard.[44] The freedman's name, which he would have acquired from his patron, is given as *Cesernius*, so the name of his patron, *Cesennius Senecio* (with N for R), must be a stone-cutter's mistake. The confusion between *e* and the diphthong *ae* is a very common 'Vulgarism'.

By dying in Britain, Caesernius Senecio (as we may now call him) was missing more than he knew. When Septimius Severus was subsequently deified at Rome, the obsequies were marked by a special cavalry parade in which the horsemen manoeuvred intricately around the imperial bier. The cavalry would have been the Emperor's mounted bodyguard, the *equites singulares Augusti*, and the cavalry of the Praetorian Guard once trained by Senecio.

Severus' strategy for Britain died with him. His sons abandoned his conquests, made peace with the northern tribes, and consolidated Hadrian's Wall as the frontier once more. The outpost forts were strongly garrisoned, as will be seen (**13.19** with

[44] *CIL* vi 1057.

note), by milliary part-mounted cohorts and new units of 'scouts' (*exploratores*). The strategy of Caracalla and Geta may have been improvised, but it was justified by the outcome: we hear of no further trouble in the north for many years. After the interval needed to implement it, the survivors of the imperial party left Britain:

<8.20> *South Shields (?Lugudunum, later Arbeia)*

Dis
Conservato-
rib(us) pro salu(te)
imp(eratoris) C(aesaris) M(arci) Aurel(i)
Antonini
Aug(usti) Brit(annici) Max(imi)
[[et imp(eratoris) C(aesaris) P(ubli) Sep(timi)]]
[[Getae Aug(usti) Brit(annici)]]
?n(umerus) Lug(u)[dun]ens<iu>m
ob reditu<m>
v(otum) s(olvit)

RIB 1054+*add.* with *Britannia* 45 (2014), 454, add. (a)

'To the Saving Gods, for the welfare of the Emperor Caesar Marcus Aurelius Antoninus Augustus, Most Great Conqueror of Britain, and of the Emperor Caesar Publius Septimius Geta Augustus Conqueror of Britain (*erased*), the military unit at Lugudunum paid its vow for their safe return.'

It will now come as no surprise that the name and titles of Geta have been erased, but their exact restoration is conjectural. The name of the dedicator(s) is almost as difficult to read, but by close examination and by identifying South Shields as *Lugudunum*, Paul Bidwell has argued strongly that the altar was dedicated by the unit which garrisoned Septimius Severus' supply-base.[45] Its members would have watched the imperial fleet sail from the Tyne estuary for the Continent: as the ships dwindled from sight, they carried with them the last chance that the Romans might have conquered the whole of Britain.

[45] Bidwell 2014.

9

SOLDIER AND CIVILIAN

The ebbing of Severus' conquests is the moment at which to pause in the history of Roman Britain, or rather to turn from the sequence of military events to the evidence of inscriptions for daily life. The island has produced fewer than three thousand inscribed stones, many of them slight or fragmentary, and the great majority come from sites with military associations, whether the northern frontier zone itself, or the other forts and legionary fortresses, or cities with military origins like Lincoln, Wroxeter and Carlisle. Civic epigraphy, celebrating a new theatre at Brough-on-Humber (**10.02**) for example, or a newly-promoted governor at Caerwent (**10.03**), is rare compared with that of other provinces. On wood, as on stone, the military dominate: 889 ink tablets from Vindolanda, 77 from Carlisle, only 3 from London.[1] But now the Bloomberg London tablets have been published, there are 108 (legible) stylus tablets from London, as against 14 from Vindolanda and 6 from Carlisle.[2] 232 lead curse tablets have also been counted, but only three come from military sites.[3] These stylus-written tablets, wood and lead, are doubly precious for being derived from civilian milieux, but it remains a truism (even if true) that Roman inscriptions of Britain, both on stone and in other media, over-represent soldiers and the army; inevitably they become a prime source for military history, the recruitment and movement of military units, the frontiers and how they were held. But let us resist this bias for a moment by turning to the civil population, or at least to its relations with the military.

The title of this chapter is taken from a text scratched on lead which a treasure-hunter found at a temple-site in Norfolk. Fortunately a tracing was made before he 'lost' it again, as this is now the only record, but it remained unread until it was seen that the original text had been enciphered by writing it from right to left in mirror-image capitals; since they cannot now be checked against the original, transcribing them entails even more brackets than usual, whether to restore letters which are [missing or defective] or to supply letters which were (wrongly formed or omitted):

1 Bowman, Thomas and Tomlin 2011; Tomlin 1998 (both totals including many 'descripta'); Tomlin 2016.

2 Tomlin 2016. The Vindolanda figure will increase, since the British Museum holds 340 stylus tablets, but most of them are uninscribed or illegible.

3 Kropp 2008 (including Uley texts incompletely published).

<9.01> *Weeting with Broomhill*

s(i) servus si [l]ib[e](r) [qu]-
i [f]uravit su[st]uli-
t [ne ei] dimitte
[male]fic(i)um d(u)m
tu vindi[c]a[s]

ante dies
nov[e](m) si pa-
[g]a[n]us si
mil[e]s [qui]
su[s]tu[l]it

Britannia 25 (1994), 296, No. 2

'Whoever has stolen or taken it, whether he is slave or free, do not forgive him his evil-doing until you punish him within nine days, whether he is a civilian or a soldier, whoever has taken it.'

This is a conventional curse against theft, which unhelpfully does not specify what has been stolen, nor even the god to whom it is addressed; but as usual it is formulaic and rhetorically repetitive, its Latin 'Vulgar' in the sense of being influenced by the spoken language. The verbs, for example, are used in senses not found in Classical Latin: *sustulit*, which supplies the perfect tense of *tollo* ('raise'), here means 'lifted' in the sense of 'stolen'; and *dimitte* ('dismiss') does not mean to 'send away', but to 'forgive', as in the Latin of 'Forgive us our trespasses' when the Lord's Prayer was first translated from Greek into Latin, a Latin which was not literary but the language of daily speech. Two formulas pin the unknown thief between pairs of mutually exclusive alternatives: 'whether he is slave or free', which is often found in curse tablets, and uniquely, 'whether he is a civilian (*paganus*) or a soldier (*miles*)'. It is a cliché to contrast the soldier-like professional with the civilian amateur. The Church Fathers, for example, use St Paul's image of putting on 'the armour of light' to preach sermons about moral rearmament, in happy ignorance of the poet Ovid's teaching that 'every lover', by which he means the successful seducer, is a 'soldier'.[4] For early Christians, the full-time soldier of Christ who renounced the world was the opposite of the non-Christian civilian, the 'pagan'.

This polarising cliché exaggerates the contrast. The title of this chapter also recalls Ramsay MacMullen's influential *Soldier and Civilian in the Later Roman Empire* (1963), which takes the image of the old Turkish Navy cemented to its quays by seaweed and barnacles, to symbolise the growing ties between the Roman army and the civilian population: 'Civilian turned soldier, soldier turned civilian, in a

[4] *Epistle to the Romans* 13.12. Ovid, *Amores* i 9.1–2, *militat omnis amans*.

rapprochement to a middle ground of waste and confusion', a thesis which must be borne in mind, even if it cannot be proved – or disproved – from British inscriptions.[5] We have already seen soldiers acting as administrators and dedicating altars like any civilian; let us now consider the ties they formed with civilians. When they married, they married civilians of course, and they also fathered civilians; but until Septimius Severus allowed serving soldiers to marry, their informal unions were not recognised under Roman Law, which is why auxiliary soldiers when they received Roman citizenship on discharge after 25 years also gained the right of Roman legal marriage to 'the wives they had at the time'.[6] The marriage ban, first introduced by Augustus, applied to long-term, professional soldiers up to the rank of centurion, but not to their superior officers, the various legates, tribunes and prefects drawn from the senatorial and equestrian aristocracy, since these only received short-term commissions. Legally they reverted to civilian status immediately their successors arrived: a surviving letter of dismissal tells the outgoing prefect to hand over to his successor and then 'attend to your own affairs'.[7]

Senators and equestrians

The altar (**4.10**) dedicated to Fortune the Home-bringer by the household (*familia*) of the legionary legate at Chester need not imply that he had a 'family' in the restricted modern sense of a wife and children, but this is explicit in an altar from York:

<9.02> *York (Eboracum), colonia baths*

deae
Fortunae
Sosia
Iuncina
Q(uinti) Antoni
Isaurici
leg(ati) Aug(usti)

RIB 644+*add.*

'To the goddess Fortune (from) Sosia Juncina, wife of Quintus Antonius Isauricus, legate of the Emperor.'

[5] MacMullen 1963, 1 and 152.

[6] *conubium cum uxoribus quas tunc habuissent*. For this privilege and the marriage ban, see Campbell 1984, 301–3, 439–45.

[7] *Digest* 29.1.21; *P. Abinnaeus* 2 (dated AD 344), concluding with *propriis attende utilitatibus*. Despite this letter, which the editors describe as 'peremptory', the recipient achieved his reinstatement by the Emperor after an interval (ibid., 11–12).

In York, as in Chester and Caerleon, there was no need to spell out the legate's command; for Isauricus it was the Sixth Legion. He was suffect consul in AD 140, as Paul Holder has shown by meticulous examination of the fragment of a military diploma recently found at Healam Bridge in North Yorkshire, so he would have been at York in the mid-AD 130s.[8] He and his wife were the only persons of senatorial rank in the whole city, approached only by Isauricus' deputy, the legion's 'senatorial' tribune (*tribunus laticlavius*), who would soon be entering the Senate. Exceptionally an equestrian officer like Antistius Rusticus (**3.01**) or Caristanius Fronto (**3.17**) might be promoted in mid-career to senatorial rank, the moment of imperial favour caught by the Benwell altar (**7.07**) which marks the dedicator's decoration with 'the broad stripe' (*latus clavus*). But although this promotion in mid-career was comparatively uncommon, senators and equestrians were not separate castes. They were closely linked, as implied by two other inscriptions from the northern frontier. The first is an altar:

<**9.03**> *High Rochester (Bremenium)*

Silvano
[Pa]ntheo
[p]ro sa[lute]
[Ru]fin[i] trib(uni) et
[L]ucillae (uxoris) eius
Eutychus
lib(ertus) c(um) s(uis)
v(otum) s(olvit) l(ibens) m(erito)

RIB 1271

'To Silvanus Pantheus for the welfare of Rufinus, the tribune, and Lucilla his wife. Eutychus his freedman, with his household, paid his vow willingly, deservedly.'

'Pantheus', literally 'all-god' in Greek, is the title of various gods regarded as 'universal'; it was applied to Victory, for example, by the long-lived centurion Maximius Gaetulicus (**6.37**). After Caracalla withdrew from Scotland to Hadrian's Wall, High Rochester became its furthest outpost-fort, a finger-tip of Empire pointing to the Cheviot. In these boundless moorlands, Silvanus was a god to be conciliated: his name identifies him as the god of 'woodland' (*silva*) in its widest sense, like the medieval 'forest' or hunting-tract, which is why he also attracted dedications from huntsmen.[9] But Eutychus' altar is quite domestic: he refers to his patron and his aristocratic

[8] *RMD* VII, forthcoming. See also Birley 2005, 250–51.

[9] **12.39** (Stanhope), **12.40**, **12.41** and *RIB* III, 3251 (Bowes). *RIB* 1905 is dedicated to Silvanus by the *venatores Banniess(es)*, the 'huntsmen of Banna' (Birdoswald).

wife by their cognomina alone, suppressing the nomen of Rufinus, although he bore it himself after his master manumitted him and made him a Roman citizen. Innocently he also implies that he had contracted with Silvanus for the welfare of his patrons; but the god's power was not universal after all:

<**9.04**> *High Rochester (Bremenium)*

[*four lines lost*]
[..] coh(ortis) I Vardul(lorum) [...]
[... praef(ecto)] coh(ortis) I Aug(ustae)
Lusitanor(um) item coh(ortis) I
Breucor(um), subcur(atori) viae
Flaminiae et aliment(orum),
subcur(atori) operum publ(icorum),
Iulia Lucilla c(larissima) f(emina) marito
b(ene) m(erenti). vix(it) an(nis) XLVIII
m(enses) VI d(ies) XXV

RIB 1288

'... of the First Cohort of Vardulli ... prefect of the First Cohort *Augusta* of Lusitani, also of the First Cohort of Breuci, sub-curator of the Via Flaminia and the *alimenta*, sub-curator of Public Works, Julia Lucilla, lady of senatorial rank, for her well-deserving husband. He lived 48 years, 6 months, 25 days.'

When this tombstone was ploughed up in 1809, the first four lines flaked away, leaving their impression in the clay, but (in Eric Birley's words) 'there was no epigraphist in attendance to recover the reading'.[10] It is obviously the epitaph of Lucilla's husband, the tribune Rufinus, even though his full name has been lost. He enjoyed an interesting mix of military and civil appointments: first he commanded a cohort in Egypt, then a cohort in Mauretania Caesariensis (western Algeria), before becoming chief of office staff to two senatorial administrators at Rome, first the Curator in charge of the Via Flaminia (the principal road linking Rome with north Italy) and the charitable endowments which supported local children, and then the Curator responsible for public buildings including temples at Rome. After this unusual interlude, he returned to an equestrian military career by commanding a double-strength (milliary) cohort in Britain, a post equivalent to a legionary tribunate; and if he had only survived Britain, he might have next commanded a cavalry *ala* before becoming an imperial procurator like Pertinax (**7.02**).

This epitaph, which is poorly inscribed but more informative than most, runs counter to three modern misconceptions. Rufinus was an equestrian careerist who married a senator's daughter. All senators pursued a public career, and so did some

[10] Birley 1961, 130–32.

equestrians; but although their careers differed in status, senators and equestrians intermarried and there was no 'class war' between them; they all belonged to the very small landowning élite. When the senatorial historian Tacitus reports public dismay that the emperor Tiberius' granddaughter should marry the grandson of an equestrian, he is being disingenuous; Tacitus' own father, like his wife's two grandfathers, was an equestrian.[11] The next misconception is the Empire's 'immoderate greatness', as Gibbon called it, a loaded phrase since it implies that the Empire was too big for its primitive structure. This is true, of course, since it was a pre-industrial State whose land-communications at least were slow and worked only by muscle-power; but the wide experience of the ruling élite, and the informal links between the periphery and the centre, mitigated such weaknesses. Rufinus, for example, an imperial 'district officer' in the far north, knew Mauretania and Egypt at first-hand, and even Rome itself, where he had recently worked for senators who themselves had governed provinces. The third misconception is that auxiliary units in the Roman army were commanded by amateurs, inexperienced young men: Rufinus, to labour the point, was a mature man of varied experience.[12]

Equestrian officers thinking of home

Since equestrian officers like Rufinus held short-term commissions of about three or four years, their province was a tour of duty, not 'home'. Four altars in Britain are dedicated to Fortune 'the Home-bringer', one by the homesick servants in Chester (**4.10**), one by the military engineer Eltaominus (**5.36**), and the other two by equestrian officers:

<9.05> *Risingham (Habitancum)*

Fortunae Reduc[i]
Iulius Severinus
trib(unus), explicito
balineo, v(otum) s(olvit) l(ibens) m(erito)

RIB 1212

'To Fortune the Home-bringer Julius Severinus, tribune, willingly and deservedly paid his vow, on completion of the bath-house.'

This was appropriately found in the bath-house, and may even imply that bathing was good for homesickness, just as St Augustine, when his mother died, was told that bathing would ease the pain of bereavement.[13] A like association of ideas is

11 *Annals* vi 27; compare *Agricola* 4.1.

12 See further E Birley 1988, 147–64, 'The equestrian officers of the Roman army'.

13 *Confessions* ix 12 (32); *balineum*, by a false etymology from the Greek, was thought to 'expel pain'.

found in the poem inscribed on stone by the centurion commanding a detachment of the Third Legion Augusta at the oasis fort of Gholaia (Bu Njem in Libya), to celebrate its new bath-house. Despite the strain of writing an acrostic poem whose initial letters would spell out his own name – Q AVIDIVS QVINTIANVS – he conveys his meaning: since he shared his men's hopes of returning home (*reditus*), he had decided to address himself to Health (*salus*). 'To the best of my ability, I have honoured her name, and I have given everyone the true Waters of Health in this heat, that in these everlasting hills of sand they may relax by swimming peacefully under the scorching heat of the southern sun.'[14]

The altar at Chester (**4.10**) also linked Health with Fortune the Home-bringer. The fourth altar is dedicated by another African officer who, while he honoured Rome and his current posting, also looked homeward:

<**9.06**> *Maryport (Alauna)*

genio loci
Fortun(ae) Reduci
Romae Aetern(ae)
et Fato Bono
G(aius) Cornelius
Peregrinus
trib(unus) cohor(tis)
ex provincia
Maur(etania) Caesa(riensi)
domo Sald[i]s
d[e]c(urio), v(otum) s(olvit) l(aetus) l(ibens) m(erito)

On the back: Volanti vivas

RIB 812+*add.*

'To the Genius of the Place, to Fortune the Home-bringer, to Eternal Rome, and to Good Fate; Gaius Cornelius Peregrinus, tribune of the cohort, from the province of Mauretania Caesariensis, his home Saldae (where he is) a town-councillor; he has paid his vow, gladly, willingly, deservedly.'

'Long may you live, Volantius.'

The combination of Eternal Rome and Fortune the Home-Bringer also occurs on a votive pillar at Maryport, but the dedicator is not named.[15] Peregrinus here is

[14] *IRT* 918, with *AE* 1976, 698. *Qua potui sanxi nomen | et cunctis dedi | veras salutis lymphas | tantis ignibus | in istis semper ha|renacis collibus | nutantis Austri solis | flammas fervidas | tranquille ut nando | delenirent corpora.* The detachment 'returned' on 26 December 205. Quintianus was succeeded by another military poet, Porcius Iasucthanus (*AE* 1995, 164, cited before **13.12**).

[15] *RIB* 840, *Romae | Aeternae | et | Fortunae Reduci.*

hedging his bets: a compliment to his place of service, but also a plea for his safe return to Saldae, where he would become a high-ranking civilian once more. Saldae (now Béjaia in Algeria) was on the sea like Maryport; it was a *colonia* founded by Augustus for legionary veterans, so one of their descendants would naturally identify with Eternal Rome; it also bungled its water-supply in the mid-second century.[16] Peregrinus does not name his cohort, and is otherwise unknown, so we cannot date him closely; but he bears a *signum*, the unique name *Volantius*, which is a second cognomen somewhat like a nickname, often formed (as here) by adding *-ius* to the stem of a present participle (*volans*, 'flying'). This type of formation, and the use of a *signum*, are fashions almost unknown until the early third century, which is the likely date of this altar, especially since Peregrinus includes his praenomen *Gaius*, and the carving is rich and accomplished. The sacrificial gear of poleaxe and knife is carved in high relief on the back, and dish (*patera*) and jug on the left-hand side; in front the inscription is framed by two fluted columns supporting an arch, supporting two pine cones(?) and surmounted by no fewer than six bolsters enclosing three curious little heads. Quite a visual catalogue, and it is tempting to fall back on Harold Nicolson's description of a social climber's dining-room: 'baroque and rococo and what-ho and oh-no-no and all that. Very fine indeed.'[17]

This splendid confection embodies the home thoughts from abroad of an equestrian officer. Here is another, but after he was safely home:

<9.07> *Travi, near Piacenza*

M(inervae) M(emori)
L(ucius) Naevius
Verus
Roscianus
praef(ectus) coh(ortis) II
Gall(orum) eq(uitatae)
votum ex
Britannia
rettulit
l(ibens) m(erito)

ILS 2603, with *AE* 1989, 318

'To Minerva the Remembrancer; Lucius Naevius Verus Roscianus, prefect of the Second Cohort of Gauls, part-mounted, brought back (this) vow from Britain, willingly, deservedly.'

Minerva 'Memor' or 'Medica' (she used both epithets) was a healing goddess at Travi, as we know from other inscriptions, for example a woman's gratitude at

[16] *ILS* 5795, summarised in the note to **5.38**.
[17] Nicolson 1966, 244, letter 19 February 1936.

'having had her hair restored to her', or a man's dedication of 'silver ears' to mark his recovered hearing.[18] Roscianus inscribed his own text on stone or marble, now lost, and we do not know if his 'vow' or 'votive' was abstract or concrete; he may have actually brought a small altar with him from Britain like the merchant who sailed from York to Bordeaux with **11.39** in his luggage, or have dedicated a plinth for the gift he was bringing to the goddess. In her own interest she would then ensure that both donor and gift arrived safely. An attractive guess is that he had visited the British healing shrine of Minerva – Sulis to the natives – at Bath, where he might have bought a souvenir. Since the inscription cannot be dated, we cannot be sure where Roscianus was stationed, but Old Penrith is likely; his cohort was already there in AD 178, and remained there during the third century.[19] We know from other inscriptions that his family, the Naevii, were landowners at Travi, and it is possible that Naevius Hilarus, who commanded the Fourth Cohort of Gauls at Vindolanda, was a kinsman.[20]

Equestrian officers and their families

Equestrian officers brought their immediate families with them; there is the touching evidence of children's shoes at Vindolanda, not to mention the famous letter of Claudia Severa, one prefect's wife writing to another, which concludes with a greeting from her husband and little son.[21] Two equestrian officers associated their sons with them in formal dedications:

<**9.08**> *Chester (Deva)*

pro sal(ute) domin-
[oru]m n(ostrorum) invi-
ct[i]ssimorum
Aug(ustorum) genio loci
Fl[a]vius Long[us]
trib(unus) mil(itum) leg(ionis) XX [V(aleriae) V(ictricis)]
[et] Longinus fil(ius)
eius domo Samosata
v(otum) s(olverunt)

RIB 450+*add.*

'For the welfare of Our Lords the most unconquered Augusti, to the Genius of the place;

[18] *ILS* 3135 (*Memori … restitutione facta capillorum*), 3136 (*aures argenteas*), 3137 (*Medicae*).
[19] **7.10**, undated but dedicated by the prefect T. Domitius Heron, who can be identified with Domitius Hiero, prefect of the cohort in *RMD* iv 193 (23 March AD 178). *RIB* 915 (AD 244/9), 916, 929 (AD 222/35).
[20] *RIB* 2062. Devijver notes Q. Naevius Q.f. Hilarus (*CIL* vi 22833) and Naevia Hilara (vi 37481).
[21] R Birley 2009, 87. **4.19**, 9–10, *Aelius meus et filiolus*.

> Flavius Longus, military tribune of the Twentieth Legion Valeria Victrix, and Longinus his son, their home Samosata, paid their vow.'

This altar, like that of Cornelius Peregrinus (**9.06**), is richly carved in high relief: the Genius stands on the right side, on the left is a vase full of acanthus leaves, and on the back a drapery enclosing fruit. It has been dated on stylistic grounds to the Severan period, which accords with the fulsome dedication, one first addressed to Severus and his sons.[22] The superlative *invictissimus* ('most unconquered') may be over the top, but it was applied to many third- and fourth-century Emperors, even though Commodus, who first assumed the title of *invictus* ('unconquered') and used it to re-name the month of February after himself, had been content – like Hercules and the Sun – with only the positive form, *invictus*. Flavius Longus, the dedicator, came from the Empire's eastern frontier where Samosata commanded an important crossing of the Euphrates; it had been the capital of Commagene until this kingdom was annexed to Syria in AD 72, after which it gained the title *Flavia* and became a legionary fortress. The immense stratigraphy of this ancient city has formed a mound-like tell, but tragically it was hardly investigated before it was drowned in the waters of the Atatürk Dam.

The other altar is less elaborate:

<9.09> *Old Carlisle (?Maglona)*

deae Bel-
lonae Rufi-
nus prae[f(ectus)]
eq(uitum) a[l]ae Aug(ustae)
et Latinia-
nus fil(ius)

RIB 890+*add.*

> 'To the goddess Bellona; Rufinus, cavalry prefect of the Ala Augusta, and his son Latinianus.'

Bellona was the goddess of war (*bellum*). A dedication at Old Carlisle (**13.15**) gives the regiment its full title, the *ala Augusta ob virtutem appellata* which previously figured at Lancaster and Chesters.[23] The well-drawn but rather

---

[22] *CSIR* i.9, No. 7. See *AE* 1944, 74 (Dacia), *pro salute d(ominorum) n(ostrorum) invictissimor(um) imp(eratorum)*, naming Septimius Severus, Caracalla and Geta as *Augusti*, but dated by consuls to AD 204. For similar dedications to Caracalla and Geta during their brief joint-reign, see *AE* 1982, 958 (Timgad); 1914, 217 (Latium/Campania).

[23] **4.01** (Lancaster) and **5.03** (Chesters).

elongated letters suggest this altar is Antonine, but earlièr than others which also locate the regiment at Old Carlisle, in AD 188 and 191.[24] Rufinus, like Longus, names his son, but other officers content themselves with a formula:

<**9.10**> *York (Eboracum)*

I(ovi) O(ptimo) M(aximo)
dis deabusque
Hospitalibus Pe-
natibusq(ue) ob con-
servatam salutem
suam suorumq(ue)
P(ublius) Ael(ius) Marcian-
us praef(ectus) coh(ortis)
aram sac(ram) et aug(ustam) de(dicavit)

RIB 649+*add.* with *Britannia* 43 (2012), 419–20

'To Jupiter Best and Greatest, to the gods and goddesses of Hospitality, to the Household Gods, for having preserved the health of himself and his family; Publius Aelius Marcianus, prefect of a cohort, dedicated this sacred and august altar.'

There is a sense of relief here: so far so good. It is most unusual for a prefect not to name his cohort unless its identity was obvious, for example by being stationed where the dedication was made, so perhaps Marcianus in York (outside the legionary fortress) was no longer in post, but on his way home; still conscious of his rank, however. The altar was given to Oxford University in 1683, but for more than a century it stood outside the Sheldonian Theatre, where acid rain and frost have reduced the magnesian limestone to something resembling a dirty snowdrift. For the missing text we depend on two independent seventeenth-century witnesses, which means that we cannot be quite sure of the unusual last line.[25] Another prefect's altar is unusual in being dated:

<**9.11**> *Housesteads (Vercovicium)*

I(ovi) O(ptimo) M(aximo)
pro salute
Desidieni Ae-
[mi]liani praef-
[ecti] et sua su[or]-
[u]m posuit vot-
[um]q(ue) solvit libe-
ns, Tusco et Bas-
so co[(n)s(ulibus)]

---

24 *RIB* 893, 894.

25 *Britannia* 43 (2012), 419–20.

RIB 1589+*add.*

'To Jupiter Best and Greatest, for the welfare of the prefect Desidienus Aemilianus, both of himself and of his (family); he set this up and paid his vow willingly, in the consulship of Tuscus and Bassus (AD 258).'

The prefect's name is probably Etruscan, but so rare that he may have belonged to a family of that name settled at Salonae, near modern Split in Croatia. Syntactically the subject of the verbs *posuit* and *solvit* must be supplied, but obviously it is the man himself, acting on his own behalf and that of his family.[26] By coincidence the year is that of a tombstone in Dorset, which itself is almost unique in being dated.[27] The evidence of equestrian officers' families is often sombre:

<**9.12**> *Birdoswald (Banna)*

D(is) M(anibus)
Aureli
Concor-
di vixit
ann(um) un-
um d(ies) V
fil(ius) Aurel(i)
Iuliani
trib(uni)

RIB 1919+*add.*

'To the Shades of the Dead (and) of Aurelius Concordius: he lived 1 year, 5 days, the son of Aurelius Julianus the tribune.'

The father is also known from **8.06** which records the building of a granary in the governorship of Alfenus Senecio (AD 205/8). Despite his son being an infant, he does not name the mother: had she died too, or was she not really his wife, or was he simply short of space on this rather crude slab? Another tribune is also reticent, but then, he was not necessarily married:

<**9.13**> *Old Penrith (Voreda)*

D(is) M(anibus)
Ylae alum-
ni karis-
simi vixi[t]
an(nos) XIII Cl(audius) Se-
verus trib(unus)
milit(um)

[26] Birley 1979, 69–70. For the formulation, compare **12.28** (Carrawburgh), dedicated by a prefect 'for himself and his (family)' (*pro se et suis*).

[27] *RIB* III, 3045; the only other dated British tombstone is *RIB* 1255 (AD 278).

RIB 937

'To the Shades of the Dead (and) of Ylas, his dearest foster-son, aged 13: Claudius Severus, military tribune, (set this up).'

Severus is a tribune, although Old Penrith normally housed a quingenary cohort commanded by a prefect (**12.47**); he may have been specially promoted like Caecilius Donatianus (**12.86**), or possibly a legionary officer commanding the legionary detachment attested there once.[28] A third tribune, however, was certainly married, and in command of an auxiliary cohort of milliary strength:

<9.14> *Chesters (Cilurnum)*

D(is) M(anibus) s(acrum)
Fabi<a>e Honor-
at<a>e Fabius Hon-
oratus tribun(us)
coh(ortis) I Vangion(um)
et Aurelia E[g]lec-
tiane fecer-
unt fili<a>e d-
ulcissim<a>e

RIB 1482

'Sacred to the Shades of the Dead (and) of Fabia Honorata. Fabius Honoratus, tribune of the First Cohort of Vangiones, and Aurelia Eglectiane made this for their sweetest daughter.'

The genitive or dative case-ending *-ae* is written *-e* throughout (the pronunciation was identical); this 'Vulgarism' has no social significance, but simply reflects the spoken language. This altar-like tombstone cannot be dated, but the nomen *Aurelia* for the wife and the absence of a praenomen for the husband suggest that it is later than the mid-second century, and is probably third-century. His name strongly suggests that he came from Africa.[29] There is no evidence that his cohort ever garrisoned Chesters, which was a cavalry fort, and in the third century it certainly garrisoned Risingham. We may conjecture, therefore, that Honorata was visiting the cavalry

[28] *RIB* 940 (fragmentary, and lost).

[29] Devijver, *PME* F 7, citing Jarrett and Kajanto. The formula D M S is also rare in Britain, but typically African. The question remains open whether he is also the Honoratus *trib(unus)* who buried his foster-son Hermagoras at High Rochester (*RIB* 1291); no wife is named (had he lost her too?), but the stone is broken here.

prefect's family at nearby Chesters (compare **4.19**, the Vindolanda letter of invitation from one prefect's wife to another), or that her parents chose to bury her in the mild and beautiful Tyne valley south of the Wall, instead of in the bleak uplands of Redesdale. Here Risingham stands at the confluence of the Chesterhope Burn with the river Rede, itself a tributary of the North Tyne which flows past Chesters. At the headwaters of the Burn, the fort's water-supply, it was probably the girl's mother who erected this crude altar:

<9.15> *Risingham (Habitancum)*

somnio prae-
monitus
miles hanc
ponere ius-
sit |
aram quae
Fabio nup-
ta est Nym-
phis vene-
randis

RIB 1228+*add.*

'Forewarned by a dream the soldier told the wife of Fabius to set up this altar to the Nymphs who are to be worshipped.'

The text is metrical, two hexameters; hence the space in line 5 after *sit*, to mark the first line-ending. But no Classical poet would have admitted *somnio* as a dactyl, or have scanned *miles* as a spondee, or have ended a line with *venerandis*. The 'soldier' and 'the wife of Fabius' are unnamed, which implies that their names were also difficult to scan. But why should a visionary soldier tell someone else's wife to erect an altar? There is an economical and appealing answer. The nomen *Fabius* is quite common, notably in Africa, but there are only two other instances in Britain. One is a legionary officer at Croy Hill[30], the other is Fabius Honoratus, who was almost certainly the commanding officer here at Risingham. His wife, Aurelia Eglectiane (**9.14**), bears a name which is metrically impossible. She is surely the 'wife of Fabius' who wrote this poem at his suggestion; by honouring the spring that made life possible in this austere and remote place, she was anticipating the realism of another woman poet, Harold Nicolson's wife Vita Sackville-West, when she was translated from Sevenoaks to the Zagros range in south-west Persia: 'Lose yourself in the mountains of Asia, and you will find that a spring or a stream is a more urgent necessity than ideal scenery.'[31]

[30] *RIB* 2160.

[31] Sackville-West 1928, 37.

Centurions and their families (i): pre-Severan

Favonius Facilis (**2.01**) was buried at Colchester by his freedmen, like another centurion at Chester[32], but the centurion at Vindolanda who was 'killed in the war' was commemorated by his son (**5.01**). This was probably soon after Hadrian's accession (AD 117), so he is the first centurion serving in Britain who is known to have started a family, long before this natural impulse was formally recognised by Septimius Severus. But four others can be identified, the first two because they were serving at forts abandoned before Severus' accession (AD 193). This altar comes from the Antonine Wall:

<**9.16**> *Westerwood*

Silvanis [et]
Quadr(i)v(i)is Ca[e]-
lestib(us) sacr(um)
Vibia Pacata
Fl(avi) Verecu[nd]i (uxor)]
(centurionis) leg(ionis) VI Vic(tricis)
cum suis
v(otum) s(olvit) l(ibens) m(erito)

RIB III, 3504

'Sacred to the celestial Silvanae and Quadriviae. Vibia Pacata, wife of Flavius Verecundus, centurion of the Sixth Legion Victrix, with her family paid her vow willingly, deservedly.'

They are 'the most northerly known married couple in the Roman Empire'.[33] As a legionary centurion at a Wall fort, Verecundus was probably the acting-commander (*praepositus*) of an auxiliary garrison. Eric Birley used this altar to suggest a Severan re-occupation of the Wall, which archaeology now denies, but his note is a model of how to illuminate one inscription from others.[34] These goddesses, of 'woodland' (*silva*) and the 'four-ways' or crossroads, were typically worshipped in Upper Pannonia; this encourages us to identify the centurion, despite his commonplace name, with the centurion Titus Flavius Verecundus from Savaria in Upper Pannonia, who dedicated an altar to Mithras at Carnuntum, where his legion (the Fourteenth Gemina) was based. But the Westerwood altar calls these Danubian goddesses 'celestial', a broad hint at Caelestis, the goddess who succeeded Tanit in Roman Carthage (**12.85**),

---

[32] *RIB* 509.
[33] Keppie 2009, 1137; unless Julia Domna accompanied Septimius Severus beyond the Wall (compare Dio 76(77).16.5).
[34] E Birley 1988, 234–6.

and thus at the origin of the dedicator herself: the name *Pacata* is popular in Africa. So it looks as if the Pannonian Verecundus served in Africa as well as Britain, and gained a wife there. Tactfully, she accommodated her own religious allegiance to her husband's.

The second centurion was buried at Birrens, which became an outpost-fort after the Antonine Wall was abandoned, but where occupation does not seem to have lasted beyond the reign of Commodus:

<**9.17**> *Birrens (Blatobulgium)*

D(is) M(anibus)
Afutiano
Bassi (filio) or-
dinato
coh(ortis) II Tung(rorum)
Flavia Baeti-
ca coniunx
fac(iendum) curavit

RIB 2115

'To the Shades of the Dead (and) to Afutianus, son of Bassus, centurion of the Second Cohort of Tungrians; Flavia Baetica his wife had this set up.'

Ordinatus (from *ordo*, meaning 'rank') is sometimes applied to auxiliary centurions in the second century; a good example is the altar dedicated by the *ordinati* of the First Cohort of Vardulli, which garrisoned Lanchester from *c.* AD 160.[35] The term becomes frequent in third-century texts, for example the Dura papyri from AD 219; and in contemporary Britain it is applied to centurions in the legionary detachment from Upper Germany based at Piercebridge in AD 217, who incidentally brought their families with them.[36]

The Pannonian Verecundus found his wife in Africa and brought her to Britain; by contrast a third centurion found his wife in Britain, but died in Africa, where she and their sons commemorated him:

[35] *RIB* 1076 with Bidwell and Hodgson 2009, 155. The unit is attested there in *c.* AD 172/4 (*RIB* 1083), but was transferred to High Rochester, where it is attested in *c.* AD 213 (*RIB* 1272, etc.).

[36] One *ordinatus* is buried by his wife (*RIB* 1026), and another dedicates an altar dated AD 217 'for himself and his household' (**12.83**); compare *RIB* III, 3258, a staff officer (*beneficiarius tribuni*) from Upper Germany, also buried at Piercebridge by his wife.

<9.18> *Lambaesis in Numidia (eastern Algeria)*

D(is) M(anibus)
T(itus) Fl(avius) Virilis (centurio) leg(ionis) II Aug(ustae)
(centurio) leg(ionis) XX V(aleriae) V(ictricis) (centurio) leg(ionis) VI Vic(tricis)
(centurio) leg(ionis) XX V(aleriae) V(ictricis)
(centurio) leg(ionis) III Aug(ustae)
(centurio) leg(ionis) III Parth(icae) Sever(ianae)
VIIII hast(atus) poster(ior)
vixit annis LXX
stip(endiorum) XXXXV Lollia
Bodicca coniux
et Flavi Victor et
Victorinus fili
heredes ex HS
I(mille)CC n(ummis) faciendum curaver(unt)

ILS 2653

'To the Shades of the Dead. Titus Flavius Virilis, centurion of the Second Legion Augusta, centurion of the Twentieth Legion Valeria Victrix, centurion of the Sixth Legion Victrix, centurion of the Twentieth Legion Valeria Victrix, centurion of the the Third Legion Augusta, centurion of the Third Legion Parthica Severiana, sixth centurion of the Ninth Cohort; lived 70 years after 45 years of service; Lollia Bodicca his wife and Flavius Victor and Flavius Victorinus his sons saw to the erection (of this) at a cost of 1,200 sesterces.'

Virilis served in all three British legions, including twice in the Twentieth, before he was transferred to the African legion. His wife's name marks her as British: *Bodicca* is a variant of *Boudica*, famously borne by the Queen of the Iceni, which appropriately means 'victory' in Celtic; Bodicca and her husband knew this, since they called their sons *Victor* and *Victorinus*.[37] Her nomen *Lollius* suggests that her father or grandfather was enfranchised by Lollius Urbicus, the builder of the Antonine Wall. The epitaph can be dated by the title *Severiana* which usually marks the reign of Severus Alexander (AD 222–35), but is occasionally borne by Septimius Severus' three new *Parthica* legions during his reign. Eric Birley justly suggested that Virilis was drafted to this legion when it was created (in *c.* AD 197) in a training capacity. We do not know whether he served in the ranks in Britain before becoming a centurion, nor why he chose to retire to Africa rather than Britain, but simple arithmetic shows that he married and fathered his sons before the accession of Severus.[38] This can also be deduced of the fourth centurion, Petronius Fortunatus, from the text he inscribed on his own mausoleum:

[37] Other variants are Bodicacia at Cirencester (*Britannia* 46 (2015), 384, No. 3) and Bodiccius, *imaginifer* of Coh(ors) I Brit(tonum *or* -taniciana) at Acumincum (*CIL* iii 3256).
[38] E Birley 1988, 209–10.

<**9.19**> *Kasserine, Tunisia (Cillium)*

[...]
militavit L annis, IV in leg(ione) I Ita[lica]
librar(ius), tesser(arius), optio, signif(er), [7 = (centurio)]
factus ex suffragio leg(ionis) eiu[sdem]
militavit 7 leg(ionis) I Ital(icae), 7 leg(ionis) VI F[erratae],
7 leg(ionis) I Min(erviae), 7 leg(ionis) X Gem(inae), 7 leg(ionis) II A[di(utricis)],
7 leg(ionis) III Aug(ustae), 7 leg(ionis) II[I] Gall(icae), 7 leg(ionis) XXX U[l]p(iae),
7 leg(ionis) VI Vic(tricis), 7 leg(ionis) III Cyr(enaicae), 7 leg(ionis) XV Apol(linaris),
7 leg(ionis) II Par(thicae), 7 leg(ionis) I Adiutricis,
consecutus ob virtutem in
expeditionem Parthicam
coronam muralem vallarem
torques et phaleras, agit in
diem operis perfecti annos LXXX,
sibi et
Claudiae Marciae Capitolinae
koniugi karissimae, quae agit
in diem operis perfecti
annos LXV; et
M(arco) Petronio Fortunato filio,
militavit ann(is) VI, 7 leg(ionis) X[X]II Primig(eniae),
7 leg(ionis) II Aug(ustae), vixit ann(is) XXXV
cui Fortunatus et Marcia parentes
karissimo memoriam fecerunt

ILS 2658+*add.*

'... served 50 years, 4 in the First Legion Italica as *librarius*, *tesserarius*, *optio*, *signifer*, made centurion by vote of the said legion; served as centurion of the First Legion Italica, and of the Sixth Legion Ferrata, the First Legion Minervia, the Tenth Legion Gemina, the Second Legion Adiutrix, the Third Legion Augusta, the Third Legion Gallica, the Thirtieth Legion Ulpia, the Sixth Legion Victrix, the Third Legion Cyrenaica, the Fifteenth Legion Apollinaris, the Second Legion Parthica, the First Legion Adiutrix; awarded the Mural Crown, the Rampart Crown, Torques and Arm-bands, for his valour in the Parthian campaign; aged 80 the day this work was finished. For himself and his dearest wife, Claudia Marcia Capitolina, aged 65 the day this work was finished; and for his son Marcus Petronius Fortunatus, who served six years, centurion of the Twenty-Second Legion Primigenia, centurion of the Second Legion Augusta, aged 35; for whom his parents Fortunatus and Marcia erected this monument to their dearest son.'

Both father and son had been centurions in Britain, the father in the Sixth Legion at York, his son in the Second Legion at Caerleon, although he may actually have died on active service. Skilful analysis of the father's career by Eric Birley, Val Maxfield and

Tony Birley, has outlined its chronology.[39] It was unusually long and geographically diverse, taking Fortunatus from the lower Danube (Legion I Italica) to Jerusalem (VI Ferrata), and then probably to the detachments of European legions which served in the Parthian campaign of Lucius Verus (AD 162–6). It is this campaign to which he refers, not that of Septimius Severus, to judge by the lavish scale of his decorations. From here he went to Africa (III Augusta), then back to Syria (III Gallica), followed by the lower Rhine (XXX Ulpia) and even Britain (VI Victrix), before returning to the eastern frontier, that is to Arabia (III Cyrenaica) and the upper Euphrates (XV Apollinaris). By now in his late 60s, he was transferred to Severus' new Second Legion Parthica (embodied *c.* AD 197), where like Virilis he may have been responsible for training recruits. Finally he served on the middle Danube with the First Legion Adiutrix. According to this chronology, he joined the First Legion Italica in the mid-AD 150s in his mid-20s, and retired 50 years later in his mid-70s. He implies that his son had died quite recently, which would place his birth (and his father's informal marriage) in the mid- AD 170s. It was a long career, although not as long as the 57 years of Maximius Gaetulicus (**6.37**).

Centurions and their families (ii): Severan and later

These centurions all fathered sons before the accession of Septimius Severus, but a somewhat later married centurion is known to us from his London tombstone, which for two centuries was the finest monument to a centurion ever found in Britain, until it was displaced by Favonius Facilis (**2.01**) in 1868. It was found on Ludgate Hill in 1669 when Christopher Wren was rebuilding St Martin's after the Great Fire, and he sent it to Oxford, where he was Professor of Astronomy, for it to stand with other classical trophies outside his new Sheldonian Theatre. The standing figure has now weathered, though less badly than the other Marcianus' ill-fated altar (**9.10**), and the centurial symbol in line 3 has broadened into what looked like a leaf-stop when it was drawn for *RIB*:

<**9.20**> *London (Londinium)*

D(is) M(anibus)
Vivio Marci-
ano (centurioni) leg(ionis) II
Aug(ustae), Ianuaria
Martina coniunx
pientissima posu-
it memoriam

[39] E Birley 1988, 208–9; Maxfield 1981, 198–9; A Birley 1988, 79, whose reading LEG II A[DI] is adopted here, together with his suggestion that Antistius Adventus, as legate of this legion, played an important part in Fortunatus' career.

RIB 17+*add.*

'To the Shades of the Dead (and) to Vivius Marcianus, centurion of the Second Legion Augusta; Januaria Martina his most devoted wife set up this memorial.'

Marcianus wears a wide military belt fastened by a ring-buckle, better evidence of third-century date than the wife who buried him.[40] He rests his right hand on the swagger-stick of his rank, like Favonius Facilis (**2.01**) at Colchester, but his left hand holds what looks like a papyrus roll, either his last will and testament or an office file, the real weapon of a military bureaucrat. Perhaps an office file, since a centurion in the provincial capital is likely to have been the governor's chief of office staff, his *princeps praetorii* like the African Saturninus (**10.28**). This imposing tombstone was finally brought under cover in the nineteenth century, but after three centuries of somewhat casual guardianship, Oxford transferred it to a more appropriate home, the Museum of London.

From Chester, more naïve in its execution, comes the standing figure of another married centurion:

<**9.21**> *Chester (Deva)*

D(is) M(anibus)
M(arcus) Aur(elius) Nepos (centurio) leg(ionis)
XX V(aleriae) V(ictricis) coniux
pientissima f(aciendum) c(uravit)
vix(it) annis L

(*on the side, below a mason's pick and square*)

sub
asci-
a d(edicatum)

RIB 491+*add.*

'To the Shades of the Dead. Marcus Aurelius Nepos, centurion of the Twentieth Legion Valeria Victrix. His most devoted wife had this made. He lived 50 years.'

'Dedicated under the mason's pick.'

Husband and wife stand side by side in their niche, but her reduced, dutiful figure is placed on a plinth to bring her up to his level. She holds a fan-like object, perhaps a weaving-comb; he rests his right hand on a swagger-stick like Marcianus (**9.20**), and likewise wears a third-century military belt fastened by a ring-buckle. Their

[40] His marriage is noted by *RIB*, but for the belt see Bishop and Coulston 2006, 182–3.

joint tombstone was dedicated 'under the *ascia*', a formality almost unknown in Britain, but which is typical of Gaul; it seems to have consecrated the monument at the moment of completion.[41] Aurelius Nepos (his name is colourless, except to suggest a third-century date) and his nameless wife were thus probably Gauls; he would have been transferred to the Twentieth from another legion. His wife and executor left a space for her own epitaph, but it was never filled; this would suggest there was no family, unless she remarried or left Chester for her native province. At York, however, we find a centurion who buried both his young wife and his son:

<9.22> *York (Eboracum)*

D(is) M(anibus)
et m{a}emoriae Iuliae Victorin<a>e
quae vixit annos XXVIIII menses II dies XV
et Constantio qui vixit annos IIII dies XXI
menses XI Septimius Lupianus (centurio) ex evoc(ato)
coniugi et f[i]lio memoriam pos{s}uit

RIB III, 3202

'To the Shades of the Dead and to the memory of Julia Victorina who lived 29 years, 2 months, 15 days; and to Constantius who lived 4 years, 21 days, 11 months. Septimius Lupianus, centurion and former *evocatus*, erected this memorial to his wife and son.'

Mother and son shared a large, handsome sarcophagus, with their joint-epitaph neatly inscribed on a peltate panel supported by a pair of Cupids. It was surely intended to be seen, but someone subsequently used it as a coffin underground to take the body of a man; hardly that of Lupianus. His nomen *Septimius* suggests that he, or his father, had been enfranchised early in the reign of Septimius Severus; as an *evocatus*

[41] The only other British example is *RIB* 204, which depicts an *ascia* between *D(is)* and *M(anibus)*. Compare **9.30** (Châlons-sur-Saône).

he was a praetorian guardsman who was retained after 16 years' service, and then promoted centurion. The Guard by this date was drawn largely from Danubian legionaries, many of them Thracians and new Roman citizens (compare **13.04**). The 'hyper-correct' spelling *maemoriae* (for Classical *memoriae*) illustrates the difficulty already seen in the epitaph of Honorata (**9.14**), that of distinguishing between [ae] and [e], since they both sounded the same. This sarcophagus was found only a few yards from another, much cruder in execution:

<**9.23**> *York (Eboracum)*

D(is) M(anibus)
Aur(elio) Supero cent(urioni)
leg(ionis) VI qui vixit an<n>is
XXXVIII m(ensibus) IIII d(iebus) XIII Aure-
lia Censorina co<n>iunx
memoriam pos{s}uit

RIB 670

'To the Shades of the Dead. To Aurelius Super, centurion of the Sixth Legion, who lived 38 years, 4 months, 13 days. His wife Aurelia Censorina erected this memorial.'

Like the previous epitaph, this concludes with the formula *memoriam possuit*, the double *s* of *possuit* (for Classical *posuit*) emphasising that the sound was a sibilant [s], not the aspirate [h] it was becoming in spoken Celtic. **12.45** is another instance. Once again, the exact age at death is recorded; this might imply a greater attention was now being paid to birthdays, but it is typical of 'late' epitaphs.

Finally, a third sarcophagus from York, eloquent of hope still-born:

<**9.24**> *York (Eboracum)*

D(is) M(anibus) Simpliciae Florentin<a>e
anim<a>e innocentissim<a>e
qu<a>e vixit menses decem
Felicius Simplex pater fecit
(centurio) leg(ionis) VI V(ictricis)

RIB 690+add.

'To the Shades of the Dead (and) of Simplicia Florentina, a most innocent soul, who lived ten months; Felicius Simplex her father made this, centurion of the Sixth Legion Victrix.'

The father's rank has been added in cruder letters, almost as an afterthought. He 'fabricated' his daughter's nomen *Simplicia* from his own cognomen, a practice typical of Britain and Gaul, from which we can deduce that his own father was called *Felix*.

The wistful phrase he applies to his daughter, although unique in Britain, is found in other epitaphs of the untimely dead, for example the Italian freedman Euhelpistus 'a most innocent soul, whom the doctors cut and killed', aged 27.[42] Simplicia is the youngest person to be commemorated in Roman Britain.

Other ranks and their families

Many tombstones refer to the wives and children of serving soldiers, but they are often difficult to date. When wives are named, *RIB* treats them as Severan or later, which is a good principle if used with caution. Caution is suggested by a handsome slab found in the seventeenth century, when a grave was being dug at a hill-top church four miles from Caerleon; it was found attached to the wall-footings, so perhaps this Norman church incorporates a Roman mausoleum:

<**9.25**> *Tredunnock, near Caerleon*

D(is) M(anibus) Iul(ius) Iulianus
mil(es) leg(ionis) II Aug(ustae) stip(endiorum)
XVIII annor(um) XL
hic situs est
cura<m> agente
Amanda
coniuge

RIB 360

'To the Shades of the Dead. Julius Julianus, soldier of the Second Legion Augusta, 18 years' service, aged 40, is buried here; the work supervised by Amanda his wife.'

The emphatic *coniuge* ('his wife') looks deliberate, for this tombstone is undoubtedly second-century, and probably Antonine. The simple ansate panel and the style of lettering resemble that of two other second-century tombstones from Caerleon, not to mention the stone tablet found in the Tyne at Newcastle (**6.28**), which is legionary work of *c.* AD 155; and it shares its unusual form of 'G' with the altar of Sosia Iuncina at York (**9.02**), legionary work of the AD 130s. Although it abbreviates *Dis Manibus*, it does not abbreviate the 'early' formula *hic situs est.*[43] To judge by its date, therefore, the concluding *coniuge* asserts that Amanda, although not a Roman citizen, is the dead man's wife in the eyes of God, if not of the Law.

This may be the earliest British stone to name the wife of a serving soldier, but an epitaph from Chester should also be considered:

42 *ILS* 9441 (near Rome), *anima innocentissima, quem medici secarunt et occiderunt.*

43 **3.07** and *RIB* III, 3098 (Caerleon), but more formal in their nomenclature. **6.28** (Newcastle) and **9.02** (York). The only other British example of *hic situs est* unabbreviated is *RIB* 932, which Eric Birley dated 'as soon as possible after A.D. 96'.

<9.26> *Chester (Deva)*

Cocce[iae]
Irene
coniugi
castis[s]im<a>e
[e]t sanctis-
[s]imae vix(it)
an(nos) XXX m(ensem)
G(aius) Val(erius) Iustus
actar[i]us
leg(ionis) XX p[os]uit

RIB 507+*add.*

'To Cocceia Irene, his most chaste and holy wife (who) lived 30 years and a month; Gaius Valerius Justus, *actarius* of the Twentieth Legion, set this up.'

It is most unusual for *Dis Manibus* and the legion's titles *Valeria Victrix* to be omitted, which would even suggest a date before the legion's arrival in the mid-AD 80s, were it not for the wife's name *Cocceia*, which indicates descent from (or manumission by) a citizen enfranchised in the brief reign of Nerva (AD 96–98). The plain, square lettering and the lack of ligatures both suit a second-century date, but they are not decisive. The *actarius* was a senior member of the legion's office staff, ranking next to the *cornicularius*. At Caerleon he even joined the *primus pilus* in celebrating the legion's birthday.[44] We know nothing of his regular duties, but since his title derives from the word *acta*, he was probably responsible for the legion's files and records. Not surprisingly, the two British altars dedicated by *actarii* (of auxiliary units) are dedicated to Minerva, the goddess of learning.[45] Also difficult to date is this tombstone from Caerleon:

<9.27> *Caerleon (Isca)*

D(is) M(anibus)
Aurelius Hercula-
nus {a}eques vixit an-
nos XXVIII coniux f-
aciendum curavi-
t

RIB 356

'To the Shades of the Dead. Aurelius Herculanus, horseman, lived 28 years; his wife had this made.'

[44] *RIB* 327.

[45] *RIB* 429 and 1101.

Aeques is a 'hyper-correction' of *eques*. The careful lettering and the non-abbreviation of *faciendum curavit* both suggest a second-century date, but the deceased is an 'Aurelius' (without praenomen), and thus likely to be the son or grandson of a veteran enfranchised by the Antonines. *faciendum curavit* is still unabbreviated in an epitaph of *c.* AD 217 from Piercebridge.[46] So Herculanus' epitaph can be accepted as Severan, but another from Caerleon is more complex:

<9.28> *Caerleon (Isca)*

D(is) M(anibus)
Tadia Vallaun[i]us vixit
ann(os) LXV et Tadius Exuper(a)tus
filius vixit ann(os) XXXVII defun<c>-
tus expeditione Germanica
Tadia Exuperata filia
ma[t]ri et fratri piiss<i>ma
secus tumulum
patris posuit

RIB 369

'To the Shades of the Dead. Tadia Vallaunius lived 65 years and Tadius Exuperatus her son lived 37 years; he died on the German expedition. Tadia Exuperata her daughter in duty to her mother and brother erected (this memorial) next to the grave of her father.'

The mother's cognomen, which is of Celtic derivation, is a rare instance of a feminine personal name in *-us*.[47] *RIB* dates this inscription to the second century, but with its wealth of ligatures it could well be early third-century. The 'German expedition' would then be Caracalla's in AD 213, dating this legionary's birth to AD 176. His sister does not name their father, but only because his much cruder tombstone was adjoining:

<9.29> *Caerleon (Isca)*

D(is) M(anibus)
Sanctinius
[E]xsuperatus
[...]

RIB III, 3099

'To the Shades of the Dead. Sanctinius Exsuperatus ...'

[46] *RIB* 1026.

[47] Two others are noted after **9.36**.

This stone was found in 1955, more than a century after its companion in *c.* 1849, and it was fifty years later still that the coincidence of name and place was spotted by Julie Reynolds, curator of the Roman Legionary Museum. Both stones were found in the civil settlement to the west of the legionary fortress, and the name *Exsuperatus* is quite rare; there is only one other instance in Britain.[48] The boy and girl were evidently given their father's cognomen, but not his nomen *Sanctinius*, itself 'fabricated' from his own father's cognomen *Sanctus*; instead they were given their mother's rare Italian nomen, this convention meaning that they were illegitimate.[49] Their father, as a serving soldier, could not contract a legal Roman marriage: in the mocking words of John Le Carré, this was a common-law marriage, unofficial but permanent. Since the man's tombstone is incomplete, we do not know whether he was still a serving soldier or a veteran when he died, nor what status his widow now claimed.

Another British legionary was on foreign service when he lost his wife, but the circumstances can only be conjectured:

<9.30> *Châlons-sur-Saône (Cavillonum)*

D(is) [M(anibus)]
et memoriae
aeternae Ve-
getiniae Ro-
manae, Mem-
mius Rusticus
miles leg(ionis) V[I]
Victricis An-
toninian(ae) con-
iugi innocentissi-
mae loco pere-
grino defunct(ae)
p(onendum) c(uravit) et sub ascia d(edicavit)

CIL xiii 2616

'To the Shades of the Dead and the eternal memory of Vegetinia Romana. Memmius Rusticus, soldier of the Sixth Legion Victrix Antoniniana, had this set up for his most innocent wife when she died in a foreign place, and dedicated it under the mason's pick.'

48 *RIB* II.8, 2503.256 (Vindolanda), again as *Exuperatus*, which was intended to 'correct' what was wrongly thought to be an intrusive [s].

49 Compare Mamercius Ianuarius, explicitly the natural son of Paccius Januarius and Mamercia Grapte, who bore his father's cognomen and his mother's nomen (*CIL* x 1138). The cognomen of Tadia Vallaunius is a rare instance of a Celtic femine name in *-us*, like that of Julia Belismicus, also of Caerleon (*RIB* 318).

This tombstone was built into the walls of Châlons, but is now lost. The only evidence of date is the title *Antoniniana* ('Antoninus' Own') borne by the York legion, referring to the reign of Caracalla (AD 211–7) or Elagabalus (AD 218–22). Memmius Rusticus' wife had accompanied him, but he gives no hint of where they were going, except that Châlons was *not* home. Châlons in the Saône valley was a major road-junction of routes leading down the Rhône valley to the Mediterranean: this would not suit Caracalla's German expedition, but perhaps Rusticus was on his way to Rome to serve as a *frumentarius* like Ulpius Quintus (**10.17**) of the same legion. The *sub ascia* formula, which is almost unknown in Britain (**9.21**), suggests that Rusticus did not compose the epitaph himself; it is typical of Gaul and especially Lugdunum (Lyon) just south of Châlons, where it often accompanies *D(is) M(anibus) et memoriae aeternae* as here.

Problems of date are less interesting than the rich glimpses of family life provided by military epitaphs:

<**9.31**> *Ribchester (Bremetennacum)*

his terris tegitur
Ael(ia) Matrona quond(am)
vix(it) an(nos) XXVIII m(enses) II d(ies) VIII
et M(arcus) Iul(ius) Maximus fil(ius)
vix(it) an(nos) VI m(enses) III d(ies) XX et Cam-
pania Dub[i]tata{e} mater
vix(it) an(nos) L Iul(ius) Maximus
s(ummus) c(urator) alae Sar(matarum) coniux
coniugi incomparabili
et filio patri p[i]entis-
simo et socaere(!) tena-
cissim<a>e memoria<m> p(osuit)

RIB 594+*add.*

'By this earth is covered the late Aelia Matrona; she lived 28 years, 2 months, 8 days. And Marcus Julius Maximus her son; he lived 6 years, 3 months, 20 days. And Campania Dubitata her mother; she lived 50 years. Julius Maximus, *summus curator* of the Cavalry Regiment of Sarmatians, as husband set up this monument to an incomparable wife, and to a son most devoted to his father, and to a most loyal mother-in-law.'

The original is lost, but it was transcribed for Camden, who assigned it to Ribchester, where another of his correspondents had reported a tombstone of the *ala Sarmatarum*.[50] In fact the copyist seems to have hesitated between ALAE SAR and ALAE SAB, so the better-known *ala Sabiniana* is a possibility. The *ala Sarmatarum* is

50 *RIB* 595.

thought to have been formed from the Sarmatian horsemen deported to Britain by Marcus Aurelius, but since the dedicator of this epitaph is a soldier who emphasises that he was married, it is probably Severan.[51] Maximus describes himself as S C, and since he belonged to a cavalry regiment (*ala*), he was probably its *summus curator*, the chief accountant.[52] His style is somewhat 'literary', with the metrical tag *his terris tegitur* (the first two and a half feet of a hexameter) and the jingle of *coniunx coniugi* and *filio patri*. His spelling exhibits the usual confusion between [ae] and [e], *socaere* being a 'hyper-correction' of *socerae*, the dative of *socera* which is the feminine form of *socer* ('father-in-law'); in Classical Latin *socrus*. Maximus evidently knew and remembered his wife's birthday – but not that of his mother-in-law.

There is certainly a Danubian echo in another epitaph from the north-west. The largest fragment was drawn in the late seventeenth century and is now lost, but two smaller fragments were identified by Ben Edwards. They came from the gable of a tomb with two niches:

<**9.32**> *Overborough (?Calacum)*

D(is)
M(anibus) s(acrum)
et perpetu<a>e sec-
uritati Aur(eli) Pus[i]-
nni ... [... vix(it)]
an(nos) LIIII mili[tavit an(nos)] XXXVI
Aur(eliae) Eubiae con[iugis] ei{i}us vix(it)
an(nos) XXXVII Aur(elius) Pr[o]p[inquus fi]l(ius) karissim(us)

RIB 612+*add.*

'Sacred to the Shades of the Dead and the Eternal Peace of Aurelius Pusinnus ... (who) lived 54 years, served as a soldier 36 years; and of Aurelia Eubia his wife, (who) lived 37 years. Aurelius Propinquus, their most beloved son, (set this up).'

Funerary busts would have stood in the niches. The name *Pusinnus* is Celtic, and well attested in other provinces; there are two instances in Britain of its feminine form *Pusinna*.[53] The formula *perpetuae securitati*, of which this is the only British example, is commonly found in the Danubian provinces. The name *Eubia* is Greek, which hints that she too was not a native of Britain. Since she was only 37, her son

[51] But earlier than the reign of Severus Alexander, when the *ala* had been reduced to a *numerus* (*RIB* 587).

[52] Davies 1976 argues that all five British instances of S C are *s(ingulares) c(onsularis)*, the governor's bodyguards on special assignment, but the other four do not name their unit, and are demonstrably in post (*statio*). A fifth is now attested by the Inveresk tombstone (*Britannia* 39 (2008), 372, No. 5), which does name the unit, but refers to the appointment as *ex n(umero) eq(uitum) sing(ularium)*.

[53] *RIB* 1667 (Cawfields) and1829 (Carvoran).

Propinquus cannot have been older than about 20', but he does not say whether he became a soldier like his father.

Finally, two of the most accomplished and opulent tombstones of Roman Britain, carved by a Palmyrene sculptor at South Shields, which both commemorate love between master and slave:

<**9.33**> *South Shields (?Lugudunum, later Arbeia)*

D(is) M(anibus)
Regina<m> liberta<m> et coniuge<m>
Barates Palmyrenus natione
Catuallauna<m> an(norum) XXX

RIB 1065+*add.*

'To the Shades of the Dead. Barates the Palmyrene (commemorates) Regina, his freedwoman and wife, by nationality a Catuvellaunian, aged 30.'

(*and in Palmyrene*) 'Regina, the freedwoman of Barate, alas.'

The odd case-endings in this epitaph have been convincingly explained by Jim Adams: they are all accusatives which have lost the (barely-sounded) final *-m*. The word *regina* means 'queen' in Latin, and is a title borne by goddesses,[54] but here it is prosaically the feminine of a common Celtic personal name. Nonetheless she sits regally in her high-backed chair, between a strong-box (its lock-plate is visible) and a basket full of balls of wool. She was the mistress of the household but, 'like the women of antiquity', she was skilled in woolwork.[55] As a Catuvellaunian (the usual spelling), a member of the tribe 'good in battle' (which is what the Celtic means), the tribe which principally resisted Caesar and the Claudian invasion, she would have been born near Verulamium (St Albans); but why was she a slave, apparently in the late second century? Perhaps she was abandoned by her parents, or was even the daughter of a slave who would have inherited her mother's status, no matter what the father was. The man who bought her – and who made her free, but not of course a Roman citizen – was an Arab from Palmyra (Tadmor), the great oasis city in eastern Syria.[56] He still

[54] *RIB* 125 with note (*dea regina*), 324 (*Salus*), 2122 (Diana).

[55] *sic priscae feminae*, in the words of Symmachus (*ep.* vi 67), thanking his daughter for 'a rich monument of (her) woolwork'. Augustus likewise wore homespun woven by his wife and the other women of his family (Suetonius, *Divus Aug.* 73).

[56] To which the poet of the first Pilgrimage (Raine 1849) likens Housesteads: 'On BORCOVICUS' walls we stand. | Hail, splendid Ruin – famous thou – | Great Tadmor of our native land!'

spoke his native language, and in his grief he commissioned a fellow-Palmyrene to carve this splendid tombstone; the style is distinctive, and the sculptor practised locally, to judge by the tombstone of Victor (**9.35**). Their native Palmyra had grown rich from international trade; there was even a moment in the AD 260s when it conquered most of the eastern Roman provinces. Perhaps Barates was a merchant like the Syrian Salmanes (**9.48**), but this is uncertain. By contrast with Regina, he was meanly buried:

<**9.34**> *Corbridge (Coria)*

[D(is)] M(anibus)
[Ba]rathes Pal-
morenus vexil<l>a(rius)
vixit an<n>os LXVIII

RIB 1171+*add.*

'To the Shades of the Dead. Barathes the Palmyrene, a *vexillarius*, lived 68 years.'

The different spelling of the name does not matter, since un-Latin [th] is often transliterated as [t]. The identification is not quite certain, since *Barathes* is a common Palmyrene name; but it cannot have been common in Britain, let alone the Tyne valley, and this would be why he is identified as 'the Palmyrene'. What then is a *vexillarius*? Something to do with a *vexillum*, a flag, which in the Roman army marked either a military detachment (*vexillatio*) whose members were each individually a *vexillarius*, or a cavalry troop (*turma*) whose flag was carried by the *vexillarius*. At Vindolanda, Tagamas or Tagomas is a well-attested example.[57] There was even a *vexillarius* in the Twentieth Cohort of Palmyrenes at Dura Europos who was called Aurelius Barathes, son of Abgar.[58] But our own Barathes is 68, much too old to be a serving soldier, and Eric Birley has suggested that he was a civilian flag-dealer (but filling a commercial niche so narrow that it is otherwise not attested); John Mann that he was a (rarely attested) 'flag-bearer' in a friendly society, a corporation of craftsmen. On balance it may be easier to suppose that Barathes was a sometime soldier, now a veteran, but that his jejune epitaph failed to make this explicit.

Regina, like Calpurnia Trifosa (**12.32**) at Bath, was 'freedwoman and wife'. This option was not yet available to the other couple at South Shields immortalised by the Palmyrene sculptor:

[57] *Tab. Vindol.* 181.14; 861.25 with note; *Britannia* 34 (2003), 377, No. 37.

[58] *RMR* 1, xxxvi.18.

<9.35> *South Shields (?Lugudunum, later Arbeia)*

D(is) M(anibus) Victoris natione Maurum
[a]nnorum XX libertus Numeriani
[e]q<u>itis ala<e> I Asturum qui
piantissime pr[ose]q<u>utus est

RIB 1064+*add.*

'To the Shades of the Dead (and) of Victor, by nationality a Moor, aged 20. (He was) freedman of Numerianus, trooper of the First Cavalry Regiment of Asturians, who most dutifully followed (his funeral).'

Victor is reclining, richly dressed, upon a couch in front of a tree symbolising paradise. A tiny slave offers him a cup of wine. The funerary banquet, like hunting for Flavius Quietus (**6.14**), symbolises life and the after-life enjoyed to the full. Numerianus' regiment, probably once commanded by Tineius Longus (**7.07**), was stationed at Benwell, on the high ground west of Newcastle. Why Victor was buried downstream at South Shields, we do not know; Jocelyn Toynbee, who has minutely described his tombstone and Regina's, conjectures that Numerianus had established him in business there.[59] The epitaph was cut by a different hand than Regina's, and the wayward syntax is much harder to explain. *Victoris* is genitive, as if the stone were dedicated to his *D(is) M(anibus)*, but his attributes are accusative (*Maurum*) and nominative (*libertus*). *ala*, which should be genitive, is also nominative. Only *piantissime* and *prosequtus* (for Classical *pientissime* and *prosecutus*) are typical 'Vulgarisms', but otherwise the writer is not at home with Latin: he knows the vocabulary, but not the case-endings.

Some veterans

We have already seen Cassius Secundus (**3.21**) at Carlisle, the legionary of the Twentieth who anticipated his next instalment of pay after surviving Mons Graupius in AD 83. His name is not distinctive, but this is probably his tombstone:

[59] Toynbee 1964, 199–200 (Victor); 206 (Regina). Also described as *CSIR* i.1, 247 and 248.

<**9.36**> *Chester (Deva)*

D(is) M(anibus)
Cassius Secun-
dus missus ho-
nesta missione
vix(it) an(nos) LXXX
[...]us con-
[iugi ...]

RIB 526, Chester (Deva)

'To the Shades of the Dead. Cassius Secundus, honourably discharged, lived 80 years. [...]us to her husband [...]'

Since *Dis Manibus* is abbreviated, the epitaph should be post-Trajanic, but it cannot be closely dated. The legion is not named, but by then at Chester it would have been the Twentieth. A veteran aged about 80 (the 'age-rounding' is obvious) would have enlisted about 60 years before, so this may well be Cassius Secundus of the Carlisle loan-note. If so, he survived Agricola's campaigns and returned with the legion to Chester, safe and (financially) sound. After discharge he married, and his widow's name apparently ends in *-us*: this is occasionally feminine, but almost always masculine, so she probably described herself as *[uxor ei]us* anonymously, simply 'his wife'.[60]

First-century veterans like Valerius Geminus (**2.03**) at Alchester tend to be buried by their comrades and heirs (mostly male), but here is one who left a widow. His cloaked figure, now headless, stands between the columns which once supported an arch or gable:

<**9.37**> *Templebrough, Yorks.*

Dis Manibus Croto Vindicis (filio) em-
erito coh(ortis) IIII Gallorum annorum
XXXX, monimentum fecit Flavia Pe-
regrina coniunx pientissima marito pientiss-
imo titulum posuit

RIB 620

'To the Shades of the Dead (and) to Crotus, (son) of Vindex, time-expired soldier of the Fourth Cohort of Gauls, aged 40. Flavia Peregrina, his most devoted wife, made this monument and set up this inscription to her most devoted husband.'

[60] Compare *RIB* 404, *coniunx eius*; 912, *co(n)iux eius*. But also note Iul(ia) Belismicus (*RIB* 318), Tadia Vallaunius (**9.28**) and Ael(ia) Comindus (*RIB* 1561), all women.

This cohort garrisoned Vindolanda in the third and fourth centuries, but the unabbreviated use of *Dis Manibus* dates Crotus' tombstone at Templebrough to the pre-Hadrianic period. Although a much later Crotus describes himself as 'German'[61], the name of this (probably) Gallic soldier is surely Celtic, just as his father's 'Roman' cognomen *Vindex* 'conceals' a Celtic name-element (compare **6.18**) His age at death has been rounded like that of Secundus, but is an under-estimate for once, since it would have included 25 years' service to qualify him as a veteran. His discharge must have been comparatively recent, but it would have been accompanied by the grant of Roman citizenship and the legal recognition of his existing but informal marriage. So it is strange that his widow gives him his old, non-Roman name, while asserting her own citizenship; presumably she acquired this in her own right, perhaps by being the daughter of another veteran.

Crotus is depicted as holding a scroll in his left hand, presumably his last will and testament: one of the privileges of citizenship was the right of making a valid Roman will. These are often quoted in Roman literature and jurisprudence, but the actual documents are quite rare. The five waxed stylus tablets which contain the will dated AD 142 of a soldier in Egypt have been called a 'marvellous survival', and this can also be said of a block of tablets found by peat-diggers in north-west Wales in the 1840s.[62] Only the first 'page' now survives, since it was taken separately to London for examination and for many years lay forgotten in a cupboard in West Kensington. The wood was originally coated in black wax which has left a black stain, but where it was penetrated by the stylus, it dried lighter, so as to preserve a brownish ghost of the writing. The text is too fragmentary to be quoted in full, but two paragraphs were indicated by the usual convention of setting the first word to the left:

<**9.38**> *Trawsfynydd, Gwynedd*

ceteri alii omnes mihi exheredes sunt[o …]
leg[e] non alia [quam] quanta quibusqu[e ...]
... ded[ero] donavi donari[q]u[e] iusser[o ...]
traces tuque
... adito ce[r]nito hereditatem meam
... centum p[ro]x{s}imis morti{s} mea(e) quibus die(bus)
[sci]es [po]t[e]risque sci[r]e te mihi esse heredem le-
{le}gitumam …

quod si ita n[on] creveris hereditatem [meam s]i aditum
noluer[is exher]es esto […]
[...] quam [ex asse mihi] here-
dem institui

61 *RIB* 1525, *German(us)*.

62 The phrase comes from Crook 1967, 131. For what follows, see Tomlin 2001.

Britannia 35 (2004), 347, No. 27

'Let all others be disinherited for me [. . .] on no other terms than that as much as I shall give, have given, shall have ordered to be given [...] and you [...] enter upon, accept my estate [... within] the next hundred days after my death in which you know or can know that you are my legitimate heir . . . '

'But if you do not thus accept my estate, if you refuse to enter upon it, be thou disinherited [. . .] whom I have instituted as my sole heir.'

These are standard phrases from a Roman will, to ensure that the whole estate be inherited by a single heir. Unfortunately the names of the testator and heir have been lost, but the gender of *legitumam* and *quam* shows that the heir was a woman. In this remote corner of Roman Britain, in the period AD 75/125 (to judge by the handwriting), Roman citizens would have been few and far between. But the find-spot is only three miles from the fort of Tomen-y-mur, and it is an easy guess that the testator was a discharged auxiliary soldier of its garrison who asserted his new citizenship by writing a will. The heir would have been his wife, or perhaps his daughter. This tablet provides a tantalising but precious glimpse of ties beginning to form between a remote garrison and local civilians. At the fortress of Caerleon, where the military presence was far greater, the process can also be seen:

<**9.39**> *Caerleon (Isca)*

D(is) [M(anibus)]
T(itus) Fl(avius) Nata[l]is
veteran[u]s
vixit an(nos) LXV curatum
per Fl(avium) Ingenuinum et Fl(avium)
Flavinum fil(ios) et Fl(aviam)
Veldiccam coniu[gem]

RIB 358+*add.*

'To the Shades of the Dead. Titus Flavius Natalis, veteran, lived 65 years. Set up by Flavius Ingenuinus and Flavius Flavinus his sons, and Flavia Veldicca his wife.'

As usual the veteran's sons do not say whether they were soldiers themselves, or indeed veterans themselves by now. The very beginning of their mother's name has been lost, and its full reading is uncertain; it is Celtic, and seems to be unique. Twelve tombstones have been found at Great Bulmore, a roadside settlement a mile to the north of Caerleon, where they almost all survive because they were convenient building materials for Romans who used them as flooring-slabs in later buildings. They indicate a community dependent upon the nearby legion, including three veterans and their families:

<9.40> *Great Bulmore, near Caerleon (Isca)*

D(is) M(anibus)
G(ai) Iuli
Decum-
ini v(eterani) l(egionis) II A(ugustae)
a(nnorum) XXXXV
c(oniunx) f(aciendum) c(uravit)

RIB 359

'To the Shades of the Dead of Gaius Julius Decuminus, veteran of the Second Legion Augusta, aged 45. His wife had this made.'

Decuminus' age is yet another example of 'rounding'. He would have enlisted at about age 18, and been discharged after 25 years, so his retirement cannot have lasted long. Like Crotus (**9.37**), the veteran who was dead at '40', perhaps he missed the support and stimulus of military discipline. Not so the next veteran:

<9.41> *Great Bulmore, near Caerleon (Isca)*

[D(is) M(anibus)]
Iul(ius) Valens vet(eranus)
leg(ionis) II Aug(ustae) vixit
annis C, Iul(ia)
Secundina coniunx
et Iul(ius) Martinus filius
f(aciendum) c(uraverunt)

RIB 363

'To the Shades of the Dead. Julius Valens, veteran of the Second Legion Augusta, lived 100 years; Julia Secundina his wife, and Julius Martinus his son, had this made.'

This was found in *c.* 1815 with seven other tombstones, including that of his widow:

<9.42> *Great Bulmore, near Caerleon (Isca)*

D(is) M(anibus) et
memoriae
Iuliae Secundi-
nae matri pi-
issim<a>e vixit an-
nis LXXV, G(aius) Iul(ius)
Martinus fil(ius)
f(aciendum) c(uravit)

RIB 373

'To the Shades of the Dead and to the memory of Julia Secundina, his most devoted mother; lived 75 years. Gaius Julius Martinus her son had this made.'

The two tombstones, although more or less contemporary, have been cut by different hands. While they share the concluding formula *f(aciendum) c(uravit)*, the first epitaph omits *D(is) M(anibus)*, whereas the second adopts a most unusual variant, *D(is) M(anibus) et memoriae*. It is unusual too to abbreviate *Gaius* as G, not C. The ages of both husband and wife are obvious estimates. Except for the anonymous Briton who resisted both Roman invasions, Julius Valens is the only professed centenarian from Roman Britain; but authentically the longest-lived is another Valens, Gaius Manlius Valens, who in AD 52 commanded a legion against the Silures (more likely the Twentieth than the Second), and died in his ninetieth year as consul for AD 96.[63] The encyclopaedist and natural historian Pliny (the Elder) quotes many fabulous and some documented claims of long life, for example that in the census of AD 74, there were 81 persons in the Eighth Region of Italy who were aged 100 and more.[64] He mentions the legendary Sattia, who lived long enough to direct that 'aged 99' be written on her tombstone; this does not survive, but her doctor's does. He was only 76.[65] Still, he beat bogey, which is three-score years and ten:

<9.43> *Great Bulmore, near Caerleon (Isca)*

[D(is) M(anibus)]
Valeri Ver[ec]undi
vet(erani) leg(ionis) II Aug(ustae) vix(it)
an(nos) LXX Onerata
con(iunx)
f(aciendum) c(uravit)

---

63 Birley 2005, 236, citing Dio 67.14.5.

64 *Hist. Nat.* vii 153ff.

65 *ILS* 9434, *medico Sattiae*, as if no further identification were needed. Pliny calls her *Statilia* 'aged 99' (*Hist. Nat.* vii 158), but the name *Sattia* is confirmed by Seneca (*ep.* 77.20), who brackets her with Nestor for longevity: *inscribi monumento suo iussit annis se nonaginta novem vixisse.*

RIB III, 3108

'To the Shades of the Dead of Valerius Verecundus, veteran of the Second Legion Augusta; lived 70 years. Onerata his wife had this made.'

This is the third of the Great Bulmore veterans, whose name is 'colonial' and colourless: *Valerii* are frequent in the legions, their ancestors having been enfranchised by various late-Republican proconsuls. *Verecundus* is popular in Britain and Gaul because it 'concealed' the Celtic name-element **uero-s* ('true'). The cognomen *Onerata* is much more unusual (it would mean 'burdened' in Latin), but need not be seen as a mistake for *(H)onorata*; in the masculine form *Oneratus* it has recently been read on a curse tablet from Kent, and is also found in sub-Roman Wales.[66] But from Caerleon let us return to the north, for one last veteran's family:

<**9.44**> *York (Eboracum), the Mount cemetery*

D(is) M(anibus) Flaviae Augustinae
vixit an(nos) XXXVIIII m(enses) VII d(ies) XI filius
Saenius Aug<u>stinus vixit an(num) I d(ies) III
[...]a vixit an(num) I m(enses) VIIII d(ies) V G(aius) Aeresius
Saenus vet(eranus) leg(ionis) VI Vic(tricis) coniugi cari-
[s]imae et sibi f(aciendum) c(uravit)

RIB 685

'To the Shades of the Dead (and) of Flavia Augustina (who) lived 38 years, 7 months, 11 days; her son Saenius Augustinus lived 1 year, 3 days; [...]a lived 1 year, 9 months, 5 days. Gaius Aeresius Saenus, veteran of the Sixth Legion Victrix had this made for his most beloved wife and himself.'

The husband holds a scroll, his last will and testament presumably, and the wife a purse. Their two children, who would have been toddlers in reality, stand in the same stiff pose as their parents, enlarged and wearing the same tunic and cloak, already miniature adults. The father's cognomen is Celtic, derived from the element **seno-s* ('old'), and he has made it into a nomen for his little son, like the centurion Felicius Simplex for his daughter Simplicia (**9.24**); this 'fabrication' is frequent in Britain and Gaul, and the son's new nomen is also found at Gloucester (**10.18**). His name is completed by the cognomen of his mother. The whole family with its interlocking names poses in a double-canopied niche with rosetted spandrels, impassively facing an uncertain future. Would Saenus, after this debâcle, try again to start a family? The wording, although formulaic, has an undertone of despair. It

[66] *Britannia* 43 (2012), 402, No. 12 (East Farleigh). Nash-Williams 1950, 170, No. 284.

is unlikely that Saenus became an ancestor: his fine tombstone was uprooted for re-use as the lid of a second-hand sarcophagus.[67]

And some camp-followers

Another group-portrait comes from Hadrian's Wall. Within a rectangular niche stand the figures of husband and wife, each resting a hand on the portrait bust of their son. His name is inscribed within the gable:

<**9.45**> *Halton Chesters (Onnum)*

Vitalis

(*and below the niche*)

[D(is)] M(anibus)
[titulu]m posu-
[erunt V]irilis e<t>
[...]s vi-
[vi filio s]uo (et) s-
[ibi ...]

RIB III, 3290

'(Tombstone) of Vitalis. To the Shades of the Dead. Virilis and [...]s erected this tombstone in their lifetime, to their son and themselves ...'

The mother's name ends in *-s*, so it was probably not Latin. The cloak worn by Virilis has been identified as a *sagum*, but this is the only hint that he was a soldier.[68] Quite often dedications and epitaphs from military sites name men and women without saying that they were soldiers or related to soldiers: at Brougham Castle, for example, five tombstones and 19 inscribed fragments come from the fort cemetery, but none of them mentions a soldier.[69] So this chapter will conclude with a selection of inscriptions from forts and fortresses which name civilian 'camp-followers' whose connection with the military can only be surmised.

At Cirencester we have already seen the spirited early tombstones of the troopers Genialis of the *ala Thracum* (**2.07**) and Dannicus of the *ala Indiana* (**2.20**). From the same cemetery comes this contemporary civilian's tombstone:

---

[67] *RIB* 683, inscribed for a woman, but the skeleton it contained was apparently male.
[68] A *sagum* is stolen at Bath (*Tab. Sulis* 62.2), but may only be a synonym for *pallium*. Several Vindolanda Tablets refer to *saga*, and a Carlisle tablet (*Tab. Luguval.* 24) even refers to 'ten military *saga*'.
[69] Note to Brougham in *RIB* III, p. 236.

<9.46> *Cirencester (Corinium Dobunnorum)*

Philus Ca-
ssavi fili(us)
civis Sequ(anus)
ann(orum) XXXXV
h(ic) s(itus) e(st)

RIB 110

'Philus, son of Cassavus, a citizen of the Sequani, aged 45. He lies here.'

All three tombstones have much the same lettering and formulation, with *h(ic) s(itus) e(st)* but no initial *Dis Manibus*. Philus wears a *caracalla*, the Celtic hooded cloak like an anorak, and is undoubtedly a civilian. He came from the canton whose capital was Vesontio (Besançon), in the upper Saône valley; their immediate neighbours to the east were the Raurici, the canton of the trooper Dannicus (**2.20**). So when the *ala Indiana* was transferred from Upper Germany to Britain, probably in AD 61, it is likely that Philus came too. Another Sequanian, a shipper, is one of the businessmen who worship at the shrine of Nehalennia in the East Scheldt estuary.[70] But he was not unique:

<9.47> *Great Chesters (Aesica)*

Dis Manib(us)
L(ucius) Novel(lius) L(uci) [f(ilius)] An(iensi tribu)
Uccus c(olonia) R(aurica) an(norum) LXX
Novel(lia) Iustina
fil(ia)
[f(aciendum)] c(uravit)

RIB 1743+*add.*

'To the Shades of the Dead. Lucius Novellius Uccus, son of Lucius, of the *Aniensis* voting-tribe, from *colonia Raurica* (Augst), aged 70. His daughter Novellia Justina had this made.'

This man was a Roman citizen, whose nomen *Novellius* (abbreviated as NOVEL)

[70] Stuart and Bogaers 2001, 67, No. 13, *cives Secuanus nauta*. For this shrine and its worshippers, see **11.34**, **11.35** and **11.36**.

was shared by his daughter. His full name is a problem, but soluble. The mason certainly cut L NOVEL LLAN|VCCVS, but **Llanuccus* is unlikely even as a Celtic name. However, *Uccus* is attested, and indeed occurs at Carrawburgh.[71] It may be conjectured that the mason, who had already cut L twice, repeated it again by mistake for F: if we read L NOVEL L **F** ANVCCVS, we achieve a conventional Roman citizen's name with patronymic and voting-tribe. The city of origin would complete it; this has been reduced to its initials C R, not a redundant *c(ivis) R(omanus)*, since his Roman citizenship was already explicit, but *c(olonia) R(aurica)*, the only Roman city in Gaul or Britain which had these initials.

Colonia Raurica was the romanised capital of the Raurici, from which non-Romans like Dannicus also came. But what was this elderly civilian, Lucius Novellius Uccus, doing on Hadrian's Wall? It is uncertain whether any tombstone which uses the formula *Dis Manibus* unabbreviated can be associated with the Hadrianic frontier.[72] Novellius' own tombstone was re-used as building material at Great Chesters, so it may have been salvaged from the Stanegate, just to the south. There is no likely connection with Dannicus' *ala Indiana*, which left Cirencester for the Continent; but two other cavalry regiments, which were still based on the upper Rhine in AD 69, came to Britain with Cerialis, the *ala Petriana* for Corbridge, and the *ala Sebosiana* for Carlisle. So it may be guessed that Novellius, like Philus with the *ala Indiana*, was a civilian camp-follower who followed the flag; they were surely merchants or sutlers: the Vindolanda Tablets strongly suggest that civilian traders played a part in supplying the army.[73]

On the Antonine Wall is another likely merchant:

<**9.48**> *Shirva (Auchendavy or Bar Hill)*

D(is) M(anibus)
Salmanes
vixit an(nos) XV
Salmanes
posuit

RIB 2182; Keppie 1998, No. 49

'To the Shades of the Dead. Salmanes lived 15 years. Salmanes set this up.'

This exotic name is repeated because it must have been given by a father to his son, but it was evidently unfamiliar

[71] *RIB* 1548 (citing *CIL* iii 5451 as another example).

[72] The only possibilities are **4.09** (Corbridge, but Flavian); 1420 (perhaps Housesteads, but probably associated with the Vindolanda Tablets: see *Tab. Vindol.* 310.1, with note); 2029 and 2030 (Stanwix). Note also *RIB* 961 (Carlisle, but only DIS); 1176 (Corbridge, but entirely restored).

[73] Bowman and Thomas 1994, 30; Bowman 1994, 46, 61–2, 78–9.

to the stonecutter. He first cut SALAMVS or SALAMNS, depending on whether he meant the zigzag to be ligatured MV or MN, but he then added E above the second S, to provide the unusual ending in *-es*. Perhaps he had assumed that a masculine name would end in *-us*. The second time he got it right, by cutting SALMANES. This is a good Semitic name, which in English becomes 'Solomon'. Among the Palmyrenes at Dura Europos, it is even more common than *Barathes* (**9.33** and **9.34**), written either as *Salman* or *Salmanes*.[74] The stone was found midway between Auchendavy and Bar Hill, where the Hamian Archers were in garrison (**6.24**), but Salmanes does not identify himself as a soldier. With a teenaged son in tow, this seems even less likely; but as a Syrian, perhaps he had gravitated towards them. But no such connection can be surmised of another exotic family, these unmilitary Greeks at Chester:

<**9.49**> *Chester (Deva)*

D(is) M(anibus)
Fl(avi) Callimor-
phi vix(it) an(n)i(s) XXXXII
et Serapioni vix(it)
ann(is) III m(ensibus) VI, Thesa-
eus fratri et filio
f(aciendum) c(uravit)

RIB 558+*add.*

'To the Shades of the Dead (and) of Flavius Callimorphus, (who) lived 42 years, and of Serapion (who) lived 3 years, 6 months. Thesaeus had this set up to brother and son.'

Two brothers, one of whom has a small son, but in the absence of a possessive pronoun, it is not clear whose son he was. No mother is in evidence. However, he is clasped affectionately by Callimorphus as he reclines on the funerary couch. In front of them is the usual tripod table on which perches a small bird – a pet, a casual visitor, the next course in the funerary banquet? – and a tapering amphora which would have contained dried fruit or sweet wine. Father and uncle, like the child, have Greek names, so they are unlikely to have been legionaries of the Twentieth; they may have been freedmen, but more likely were merchants, or specialist craftsmen such as doctors.[75]

---

[74] Fink 1971, Index 1 (p. 490). Keppie (1998, No. 49) collates the names as *Salamanes*, which is possible by reading more ligatures, but this form is less well attested.

[75] Two altars are dedicated at Chester by Greek doctors, *RIB* 461 and III, 3151. The doctor at Binchester also has a Greek name (*RIB* 1028), but not the doctor at Housesteads (**11.19**).

There is only one epitaph in Greek from Roman Britain and, for all its length, it does not say much:

<9.50> *Brough-under-Stainmore (Verteris)*

ἑκκαιδεχέτη τις
ἰδών τύμβω<ι> σκεφθέντ'
ὑπὸ μοίρηϲ | Ἑρμῆ<ν>
Κομμαγηνὸν ἔποϲ
φραϲάτω τόδ' ὁδείτηϲ· | χαῖρε ϲύ
παῖ, παρ' εμοῦ,
κἤνπερ θνητὸν βίο<ν>
ἕρπη<ι>ϲ, | ὠκύτατ' ἔπ-
τηϲ γὰρ μερόπων ἐπὶ
Κιμμερίων γῆ<ν>. | κοὺ ψεύ-
ϲει αγ[αθὸϲ] γὰρ ὁ παῖϲ, ῥέξειϲ
δὲ σὺ [καλόν]

RIB 758+*add.*

'Let a passer-by, on seeing Hermes of Commagene, aged sixteen years, sheltered in the tomb by fate, speak this word: fare well from me, boy, even though you walk a mortal life, for you have made your way swiftly to the land of the Cimmerians. And you will not lie, for the boy is good, and you will do him well.'

This epitaph is metrical, five Homeric hexameters to inform well-read passers-by that the deceased was called Hermes, that he was male, aged 16, and came from the province of Commagene (in south-east Turkey).[76] Its capital was Samosata (**9.08**). The half-legendary Cimmerians, 'on whom the sun never shines', lived somewhere north of the Caucasus, and Odysseus sailed into the darkness there to make contact with the dead.[77] This epitaph, like the Risingham text of Aemilius Salvianus (**8.07**), was surely intended to be decorative – and difficult to read. It thus drew the attention of a pioneering expert in cuneiform, the first Professor of Assyriology at Oxford, A H Sayce, who concluded that it was evidence of a 'Celtic-Greek' dialect persisting in sub-Roman Britain; writing to Bodley's Librarian, he 'was amused to see how you and I triumphed over the dogmatism and sneers of the Cambridge scholars who nevertheless had not the decency to confess in public that our readings were right.'[78]

In fact their readings were wrong, but when we turn to the economy of Roman Britain, we will see another metrical inscription, mercifully in Latin, which prays for

[76] Wilhelm's emendations (*SEG* 30 (1980), 340, No. 1241) would improve the verse, but they are not supported by the published drawing.
[77] *Odyssey* xi, 15–16.
[78] Sayce to E W B Nicholson, 25 September 1900, quoted by Tomlin 1994, 96.

a return on investment (**11.23**). And at York a Gallic businessman commemorated his wife with this metrical tag:

<**9.51**> *York (Eboracum)*

Iul(iae) Fortunat<a>e domo
Sardinia Verec(undio) Dio-
geni fida coniuncta
marito

RIB 687

'For Julia Fortunata, her home Sardinia; a loyal wife to her husband Verecundius Diogenes.'

The last two words are the end of a Latin hexameter. They were inscribed on a handsome stone coffin, matched in style by the sarcophagus which Diogenes commissioned for himself:

<**9.52**> *York (Eboracum)*

M(arcus) Verec(undius) Diogenes IIIIIvir col(oniarum)
Ebor(acensis) idemq(ue) Mor(inorum) [e]t cives(!) Biturix
Cubus haec sibi vivus fecit

RIB 678+*add.*

'Marcus Verecundius Diogenes, sevir of the *colonia* of York and also of the Morini, and citizen of the Bituriges Cubi; made these for himself in his own lifetime.'

The neuter plural *haec* ('these') is unusual, and must refer to both sarcophagi. Diogenes' coffin was unfortunately taken to Hull, where (in Horsley's words) it was 'converted into a watering trough for horses at a publick inn'. It is now lost, so we depend upon Camden's reading and a drawing published in 1709. This shows that the text was flanked by the same *peltae* as **9.51**, 'B'-shaped with a horizontal lobe in the centre. *item* ('also') is often confused with *idem* ('the same'), just as we have already seen (**2.08**) *cives* for *civis*. The interpretation adopted here is by Jules Bogaers, who also improved the Togidubnus inscription at Chichester (**2.15**). Diogenes was a Gaul from Avaricum in Aquitania (modern Bourges), who became a minor dignitary in two cities, York and Taruenna (now Thérouanne, east of Boulogne): if by *sevir* he means that he was a *sevir Augustalis*, he would have belonged to the association responsible for the local imperial cult (compare **11.39**). It was virtually confined to rich freedmen, for whom it was equivalent to membership of the Council. A rather more humble association is revealed by this tombstone:

<**9.53**> *Halton Chesters (Onnum)*

[D(is) M(anibus)]
Hardalio-
nis
collegium
conser(vorum)
b(ene) m(erenti) p(osuit)

RIB 1436

'[To the Shades of the Dead] (and) of Hardalio; the guild of his fellow-slaves set this up to him, well-deserving.'

The name *Hardalio* is unique, and is apparently derived from Greek *ardalos* (a mild obscenity which Liddell and Scott are unable or unwilling to translate) or Latin *ardelio*, a 'busybody': slaves, like most of us, did not choose their own names.[79] The Vindolanda Tablets quite often refer to slaves in the military world; Clodius Super, for example, orders more than a dozen cloaks and seven tunics 'for the use of my boys'.[80] *puer* ('boy') is used informally of slaves, but their formal status was that of *servus*; one of the Bloomberg London tablets is a receipt from a slave (*servus*) who writes 'by order of my master'.[81] But here are three slaves who really were boys:

<**9.54**> *Chester (Deva)*

Dis Manibus
Atiliane [a]n(norum)
I At[i]lianus an(norum) X
Protus an(norum) XII
Pompeius Optatus do-
minus f(aciendum) c(uravit)

RIB 560+*add.*

'To the Shades of the Dead. Atiliane, aged 1; Atilianus, aged 10; Protus, aged 12. Pompeius Optatus, their master, had this made.'

Alföldy's reading has been adopted here of the badly damaged lines 2–3, although the variant *Atiliane* (whether male or female) is otherwise unknown. Since Optatus describes himself as their *dominus*, they were evidently his slaves. Also in the military world are women of unspecified status:

---

79 Birley 1979, 208, first recognised it as the slave's name.

80 *Tab. Vindol.* II, 255.7, *usibus puerorum meorum* (with the editors' note).

81 *Tab. Lond. Bloomberg* 50, *scrips[i] iussi domini mei.*

<9.55> *Old Carlisle (?Maglona)*

Tancorix
mulier
vigsit(!) annos
segsaginta(!)

RIB 908+*add.*

'Tancorix, a woman, lived sixty years.'

The voicing of [k] to [g], in *vigsit* (for *vixit*) and *segsaginta* (for *sexaginta*), is a 'Vulgarism' which carries into the Romance languages; another example is the dedication by Lunaris (**11.39**) to Tutela Boudiga (for *Boudica*). The description of Tancorix as 'a woman' suggests that she was alone – that she was no one's widow, mother, aunt or grandmother – unless it only qualifies one of the rare feminine names compounded from *rix* ('king'); *Manduorix* at Vindolanda is another.[82] But writing to the god at Uley, Saturnina (**12.36**) was content to describe herself as 'a woman' (*mulier*).

At a fort on Hadrian's Wall, one household seems to have been limited to two young women:

<9.56> *Great Chesters (Aesica)*

D(is) M(anibus)
Aureliae
Caula[e]
Aur[e]lia
S[en]illa
[s]orori [ca]-
rissim<a>e
vixit an(nos)
XV m(enses) IIII

RIB 1745

'To the Shades of the Dead (and) to Aurelia Caula: Aurelia Senilla to her dearest sister (who) lived 15 years, 4 months.'

Since the sisters are *Aureliae*, they may have been the orphaned daughters of an auxiliary veteran. An earlier veteran at the same fort may have fathered the senior military clerk (*cornicularius*) called Aelius Mercurialis, who is buried by his sister Vacia.[83] Yet another deceased veteran may be implied by this altar from the next fort to the east:

[82] *Tab. Vindol.* IV.1, 863, *Manduorix Vastini filia.*
[83] *RIB* 1742.

<9.57> *Carvoran (Magnis)*

deabus Nym-
phis Vetti[a]
Mansueta e[t]
Claudia Turi[a]-
nilla fil(ia) v(otum) s(olverunt) l(ibentes) [m(erito)]

RIB 1789

'To the Goddesses the Nymphs, Vettia Mansueta and Claudia Turianilla her daughter paid their vow, willingly and deservedly.'

The daughter would have been fathered by a *Claudius*. These examples could be multiplied, to reinforce the impression that some civilians at least felt no need to spell out their relationship to the military. But they belonged to the population of the *vicus*, the village which soon developed outside a fort, to judge by this example from the Antonine Wall:

<9.58> *Carriden (Veluniate)*

I(ovi) O(ptimo) M(aximo)
vikani consi[s]-
tentes castel[lo]
Veluniate, cu[ram]
agente Ael(io) Man-
sueto, v(otum) s(olverunt) l(aeti) l(ibentes) m(erito)

RIB III, 3503

'To Jupiter Best and Greatest, the villagers living at the fort of Veluniate (*or* Velunias) paid their vow joyful and willing, deservedly; Aelius Mansuetus taking care of the matter.'

The Antonine Wall lasted less than 20 years, and was abandoned two and a half centuries before the Notitia Dignitatum was compiled (see note to **5.15**). **9.58** is the only inscription to name a fort on this Wall, but the Ravenna Cosmography lists 'ten places in Britain in a straight line from sea to sea, just where Britain is narrowest'. We do not know how many of these were also forts, but the first is called *Velunia*.[84]

[84] Rivet and Smith 1979, 211 (with commentary), *civitates in ipsa Britania recto tramite una alteri conexa, ubi et ipsa Britania plus angustissima de oceano in oceano esse dinoscitur.* The Cosmographer uses *civitas* ('city', 'tribe') broadly in the sense of 'place(-name)'.

10

GOVERNMENT AND ADMINISTRATORS

Local government: the *vicus*

The *vicus* ('village'), an example of which we have just seen on the Antonine Wall, was the smallest unit of government. Outside a fort it was under the commandant's eye, but it might act like a small corporation with funds of its own:

<10.01> *Old Carlisle (?Maglona)*

I(ovi) O(ptimo) M(aximo) et
V<u>lk(ano) pro sa-
lute d(omini) n(ostri) M(arci) Anto(ni)
Gordiani P(ii)
F(elicis) Aug(usti) vik(ani)
Mag(...) aram
a(ere) col(lato) a v(ikanis) d(edicaverunt)

RIB 899+*add.*

'To Jupiter Best and Greatest, and to Vulkanus, for the welfare of Our Lord Marcus Antonius Gordianus Pius Felix Augustus; the villagers of Mag(...) dedicated this altar from money collected by the villagers.'

Vulkanus is an alternative spelling of Vulcan, the smith-god whom we will see at Stony Stratford (**12.06**) and Vindolanda (**12.73**). The Emperor is Gordian III (AD 238–44), whose titulature is typical of Septimius Severus and his successors: an emperor was now not only 'august', he was conscientious (*pius*) and successful (*felix*) as well. MAG has been convincingly explained by Mark Hassall as an abbreviated place-name; the Notitia Dignitatum offers two possible forts in the north-west, either *Maglone* or *Magis* (both locatives, nominative case unknown). The other problem is line 7, since the altar is broken here, and we do not know if this was actually the last line. But the reading and interpretation in *RIB* are quite acceptable, since *vicani* (the usual spelling) also dedicated altars at Leintwardine and Vindolanda, and passed a 'decree' at Housesteads.[1] They were the civil inhabitants, and here at Old Carlisle they were acting in concert with the garrison, which dedicated an altar of its own to Jupiter for the 'welfare' of Gordian (**13.15**).

Modern writers mostly apply the term *vicus* to the civil settlement outside a fort, but the Romans also applied it to two other administrative units: a 'ward' within a town or city (Rome had 265), of which there are only two uncertain examples[2] in Britain, and a dependent 'village' in the territory of a tribe organised as a *civitas* ('canton'), of which there is just one example. It is named in this inscription from Yorkshire, which celebrates a civic amenity:

<**10.02**> *Brough-on-Humber (?Petuaria)*

ob honor[em]
domus divi[nae]
imp(eratoris) Caes(aris) T(iti) Aeli H[adri]-
ani Ant[o]nini A[ug(usti)]
p(atris) p(atriae) co(n)s(ulis) I[I]
et numinib(us) A[ug(ustorum)]
M(arcus) Ulp(ius) Ianuar[i]u[s]
aedilis vici Petu[ar(iensis)]
proscaen[ium ...]
de suo [dedit]

RIB 707+*add.*

'In honour of the divine house of the Emperor Caesar Titus Aelius Hadrian Antoninus Augustus, Father of his Country, consul for the second time (AD 139), and to the Divinities of the Emperors, Marcus Ulpius Januarius, aedile of the village of Petuaria, gave (this) theatre-stage at his own expense.'

Petuaria is said to be a *vicus*, which is puzzling, since it is the only 'city' of the Parisi named by the geographer Ptolemy, and we would have expected it to be the *civitas* capital. There have been various attempts to resolve this problem.[3] The original location of the slab is unfortunately unknown, since it was taken to the fortified site at Brough-on-Humber for re-use as building material. Another puzzle is that Antoninus Pius is correctly called *pater patriae*, but not given his accession title of *Pius*; but this was probably an oversight.

Theatres in Britain have been excavated at Verulamium and Canterbury, but this is the only epigraphic mention. Roman taxation was not progressive, but instead

---

1 *RIB* III, 3117 (Leintwardine). **12.73** (Vindolanda). *RIB* 1616 (Housesteads), *d(ecreto) vica[norum].*

2 *RIB* 270 (Lincoln), *vic(us) HRAPO Mercur(i)e(n)sium*); *RIB* II.3, 2436.9 (London), *vico Iovio.*

3 Discussed by Rivet and Smith 1979, 437–8. *RIB* takes 'C' within the left-hand *pelta* to be *c(ivitas)*, corresponding to *P(arisorum)* in the missing *pelta*, but it looks more like a piece of decoration.

the rich men who monopolised local office were under moral pressure to pay for their prestige by funding public amenities. Januarius was joint-mayor for the year, his full name indicating that he or his father had been enfranchised in the reign of Trajan. The reference to imperial 'Divinities' (*numina*) in the plural, as at Benwell (**6.32**), associates Antoninus Pius with his predecessors who had already become gods (*divi*).[4]

The *civitas*

When the Romans organised a new province, they delegated some power to local authorities; in Britain, these included well-behaved 'client kings' like Togidubnus (**2.15**). But with longer-lasting effect, they also delegated power to tribal aristocracies. The Romans came from a Mediterranean world in which city-life was, literally, civilisation. For administrative convenience, if for no other reason, they imposed this pattern on the tribes they found in their western provinces. Each *civitas* was now governed by annual magistrates and a council of decurions elected from local landowners, whose own property and position depended on their maintaining Roman rule, with its public order and collection of taxes. Naturally they would conciliate important Roman officials in the area, for example the Silures in south-east Wales:

<10.03> *Caerwent (Venta Silurum)*

[Ti(berio) Claudio]
Paulino
leg(ato) leg(ionis) II
Aug(ustae) proconsul(i)
provinc(iae) Nar-
{r}bonensis,
leg(ato) Aug(usti) pr(o) pr(aetore) provin(ciae)
Lugudunen(sis),
ex decreto
ordinis res-
publ(ica) civit(atis)
Silurum

RIB 311+*add.*

'To Tiberius Claudius Paulinus, legate of the Second Legion Augusta, proconsul of the province of Narbonensis, imperial propraetorian legate of the province of Lugudunensis; by decree of their council, the commonwealth of the Canton of the Silures.'

[4] Fishwick 1994.

This block of oolitic limestone, its inscribed surface flaking where it has been weakened by fossils, now stands in the porch of Caerwent church. It once carried a statue of Paulinus, and is the only British example of the senatorial career-inscriptions frequent in Italy and the provinces; many have been quoted already. The Caerwent stone summarises Paulinus' career after his praetorship in Rome: a minor province in the gift of the Senate (its name perpetuated in modern Provence), next the legionary command at nearby Caerleon, and then a larger province in Gaul as the Emperor's appointee. This statue would have been erected when news came of his promotion. Paulinus' second Gallic province was succeeded by a brief suffect consulship in Rome, and then by his return to Britain, or rather Lower Britain and its legion at York (**10.39**).

Civic initiative was also responsible for one of the finest British inscriptions to survive, albeit in some 300 fragments after the building to which it belonged caught fire and collapsed. Wroxeter, unlike Colchester, Lincoln and Gloucester, did not become a Roman *colonia* when it ceased to be a legionary fortress in the early AD 90s; instead, the site was developed as the capital of the Cornovii. A forum was created with adjoining civic buildings, including the baths of which a large fragment, the Old Work, looms over the grass and gravel of English Heritage.[5] Above the main entrance to the forum was this inscription, its lettering exceptionally well-drawn and executed, although close examination has revealed some minor slips in cutting.[6] Its quality can be seen in the abbreviation TRIB (for *tribunicia*) illustrated here. It consisted of two slabs of very fine-grained buff sandstone butted together:

<10.04> *Wroxeter (Viroconium)*

imp(eratori) Ca[es(ari)] divi Traiani Parthi-
ci fil(io) di[vi N]ervae nepoti Tra-
iano H[a]driano Aug(usto) ponti[fi]-
ci maximo trib(unicia) pot(estate) XIII[I co(n)suli III p(atri) p(atriae)]
civitas Cornov[iorum]

RIB 288

'For the Emperor Caesar Trajan Hadrian Augustus, son of the deified Trajan Conqueror of Parthia, grandson of the deified Nerva, pontifex maximus, in the fourteenth year of tribunician power (AD 130), three times consul; the Canton of the Cornovii (erected this).'

Hadrian was actually Trajan's cousin once removed, but when Trajan died, he was the prime candidate to succeed him, and was duly declared to have been adopted by the dying Emperor as his son and successor; this made him, again by adoption, the grandson of Nerva. These five lines amount to little more than a foundation-date, but they handsomely record the two authorities: the Emperor himself, and the *civitas*. A fragmentary military diploma of much the same date, probably found

5 White and Barker 1998, esp. Chs. 4 and 5.

6 Grasby 2012, Study 5.

in Bulgaria, was issued by Hadrian to a veteran who originated from this tribe; he is described as *Cornov(io)*.[7]

A century later, in the north-west, three inscriptions reveal a new *civitas*. The first is a columnar milestone:

<10.05> *Langwathby (near Brougham)*

imp(eratori) Caes(ari) M(arco) Aur(elio)
Sev(ero) Alexandro
p(io) f(elici) Aug(usto) pont(ifici)
max(imo), tr(ibunicia) p(otestate) II, co(n)s(uli),
p(ro)co(n)s(uli), p(atri) p(atriae), c(ivitas) Car(vetiorum)
Lug(uvalio) m(ilia) p(assuum)
XVIIII

RIB III, 3526

'For the Emperor Caesar Marcus Aurelius Severus Alexander Pius Felix Augustus, pontifex maximus, in his second year of tribunician power (10 Dec. 222 – 9 Dec. 223), consul, proconsul, Father of his Country, the Canton of the Carvetii (set this up). From Carlisle, 19 miles.'

Like some other third-century inscriptions, this calls the Emperor proconsul (of Britain), but the title is omitted by another milestone of the same year.[8] The authority responsible, the *civitas Carvetiorum*, later erected another milestone on the same road, less than two miles away; not columnar this time, but a Red Sandstone slab crudely inscribed:

<10.06> *Brougham (Brocavum)*

imp(eratori) Caes(ari) Ma-
r(co) Cas<s>ianio
Latin{ian}io
Postimo(!)
Aug(usto) Pio
Felici r(es)p(ublica) c(ivitatis)
Car(vetiorum)

RIB III, 3525

'For the Emperor Caesar Marcus Cassianius Latinius Postumus Augustus Pius Felix; the Commonwealth of the Canton of the Carvetii.'

---

[7] *AE* 2007, 1772 = *ZPE* 162 (2007), 223–34, dated by its formulation to AD 126/40. For the spelling of the tribal name, see Rivet and Smith 1979, 324–5.

[8] *RIB* 2306 (Cawfields).

Postumus was the 'Gallic' Emperor who seized control of Britain, Gaul and Spain in AD 260. An altar at Birdoswald (**13.27**) duly acknowledged his new authority. All three of his names have been mis-spelt: the Carvetii seem to have been in a hurry to express their loyalty. When their milestones were found, in 1964 and 2004, they resolved an old problem:

<**10.07**> *Old Penrith (Voreda)*

D(is) M(anibus)
Fl(avio) Martio sen(atori)
in c(ivitate) Carvetior(um)
qu<a>estorio
vixit an(nos) XXXXV
Martiola filia et
heres ponen-
[dum] curavit

RIB 933+*add.*

'To the Shades of the Dead (and) to Flavius Martius, *senator* of quaestorian rank in the Canton of the Carvetii, (who) lived 45 years. Martiola, his daughter and heiress, had this set up.'

This tombstone was seen by Camden in 1600, but was lost soon after. It was published in *RIB* just before **10.06** was found in 1964, too late to resolve the abbreviations SEN | IN C (lines 2–3): did they refer to a *c(ohors)* or a *c(ivitas)*? With the benefit of hindsight, we can see that C E Stevens was right to deduce from another milestone on this road that distances were being measured from Carlisle, which suggested that it was a *civitas* capital.[9] Martius was a local senator, a member of the council, who had previously been *quaestor*, the annual magistrate responsible for finance. His tribe the Carvetii are otherwise unknown, but they can be located in the Eden valley, and may reasonably be seen as part of the Brigantes which was 'devolved' some time after being governed by a Roman district officer, the *centurio regionarius* at Carlisle.[10] This would have then become their capital.

To judge by these milestones, and others in Herefordshire and Hampshire, *civitas* authorities were responsible for road-maintainence by the third century.[11] Another encroachment on the military sphere is suggested by five small *civitas* inscriptions from Hadrian's Wall, one of which can be exactly located:

---

9 *RIB* 2283, cited in the note to *RIB* 933.

10 *Tab. Vindol.* II, 250.8–9. Two other *centuriones regionarii* are attested at Ribchester in the third century (**7.04** and *RIB* 587), where they also commanded the local garrison, but there is no other evidence of such a combination of duties. The only other *centurio regionarius* attested (**12.33**) is likely to have been a casual visitor to Bath.

11 **10.16** (the Dobunni); *RIB* 2222+*add.* and III, 3516 (the Belgae). Note also *RIB* 2240, a milestone of AD 253/59 erected by the *r(es) p(ublica) Lindinensis* (Lincoln).

<10.08> *Cawfields (milecastle 42)*

[c(ivitas) Durot]rac(um)
[Lendine]<n>sis

RIB III, 3376

'The *civitas* of the Durotraces of Lendin(...) (built this).'

This was found in the remains of a mediaeval kiln set into the north mound of the Vallum. Its reading can be restored from two other Cawfields stones of the same *civitas*, their consensus incidentally suggesting that the tribe called 'Durotriges' by Ptolemy was really the 'Durotraces'. Its capital was Dorchester in Dorset, but the addition of *Lendine<n>sis* would indicate a devolved tribe with its capital at Ilchester (*Lindinis*).[12] This stone is a thin slab only 65 mm thick, not a facing-stone like the 'centurial stones' from the Wall itself, and is comparable with the thin slabs found in the Vallum at Benwell.[13] These, however, record the work of an auxiliary cohort, while the date of this contribution by civilians is quite uncertain (see note to **14.22**).

The cities: *municipium*

Most urban centres of any size were *civitas* (tribal) capitals, and the term *civitas* (but only in the sense of 'city', and informally at that) seems also to be used of London:

<10.09> *London (Londinium)*

. . .
[... ad] civita-
tem IIX K(alendas) Ianuarias venit
Atigniomarus ...
accipere et dicebat se (h)abere
abs te (denarios) CCC rite cum me
rogabat (*writing ends here*)

Tab. Lond. Bloomberg 37

'... Atigniomarus came to the city on the eighth day before the Kalends of January (25 December) ... he was saying that he is in receipt and has from you the 300 *denarii* properly. When he was asking me ...'

This is the bottom of a 'page' from a letter written on a stylus writing-tablet from an archaeological context of AD 65/70–80 in the Walbrook, which refers obscurely

12 *RIB* 1672 and 1673. Rivet and Smith 1979, 352–3.

13 **5.42** and *RIB* 1361–4. The other two *civitas* stones are **14.22**, *civitas Dumnoni(orum)*.

to a business transaction of which nothing more is known. Atigniomarus is likewise unknown, but his name is Celtic and occurs in Gaul. Since this fragment was found in London, the implication is that the 'city' (*civitas*) is London itself, but this was not necessarily where the letter was written, so the inference cannot be certain.

A few urban centres ranked higher as a Roman chartered city, either *municipium* or *colonia*. Only one *municipium* is actually known, Verulamium (St Albans), and this from a passing remark by Tacitus. He has just said that London, when destroyed by Boudica in AD 60 or 61, was not a *colonia* like Camulodunum, so when he refers to Verulamium as a *municipium*, he is surely being specific.[14] He would have been corroborated – or corrected – by the great inscription from its forum on panels of Purbeck marble altogether some four metres wide, if only it were better preserved; but the four fragments enable us to reconstruct all but the crucial last line:

<10.10> *St Albans (Verulamium)*

[imp(eratori) Tito Caesari divi] Vespa[siani] f(ilio) Ves[pasiano Aug(usto)]
[p(ontifici) m(aximo) tr(ibunicia) p(otestate) VIIII imp(eratori) XV co(n)s(uli) VII]
desi[g(nato) VIII censori patri patriae]
[et Caesari divi Vesp]asian[i f(ilio) Do]mi[tiano co(n)s(uli) VI desig(nato) VII principi]
[iuventutis et] omn[ium collegiorum sacerdoti]
[Gn(aeo) Iulio A]gric[ola legato Aug(usti) pro] pr(aetore)
[...]*VE.*[...]*NATA*[...]

RIB III, 3123

'For the Emperor Caesar Titus Vespasian Augustus, son of the deified Vespasian, pontifex maximus, in the ninth year of tribunician power, acclaimed Emperor fifteen times, consul for the seventh time (AD 79), designated for the eighth time (for AD 80), Censor, Father of his Country; and to the Caesar Domitian, son of the deified Vespasian, consul for the sixth time (AD 79), designated for the seventh time (for AD 80), *princeps iuventutis*, member of all the priestly colleges; when Gnaeus Julius Agricola was imperial propraetorian legate ...'

[14] *Annals* xiv 33, *cognomento quidem coloniae non insigne*. Confusingly, Suetonius (*Nero* 39.1) refers only to the destruction of two *oppida* in the Boudican revolt, but whether he means London, Verulamium or Colchester (a *colonia*), his language is non-technical.

Since the name *Vespasianus* occurs twice in the first line, this cannot be a dedication to Vespasian alone, nor to Vespasian *and* Titus. Instead, it belongs to the short reign of Titus alone (23 June AD 79–13 September 81), with just enough to show that his younger brother, Domitian, was named as well. The latter's titles mark him as heir-presumptive: the Republican title of 'youth-leader' (*princeps iuventutis*), the leading young equestrian of military age, was revived by Augustus to mark princes of the imperial family. According to the biographer Suetonius, who accompanied Hadrian to Britain, there were many statues and inscriptions of Titus there. This is the only survivor.[15] The date can be restored as AD 79 or 81, but *RIB* follows Sheppard Frere in preferring AD 79 because of the coincidence with Tacitus, who dates Agricola's encouragement of temples, fora and private houses, to his second winter (almost certainly AD 79/80).[16] All that remains of the dedicator in line 6 is the tantalising fragment below Agricola's name, the letters VE and a vertical stroke. This should be *Ver[ulamium]* (compare **2.21**) identified as a *municipium*, but we cannot be quite sure it was not just *[civitas Catu]vel[launorum]*, the name of the tribe whose capital it was.[17]

The cities: *coloniae*

There were at least four *coloniae*, three of them founded for legionary veterans after the legion had moved on. The first was Colchester (Camulodunum), described by Tacitus as intended to protect the province from rebellion, and to promote law and order among the provincials.[18] It was an immediate failure in both respects, since it became a focus of resentment, and was sacked by Boudica. But it was rebuilt, and this legionary was born there:

<**10.11**> *Carnuntum (Petronell, east of Vienna)*

T(itus) Statius T(iti filius)
Cla(udia tribu) Vitalis Ca-
muloduni, sti(pendiorum)
III an(norum) XXIII, (centuria) Arru-
nti Expectati

CIL iii 11233

'Titus Statius Vitalis, son of Titus, of the *Claudia* voting-tribe, from Camulodunum, of three years' service, aged 23; in the century of Arruntius Expectatus.'

---

15 Suetonius, *Titus* 4.1.

16 *Agricola* 21. But strictly speaking, this is only a terminus post quem.

17 Possible restorations (after Frere) are shown in *RIB* III, p. 130, where the question is discussed. The slave Regina (**9.33**), *natione Catuallauna*, probably came from the territory, not the city itself.

18 *Annals* xii 32, *subsidium adversus rebellis et imbuendis sociis ad officia legum.*

Vitalis was buried at a legionary base on the upper Danube, but his legion is not named, and we do not know why he died so far from home when he might have enlisted in a British legion like Pomponius Valens (**10.12**). Possibly he belonged to one of the British legionary detachments which fought for Vitellius in north Italy in AD 69, which perhaps (but we do not know) were then sent to the Danube. Or he may have belonged to an expeditionary force like 'the detachment from Britain' which appears at Carnuntum (**4.05**) somewhat later. His tribe incidentally was *Claudia*, which would have been the tribe of Claudius' new foundation, and its original name may thus have been *Colonia Claudia*. However, it was amplified after the defeat of Boudica:

<**10.12**> *London (Londinium)*

Dis Manibus
G(ai) Pomponi
G(ai) f(ilii) Valentis
Victricens[is]
[b(ene)f(iciarii)] t[r]ib(uni) [leg(ionis) ...]
[...]

RIB III, 3005

'To the Shades of the Dead (and) of Gaius Pomponius Valens, son of Gaius, of (*colonia*) *Victricensis*, [*beneficiarius*] of a tribune of the Legion ...'

This is the tombstone of the other known legionary from Colchester, who died on detached service as a junior staff officer; he belonged to a British legion, but its identity is lost. That he came from Colchester is shown by this senatorial career-inscription:

<**10.13**> *Nomentum*

Gn(aeus) Munatius M(arci) f(ilius) Pal(atina tribu)
Aurelius Bassus
proc(urator) Aug(usti),
praef(ectus) fabr(um), praef(ectus) coh(ortis III
sagittariorum, praef(ectus) coh(ortis) iterum II
Asturum, censitor civium
Romanorum coloniae Victri-
censis quae est in Brittannia
Camaloduni, curator
viae Nomentanae, patronus eiusdem
municipi, flamen perpet<u>us
duumvirali potestate,
aedilis, dictator IIII

ILS 2740

'Gnaeus Munatius Aurelius Bassus, son of Marcus, of the *Palatina* voting-tribe, imperial procurator; aide-de-camp, prefect of the Third Cohort of Archers, prefect again of the Second Cohort of Asturians, Census Officer for the Roman citizens of the Victricensis *colonia* which is in Britain at Camalodunum, Curator of the Road to Nomentum, Patron of the said town, Priest for life of the Imperial Cult, (granted) the powers of Duumvir, Aedile, Dictator four times.'

Bassus was a much bigger fish than Valens, but in quite a small pond, even if it was better than living in Britain.[19] He held the various local magistracies, and he represented the town in its dealings with the wider world, both as its Patron and as the imperial official responsible for the road which connected it with Rome, fourteen miles away. This appointment seems to have carried the extraordinary title of Imperial Procurator. His outside career had begun with the *praefectura fabrum*, originally an important military post on the staff of provincial governors, but which from the mid-first century declined into a junior appointment held at the outset of an equestrian career (**1.02**). The Second Cohort of Asturians, as we have seen (**3.20**), fought in a 'British War', but Bassus may not have seen active service; at all events he was available for a special assignment, compiling the citizen-lists and property returns for the *colonia* at Camulodunum (as it is usually spelt). Its title is uniquely derived from *Victrix*, 'Victorious', which was part of the title gained by the Fourteenth Legion Gemina for its defeat of Boudica (**1.04**); perhaps too by the Twentieth Legion, which contributed a detachment to the victory. *Victricensis* would then have been a complimentary allusion to the veterans of the Boudican war who were settled there.[20]

The other veteran *coloniae* were Lincoln (Lindum) and Gloucester (Glevum). Two legionaries from Lincoln are known; one died young in Africa:

<10.14> *Albulae in Mauretania Caesariensis (western Algeria)*

D(is) M(anibus)
M(arcus) Iuni-
us Capi-
to Lin-
do m<i>l(es)
leg(ionis) X G(eminae)
st(ipendiorum) X, Iul(ius)
Primus
sig(nifer) h(eres) f(aciendum) c(uravit)

---

[19] Martial tells his friend Ovidius, who was leaving the leisures of Nomentum (*Nomentana otia*) for a visit to Britain, that he would be his own best friend if he returned as soon as possible (*ep.* 10.44).

[20] There is another instance, *[Vi]ctrice(nsi)* for a centurion of the Fourth Legion Flavia in Dacia (*IDR* 35).

CIL viii 21669

'To the Shades of the Dead. Marcus Junius Capito of Lindum, soldier of the Tenth Legion Gemina, with ten years service; Julius Primus the standard-bearer, his heir, saw to this being made.'

The legion, which by then was based at Vienna (Vindobona), is thought to have contributed to the expeditionary force which suppressed the Moorish revolt in the reign of Antoninus Pius; Flavius Quietus, sometime *primus pilus* of the Twentieth Legion, also participated (**6.14**). Capito would have been less than 30 when he died, but the other legionary from Lincoln, like Quietus, climbed to the very top of the greasy pole:

<10.15> *Mainz (Mogontiacum)*

Fortunam
Superam ho-
nori aquilae
leg(ionis) XXII Pr(imigeniae) p(iae) f(idelis) M(arcus)
Minicius M(arci) f(ilius)
Quir(ina tribu) Lindo Mar-
[cel]li[nus p(rimus)] p(ilus) leg(ionis) ei[us]-
[dem ...]

CIL xiii 6679

'Higher Fortune, in honour of the Eagle of the Twenty-Second Legion Primigenia Dutiful and Loyal, Marcus Minicius Marcellinus, son of Marcus, of the *Quirina* voting-tribe, from Lindum, first-ranking centurion of the same legion ...'

This is a statue-base of 'Higher' Fortune; two other dedications to her are known, but not why she was superior to other Fortunes. The handsomely-lettered block is carved with her attributes on one side, a rudder and a horn of plenty (*cornucopia*); on the other is the Eagle with a laurel wreath in its beak.[21] The *primus pilus* marked his year in office by making a dedication in honour of the Eagle for which he was responsible: the practice is well known at Mainz, and is found elsewhere, perhaps including Caerleon.[22] Dated examples are Severan or later (AD 192–235), so it is difficult to connect this Marcellinus (assuming his cognomen has been correctly restored) with the much earlier equestrian Marcus Minicius Marcellinus who commanded the *ala Brittonum* in Dacia in AD 123.[23] Were the centurion his descendant, this would imply a family at Lincoln which enjoyed equestrian rank, but the coincidence of names cannot be pressed.

---

21 *CSIR Deutschland* ii.4, 77–8, No. 33 (with Taf. 30). The other dedications to Higher Fortune are *ILS* 3713 and 9254.

22 *RIB* 327+*add.* (Caerleon). The dedications are collected by Dobson 1978, 155–60, to which now add *AE* 1982, 849 and *AE* 1988, 984 (Kolendo and Bozilova 1997, Nos. 47 and 33) from Novae.

23 *RMD* I, 21.

At Lincoln such a family, if it existed, would indeed have been among the 'colonial élite', but only one councillor (*decurio*) of Lincoln is actually known, from the enigmatic tombstone he erected to his wife; it carries the portrait busts of two women, and below them two epitaphs side by side:

<**10.16**> *Lincoln (Lindum)*

D(is) M(anibus)	D(is) M(anibus)
Volusia	Cl(audia) Catiotui (filia)
Faustina	vixtt(!) a[n(nos)]
c(ivis) Lind(ensis) v(ixit)	LX[...]
ann(os) XXVI	
m(ensem) I d(ies) XXVI	
Aur(elius) Sene-	
cio dec(urio) ob	
merita c(oniugi) p(osuit)	

RIB 250+*add.*

'To the Shades of the Dead. Volusia Faustina, a citizen of Lindum (Lincoln), lived 26 years, 1 month, 26 days. Aurelius Senecio, a councillor, set this up to his deserving wife.'

'To the Shades of the Dead. Claudia, daughter of Catiotuus, lived 60 [or more] years.'

Why this tombstone commemorated two unrelated women is unstated. Senecio only tells us that he married a local woman – to judge by her good Roman name, probably descended from a veteran colonist – and remembered her birthday. Also a mystery is our only record of civic business at Lincoln, a scrap of Purbeck marble handsomely lettered, which may honour an imperial freedman for his public generosity.[24]

Gloucester was the birthplace of an auxiliary soldier who however chose Colchester for his retirement, since his military diploma was found here.[25] Another soldier from Gloucester died on service in Rome:

<**10.17**> *Rome*

D(is) M(anibus)
M(arco) Ulpio Ner(viana tribu)
Quinto Glevi
mil(es) fr(umentarius) leg(ionis) VI V(ictricis)
Calidius
Quietus collega
fratri observato
piissimo b(ene) m(erenti) f(aciendum) c(uravit)

---

24 *RIB* III, 3173, with discussion. It is too fragmentary to be quoted here, but a possible sequence is *[...]annus | [Au]g(usti) lib(ertus) o[b] | [ho]norem [...]*

25 *RIB* II.1, 2401.12 (Saturninus of the First Cohort of Vardulli).

ILS 2365

'To the Shades of the Dead (and) to Marcus Ulpius Quintus of the *Nerviana* voting-tribe, of Glevum (Gloucester), commissariat soldier (*frumentarius*) of the Sixth Legion Victrix; Calidius Quietus his colleague saw to this being done for his respected, most dutiful and well-deserving brother.'

This tablet was found in a *columbarium* on the southern edge of Rome, a communal mausoleum like a dovecot with pigeon-holes for cremated ashes. Quintus was not literally Quietus' brother: 'brother' is an affectionate term often used in letters between friends and colleagues (compare **10.27**). Nor was there a *Nerviana* voting-tribe: like *Ulpia* in the nomenclature of Aurelius Syrio at Carlisle (**13.04**), it is a 'pseudo-tribe' fabricated from the imperial title of a legionary's place of origin.[26] It is the only evidence that the *colonia* bore this title, which would imply that it was founded by Nerva. But Nerva's reign was brief (AD 96–98), and the Twentieth must have left Gloucester by the early AD 80s. Since Colchester and Lincoln became *coloniae* soon after the legion left, it has been suspected that Gloucester was actually refounded by Domitian; but that when his 'memory' was condemned in AD 96, it was forced to change its title. Quintus in any case, with the imperial nomen of *Ulpius*, cannot be descended in the male line from one of the original veterans; his ancestor was probably an auxiliary veteran enfranchised by Trajan. We will see other *frumentarii* from Britain (after **10.30**). The title suggests they were originally responsible for their legion's food supply (*frumentum*), but they actually served as couriers between Rome and the provinces, and like their successors the late-Roman 'agents' (*agentes in rebus*), they gained a dark reputation as secret policemen.

A councillor of the *colonia Glev[ensis]* was buried at Bath, a gouty alderman taking the waters perhaps, but his name is lost.[27] However, the abbreviated names of some of Gloucester's annual pairs of magistrates are preserved by stamped tiles from a second-century tilery outside the walls; here is an example:

<10.18> *Gloucester (Glevum)*

D(ecimi) Senni V<i>t(alis)
G(ai) [V]aleri An(...) R(es) P(ublica) G(levensis)

RIB II.5, 2487.6

'(Year) of Decimus Sennius Vitalis and Gaius Valerius An(...), the Commonwealth of the people of Glevum.'

---

[26] The only examples from Britain are **13.04** and *RIB* 671.
[27] *RIB* 161.

There are many such tiles.[28] The names of these magistrates hint at the composition of the local oligarchy. *Sennius* incorporates the Celtic element **seno-s* ('old') found in *Saenus* (**9.44**), and Vitalis' ancestor is likely to have been a tribal aristocrat turned landowner; he even has a namesake buried at Cologne, who is an auxiliary soldier of British origin.[29] But *Valerius* is frequent in Spain and Southern Gaul, and is typical of legionaries; this man's ancestor would have been a veteran.

The fourth *colonia* was of course York (Eboracum). The legion moved here from Lincoln in *c.* AD 71, but a connection persisted, to judge by the veteran of the Sixth Legion who retired from York to Lincoln, and the two merchants who enjoyed civic rank in both cities.[30] But York, unlike Lincoln, was not a true veteran *colonia*, although many veterans of the Sixth Legion must have retired there from the fortress across the river. By the date of its promotion, most likely when Septimius Severus resided here in AD 208–11, the title of *colonia* had long been a distinction sought by leading cities; when he bestowed it on the civil settlement at York, London may have possessed it already.[31]

The new council donated the site for a temple-extension in AD 221, and the names are known of two or three councillors.[32] Like other successful citizens of third-century York, they were buried grandly in stone coffins:

<**10.19**> *York (Eboracum)*

D(is) M(anibus)
Fl[a]vi Bellatoris dec(urionis) col(oniae) Eboracens(is)
vixit annis XXVIIII mensib[us ...]
[...]

RIB 674

'To the Shades of the Dead (and) of Flavius Bellator, councillor of the *colonia* of Eboracum; he lived 29 years, [...] months, [... days].'

The skeleton of Bellator still wore its gold ring on one finger, traditionally the mark of an equestrian: we have already seen the gold ring of Claudius Catuarus at Fishbourne (**2.16**), and another Roman *eques* is known from Colchester.[33] A fourth is known from York:

---

28 *RIB* II.5, 2486 (*r(es) p(ublica) G(levensium)*); 2487 (annual magistrates); 2488 (5-yearly magistrates).

29 *ILS* 2572+*add.*, *D(ecimo) Sen[i]o Vital[i] mil(iti) [coh(ortis) VI In]genuorum c(ivium) R[o]m(anorum) civi Brit[to(ni)].*

30 *RIB* 252 (the veteran); **11.39** and **9.52** (the merchants).

31 Tomlin 2006(a) (deduced from *RIB* III, 3006).

32 **11.37**, *d(ecreto) d(ecurionum)*. The name of the *dec(urio) col(oniae) Ebor(acensis)* of *RIB* III, 3203, is lost, but the informal title of Aelia Severa, *honesta femina* (*RIB* 683), probably implies that her husband Caecilius Rufus was a decurion.

33 *RIB* 202.

<10.20> *York (Eboracum)*

D(is) M(anibus) [A]nt(oni) Gargiliani equ(o)
publ(ico) e[x pr]a[e]f(ecto) leg(ionis) VI V(ictricis) an(norum) LVI
m(ensium) VI Cla(udius) Florentinus
dec(urio) gener eius

RIB III, 3201

'To the Shades of the Dead (and) of Antonius Gargilianus, (allotted) a public horse, sometime prefect of the Sixth Legion Victrix, aged 56 years, 6 months. Claudius Florentinus, councillor, his son-in-law, (set this up).'

The inscription is badly worn, since the front of this stone coffin was re-used as an Anglo-Saxon grave slab in York Minster. Like Maenius Agrippa (**5.12**) and other officers we have seen, Gargilianus was an equestrian by birth, his status being marked by the grant of a notional '(cavalry) horse' at Rome.[34] He chose to retire to York, which does not mean that he originated from here; his nomen is more often found in Africa. But although a very senior officer, he integrated with local society well enough to marry his daughter to one of its leading members; it is a late, but striking, instance of the developing ties between Soldier and Civilian.[35]

Central government: the legate of Britain

The splendid inscriptions at St Albans and Wroxeter were erected by local authorities, but they were dedicated to the Emperor who personified central government. He governed the whole province on behalf of the Roman Senate and People (the famous acronym S P Q R, which is never found in Britain), and in some third-century inscriptions like **10.05** he is actually called the proconsul, but he delegated his immediate powers to an imperial legate (*legatus Augusti pro praetore*) whom he chose from senators who had been consul. This Viceroy or Lord Lieutenant was commander-in-chief, with authority over the less senior senators (ex-praetors) whom the Emperor appointed as legates of the legions. He was responsible for public order, the administration of justice, the whole government of the province except its finances, which were supervised by an equestrian procurator also appointed by the Emperor. The legate's powers were thus very great, but he was bound by the Emperor's standing orders (*mandata*), he corresponded with him and received his instructions and guidance, he held office only during his pleasure; also, he needed to

[34] The others are Stlaccius Coranus (**2.09**), Julius Quadratus (**5.11**) and Pertinax (**7.02**).

[35] See chapter 9. It is unclear whether Gargilianus was *praefectus castrorum*, or actually commanded the legion after Gallienus' reform. The last-known legionary legate is attested at Caerleon in *c.* AD 255–60 (**13.22**).

take account of the procurator,[36] the minority of Roman citizens who lived there, and even public opinion as represented by the Council of the province (compare **10.39**).

When Britain was divided into two provinces, Lower Britain was governed by the legate of the Sixth Legion at York, for example Claudius Paulinus (**10.39**). Governors were still chosen from the senatorial aristocracy until *c.* AD 260, when Gallienus appointed equestrian prefects to command the legions, and subsequently (but the exact chronology is unclear) equestrians were also appointed governor with the title of *praeses*. Aurelius Arpagius (**14.06**) is an example. This hierarchy was modified in the fourth century, but the epigraphic evidence for Britain is slight, the most notable item being the allusion to Britannia Prima at Cirencester (**14.07**). By dividing Britain into two provinces, and later into four, the Emperors would have reckoned that a governor was less likely to rebel if he had a smaller army at his disposal. But this was only the political dividend from an administrative reform: if the governor's work-load were reduced, he could pay closer attention to what remained.

This may only seem to be the principle well known to administrators, that administration improves as administrators grow in number, but two more stylus tablets from London reveal how minute the detail might be that confronted them. The wax is lost as usual, but the stylus has left legible traces. The first tablet was written in the very year that lead ingots (**3.11**) reveal that Wales had been conquered at last:

<**10.21**> *London (Londinium)*

imper(atore) Ca[e]sare Vespasiano VII
Tit[o] V c[o](n)s(ulibus) XI K(alendas) Nov(embres)
opera in V Id(us) Novembres
inter Litugenum et
Magunum data ab
Ca[e]sare, praeiudico
. . .

Tab. Lond. Bloomberg 51

'In the consulship of the Emperor Caesar Vespasian for the seventh time (and) of Titus for the fifth time, on the eleventh day before the Kalends of November (22 October AD 76). Responsibility (for the case) between Litugenus and Magunus on the fifth day before the Ides of November (9 November) having been given by the Emperor, my preliminary judgement is [...]'

[36] Classicianus (**2.19**) is said by Tacitus (*Ann.* xiv 38–9) to have achieved the recall of Suetonius Paulinus, whose protégé Agricola when legate of Aquitania took care not to quarrel with the procurator (*Agric.* 9.4, the plural *procuratores* being rhetorical).

This is the carefully dated preamble to a *praeiudicium*, the ruling given by the judge appointed to hear a lawsuit, relating to a legal point which had arisen before the hearing began. The litigants, who are otherwise unknown, both have Celtic names and are not Roman citizens. The judge himself, although formally appointed by the Emperor, must in fact have been appointed by the provincial governor, who was then Agricola's immediate predecessor, Sextus Iulius Frontinus, who conquered Wales.[37] The implication is that London was still directly administered, that it did not have the annually elected magistrates with judicial powers (*duumviri iuri dicundo*) who might have made such an appointment.

Unfortunately the text breaks off at the crucial point, as it does in the second tablet, which nonetheless is precious for its minute detail of land-tenure in the new province:

<10.22> *London (Londinium)*

imp(eratore) Traiano [Had]ri[ano] Caesare Aug(usto) II, Gn(aeo)
Fusco Salinatore co(n)s(ulibus) pr(idie) idus Martias.
cum ventum esset in rem praesentem,
silvam Verlucionium, arepennia de-
cem quinque, plus minus, quod est in ci-
vitate Cantiacorum pago [*illegible*]
[*illegible*] adfinibus heredibus
7a (*interlineated) traces of half a line*
et heredibus Caesenni Vitalis et via
vicinale, quod se emisse diceret L(ucius)
Iulius Bellicus de T(ito) Valerio Silvino
(denariis) quadraginta sicut emptione con-
tinetur.
L(ucius) Iulius Bellicus testatus est se

Britannia 25 (1994), 302, No. 34 = Tomlin 1996

'In the consulship of the Emperor Trajan Hadrian Caesar Augustus for the second time, and Gnaeus Fuscus Salinator, on the day before the Ides of March (14 March AD 118). Whereas, on arriving at the property in question, the wood *Verlucionium*, fifteen *arepennia*, more or less, which is in the Canton of the Cantiaci in [...] parish, neighboured by the heirs [of ...] and the heirs of Caesennius Vitalis and the vicinal road, Lucius Julius Bellicus said that he had bought it from Titus Valerius Silvinus for forty *denarii*, as is contained in the deed of purchase. Lucius Julius Bellicus attested that he [...]'.

This is the first 'page' of the record of an inquiry into the ownership of a wood in Roman Kent, which breaks off in mid-sentence. Coincidentally it is dated only

37 The appointment may have been delegated to the *iuridicus* (see below), if there was already one; the first attested is Salvius Liberalis, probably in AD 78.

seven months after Hadrian's accession, the moment when his biographer says that Britain could not be kept under control.[38] The punctuation, word-separation and capitalisation of proper names have been modernised, but the paragraphing is original: the writer began lines 1, 3 and 13 to the left. It is full of technical terms found in other Roman legal documents. 'On arriving at the property in question' refers to the arrival of the judge and interested parties. *arepennia* were units of land-measurement in Celtic-speaking provinces, each 120 (Roman) feet square, nearly one-third of an acre. The property is correctly located, first of all by the administrative unit of the *civitas* and then by its territorial sub-unit the *pagus*, in anachronistic terms by the 'county' and the 'parish' (its name illegible), and then by the names of the two neighbouring proprietors: the puzzling repetition of that phrase 'the heirs of' is apparently due to the scribe having omitted the first name, and then inserting it illegibly between the lines. By implication there was a land-register of all the properties in Roman Kent, which would have been needed for the land-tax (*tributum*); however, it was being allowed to get out of date as the original owners died. The other boundary, the 'vicinal' road, was a branch road whose upkeep was the responsibility of local landowners under the supervision of the 'parish' authorities.

The three landowners, to judge by their names, were not of British origin: *Caesennius* is an Italian name, but *Iulius* and *Valerius* suggest the descendants of provincials enfranchised in the late Republic; both names are very common among legionaries. In the 75 years since the Claudian invasion, with the influx of Roman capital and the settlement of veterans, much British land must have been confiscated or sold, and have found new owners from abroad. This is the first land-price recorded from Roman Britain: it does seem rather low (a legionary was now earning 300 *denarii* a year before stoppages), but unless a numeral has been omitted it may mean that the fortunate minority who had ready cash could piece together landed estates on the cheap. One of the Bloomberg London tablets acknowledges two payments (*pensiones*) in respect of a farm.[39] There may be a hint of this activity, and indeed of cultural discontinuity, in the Celtic name of the wood, *Verlucionium*, which contains an intensive form of the adjective *leuco-s, 'bright, shining, white', cognate with Latin *lux* ('light') and *lucus* (a small wood, especially in the sense of a 'sacred grove'). Was *Verlucionium* a pre-Roman sacred grove which had fallen into private hands? According to a Roman treatise on land-surveying, this tended to happen, and imperial governors were expressly told to see that sacred places remained in public ownership.[40]

By the time of this document, the principle of reducing the governor's work-load

---

[38] Hist. Aug. *Hadrian* 5.2, *Britanni teneri sub Romana dicione non poterant*. This is the likely occasion of **5.01**, the centurion's tombstone at Vindolanda.

[39] *Tab. Lond. Bloomberg* 50. The farm (*fundus*) is named, but unfortunately is illegible.

[40] Tomlin 1996. *Cantiaci* is the form read by the Ravenna Cosmography, although it is often inferior to Ptolemy, who here reads *Cantii* or *Cantici* (Rivet and Smith 1979, 299).

was long established. After the conquests of Cerialis, Frontinus and Agricola doubled the size of the province, campaigning and consolidation would have taken much of the legate's time and energy, so it is not surprising to find that a junior legate was now appointed, the *iuridicus*, who deputised in the administration of justice:

<**10.23**> *Nadin, Croatia (Nedinum)*

G(aio) Octavio
Tidio Tossia{a}no L(ucio) Ia<v>oleno
Prisco, leg(ato) leg(ionis) IV Flav(iae), leg(ato) leg(ionis) III Aug(ustae),
iuridic(o) provinc(iae) Brittaniae, leg(ato)
consulari provin[c(iae)] Germ(aniae) superioris,
legato consulari provinc(iae) Syriae,
proconsuli provinc(iae) Africae, pontifici
P(ublius) Mutilius P(ubli) f(ilius) Cla(udia tribu) [C]rispinus t(estamento) p(oni) i(ussit)
amico carissimo

ILS 1015+*add.*

'To Gaius Octavius Tidius Tossianus Lucius Javolenus Priscus, legate of the Fourth Legion Flavia, legate of the the Third Legion Augusta, Chief Justice of the province of Britain, consular legate of the province of Upper Germany, consular legate of the province of Syria, proconsul of the province of Africa, pontifex; Publius Mutilius Crispinus, son of Publius, of the *Claudia* voting-tribe, in his will ordered this to be set up to his most dear friend.'

The inscription omits any post Priscus may have held before his first legionary command, perhaps because Vespasian and Titus had enrolled him in the senate like Caristanius Fronto (**3.17**), Antistius Rusticus (**3.01**) and Curiatius Maternus;[41] but his consulship is also omitted, and this we know was towards the end of AD 86; since we also know that he was still commanding the Third Legion in Africa in AD 83, his British appointment can be quite closely dated to *c.* AD 84/6, just after Agricola left the island. His successor was undoubtedly busy with consolidating the Roman hold on northern England and the lowlands of Scotland, which would have included building the new legionary fortress at Inchtuthil. Domitian next chose Priscus to govern Upper Germany after the failure of Saturninus' coup in AD 89, and when, in the last months of Nerva's reign the legate of Syria came under suspicion, Priscus seems to have been Trajan's choice to replace him.[42] It is evident that two very different emperors both regarded him as a safe pair of hands. As *pontifex*, he belonged to the senior college of priests who supervised the Roman State religion, a high social distinction, but he was remembered as a classical jurist.[43]

[41] *AE* 1973, 283.
[42] Syme 1958, 52 and 631–2 (commenting on Pliny, *ep.* ix 13.11).
[43] Birley 2005, 270–72.

It is likely that the juridicate, first attested in *c.* AD 78, became a regular appointment, but later *iuridici* were senators of less seniority: the next example, a man whose name we have seen already in the earliest days of the province, came to Britain *before* his legionary command:

<**10.24**> *Rimini (Ariminum)*

M(arco) Vettio M(arci) f(ilio)
An(iensi tribu) Valenti
quaestori provinc(iae)
Macedon(iae), quaestori(!) pleb(is),
seviro eq(uitum) [R]om(anorum), praet(ori),
leg(ato) provinc(iae) [N]arbonens(is),
[iuridic(o)] provinc(iae) Britan(niae),
[leg(ato)] leg(ionis) XV Apollinar(is)
provincia Brittannia
patrono

CIL xi 383

'To Marcus Vettius Valens, son of Marcus, of the *Aniensis* voting-tribe; quaestor of the province of Macedonia, [tribune] of the people, one of the Six troop-commanders of the Roman *equites,* praetor, legate of the province of Narbonensis, Chief Justice of the province of Britain, legate of the Fifteenth Legion Apollinaris. The province of Britain to its Patron.'

This dedication comes from the same Italian city as the inscription which honoured the imperial procurator Marcus Vettius Valens, the sometime guardsman who escorted Claudius to Britain (**1.04**). The second Marcus Vettius Valens is probably his grandson, who has carried the family another step up the ladder, from the equestrian to the senatorial aristocracy. (*quaestori* has been repeated by mistake, instead of *tribuno.*) His service in Britain can be dated by the legionary command he held next, at Satala in its remote and beautiful location on the upper Euphrates; this coincided with the threat of a nomad invasion of eastern Anatolia in the mid-AD 130s, so Vettius Valens must have been *iuridicus* of Britain while the provincial legate and the army were busy in the north, building Hadrian's Wall. He maintained his connection with Britain, since he became its 'patron'; this would have entailed representing the province in legal proceedings at Rome, whether to defend provincials or even to prosecute a governor for misconduct.[44]

Valens was presumably chosen as patron by the provincial Council (*concilium provinciae*), a body of which we know almost nothing in Britain. In other provinces,

---

[44] The only other known patron of Britain is Julius Asper (*CIL* xiv 2508), for whom see Birley 2005, 181–3.

cities and tribes sent delegates each year to the capital to celebrate the imperial cult, and this must have been the practice in Britain:

<**10.25**> *London (Londinium)*

num(ini) C[aes(aris) Aug(usti)]
prov[incia]
Brita[nnia]

RIB 5

'To the Divinity of the Emperor, the province of Britain (set this up).'

This incomplete slab was found in 1850, but was soon lost. It embodied a decision by the Council on behalf of the province, and what was dedicated would have been obvious at the time; most likely a statue of the Emperor. Its location in London indicates that this was now the capital; in earliest years, the Council probably met in Colchester, at the Temple of Claudius. The meeting would dutifully thank the governor or, in dire cases, might pass a vote of censure, an embarrassment that Claudius Paulinus escaped in Gaul (**10.39**). One of its officers is thought to have erected this hexagonal column in the cemetery on Ludgate Hill, probably to support a memorial statue:

<**10.26**> *London (Londinium)*

D(is) M(anibus)
Cl(audiae) Marti-
nae an(norum) XIX
Anencle-
tus
provinc(ialis)
coniugi
pientissimae
h(ic) s(ita) e(st)

RIB 21+*add.*

'To the Shades of the Dead (and) to Claudia Martina, aged 19; Anencletus, ?slave of the province, (set this up) to his most dutiful wife; she lies here.'

Anencletus (his name is Greek, meaning 'without reproach') describes himself as PROVINC. The obvious expansion is *provincialis*, but why stress that he came 'from the province' (of Britain, by implication), which is the natural meaning of *provincialis*? *RIB* therefore accepts the conjecture of Hübner that he was *provinc(iae servus)*, '(the slave) of the province', although it prefers the form *provinc(ialis)*. *RIB* is followed by Tony Birley, who aptly calls Anencletus 'the first known British civil servant'.[45] He would have been the provincial Council's Most Humble Servant, literally so, since it owned him; but in practice, like the slaves and freedmen of the Emperor, he would have been influential and rich.[46] Incidentally he married a Roman citizen, his wife being the youngest at death yet recorded from Roman Britain. But his status must remain a conjecture, although an attractive one, since although 'public slaves' (*servi publici*) are well attested, as slaves owned by a corporate body, there is no sure instance of a slave being owned by a province and called *provincialis*.[47] The use of *h(ic) s(ita) e(st)* with *D(is) M(anibus)* abbreviated suggests an early second-century date, contemporary with this fragment of a letter from Carlisle, which contains the only other instance of his rare name in Britain:

<10.27> *Carlisle (Luguvalium)*

Primu<s> et Anoncletus Eu-
phemio <e>t Secundo et Rusti-
[co] fratribus su{i}is sal[ut]em
...

Tab. Luguval. 18

'Primus and Anoncletus to Euphemius and Secundus and Rusticus their brothers, greetings. ... '

The term 'brothers' again is not to be taken literally. *Euphemius* like *Anoncletus* (as it is spelt here) is a Greek name, so they do not sound like soldiers; it is tempting to see them as two 'slaves of the province' (if we accept Hübner's conjecture), writing from London to fellow-bureaucrats at Carlisle. The text breaks off in the fourth line, which has been damaged by woodworm, but it may contain the word *precatio* ('plea'); just possibly this fragment, though grievously shredded, is the first known British inter-departmental memorandum.

The governor's staff

The governor drew his bodyguard (*singulares*) of cavalry and infantry from the auxiliary *alae* and cohorts, his secretariat and staff from the legions. None of them were civilians, and the bodyguard at least (perhaps 1000-strong) was probably based

[45] Birley 1979, 145, adding Tertullus from the die TERTVLLI | PROVINC (*RIB* II.1, 2409.35) found at Cramond 'in the far north'. But *Provincialis* is quite frequent as a cognomen (in Britain, *RIB* 1085), and should be so understood here, since there was a prefect at Cramond called Tertullus; Provincialis would have been his slave, not his freedman.

[46] Compare **10.37**, **10.38** and *RIB* III, 3173, noted after **10.16**.

[47] Fishwick 1961, 165–6.

in the unusually large fort on the north-west edge of London.[48] The Vindolanda strength report itemises 46 soldiers absent as *singulares leg(ati)*, and the letter has already been quoted in which an Egyptian legionary tells his father that he has escaped stone-breaking by becoming a clerk instead.[49] Soldiers of all three British legions are buried at London, no doubt because they had been seconded in this way. We have already seen the imposing tombstone of the centurion Marcianus (**9.20**), who was probably the chief of office staff (*princeps praetorii*). We can put a name (his cognomen at least) to another holder of this senior post:

<10.28> *Madauros in Numidia (eastern Algeria)*

[... f(ilius)] Quirina Saturninus c[enturio]
e[xercitus p]rovinciae Britan[n]i[ae .....]
prin[c(eps)] offici praesidis, bene[ficiarius]
consularis, optioni(!) praetori,
monymentum(!) sepul[turae]
sibi ex (sestertium) XXX m(ilibus) nummu[m] fecit
et se vivo dedicavit et decessit
annorum LXXXV. h(ic) s(itus) e(st)

Alföldy 1988 (*AE* 1989, 830)

'... Saturninus, son of [...], of the *Quirina* voting-tribe, centurion of the army of the province of [...] Britain; chief of office staff to the governor, seconded to the governor's staff, deputy-chief of his residence; made this burial monument for himself at a cost of 30,000 sesterces, and dedicated it in his lifetime; and died aged 85; he lies here.'

The mausoleum of Saturninus was quarried for stone to build a Byzantine fort, but part of its inscription survives on this re-used limestone block, now badly worn, which was originally butted to another to the left, now lost; its line-endings on the present block suggest it commemorated a woman related to Saturninus, his wife or daughter. The word missing after *Britan[n]i[ae]* is likely to be SVPER or INFER, which would date this monument to the third century, after Britain had become two provinces, Upper and Lower. This is also suggested by the use of *praeses*.[50] The anomalous dative *optioni*, where the nominative is required, is simply a mistake. Saturninus came from Madauros in Numidia (now Mdaourouch in Algeria), a *colonia* of veterans enrolled in his own voting-tribe *Quirina*, which indicates that he returned home after his legionary service in Britain, unlike the other Saturninus from Numidia, soldier of

---

48 Hassall 1973.

49 *Tab. Vindol.* II, 154.5 (with the editors' note). *P. Mich.* VIII 466, quoted after **4.18**.

50 The concluding formula *h(ic) s(itus) e(st)* might suggest an earlier date, but to judge by the published photograph, this reading is by no means certain.

the Sixth Legion, who was buried at Birdoswald.[51] Madauros is best known as the birthplace of the novelist Apuleius, author of *The Golden Ass*, and as the still-pagan university town where St Augustine was a student. It seems an appropriate origin for a bureaucrat, not a fighting soldier, to judge by the career which took Saturninus from quite a junior post in the governor's entourage (the sense of *praetorium* here) to being out-posted as *beneficiarius consularis*, and ultimately returning as the chief of office staff. Like the *speculator* of the British army who died on secondment at Rome (**10.30**), he felt no need to specify his legion: the connection would have become tenuous. His career also reflects the separate evolution of army and 'civil service', as they diverged from their common origin. But even in the fourth century and later, when civil servants were genuine civilians, they still wore a military belt, were known as *cohortales*, and enrolled in fictive legions.[52]

Another inscription from Numidia lists the staff officers in the Third Legion Augusta by grade, notably the *speculatores* and *beneficiarii consularis*.[53] It prompts comparison with the fragmentary marble panels at Southwark which list legionaries by cohort, not century, but unfortunately the heading is almost entirely lost, and their status is unknown; we can only guess they were attached to the governor's staff.[54] When the first Vettius Valens was promoted from the Fourteenth Legion to become procurator of Lusitania, he was honoured by the legion's ten *speculatores* (**1.04**), from which it has been assumed that this number was a legion's regular contribution to the staff. Three or four British *speculatores* are named by a tombstone from London which, like that of Marcianus, once depicted a standing figure within a niche; only the silhouette of his head remains, with this epitaph above:

<**10.29**> *London (Londinium)*

[Dis Mani]bus
[?L(ucius) Vale]r(ius) L(uci) f(ilius) C[l(audia tribu) Celsu[s]
[... s]pec(ulator) leg(ionis) [II A]ug(ustae) A[...]
[...]n(ius) Dardanus cu[...]
[... Val]erius Pudens [...]
[...u]s Probus sp[e]c(ulatores) l[eg(ionis)]

RIB 19+*add.*

---

51 *RIB* III, 3445. Other African legionaries in Britain are C. Aelius Tertiolus (*CIL* viii 2401) and T. Flavius Ingenuus (*CIL* viii 5180), both likewise of the Sixth Legion, and Julius Victor of the Twentieth (*CIL* viii 2080), who may have been drafted there by Septimius Severus from the Third Legion Augusta (Mann 1993, 262). *RIB* II.8, 2502.14 (Holt) is the signature in neo-Punic script of Macrinus, who is likely to have been an African in the Twentieth. The evidence, especially ceramic, is collected by Swan 1992 and 1999.

52 Jones 1964, ch. 16 ('The Civil Service'), esp. 566.

53 *ILS* 2381 (Lambaesis): two *cornicularii* (*RIB* 659 is the only British example), two *commentarienses*, four *speculatores*, 30 *beneficiarii consularis*, five *quaestionarii*, five *beneficiarii tribuni*, and an *haruspex*.

54 *RIB* III, 3016, where this question is discussed.

'To the Shades of the Dead. ?Lucius Valerius Celsus, son of Lucius, of the *Claudia* voting-tribe, [from ...], *speculator* of the Second Legion Augusta. A[...]nius Dardanus [...], Valerius Pudens, [...]ius Probus, *speculatores* of the legion, (set this up).'

The name of Valerius Celsus is given in full, so it would have been followed by his place of origin, abbreviated to three letters; for example LVG for *Lug(duno)*. The names of his three executors cannot be restored so easily, but two at least were *speculatores*; Dardanus seems to have held a different post. The use of *Dis Manibus* unabbreviated suggests a date no later than Trajan; the presence of *speculatores* in London shows that it was by now the provincial capital.[55] Their duties are little known, but anecdotally they served as executioners and confidential emissaries; they were also posted to the imperial capital:

<10.30> *Rome*

D(is) M(anibus)
Val(eri) Paterni
specul(atoris) exercit(us)
Britann(ici),
cura<m> agentibus
Sem(pronio) Pudente
mil(ite) frum(entario)
et Cutio Euplu
ministro spec(ulatorum),
b(ene) m(erenti) fecerunt.
In fr(onte) p(edes) VII, in ag(ro) p(edes) V.

ILS 2372

'To the Shades of the Dead (and) of Valerius Paternus, *speculator* of the British army; (memorial) supervised by Sempronius Pudens commissary soldier, and Cutius Euplus, agent to the *speculatores*; they did this for a well-deserving man. Frontage 7 feet; depth 5 feet.'

The dimensions are those of the burial plot. This elegant marble slab was bought in Rome for the Earl of Arundel's collection and thus came to London, unlike Paternus himself; in 1667, at the prompting of the diarist John Evelyn, it was presented to the University of Oxford. Paternus' executor, Sempronius Pudens, was a *frumentarius* like Quintus of Gloucester. His own tombstone happens also to survive, as well

[55] Hassall 1996. The term 'capital' is used informally (compare Haensch 1997, 120–30), but London was Britain's largest city and centre of communications; evidence is found there of the staffs of legate and procurator.

as the tombstone he erected to his 'excellent friend' Aemilius Flaccus; they both belonged to the Twentieth Legion Valeria Victrix, which may also be assumed of Paternus.[56] The three comrades had been seconded from a British legion to the élite unit of couriers and special agents housed in the *castra peregrina* ('foreign barracks') at Rome, commanded by the *princeps peregrinorum*. One of their commanders we have seen already, Oclatinius Adventus (**8.07**), the sometime procurator of Britain who nearly became Emperor.

The *speculatores* were senior to the *beneficiarii consularis* on the governor's staff, who considerably outnumbered them. Their cumbersome title (often abbreviated to BF COS) only meant that they had been seconded from their legion by 'the favour' (*beneficium*) of the governor; the addition of *consularis*, the informal term for the governor (an ex-consul), distinguished them from lower-ranking *beneficiarii* chosen by other officers to assist them, in particular the legionary legate (**3.02**) and tribunes (**10.12**), and the prefects of auxiliary units. *beneficiarii* are mentioned in writing-tablets from Vindolanda and Carlisle, without the nominating officer being clear, but fourteen stone inscriptions refer to *beneficiarii consularis*, twelve of them the altars they dedicated at forts to which they were outposted.[57] Here is an example from the far north:

<**10.31**> *Risingham (Habitancum)*

deo Mogonito Cad(...)
et n(umini) d(omini) n(ostri) Aug(usti)
M(arcus) G(...) Secundinus
[b(ene)]f(iciarius) co(n)s(ularis) Habita-
nci prima stat(ione)
pro se et suis posu[it]

RIB 1225

'To the god Mogonitus Cad(...) and to the Divinity of Our Lord the Emperor, Marcus G(...) Secundinus, *beneficiarius consularis*, on his first posting at Habitancum, set this up for himself and his family.'

The god Mogons spelt his name in various ways; the evidence for his cult is mostly British, but it was probably imported from the Rhineland, to judge by the Roman name for Mainz, *Mogontiacum*.[58] The abbreviated epithet CAD occurs twice at Risingham, but nowhere else, and its expansion is unknown. The dedicator has also

[56] *CIL* vi 3359 and 3357 (*amico optimo*).

[57] The altars are **10.31** (Risingham), **10.32** (Catterick) and **12.13** (Winchester); *RIB* 235 (Dorchester-on-Thames), 602 (Lancaster), 726 (Catterick again), 745 (Greta Bridge), 1031 and 1032 (Binchester), 1085 (Lanchester), 1696 (Vindolanda) and 1894 (Birdoswald). Two other dedications mark their 'promotion': *RIB* 783+add. (Brougham) and III, 3193 (York).

[58] The derived personal name *Mogontius* is also found, for example in *Tab. Lond. Bloomberg* 6.

abbreviated his own nomen, but there are various possibilities, including *Gabinius* and *Geminius*. By referring to his 'first posting', he implies that other postings would follow: evidently *beneficiarii consularis* expected to be out-posted, and much of what we know about them comes from such altars, which tell us where they were posted, but not really why.[59] The same is true of *stratores consularis*, legionaries seconded to the governor's staff as 'grooms'.[60] Their distribution reflects the strategic network of roads, notably the three altars at Catterick and Greta Bridge, the forts nearest to Scotch Corner where the road to Hadrian's Wall forked for Carlisle and Corbridge. Since Risingham was an outpost of Hadrian's Wall and Caracalla later based 'scouts' (*exploratores*) there, it has also been conjectured that Secundinus was collecting military intelligence. The importance of road-communications is explicit in this altar already mentioned from Catterick:

<**10.32**> *Catterick (Cataractonium)*

deo qui vias
et semitas com-
mentus est T(itus) Aur(elius)
Dasso s(ingularis) c(onsularis) f(ecit) v(otum) l(aetus) l(ibens) m(erito);
Q(uintus) V(arius) Vita-
lis b(ene)f(iciarius) co(n)s(ularis) aram
sacram resti-
tuit
Aproniano et Bra-
dua co(n)s(ulibus)

RIB 725+add.

'To the god who devised roads and paths, Titus Aurelius Dasso, *singularis consularis*, made his vow gladly, willingly, deservedly; Quintus Varius Vitalis, *beneficiarius consularis*, restored this sacred altar in the consulship of Apronianus and Bradua (AD 191).'

This altar, which is one of two dedicated by *beneficiarii consularis* at Catterick, was found in 1620, and has long been lost; the reading depends on a contemporary transcript, but there was apparently a primary inscription to which Vitalis added his own. Dasso's unusual name, which is Illyrian, has been reconstructed from the transcript. He may not have known which god to honour, but a veteran at Cologne could have told him; this man made a dedication to 'Jupiter and the gods of cross-roads, road-forks, roads and paths.'[61] Dasso's altar was renewed by Vitalis,

---

[59] Comprehensively collected by Schallmayer 1990. In general see Austin and Rankov 1995.

[60] Only one of their altars is known (*RIB* III, 3031, with note), at Dover; but a fragment also from Dover (*Britannia* 43 (2012), 396, No. 2) may have been another.

[61] *CIL* xiii 8243, *Quadrivii[s] Trivis Viis Semitis*; compare xiii 202, *Biviis Triviis Quadriviis*. The only British dedication to the *Quadriviae* is **9.16**.

who was evidently a *beneficiarius consularis* replacing a *singularis consularis*, with the implication that their duties were similar and concerned the 'roads and paths'.[62] In Britain, lead sealings of the *eq(uites) s(ingulares)* have been found, not in London, but at Catterick, Carlisle and Brough-under-Stainmore.[63] A *singularis consularis* was buried at Vindolanda, where *beneficiarii* are well attested by the Tablets; but at the age of 55, after 26 years' service, he was surely retired.[64]

The procurator and his staff

Provincial finance, which included the management of imperial estates, taxation and State expenditure, such as paying soldiers and officials, was the responsibility of the imperial procurator (*procurator Augusti*) of Britain, who was directly appointed by the Emperor; although only equestrian in rank, he was independent of the senatorial legate. We have already seen the great tombstone of Classicianus (**2.19**), who achieved the dismissal of a governor, the altars dedicated by Lusius Sabinianus (**6.15**) which probably mark his tour of the new Antonine frontier, and the evidence of Oclatinius Adventus (**8.07**) directing building-work at a Severan outpost-fort. A little later, in the reign of Caracalla, the procurator Cocceius Nigrinus dedicated an altar to a 'goddess-nymph' on Hadrian's Wall.[65] These are four of the thirteen imperial procurators known to us.[66] Their most senior subordinates also enjoyed the title of *procurator*, a word which only means 'manager'. Here is a stylus writing-tablet from London, branded with a circular stamp:

<**10.33**> *London (Londinium)*

proc(uratores) Aug(usti) dederunt
[Br]it(anniae) prov(inciae)

RIB II.4, 2443.2

'The imperial procurators of the province of Britain issued (this).'

This was official stationery 'supplied for the public service', but unfortunately any traces of text inside are illegible. The plural *proc(uratores)* is required by the

---

62 Speidel 1978(a), 126, expands S C as *s(ummus) c(urator)*, because Vitalis uses the explicit abbreviation COS; but his practice cannot have influenced his predecessor. *singulares consularis* were many times more numerous than *summi curatores* (Davies 1976), and to connect the chief accountant of a cavalry unit with 'roads and paths' requires special pleading.

63 *RIB* II.1, 2411.91 (Catterick); *Britannia* 22 (1991), 298, No. 14 (Carlisle); *RIB* II.1, 2411. 254 (Brough-under-Stainmore, reading EQS).

64 *RIB* 1713. *Tab. Vindol.* II, 180, 244; III, 581, ?642, 643. ?App. 263.

65 *RIB* 2066 (Brampton); the attribution to Brigantia is rightly doubted by Birley (2005, 314–15).

66 Birley 2005, 298–300; 302–15. A fourteenth has been deduced from *RIB* 752, but the restoration is unlikely (see *add.*).

verb *dederunt*, but does not make it clear whether just two procurators are meant, the *procurator Augusti* himself and his most senior freedman subordinate, who was confusingly called the *procurator provinciae Britanniae*.[67] Just one of these is known by name, with the outline of his career:

<**10.34**> *Kaimaz, Turkey (Tricomia in Phrygia)*

M(arco) Aur(elio) Aug(usti) liber(to)
Marcioni proximo
rationum, proc(uratori)
marmorum, proc(uratori)
prov(inciae) Britanniae,
proc(uratori) summi chorag(ii),
proc(uratori) prov(inciae) Fryg(iae),
Senecianus collib(ertus)
ex tabular(io)
h(onoris) c(ausa)

ILS 1477

'To Marcus Aurelius Marcio, imperial freedman, deputy in the department of Finance, procurator of marble quarries, procurator of the province of Britain, procurator of the principal stage properties, procurator of the province of Phrygia; (from) Senecianus his fellow-freedman, sometime accountant, in his honour.'

Marcio, like Senecianus, was an imperial slave who had achieved manumission, probably in his 30s. He then reached the highest grade (that of *proximus*) open to freedmen in the *rationes*, the 'ministry' in Rome which administered the Emperor's finances (compare **10.34**), before embarking on a series of provincial appointments, of which Britain was only one. Phrygia, his present appointment, was not really a 'province', but a vast tract of central Anatolia divided between the provinces of Asia and Galatia; Marcio was probably responsible for the Emperor's landholdings there, which would have included mines and quarries.

A freedman 'assistant' (*adiutor*) to the procurators is also known:

[67] Birley 2005, 328–9 (Aurelius Marcio). Seven junior equestrian procurators are known (ibid., 321–8), but they were appointed for special purposes, and we do not know how many there were at a time.

<**10.35**> *Combe Down, near Bath*

pro salute imp(eratoris) C(a)es(aris) M(arci) Aur(eli)
Antonini Pii Felicis Invic-
ti Aug(usti) Naevius Aug(usti)
lib(ertus) adiut(or) proc(uratorum) princi-
pia ruina op<p>ress<a> a solo res-
tituit

RIB 179+*add.*

'For the welfare of the Emperor Caesar Marcus Aurelius Antoninus Pius Felix Unconquered Augustus, Naevius, imperial freedman, assistant of the procurators, restored (these) ruined headquarters from ground-level.'

The emperor is Caracalla (AD 211–17) or his cousin Elagabalus (AD 218–22), both of whom claimed a fictive descent from Marcus Aurelius; Marcus' real and regrettable son Commodus added *Felix* to the imperial titulature, so that his successors such as Caracalla (**13.02**) became *Pius Felix*, meaning 'Conscientious and Dutiful, and (in consequence) Happy and Successful'. Gordian III is an example (**10.01**). Naevius would have managed imperial estates, which here probably included stone-quarries. Forts also have *principia* (**14.06**), but there is no question of Combe Down being military; and although reference to 'ruin' and 'collapse' in military building inscriptions has been suspected to be a euphemism for enemy destruction, this inscription shows it should be taken literally. The same building produced another 'official' document, a lead sealing with the device of a stag couchant:

<**10.36**> *Combe Down, near Bath*

p(rovinciae) Br(itanniae) s(uperioris)

RIB II.1, 2411.37

'(Seal) of the province of Upper Britain'

This once sealed some official package, like the lead tags clipped onto carpets exported from Turkey and Persia. Lower Britain is represented by four lead sealings, each with the device of a bull as its symbol, so it would seem by analogy that a stag symbolised Upper Britain.[68]

Other inscriptions advertise the wealth and power of imperial freedmen, for example the civic honour already mentioned at Lincoln.[69] Another dedicated a statue of 'Holy Britannia' at York (**12.15**). In London this altar was re-used as building material in the Roman Thames embankment:

---

[68] *RIB* II.1, 2411.34 (with note), 35, 36 and *Britannia* 19 (1988), 504, No. 97.

[69] *RIB* III, 3173.

<10.37> *London (Londinium)*

[I(ovi) O(ptimo)] M(aximo)
[templum] vetus-
[t]ate conlabsum
Aquilinus Aug(usti)
lib(ertus) et Mercator
et Audax et Graec(us)
restituer(unt)

RIB III, 3002

'For Jupiter Best and Greatest, Aquilinus freedman of the Emperor, and Mercator and Audax and Graecus, restored (this) [temple] collapsed from age.'

The status of Mercator, Audax and Graecus is not specified, but they were probably imperial slaves, junior colleagues of Aquilinus. This quartet of civil servants, it would seem, had the resources to rebuild a temple. A letter found at Vindolanda alludes to 'business' with imperial freedmen or slaves[70], but there is more human interest in a deed of sale from London, of which the first page survives. The 'girl in question' is bought by an imperial slave:

<10.38> *London (Londinium)*

Vegetus Montani imperatoris Aug(usti) ser(vi) Iucun-
diani vic(arius) emit mancipioque accepit pu-
ellam Fortunatam sive quo alio nomine
est natione Diablintem de Albiciano
LEG[...] (sestertiis) sescentis
ea<m>que puella<m> de qua agitur sanam tradi-
tam esse erronem fugitivam non esse
praestari quod si qu[i]s eam puellam de
qua agitur part[em]ve quam [quis ex] ea e[vi]-
cerit quo m[i]nu[s Vege]tum M[ontani imp(eratoris)]
Caesaris ser(vi) [vi]c(arium) eu[mv]e [a]t que[m] ea res

Tomlin 2003 with Camodeca 2006

'Vegetus, assistant slave of Montanus the slave of the August Emperor and sometime assistant slave of Jucundus, has bought and received by *mancipium* the girl Fortunata, or

---

70 *Tab. Vindol.* III, 645.8, *negotium cum Caesarianis.* The *vikarius* in IV.1, 879.4, may be an imperial slave like Vegetus (**10.38**).

by whatever name she is known, by nationality a Diablintian, from Albicianus [...] for six hundred *denarii*. And that the girl in question is transferred in good health, that she is warranted not to be liable to wander or run away, but that if anyone lays claim to the girl in question or to any share in her, so as to prevent ownership by Vegetus, assistant slave of Montanus the slave of Caesar, or by him to whom the matter [will pertain ...]'

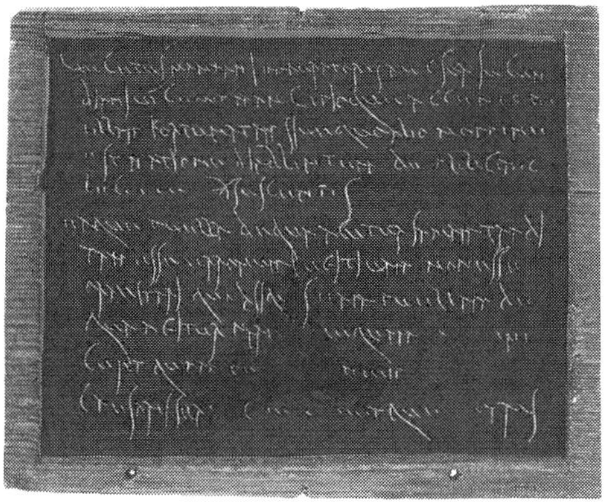

This is another Walbrook discovery, a stylus writing-tablet with part of a deed of 'mancipation', the archaic process by which Roman citizens transferred ownership of land and houses, transport animals and slaves. Its formulaic language is found in other deeds detailing the sale of slaves.[71] The purchaser was not in fact a Roman citizen, but he was rich and influential: despite being the slave of a slave, he could buy his own slave for 600 *denarii*, equal to 2 years' legionary pay before deductions. Vegetus' complicated nomenclature means that he had been bought by the imperial slave Montanus as his assistant, with the prospect of replacing him when Montanus was allowed to purchase his own freedom and rise to higher posts. Montanus incidentally stood in the same relationship to Jucundus, one which made the Emperor's household or 'family' (*familia Caesaris*) almost self-perpetuating. The Emperor is not named, but the formulation suggests Vespasian or his immediate successors, since the term *imperatoris* is not used in the titulature of imperial slaves until after the Julio-Claudian period, and the use of 'agnomina' like *Iucundianus* (the second cognomen which identified their 'owner' within the family) is not found later than Trajan.[72]

Vegetus does not specify his post, but there is the intriguing possibility that he later gained the status of imperial freedman from Nerva, if we identify him with

71 Camodeca 2006, who corrects the reading of the last two lines.

72 Weaver 1972, chs. 12 (Vicarii) and 14 (Vicariani).

the Cocceius Vegetus addressed in a letter at Vindolanda.[73] His new acquisition came from north-western Gaul; Noviodunum, the capital of her tribe the Diablintes, is usually identified with Jublains (dépt. de la Mayenne). Imperial freedmen quite often manumitted and married their own slaves; one day, perhaps, an inscription will attest this 'Cocceia Fortunata', and give her story a happy ending.[74]

The Thorigny Marble

Tiberius Claudius Paulinus, the legate of Lower Britain in AD 220, is unusually well served by inscriptions: we have already seen the Silures marking his promotion from a British legion to a Gallic province (**10.03**), and it is in Gaul that he features in the famous 'Thorigny Marble', the longest and most revealing inscription of the Roman government of Britain.[75]

This is a tall statue-base of pink marble found in Normandy at Vieux, ancient Aragenua, the capital city of the Viducasses, which once supported the statue of a local notable, Titus Sennius Sollemnis. The statue is lost, but the base was found in the seventeenth century and taken to Thorigny (now Torigni-sur-Vire), hence its name, where it survived neglect and mistreatment which included being used as a chopping-block for cutting roof-slates; in 1814 it was taken to Saint-Lô, where from 1852 was housed in the Hotel de Ville and suffered the nadir of its fortunes in 1944, when Saint-Lô was bombed after D Day and the building collapsed upon it. Not surprisingly, the text is now badly damaged, especially on the front where those slates were cut; but most of it has been read or at least restored by the devoted labour of modern scholars, notably Hans-Georg Pflaum and Pascal Vipard, whose edition has been followed here.

Unusually, the base is inscribed on three of its four sides. From the Romano-British perspective, it is the left-hand side which is the most interesting, since it carries the only known example of a letter written by a governor of Britain. But this is only an appendix to the main text on the front, which describes the honorand and his career, and concludes with an emphatic reference to his influential patrons:

[73] *Tab. Vindol.* III, App. 352. Imperial freedmen took the nomen of the Emperor who manumitted them, which in this case would be Nerva.

[74] Three women called *Cocceia Fortunata* are known in Rome (*CIL* vi 3542, 34442) and Puteoli (*Notizie degli Scavi di Antichità* 1913, 25), but none can be identified with 'our' Fortunata.

[75] This phrase is used in tribute to Birley 2005, but also invaluable is Frere 1987, ch. 9, 'The administration of Roman Britain'.

<10.39> *Vieux (Aregenua Viducassium)*

T(ito) Sennio Sollemni Sollem-
nini fil(io) IIvir(o) sine sorte quater, [a]ug(uri)
[o]mnib(us) honorib(us) mun[eribus]que i[n]
[... functo ... flamen] m[unera?]r[i]us in
[s]ua c[i]vitate eodemq(ue) tem[po]re sacerdo[s]
R[om]a[e] e[t Aug(usti) ?fuit] et [o]mne genus spec-
taculorum e[did]it. [fu]erunt gladia[to]-
r[um c]ertam(ina) n(umero) XXXII, ex quibus per quad-
riduum [n(umero)] V[III] s[i]n[e] missione edideru[nt].
[bal]neum, quod [pop]u[lar]ibus coloniae s[uae]
pr[ofutu]rum S[ollemninus inferio?]ribus
fundam[en]tis inst[i]tut[is? pae]ne [reli]querat
consumm(avit) d[e]s[tin(avitque ?conc]edere fructum unde
in perpetuum instauraretur. is Sollemnis
amicus Tib(erii) Claud(ii) Paulinus, leg(ati) Aug(usti) pro pr(aetore) pro-
vinc(iae) Lugd(unensis) et cliens fuit, cui postea
[l]eg(ato) Aug(usti) p(ro) p(raetore) in Brit(annia) ad legionem sext[am]
adsedit, cuique(!) ei salarium militiae
in auro aliaque munera longe pluris miss[it].
fuit cliens probatissimus Aedini Iuliani
leg(ati) Aug(usti) prov(inciae) Lugd(unensis), qui postea praef(ectus) praet(orio)
fuit, sicut epistula, quae ad latus scripta es[t]
declaratur. adsedit etiam in provincia Num[id(ia)]
Lambense M(arco) Valerio Floro trib(uno) mil(itum) leg(ionis) III Aug(ustae).
iudici arcae ferrar(iarum)
tres prov(inciae) Gall(iae)
primo umquam in sua civitate posuerunt.
locum ordo civitatis Viducass(ium) libera(e) dedit.
p(osita) XVII K(alendas) Ian(uarias) Pio et Proculo
co(n)s(ulibus)

CIL xiii 3162; Vipard 2008 (*AE* 2008, 909)

'To Titus Sennius Sollemnis, son of Sollemninus, four times joint-mayor without drawing lots, augur, after fulfilling all honours and duties ... he was Priest (of the Imperial Cult) in his own city, and at the same time Priest of Rome and Augustus (at Lyon), and presented every sort of spectacles: there were 32 gladiatorial combats in four days, 8 of which ended without reprieve. He completed the baths which Sollemninus had left for the benefit of his

> fellow-citizens with only the lower foundations laid, and he undertook to provide the interest for their upkeep in perpetuity.
>
> 'Sollemnis was the friend and client of Tiberius Claudius Paulinus, imperial propraetorian legate of the province of Gallia Lugdunensis, whom he served as assessor in the Sixth Legion when he was subsequently propraetorian legate in Britain, and who sent him his salary in gold and other gifts worth much more. He was the valued client of Aedinius Julianus, imperial propraetorian legate of the province of Gallia Lugdunensis, who subsequently became Praetorian Prefect, as the letter which is written on the side makes clear. He was also assessor in the province of Numidia, at Lambaesis, to Marcus Valerius Florus, military tribune of the Third Legion Augusta.
>
> 'To the Judge of the Treasury of the Iron Mines, the first to be given a statue in his own city by the Three Provinces of Gaul. The site was given by the Council of the Free City of the Viducasses. Erected 17 days before the Kalends of January in the consulship of Pius and Proculus (16 December AD 238).'

Sollemnis was elected joint-mayor (*duumvir*) without the need to draw lots in the event of a tied vote. He held a local priesthood, the augurate, and also the priesthood of the Imperial Cult. He was also elected as his city's delegate to the annual Council of the three Gallic provinces which met at Lyon to celebrate the Imperial Cult; here he was even elected High Priest for the year. The text emphasises the expensive games he gave to mark these priesthoods, implying that he was rich as well as influential. His influence culminated in cordial relations with successive governors of Gallia Lugdunensis, whose 'client' or follower he was, meaning that he repaid their patronage with his loyal support. This nexus of reciprocal obligation between persons of different status was fundamental to Roman society, and is substantiated here by two letters quoted verbatim; the first is inscribed on the left-hand side:

> [e]xemplum epistulae Cl(audii)
> [Pa]ulini leg(ati) Aug(usti) pr(o) pr(aetore) prov(inciae)
> [B]ritanniae ad Sennium Soll[em]-
> nem a Tampio.
> 'licet plura merenti tibi h[aec]
> a me pauca tamen quonia[m]
> honoris causa offeruntu[r],
> velim accipias libente[r]:
> chlamidem Canusinam,
> dalmaticam Laodiciam, fibulam
> [au]ream cum gemmis, rachanas
> duas, tossiam Brit(annicam), pellem vit[uli]
> [m]arini. semestris autem epistulam,
> ubi prope diem vacare coeperi[t],
> mittam, cuius militiae salarium
> [i]d est (sestertium) XXV (millia) n(ummum) in auro suscip[e],

[d]is faventibus et maiestate sànct[a]
[i]mp(eratoris) deinceps pro meritis
adfectionis magis digna
consecuturus. concordit(er).'

'Copy of the letter of Claudius Paulinus, imperial propraetorian legate of the province of Britain, to Sennius Sollemnis, from *Tampium*.

'Although you deserve more, I would that you willingly accept these few things from me, since they are offered to do you honour: a cloak from Canosa, a sleeved tunic from Laodicea, a gold brooch with gemstones, two mantles, a British rug, a seal skin. I shall send the commission of a six-month tribunate just as soon as it falls vacant, and you are to receive the salary of this post, that is 25,000 sesterces, in gold; if the gods and the Emperor's holy majesty allow, you will receive hereafter rewards more worthy of what your affection deserves. Cordially yours.'

Paulinus is misleadingly described as governor of Britain, since it is clear from the context, as indeed from **13.06** at High Rochester, that he was actually legate of Lower Britain with its capital at York, the base of its only legion, the Sixth, in which he was offering Sollemnis a short-term commission. He writes from *Tampium*, which must be somewhere in northern Britain; a connection has been surmised with the *ala Tampiana*, which had left Britain by the AD 130s, but this regiment was named after its first prefect who was called *Tampius*, not a place, and there is no instance in Britain of an auxiliary unit giving its name to its station.

The principal inscription says that Sollemnis served as an 'assessor' in the Sixth Legion, which strictly speaking would mean that he served as an adviser in legal matters to a senior officer, as he undoubtedly did in Africa. Paulinus of course was legate of the Sixth Legion, and as such might have appointed his own 'assessor' (a term which carries some of the overtones of 'adviser' in modern public life) if a tribunate had been unavailable; so it is unclear whether Sollemnis actually achieved the commission he had been promised, but this was certainly Paulinus' intention, since his personal gifts of jewellery and clothing amounted to the 'uniform' of a newly-appointed officer. It was a lavish act of patronage like Pliny's, who records his own generosity in giving a fellow-townsman 40,000 sesterces to 'equip and adorn' himself for the post of centurion which he had just secured for him.[76] Other examples are known of such 6-month tribunates, which would have given Sollemnis formal equestrian status (he was obviously rich enough to qualify), and might even have prefaced a career in the Emperor's service. The payment of his salary 'in gold' is stressed, since it implies the progressive depreciation of the 'silver' coinage; by now 100 sesterces or 25 silver denarii, equivalent to one gold *aureus* in

[76] Pliny, *ep.* vi 25, *ad instruendum se ornandumque*. But his protégé disappeared en route to his appointment, and Pliny feared the worst. The Augustan History provides parodies of letters in which a patron, in this case the Emperor himself (*Claudius* 14; *Probus* 4), equips a deserving officer on appointment.

theory, were actually worth less than half of one. If then we assume that Caracalla doubled legionary pay from 1200 sesterces to 2500, it means that Sollemnis was being offered more than twice 10 years' pay for just 6 months of ornamental service on the staff.

Paulinus was thus repaying a deserving follower out of public funds as well as from his own pocket. His letter, with its elegant and Ciceronian turn of phrase, ignores the nature of the debt; this is artlessly revealed by the other letter, inscribed on the right-hand side:

exemplum epistul(ae) Aedini[i]
Iuliani, praefecti praet(orio),
ad Badium Comnianum pr[o]-
cur(atorem) et vice praesidis agen[t(em)]:
'Aedinius Iulianus Badio
Comniano, sal(utem). in provincia
Lugdune<n>s{s}(i) quinque fascal(is)
cum agerem, plerosq(ue) bonos
viros perspexi, inter quos
Sollemnem istum oriundum
ex civitate Viduc(assium) sacerdote[m]
quem propter sectam, gravitat[em]
et honestos mores amare coepi.
his accedit, quod, cum Cl(audio) Paulin[o],
decessori meo in concilio
Galliarum instinctu quorund[am]
qui ab eo propter merita sua laes[i]
videbantur, quasi ex consensu provin[c(iarum)]
accus{s}ationem instituere tem(p)tare[nt],
Sollemnis iste meus proposito eor[um]
restitit, provocatione scilicet inter[po]-
[s]ita, quod patria eius cum inter ce[ter(os)]
legatum eum creasset, nihil de ac-
tione mandassent, immo contra laud[as]-
[se]nt, qua ratione effectum est, ut o[mnes]
[a]b accus{s}atione desisterent: que[m]
magis magisque amare et compro[bare]
coepi. is certus honoris mei erg[a se]
ad videndum me in urbem venit [atq(ue)]
proficiscens petit, ut eum tibi [com]-
mendarem. recte itaque feceris, [si]
de[si]d[e]rio illius adnueris. et reliqua.'

'Copy of the letter of Aedinius Julianus, Praetorian Prefect, to Badius Comnianus, Procurator and acting-Governor:

> 'Aedinius Julianus to Badius Comnianus, greetings. When I was propraetorian legate of the province of Lugdunensis, I got to know many good men, including Sollemnis, the Priest from the city of the Viducasses, whom I grew to like for his high principles, his seriousness, and his moral character. A further reason was that when my predecessor Claudius Paulinus was threatened with prosecution in the Council, ostensibly on behalf of the provinces but instigated by certain persons who thought they had been injured by him for what they deserved, my friend Sollemnis opposed their purpose, by objecting that his own city, when it made him one of the delegates, had given him no such mandate, and that on the contrary it had commended Paulinus. The result was that everyone abandoned the prosecution, and I begun to like and esteem Sollemnis more and more. Being assured of my respect for him, he came to see me at the City (Rome); and when he was leaving, he asked me to recommend him to you. So you will do rightly in acceding to his wish. (etc.)'

The writer of this letter, Aedinius Julianus, was praetorian prefect when the statue-base was erected; Badius Comnianus was the imperial procurator and acting-governor of Lugdunensis at the time. Sollemnis, a small-town magnate, had thus developed contacts which extended far beyond Gaul in AD 238, as far as the new Emperor Gordian III, since Aedinius Julianus had just become his virtual vicegerent. Gordian's recent accession explains why so little is made of Sollemnis' connection with the Third Legion Augusta: embarrassingly, it was being disbanded for having caused the deaths of Gordian's grandfather and uncle, Gordian I and II, when they rebelled against Maximinus in AD 238 (compare **13.15**). The imperial politics of AD 238 have been much discussed in the light of this inscription, but from the perspective of Britain its principal interest is to illustrate the working of patronage. Paulinus in Gaul had been in danger of a vote of censure (Julianus tactfully does not say whether he deserved it or not), which might have resulted in his prosecution for misgovernment; this would have been embarrassing, to say the least, and would have interrupted his smooth progress to Lower Britain. Here he was at once able to reward his saviour.

Educated persons who read this story will object that important posts should go to educated persons, perhaps after the formality of interview or competitive examination, but to understand Roman values they should ponder another of Pliny's letters.[77] Pliny successfully asked the governor of Britain, Neratius Marcellus, to appoint his own follower, the scholarly Suetonius Tranquillus, to a military tribunate; but Suetonius (the future biographer of Claudius and the other Caesars) now asked him to transfer his commission to a kinsman, Caesennius Silvanus. Pliny's letter to Suetonius makes no reference to military ability or experience, only to unspecific 'merits' (*merita*) and 'distinction' (*honores*). He congratulates Suetonius on his family loyalty, and himself on having friends who were not only able to gain commissions, but could give them to others.

[77] Pliny, *ep.* iii 8. The importance of patronage, or at least recommendation, in the appointment of equestrian officers is well illustrated by Birley 2003.

11

ECONOMY AND SOCIETY

The land and its products

In Roman Britain, as in every pre-industrial society, most people got their living from the land. In their turn they supported a small service sector, craftsmen of all kinds, shopkeepers, businessmen and traders, prostitutes, domestic servants and slaves, doctors, teachers and other professional men, and in particular what peasants might have called the 'idle mouths' responsible for so many of our inscriptions: landowners and administrators, priests and soldiers. Romano-British herdsmen and ploughmen were illiterate, so far as we know, which lends interest to this curse tablet, the second most northerly[1] yet found:

<11.01> *Ratcliffe-on-Soar, near Nottingham*

annoto de duas
ocrias ascia<m> scal-
pru<m> ma<n>ica<m> si m(ulier) au[t] si
b(aro) *RIANTINE* duas
partis deo *AC CEVM*

Britannia 35 (2004), 336, No. 3

'I take note of two gaiters, an axe, a knife, a glove; whether woman or if man ... two parts to the god ...'

The scribe used the accusative case, not the ablative, with the preposition *de*. He omitted the final *-m* (unsounded) from the words for 'axe', 'knife' and 'glove', incidentally reducing the latter (*manicam*) to MACIA. The formula 'whether man or woman' was so familiar to him, or space so short, that he reduced it to its initials, *m(ulier)* and *b(aro)*. He added a redundant *aut* ('or'). Some of his text cannot be resolved, so it has been left in italic capitals, but the general sense is clear: he is listing stolen property, and offering the unnamed god a proportion for its recovery. Gloves and gaiters were used

[1] The most northerly is the Rothwell tablet (*Britannia* 43 (2012), 403, No. 13). Not one has been found in the forts of Hadrian's Wall and its hinterland; their distribution is almost entirely 'civilian'.

for heavy work in brambles and woodland: a farmworker or a woodman, hedging or coppicing perhaps, has lost his working-gear.[2] He may have been illiterate, but he had access to literacy, just as other peasants, if they were estate-workers or tenant-farmers, would have had literate masters: styluses are quite often found at villas, one of which has even produced a fragmentary land-conveyance, inscribed in ink on a re-used waxed tablet; tantalising scraps of ink text have also been found in the Thames valley near Lechlade.[3] Occasionally a villa mosaic incorporates an inscription, and here is the most sophisticated of them, just two lines of verse incorporated in the dining-room floor:

<11.02> *Lullingstone Roman villa*

invida si ta[uri] vidisset Iuno natatus
iustius Aeolias isset adusque domos

RIB II.4, 2448.6

'If jealous Juno had seen the swimmings of the bull, she would have been more justified in going to the halls of Aeolus.'

This allusive couplet captions a picture of the mythical princess Europa being carried off from the Lebanon, across the sea to Crete, by Jupiter who has turned himself into a bull. The story comes from Ovid's *Metamorphoses*, and in Ovidian verse the anonymous poet – perhaps even the villa's owner, showing off to his dinner guests – is also recalling an episode in Virgil's *Aeneid*, Juno's visit to the God of the Winds for a storm to wreck Aeneas: he comments that she might have used the opportunity to sink her errant husband instead. But the poet Martial also saw a picture of Europa, and he comments that Jupiter should have become a bull when he deceived Juno by turning the nymph Io into a cow. His epigram sounds like the coarse but witty riposte of a guest at Lullingstone, rather than a third source of the host's inspiration.[4] At all events, the mosaic is striking evidence that books were read in Roman Britain, even if none survives.[5]

---

[2] Palladius I 42(43), 4, *ocreas manicasque* (etc.), quoted in the commentary to *Tab. Sulis* 5, which also relates to the theft of gloves; note also Ionas, *vita Columbani* I 15, for the Saint cursing the thief who stole his gloves (in fact a raven). Gloves were also stolen at Uley (*Britannia* 27 (1996), 439, No. 1).

[3] *Tab. Vindol.* I, p. 35, British tablets (f) (now *RIB* II.4, 2443.13) and (k). Hanson and Conolly 2002.

[4] Cosh 2016 notes the relevance of Martial *ep.* 14.180, which he argues is parodied by **11.02**. But if both epigrams had been anonymous, Martial's would seem to have been prompted by **11.02**, not vice versa, as if it were intended to puncture a literary conceit. Although Martial claimed to have British readers (*ep.* 11.3), it is safer to see both epigrams as responding independently to a well-known picture.

[5] Barrett 1978; Tomlin 2012(a).

Nonetheless, despite this evidence of high education, inscriptions and graffiti are uncommon from villas. Another precious glimpse of country life and manners is offered by the curse tablets from the rural temple of Mercury at Uley on the Cotswold escarpment, about 80 in total.[6] When they have all been published, they should reflect the interests and anxieties of an agricultural community, but here are two which illustrate the human element involved in animal husbandry:

<11.03> Uley

deo Mercurio
Docilinus ...
Varianus et Peregrina
et Sabinianus qu[i] peco-
ri meo dolum malum in-
tulerunt et ... pro-
locuntur(!), rogo te ut eos
max[i]mo [le]to adigas nec
eis sanit[atem nec] som-
num perm[itt]as nisi
a te quod m[ihi] ad[mi]-
ni[strav]erint
redem[e]rint

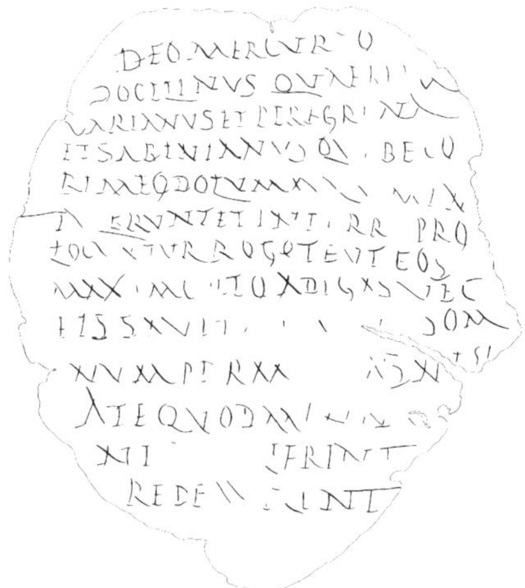

Britannia 20 (1989), 329, No. 3

50 mm

'Docilinus to the god Mercury. [...] Varianus and Peregrina and Sabinianus, who have brought evil harm on my beast and are [...] I ask that you drive them to the greatest death, and do not allow them health or sleep unless they redeem from you what they have administered to me.'

Docilinus has a farm animal which has fallen sick, and he knows whom to blame: two men and a woman, a neighbouring family no doubt. But although this is the countryside, these people all have colourless 'Roman' names, even if *Docilinus* 'conceals' the Celtic name *Docca*. Like many British curse tablets, it appeals to the deity to punish the guilty person (whether named or anonymous) with ill-health until the wrong is put right. Here is another such petition:

[6] Tomlin 1993, with additions in *Britannia* 20 (1989), 327, No. 2; 329, No. 3; *Britannia* 23 (1992), 310, No. 5; *Britannia* 26 (1995), 371, No. 1; 373, No. 2; 376, No. 3; 378, No. 4; *Britannia* 24 (1993), 310, No. 1; *Britannia* 27 (1996), 439, No. 1; *Britannia* 29 (1998), 433, No. 1; *Britannia* 46 (2015), 398, No. 21.

<11.04> *Uley*

deo sancto Mercurio Honoratus.
conqueror numini tuo me per-
didisse rotas duas et vaccas quat-
tuor et resculas plurimas de
hospitiolo meo.
rogaverim genium nu-
minis tu{u}i ut ei qui mihi fraudem
fecerit sanitatem ei non per-
mittas nec iacere nec sedere nec
bibere nec manducare, si baro
si mulier, si puer si puella, si servus
si liber, nis{s}i meam rem ad me
pertulerit et meam concordiam
habuerit. iteratis pr{a}ecibus ro-
go numen tuum ut petitio mea
statim pareat me vindica-
tum esse a maiestate tua

Britannia 23 (1992), 310, No. 5

'Honoratus to the holy god Mercury. I complain to your divinity that I have lost two wheels and four cows and many small belongings from my house.

'I would ask the genius of your divinity that you do not allow health to the person who has done me wrong, nor allow him to lie or sit or drink or eat, whether he is man or woman, whether boy or girl, whether slave or free, unless he brings my property to me and is reconciled with me. With renewed prayers I ask your divinity that my petition may immediately make me vindicated by your majesty.'

Roman agricultural writers speak of cows being used for ploughing: the 'two wheels' belonged perhaps to a cart or heavy plough. Another Uley tablet complains of two villains called Vitalinus and Natalinus, his son, who have stolen a transport animal (*iumentum*).[7] Honoratus' neatly-written text is a mixture of the colloquial, the formulaic and the 'literary'. His vocabulary may offend Classical Latinists, who will meet words that were current in spoken ('Vulgar') Latin, such as the diminutives *resculas* ('little things') and *hospitiolum* ('little lodgings', here meaning 'house'), and the word *baro* which means 'fool' in Classical Latin, but here quite obviously means 'man'. In this sense it seems to have been a loan-word from Celtic or (more likely) German; the English word 'Baron' is descended from it. But in writing *nissi* for *nisi* and *praecibus* for *precibus*, Honoratus was trying unsuccessfully to avoid Vulgarisms.

[7] Tomlin 1993, 118, No. 1.

Despite repeating formulas found in other curse tablets, he was also trying to write a mannered, impressive Latin. Note the polite subjunctive *rogaverim* (line 6) equivalent to the indicative *rogo* (14–15), the polite periphrases addressed to the god's 'divinity', the pompous references to 'reconciliation', 'renewed prayers' and 'vindication'. Those stolen cows inspired a rustic litterateur.

Another Uley tablet refers to 'linen' (**12.36**), and unpublished tablets to 'wethers' (castrated sheep) and to 'property, i.e. wool', just as we have seen the balls of wool on Regina's tombstone at South Shields (**9.33**).[8] Woollen textiles are the only British products to be mentioned in the enormous catalogue of goods and services with which the Emperor Diocletian tried to fix prices in AD 301. This famous edict was inscribed on stone, and copies in Latin and Greek translation, all of them fragmentary, survive from the eastern Empire. Here are the two relevant entries:

<11.05> Diocletian, *Edict of Maximum Prices*

[tap]ete Britannic[u]m prim(ae) form[ae (denariorum) quinqu]e mili[b]us
[for]ma[e] secundae [(denariorum) quattuor] milibus

burrus(!) Britanni[cus] (denariorum) sex milibus

Lauffer 1971, chs. xix 28–9 and 48

'Rug, British, first quality: 5,000 *denarii*
ditto, second quality: 4,000 *denarii*

Hooded cloak, British: 6,000 *denarii*'

The Greek text spells *birrus* ('hooded cloak') correctly; like *caracalla* (**11.06**), it was probably a Celtic loan-word. Since Diocletian was vainly trying to freeze inflation, it is difficult to say how 'real' his prices were. He prices gold bullion at 72,000 *denarii* to the pound, which would have made the *birrus* worth six *solidi* in terms of the gold coin first struck by Constantine at 72 to the pound; oddly enough, this is the price quoted by the poet Claudian a century later for his own *birrus*.[9] It would have been a considerable sum, beyond the reach of many: the five-yearly bonus (*donativum*) issued to soldiers in the fourth century was only five *solidi*.

Many of the Bath curse tablets refer to stolen clothing, which includes the hooded cloak favoured by Antoninus, the elder son of Septimius Severus, which gave him the name 'Caracalla':

---

[8] Tomlin 1993, 129, No. 58 (*res, id est lanam*); 130, No. 83 (*uerbeces*).

[9] *carm. min.* 10 (92), *de birro castoreo: sex emptus solidis*.

<11.06> *Bath (Aquae Sulis)*

Docilianus
Bruceri (filius)
deae sanctissim<a>e
Suli.
devoveo eum [q]ui
caracellam(!) meam
involaverit, si
vir si femina, si
servus si liber,
ut [e]um dea Sulis
maximo letum(!)
[a]digat nec ei so-
mnum permit-

(*overleaf*)
tat, nec natos nec
nascentes, do-
[ne]c caracallam
meam ad tem-
plum sui numi-
nis per[t]ulerit.

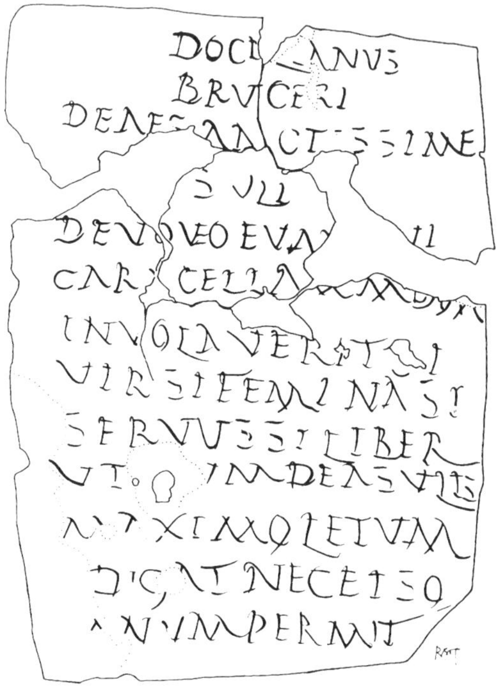

Tab. Sulis 10

'Docilianus son of ?Brucetus to the Most Holy Goddess Sulis. I curse him who has stolen my hooded cloak, whether man or woman, whether slave or free, that the goddess Sulis may drive him to the greatest death, and not allow him sleep or children now and in the future, until he has brought my hooded cloak to the temple of her divinity.'

The first-century tombstone of Philus (**9.46**) shows him wearing such a cloak, and this text is probably not much later. Its 'rustic capitals' are beautifully inscribed, but they contain what seem to be copying mistakes: probably *Bruceri* for *Bruceti* (compare **11.07**), since in cursive writing *t* can look like *r*; and certainly *devovo* for *devoveo* (the second *e* was inserted afterwards by ligature), and the false diminutive *caracellam* for *caracallam* (spelt correctly the second time); also *maximo letum* is ungrammatical. This tablet is not only the earliest written reference to a *caracalla*, the garment later affected by the Emperor Aurelius Antoninus, it is the first and only document to name the goddess in the nominative case: she was indeed *Sulis*, not *Sul*, as some scholars once thought.[10] But it poses a new question. The script resembles that of Docilinus' Uley tablet (**11.03**), with which it shares a formula otherwise unknown,

[10] Scarth (1864), for instance, always refers to her as 'Sul', which in turn he takes to be a confusion of *Sol* (the Sun); hence the title of his book, *Aquae Solis*, which reproduces a variant in the manuscript tradition of the Antonine Itinerary.

the curse of 'the greatest death', although Docilianus writes *letum* ungrammatically for *leto*. Does this similarity of handwriting, the coincidence of formula, the near coincidence of the petitioners' names, all mean that these two texts, from two quite different sites, are closely related? It looks like it.

Stone, metal and clay

Docilianus' very accomplished lettering (**11.06**) raises another question: was he the brother of a local stone-cutter? This craftsman dedicated two altars to female divinities which he may have thought were akin to Sulis, although their cult actually came from the Rhineland:

<11.07> *Bath (Aquae Sulis)*

Sulevis
Sulinus
scul<p>tor
Bruceti f(ilius)
sacrum f(ecit) l(ibens) m(erito)

RIB 151

'To the Suleviae, Sulinus the stone-cutter, son of Brucetus, willingly and deservedly made (this) offering.'

And in another city, but by the same hand:

<11.08> *Cirencester (Corinium Dobunnorum)*

Sule<v>is
Sulinus
Bruceti (filius)
v(otum) s(olvit) l(ibens) m(erito)

RIB 105

'To the Suleviae, Sulinus son of Brucetus willingly and deservedly paid his vow.'

Brucetus, the father of Sulinus, named him after the local goddess Sulis, so he can safely be attributed to Bath, like the 'Sulinus son of Maturus' who honoured

Sulis with an altar there.[11] The name *Brucetus* is otherwise unknown, but it should surely be restored in Docilianus' tablet. Does it then follow that he and Sulinus were brothers, and that it was Sulinus' professional skills which inscribed the tablet? These questions cannot really be answered, but Sulinus must have worked the famous Bath freestone, like this immigrant mason who joined the local cult:

<11.09> *Bath (Aquae Sulis)*

Priscus
Touti f(ilius)
lapidariu[s]
cives(!) Car[nu]-
tenus Su[li]
deae v(otum) [s(olvit) l(ibens) m(erito)]

RIB 149

'Priscus, son of Toutus, stonemason, a tribesman of the Carnutes, to the goddess Sulis willingly and deservedly paid his vow.'

Priscus was a Gaul who came from what is now Chartres. *cives* is a frequent confusion for *civis*, as in **2.08** and **11.36**. For the dedicator to be named before the deity is most unusual in the epigraphy of Roman Britain, and would suggest Gallic influence.[12] The quarries which produced this mason's stone may well have been imperial property, to judge by the Combe Down inscription (**10.35**) which reveals a government 'headquarters' in the area.

After the conquest, as we have seen, the Roman government promptly extracted British lead from the Mendips (**2.17**), north Wales (**3.11**) and Yorkshire (**3.18**); later this mining and smelting was contracted out, to judge by this ingot from the Derbyshire field:

<11.10> *Tansley Moor, Derbys.*

P(ubli) Rubri Abascanti metalli Lutudare<n>s(is)

RIB II.1, 2404. 51

'(Product) of Publius Rubrius Abascantus, of the mine at Lutudarum.'

The mould-maker used ligatures to cram in the lessee's name, with AN inside C, and L inside L, and he contracted the place-name: in spoken Latin there was a

---

[11] *RIB* 150.

[12] Compare the Vindolanda dedication (**12.16**) to the goddess Gallia by 'the citizens of Gaul', who name themselves first.

tendency to reduce [ns] to [s], as in *Lugduness* (**10.39**, right face), *fabriciesis* (**11.16**) and *Vindolandesses* (**12.73**). *Lutudarum* is named by some 20 ingots, but its exact location is unknown.

Bricks and tiles were often stamped by military units, or by private manufacturers with their name or initials, like British mixing bowls (*mortaria*) or Gallic samian ware. More than 200 graffiti are also known on brick and tile, inscribed with a stylus, stick or finger, in the damp clay before it was fired.[13] They are numerals (batch-totals), dates (of manufacture), personal names (of the workmen presumably), occasionally scraps of literature like a Virgilian tag at Silchester[14] and this mysterious line:

<**11.11**> *Binchester (Vinovia)*

Armea me docuit recte
<ti>bi dicere cunctis

RIB II.5, 2491.146

'Armea has taught me to say "No, thank you" to everyone (else).'

This hexameter is otherwise unknown. The scribe wrote quite elegant capitals, but omitted TI from *tibi* by mistake for the TE he had just written in *recte*. His Latin is idiomatic: other poets use *me docuit* of some woman 'teaching' them to change their habits, and *recte tibi* is a colloquialism like 'All right', a politely evasive formula. But we do not know who this angel of the North was, nor whether she really succeeded in teaching her leopard to change his spots. The reference is quite obscure, like this metrical jingle from London:

<**11.12**> *London (Londinium)*

Austalis
dibus XIII
vagatur sib<i>
cotidim

RIB II.5, 2491.147

'Austalis has been wandering by himself every day for 13 days.'

Austalis is a 'Vulgar' spelling of *Augustalis*, the medial *g* having become [y] by lenition, just as St Augustine was dismissed by Chaucer's monk as 'Austin'.[15] *cotidim*

[13] Tomlin 1979, now collected in *RIB* II.5, 2491.

[14] *RIB* II.5, 2491.148, *conticuere omnes* (*Aen.* ii 1); also inscribed by a Verulamium potter (*RIB* II.8, 2502.51 with *Britannia* 46 (2015), 419, add. (i)).

[15] *Prologue* 188, 'Let Austin have his swynk [toil] to him reserved'.

is a variant of Classical *cotidie*. The metre is 'accentual' and depends on the spoken stress, not 'quantitative' like the Binchester hexameter (**11.11**) which depends on whether vowels are 'short' or 'long'; it is a pair of iambic dimeters which rhyme, unlike the whole of Virgil.

These graffiti are little more than evidence of literacy – or rather, of pride in literacy – but here are three fine examples from the Twentieth Legion's works-depot at Holt which say something of the makers; the first is a roof-tile (*tegula*) which also bears the legion's stamp:

<11.13> *Holt (?Bovium)*

Iulius Aventinus milis(!)
co<h>ortis p[r]ima<e> Sunicor(um)

RIB II.5, 2491.96

'Julius Aventinus, soldier of the First Cohort of Sunici.'

Aventinus was an auxiliary soldier, whose cohort was based at Caernarvon (**8.03**). Without being a legionary, he was a Roman citizen and wrote in well-practised capital letters, like those used for public notices and the headings of military documents. He also wrote Latin as he pronounced it: the influence of the spoken language is apparent in *milis* for *miles* (like *cives* for *civis* in **11.09**), and in the failure to sound the *h* which contracted *cohortis* to *cortis*, the confusion over the case-ending of *prima*, and the 'clipping' of the lightly-sounded *-um* from *Sunicorum*.

The second graffito is unfortunately incomplete, since it is a unique military document. It was inscribed on a bonding brick, 18 (Roman) inches by 12 (*c.* 44.4 × 29.6 cm), of which only half the surface survives. There are six lines of cursive writing, all by different hands, and thus of particular interest for showing a cross-section of contemporary handwriting:

<11.14> *Holt (?Bovium)*

sum<p>tu[aria ...?]
Iuniu[s ...?]
(denarios) IIII [...?].[...]
Maternu[s]
sum<p>tuaria [...?]
Bellettus

Britannia 26 (1995), 387, No. 28

'Expenses ...Junius ... , 4 *denarii*; Maternus, expenses ... Bellettus.'

Here are the names of three workmen, probably legionaries, two of them bearing commonplace Roman names that may 'conceal' Celtic name-elements, the third a name that may be a variant of *Bellicus* (etc.), which is popular in Celtic-speaking provinces. The hands are different, meaning that these are signatures – and that the sub-unit concerned contained at least three literate members (compare **5.25** and **5.26**). The neuter noun *sumptuarium*, which here has lost its [p] like Sulinus' *scultor* for *sculptor* (**11.07**), is one of those words that must have been common but which has almost disappeared from the written record: the only other instance occurs in a Roman legionary's pay-sheet at Masada in Israel, where it means 'food expenses'.[16] So this brick can be seen as a note of expenses: the three soldiers, each of whom signs his name, had presumably been outposted to Holt, and were expecting to be reimbursed by Chesters HQ at a later date. But were they also expected to bring the brick with them?

The third graffito may also be from Holt, since it is the signature of a legionary on the underside of the jar he had made from a reddish tile-like fabric:

<**11.15**> *Chester (Deva)*

G(aius) V[al(erius) G(ai) f(ilius)]
Pud[ens]
Maceia(!) (tribu)

Britannia 40 (2009), 321, No. 14

'Gaius Valerius Pudens, son of Gaius, of the *Maceia* voting-tribe.'

This graffito is also incomplete, but the restoration is probable. Nomen and cognomen are typical of legionaries, and a 'Lucius (*not* Gaius) Valerius Pudens' is actually known from Chester.[17] The voting-tribe (properly *Maecia*) is mis-spelt, but the writer has insisted on it, as if to emphasise that he was a Roman citizen with voting-rights at Rome.

There was a guild of craftsmen (*collegium fabrorum*) at Chichester (**2.15**), but similar associations existed within the army; here again is the Twentieth Legion:

16 Cotton and Geiger 1989, 35–56, No. 722, line 7, *sumtuarium* (same spelling).

17 *RIB* 542, only a fragment, but the lettering and the use of *Dis Man(ibus)* suggests it is legionary and quite early.

<11.16> *Bath (Aquae Sulis)*

Iulius Vita-
lis fabricie<n>s-
is leg(ionis) XX V(aleriae) V(ictricis)
stipendior-
um IX an<n>or(um) XX-
IX natione Be-
lga, ex col<l>egio
fabrice(nsium) elatu-
s h(ic) s(itus) e(st)

RIB 156+*add.*

'Julius Vitalis, armourer of the Twentieth Legion Valeria Victrix, of 9 years' service, aged 29, by nation Belgic, carried out (to his funeral) by the guild of armourers; he lies here.'

Fabriciensis (with a 'Vulgar' reduction of [ns] to [s]) is conventionally translated as 'armourer', but this should not be understood too narrowly: Vitalis worked in a legionary workshop (*fabrica*) which worked iron and produced metalwork as required, not just arms and armour. This is shown by the Vindolanda worksheet (*opus fabricae*) for '20 April' which itemises iron-working and metal parts for vehicles.[18] The formulation of the epitaph – its use of *h(ic) s(itus) e(st)* without *Dis Manibus*, and of *stipendiorum* unabbreviated – suggests it is first-century, but later than AD 61, the likely date when the legion earned its title of *Valeria Victrix*. There was a British tribe of Belgae with its capital at Venta (Winchester), one of whom became an auxiliary soldier and was discharged in AD 110 after 25 years' service (**4.12**), but this was in Dacia; it is unlikely that Belgae were also being recruited at this early date for legionary service within Britain itself. Vitalis probably came from Gallia Belgica: his executors, who evidently guessed his age, also did not know which of its tribes to name.

His epitaph, like the signatures of the tile-makers at Holt, reminds us that the army had its own craftsmen. But a detailed list of British craftsmen and manufacturers would be little more than a catalogue of names and trademarks. Stamped tiles, *mortaria* and samian ware have been mentioned already. Imported amphoras, iron tools and bronze vessels are stamped with their makers' names.[19] Some British craftsmen sign their work, for example Glaucus, who made a bronze statuette of Mars Corotiacus

[18] *Tab. Vindol.* IV.1, 826 with commentary, including the Egyptian papyrus which records work *in fabricam legionis*.

[19] *RIB* II.2, 2415 (notably Campanian bronzesmiths); II.3, 2428 (iron tools). *RIB* does not include amphora-stamps, for which see Peacock and Williams 1986, 10ff.

(**12.43**). Another statuette of Mars is more informative; the inscription is engraved on two sides of the integral square base:

<11.17> *Torksey, Lincs. (on the Foss Dike Roman canal)*

deo Mar(ti) et
nu(mini)b(us) Aug(ustorum) Col-
asuni Brucci-
us et Caratius de
suo donarunt

ad sester(tios) n(ummos) C
Celatus aerar-
ius fecit et aera-
menti lib(ram) donav-
it factam (denariis) III

RIB 274

'To the god Mars and the Divinities of the Emperors, the Colasuni Bruccius and Caratius gave (this) at their own expense at (a cost of) 100 sesterces; Celatus the bronzesmith made it and gave a pound of bronze made for 3 *denarii*.'

NVB for *nu(mini)b(us)* is a rare instance of abbreviation by contraction. The lettering looks as if it was drafted with pen and ink: it is pleasantly relaxed, as if the engraver, although skilled, felt there was no need to be consistent, either in letter-height or in form. The weight is 5 (Roman) pounds (*c.* 1645 g), so the metal of which it was made cost 15 *denarii* or 60 sesterces. (One silver *denarius* was worth four brass sesterces.) It follows that Celatus' fee was only 40 sesterces, of which 12 went on the pound of bronze he donated. It is hardly surprising, therefore, that 'his' inscription occupied as much space as that of the dedicators. Their names are Celtic, superficially Latinised: *Bruccius* is cognate with *Brucetus* (**11.08**), and *Caratius* derives from *Caratus* embodying the element **caro-s* ('dear'); but *Colasunius*, the name they share, whether as brothers or father and son, is otherwise unknown. The name *Celatus* is found in other provinces, but is also of uncertain derivation; coincidentally, *c(a)elatus* means 'engraved'.

The raw materials cost more than the excellent workmanship. The differential would have been still more extreme in goldsmith's work, but the only stone inscription (a simple ansate panel) is silent on this point:

<**11.18**> *Malton (Derventio)*

feliciter sit
genio loci.
servule, utere
felix tabern-
am aurefi-
cinam

RIB 712

'Good luck to the spirit of the place. Little slave, use the goldsmith's shop (and be) happy.'

Like the previous inscription, this carries a redundant leaf-stop; two, in fact, interrupting the word LOCI. The *genius loci* was the distinctive personality of a place, almost its guardian spirit.[20]

Servulus is a diminutive like *resculas* and *hospitiolum* (**11.04**), used with affection or condescension. The ultimate in this respect is the poem attributed to the dying Hadrian as he questioned his 'poor little wandering Soul'.[21] But the 'little slave' is not named, nor why he merited this handsome inscription. We are only told that there was a goldsmith's shop in Malton.

Medicine

Doctors would regard themselves, not as craftsmen, but as members of a profession. In Britain there is evidence only of military doctors: one dedicates a carved stone relief to Aesculapius and Salus for the welfare of the cavalry regiment at Binchester, two others dedicate altars in Greek at Chester.[22] There is also this tombstone from Hadrian's Wall:

<**11.19**> *Housesteads (Vercovicium)*

D(is) M(anibus)
Anicio
Ingenuo
medico
ord(inario) coh(ortis)
I Tungr(orum)
vix(it) an(nos) XXV

---

20 For *genius* see further **12.18–25.**

21 Hist. Aug. *Hadrianus* 25.9, *animula vagula blandula ... pallidula rigidula nudula.*

22 *RIB* 1028 (Binchester); *RIB* 461 and III, 3151 (Chester). In general, see Davies 1970.

RIB 1618+*add*.

'To the Shades of the Dead (and) to Anicius Ingenuus, commissioned doctor of the First Cohort of Tungrians; he lived 25 years.'

The meaning of *medicus ordinarius* is uncertain, but the best explanation is by Roy Davies, that he was a qualified physician who ranked as centurion (*ordinatus*). Above the inscribed panel is carved a crouching hare; this too is of uncertain significance, but the animal's known fecundity may have made it a symbol of life and immortality.[23] Hospitals (*valetudinaria*) have been identified in many forts and fortresses, so it is not surprising to find other medical staff; this stylus writing-tablet is addressed to one:

<11.20> *Carlisle (Luguvalium)*

Albano seplasiario

Britannia 22 (1991), 299, No. 24

'To Albanus the pharmacist.'

The unusual word *seplasiarius* derives from a street of dealers in Capua who specialised in cosmetics, but in this military context the translation of 'pharmacist' or 'chemist' seems appropriate: we hear of a *seplasiarius* in the First Legion Adiutrix, and of buying medicines from a *seplasiarius*. There was another at Vindolanda, who was called Vitalis.[24]

The itinerant oculist in Roman Britain has been a good friend of historical novelists: the passage across the Brentwood marshes is revealed to the invading Romans by 'a travelling Spanish oculist' in Robert Graves' *Claudius the God*, 'who goes about the country curing the people of marsh-ophthalmia'; and the hero of Rosemary Sutcliffe's *The Eagle of the Ninth* disguises himself as an itinerant oculist to penetrate Caledonia (Scotland). In reality we cannot be sure that he existed, only that some 30 so-called oculists' stamps have been found in Britain, their distribution relating to the road-system.[25] They are small stone tablets with a retrograde inscription on all four edges, used apparently for stamping cakes of eye-salve (*collyrium*):

---

23 Davies 1970. *CSIR* i.6, No. 198 (with note). See also the note to *CSIR* i.9, No. 73 (Chester).

24 References with discussion in *Britannia* 22 (1991), 300, n. 35. For Vitalis see *Tab. Vindol.* II, 586 i.7; IV.2, 871.

25 *RIB* II.4, 2446, with Jackson 1996; Cruse 2004, 166–70 (largely accepting 'the idea of the itinerant eye-doctor').

<**11.21**> *Biggleswade (Beds.)*

G(ai) Val(eri) Amandi
dioxum ad reumatic(a)

G(ai) Val(eri) Amandi
stactum ad cal(iginem)

G(ai) Val(eri) Valentini
diaglauc(ium) post imp(etum) lip(pitudinis)

G(ai) Val(eri) Valentini
mixtum ad cl(aritatem)

RIB II.4, 2446.2

'Gaius Valerius Amandus' vinegar salve for running eyes.'
'Gaius Valerius Amandus' drops for dim sight.'
'Gaius Valerius Valentinus' celandine (*or* poppy) salve after the onset of ophthalmia.'
'Gaius Valerius Amandus' mixture for clear sight.'

The two oculists are obviously related, but we do not know whether they were father and son, brothers, or only freedmen of a Gaius Valerius; nor whether they travelled with this stamp, or it was only used to authenticate blocks of *collyrium*. 'Dim sight' and 'clear sight' may sound like claims made by patent medicines, but this was when cataracts were 'couched' with a needle, and spectacles had not yet been invented. There were also infectious illnesses such as trachoma: ten soldiers at Vindolanda were 'off sick' (*aegri*) because of inflammation of the eyes.[26]

The Vindolanda strength report counts 296 men as being present (*praesentes*) but not altogether correct: 31 in all were 'off sick' (*aegri*). Good health and bad is the preoccupation of many curse tablets, which know that it can be altered by divine intervention. Here is a reminder that scientific medicine merged into alternative therapies, or rather what critics might dismiss as 'magic'. It was found at a Roman villa, and is a lead or pewter tablet rolled into a cylinder for fitting into an amulet-case worn at the neck:

[26] *Tab. Vindol.* II, 154.24, *lippientes*, confirming Boon's emphasis (1983) on the threat to the army of eye-infections.

<**11.22**> *West Deeping, Lincs.*

ma[t]r[i]x, [t]i[bi]
dico: sede in
tuo loco *VO..*
..S dedit tibi. ad-
iuro te per Iaω
et per Sabaω et
per Adωnai ne
latus teneas, se-
d sede in tuo lo-
co nec nocea[s]
Cleuomedem
[f]iliam A[...]
[...]

Britannia 27 (1996), 443, No. 10

'Womb, I say to you, stay in your place [...] has given to you. I adjure you by Iaô, and by Sabaô and by Adônai, not to hold onto the side; but stay in your place, and not to hurt Cleuomedes(?) daughter of A[...].'

This is an uterine phylactery, a translation into Latin of a well-attested Greek spell against the medical condition of displacement of the womb; or, more likely, against spontaneous movement of the womb, in the ancient belief that it was a separate living creature liable to move about a woman's body and cause her various illnesses, notably 'hysteria', which embodies the Greek word for 'womb'. Like other amulets, it names the bearer, the patient so to speak, but not the consultant. He writes his prescription in fourth-century New Roman Cursive, but the three divine names retain an omega (ω) from the Greek original. Ultimately they derive from attributes of the Hebrew God Jehovah, Jahweh the Lord of Hosts, but they are frequent in Greco-Roman magic as independent deities who can be invoked to protect the bearer.[27]

Imported foods and wine

In the commanding officer's cellar at Newstead there once stood an amphora containing the equivalent of three dozen bottles of wine from southern Gaul (**4.07**). The Roman army in Britain, and indeed anyone with the money, depended for wine, olive oil and other exotic foodstuffs, on sea-borne imports. This was a lottery in which merchants might make a fortune, and they knew that 'luck' or divine favour was all-important. Hence they had the means and the motive to inscribe stones, for example this metrical dedication from the province's north-western corner:

[27] Tomlin 1997(a). For another gynaecological amulet, see **12.05**.

<**11.23**> *Bowness-on-Solway (Maia)*

[Matribus deabus aed]em
[Ant]onianus dedico:
[se]d date ut fetura quaestus
suppleat votis fidem;
aureis sacrabo carmen
mox viritim litteris

RIB 2059

'To the Mother Goddesses, I, Antonianus, dedicate [a shrine]. But grant that increase of profit give assurance to my prayers, and I will hereafter consecrate my poem by gilding the letters one by one.'

The first line is almost entirely lost, but plural deities are being addressed, and it is quite likely that they were the 'Mothers'. This is verse of sorts, trochaic tetrameters catalectic to be precise; somewhat on the lines of 'Hello, Hello, who's your Lady Friend?' It was a popular marching metre, not great poetry. But in Britain, like a woman's preaching (at least according to Dr Johnson), you are surprised to find it done at all.[28] Still more surprising, the author seems to have read Virgil.[29] His poem is a frank expression of the Roman idea that religion is a contract between man and god which imposes obligations on both parties. He was casting his bread upon the waters, but he did not find it after many days: there is no trace of gold in the letters.

The sea was notoriously unreliable: 'Neptune gobbled up thirty million sesterces that day', comments the fictional businessman and speculator Trimalchio after losing five ships with their cargoes of wine.[30] Here is an early epitaph also from the north-west, inscribed above a schematic picture of a mausoleum in a cemetery planted with shrubs:

[28] Other verse inscriptions are **2.11** (Wroxeter), **12.72** (York), **9.15** (Risingham), **12.86** (Carvoran) and **14.07** (Cirencester). **11.11** (Binchester) and **11.12** (London) are written on tile, **12.96** (Water Newton) on silver. **9.50** (Brough-under-Stainmore) is even in Greek. But *RIB* 1253 (Risingham) is a puzzle unsolved, the right-hand portion of a long metrical epitaph which became a gatepost.

[29] In *Eclogue* vii, 35–6, a shepherd dedicates a marble statue of Priapus, and promises to gild it if his flock increases: *nunc te marmoreum pro tempore fecimus; at tu | si fetura gregem suppleverit, aureus esto.*

[30] Petronius, *Satyricon* 76, *uno die Neptunus trecenties sestertium devoravit.*

<11.24> *Chester (Deva)*

[...]
op<t>ionis ad spem
ordinis, (centuria) Lucili
Ingenui, qui
naufragio perit
<h(ic)> s(itus) e(st)

RIB 544

'... an *optio* with the prospect of becoming centurion, in the century of Lucilius Ingenuus, who died in shipwreck; he lies (here).'

The dead man was not a merchant, but a legionary, and we do not know what he was doing on the sea. Maybe he was another casualty of Agricola's campaigns, in which the fleet played its part.[31] As an *optio* he was the second-in-command of the century (compare **12.37**), explicitly marked for promotion. The stone-cutter seems to have missed out T from OPTIONIS by mistake, but ligatured TI may have been lost where the edge is now broken. What is remarkable is that a space has been left for the H in the H S E formula, in case the body were found and could be buried 'here' (*hic*). The stone is thus a cenotaph, for one whose body (in Virgil's phrase) 'will lie naked on an unknown beach'. Horace likewise envisages a drowned sailor asking a passing merchant to throw three handfuls of sand into the sea, to give him symbolic burial.[32]

George Boon, who united much learning with true historical imagination, once published a Greco-Roman anchor stock found underwater off the cliffs of the Lleyn peninsula in North Wales. It was unmistakable evidence of the ancient shipwreck of a vessel trading from the Mediterranean, and it prompted him to re-interpret a curious graffito. This is the drawing of an otter scratched underneath a grey pottery jar not of Romano-British origin, with the caption in cursive letters:

<11.25> *Porcupine Bank*

G(ai) Pisci
Fagi

RIB II.8, 2503.379

'(Property) of Gaius Piscius Fagus.'

[31] Tacitus, *Agricola* 10.4, 25.1, 38.4.

[32] Virgil, *Aen.* v 871, *nudus in ignota, Palinure, iacebis harena.* Horace, *Odes* i 28. Compare **5.01** with note.

At first sight this is an ordinary ownership graffito; there are more than a thousand of them scratched on samian ware and coarse pottery in Britain. But this name is unparalleled, and it is best explained as one of the Roman facetious names derived from eating and drinking: *Piscius* from *piscis*, a fish, and *Fagus* from Greek φαγεῖν, to eat. In other words, 'Gaius the Fish-eater'; hence the otter. But there is also an unintended poignancy to the joke: the jar was trawled up in 150 fathoms of water, 150 miles (*c.* 240 km) off the west coast of Ireland, and it 'aptly illustrates the dangers facing a simple, square-rigged vessel in the merciless Atlantic'.[33]

The moralising poet Juvenal thinks it crazy to be shipping Cretan amphoras of full-bodied Cretan raisin wine across the Mediterranean and out of the Straits of Gibraltar, all for the sake of making a fortune among the seals and sea-monsters of the Atlantic, where the hot sun sets with a hiss. Safer to earn one's living as a tight-rope dancer.[34] But here is part of the painted inscription ('dipinto') on an Aegean amphora, probably from Crete:

<**11.26**> *London (Londinium)*

Ηλιοδωρου μέλι

Dipinto (unpublished) in the Museum of London

'Heliodorus' honey.'

Heliodorus is an ordinary Greek name, but appropriately means 'gift of the Sun'. Moralists now blame sugar for obesity, tooth decay and the slave trade, but Roman Britain could not get enough of it. Another welcome additive was fish sauce imported from southern Spain in a characteristic amphora (Peacock and Williams 17), the neck of which was 'labelled' with the contents in neat black letters. There is no complete such 'label' from Britain, but two fragments conveniently overlap. The first comes from Carlisle, and each line is written on a separate panel of white slip:

<**11.27**> *Carlisle (Luguvalium)*

CO[D] T[i]ng(itanum) v[e(tus)]
penuar(ium)
ex{s}cel[l(ens)]
[SV]MAVR
[...]

Britannia 33 (2002), 361, No. 7

[33] Boon 1977, 25 with n. 103.

[34] Juvenal, *Sat.* xiv 265–83.

The second is from London, and is written on overall white slip:

<**11.28**> *London (Londinium)*

[...]
SVMAVR
AIAA
LXXX
G(ai) Asici Probi

Britannia 31 (2000), 440, No. 32

(*Combined*) 'Old Tangiers tunny relish, "provisions" quality, excellent, top-quality, (matured) four(?) years, '80', (product) of Gaius Asicius Probus.'

These two incomplete 'labels' can be collated and largely understood with the help of others found elsewhere which are more complete. The product is always abbreviated to COD or CORD, which derives from *cordyla*, a young tuna. These fish migrate seasonally through the Straits of Gibraltar, and in the Roman period they unwittingly provided the raw material for an industry in the Cadiz area which chopped them up and put the pieces into tanks, where they were digested by their own enzymes into fish sauce. The brand-name *penuar(ium)* incorporates the word meaning 'provisions' in the London–Verulamium contract (**2.21**). SVMAVR like COD is always abbreviated, but might well be the composite *sum(mum) aur(eum)* ('top' and 'golden'). A is for *a(nnorum)*, the 'years' of maturing; probably '4', but the number is uncertain. '80' is the quantity, but unfortunately it is unclear what unit was being used. Finally the producer's name in the genitive case, in this instance Gaius Asicius Probus; another *Asicius* is known at Gades (Cadiz).[35]

Southern Spain also exported olive oil in large globular amphoras which are frequent site-finds, since they were convenient for secondary bulk storage; often they are scratched with a note of capacity and the owner's name.[36] Before being exported, they were painted with names and numerals, the producer and the number of 'pints' (*sextarii*). These dipinti[37] are usually damaged and difficult to read, but here is quite a legible first-century example:

<**11.29**> *Vindolanda*

AEMILIORVM ET
CASSIORVM

RIB II.6, 2492.5

'(Product) of the Aemilii and the Cassii.'

---

[35] See further *Britannia* 31 (2000), 441, n. 56. Other British examples are cited in *Britannia* 33 (2002), 361, n. 17. For *liquamen* from Antibes, a similar product, see *RIB* II.6, 2492.24.

[36] Dressel 20 (Peacock and Williams 25). Graffiti made after firing (and thus by owners) are collected in *RIB* II.6, 2493.

[37] *RIB* II.6, 2492. Funari 1996, 7–15.

Above this are painted two numerals, both of uncertain reading and interpretation: CIII, '103', and VLXXVI, '[ ]26'. The 'Aemilii and the Cassii' were a *societas*, a partnership formed by two families or groups of freedmen. Their names, like *Domitius* and *Valerius*, are 'colonial' and suggest they were descended from provincials important enough to be enfranchised by Republican proconsuls.

More informative than dipinti are the monumental inscriptions on stone of merchants who travelled between Britain and the estuaries of the Continent. The Sixth Legion gave thanks to Neptune and Ocean (**5.07** and **5.08**) when it arrived safely in the Tyne estuary from the Rhineland. By contrast, here is the tombstone of a soldier who sailed in the other direction:

<**11.30**> *Cologne (Colonia Agrippinensis)*

Aemilio Sae-
ni f(ilio) mil(iti) ex classe
G(ermanica) p(ia) f(ideli) pl(eromate) Euhodi n(avarchi) ci-
vi Dumnonio an(norum)
[...]

AE 1956, 249

'To Aemilius son of Saenus, soldier of the German Fleet Dutiful and Loyal, in the crew of Captain Evodius, a tribesman of the Dumnonii, aged ...'

Aemilius is a 'colonial' nomen, but also popular among non-citizens as a cognomen; in Africa it may even have 'concealed' the Punic name *Himilis*.[38] But Saenus, the father of this Aemilius, like the veteran who buried his whole family at York (**9.44**), is Celtic by name. The Dumnonii were the south-western tribe whose capital was at Isca (Exeter). A *pleroma* was a transport vessel attached to the Fleet, which was really a river flotilla based at Alteburg just south of Cologne. The irony of all this does not escape Tony Birley: 'The first recorded British sailor was a man from Devon who served in the German fleet.'[39]

More evidence of the British presence at Cologne is inscribed on this slab of black marble:

<**11.31**> *Cologne (Colonia Agrippinensis)*

Apollini
G(aius) Aurelius G(ai) l(ibertus)
Verus negotiator
Britannicianus,
moritex, d(ono) d(edit)
l(oco) d(ato) d(ecreto) d(ecurionum)

[38] A R Birley 1988(b), 4–5.

[39] Birley 1979, 104. Another Briton in the *classis Germanica* is now recorded by the diploma of AD 150 found near Lanchester in 2016, but not yet published.

ILS 7522

'To Apollo. Gaius Aurelius Verus, freedman of Gaius, merchant with Britain, *moritex*, gave (this) as a gift. The site was given by decision of the Council.'

Britannicianus does not mean that Verus was necessarily British, only that he was a businessman associated with Britain. Two other merchants describe themselves as *negotiator Britannicianus*, and a fourth is known, which would imply that they belonged to an association (*collegium*) of traders with Britain.[40] Parts have been found of three pipeclay figurines in Britain which are metaphorically 'a present from Cologne', since they were incised[41] before firing:

<11.32> *South Shields (?Lugudunum, later Arbeia)*

Servan-
dus c(oloniae) C(laudiae) A(rae) A(grippinensium)
fecit

RIB II.4, 2456.6

'Servandus made (this) at Colonia Claudia Ara Agrippinensium (Cologne).'

'Cologne' has been abbreviated to its initials, C C A A. Its full name identified it as the location of the altar (*ara*) for the Imperial Cult in Lower Germany, of which it was the capital, refounded as a *colonia* by Claudius in honour of his wife Agrippina, whose grandfather Agrippa had founded it originally. The question of what Aurelius Verus meant by describing himself as a *moritex* was renewed when this marble plaque was found in Southwark, buried in a pit between two Romano-Celtic temples:

<11.33> *London (Londinium), Southwark*

num(inibus) Aug(ustorum)
deo Marti Ca-
mulo Tiberini-
us Celerianus
c(ivis) Bell(ovacus)
moritix
Londiniensi-
um
primus [...]
[...]*VA*[...]
[...].

[40] *ILS* 5751 and **11.35** (Secundinius Silvanus, at Colijnsplaat and Domburg); **11.38** (Solimarius Secundus, at Bordeaux); *AE* 1983, 721 (Arisenius Marinus, at Colijnsplaat). See further, Hassall 1978.

[41] On the base, which is all that survives, like the lost fragment from Lancaster (*RIB* II.4, 2456.8). The head of a third from Colchester (ibid., 7) carries the same inscription.

RIB III, 3014

'To the Divinities of the Emperors (and) to the god Mars Camulus. Tiberinius Celerianus, a citizen of the Bellovaci, *moritix*, of Londoners the first [...].'

The emperors are probably Marcus Aurelius and his colleagues (in AD 161–9 or 177–80). The Celtic war-god *Camulos* gave his name to *Camulodunum* (Colchester), but this is only the second dedication from Britain; its well-drawn letters are unusually well provided with different sorts of leaf-stop (*hedera*). Mars Camulus was very much the god of the Remi in Gallia Belgica, so it is not surprising that the dedicator should be one of the Bellovaci, a tribe somewhat to the west of modern Reims. Like Aurelius Verus, he describes himself as a *moritix* (the difference in spelling is trivial) which is a Celtic loan-word meaning 'seafarer', but the specific reference is uncertain. Verus and Celerianus were both apparently shipmasters engaged in trade with the Continent, but we do not know whether *moritex* meant that they were trade officials of some sort, or (more likely) members of a trade association (*collegium*).[42] It is also notable that Celerianus should call himself a 'Londoner' (*Londiniensis*), the first occurrence of this word as a noun: he was not British-born, but he lived in London, and regarded himself as belonging there. Unfortunately the rest of his plaque is missing after *primus* ('the first'), so we do not know whether he was 'the first *moritex* of the Londoners' or (more likely) the first Londoner to hold a new office or to introduce a new cult, perhaps that of Mars Camulus himself.

Before Celerianus' fellow-*moritex* Aurelius Verus ventured onto the North Sea, he prayed en route to another deity, the goddess Nehalennia, who had two shrines in the Scheldt estuary, one facing the open sea at Domburg on the island of Walcheren and the other, up-river and to the east, at Colijnsplaat on the East Scheldt. Colijnsplaat is an epigraphic time-capsule, a collection of stones untouched since the fourth century, when the shrine and its contents collapsed into the sea. In 1970–71, after its chance discovery by a fishing trawler, 122 altars and three statues were systematically dredged up from the site.[43] Many of the altars like **11.36** depict the goddess on her throne between horns of plenty and, to her left, a basket of apples, and to her right, the regular companion of healing deities, a seated dog.[44] In 1981 another such altar was found by a diver:

42 Adams 2003.

43 Stuart and Bogaers 2001.

44 Boon 1989.

<11.34> *Colijnsplaat*

deae
Nehalenniae
G(aius) Aurelius
Verus
negotiator
Britannicianus
ex voto l(ibens) m(erito)

AE 1983, 722

'To the goddess Nehalennia. Gaius Aurelius Verus, merchant with Britain, (gave this) as promised, willingly and deservedly.'

Once again Verus describes himself as *negotiator Britannicianus*. He was repaying Nehalennia for her protection, and another altar from the shrine is still more explicit:

<11.35> *Colijnsplaat*

deae N[e]halenniae
ob merces recte conser-
vatas M(arcus) Secund(inius?) Silvanus
negotiator cretariu[s]
Britannicianu[s]
v(otum) s(olvit) l(ibens) m(erito)

AE 1973, 370

'To the goddess Nehalennia, for goods successfully preserved. Marcus Secundinius Silvanus, pottery merchant with Britain, paid his vow willingly, deservedly.'

The text is identical with that of an altar dedicated at the other shrine, Domburg, which was unexpectedly found in 1647 when a hurricane first swept away sand dunes, and then the sea exposed its remains.[45] This altar, like more than twenty others, was salvaged before the site was swallowed by the scouring sea. Secundinius was exporting fragile goods, figurines from Cologne perhaps, Rhenish colour-coated pottery or eastern-Gaulish samian, and felt double cause to be grateful.

Two other stones, if taken together, reveal that some of these cargoes were bound for the Humber estuary. First, another altar from the East Scheldt:

[45] *ILS* 4751.

<**11.36**> *Colijnsplaat*

deae Nehalenniae
Placidus Viduci fil(ius)
cives(!) Veliocassinius
negotiat(or) Britann(icianus)
v(otum) s(olvit) l(ibens) m(erito)

AE 1975, 651

'To the goddess Nehalennia. Placidus the son ofViducus, citizen of Rouen, merchant with Britain, paid his vow willingly and deservedly.'

This was dredged up in 1970. *cives* is a frequent confusion for *civis*, as in **2.08** and **11.09**. The Veliocasses were the north-Gallic tribe whose capital was Rotomagus (Rouen). Six years later a slab was found at York, badly worn from being re-used in a medieval lime-kiln; it is the right-hand half of a large ansate panel:

<**11.37**> *York (Eboracum)*

[...] et genio loci
[et numinibus Au]g(ustorum) L(ucius) Viducius
[?L(uci) f(ilius) Pla]cidus domo
[civitate] Veliocas[s]ium
[... n]egotiator
[?Britann(icianus) a]rcum et ianum
[?d(ono) d(edit) l(oco) d(ato)] d(ecreto) [d(ecurionum)] Grato et
[Seleuco co(n)s(ulibus)]

RIB III, 3195

'To ... and the Genius of the Place and to the Divinities of the Emperors. Lucius Viducius Placidus ... his home Rouen, merchant [with Britain] gave (this) arch and passage-way as a gift, [the site being given by vote of the Council]. In the consulship of Gratus and [Seleucus] (AD 221).'

The prime deity's name is lost, but it was probably not Nehalennia, since her cult was localised: when her votary Aurelius Verus was in Cologne, he paid his respects to Apollo.[46] Everywhere had its *genius loci*, as we have seen at Malton (**12.20**). The emperors are Elagabalus and Severus Alexander, who was in fact only *Caesar* at the time. The name of the dedicator, Lucius Viducius Placidus, recalls that of 'Placidus son of Viducus', who dedicated the Colijnsplaat altar; they both describe themselves as a *negotiator* from Rouen, and *Britannicianus* can be restored in the York inscription. Although doubt is possible, they are probably the same man, the non-Roman Placidus 'son of Viducus' having subsequently become a Roman citizen: in the Gallic style he would then have 'fabricated' his nomen *Viducius* from his father's cognomen *Viducus*, emphasising it with a fictive patronymic, *L(uci) f(ilius)*, 'the son of Lucius'.

This slab was incorporated in the arch which led to the unknown deity's temple precinct, its size and elaboration reflecting the prosperity of York in the third century, after the legionary base had become a provincial capital with the rank of *colonia*, even on occasion the imperial headquarters: two campaigning emperors died there, Septimius Severus in AD 211 and Constantius I in AD 306. Another index of prosperity is its inscribed stone coffins; although these are quite frequent in Italy and the western provinces, they are almost unknown in Britain except at York. We have already seen the pair of coffins (**9.51** and **9.52**) which commemorate the Gaul Verecundius Diogenes and his Sardinian wife, a man who was probably a successful merchant.

Two inscriptions from Bordeaux, which was 'famous for its wine, its rivers and its men' according to the local poet and vine-grower Ausonius, reveal its commercial links with York.[47] The first is a tombstone:

<11.38> *Bordeaux (Burdigala)*

D(is) M(anibus)
L(ucio) Solimario
Secundino
civi Trevero
neg(otiatori) Britan(niciano)

ILS 7523

'To the Shades of the Dead (and) to Lucius Solimarius Secundinus, a tribesman of the Treveri, merchant with Britain.'

He is another *negotiator Britannicianus*, but originally from Trier. The other inscription

[46] Compare **11.34** (Colijnsplaat) with **11.31** (Cologne).

[47] *patria, insignem Baccho fluviisque virisque* (*ord. urb. nobilium*. 20.2). Ausonius inherited 100 *iugera* of vines, traditionally the origin of Château Ausone.

is a third-century altar which was subsequently built into the late-Roman walls of Bordeaux:

<11.39> *Bordeaux (Burdigala)*

deae Tutel<a>e Boudig(ae)
M(arcus) Aur(elius) Lunaris IIIIII
vir Aug(ustalis) col(oniarum) Ebor(acensis) et
Lind(ensis) prov(inciae) Brit(anniae) Inf(erioris)
aram quam vover(at)
ab Eboraci(!) avect(us)
v(otum) s(olvit) l(ibens) m(erito)
Perpetuo et Corne(liano consulibus)

JRS 11 (1921), 102 (*AE* 1922, 116)

'To the goddess Tutela Boudiga. Marcus Aurelius Lunaris, *sevir Augustalis* of the colonies of York and Lincoln, in the province of Lower Britain, (set up) the altar which he had promised when he sailed from York. He paid his vow willingly and deservedly, in the consulship of Perpetuus and Cornelianus (AD 237).'

The stone is millstone grit from Yorkshire, not the local limestone, and Lunaris must have brought it with him to be dedicated to Tutela if he (and the altar, of course) arrived safely. He gives her the unique title of *Boudig(a)*, Celtic for 'victorious', which recalls the great Boudica, widow of a king, and the centurion's lady, Lollia Bodicca (**9.18**). Above the text there is a damaged relief of Tutela – the Protecting Goddess – who had a temple at Bordeaux. Other altars to her have been found here, including one with the same iconography, the goddess flanked by a bull (whether symbolising strength or for sacrifice) and a horn of plenty. A figure is carved in high relief on either side of Lunaris' altar: a river god, presumably the Garonne, and a wild boar, which may have been intended for York. This remains uncertain, since Lower Britain, of which York was the capital, was represented by a bull;[48] and the wild boar was actually the symbol of the Twentieth Legion (**6.13**) based at Chester. The answer, it has been suggested, was that *Eboracum* gained a popular but unfounded etymology from Germanic *Eber*, the wild boar.

Eboraci was familiar as a locative ('at York'), which misled Lunaris: he should have written *Eboraco* (ablative, 'from York'), especially after the preposition *ab*. He emphasises that he was a civic dignitary of two British cities, both of them ranking as a *colonia*: as *sevir Augustalis*, he belonged to an élite association of rich freedmen responsible for the local Imperial Cult. So he would have been born a slave, but the name *Lunaris* is unusual though found in Britain, so he was probably born here. It would have been in partnership with his former owner, now his patron, that he

[48] *RIB* II.1, 2411.34 (with note), 35, 36 and *Britannia* 19 (1988), 504, No. 97.

began to make his money, evidently trading with south-west Gaul; his connection with Bordeaux suggests that he was a wine merchant and shipper, a *negotiator vinarius*.

We began with the wine stored in the commanding officer's cellar at Newstead, so let us conclude by guessing at the vintage. Not in fact claret from Bordeaux, if that is what Lunaris imported, but Burgundy from the Rhône. The evidence is a barrel-head from London which survives because it was re-used in the sump of a well. The cooper (*a*) branded it twice, then someone else (*b*) added a series of graffiti:

<11.40> *London (Londinium)*

(*a*) Sex(ti) Servandi
(*b*) Capriacum

CVXIS, for *(modios) CV (sextarios) XI s(emis)*[49]

Britannia 40 (2009), 337, No. 36

'(Work) of Sextius Servandus.'
'Capriacum. 105 (*modii*), 11½ (*sextarii*).'

Capriacum is a place-name, as the termination *-acum* indicates, which derives from the name *Caprius*, presumably that of the estate-owner. This is Latin, but well attested in Gaul, where it 'conceals' the Celtic element **gabro-s* ('goat'). The place-name is not anciently attested, but many place-names in France are thought to be derived from it, the most attractive identification being Gevrey-Chambertin (dép. Côte d'Or) in Burgundy, *Gibriacus* in AD 630 and *Gebriacus* in AD 858, when its vineyards were already well known. It was Napoleon's favourite wine (he drank it in the Kremlin), and 'it has long been an English favourite'.[50] That London barrel contained 925.45 litres of this nectar, which is equivalent to just over 100 dozen bottles.

Beer

The emperor Julian, a Greek-speaking intellectual who campaigned against the Germans in the late AD 350s, contrasts the 'nectar' of wine with German beer made of barley, which smells of 'goat'.[51] The worst insult thrown by easterners at the Pannonian emperor Valens in AD 365 was 'beer-drinker' (*sabaiarius*), *sabaia* being a poor man's drink in the Danubian provinces made of wheat or barley.[52]

---

49 Two separate annotations, CIP(?) by another hand, and VIIII ('9'), have not been explained.

50 Dauzat and Rostaing 1978, s.v. *Gabriac*. Morton Shand 1964, 215–6.

51 *Epigram* 1. Attributed to the 'Celts', by whom he probably means 'Germans'.

52 Ammianus Marcellinus xxvi 8.2, *est autem sabaia ex ordeo vel frumento in liquorem conversis paupertinus in Illyrico potus.*

But in Britain, where there was plenty of barley but no wine unless imported, it was inevitable that a brewing industry should develop. Here are two stylus writing-tablet letters addressed to the first known beer baron:

<11.41> *Carlisle (Luguvalium)*

Domitio Tertio
braceario Luguvalio
. . .

RIB II.4, 2443.4

'To Domitius Tertius the brewer, at Luguvalium (Carlisle) ...'

<11.42> *London (Londinium)*

Tertio bracea-
rio

Tab. Lond. Bloomberg 12

'To Tertius the brewer.'

The coincidence of the cognomen *Tertius* (itself quite common) with the rare word *bracearius* guarantees that both letters were written to the same man, despite being found at opposite ends of the province. His empire must have been extensive. He may even be the 'Tertius' whose name is scored on a barrel head found in London.[53] A second *bracearius* called Optatus is found at Vindolanda, the term being derived from *bracae*, a type of grain; its meaning is not certain, but was probably 'maltster' or 'brewer'.[54] Vindolanda has also produced the letter written by a decurion commanding an outposted detachment to his prefect; it ends with this postscript:

<11.43> *Vindolanda*

cervesam commilitones
non habunt(!) quam
rogo iubeas mitti

Tab. Vindol. III, 628.ii.4–6

'My fellow-soldiers have no beer. Please order some to be sent.'

---

[53] *Britannia* 37 (2006), 478, No. 33(g), TIIRTIVS. The Bloomberg London tablets include a fragmentary account (No. 72) relating to large quantities of beer (*ceruesa*) and a letter (No. 14) addressed to the cooper (*cuparius*) Junius.

[54] *Tab. Vindol.* III, 646, with Adams 2003(b), 562–3.

12

GODS AND MEN

Altars

When Julius Caesar visited Troy, the home of his mythical ancestors, he improvised an altar from blocks of turf, burnt incense on it, and promised that if the gods gave him success, he would repay them.[1] This is poetic fiction, but true to the contract at the heart of Roman religion: *do ut des* is the Latin phrase, 'I give, that you may give in return'. We have already seen the dedication of a statue for Claudius' safe return from Britain (**1.08**), the unsuccessful prayers for the welfare of Aelius Caesar (**5.46**) and the prefect Rufinus (**9.03**), and a merchant's unfulfilled promise to gild the stone if he made a profit (**11.23**). Soon we will see a certificate written on silver (**12.06**) which embodies the payment of six *denarii*, as promised in return for divine protection.

Inscribed stones are more permanent than the turf altar dear to Roman poets: Horace, for example, celebrated the anniversary of his escape from a falling tree with a thanksgiving service, a sacrifice of 'flowers, incense, and embers on the living turf'.[2] No turf altar has yet been excavated, but an improvised stone altar survives in high relief, carved into the living rock from which Hadrian's Wall was being quarried; the masons cut their names nearby:

<**12.01**> *River Gelt quarries near Brampton*

ara(m) fecit et Amio
Eustus legione sex{s} et

RIB 1016

'Eustus made (this) altar, and Amio (did) ... from Legion Six.'

The letters were cut with a mason's pick and are irregular, like most quarry-face graffiti. *sexs* is for *sex*: the numeral VI, or perhaps the abbreviated ordinal *sexta* ('sixth'). The speakers (there seem to be two or three hands at work) as usual did

---

1 Lucan, *Pharsalia* ix 989–90.

2 *Odes* iii 8, 1–3, *flores et acerra turis … positusque carbo in caespite vivo.*

not sound the final [m] in *aram*, but they knew that *sex* ended in the sound [ks] not [ss] (compare **2.14**).

Another rock-cut altar of the Sixth Legion used to be visible five miles to the north-east, in Lodge Crag quarry, but this was in 1694; by the time Horsley made inquiries, it had been destroyed.[3] When the Second Legion inaugurated the Antonine Wall, it carved its own altar in high relief on the Bridgeness distance slab (**6.07**). The celebrant was probably the legate, Claudius Charax (**6.08**). At home in Greek-speaking Pergamum (now Bergama in north-west Turkey), he paid for the entrance portico at the great sanctuary of the healing god Asclepius. His name was inscribed within a roundel on the pediment in the foreground:

<**12.02**> *Bergama (Pergamum)*

Κλ(αύδιος)
Χαραξ
τὸ πρό-
πυλο[ν]

Habicht 1969, 142, No. 141

'Claudius Charax (donated this) portico.'

[3] *RIB* 1953, inscribed *leg(io) VI Vict(rix) p(ia) f(idelis).*

This human link between two inscriptions far removed, one now in Scotland, the other in Turkey, speaks of the breadth of the Empire, the 'international' recruitment of its ruling class, and the easy movement of religious ideas from east to west. Charax's god Asclepius (in Latin, Aesculapius) is also found in Britain; other exotics are Mithras, ultimately from Persia; Jupiter Dolichenus, from south-eastern Anatolia; Caelestis, the Juno of Roman Carthage, but ultimately Tanit from the Lebanon; Atargatis from Syria, and worshipped as the Syrian Goddess; Isis and Serapis from Egypt. Auxiliary soldiers introduced their native cults, notably from Germany, and from within the Greco-Roman world came 'public' gods such as Jupiter and Minerva who also attracted private devotion, personifications such as Victory and Fortune, and the divine attributes (*numina*) of living emperors. When Roman Britain came to an end, these cults were being displaced by the most successful immigrant of them all, Christianity.

Altars are free-standing, squared stone pillars with an integral base and capital, which translate turf into stone, and the faggots of the sacrificial fire into the cylindrical 'bolsters' of the capital. On top there is often a *focus*, the hemispherical hearth in which the fire was kindled. Some altars are elaborately carved and decorated (**9.06**), others are simple slabs with the middle portion, the die, crudely indicated by scored lines. They all commemorate a sacrifice, and were intended for future sacrifices, but they did not have to be inscribed. When Coventina's Well was emptied in 1876, at least 22 altars were found, but only half of them are inscribed.[4] Another disappointment has been the altar which was found in 1891 near the dam which headed the Lanchester aqueduct. It was lost again, with 'no text recorded' according to *RIB*; but when it was rediscovered in 1984, it proved to be uninscribed.[5] Fortunately for us, however, monumental altars often bear inscriptions which name the god(s) and the dedicator(s), and usually conclude with an abbreviated formula like V S L M for *v(otum) s(olvit) l(ibens) (m)erito*: 'he paid his vow willingly, deservedly'. The dedicator often adds information about himself, his office or military rank, sometimes even the source of his inspiration, instances of which are the Carvoran altar dedicated for the safety of Aelius Caesar after a vision (**5.46**), a foreboding well founded, and the Risingham altar to the nymphs after the commandant had a dream (**9.15**). Other votaries respond to a 'vision', a 'message', a 'warning', an 'order', the 'interpretation of an oracle', a 'reply from the god', but unfortunately they give no further details. They had not necessarily slept the night in a temple.[6] The gods communicated with receptive minds in many ways, just as St Augustine's Christian mother knew 'by a sort of taste which she could not express in words' which of her dreams was

[4] Allason-Jones and McKay 1985, 14–19. The inscribed altars are *RIB* 1522–1535.

[5] *RIB* 1090+add.

[6] *RIB* 153, *ex visu*; 760, *ex viso*; III, 3499 (b), *ex nuntio*; 320, *monitu*; **12.83**, *ex iussu*; *RIB* 1131, *iuss(u) dei*; **12.17**, *ex imperio*; *RIB* 1579, *secundum interpretationem oraculi Clari Apollinis*; 587, *ex responsu [dei]*. But Renberg (2006) shows that there is little reliable evidence of 'incubation' in the West.

authentic.[7] But the presence of a 'diviner' at Bath and an 'interpreter' at Lydney Park suggests that professional help might be available to the perplexed.[8] Whatever their medium, divine messages could be answered by inscribed altars which were prayers in stone; brief and stereotyped though they are, they justify the ways of Man to God.

The need for protection

The gods, however, were less amenable than Man. A brief but ominous message was found in 1848 inscribed on a small stone slab, two or three hundred yards south of Hadrian's Wall on the hillside between Dere Street and Halton Chesters. It is only two words:

<12.03> *near Halton Chesters (Onnum)*

fulgur divom

RIB 1426+*add.*

'The lightning of the gods.'

This is a *bidental*, the only one ever found in Britain, a stone which marked the place where someone had been struck dead by lightning; in the words of Collingwood Bruce, where a Roman soldier was 'arrested on life's journey and summoned to his great account'.[9] Life is uncertain, the gods unpredictable; we can only pray:

<12.04> *Billingford*

Iao
Abrasax
... ablan-
{n}athanalba
date salutem
et uic{t}oriam
Tib(erium) Clau<diu>m Similem quem pe-
perit Heren<n>ia Marcellina

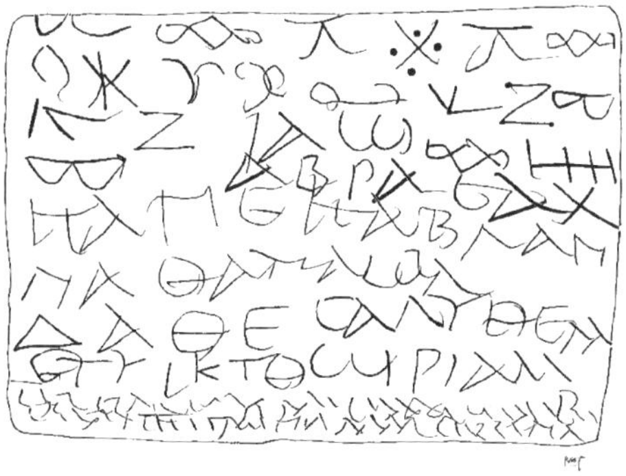

Britannia 37 (2006), 481, No. 51

'Iao, Abrasax [...], ablanathanalba, give health and victory (to) Tiberius Claudius Similis whom Herennia Marcellina bore.'

---

7 Augustine, *Confessions* vi 13 (23), *nescio quo sapore quem verbis explicare non poterat.*

8 **12.31** (*haruspex*); **12.45** (*interp(r)[e]tiante*). There is even a surviving handbook on the interpretation of dreams, Artemidorus' *Onirocritica.*

9 Tomlin 1986.

This text has been scratched onto a rectangle of gold leaf no larger than a postage stamp, rolled into a cylinder after being inscribed, and worn at the neck in a carrying-case as an amulet. The words are Latin, but were transcribed into Greek letters (with some lapses into Roman), to conceal it from profane eyes. Only the last two lines are actually written in Roman letters, tiny letters because space was running out, and they name the bearer. He is identified by his mother's name, a practice often found in protective spells and curses, since it is infallible: one's father may be in doubt, but not one's mother. The names of the two protective deities, Iao (ultimately derived from Yahweh or Jehovah) and Abrasax (sometimes depicted with a cock's head and snake-legs) are preceded and surrounded by 'characters': these are geometrical patterns and elaborations of Greek letters known to have binding powers. 'ablanathanalba' is a magical palindrome, *th* being a single letter (theta) in Greek. Altogether, great power is packed into a tiny space, as into another gold amulet, which was found in 2007 just south of Oxford, in ploughsoil beside the railway to London; many Classical scholars have passed it unknowing:

<12.05> *south of Oxford*

characters
characters
characters ϲαμιου
ηριϲφαλμα χνουν
ιαχματιαν φνε
φνε ωχ ποιήϲα-
τε τοῖϲ <ὑ>μετέροιϲ
ἁγίοιϲ ὀνόμαϲι
ἵνα τὸ ἔ<γ>κυον
κρατήϲ<ει> καὶ τέξετ<αι>
ὁλοκληροῦϲα καὶ
ὑγι<αί>νουϲα Φάβι-
α ἣν ἔτεκεν Τερέ<ν->
τια μήτηρ εη [=αἰεί] ὀνό-
ματοϲ τοῦ κυρίου
καὶ μεγάλου θεοῦ

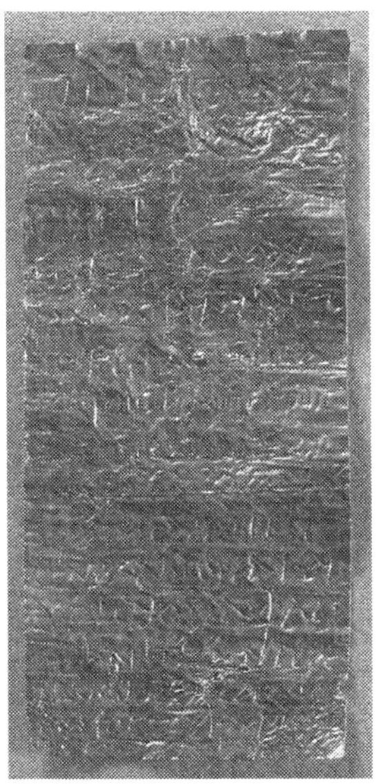

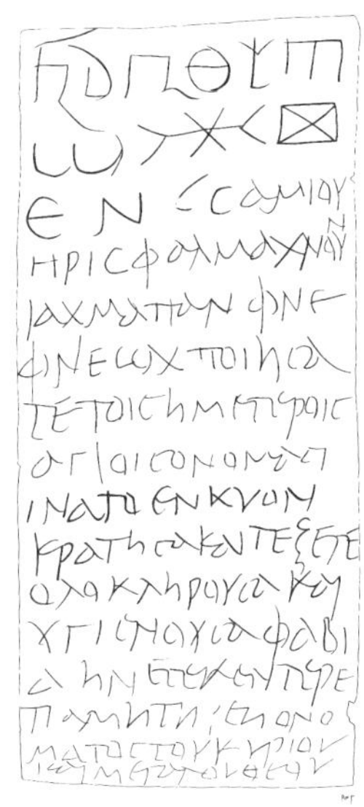

Britannia 40 (2009), 353, No. 97

'*Characters. Magical names.* Make with your holy names that Fabia whom Terentia her mother bore, being in full fitness and health, shall master the unborn child and bring it to birth; the name of the Lord and Great God being everlasting.'

This is another gynaecological amulet, like the one against 'hysteria' (**11.22**). The Greek is post-Classical, and is preceded by two rows of magical 'characters' (elaborated letters) and six magical 'names', great words of power. The concluding phrase has a

'Christian' ring, but this is misleading; the words are often found in non-Christian magical papyri. The bearer once again is identified by maternal lineage, and the charm is preoccupied with health, but this time it is specific, to ensure an easy childbirth. It embodies the popular belief that the embryo was active, the womb passive, and that the unborn child understandably resisted being born. The ancient gynaecologist Soranus, in his own scientific and very practical treatment of difficulties in childbirth, allows the use of amulets: they have no direct effect, he says, but they may be good for the patient's morale.[10] This is some answer to the question moderns often ask, whether ancient amulets 'worked'. One votary at least knew they did:

<12.06> *Stony Stratford*

deo
Iovi et [Vo]lca(no)
Vassinus
cum vell[e]-
nt me con-
sacratum
con[ser]va[r]e
promisi dena-
rios sex pro vo-
to lam[ell]a p(osita est)

RIB 215, with Tomlin forthcoming, SS6a

'Vassinus to the god Jupiter and Volcanus. Since they were willing to sanctify and preserve me, I promised them six *denarii*. This plaque is placed to represent my vow.'

This text, now badly worn, was neatly but shallowly inscribed with a stylus within a rectangular panel which was probably the lower portion of a silver votive 'leaf', found in 1789 stuffed into an urn with more 'leaves' and other temple treasures. Like two of the Ashwell plaques[11], it describes itself as a *lamella*. The sum of 'six *denarii*' apparently represents the cost of the metal from which it was made, if not the actual source. It is Vassinus' payment for the protection he has received. His protector is the god Vulcan (see also **10.01** and **12.73**), whom a silver 'leaf' from a nearby shrine depicts as a smith with anvil.[12]

The Romans come to Britain, but take a backward glance

In reading the inscriptions which follow, we should keep these amulets in mind and not lose sight of man's uncertainty and his will to believe, but no analysis will be

[10] Further commentary in Tomlin 2008(b).
[11] Tomlin forthcoming, A 11 and A12.
[12] *RIB* 220 (Barkway).

attempted of religious belief, nor any comprehensive account given of religion in Roman Britain and the role of individual gods, for this has already been provided by Martin Henig, while the epigraphy itself until the mid-1980s was assembled by Eric Birley.[13] Their achievements are possible because the Romans brought to Britain a written language, in which they conciliated both the divine powers they found here and the more familiar powers whose protection they wished to retain. A sample of such texts follows, cutting like an archaeological section through the man-made strata imposed upon the subsoil: first the cult of natural features like springs and the local 'genius', next the native Celtic deities of Britain and Gaul, often quite localised, and then the foreign deities and personifications introduced by the Romans, whether by origin Germanic, Greco-Roman, or oriental. The strata are inevitably 'disturbed', since cults did not exist in isolation: gods were identified with one another, and even to worship them in writing was to 'Romanise' them.

The Romans in Britain had crossed the sea to another world. The Sixth Legion, after landing safely in the Tyne estuary, thanked Ocean and Neptune with splendid altars (**5.07** and **5.08**). Here are two bronze tablets in much the same spirit, inscribed at York by a seafaring Greek intellectual:

<12.07> *York (Eboracum)*

θεοῖc
τοῖc τοῦ ἡγε-
μονικοῦ πραι-
τωρίου Σκριβ(ώνιοc)
Δημήτριοc

RIB 662+*add.*

'To the gods of the legate's Residence, Scrib(onius) Demetrius.'

The Greek words for 'legate' and official 'residence' (which transliterates Latin *praetorium*), like their Latin equivalents, are ambiguous: the legate is either the provincial governor himself – but York was not a provincial 'capital' until the creation of Lower Britain in the early third century – or the general officer commanding the legion at York, both of whom as deputies of the proconsul Emperor were 'praetorian' in authority. Since this plaque and the next were found, not in the legionary fortress where the legionary legate resided, but across the river in the area of what became the civil *colonia*, it is quite possible that the 'residence' is an official building intended for the governor in his tours of duty. This tablet was accompanied by another:

13 Henig 1984; Birley 1986.

<12.08> *York (Eboracum)*

Ὠκεανῶι
καὶ Τηθύι
Δημήρι[οϲ]

RIB 663

'To Ocean and Tethys (from) Demetrius.'

Tethys in Greek mythology was the sister and consort of Ocean, and the mother of rivers. Alexander the Great dedicated altars to them both at the mouth of the Indus, after his army forced him to turn back from the conquest of India. It is likely that Demetrius was Demetrius 'of Tarsus', a professional teacher of Greek who visited Britain during Agricola's campaigns. Later at Delphi in AD 83, at the 'navel' or centre-point of the world, he reminisced about the offshore islands he had visited in distant Britain. This dedication at York identified him as an explorer in the mould of Alexander, exploring the watery western edge of the world.[14] At much the same date, the poet Martial was writing to an Italian friend and neighbour who was about to visit Britain, which he couples with 'green' Tethys and 'father' Ocean: this would imply that the association had become a cliché.[15] Britain was so remote that it might be difficult to put a name to the local gods:

<12.09> *Risingham (Habitancum)*

dis culto-
ribus huiu[s]
loci Iul(ius)
Victor trib(unus)

RIB 1208+*add.*

'To the gods who tend this place, (from) Julius Victor the tribune.'

Despite his colourless name, Julius Victor was a Roman aristocrat, an equestrian serving a short-term commission as the commandant. He dedicated another altar with a splendid chip-carved capital. Like those[16] dedicated to Fortune 'the Home-bringer', it is redolent of home-thoughts from abroad:

[14] Note to *RIB* 662–3, citing Diodorus Siculus xvii 104.1 and Plutarch *de defectu oraculorum* 410A.
[15] Martial, *ep.* 10.44, *Britannos | et viridem Tethyn Oceanumque patrem.*
[16] **4.10**, **5.36**, **9.05** and **9.06**.

<12.10> *Risingham (Habitancum)*

Matribu-
s Trama-
rinis Iul(ius)
Victor v(otum) s(olvit) l(ibens) m(erito)

RIB 1224

'To the Mothers Overseas, Julius Victor the tribune paid his vow willingly, deservedly.'

This is one of about 60 British dedications to the Mothers, protective mother-goddesses whose cult seems to have radiated from the Rhineland, where it is best represented; the Mothers are often qualified by titles indicating where the dedicator felt most at home.[17] In Manchester, for example, Aelius Victor dedicated an altar to Mothers whose Germanic names associate him with the lower Rhine:

<12.11> *Manchester (Mamucium)*

deabus
Ma[t]ribus
Hananeftis
et Ollototis
Aelius
Victor
v(otum) s(olvit) l(aetus) l(ibens) m(erito)

Britannia 40 (2009), 315, No. 3 with 42 (2011), 463–4, add. (m)

'To the Mother Goddesses Hananeftae and Ollototae, Aelius Victor gladly, willingly, and deservedly paid his vow.'

This Victor does not specify his status. Conversely, but in the same spirit, a British legionary on the lower Rhine remembered the Mothers back home:

[17] Birley 1986, 49–51; to which now add *RIB* III, 3183 (Ribchester), 3484 (Birrens) and **12.11** (Manchester).

<**12.12**> *near Xanten*

Matribus
Brittis
L(ucius) Valerius
Simplex
mil(es) leg(ionis) XXX
U(lpiae) V(ictricis)
v(otum) s(olvit) l(ibens) m(erito)

ILS 4789

'To the British Mothers, Lucius Valerius Simplex, soldier of the Thirtieth Legion Ulpia Victrix, paid his vow willingly, deservedly'.

Like the names *Julius Victor* and *Aelius Victor*, this dedicator's name is colourless, but his unusual dedication reveals him to be one of the few legionaries in other provinces attributable to Britain.[18] Another altar suggests a series of postings:

<**12.13**> *Winchester (Venta Belgarum)*

Matrib(us)
Italis Ger-
manis Gal(lis)
Brit(annis)
[A]ntonius
[Lu]cretianus
b(ene)f(iciarius) co(n)s(ularis) rest(ituit)

RIB 88

'To the Italian, German, Gallic and British Mothers, Antonius Lucretianus, *beneficiarius consularis*, restored this.'

The *genius* of Britain and other entities

Lucretianus, whose loyalties were thus divided among Italy, the Rhineland, Gaul and Britain, was a junior officer seconded from his legion to the governor's staff; *beneficiarii consularis* like him managed posts (*stationes*) on the lines of communication, and one of them may have dedicated this altar at a principal port of entry:

[18] *CIL* xiii 8632 (also Xanten) is also dedicated to the British Mothers by a legionary of the Thirtieth. Tony Birley (1979, 104–5) finds 16 legionaries of British origin, including *frumentarii* seconded from the British legions, but not centurions of British origin like Quintius Petrullus at Bostra, *dom(o) Britan(nia)* (*IGLS* 9188 with Tacoma, Ivleva and Breeze 2016).

<**12.14**> *Dover (Dubris)*

deae
Britani-
[ae ...]

Britannia 43 (2012), 396, No. 2, Dover (Dubris)

'To the goddess Britania ...'

The spelling of *Britannia* with only one T and one N is hardly found in Britain – the only other exception is a stylus-tablet letter found at Carlisle[19] – which suggests that this altar was dedicated by a new arrival. Unfortunately his name and status have been lost, but perhaps he was an incoming official like the courier (*strator consularis*) who dedicated an altar made of the same stone to the Mother Goddesses of Italy.[20] Britannia was personified as a Victory-like figure on the Antonine Wall (**6.13**), and there was also a statue of her at York:

<**12.15**> *York (Eboracum)*

Britanniae
sanctae
p(osuit) ?Nikomedes
Aug(ustorum) n(ostrorum)
libertus

RIB 643+*add.*

'To Holy Britannia, Nikomedes, freedmen of our Emperors, set (this) up.'

This is only the statue-base, which was found in 1740 and like the statue itself is now lost; its reading depends on contemporary reports, but only the dedicator's name is uncertain.[21] He was an imperial freedman like Vegetus in London (**10.38**), and thus a senior official in the financial administration of the province. Further north, at Vindolanda, is the personification of another province:

<**12.16**> *Vindolanda*

cives Galli
de<ae> Galliae
conco[r]des-
que Britanni

[19] *RIB* II.4, 2443.5, *in Britania.*

[20] *RIB* III, 3031 (Dover), *[Mat]ribus (I)talic[is].*

[21] Birley rightly observes (2005, 300 n.7) that '[a] name beginning Philo- is perhaps likelier'.

RIB III, 3332

'The citizens of Gaul to the goddess *Gallia*, and the (citizens) of Britain in concord, (dedicated this).'

This again is only a statue-base, re-used in a late-Roman drain, but made of stone used in third-century work at Vindolanda. There is an iron tag in the top which would have secured the statue of Gaul, personified as a goddess. The lettering is quite poor, and DE for *deae* is a trivial 'Vulgarism', yet another example of the confusion between [ae] and [e], both of which were pronounced the same. In his commentary on this brief but pregnant text, Tony Birley has shown that 'the citizens of Gaul' were recruits from the central Gallic province of Gallia Lugdunensis drafted into the Fourth Cohort of Gauls, the third-century garrison of Vindolanda.[22] By now it had been in Britain for more than a century, as we know from early tombstones and other evidence, so this goes against the assumption that auxiliary units, once established in garrison, altogether lost their original ethnic composition by recruiting locally. Here Gauls were still serving alongside native Britons, and this inscription gives more prominence to 'the citizens of Gaul' than to their 'British' colleagues. This may betray outside influence, since in Britain it is very rare for dedicator(s) to be named before deity. Even if this is only a lapse due to careless drafting and execution, it should be remembered that, as at Corbridge (**12.53**) and Carlisle (**12.54**) where garrisons were drawn from two different legions, Concord was a deity honoured when discord was to be feared.

The largest tribe in the north was the Brigantes, which is also personified:

<12.17> *Birrens (Blatobulgium)*

Brigantiae s(acrum) Amandus
arc<h>itectus ex imperio imp(eratum fecit)

RIB 2091+*add.* with *CSIR* i.4, No. 12

'Sacred to Brigantia: Amandus the engineer by (her) command did what was commanded.'

This is the inscribed base of a gabled niche within which stands the figure of Brigantia in high relief, represented as a goddess with wings like Victory but wearing as a badge the gorgon's head of Minerva, the goddess of wisdom and technology who might be expected to give orders to a military engineer. Other devotees identify her with Victory, or with the Carthaginian

[22] Birley 2007, 104–12. The Fourth Cohort is first attested at Vindolanda in AD 213 (*RIB* 1705).

goddess Caelestis, or even as masculine.[23] She was much more than a geographical expression; she had varying divine attributes like Britannia herself, whose 'genius' or distinctive quality is recognised in this altar from the Antonine Wall:

<12.18> *Auchendavy*

genio
terrae
Brita-
nnicae
M(arcus) Coccei(us)
Firmus
(centurio) leg(ionis) II Aug(ustae)

RIB 2175+*add.* Keppie 1998, No. 34

'To the Genius of the land of Britain (from) Marcus Cocceius Firmus, centurion of the Second Legion Augusta.'

This altar is one of five found in a pit in 1771, when the Forth and Clyde Canal was being dug, at least four of them dedicated by Firmus.[24] He does not say whether he was acting-commander (*praepositus*) of an auxiliary unit in garrison at Auchendavy, or in charge of a legionary detachment there; but the latter is more likely, since it is attested in the area.[25] By honouring the 'genius' of Britain, however, he was not praising his new posting but conciliating it: he was mindful of Roman gods, as we will see, but he also knew that everywhere has its own personality which should be conciliated. Here is the idea at its simplest:

<12.19> *York (Eboracum)*

genio loci
feliciter

RIB 647

'Good luck to the Genius of this place.'

---

[23] The conical stone to the left of Brigantia hints at Caelestis, an identification made explicit in **12.85** (Corbridge). She is identified with Victory in **8.14** (Greetland) and *RIB* 628 (Castleford), and masculine in *RIB* 623 (Slack), *deo Breganti*. *RIB* identifies Amandus with AR VAL AMAN DISCENTE in *ILS* 2459+*add.*, but *Amandus* is quite a common name, the expansion of AR is quite uncertain, and this inscription is dated to AD 209, long after Birrens had been abandoned.

[24] The others are **12.58**, **12.59** and **12.60**. The fifth is *RIB* 2178, but the dedicator's name is lost: it was probably Firmus.

[25] *RIB* 2180 and 2181, both found a mile to the east; recording a detachment of the legion, and one of its legionaries (his tombstone).

We have already seen another dedication to the *genius loci* at York (**11.37**). The idea of *genius* was extended to one's work-place, for example a goldsmith's shop at Malton (**11.18**), or to one's military unit:

<12.20> *Chester (Deva)*

genio
sancto
centuri<a>e
Aelius
Claudian(us)
opt(io) v(otum) s(olvit)

RIB 448

'To the holy Genius of the century. Aelius Claudianus the *optio* paid his vow.'

Claudianus was the century's second-in-command; his altar is one of three dedicated to the *genius* of centuries of the legion at Chester.[26] Even its standard-bearers possessed a collective personality:

<12.21> *Chester (Deva)*

genio signi[f(erorum)]
leg(ionis) XX V(aleriae) V(ictricis)
T(itus) Fl(avius) Valerianus
collegis d(ono) d(edit)

RIB 451

'To the Genius of the standard-bearers of the Twentieth Legion Valeria Victrix; Titus Flavius Valerianus gave (this) as a gift to his colleagues.'

The freely-drawn letters suggest an ink-drawn draft, notably the flourish of T FL in the third lines. There is lavish provision of leaf-stops. Each century had its standard-bearer, who also kept the accounts, and collectively they formed a *collegium* or association. At Carlisle there is the statue of such a Genius, a standing figure with a horn of plenty over his left shoulder, making an offering on the altar from a dish in his right hand:

[26] The others are *RIB* 446 (century un-named) and 447 (century of Aurelius Verinus). Note also *RIB* 449, a fragment apparently dedicated to the *genius* of the legion.

<12.22> *Carlisle (Luguvalium)*

geni[o cent]uria[e]
[(centuria)] Bassi[li] Cresce[ntis]
don[o d]onavit

RIB 944

'To the Genius of the century, the century of Bassilius Crescens gave (this) as a gift.'

This is the reading of *RIB*, which for once does not provide a drawing. Its photograph and other photographs[27] are not very helpful, but they do suggest that the centurion's nomen should be read as BASSII, for *Bassius* rather than *Bassilius*, which is very rare; but the difficulty remains that dedicators to the Genius of a century (**12.20** for example) are usually individuals, not the century as a whole. That the centurion, if not the dedicator, is a Roman citizen may be noted: legionaries are well attested at Carlisle.[28] At Lanchester there would have been a similar statue, now lost, which stood on this inscribed pedestal:

<12.23> *Lanchester (Longovicium)*

genio praetori
Cl(audius) Epaphroditus
Claudianus
tribunus c(o)ho(rtis)
I Ling(onum) v(otum) s(olvit) l(ibens) p(osuit) m(erito)

RIB 1075+*add.*

'To the Genius of the commanding officer's house. Claudius Epaphroditus Claudianus, tribune of the First Cohort of Lingones, paid his vow willingly, erected (this) deservedly.'

We have already seen Demetrius' early dedication in Greek (**12.07**) to the divinities of an official residence (*praetorium*), but the idea is found most richly at Vindolanda, in four large altars which stood in the commandant's house. Their dedications are closely related, but detail of two dedicators has been lost.[29] The other two texts are well preserved:

---

[27] Toynbee 1962, Pl. 30; *CSIR* i.6, Pl. 107.

[28] **3.21**, **13.04** and **12.54**.

[29] *RIB* 1687+add., dedicated to Jupiter, *genius* and 'the guardian gods', apparently of the cohort and Vindo(landa); *RIB* III, 3333, to Jupiter and the *genius* of the *praetorium*.

<12.24> *Vindolanda*

genio
praetori
sacrum Pi-
tuanius Se-
cundus prae-
fectus coh(ortis) IIII
Gall(orum)

RIB 1685+*add.*

'Sacred to the Genius of the commandant's house, (from) Pituanius Secundus, prefect of the Fourth Cohort of Gauls.'

To the left of the die are carved in relief the instruments of sacrifice, a poleaxe and a butcher's cleaver; below them, a sacrificial ox or bull. The dedicator's nomen is unusual, and probably Italian; there was a family of *Pituanii* at the small Sabine town of Reate, incidentally the birthplace of the Emperor Vespasian, whose members included Pituania Secunda; she may have been related to the prefect, or even his daughter.[30] The other prefect is avowedly Italian, and names his home-town:

<12.25> *Vindolanda*

I(ovi) O(ptimo) M(aximo)
ceterisque
diis immort(alibus)
et gen(io) praetor(i)
Q(uintus) Petronius
Q(uinti) f(ilius) Fab(ia tribu) Urbicus
praef(ectus) coh(ortis) IIII
Gallorum
two lines deleted
ex Italia
domo Brixia
votum solvit
pro se
ac suis

RIB 1686+*add.*

'To Jupiter, Best and Greatest, and the other immortal gods and to the Genius of the commandant's house, Quintus Petronius Urbicus, son of Quintus, of the *Fabia* voting-

[30] *CIL* ix 4694.

tribe, prefect of the Fourth Cohort of Gauls [...], from Italy his home Brixia (Brescia), paid his vow on behalf of himself and his family.'

This altar probably dates from AD 222–35, since the title assumed by the cohort in honour of the reigning Emperor, but deleted after his 'memory' was condemned, apparently occupied two lines; this would exclude *Antoninianae*, but would suit *Severianae Alexandrianae* very well.[31] There is a crane carved in relief on either side of the die, a bird which also features on this imposing slab dedicated by the same cohort at a previous posting:

<**12.26**> *Risingham (Habitancum)*

numinib(us)
Augustor(um)
coh(ors) IIII Gal(lorum)
eq(uitata)
fec(it)

RIB 1227+*add.* with *CSIR* i.1, No. 215

'To the Divinities of the Emperors, the Fourth Cohort of Gauls, part-mounted, set (this) up.'

Oaths were sworn by the *genius* of the Emperor, and later we will see an altar (**13.19**) dedicated to it, but his god-like power implied that like Mercury (**11.04**) and Sulis Minerva (**12.34**), he also had a god-like will, his *numen*, which naturally became an object of worship in itself. It is often linked with other deities. This dedication from Risingham is the grandest of all such expressions of loyalty found in Britain.[32] The crane at the feet of Victory was a bird which symbolised vigilance and devotion, but since it is repeated on the Vindolanda altar, it may have been regarded by the cohort as its totem. However, since it is balanced by the goose at the feet of Mars, one of his regular attributes, the sculptor probably meant rather to convey that Victory depends on vigilance and devotion.

Springs, nymphs and water goddesses

Believers in *genius* like Cocceius Firmus sensed a divine element in everyone and

[31] Bidwell 1985, 50. It was probably also deleted on *RIB* 1706 (now lost) at Vindolanda, but not on **12.50** at Housesteads.

[32] Collected by Birley 1986, 34–6.

everything: 'everything is full of Jupiter', as Virgil wrote, in a phrase echoed by the pagan apologist Symmachus who tactfully changed 'Jupiter' to 'God' when addressing a Christian emperor.[33] Virgil's commentator Servius also remarks that every spring is sacred, so it is natural that altars should mark where the life-giving water wells up. At Risingham the nymphs were celebrated in a poem by the prefect's wife (**9.15**), and at Chester the Twentieth Legion honoured the source of its own water-supply with this altar inscribed on front and back:

<**12.27**> *near Chester (Deva)*

Nymphis
et
Fontibus
leg(io) XX
V(aleria) V(ictrix)

RIB 460+*add.*

'To the Nymphs and Springs (from) the Twentieth Legion Valeria Victrix.'

This was found near springs which would have fed an aqueduct. At Carrawburgh on Hadrian's Wall, an altar was found still standing on its pedestal beside a spring-fed cistern; it too is inscribed on front and back:

<**12.28**> *Carrawburgh (Brocolitia)*

Nymphis et genio
loci M(arcus) Hispanius
Modestinus praef(ectus)
coh(ortis) I Bat(avorum) pro se
et suis l(ibens) m(erito)

RIB III, 3316

'To the Nymphs and the Genius of this place. Marcus Hispanius Modestinus, prefect of the First Cohort of Batavians, (erected this) for himself and his (family), willingly, deservedly.'

The prefect's name *Hispanius* has been 'fabricated' from the cognomen *Hispanus*; as one might expect, it is mostly found in the Spanish provinces, but two of the Ashwell silver 'leaves'

[33] *Eclogues* 3, 60, *Iovis omnia plena*. Symmachus, *rel.* 3.5, *omnia quidem deo plena sunt.*

were dedicated by the son of an Hispanus.[34] A cult of the nymphs is surprising at Carrawburgh, however, since it already had its own water goddess, Coventina, who was virtually the presiding genius. The Romans captured her spring with a square, stone-lined reservoir, and surrounded it with a small walled precinct in which they dedicated altars and other votive objects. These were the 'rubbish' which almost filled the the well when it was first noticed by Horsley, and in 1876 they were salvaged by John Clayton and taken to his museum at Chesters.[35] Much the most delightful is the carved relief, shaped somewhat like a gabled tombstone, which shows the divinity basking half-naked on what looks like a water-lily leaf, a scene which an irreverent but distinguished archaeologist (a woman, it may be added) once called the 'Prawn Cocktail'. Closer inspection suggests that the lettuce leaf is really the lapping waves of a stream. In her right hand the lady holds the leaf of some plant, perhaps a water-lily, which by rights should have been the wild musk which now chokes her Well in summer with its rank yellow flowers. Here is the inscription:

<12.29> *Carrawburgh (Brocolitia)*

deae
Covventinae
T(itus) D(...) Cosconia-
nus pr(aefectus) coh(ortis)
I Bat(avorum) l(ibens) m(erito)

RIB 1534

'To the goddess Covventina. Titus D(...) Cosconianus, prefect of the First Cohort of Batavians (paid his vow) willingly, deservedly.'

Latin did not have the letter 'w', but sometimes intervocalic 'u/v' is doubled in Vulgar usage to guarantee the [w] sound; writing a tribal name as *Corieltauui* is a good example.[36] The prefect's nomen is abbreviated to a single letter, but it may have been *Domitius*. His cognomen, which is derived from the rare Italian name *Cosconius*, is so unusual that he probably thought it was distinctive enough.[37]

Other sites in Britain also had their own water goddess, notably Ilkley on the river

34 Tomlin 2008(a), 312–13, Nos. 21 and 22, *Servandus Hispani*.

35 Horsley, *Britannia Romana* (1732), 145–6. Allason-Jones and McKay 1985.

36 *RIB* II.5, 2491.150 with *Britannia* 34 (2003), 382, add. (c).

37 Like Herbonianus (**12.30**); but note also **10.31** where the dedicator, in spite of his cognomen *Secundinus* being so common, abbreviates his nomen to 'G'.

Wharfe (Verbeia), the 'Waters of Arnemetia' at Buxton, and Sulis Minerva at Bath (Aquae Sulis).[38] The latest addition is Ashwell, where the richest temple-treasure ever found in Britain was found about a mile away in 2002, and includes a silver statuette and twenty votive 'leaves' of gold or silver dedicated to the goddess Senuna, who was previously unknown.[39] These 'leaves' are similar in style to those in the Stony Stratford treasure (**12.06**) and at Barkway, both quite near to Ashwell, and they show Senuna standing within her gabled shrine, armed with helmet, spear and shield. The statuette and ten 'leaves' are inscribed with her name and the names of votaries, for example this silver 'leaf':

<**12.30**> *near Ashwell, Herts.*

d(eae) Senu-
nae L(ucius) L(...)
Herboni-
anus v(otum) s(olvit) l(ibens)
m(erito)

Tomlin 2008, 310, No. 17 = Tomlin forthcoming, A17

'To the goddess Senuna, Lucius L(...) Herbonianus has paid his vow willingly, deservedly.'

Unlike the other 'leaves', which are lettered with a maze of punched dots difficult to decipher, this one has been fluently inscribed with a stylus in literally stylish 'rustic capitals'. Like Cosconianus (**12.29**), Herbonianus may have reduced his nomen to its initial letter since his cognomen was distinctive; it suggests his place of origin since it derives from the nomen *Herbonius* or *Erbonius* which is virtually confined to the north-east corner of Italy. We cannot be quite sure that Senuna was a water goddess like Verbeia and the others, but there was certainly a river in southern Britain called the *Sena* or *Senua*, and her treasure was found almost on the bank of the small river which issues from the copious and still-numinous springs at Ashwell.[40]

Sulis Minerva at Bath

Senuna is given the attributes of Minerva, and thus resembles the great Sulis, the eponymous goddess of Bath (Aquae Sulis): the 'waters of Sulis' are the only thermal springs in Britain, and make it Britain's most important spa. A consultant physician there once admitted to a visiting lecturer over dinner afterwards that there was no need actually to drink the disgusting hot water: the real therapeutic benefit comes from bathing in it, and simultaneously drinking lots of nice clean water. To

---

[38] *RIB* 635 (Ilkley), 281 (Brough-on-Noe, *Arnomecta*); for Bath, see below.
[39] Tomlin 2008 and forthcoming.
[40] Jackson and Burleigh forthcoming.

supply these baths, the Romans captured the principal hot spring with a reservoir of massive masonry and lead sheeting, now covered by the medieval King's Bath at the Pump Room, and beside it they built a classical temple for Sulis Minerva. At the foot of its steps was the cult-altar which was not inscribed, so far as we can tell from its surviving fragments, but on the pavement nearby was found this altar-like statue-base still in position:

<12.31> *Bath (Aquae Sulis)*

deae Suli
L(ucius) Marcius Memor
harusp(ex)
d(ono) d(edit)

RIB III, 3049

'To the goddess Sulis, Lucius Marcius Memor, soothsayer, gave (this) as a gift.'

Memor is the only *haruspex* known from Britain, a professional diviner who interpreted the gods' will by inspecting the entrails of animals sacrificed. At first he described himself as HAR (since this abbreviation has been centred), but someone then added the letters VSP to make it clear that he was not just any old *har(iolus)*, an unqualified 'soothsayer', even if this upset the balance of his well-lettered inscription.

Another standing stone from Bath also resembles an altar, but it was found with two cinerary urns by the roadside outside the Roman city, and in fact it is a tombstone:

<12.32> *(Aquae Sulis)*

D(is) M(anibus)
G(aius) Calpurnius
[R]eceptus sacer-
dos deae Su-
lis vix(it) an(nos) LXXV,
Calpurnia Trifo-
sa libert(a) coniunx
f(aciendum) c(uravit)

RIB 155

'To the Shades of the Dead. Gaius Calpurnius Receptus, priest of the goddess Sulis, lived 75 years. Calpurnia Trifosa, his freedwoman (and) wife, had this made.'

The infant Fabia Honorata (**9.04**) and the imperial procurator Classicianus (**2.19**) were also commemorated by altar-tombstones, but this memorial form was particularly appropriate for a priest. His widow's name *Trifosa* is Greek and means, more or less, 'De Luxe'. It was her given name when she was a slave, and she retained it as her cognomen when she was freed by her owner, Receptus. Since he was a Roman citizen, she gained citizenship herself and – more than this, Reader – she married him. This is more surprising to us moderns than it would have been to a Roman. The tombstone was found in 1795, 60 years before Trollope began his 'Barchester' novels, and if he had been a historical novelist, we might have had the story of the ageing Dean of Sulis who married his parlour-maid. But the Roman combination of 'freedwoman' and 'wife' is quite common – Regina (**9.33**) springs to mind – and is evidence that the peculiar institution of ancient slavery might be mitigated by human affection. Trifosa buried her late husband, her sometime lord and master, in proper style. Her own ashes no doubt filled the second urn.

Curse tablets

Trifosa's marriage was no scandal, therefore, but we may wonder what prompted this altar:

<12.33> *Bath (Aquae Sulis)*

locum reli-
giosum per in-
solentiam e-
rutum
virtuti et n(umini)
Aug(usti) repurga-
tum reddidit
G(aius) Severius
Emeritus (centurio)
reg(ionarius)

RIB 152+*add.*

'This holy place, spoiled by vandals and purged again, Gaius Severius Emeritus, district centurion, has given back to the Virtue and Divinity of the Emperor.'

Like the great Risingham slab (**12.26**), this is one of many dedications which extend the idea of *genius* to honour the superhuman personality and inspiration of the Emperor, his *numen*, without going so far as to call him a god. It was found near the precinct of Sulis, but probably derives from another shrine.[41] A 'district centurion'

[41] Altars found with it in 1753 are dedicated to Mars Loucetios and Nemetona (*RIB* 140) and the Suleviae (**11.07**).

is also known at Carlisle, but we do not know whether Bath was in the 'district' of Emeritus, or whether he was just another officer visiting the baths, like the centurion Aufidius Maximus of the Sixth Legion and a junior officer of the Second Legion, whose freedmen dedicated altars to Sulis on their behalf. Other altars were dedicated to her by a centurion of the Second, and a Gallic stonemason (*lapidarius*).[42] Roman Bath was full of 'ultra-Roman Britons, and ultra-British Romans, and tame tribesmen pretending to be civilised', according to Kipling's centurion[43], where 'the old gluttons sit in hot water, and talk scandal and politics', but the richest source of scandal is now its treasury of letters of complaint addressed to the goddess on small sheets of lead and pewter, one of which has already been quoted (**11.06**). The first two were discovered in 1880 when the City Engineer investigated the sacred spring, and incidentally stripped it of its lead sheeting. A century later, in 1979, their number was multiplied when Barry Cunliffe excavated the gravels that filled the spring. As well as votive objects including 12,500 coins which provide a rich cross-section of the Roman money-supply, another 125 tablets were found, perhaps the richest archive anywhere of letters written to a Roman god.[44] In 2014 they were adopted by UNESCO as part of the Memory of the World. They are precious documents, down to earth but inspired by a sense of divine power and justice. The writers have been wronged, but they believe the goddess to be their protector; consequently they ask her to deny protection to the villains, even if the occasion tends to be disarmingly trivial, the theft of clothing, jewellery, or small sums of money, often no doubt in the adjoining baths:

<**12.34**> *Bath (Aquae Sulis)*

deae Suli Minerv<a>e Soli-
nus dono numini tuo ma-
iestati pax{s}a<m> ba<ln>earem et [pal]-
leum [nec p]ermitta[s so]mnum
nec san[ita]tem {e}ei qui mihi fr<a>u-
dem [f]ecit, si vir si femi[na], si servus
s[i] l[ib]er, ni{s}si [{s}s]e retegens istas
s[p]ecies ad [te]mplum tuum detulerit
[.. li]beri sui vel son.. sua e[t?] qui
illegible
ei quoque [...]
[... so]mnum ne[c sanitate-]
[m ... p]all[e]um
et reli{n}q[ua]s ni{s}si ad [te]mplum tu-
um istas res retulerint

42 *Tab. Vindol.* II, 250.8–9 (district centurion). *RIB* 143 and 144 (legionary centurion); 147 (*imaginifer*); 146 (second legionary centurion); **11.09** (*lapidarius*).

43 Kipling 1906, 'A centurion of the Thirtieth'.

44 Tomlin 1988.

Tab. Sulis 32

'Solinus to the goddess Sulis Minerva. I give to your divinity (and) majesty (my) bathing tunic and cloak. Do not allow sleep or health to him who has done me wrong, whether man or woman, whether slave or free, unless he reveals himself and brings these things to your temple ... his children or his ... and(?) who ... to him also ... sleep or [health] ... cloak and the rest, unless they bring those things to your temple.'

The *paxsa balnearis* was a casual garment like a caftan, worn before and after bathing. Solinus evidently returned from the baths to find his peg or locker empty, and was lost for words in which to clothe his indignation. By spelling *pexa* as *paxsa* and *nisi* as *nissi*, he simply strengthened his sibilants. Since he also used formulas which are found in other tablets, he must have sought advice, but we have no evidence yet (in the duplication of texts, for example, let alone of handwriting) that the Bath tablets were actually written to order by professional scribes. The wide spectrum of hands and literacy, which extends even to illiterate tablets with scribbled patterns to look like writing, suggests that one was expected to write one's own. They are mostly appeals for justice to the divine patron, but there is also an unique request that she guarantee an oath, which incidentally gives us the Roman name of her cult-site:

<12.35> *Bath (Aquae Sulis)*

Uricalus, Do[c]ilosa ux[or] sua,
Docilis filius suus et Docilina,
Decentinus frater suus, Alogiosa:
nomina {a}eorum qui iuraverunt
{qui iuraverunt} ad fontem deae Suli<s>
prid<i>e idus Apriles. quicumque illic per-
iuraverit deae Suli, facias illum
sanguine suo illud satisfacere.

Tab. Sulis 94

'Uricalus, Docilosa his wife, Docilis his son and Docilina, Decentinus his brother, Alogiosa: the names of those who have sworn who have sworn [*repeated by mistake*] at the spring of the goddess Sulis on the day before the Ides of April (12 April). Whosoever has perjured himself there, you are to make him give satisfaction for it to the goddess Sulis in his own blood.'

This tablet is the only evidence from Britain of a belief which was widespread in the Roman world, that hot springs punish perjury. In Sicily, for example, there were famous seething pools which received oaths in writing: if they floated, the oath was truthful, but if they sank, the perjurer was scalded to death.[45] This Bath tablet also contains the only date in the whole archive – the day, month, but unfortunately not the year – which otherwise is dated only by the handwriting of individual tablets, which ranges from the 'Old Roman Cursive' of the second and third centuries to the 'New Roman Cursive' which replaced it by about the beginning of the fourth. This shows that they continued to be inscribed for at least two centuries, and implies that they were known to work. We have already seen the belief in amulets (**12.06**), but unfortunately at Bath no petitioner thought to leave a note of thanks to the goddess.[46]

Identifying an unfamiliar god

The cult of Sulis should not therefore be considered in isolation; although localised, she lived in a classical temple and looked like Minerva. A very fine bronze head of Minerva was found there in 1727, which may have belonged to her cult statue.[47] Like Apollo, she presided over hot springs which punished perjury.[48] It was easy to 'identify' a local god on the evidence of shared characteristics, the classic statement of this *interpretatio Romana* being Julius Caesar's remark that the Celts worship Mercury most of all, then Apollo, Mars, Jupiter and Minerva.[49] Minerva we have just seen, identified with Senuna and Sulis, but the others were also identified with British gods. At Uley, for example, there was another cult-site previous to the Romans, who built a temple of Mercury which has produced the other British archive of inscribed lead tablets.[50] The head survives of the cult statue, which is a Celtic sculptor's masterpiece of classicising art to identify the local god with Mercury, as indeed do most of the tablets, three of which we have seen already (**11.03**, **11.04** and **11.06**), but one of his correspondents was in two minds about how to address him:

[45] Macrobius, *Sat.* 5.19, 15–31.

[46] This question is discussed further below, after **12.46** (Lydney Park). See also 'The power of the goddess' (Sulis) in Tomlin 1988, 101–05.

[47] *CSIR* i.2, No. 26.

[48] *Pan. Lat.* vi 21.6, with Nixon and Rodgers 1994, 251. For Apollo (Grannus) see **6.15**.

[49] *Gallic War* 6, 17. The term is that of Tacitus (*Germania* 43.3).

[50] Tomlin 1993.

<12.36> *Uley*

commonitorum deo
Mercurio [*written over* Marti Silvano] a Satur-
nina muliere de lintia-
mine quod amisit. ut il-
le qui ho[c] circumvenit non
ante laxetur nissi quand[o]
res s(upra)dictas ad fanum s(upra)d[ic]-
tum attul[e]rit, si vir si [m]u-
lier, si servus si liber.

deo s(upra)dicto tertiam
partem [d]onat ita ut
ex{s}igat istas res quae
s(upra)s(crip)ta sunt,
... quae per<i>t deo Silvano
tertia pars donatur ita ut
hoc ex{s}igat, si vir si femina, si s[erv]-
us si liber ...

Tomlin 1993, 121, No. 2

'A memorandum to the god Mercury (*or* Mars Silvanus) from Saturnina a woman, concerning the linen cloth which she has lost. May the person who stole it not have any rest unless (and) until he brings the aforesaid property to the temple aforesaid, whether (he be) man or woman, slave or free. She gives to the aforesaid god one-third part on condition that he exact this property which has been written above ... one-third of what has been lost is given to the god Silvanus, on condition that he exact it, whether (the thief be) man or woman, whether slave or free ...'

Saturnina writes in the same spirit as the petitioners of Sulis, calling her appeal a 'memorandum' (*commonitorium* is one of many 'legal' words and phrases in these texts) and addressing it to the god 'Mars Silvanus'. She corrected this to 'Mercury', but overleaf she wrote 'Silvanus' again and did not correct it. In the same way we find another localised god, Cocidius in the north-west, variously identified at two different military sites:

<12.37> *Hadrian's Wall near Carlisle*

Marti Coc(idio) m(ilites)
leg(ionis) II Aug(ustae)
(centuria) Sanctiana
(centuria) Secundini
d(ono) sol(verunt) sub cu-
ra Aeliani (centurionis),
cura(vit) Oppius
Felix optio

RIB 2024+*add.*

'To Mars Cocidius the soldiers of the Second Legion Augusta, from the Sanctian century (and) the century of Secundinus, with this gift paid their vow under the command of the centurion Aelianus. Oppius Felix, *optio*, had charge of the task.'

The dedicators are a legionary detachment consisting of two centuries, one of which has lost its centurion Sanctus by death or promotion; Oppius Felix the *optio* was probably its second-in-command. The two centuries are jointly commanded by another centurion, Aelianus. Cocidius here is identified with Mars, but not so at Housesteads:

<12.38> *Housesteads (Vercovicium)*

deo
Silvano
Cocidio
Q(uintus) Florius
Maternus
praef(ectus) coh(ortis)
I Tung(rorum)
v(otum) s(olvit) l(ibens) m(erito)

RIB 1578+*add.*

'To the god Silvanus Cocidius; Quintus Florius Maternus, prefect of the First Cohort of Tungrians, paid his vow willingly, deservedly.'

This time Cocidius is identified with Silvanus, whom we have already seen as the god of woodland (*silva*) in its widest sense (**9.03**). This identification is a little surprising, since Cocidius looked more like

Mars, being represented as a standing warrior on a silver plaque from his temple at Bewcastle (*fanum Cocidi*).[51] Silvanus was more naturally worshipped as the patron of hunting:

<**12.39**> *near Stanhope in Weardale*

n[u]mi[ni]b(us) [August]orum
et Silvano invicto sacr(um)
G(aius) Tetius Veturius Micia-
nus pr[<a>e]f(ectus) alae Sebosian-
nae ob aprum eximiae
formae captum quem
multi antecesso-
res eius praedari
non potuerunt v(otum) s(olvit) l(ibens) p(osuit)

RIB 1041+*add.*

'Sacred to the Divinities of the Emperors and to Unconquered Silvanus. Gaius Tetius Veturius Micianus, prefect of the Cavalry Regiment Sebosiana, paid his vow willingly (and) erected (this), because of taking a wild boar of outstanding beauty, which many of his predecessors had been unable to bag.'

The *ala Sebosiana* was at Carlisle in the late first century (**3.14**), and in the mid-second century at Inveresk (**6.16**). In the AD 260s it is found at Lancaster (**13.28**), but its movements in the previous century are unknown. This altar with its crowded text looks Severan rather than Antonine, and if we press the prefect's reference to his 'many predecessors', we might suppose the *ala Sebosiana* had occupied the nearest cavalry fort, Binchester, for quite some time. But perhaps he also meant the prefects of the *ala Vetttonum*, which is well attested at Binchester.[52] The Etruscan nomen *Veturius* implies that he was Italian, even perhaps the son or grandson of the influential Roman *eques* Gaius Veturius Testius Amandus, who was honoured at Ostia in AD 146 by local guilds as their patron.[53]

This altar was found in 1747, but without any associated building being reported: its remains are still to be sought in the wilder parts of Weardale. Two such shrines were found two centuries later, in about 1936 and in 1946, in purple moorland south of the fort at Bowes. Appropriately there are modern grouse butts a few yards away. Both shrines contained altars dedicated to the local god Vinotonus, whom a centurion of the third-century garrison identified with Silvanus:

---

[51] *RIB* 986.

[52] *RIB* 1028, 1035, III, 3260; compare **8.02** (Bowes).

[53] *ILS* 6173. *Tetius* would then be a stone-cutter's error for *Testius*.

<12.40> *near Bowes (Lavatris)*

[deo]
Vinotono
Silvano Iul(ius)
Secundus (centurio)
coh(ortis) I Thrac(um)
v(otum) s(olvit) l(aetus) l(ibens) m(erito)

RIB 732+*add.*

'To the god Vinotonus Silvanus, Julius Secundus, centurion of the First Cohort of Thracians, paid his vow, gladly, willingly, deservedly.'

Contrast this with an altar from the other shrine, also third-century but with notably more handsome lettering:

<12.41> *near Bowes (Lavatris)*

deo Vin-
otono
L(ucius) Caesius
Frontinus pr-
aef(ectus) coh(ortis) I Thrac(um)
domo Parma
v(otum) s(olvit) l(aetus) l(ibens) m(erito)

RIB 733

'To the god Vinotonus, Lucius Caesius Frontinus, prefect of the First Cohort of Thracians, his home Parma, paid his vow, gladly, willingly, deservedly.'

This commanding officer was an Italian, from Parma in north Italy, and of much higher social class than the centurion, but he did not associate Vinotonus, who is unknown elsewhere, with any Roman god. Such an 'identification', therefore, although it is made by another prefect[54], is not necessarily an index of sophistication or 'imperialism'. At Benwell, for example, three altars were dedicated by Roman officers to the local god Antenociticus without qualification.[55]

A fragmentary altar dedicated to Silvanus[56] was found in a temple which belonged to Apollo, according to another altar from the same site:

[54] *RIB* III, 3251.

[55] **7.07,** *RIB* 1327 and 1328. Localised gods who receive worship without 'identification' include Ancasta at Bitterne (*RIB* 97), Setlocenia at Maryport (841), Saiiada(?) at Vindolanda (1695).

[56] *RIB* III, 3054 (Nettleton Shrub).

<**12.42**> *Nettleton Shrub, West Kington (Wilts.)*

deo Apol-
lini Cuno-
maglo Co-
rotica Iu
ti fil(ia)
v(otum) s(olvit) l(ibens) m(erito)

RIB III, 3053

'To the god Apollo Cunomaglos, Corotica, daughter of Iutus, paid her vow, willingly, deservedly.'

This is the first instance of the cult-title *Cunomaglus*, which is compounded from two well-known Celtic elements, **cunos* ('hound') and **maglos* ('prince'), which are reversed in the sub-Roman personal name *Maglocun*. 'Hound-prince' is the name or title of a Celtic god identified with Apollo, who in some respects also recalled Silvanus.[57] The dedicator's name *Corotica* is also Celtic, and should be restored on a tombstone from Caerleon.[58] A derived form occurs on the base of this bronze statuette:

<**12.43**> *Martlesham, Suffolk*

deo Marti
Corotiaco
Simplicia
pro se v(otum) p(osuit) l(ibens) m(erito)

(*underneath*) Glaucus fecit

RIB 213

'To Mars Corotiacus, Simplicia placed her vow on her own behalf, willingly, deservedly.'
'Glaucus made this.'

The cult-title *Corotiacus* is probably the name of another local god, this time identified with Mars. It too survived the Roman period, since it is the name of an obstreperous British king to whom St Patrick addressed his *Epistle to Coroticus*. Mars, with whom Saturnina thought of associating the god of Uley, is associated with many Celtic gods in Britain.[59] We have already seen Cocidius (**12.37**), and here is another:

---

[57] Merrifield 1996. For *Maglocun*, see Edwards 2007, 390, P70.
[58] *RIB* 371 with *Britannia* 44 (2013), 395, add. (a), *Caesoria Coro[ti]ca*.
[59] Birley 1986, 47–9.

<12.44> *Nettleham, Lincs.*

deo Marti Rigo-
nemeti et numini-
bus Augustorum
Q(uintus) Nerat(ius) Prox{s}i-
mus arcum de suo
donavit

RIB III, 3180

'To the god Mars Rigonemetis and the Divinities of the Emperors, Quintus Neratius Proximus gave (this) arch at his own expense.'

This cult-title means 'Lord of the Grove'. The handsome slab, with its well-drawn lettering cut within a recessed panel flanked either side by a *pelta*, is Antonine in style. The dedicator's nomen is rare, and suggests that his father or grandfather was a local magnate enfranchised by Lucius Neratius Marcellus, governor of Britain in AD 103. The slab would have been inserted above the entrance to the god's precinct, such an 'arch' being the British equivalent of the portico Charax gave to Pergamum at about the same time (**12.02**); others were given to an unknown deity coupled with the Genius of the place at York (**11.37**), and to the god Viridius at Ancaster.[60]

At Lydney Park, a mosaic pavement was given to yet another god identified with Mars, his name being so familiar locally that it could be reduced to its initials. Sadly it is now destroyed, but a drawing survives. The dedication was picked out in blue tesserae on a white ground:

<12.45> *Lydney Park, Glos.*

d(eo) M(arti) N(odenti) T(itus) Fl(avius) Senilis pr(aepositus) rel(igionis) ex stipibus pos{s}uit | o[pitu]lante Victorino interp(r)[e]tiante

RIB II.4, 2448.3

'To the god Mars Nodens. Titus Flavius Senilis, superintendent of the cult, laid this from donations, with the help of Victorinus, interpreter.'

The romantic site of the temple of Nodens is a wooded hilltop overlooking the Severn estuary; locally its ruins were known as the Dwarfs' Chapel, because the under-floor heating channels seemed to be a series of low-ceilinged rooms. No less mysterious is the abbreviation of the office held by Senilis, PR REL. Since he was handling temple funds – the reference to 'donations' (*stipes*) implies that Nodens had his own treasury, like that of Mercury at Uley[61] – he was surely a temple-officer; which makes Mark Hassall's conjecture of *pr(aepositus) rel(igionis)* more appropriate

[60] *RIB* III, 3170.

[61] Tomlin 1993, 130, No. 78, *thesaurum potententis[imi](!) dei.*

than Mommsen's *pr(aepositus) rel(iquationis)*, the officer in charge of naval stores. Likewise, although the Roman army had 'interpreters', in this context an 'interpreter' of divine messages seems more likely.[62] The spelling *possuit* is for *posuit*, as in **9.22** and **9.23**. The god's unabbreviated name can be recovered from other inscriptions, including the first curse tablet ever found in Britain:

<**12.46**> *Lydney Park, Glos.*

de{u}o
Nodenti Silvianus
anilum perdedit
demediam partem
donavit Nodenti.
inter quibus nomen
Seniciani no<n i>llis
petmittas(!) sanita-
tem donec perfera<t>
usque templum [No]-
dentis

RIB 306+*add.*

'To the god Nodens.[63] Silvianus has lost his ring and has given half of it to Nodens. Among those who have the name *Senicianus*, do not allow them health until he bring it to the temple of Nodens.'

This was found in 1805, and Charles King in 1879, its first real editor, not only saw that a thief was being cursed but astutely compared it with lead tablets from the Greek-speaking East recently acquired by the British Museum which 'dedicated' wrongdoers to the goddess Demeter. The special character of such curses has now been illuminated by the Dutch scholar Henk Versnel, who aptly calls them 'prayers for justice'.[64] Britain for some reason has been especially productive, the *commonitorium* of Saturnina (**12.36**) being a good example. As already observed, they are not infallible spells against enemies, but petitions addressed to a divine patron like Sulis Minerva to right a wrong. They have their earthly counterparts, notably in the correspondence of Abinnaeus, the fourth-century commandant of a fort in Egypt who receives complaints of wrongdoing (housebreaking, for example, and cattle-theft) followed by this formula: 'Wherefore I request and beg of your philanthropy to apprehend this man and compel him to restore to me what he has

[62] These conjectures are rejected by Renberg 2006 since they run counter to the rest of his paper, and it is true that *RIB* 305 was dedicated at Uley by a weapons-instructor (*armatura*), but the 'interpreter' (of Aesculapius) is attested on the Tiber Island (*CIL* vi 33864), and the 'interpretation' of an oracle of Apollo at Housesteads (*RIB* 1579).

[63] *Nodons* in *RIB* 305 and 316; *Nudens* in 307. *deuo* for *deo*, unless it was prompted by *devoveo* (compare **11.06**), may represent a [w] glide between two vowels in hiatus.

[64] Versnel 2005.

wickedly seized.'[65] Modern readers may even think of Don Corleone and his clients in the first chapter of *The Godfather*, but old-fashioned gods of the countryside like Nodens and Mercury at Uley would have deplored this comparison; they were too polite to say so, but they felt more like the aristocratic and conventional Pliny on his Tuscan estate: 'I am beset on all sides by the peasants with all their petitions full of complaints.'[66]

Some scholars have supposed that Nodens was unsuccessful on this occasion, since a handsome gold ring has been found at Silchester bearing the name *Senicianus*, but this 'conceals' the same Celtic name-element as *Saenus* (**9.44**) and is quite a common name in Britain. So the identification is unnecessary.[67] But an inscribed altar found in Turkey is eloquent of divine power in these matters: after a ritual curse was placed on persons who stole from the bath-house, a cloak was stolen (as so often at Bath), and the local god punished the thief; he was compelled to bring the cloak back to the god, and to confess his crime. A divine messenger then ordered that the cloak be sold, and the history be inscribed on stone; the altar carries a picture of the cloak lying at the feet of the god.[68]

These precious scraps of literacy document the role played by British gods in their communities, but the buildings round the temple of Nodens, the inscribed archway at Nettleham, the great temple of Sulis Minerva, the gold and silver leaves of Senuna, all show that localised cults in the south of Britain might attract money and influential persons from elsewhere. They contrast in this respect with two northern cults, which nonetheless attracted many humble altars.

Belatucadrus and 'Veteres'

The grandest monument of the cult of Belatucadrus is this amateurish altar:

<12.47> *Old Penrith (Voreda)*

deo
Marti
Belatucad-
ro et numi-
nib(us) Aug(ustorum)
Iulius Au-
gustalis,
actor
Iul(i) Lu-
pi pr<a>ef(ecti)

[65] *P. Abinnaeus* 44, and similar in 45–57 (with the editors' introduction to these 'Petitions').

[66] Pliny, *ep.* ix 15.1 (trans. Radice), *tam multis undique rusticorum libellis et tam querulis inquietor.*

[67] *RIB* II.3, 2422.14 with note.

[68] Tomlin 1988, 104, summarising *CMRDM* I, No. 69. It is not clear whether the thief was actually revealed, or only returned a cloak anonymously.

RIB 918

'To the god Mars Belatucadrus and to the Divinities of the Emperors, Julius Augustalis, agent of Julius Lupus the prefect, (erected this).'

This is one of 28 altars dedicated to Belatucadrus in north-west Britain; but unlike Cocidius, whose distribution is geographically similar without overlapping at individual sites, Belatucadrus does not attract any Roman officer more important than an *optio* at Maryport.[69] Also there are twelve ways of writing his name, which implies that it was transmitted verbally, like that of the other god:

<12.48> *Carvoran (Magnis)*

deo sanct[o]
Veteri
Iul(ius) Pastor
imag(inifer) coh(ortis) II
Delma(tarum) v(otum) p(osuit) l(ibens) m(erito)

RIB 1795+*add.*

'To the holy god Veteris, Julius Pastor *imaginifer* of the Second Cohort of Delmatians paid his vow willingly, deservedly.'

The mysterious 'Veteres' is the most prolific god in Britain, being attested by some 60 altars almost entirely in the mid-Wall area with outliers to the south-east.[70] They cluster at Vindolanda (with 11) and Carvoran (with 13), but except for the pretty altar from Netherby[71] carved with two of the Labours of Hercules, and a silver 'leaf' from Rutland,[72] they are all crudely made, and only two votaries reveal more about themselves than their names; Pastor, the most informative, was only the under-officer who carried an image of the Emperor. 'Delmatians' is an alternative spelling of 'Dalmatians', who came from what is now Croatia, but the god's name is written in some eighteen different ways, masculine or feminine, singular or plural; the initial *u* or *v* is quite often aspirated like a Germanic personal name,[73] but we cannot be certain that he (or she, or even they) was German. The cult does not occur in Germany itself, and hardly any of the votaries' names are German.

Other gods undoubtedly were German.[74] Some are only names attested once, for

69 *RIB* 809.
70 Birley 2008, 35–44.
71 *RIB* 973.
72 *RIB* II.3, 2431.3.
73 For example *Huitiris* in *RIB* III, 3335.
74 Birley 2008, 31–35.

example the goddesses Harimella and Ricagambeda at Birrens,[75] and this goddess at Lanchester:

<**12.49**> *Lanchester (Longovicium)*

deae Gar-
mangabi
et n(umini) [[Gordi-]]
[[ani]] Aug(usti) n(ostri), pr[o]
sal(ute) vex(illationis) Suebo-
rum Lon(govicianorum) Gor(dianae) (vexillarii) vo-
tum solverunt m(erito)

RIB 1074

'To the goddess Garmangabis and to the divinity of our August Emperor Gordian, for the welfare of the detachment of Suebi, Gordian's Own, at Longovicium; its members deservedly paid their vow.'

German philologists explain *Garmangabis* as meaning 'wish-giver', but this is her only monument, a splendid altar with 'romanesque' chip-carving on the capital that now stands in the porch of the church at Lanchester, which itself is built of stones from the Roman fort. Gordian's name was deleted after his 'memory' was condemned, but the revisionists missed the abbreviated form of GOR in the titulature of the unit which dates this altar to AD 238–44. The German unit is a *vexillatio*, but not in the sense of earlier 'detachments' which implied a parent-unit to which they would return; instead it anticipates fourth-century usage, when independent units (now cavalry) were known as *vexillationes*.[76] Another usage which anticipates the late-Roman army is that the unit has taken the name of its station, Longovicium. In Britain this practice begins in the third century – we have already seen it of the contemporary unit at Ribchester (**7.04**) – and is characteristic of the new-style 'units' (*numeri*) such as 'scouts' (*exploratores*) and 'squadrons' (*cunei*).

At Housesteads, the existing garrison was reinforced in the third century by a draft of Germans. The internal organisation of this 'squadron' (*cuneus*), and how it was 'brigaded' with the Tungrians, remains unclear, despite a wealth of epigraphic evidence from a shrine outside the fort.[77] This shrine was dedicated to at least three German deities:

[75] *RIB* 2096 and 2107.

[76] Diocletian's legislation (*Cod. Just.* 7.64.9 and 10. 55(54).3) distinguishes them from (infantry) legions, and implies that they were 'detachments' from a cavalry army which no longer existed as an entity. This is usually dated to Gallienus in the AD 260s.

[77] The best treatment is by Rushworth 2009, but he sees the draft as consisting of 'detachments' (*cunei*, plural) of Frisii named after Housesteads, despite there being only single 'detachments' (*cuneus*, singular) named after other forts: at Papcastle, the *cuneus Frisionum Aballauensium* (*RIB* 882 and 883); at Brougham, the *cuneus [. . .]rum* (*RIB* 722); at Binchester, the *c(uneus) Fris(iorum) Vinovie(nsium)* (*RIB* 1036).

<12.50> *Housesteads (Vercovicium)*

deo
Marti et duabus
Alaisiagis et n(umini) Aug(usti)
Ger(mani) cives Tuihanti
cunei Frisiorum
Ver(covicianorum) Se<ve>r(iani) Alexand-
riani votum
solverunt
libent[es]
m(erito)

RIB 1594+*add.*

'To the god Mars and the two Alaisiagae and the Divinity of the Emperor, the German tribesmen of Twenthe, of the squadron of Frisii at Vercovicium, Severus Alexander's Own, willingly and deservedly paid their vow.'

The dynastic title, which incidentally was not deleted after Alexander's 'memory' was condemned, dates this altar to AD 222–35. It was found in 1883 together with two-thirds of the monumental entrance to the shrine, the left-hand pillar carved with a stately female figure, her right hand raised in greeting (just visible behind **12.25**), and the arch carved with a standing figure of Mars attended by two cupids(?) holding wreaths. The lady must be an Alaisiaga, since the pillar is inscribed by the 'German tribesmen of Twenthe' again, who give Mars the German title of *Thincsus* (god of the *Thing*, the tribal assembly), and name the two Alaisiagae as Beda and Fimmilena.[78] The right-hand pillar has not yet been found, but it would have been inscribed by another constituent of the *cuneus*, quite likely 'Notfried's unit' (*n(umerus) Hnaudifridi*), which dedicated its own altar nearby to the Alaisiagae *Baudihillia* and *Friagabis*.[79] The difference of name here is surprising, but it may mean that there were actually four Alaisiagae, worshipped in pairs. *numerus* in military usage is a general term like English 'unit', but *cuneus* (literally 'wedge', and originally a battle-formation) is more specific; in the fourth century at least, it was applied to a cavalry unit smaller than the 'vexillation' but often derived from one.[80] Like the Longoviciani at Lanchester, the Frisii have adopted the name of their fort; the abbreviation VER preserves the correct spelling of what the Notitia Dignitatum transmits as *Borcovicium*.[81]

[78] *RIB* 1593, illustrated as *CSIR* i.6, No. 159. The arch is *CSIR* i.6, No. 161. The name of the *Tuihanti* (although *Tuihauti* could also be read) has usually been deduced from what is now Twenthe in the southern Netherlands.

[79] *RIB* 1576.

[80] Hoffmann 1969, 211, 253. Likewise the *ala Sarmatarum* at Ribchester (**9.31** and *RIB* 595) had become a *cuneus* by the time of the Notitia (*Occ.* 40.54).

[81] *ND Occ.* 40, 40, with Rivet and Smith 1979, 493.

Rome personified

These German gods were all brought to Britain by Germans serving in the Roman army, but if we turn now to imported cults, we should begin with that of Rome herself:

<12.51> *High Rochester (Bremenium)*

d(eae) R(omae) s(acrum)
dupl(icarii) n(umeri) Explor(atorum)
Bremen(iensium) aram
instituerunt
n(atali) eius, c(urante) Caep(ione)
Charitino trib(uno),
v(otum) s(olverunt) l(ibentes) m(erito)

RIB 1270+*add.*

'Sacred to the Goddess Roma. The *duplicarii* of the unit of Scouts of Bremenium set up (this) altar on her birthday under the charge of Caepio Charitinus, tribune, (and) willingly and deservedly paid their vow.'

The dedicatee has been reduced to its initial letters D R S on the capital, for decorative reasons perhaps, or to save space, although the dedicators might have suppressed the redundant verb *instituerunt* ('set up') instead.[82] This unique abbreviation was convincingly solved by Horsley, but his *Britannia Romana* (1732) seems to have been unknown to the Revd Dr Surridge more than a century later, when he visited High Rochester for the excavations of 1852.[83] He was the resident clergyman in the nearby parish of Thorneyburn, which made him scornful of critics who enjoyed 'ample metropolitan references'. Reading Caesar's *Gallic War* had convinced him that Julius Caesar succeeded in conquering Britain, in spite of Tacitus' attempt to steal the credit for Agricola, and he used this inscription to prove it. After expanding D R S to *d(ominis) R(omanis) s(uis)*, 'the Romans being their Lords or Masters', he took N EIVS C CAEP to be the dedication: *n(umini) eius C(aio) Cae(sari) p(onendam)*, 'to its presiding deity Caius Caesar'. Then, to avoid identifying High Rochester as *Bremenium*, another of his obsessions, he expanded BREMEN to *Br(itanniam) emen(si)*, 'having completed their Survey of Britain', so as to understand the whole as a dedication to Caesar by the engineers who made the first military survey of Britain. An epigraphist needs imagination, of course, but

[82] Compare **13.19** (also from High Rochester), which likewise reduces the dedicatee to its initials (G D N) on the capital, but does not express the verb of dedication, for which there was no room any way.
[83] Horsley 1732, 243, and *Northumberland* XCV. Surridge 1853.

Surridge offers an object-lesson in how to solve epigraphic abbreviations by pure guesswork rooted in spleen and prejudice.

The *duplicarii* who dedicated this altar were collectively the junior officers of a unit of *exploratores* ('scouts') which, like the Germans at Lanchester and Housesteads, took the name of its fort. Another altar records them at High Rochester in AD 238/44, and as 'brigaded' with the milliary cohort in garrison; a similar unit of 'scouts' is found at Risingham in AD 211/17.[84] They have been seen by analogy with units of *exploratores* on other frontiers as providing long-range surveillance from the outpost forts, an 'early warning' system which would mitigate the loss of the initiative that followed the decision by the sons of Septimius Severus to fall back on Hadrian's Wall.

N EIVS was read by Horsley and his successors as *n(umini) eius* ('to her divinity'), of which there are many examples, but a better reading is *n(atali) eius*, 'on her birthday', which only became possible when the *feriale Duranum* was excavated in 1931/2. This is a fragmentary papyrus calendar of official religious observances dating from *c.* AD 223/27, which was found in the dry, dusty soil of Dura Europos on its coffee-coloured cliffs above the Syrian Euphrates. The birthday of Rome was 21 April; its formal celebration, which displaced an earlier festival, was introduced by Hadrian. Every year on that day the garrison of Dura, the Twentieth Cohort of Palmyrenes, sacrificed a heifer *ob natalem urbis [R]omae [a]ete[rnae]*, 'for the birthday of the Eternal City of Rome'.[85]

Victory and Concord

These Arabs in the service of Rome on her eastern frontier were thus able to worship as a goddess the capital city they never saw. In Britain the geographical entities Britannia, Gallia and Brigantia, were also treated as goddesses, and even institutions and social organisms could be personified by the concept of *genius*. Ideal qualities were also personified, for example Discipline at Chesters (**5.03**), Bertha (**6.27**), Corbridge and Birrens.[86] Victory is understandably frequent, with 21 dedications and many sculptured reliefs; they include this silver statuette identified by the silver tag attached to its arm:

<**12.52**> *Milnrow, Lancs.*

Victoriae
leg(ionis) VI Vic(tricis)
Val(erius) Rufus
v(otum) s(olvit) l(ibens) m(erito)

---

84 **13.19** (High Rochester). *RIB* 1235 with 1243 and 1244 (Risingham).

85 Fink, Hoey and Snyder 1940, Coll. II, 5.

86 *RIB*1127 and 1128 (Corbridge); 2092 (Birrens).

RIB 582+*add.*

'To the Victory of the Sixth Legion Victrix, Valerius Rufus paid his vow, willingly, deservedly.'

The find-spot in Lancashire, far from the legion's base at York, suggests that the statuette was stolen from a shrine there, perhaps as loot in a barbarian incursion. There is no instance of 'Victory' being linked with 'Concord' – in Britain this must wait until the end of the Seven Years War in 1763 and the dedication of the largest temple in the landscape gardens at Stowe – but we do find specific 'concords':

<**12.53**> *Corbridge (Coria)*

Concordi-
ae leg(ionis) VI
Vi(ctricis) p(iae) f(idelis) et
leg(ionis) XX [V(aleriae) V(ictricis)]

RIB 1125+*add.*

'To the Concord of the Sixth Legion Victrix Dutiful and Loyal, and the Twentieth Legion Valeria Victrix.'

After Britain was divided into two provinces, Lower Britain included the northern frontier despite having only one legion, whereas two legions garrisoned Upper Britain in the south, where the external threat was less. The military balance was restored by the south contributing detachments to the northern frontier, hence this double unit at Corbridge. Its constituents occupied separate compounds, for better discipline presumably, but also a sign that 'discord' was feared if they got too close to each other. This would explain the self-conscious concord of Gauls and Britons at Vindolanda (**12.16**), and the same is true of a statue-base from Carlisle; only the feet remain of two standing figures, but they are explained by the inscription below:

<**12.54**> *Carlisle (Luguvalium)*

Concord[iae]
leg(ionis) II Aug(ustae) et (legionis) XX V(aleriae) [V(ictricis)]

RIB III, 3459

'To the Concord of the Second Legion Augusta and the Twentieth Legion Valeria Victrix.'

These figures were two legionaries standing arm-in-arm, like Diocletian and his colleagues in the famous porphyry statue-group now in Venice,[87] and soon we will see an altar dedicated by their commanding officer (**13.04**). They represent detachments of the two legions of Upper Britain in the south, 'brigaded' together on the northern frontier.

Fortune and Nemesis

Modern visitors to Stowe may regard the Temple of Concord as a piece of eighteenth-century Classical sentiment paying homage to an artificial abstraction, but they might still accept two ideas of causation as personalities beyond their control: Fortune (or perhaps Luck) as the blind force of Chance, and Nemesis as the workings of divine retribution. We have already seen altars dedicated to Fortune at Chester (**4.10**), Binchester (**5.36**), Carvoran (**5.46**), Bowes (**8.02**), York (**9.02**), Risingham (**9.05**) and Maryport (**9.06**); here is yet another, from the Antonine Wall:

<12.55> *Castlecary*

Fortunae
vexilla-
tiones leg(ionis) II Aug(ustae)
leg(ionis) VI Vic(tricis)
p(iae) f(idelis) p(osuerunt) l(aetae) l(ibentes)

RIB 2146; Keppie 1998, No. 27

'To Fortune, detachments of the Second Legion Augusta and the Sixth Legion Victrix Dutiful and Loyal gladly and willingly set (this) up.'

This was found in the bath-house, with a small figure of Fortune nearby. The mason undoubtedly cut S, not F, in the last line, but he might have been expected to complete the legion's title as in the Corbridge inscription (**12.53**), so he probably mis-read a handwritten draft. No doubt also he belonged to the other legion. Why altars to Fortune are so often found in military bath-houses is uncertain; at Kirkby Thore and in Spain and Germany she is actually called *balinearis* ('of the bath-house').[88] An allusion to gambling has been cynically suggested, but it seems more likely that Roman soldiers felt most at risk when they were naked. At Bath, as we have seen (**11.06**), bathers risked losing their clothes and other valuables. Whatever the compulsion, it was shared by women: the general's wife at York dedicated a fine

[87] Illustrated in Brown 1971, 23, and one of Kenneth Clark's favourite works of art (Clark 1977, 92).

[88] *RIB* 764; *ILS* 2605 and 3719. Macdonald 1934, 419–20.

altar in the bath-house (**9.02**). Soldiers also knew (who better?) that pride goes before a fall:

<12.56> *Chester (Deva)*

deae Nemesi
Sext(ius) Marci-
anus (centurio) ex visu

RIB III, 3149

'To the goddess Nemesis (from) Sextius Marcianus, centurion, as the result of a vision.'

The idea of Nemesis as divine retribution for 'presumption' is ultimately Greek; as late as AD 380, a Roman proconsul of Asia who had persecuted pagan Greek intellectuals is gleefully reported – by a pagan Greek intellectual – to have fallen dead as he left her temple.[89] The Chester altar was found in the legionary amphitheatre, in a small room which was presumably her shrine, and others come from amphitheatres in other provinces; she is invoked by this curse tablet from the legionary amphitheatre at Caerleon:

<12.57> *Caerleon (Isca)*

dom<i>na Ne-
mesis do ti-
bi palleum
et galliculas,
qui tulit non
redimat ni<si>
v[i]ta sanguine
sua

RIB 323+*add.*

'Lady Nemesis, I give you (my) cloak and sandals; let the person who took them not redeem them except by his own life and blood.'

This lead tablet was found in a small room which again is likely to have been her shrine. It is scratched with a stylus in handwriting which resembles that used on waxed writing-tablets; in particular E is made with two diagonal strokes ('II'), a form

[89] Eunapius, *Lives of the Sophists*, 481.

which is typical of such tablets and owners' signatures on pottery, but is not used in the ink leaf-tablets from Vindolanda[90] and almost never in stone inscriptions. This is the only true curse tablet from a military site in Britain, and like the Lydney tablet (**12.46**) it devotes a thief to a god, but when it was found in 1927 it was almost unparalleled in Britain, and for many years it was misunderstood. It was thought to curse a gladiator or charioteer, but the discovery of the Bath tablets has now made its purpose only too obvious.

Roman gods

Nemesis, like Fortune and the others, is a personification; but to return to Roma and the *feriale Duranum*, we read that every year on 3 January, animals were sacrificed because vows were paid and renewed for the welfare of the Emperor and the eternity of the Roman Empire; the list includes an ox for Jupiter, a cow for his consort Juno, a cow for Minerva, a bull for Father Mars, and a bull for Victory.[91] These Roman gods all feature on the contemporary altar dedicated at Carlisle by Aurelius Syrio (**13.04**), the commander of the two legionary detachments whose 'concord' we have just seen (**12.54**). As a Thracian recruit who rose through the Guard to independent command, Syrio foreshadows the great 'Illyrian' emperors of the third century, but he also recalls an earlier officer, the Antonine centurion Cocceius Firmus at Auchendavy, who dedicated that altar to the *genius* of Britain (**12.18**). Firmus' other altars name all the gods of the Carlisle altar except Juno, beginning with her consort Jupiter:

<12.58> *Auchendavy*

I(ovi) O(ptimo) M(aximo)
Victoriae
Victrici pro salu-
te imp(eratoris) n(ostri) et sua
suorum, M(arcus) Coccei(us)
Firmus
(centurio) leg(ionis) II Aug(ustae)

RIB 2176+*add*. Keppie 1998, No. 35

'To Jupiter Best and Greatest, and to Victorious Victory, for the welfare of our Emperor and of himself and his family, (from) Marcus Cocceius Firmus, centurion of the Second Legion Augusta.'

[90] *Tab. Vindol.* I, pp. 62–3.

[91] Fink, Hoey and Snyder 1940, Coll. I, 1–6.

Next Jupiter's colleagues are named, but with significant additions:

<12.59> *Auchendavy*

Dianae
Apollini
M(arcus) Cocce[i(us)]
Firmus
(centurio) leg(ionis) II Aug(ustae)

RIB 2174+*add.* Keppie 1998, No. 33

'To Diana and Apollo, (from) Marcus Cocceius Firmus, centurion of the Second Legion Augusta.'

<12.60> *Auchendavy*

Marti
Minervae
Campestri-
bus Herc<u>l(i)
Eponae
Victoriae
M(arcus) Coccei(us)
Firmus
(centurio) leg(ionis) II Aug(ustae)

RIB 2177+*add.* Keppie 1998, No. 36

'To Mars, Minerva, the Goddesses of the Parade-ground, Hercules, Epona, Victory, (from) Marcus Cocceius Firmus, centurion of the Second Legion Augusta.'

A fifth altar is dedicated to Silvanus.[92] Firmus' unique devotion to more than ten deities inspired a classic study by Eric Birley, who showed that his selection implied previous service as a decurion (troop-commander) in the *equites singulares Augusti*, the Emperor's mounted guards at Rome. Epona was the Celtic goddess of horses, her name being cognate with Latin *equus*. That Firmus came from Thrace like Aurelius Syrio is implied by his naming Diana before Apollo, an allusion to the principal goddess and god of this area, and it is confirmed by his retirement to Histria, a

[92] *RIB* 2178. Only the dedication survives, but since it was found with his other altars, the dedicator was surely Firmus.

Black Sea port near the Danube delta, where he is attested in AD 169 as a local magistrate. In addition we know, from a legal decision cited by the Digest, that after being promoted centurion he owned a female slave who was stolen by raiders after being condemned to the salt-works; where this happened is unknown, but it may well have been in Britain itself.[93]

Jupiter

By dedicating his altar to Jupiter 'Best and Greatest', Firmus was following the practice of unit-commanders on 3 January, for example Julius Candidus at Old Kilpatrick (**6.26**). Such altars have been found at many forts, but in particular at Birdoswald with at least 23, and Maryport with 22. At Maryport the first of these was found shortly before 1665, and no fewer than 12 were found in 1870; others (including some to other 'official' deities) have been found casually ever since the sixteenth century. They were preserved by the Senhouse family, which with some exceptions[94] accumulated the inscriptions found on their land now housed in the museum which worthily commemorates their name. The altars dedicated to Jupiter include **5.13** and three others by Maenius Agrippa (**5.12**), four by another tribune, Caballius Priscus, and three by Cammius Maximus. A second altar dedicated to Jupiter by Attius Tutor (who also dedicated one to Mars Militaris) was found as recently as 2012.[95] They are usually thought to have been annual dedications, and the unweathered state of the lettering suggests that they were kept under cover. Also found at Maryport in 1870 was this splendid dedication-slab:

<12.61> *Maryport (Alauna)*

Iovi Optim(o) Maxi(mo)
Capitolino
pro salut(e) An-
tonini Aug(usti)
Pii Postumi-
us Acilianus
praef(ectus) coh(ortis) I Delm(atarum)

RIB 832

'To Jupiter Best and Greatest, Capitolinus, for the welfare of Antoninus Augustus Pius, Postumius Acilianus, prefect of the First Cohort of Delmatae, (set this up).'

93 Birley 1961, 87–103.

94 Apart from a few stones which were lost after being recorded, the Senhouses loaned or gave away **9.06** (now in the British Museum), *RIB* 814 (to Carlisle Museum) and 831 (now in the Museo della Civiltà Romana, Rome). In more recent years the stones were neglected, but they were rescued by Roger Senhouse and Brian Ashmore before the Senhouse Museum was founded in 1990.

95 Respectively **5.12** and *RIB* 824, 825 and 826; *RIB* 817, 818, 819 and 820; *RIB* 827, 828 and 829; *RIB* 830 (compare 837), *Britannia* 44 (2013), 382, No. 3. Re-excavation in 2012 (*Britannia* 43 (2012), 294) disproved the idea that they were ritually buried. As noted after **5.13**, the idea that they were annual dedications has been questioned.

This was found in a pit like the altars, and may have been part of an associated structure which once sheltered them, perhaps a reviewing-platform or a temple. Jupiter is 'Capitoline' since his most important shrine was on the Capitoline Hill in Rome, but this is the only instance of the title from Britain.[96] The emperor is Antoninus Pius (AD 138–61), and the eagle-headed *peltae* are typical of contemporary building-inscriptions, notably a three-mile slab of the Twentieth Legion from the Antonine Wall.[97] Four other dedications by this prefect have been found, including this altar:

<**12.62**> *Maryport (Alauna)*

dis deabusq(ue)
P(aulus) Postumius
Acilianus
praef(ectus)
coh(ortis) I Delm(atarum)

RIB 810+*add.*

'To the gods and goddesses, (from) Paulus Postumius Acilianus, prefect of the First Cohort of Delmatae.'

The text is now largely lost, but was recorded by Horsley. The figures of Hercules and Mars stand in high relief on each side of the die, whether they were the deities originally intended, or were meant to represent the whole crew. In the prefect's name the initial letter P does not abbreviate the common praenomen *Publius*, but the very rare *Paulus* (or *Paullus*), as we know from another slab he dedicated for the welfare of Antoninus Pius. This has unfortunately lost the name(s) of the god or gods concerned, but gives the prefect's full name as Paulus Postumius Acilianus, son of Paulus, of the *Palatina* voting-tribe. There must be a connection with the procurator of Syria in AD 102, since he has the same unusual name; he came from southern Spain (Baetica), but was not necessarily related by blood.[98]

Mars

The warrior-god Mars is often identified with Celtic gods, as we have seen, and the Maryport altars include two dedicated to Mars Militaris; like Hercules, he was understandably popular with soldiers. Two inscribed bronze statuettes have already been noted (**12.43** and **11.17**), and another has been lost, to judge by its surviving label:

[96] Unless it has been abbreviated in the dedication of *RIB* 898 (Old Carlisle) to *I(ovi) O(ptimo) M(aximo) C(onservatori)*.

[97] *RIB* 2173 (Keppie 1998, No. 1).

[98] Devijver, *PME* P 100 with P 101. The procurator's voting-tribe (*Papiria*) is different, as Birley noted, and implies that the prefect's father was a freedman of the procurator. The slab is *RIB* 850, and the other dedications are *RIB* 833 (to Jupiter, probably a statue-base) and 847 (the fragment of an altar).

<**12.63**> *Lanchester (Longovicium)*

Marti
Aug(usto)
Auffidi-
us Aufi-
dianus
d(ono)
d(edit)

RIB 1077

'To August Mars, Auffidius Aufidianus gave (this) as a gift.'

Five small altars to Mars have also been found at Lanchester, but this little ansate plaque is made of gold, 'the same weight as two guineas', according to Collingwood Bruce.[99] Fortunately it was not melted down when found in 1716, and later found refuge in a matchbox in the Chapter Library, Durham. Its lettering is in relief, unlike the incised letters of a stone inscription, since it was made by punching the reverse with a fine point. Three holes driven through the first word show that it was attached to a votive statuette.

Minerva

Dedications to Jupiter's wife and consort Juno are rare in Britain, but the third member of the Capitoline triad, Minerva, was identified with British goddesses such as Sulis (**12.31**) and Senuna (**12.30**). A group of three altars from the northernmost outpost of Hadrian's Wall honours her in her own right:

<**12.64**> *High Rochester (Bremenium)*

deae Mi-
nerv<a>e Iul(ius)
Carantus
s(ingularis) c(onsularis)

RIB 1266

'To the goddess Minerva, Julius Carantus, *singularis consularis*, (set this up).'

99 Bruce 1875, 355, No. 676

<12.65> *High Rochester (Bremenium)*

deae sanctae
Minervae
Flavius Se-
verinus
trib(unus) aram
dedit

RIB 1267

'To the holy goddess Minerva, Flavius Severinus, the tribune, gave this altar.'

<12.66> *High Rochester (Bremenium)*

deae Mi-
nervae et
genio col-
legi Caecil(ius)
Optatus trib(unus)
v(otum) s(olvit) l(aetus) m(erito)

RIB 1268

'To the goddess Minerva and the Genius of the Association, Caecilius Optatus, the tribune, paid his vow willingly, deservedly.'

These altars were found in the remains of a Roman building outside the fort, the temple of Minerva itself, or a 'club-room' built by the association (*collegium*) of her worshippers; other such associations are attested for Mercury and Apollo at Lincoln, Mars at Caerwent, Silvanus at Corbridge, and Mercury at Birrens.[100] The dedicators were the leaders of society at High Rochester: the tribunes commanded the large garrison, and the *singularis consularis* an important post (*statio*) in the provincial road-system. In this he resembled the *beneficiarii consularis* (**10.31**). Optatus' altar can be closely dated by his other two dedications, to Matunus (who is Celtic, but otherwise unknown) and to Mithras, for the welfare of Caracalla in AD 213.[101] Its capital is decorated with two small swastikas, like another altar from High Rochester,

[100] *RIB* 270, 271, 309, 1136+add., 2102 and 2103.

[101] *RIB* 1272 and 1265. For the role of the *singularis consularis* in road-communications, see **10.32**.

which was dedicated to the *genius* and the standards (*signa*) of the First Cohort of Vardulli. This motif, although sometimes regarded as a solar 'wheel'-symbol and associated with Jupiter, was not specific to a single god.[102]

Apollo

Apollo, the god of healing, music and the arts including poetry, was exceptional in being a Greek god directly adopted by the Romans: unlike Zeus (Jupiter), Ares (Mars) and Athena (Minerva), he did not have a Roman counterpart, but even in Britain might inspire Greek hexameters. At Chester, for example, he was indirectly responsible for two metrical Greek altars dedicated by doctors called Hermogenes and Antiochus, one to 'the mighty Saviour Gods', the other which names them as Asclepius (the son of Apollo), Hygeia ('health') and Panakeia ('all-healing'), healing deities associated with Apollo in the Hippocratic Oath.[103] At Vintry in London, where the Walbrook meets the Thames, a pewter amulet has been found which invokes Great Iao and Great Sabaoth, in effect avatars of Jahweh, the Lord of Hosts, to protect a certain Demetrius against 'raging plague'. The 30-line metrical text is too complex to be quoted in full, but here is the highlight:

<12.67> *London (Londinium)*

Φοῖβε
ἀκερcικόμα, το-
ξότα, λοιμοῦ νε-
φέληcι(!) ἀπέλαυ-
νε

Britannia 44 (2013), 390, No. 21, lines 19–23

'Phoebus of the unshorn hair, archer, drive away the cloud of plague.'

'Phoebus' is the regular name or title of Apollo, whose arrows cause the plague in Homer's Iliad; by an easy inversion, he could be invoked against epidemics. These words have been adapted from two hexameters which addressed him by his attributes, one of them a variant of the metrical charm 'Phoebus of the unshorn hair keeps off the cloud of plague' which is quoted by the satirist Lucian in his essay on Alexander of Abonuteichos (on the Black Sea coast of Asia Minor).[104] This

---

[102] *RIB* 1263. Other instances are *RIB* 1024 (Mars Condates) and 1877 (Jupiter), but it also occurs on a tombstone (1641). There are swastikas in the mosaic immediately above the picture of Europa and the bull (**11.02**), but they need only be decoration.

[103] *RIB* 461 and III, 3151 (Chester). Also at Chester (**4.10**), the household of the legate associates Aesculapius with Salus ('health').

[104] Lucian, *Alexander* 36. νεφέληcι (dative) is a copying-error for νεφέλην (accusative).

'false prophet' invented an oracular god called Glycon, Apollo's son Asclepius made manifest in the form of a snake, for whom he wrote this oracle as a charm against the great Antonine Plague in the late AD 160s. It was circulated everywhere, according to Lucian, but proved a failure. Alexander may have been paying a compliment to the genuine oracle of Apollo at Claros in western Anatolia, which Lucian says he conciliated. It should be added that Britain has produced the only dedication by a military unit 'according to the oracle of Clarian Apollo', whose wording identifies it as one of the group of dedications in Italy and the western provinces which seem to have been prompted by the great plague out of the East.[105]

Some dedicators, like Maximius Gaetulicus at Newstead (**6.39**), invoke Apollo in his own right, but others identify him with British gods. He is identified with a hunter-god at Nettleton Shrub (**12.42**) and further north, at Ribchester (**7.04**) and Corbridge, with the local god Maponus. At both these forts, Maponus' votaries were officers of the Sixth Legion Victrix, the most senior being its camp commandant:

<12.68> *Corbridge (Coria)*

Apollini
Mapono
Q(uintus) Terentius
Q(uinti) f(ilius) Ouf(entina tribu)
Firmus Saen(a)
praef(ectus) castr(orum)
leg(ionis) VI V(ictricis) p(iae) f(idelis)
d(edit) d(edicavit)

RIB 1120

'To Apollo Maponus, Quintus Terentius Firmus, son of Quintus, of the *Oufentina* voting-tribe, from Saena, camp prefect of the Sixth Legion Victrix Dutiful and Loyal, gave and dedicated (this).'

Firmus came from Saena or Sena Iulia, an obscure Roman *colonia* in Etruria which is now Siena. The other officers at Corbridge were a centurion of the Sixth, and a tribune whose legion is unstated.[106] Still further north, at Inveresk, an even more important votary – the imperial procurator Quintus Lusius Sabinianus (**6.15**) – identifies Apollo with a Celtic god whose cult extended across northern Gaul and Germany to the Danube. Sabinianus does not say what religious experience prompted his choice of deity, but when one of his altars was re-used, the new dedicator referred to a 'message' (*nuntium*). Grannus was a god associated with healing springs, notably at Aachen (*aquae Granni*) and Grand in the Vosges, which may derive its modern

[105] *RIB* 1579 (Housesteads), with Jones 2005.

[106] *RIB* 1122 and 1121 respectively. For Maponus see Birley 1986, 55–58.

name from *Grannus*; the hot springs at Grand were graced by 'the most beautiful temple in the whole world', where the emperor Constantine, not yet a Christian, is said to have seen Apollo and Victory bringing him garlands in the 'pagan vision' which anticipated his momentous dream later of the Christian god.[107]

Diana

One of the Corbridge altars depicts Apollo with his twin-sister Artemis, the virgin huntress whom the Romans identified with Diana.[108] Diana and Apollo, in that order, were jointly honoured by Cocceius Firmus (**12.59**). Like Nemesis, Diana was associated with amphitheatres, so she is the appropriate recipient of a message scratched on a piece of lead found in the Roman arena under Guildhall Yard in London. It is a typical curse tablet, inscribed in laboured capitals:

<**12.69**> *London (Londinium)*

[d]eae Dea[na]e dono
capitularem et fas-
[c]iam minus parte
tertia. si quis hoc feci[t],
[s]i p[u]er si [p]uella, s[i]
[s]er[vus] s[i liber],
don[o eum] nec p[er]
me [vi]v[ere] possit

Britannia 34 (2003), 362, No. 2, with 36 (2005), 496, add. (d)

'I give to the goddess Deana (my) headgear and band, less one-third. If anyone has done this, whether boy or girl, whether slave or free, I give him; and through me let him be unable to live.'

Deana is the alternative spelling of her name. Like the tablet to Nemesis in the Caerleon amphtheatre (**12.57**), this was prompted by the theft of clothing. As usual it is formulaic: the thief is defined as A or not-A, and is 'given' to the god, who is promised a percentage of the stolen property in return as commission for recovering it. An altar found nearby in 1830, not inscribed but depicting a male hunting-god with bow and hound, was for long identified with Diana.[109] It would have implied she had a temple, which at Caerleon is explicit:

---

107 *Pan. Lat.* vi 21, with Nixon and Rodgers 1994, 248–51.
108 *RIB* 1121, illustrated in *CSIR* i.6, No. 60, Plate 18.
109 *CSIR* i.10, No. 73.

<**12.70**> *Caerleon (Isca)*

T(itus) Fl(avius) Postumius
[V]arus v(ir) c(larissimus) leg(atus)
templ(um) Dianae
restituit

RIB 316+*add.*

'Titus Flavius Postumius Varus, a Senator by rank, the legate, has restored (this) temple of Diana.'

Varus commanded the Second Legion Augusta, but there was no need to spell this out at Caerleon. His ansate slab is quite a stylish inscription, with the symmetrical enlargement of the first and last letters in line 1, and the swaggering stroke of L in line 3. It can be dated to the mid-third century with the help of two inscriptions from Rome. In the first, Varus commemorates his great-grandfather, Postumius Festus, an orator of African origin in the reign of Marcus Aurelius who is credited by the encyclopaedist Aulus Gellius with some learned comments on the Latin word for 'dwarf'.[110] The second inscription is Varus' own epitaph:

<**12.71**> Rome

D(is) M(anibus)
T(itus) Fl(avius) Postumius Varus
v(ir) c(larissimus), co(n)s(ul), orator, aug(ur), XVvir, praef(ectus) urb(i)
vixi beatus diis amicis literis.
Manes colamus, namque opertis manibus
divin[a] vis est ae[vi]terni temporis

ILS 2940

'To the Shades of the Dead. Titus Flavius Postumius Varus, senator, consul, orator, augur, member of the Board of Fifteen, Prefect of the City. I have lived happily, blessed by the gods, my friends, and literature. (Now) let us pay our respects to the Shades, for to the hidden Shades belongs the divine power of eternal time.'

Varus was by now an elder statesman, Prefect of Rome in AD 271; this gives an approximate date to his mid-career command at Caerleon. He also belonged to two of the four major boards of priests at Rome (see note to **5.02**), which was a rare social distinction (his great-grandfather only belonged to one), but may also hint that they were now less sought after. Certainly it gives point to the family's later change of allegiance: the epitaph also survives at Rome of another senator called

110 *ILS* 2929. Aulus Gellius, *Noctes Atticae* xix 13, whether *nanus* or *pumilio*.

Postumius Varus, who was probably his grandson; he died a Christian.[111] The elder Varus' epitaph ends with three lines of verse in the first person, the metre of which (iambic trimeters) forced him to use the unusual adjective *aeviternus* ('eternal'), the archaic form of Classical *aeternus*. The dying senator was addressing the Shades of the Dead, like this bereaved father in York, who wrote in hexameters:

<12.72> *York (Eboracum)*

[D(is)] M(anibus)
Corellia Optata an(norum) XIII.
secreti Manes qui regna
Acherusia Ditis | incoli-
tis, quos parva petunt post
lumina vit<a>e | exiguus cinis
et simulacrum corpo<r>is um-
bra. | insontis gnat<a>e geni-
tor spe captus iniqua |
supremum hunc nat<a>e
miserandus defleo finem.
Q(uintus) Core(llius) Fortis pat(er) f(aciendum) c(uravit)

RIB 684+*add.*

'To the Shades of the Dead. Corellia Optata, aged 13. You remote Shades who inhabit the Underworld kingdom of Pluto, whom a few ashes and the ghost of our body seek after life's short light; I am the father of an innocent daughter, unfairly robbed of my hopes, who grieve pitifully for my daughter's final end. Quintus Corellius Fortis, her father, had this set up.'

Vulcan and Neptune

There were more gods than this in the Roman pantheon – Eric Birley collects no fewer than 46 'Strictly Roman cults' – but we may conclude with a contrasting pair at Vindolanda, the gods of fire and water. The first is the smith-god Vulcanus or Volcanus, recipient of the silver 'certificate' at Stony Stratford (**12.06**). As a divine craftsman, he would have appealed to civilians, like the 'villagers' at Old Carlisle (**10.01**, as *Vulkanus*). At Vindolanda this was also true:

---

111 *CIL* vi 31985. Birley 2005, 362.

<12.73> *Vindolanda*

pro domu
divina et nu-
minibus Aug-
ustorum Volc-
ano sacrum
vicani Vindol-
ande<n>s{s}es, curam
agente [...]o[...],
v(otum) s(olverunt) l(ibentes) m(erito)

RIB 1700+*add.*

'For the Divine House and the Divinities of the Emperors, sacred to Volcanus; the villagers of Vindolanda paid their vow willingly, deservedly, under the charge of ...'

The 'Divine House' is the imperial family, probably that of Septimius Severus, since it comprised more than one reigning Emperor. *Volcanus* is the alternative spelling of the god's name, as in 'volcano'. In Britain it would be pleasant to think of him as the God of Central Heating, but his cult is more likely to have been a precaution against fires: Domitian revived it at Rome 'for the sake of preventing fires', and prescribed an annual sacrifice on the Volcanalia, 23 August; he was also the favourite god of the Vigiles, the Watch or fire brigade of Rome.[112] This Vindolanda altar was found in 1914, and for many years, until the famous tablets were discovered from 1973 onward, its coarse lettering was the best evidence of the Roman place-name.[113] In *RIB* the site is still called 'Chesterholm', the name invented by its first excavator Anthony Hedley for his cottage there in 1831; and where, according to the poem which celebrated the first Pilgrimage of Hadrian's Wall (1849), 'art with nature reigns serene, amid thy beauties, Chester Holme'.[114] But since the publication of *RIB* in 1965, after extensive excavation and publication by three generations of the Birley family – Eric, Robin and Andrew, who merit comparison with the Senhouses at Maryport – the original name 'Vindolanda' has now displaced it.

Vindolanda has also produced an altar to Neptune[115] which, like **6.22** at Castlecary, shows that he was the god of water everywhere, not just the sea. His finest memorial is the Sixth Legion's altar (**5.07**) from the river Tyne, but another altar, re-used as building material in a Kentish shore fort, carries the remains of barnacles from previous immersion in the sea; it was dedicated by a Roman admiral:

---

[112] *ILS* 4914, *incendiorum arcendorum causa.*

[113] *Vindolandesses* is for *Vindolandenses* by assimilation of [ns] to [s] (see note to **11.10**). The place-name is transmitted by the Notitia Dignitatum (*Occ.* 40.41) as *Vindolana*, but the Ravenna Cosmography (107.12), despite its poor record with place-names, preserves the form *Vindolande.*

[114] Raine 1849.

[115] *RIB* 1694.

<**12.74**> *Lymne (Lemanis)*

[N]ept[no]
aram
L(ucius) Aufidius
Pantera
praefect(us)
clas(sis) Brit(annicae)

RIB 66

'To Neptune, Lucius Aufidius Pantera, prefect of the British Fleet, (set up this) altar.'

Panthera (as his name is better spelt), like his predecessor Maenius Agrippa (**5.12**), was not an old sea-dog. A military diploma of AD 133 shows that his previous appointment was the command of a milliary *ala*, a double-strength cavalry regiment in Upper Pannonia. There were only a dozen of these formidable units in the Roman army, and they were commanded by an élite among equestrian officers who had already held the usual three commands.[116] Panthera, a very experienced soldier by land, was conciliating the god of his new element. A less formal relationship with Neptune is implied by the four curse tablets addressed to him which have been recovered from British rivers.[117] The most detailed was found in a creek near Southampton:

<**12.75**> *Hamble estuary*

domine Neptune,
t<i>b<i> d<o>no <h>ominem qui
(solidum) involav(it) Mu-
coni et argenti[olo]s
sex. ide<o> dono nomi<n>a
qui decepit, si mascel si
femina, si pu{u}er si pu{u}e-
lla. ideo dono tibi, Niske,
et Neptuno vitam, vali-
tudinem, sangu<in>em eius
qui conscius fueris eius
deceptionis. animus
qui hoc involavit et
qui conscius fuerit ut
eum decipias. furem
qui hoc involavit sangu<in>em
ei{i}us consumas et de-
cipias, domin[e] Ne[p]-
tune.

[116] *CIL* xvi 76, with Birley 2005, 317. E Birley 1988, 250.

[117] The other three are *Britannia* 13 (1982), 408, No. 9 (the Tas at Caister St Edmund); 18 (1987), 360, No. 1, as *Metunus* (the Thames at London Bridge); 25 (1994), 293, No. 1 (the Little Ouse at Brandon).

Britannia 28 (1997), 455, No. 1

> 'Lord Neptune, I give you the man who has stolen Muconius' coins, one gold (*solidus*) and six silver (*argentioli*). Also I give the names who took them away, whether male or female, whether boy or girl. Also I give to you, Niskus, and to Neptune the life, health, blood of him who has been privy to that taking-away. The mind which stole this and which has been privy to it, may you take it away. The thief who stole this, may you consume his blood and take it away, Lord Neptune.'

The handwriting is fourth-century, as might be expected from the reference to a *solidus*, the gold coin first struck by Constantine. 'Niskus' is unknown, but he may be a Celtic water-deity, the male counterpart of water-nymphs called *Niskae* invoked in tablets found in a Gallic spring. Like many curse tablets, this text is rhetorical and repetitive; its Latin echoes the spoken language, for example in writing *sanguem* for *sanguinem* ('blood', as in French *sang*, Italian *sangue*); and the thief is 'given' to the god, but since he can only be defined, not identified, his 'name' is cursed as well.[118]

Some oriental cults: Mithras

The Roman pantheon was reinforced by cults originating further east; on Hadrian's Wall at Rudchester, for example, Apollo 'the Unconquered' was identified with the Sun and Mithras.[119] Mithraism was a saviour cult which saw the universe in 'dualist' terms as a battleground between good and evil symbolised by light and darkness. Its followers were exclusively men – its ethos undoubtedly appealed to soldiers – who met for ritual meals in a 'cave', a windowless chapel sometimes literally undergound. Its central myth was the slaughter of a bull by Mithras, the divine emissary of the Sun, and it is carved in high relief on a marble panel from the London Mithraeum. At the corners are the chariots of Sun and Moon, and the heads of two Winds, surrounding the circle of the Zodiac, within which Mithras in Persian costume straddles the bull and cuts its throat. As usual he is attended by a scorpion, snake, dog and raven (now lost), and flanked by the standing figures of Cautes and Cautopates whose torches symbolise the rising and the setting sun. The dedicatory inscription has been awkwardly inserted into the flat areas round the edges. Reading from left to right:

<12.76> *London (Londinium)*

Ulpi|us | Silva|nus
fac|tus Arau|sione
emeri|tus leg(ionis) | II Aug(ustae) | votum | solvit

RIB 3+*add.*

[118] For a full commentary see *Britannia* 28 (1997), 455–8, n. 4.

[119] *RIB* 1397. His attributes also occur on the Sun altar at Inveresk (**12.80**).

'Ulpius Silvanus, promoted at Arausio; veteran of the Second Legion Augusta, paid his vow.'

The meaning of *factus* ('made') is uncertain. In epigraphic records of soldiers' careers it usually means 'promoted' (centurion, etc.), but in this Mithraic context it may have been extended to mean that Silvanus had achieved one of the seven successive grades of initiate; perhaps even that of 'Father' (*pater*). Arausio in Gallia Narbonensis is now Orange, which Augustus refounded as a *colonia* for veterans of Julius Caesar's old legion, the Second Gallica. This did not survive into the imperial Roman army, but Augustus may have reconstituted it as his new Second Legion Augusta.[120]

The liturgies of Mithraism are almost entirely lost, but the gap is partly filled by surviving iconography and other archaeological remains. The London Mithraeum was wilfully demolished to accommodate the quadrangular pile of Bucklersbury House, itself now demolished in its turn, and Britain's best-preserved Mithraeum is at Carrawburgh on Hadrian's Wall, where visitors can still go through the doorway and between the timber posts (now cast in concrete) which revetted the platforms on which the congregation reclined, and where they can still read the three altars at the further end. These were not removed when the chapel was dismantled in the fourth century, perhaps because they had been dedicated by previous commanding officers. They were still there in 1950, when Richard Wright drew them for *RIB*, but they have now been replaced by replicas; reading from right to left:

<12.77> *Carrawburgh (Brocolitia)*

d(eo) in(victo) M(ithrae) s(acrum)
Aul(us) Cluentius
Habitus pra<e>f(ectus)
coh(ortis) I
Batavorum
domu Ulti-
n<i>a (tribu) colon(ia)
Sept(imia) Aur(elia) L(arino)
v(otum) s(olvit) l(ibens) m(erito)

RIB 1545+*add.*

'Sacred to the Unconquered God Mithras. Aulus Cluentius Habitus, prefect of the First Cohort of Batavians, of the *Ultinia* voting tribe,[121] his home Colonia Septimia Aurelia Larinum, paid his vow willingly, deservedly.'

[120] Keppie 1984, 205. Silvanus did not necessarily originate from Arausio; with the name *Ulpius* implying enfranchisement by Trajan, he cannot have been directly descended from a legionary veteran there.
[121] Alternative spelling of the usual *Voltinia (tribu)*.

<12.78> *Carrawburgh (Brocolitia)*

deo inv(icto) M(ithrae)
L(ucius) Antonius
Proculus
prae(fectus) coh(ortis) I Bat(avorum)
Antoninianae
v(otum) s(olvit) l(ibens) m(erito)

RIB 1544+*add.*

'To the Unconquered God Mithras, Lucius Antonius Proculus, prefect of the First Cohort of Batavians Antoninus' Own, paid his vow willingly, deservedly.'

<12.79> *Carrawburgh (Brocolitia)*

deo invicto
Mitrae M(arcus) Sim-
plicius Simplex
pr<a>ef(ectus) v(otum) s(olvit) l(ibens) m(erito)

RIB 1546+*add.*

'To the Unconquered God Mit(h)ras, Marcus Simplicius Simplex, prefect, paid his vow willingly, deservedly.'

This is probably the order in which the altars were dedicated: **12.77**, by emphasising the new titles of Larinum in southern

Italy, during the joint-reign of Septimius Severus and his son Aurelius Antoninus ('Caracalla'); **12.78**, conveniently dated by the unit-title *Antoniniana* to the period AD 213/22; and **12.79**, whose dedicator Simplicius Simplex did not need to name his cohort, since it had already been named twice by the others.[122] His altar (on the left) incorporated a bust of Mithras whose radiate crown was pierced through to a recess behind, so that a lamp could be placed there to make the rays shine in the dark. This had already been done at Inveresk (**12.80**). The central altar was dedicated by Lucius Antonius Proculus, whose name is not distinctive, but is shared by a deputy-governor (*epistrategus*) in southern Egypt; they could well be the same man, another instance of an officer who was promoted from Britain to Egypt. The altar on the right is the most remarkable, since it is Roman Britain's prime instance of literary snobbery. The prefect, Aulus Cluentius Habitus, emphasises that his home-town has been promoted to the rank of *colonia* by Septimius Severus and Caracalla, but he abbreviates its name to the initial letter, L. This is like a crossword-puzzle clue: his name *Aulus Cluentius Habitus* is that of Cicero's client in the *pro Cluentio* – in 66 BC, Cicero defended him successfully on a charge of poisoning his stepfather, incidentally exposing a farrago of small-town politics and intrigue – and this Aulus Cluentius Habitus was a leading citizen of … Larinum.

The family is otherwise virtually unknown, but here is evidence that it persisted for at least another two centuries and a half, still equestrian in rank, not senatorial, still conscious of its one moment in the glare of history. Altars dedicated to Mithras have also been found in two other Mithraea on Hadrian's Wall, at Rudchester and Housesteads, and imply the existence of a fourth at Castlesteads.[123] At High Rochester the tribune Caecilius Optatus, who also dedicated an altar to Minerva (**12.66**), does not actually name Mithras, but by speaking of 'the Unconquered God (and) the Sun his ally', and by referring to his 'fellow-worshippers' (*consecranei*) and the construction of a building 'from ground-level' (*a solo*), he broadly implies that there was a Mithraeum here too.[124] More striking evidence has recently been found at Inveresk, in 2010, consisting of two superb altars buried, face down, in a rectangular pit.[125] They are both richly carved, the first with a radiate head of the Sun filling the die, its rays, eyes and mouth pierced as at Carrawburgh (**12.79**), for illumination from behind. On the capital above are four differentiated female busts, the Seasons of Spring, Summer, Autumn and Winter, with the dedication crammed into a panel beneath them:

---

[122] Birley 1961, 172–8 (and for what follows).

[123] *RIB* 1395, 1396, 1397, 1398 (Rudchester). *RIB* 1599, 1600 (dated AD 252), 1601 (from the mithraeum, but dedicated to the Sun) (Housesteads). *RIB* 1992, 1993 and 1994 (Castlesteads), dedicated to Mithras and the Sun.

[124] *RIB* 1272, *deo invicto Soli soc(io)*, where *et* was apparently deleted before *Soli* to limit the dedication to the Sun alone, but *soc(io)* ('ally') remained to show that Mithras had originally been included.

[125] Hunter 2016.

<12.80> *Inveresk (?Coria)*

Soli G(aius) Cas(sius?) Fla(vianus?) (centurio)

Britannia 42 (2011), 443, No. 6

'To the Sun, the centurion Gaius Cassius Flavianus (dedicated this altar).'

Flavianus' second altar is almost as exuberant: its capital is richly carved with a leaf-frieze above arcading and a rope-moulding, and on the left side of the die is a griffin in high relief above a ram-headed patera; on the right side a lyre above a plectrum and a jug. These are attributes of Apollo, implying another identification with Mithras. The dedication is well cut but unnecessarily abbreviated, since it occupies only half of the die:

<12.81> *Inveresk (?Coria)*

d{a}eo
invicto My(thrae)
G(aius) Cas(sius?) Fla(vianus?)

Britannia 42 (2011), 441, No. 5

'To the Unconquered God Mythras, Gaius Cassius Flavianus.'

Daeo is a 'hyper-correction' of *deo*, an over-reaction to the 'Vulgar' tendency to reduce [ae] to [e] since they were both pronounced the same. The letter Y is only used in Latin to transliterate Greek 'u', but this variant spelling of 'Mithras' is found elsewhere. The letter A with chevron (V-like) cross-bar, although common in the Greek world, is rare in imperial Roman inscriptions; in Britain it is virtually confined to the 'distance slabs' of the Twentieth Legion on the Antonine Wall, which identifies Flavianus' legion and dates his altars to the early AD 140s. He not only omits to name his legion like Maximius Gaetulicus at Newstead (**6.39**), he abbreviates his own name as ruthlessly as that of his god. Since he is otherwise unknown, we cannot be quite sure how to expand it, but the contrast between the richness of the altars and the brevity of their inscriptions argues a certain conceit. Flavianus is like Aulus Cluentius Habitus many years later (**12.77**): no need to spell it out, he seems to be telling us; you will know who I am.

Jupiter Dolichenus

The other oriental cult which appealed most to officers and their men, to judge by the number of dedications, was that of the sky-god Jupiter Dolichenus, whom we have already seen at Benwell (**6.32**). Except for a slab found at Caerleon in 1635, but now lost, the evidence all comes from the northern frontier.[126] A temple has recently been excavated at Vindolanda, and probably another at Piercebridge; two more can be deduced at Corbridge and Chesters. This statue-base was found outside the fort at Piercebridge:

<**12.82**> Piercebridge

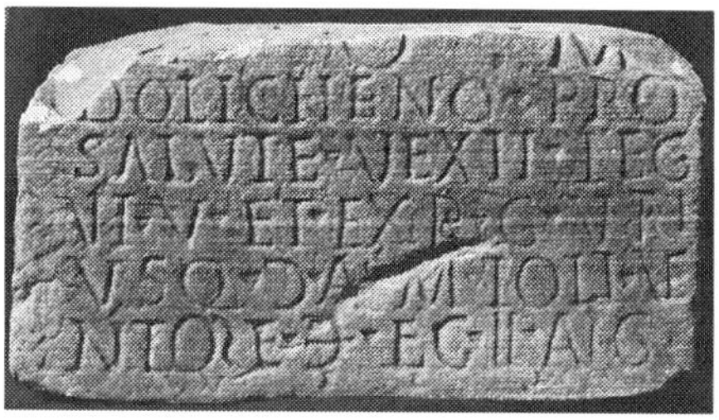

I(ovi) O(ptimo) M(aximo)
Dolicheno pro
salute vexil(lationum) leg(ionis)
VI V(ictricis) et exer(citus) G(ermaniae) utri-
usq(ue), c(uram) a(gente) M(arco) Loll(io) Ve-
n<a>tore (centurione) leg(ionis) II Aug(ustae),
v(otum) s(olverunt) l(ibentes) m(erito)

RIB III, 3253

'To Jupiter Dolichenus Best and Greatest, for the welfare of the detachments of the Sixth Legion Victrix and of the army of both Germanies under the charge of Marcus Lollius Venator, centurion of the Second Legion Augusta. They paid their vow willingly, deservedly.'

In line 6, unusually, R has been ligatured to O, and the centurial symbol is a reversed C reinforced by a cross-bar. The letter-cutter made mistakes such as VEXII for VEXIL in line 3, and because he ran out of space towards the bottom, he was forced to cut tiny letters to cram in the last line. This inscription is prime evidence of Caracalla's reinforcement of the army of Lower Britain (compare **13.04**), the date being deduced from an altar which was re-used as a building-block in a nearby church:

<**12.83**> *Piercebridge*

[I(ovi)] O(ptimo) M(aximo)
Dolychen[o]
Iul(ius) Valentin[us]
ord(inatus) Ger(mania) Su[p(eriore)]
ex iussu ipsius
posuit pro se et
suis l(aetus) l(ibens) m(erito)
[Pr]aesente et Extricato II co(n)[s(ulibus)]

RIB 1022+*add.*

---

126 *RIB* 320. The others all come from Hadrian's Wall and its hinterland, except for two fragments from the Antonine Wall (*RIB* 2158). In general, see Speidel 1978(b) and Birley and Birley 2010.

> 'To Jupiter Dolichenus Best and Greatest, Julius Valentinus, centurion from Upper Germany, by order of the god gladly, willingly and deservedly, set this up for himself and his household, in the consulship of Praesens and Extricatus for the second time (AD 217).'

Upper Germany was garrisoned by two legions, the Eighth Legion Augusta and the Twenty-Second Primigenia, detachments of which built the fort of Birrens many years earlier (**6.01**). Once again they contributed to the army in Britain, and Valentinus by implication was commander of the paired detachments, but he does not reveal the way in which Jupiter Dolichenus 'ordered' him to erect this altar. The god was discredited in the mid-AD 250s, when his eponymous shrine at Doliche was captured and destroyed by Persian invaders, but the cult lingered on. It was even responsible for the latest consular date on a Roman inscription from Britain, part of a slab found in the river at Chesters which is too fragmentary to be quoted in full, but which refers to a temple of Jupiter Dolichenus in AD 286, *[Maxi]mo et Aqui[lino co(n)s(ulibus)]*. Its existence comes as no surprise: the pedestal of the cult-statue, and the matching statue of his consort, Juno Regina, were found at Chesters two centuries ago.[127]

The goddess at Chesters is gracefully robed and imperious, despite having lost her head, but even more remarkable is a recent discovery from Vindolanda. It is a complete altar found in 2009, still standing within a third-century building just inside the northern rampart, which must have been the Dolichenum. Jupiter Dolichenus is carved in high relief on the left side of the die, holding his axe and thunderbolt, and standing on a bull; on the right side, there is a jug and patera. The front of the die is inscribed:

<12.84> *Vindolanda*

I(ovi) O(ptimo) M(aximo)
Dolocheno(!) | Sulpicius Pu-
dens praef(ectus)
coh(ortis) IIII Gall(orum)
v(otum) s(olvit) l(ibens) m(erito)

Britannia 41 (2010), 444, No. 4

> 'To Jupiter Dolochenus Best and Greatest, Sulpicius Pudens Prefect of the Fourth Cohort of Gauls, paid his vow willingly, deservedly.'

The mis-spelling 'Dolochenus' is rare, but Horsley saw it on a Risingham altar which is

[127] *RIB* III, 3299, also referring apparently to *[sy]mmachar[ii]*, un-Roman 'allied troops' hitherto unattested in Britain. *CSIR* i.6, Nos. 117 and 118.

now lost.[128] The prefect Sulpicius Pudens is otherwise unknown, but his name can now be recognised on an illegible altar from Vindolanda, thanks to the drawing which Wright made for *RIB* in 1950. His cohort was the third-century garrison, and we have already seen its dedications to the goddess Gallia (**12.16**) and the *genius* of the commandant's house (**12.24** and **12.25**).

Caelestis and the Syrian Goddess

A centurion at Corbridge obeyed another 'order' from Jupiter Dolichenus when he dedicated this altar to him. The god keeps interesting company:

<**12.85**> *Corbridge (Coria)*

Iovi aeterno
Dolicheno
et Caelesti
Brigantiae
et Saluti
G(aius) Iulius Ap-
olinaris
(centurio) leg(ionis) VI iuss(u) dei

RIB 1131+*add.*

'To eternal Jupiter Dolichenus, and to Caelestis Brigantia, and to Salus, (from) Gaius Julius Apolinaris, centurion of the Sixth Legion, by order of the god.'

Welfare or health (*salus*) personified (**4.10**), and the Brigantes as a goddess (**12.17**), we have seen already. The epithet identifies Brigantia with Caelestis, the 'heavenly goddess' who succeeded the Punic goddess Tanit in Roman Carthage.[129] In her different aspects she is the subject of the longest poem to survive from Roman Britain:

---

128 *RIB* 1220. Outside Britain, it occurs at Rome (*ILS* 4314) and Sacidava (*AE* 1998, 1144).

129 Halsberghe 1984. Brigantia is accompanied by an attribute of Caelestis in **12.17** (with note), and Vibia Pacata identifies her husband's Pannonian deities with Caelestis (**9.16**).

<12.86> *Carvoran (Magnis)*

imminet leoni Virgo caeles|ti situ
spicifera iusti in|ventrix urbium conditrix |
ex quis muneribus nosse con|tigit deos:
ergo eadem mater divum | Pax Virtus Ceres
dea Syria | lance vitam et iura pensitans.
in caelo visum Syria sidus edi|dit
Libyae colendum: inde | cuncti didicimus. |
ita intellexit numine inductus | tuo
Marcus Caecilius Do|natianus militans
tribunus | in praefecto dono principis

RIB 1791+*add.*

'The Heaven-placed Virgin rides upon a lion; corn-bearer, inventor of justice, founder of cities, from whose gifts it follows that we know the gods: in fact she is the Mother of the Gods, Peace, Virtue, Ceres, the Syrian Goddess, weighing life and justice in her scales. Syria produced this heaven-seen star for Africa to worship. Marcus Caecilius Donatianus, serving by gift of the Emperor as tribune instead of prefect, has been enlightened by her inspiration.'

The metre is 'iambic senarii', six-foot accentual iambics somewhat like English blank verse which has five. It is transcribed here as verse, but in the original it was inscribed as an intimidating block of prose with the verse-endings marked by a space. According to the African novelist Apuleius,[130] Caelestis rode in a car drawn by lions, and in iconography like the pediment of a shrine from Rome, she rides upon a lion, but the reference here to a 'heaven-seen' star may be to the constellation of Leo (the Lion) which in astrology succeeds Virgo (the Virgin). The poet Donatianus was undoubtedly African: his cognomen is mostly found there, and the choice of an African goddess confirms it. But he identifies her with other goddesses including Cybele, the Anatolian 'Mother of the Gods', and in particular with Atargatis, the 'Syrian Goddess' par excellence, who like Caelestis was a goddess of fertility associated with lions.

This identification has been seen as a compliment to Julia Domna, the Syrian wife of the African emperor Septimius Severus, but it seems unlikely.[131] Julia Domna is indeed identified with Caelestis, but only once[132] apparently, and although Severus struck coins which showed Caelestis riding on a lion when he visited Carthage in AD 202/3, this was in compliment to Carthage. To identify Julia Domna not only

130 *Metamorphoses* (the Golden Ass) vi 4.
131 Stephens 1984; Birley 1986, 78–9.
132 *CIL* xiii 6671 (Mainz).

with Caelestis but with the Syrian Goddess would be forced: she was actually the daughter of the high-priest of the Sun-god of Emesa (Homs), Sol Invictus or Elagabal. Unless Donatianus is making the learned point that Tanit derived ultimately from Syria (the Lebanon, to be precise), he is only engaging in amateur theology, like another dedicator who gives the Syrian Goddess the titles of Cybele and Caelestis. This man has a Semitic name, and his syncretism is typical of the Antonine age and later.[133] Donatianus does not name the auxiliary cohort he was commanding with the superior title of 'tribune' appropriate to a cohort of double strength, but it can be deduced from this altar:

<12.87> *Carvoran (Magnis)*

deae Suri-
ae, sub Calp-
urnio Ag[r]-
ico[la] leg(ato) Au[g(usti)]
pr(o) pr(aetore), Lic[in]ius
[C]lem[ens praef(ectus)]
[co]h(ortis) I Ha[miorum]

RIB 1792+*add.*

'To the Syrian Goddess, under Calpurnius Agricola, imperial propraetorian legate, (dedicated by) Licinius Clemens, prefect of the First Cohort of Hamians.'

Calpurnius Agricola (**7.03**) governed Britain in the early AD 160s. Except for a crude altar at Catterick,[134] this is the only British dedication to the Syrian Goddess, who would have had special significance for the Hamian archers, since they originally came from Syria. It was they who made the unsuccessful dedication at Carvoran (**5.46**) for the welfare of Aelius Caesar in AD 136/8, and **12.87** shows that they returned there from Bar Hill[135] when the Antonine Wall was abandoned. Carvoran has also produced altars to their eponymous goddess Hammia, and to Jupiter Heliopolitanus, the god worshipped at Heliopolis (Baalbek). So it is tempting to conclude that the Hamians, like the Gauls at Vindolanda, continued to draw some recruits from their homeland.[136] Donatianus does not actually name them, but his linking of Africa with Syria gains point if he was an African commanding Syrian troops.

Two Egyptian gods: Isis and Serapis

More than a dozen officers are known to have served in both Egypt and Britain, so it is not surprising to find Egyptian gods in Britain who attract important worshippers:

---

133 *AE* 1965, 30 (Apulum in Dacia), *deae Suriae Magnae Caelesti*, dedicated by Flavius Barhadadi ('son of Hadad').

134 *RIB* 726.

135 **6.24** and *RIB* 2172.

136 *RIB* 1780 and 1783. But Haynes 1993 (esp. 149–50) is sceptical.

<12.88> London (Londinium)

in h(onorem) d(omus) d(ivinae)
M(arcus) Martian-
{n}ius Pulch-
er v(ir) c(larissimus) leg(atus)
Aug(ustorum) pro
praet(ore) templ<u>m
Isidis .[...]
tis vetustate
collabsum(!)
restitui pr<ae>-
cepit

RIB III, 3001

'In honour of the Divine House, Marcus Martianius Pulcher, senator and imperial propraetorian legate, ordered the restoration of the temple of Isis which had collapsed from ... age.'

The 'Divine House' is the imperial family again (compare **12.74**), at a time when there were two emperors related to each other. The governor's nomen was probably 'Martianius', with N repeated by mistake; it has been 'fabricated' from the cognomen *Martianus*, which was probably his father's cognomen, this being a practice typical of Britain and Gaul. Pulcher is otherwise unknown, but his titulature suggests that he is a third-century governor of Upper Britain before *c.* AD 260, when senatorial governors were phased out. His altar was re-used by the Romans in their Thames embankment, so the site of the temple is unknown, but it was probably south of the river:

<12.89> *London (Londinium), Southwark*

Londini ad fanum Isidis

RIB II.8, 2503.127

'London, at the temple of Isis.'

This is scratched on a jug found in Southwark, to locate the tavern from which it came. The Egyptian goddess Isis was popular with sailors, so it is appropriate that Southwark has also produced London's only reference to a 'seafarer' (*moritix*) (**11.33**). The consort of Isis was Osiris, who is not yet attested, but a temple was erected in York to his close relative:

<12.90> *York (Eboracum)*

deo sancto
Serapi
templum a so-
lo fecit
Cl(audius) Hierony-
mianus leg(atus)
leg(ionis) VI Vic(tricis)

RIB 658+*add.*

'To the holy god Serapis. Claudius Hieronymianus, legate of the Sixth Legion *Victrix*, has built this temple from ground-level.'

Serapis was a saviour god identified with Zeus or Jupiter, but originally conflated from Osiris and Apis by the Macedonian kings of Egypt, who successfully exported his cult all over the Greco-Roman Mediterranean. By courtesy of Serapis, Vespasian even performed embarrassed miracles of healing in Alexandria soon after his proclamation there.[137] At the Pergamum of Claudius Charax (**6.08**), the main building of the Hadrianic Serapeum is 60 m long, its ruins the size of a cathedral; a whole Turkish mosque fits into one of its adjoining towers. A fine marble head of Serapis was found in the London Mithraeum.[138] This lavish 'international' cult obviously appealed to Hieronymianus, who is cited by a Christian propagandist in AD 212 as evidence of the wrath of God: he became governor of Cappadocia in eastern Anatolia (this might have been 10 years after York, but we do not know exactly when), where he persecuted the Christians because his own wife had defected to them. There was then an epidemic, but Hieronymianus was the only member of his household to fall ill. Eaten alive by worms (an occupational hazard for persecutors in Christian legend), he repented and died 'almost a Christian'.[139]

Christianity

The most successful oriental cult was Christianity, which ultimately displaced or absorbed ancient paganism, but in Roman Britain the epigraphic evidence is surprisingly slight. Whereas the standard corpus for Rome has now achieved 27,500 entries, Roman Britain can claim only four possible Christian tombstones, which depend on how key words and phrases are evaluated: they make no explicit reference to Christianity, they display no visual symbolism such as the Cross or the Chi-Rho monogram derived from the initial letters of 'Christ' in Greek, and they

137 Tacitus, *Histories* iv 81.
138 *CSIR* i.10, No. 16
139 Tertullian, *Ad Scapulam* 3.4, *paene Christianus decessit.*

all begin with the old pagan formula *D(is) M(anibus)*, which however does occur in some Christian epitaphs.

We have already seen Simplicia (**9.24**), 'a most innocent soul' who was buried at York, aged ten months. This phrase, like *anima innocens*, is found in Christian epitaphs, but is far from exclusive to them; rather it emphasises her premature death. Then there is this tombstone from Carlisle:

<12.91> *Carlisle (Luguvalium)*

D(is) M(anibus)
Fla(vius) Antigon<u>s Papias
civis Gr<a>ecus vixit annos
plus minus LX quem ad
modum accom<m>odatam
fatis animam revocavit
Septimia Do[...]

RIB 955

'To the Shades of the Dead. Flavius Antigonus Papias, a Greek citizen, lived 60 years, more or less, (and) recalled to the fates a soul which had been lent for that measure (of time). Septimia Do[...] (set this up).'

The heavily-stressed horizontal lines are most unusual in Britain, and suggest that this epitaph is fourth-century. It was compiled like many a curse tablet from stock formulas at the expense of syntax, and its full meaning has died with the author. The idea of 'the fates' is of course not Christian, but as a poetic cliché it does occur in Christian epitaphs; however, the idea of 'returning' a soul to them occurs only in a non-Christian epitaph of AD 310 found in Hungary, so it is not distinctively Christian.[140] Age at death 'more or less' is typical of Christian epitaphs, as if the exact length of our pilgrimage in this vale of tears were unimportant, but again it not exclusively Christian.[141] Elsewhere in Britain it occurs only in a fragment from Brougham Castle, which there is no other reason to see as Christian.[142]

The fourth stone comes from Carvoran, and like that of Papias, commemorates an immigrant:

[140] *CIL* iii 3335, *fatis animam reddidit*, cited in Hartley, Hawkes, Henig and Mee 2006, 207, which illustrates **12.91** in colour.

[141] Pagan examples: *ILS* 1523 (tombstone dedicated *deis et genio*); 2055 (third-century Thracian cavalryman in the Praetorian Guard); 7518 (*qui vixit sine macula an(nos) p(lus) m(inus) LXVIII*, his spirit received *inter deos*); 8499 (a casualty in AD 238).

[142] *RIB* 787+*add.* with Fitzpatrick 2004, 427. It concludes with the *titulum posuit* formula which is typical of this cemetery.

<12.92> *Carvoran (Magnis)*

D(is) M(anibus)
Aur(eliae) T(iti) f(iliae) Aiae
d(omo) Salonas
Aur(elius) Marcus
(centuria) Obseq(uentis) con-
iugi sanctis-
simae quae vi-
xit annis XXXIII
sine ulla macula

RIB 1828

'To the Shades of the Dead (and) to Aurelia Aia, daughter of Titus, from Salonae; Aurelius Marcus of the century of Obsequens (set this up) to his most holy wife, who lived 33 years without a single stain.'

This stone is more likely to be third-century than fourth: Marcus is a serving soldier who is married, but he is not *Fl(avius)* as one might expect of a fourth-century soldier; his father-in-law's nomenclature, *Titus Aurelius*, implies that he gained Roman citizenship in the reign of Antoninus Pius (AD 138–61), or at least that an immediate ancestor did. The language of *sanctissima* ('most holy') and *sine ulla macula* ('without a single stain') does indeed have 'a Christian flavour', as *RIB* notes, but it also occurs in pagan contexts; these even include an epitaph cited by *RIB* as Christian, which commemorates one of the Faithful whose 'spirit was received among the gods' (*plural*).[143]

This problem of language common to pagans and Christians is like that posed by the famous word-square, of which there are two British examples; at Cirencester it is scratched on wall-plaster of unknown date:

<12.93> *Cirencester (Corinium Dobunnorum)*

R O T A S
O P E R A
T E N E T
A R E P O
S A T O R

RIB II.4, 2447.20

'Arepo the Sower holds the wheels with care.'

[143] *ILS* 7518 (Rome), *cuius spiritus inter deos receptus est ... homo super omnes fidelissimus, cuius fama in aeterno nota est, qui vixit sine macula.*

More than 200 books and articles have been written about this enigmatic palindrome, especially since it was noticed in 1926 that it is an anagram of *Pater Noster* ('Our Father') written twice as a cross centred on N, with the letters A A O O left over, which can be interpreted as 'Alpha' and 'Omega' twice. Unfortunately for the romantic thesis that it is a Christian cryptogram, the word-square does not occur in early-Christian contexts but rather where it is unlikely there was any Christian presence at all; it has also been claimed for other religions; and the truth may be that it is simply a word-square, the only five-letter word-square possible in Latin, which could only be achieved by inventing the arbitrary name *Arepo*.[144]

'Crosses' occur too often on ordinary building-stones, for example in the curtain of Hadrian's Wall itself, for them to be seen as Christian. The Chi-Rho monogram, however, is also found on building-stones, but it remains a problem how far to press intersecting lines as evidence of Christianity.[145] Firmer ground is provided by jewellery like Senicianus' ring (see note to **12.46**), which hopes that he will 'live in God', and items of tableware, spoons in particular, which bear the Chi-Rho; and there is an interesting group of lead tanks with integral moulded inscriptions which are Christian.[146] But the most important evidence of all is the Water Newton treasure, which like the Ashwell treasure seems to have been rescued from a shrine.[147] It consists of nine silver vessels, four of which are inscribed, a detached gold disc with a Chi-Rho, and 17 silver plaques shaped like leaves or feathers, nine of which incorporate a Chi-Rho. One of these plaques also carries an inscription:

<12.94> *Water Newton / Chesterton (Durobrivae)*

amcilla(!) votum quo[d]
promisit conplevit

RIB II.3, 2431.1

'(His) handmaid has paid the vow which she promised.'

The first word has been read as a personal name (*Iamcilla* or *Anicilla*), but it is more likely that the silversmith (who was working from behind, and reversed other letters as a result), simply made a mistake for *ancilla* ('handmaid'). This term is frequent in Christian texts and inscriptions, and is often qualified by *Dei* ('of God') or *Christi* ('of Christ'), but there is a comparable inscription from Rome; it encircles a pierced silver hanging-bowl intended as a lamp in a church built by the Pope who is said to have baptised Constantine: *sancto Silvestrio ancilla sua votum solvit*. 'His handmaid has

144 The other example is scratched on a late second-century sherd from Manchester (*RIB* II.6, 2494. 98). See further, the note to *RIB* II.4, 2447. 20.

145 *RIB* 128 (Chedworth), 856 (Maryport), but contrast *RIB* III, 3214 (Catterick) with note.

146 *RIB* II.2, 2416, with Penny and Shotter 1996.

147 Painter 1977, and for what follows.

paid her vow to St Silvester.'[148] Her phrase 'has paid the vow which she promised' is the Christian equivalent of the old pagan formula V S L M.[149]

Two of the Water Newton vessels only incorporate a Chi-Rho, but the other two are fully inscribed. They are bowls or cups, which may have been the chalices of a Christian community. Only half survives of one, which has this inscription around the rim:

<12.95> *Water Newton / Chesterton (Durobrivae)*

alpha Chi-Rho omega Innocentia et Viventia ?lib[enter dede]runt

RIB II.2, 2414.1

'Innocentia and Viventia gave (this) willingly.'

Like *Volantius* (**9.06**), the ladies' names are formed from present participles; they are probably fourth-century. Without being exclusively Christian, they embody Christian concepts, 'innocence' and 'living (in God)', so their parents may also have been Christian. The other bowl or cup carries a more elaborate text, which is likewise inscribed around the rim in capitals:

<12.96> *Water Newton / Chesterton (Durobrivae)*

sanctum altare tuum, Domine, subnixus honoro

It is broken twice by the formula *alpha Chi-Rho omega*. Around the base is inscribed in the same lettering:

Publianus

RIB II.2, 2414.2

'Prostrating myself, O Lord, I honour your sacred sanctuary. Publianus.'

148 *AE* 2005, 208.

149 Compare *ILCV* 1636 (Numidia), *in nomine Patris et Filii* ('in the Name of the Father and Son') ... *quod promisit complevit.*

Publianus was probably the subject of this line of verse (it is a hexameter, but with the third syllable of *domine* stressed as if long), and was thus the donor; his gift offers a tantalising glimpse of a Christian community with its own meeting-place once adorned with silver 'leaves', a motif which it adopted from pagan sanctuaries like that of Senuna at Ashwell (**12.30**). But quite as tantalising is this curse tablet from the spring of Sulis at Bath, which hints at how far the new cult had encroached. The handwriting is fourth-century, the New Roman Cursive which developed into post-Roman 'Insular' scripts. At first sight it is unreadable, which is what the scribe intended, but then the persevering reader realises that the sequence of letters has been reversed; so he starts at the bottom right-hand corner, and works back:

<**12.97**> *Bath (Aquae Sulis)*

seu gens seu C-
h<r>istianus, quaecumque, utrum vir
[u]trum mulier, utrum puer utrum puella,
utrum s[er]vus utrum liber, mihi Annia[n]-
o Mantuten<a>e de bursa mea s<e>x argente[o]s
furaverit, tu, d[o]mina dea, ab eo perexi[g]-
[ ]. si mihi per [f]raudem aliquam ...
... dederit, nec sic ipsi dona, sed ut sangu-
inem suum <r>eputes qui mihi hoc inrogaverit

Tab. Sulis 98

'Whether pagan or Christian, whoever, whether man or woman, whether boy or girl, whether slave or free, has stolen six pieces of silver from my purse, from me, Annianus son of Mantutena(?), you, Lady Goddess, are to exact (them) from him. If through some deceit he has given me [...], do not give thus to him, but reckon it as the own blood of him who has invoked this upon me.'

Overleaf, 18 personal names have been inscribed, also in reverse letter-sequence: they are presumably the persons suspected of theft. The aggrieved victim is identified by his mother's name, in contrast with usual Celtic naming-practice; but this 'female lineage' is found in another Bath text,[150] and its 'magical' significance is obvious in the gold amulets from Billingford (**12.04**), West Deeping (**11.22**) and south of Oxford (**12.05**). What is unique is the initial formula, the first of the series of mutually-exclusive alternatives which otherwise are conventional: the thief is cursed 'whether pagan or Christian'. Since the writer continues with the usual alternatives 'whether man or woman', 'whether slave or free', he is surely parodying the words of St Paul to the Galatians: 'There is neither male nor female, there is neither slave nor free ... in Christ Jesus.' Obviously he is not a Christian, since he pays tribute to

[150] *Tab. Sulis* 30.

the power of Sulis Minerva which transcends religious differences, but he does take Christianity for granted: there could be no more striking evidence of its successful intrusion into late-Roman Britain than this admission that 'pagans' lived in harmony, or at least in balance, with 'Christians'. Its visual counterpart is the mosaic floor, sadly now destroyed, of the Frampton villa in Dorset, which depicted the bearded head of Neptune above a Chi-Rho.[151]

Although Christianity was evidently taken for granted in late-Roman Britain, it is frustrating that the epigraphic evidence should be comparatively so slight. It is not surprising, therefore, that supply has sometimes tried to meet demand. Roman sherds were found on the beach at Fishbourne (Isle of Wight) which had been used as devotional writing-tablets, being scratched with the Christian symbols of Chi-Rho and the Fish (a rebus of Christ's initials in Greek), *sator* ('the Sower', a reminiscence of **12.93**), and even Chi-Rho with the words *ex hoc amici bibunt*, 'Friends drink out of this' (as if from a chalice). The angular letters of these graffiti – O, for example, is made with four straight cuts like a 'diamond' – are quite unlike genuine Roman cursive writing, but a pious forger may have wanted to extend the history of nearby Quarr Abbey back into the Roman period.[152]

A still more appealing instance, since quite unconscious, comes appropriately from Bath. When the sacred spring of Sulis was exposed in 1880, two lead tablets were found.[153] The first, which was inscribed in capitals in reverse order, was quickly deciphered as a curse against theft, but the second was inscribed in a difficult cursive which resisted decipherment until the energetic Librarian of the Bodleian Library in Oxford, E W B Nicholson, took his summer holiday in 1904. Working at first from photographs, he found the tablet to be written in a mixture of capitals and lower-case letters complicated by ligatures and contractions, and protected himself by adding: 'The same letter of the alphabet has various shapes'. He duly published the result as 'a complete 4th cent(ury) Latin letter written by a Christian man in Britain to a Christian woman in Britain.' Vinisius tells Nigra to be brave about her husband's faults, and warns her that a heretic is coming to Bath: 'Christ's enemy has sent Biliconus from Viriconium that ye may take (him) in the sheepfold, although a dog of Arius. Do thou pray Christ for light.' (An obituarist later described Nicholson as 'in religion an agnostic, who throughout life believed in the efficacy of prayer.') Vinisius' letter ends with a note that 'A(p)ulicus carries these sheets', and one of Nicholson's reviewers expressed sympathy with 'the unfortunate postman who carried letters of lead from Viriconium to Aquae Sulis.' With hindsight after 1979, when the Sacred Spring yielded many more lead curse tablets, it becomes more difficult to believe in long-range correspondence conducted on sheets of lead, although a recent historian of the world has supposed the Vindolanda Tablets to be made of

151 *RIB* II.4, 2448.8.

152 *Britannia* 22 (1991), 307, No. 57.

153 *RIB* 154 and 2349*, now *Tab. Sulis* 4 and 100.

stone.[154] Nicholson himself, who understandably read his text from left to right, should have noticed that its letters cut those just ahead of them, which might have prompted him to try them the other way round. Had he then inverted the tablet, he would have read quite a different text, even if it was still written in New Roman Cursive: it denounced just another thief, 'whether man or woman', not a Christian heretic however dogged.[155]

[154] Frankopan 2015, 13, citing Bowman 1994 for evidence that Britain was not worth conquering: 'as slate letters sent home by soldiers stationed in Britain attest, this province was a byword for grim and fruitless isolation.'

[155] Tomlin 1994, quoting Nicholson 1904 and its review in *The Scotsman*, and Gibson's obituary in 1912. Tomlin's ironical choice of title led to Vinisius being added to the second edition of Ireland 1986, where he remains (2008, 198–9, No. 448), prefaced by the comment: 'Recent finds of letters, however, begin to reveal more personal concerns and the problems caused by heresy.'

13

THE THIRD CENTURY

Caracalla (AD 211–17)

When Septimius Severus died, we turned from the sequence of military events to consider inscriptions as evidence for the society and economy of Roman Britain, its government and religious beliefs. Chronology resumes with this altar, which was dedicated to the good order personified by Septimius Severus and his sons:

<**13.01**> *Castlesteads (Camboglanna)*

Discipu-
[l]inae
[A]ug(ustorum trium)

RIB 1978

'To the Discipline of the (three) Augusti.'

The cult of 'Discipline' was introduced by Hadrian (**5.03**), and meant more than just the military obedience imposed by an emperor. When Severus was about to promote his elder son Antoninus ('Caracalla') to the rank of *Augustus*, he was celebrated in the Numidian *colonia* of Thamugadi (Timgad) as 'the champion and the founder of Roman Discipline'.[1] The Castlesteads altar, in being dedicated to three *Augusti*, would have been prompted by Geta's belated promotion to this rank in AD 210 when Severus, now in failing health, tried to reinforce the future of his dynasty.[2] The (three) *Augusti* are neatly abbreviated to AVGGG, the double repetition of the final letter indicating as usual how many of them there were.

However, when this altar was found in 1791, during the ruthless clearance of the Roman site to make gardens, the final GG of AVGGG had been deleted, and replaced

1 *ILS* 446 (AD 197, in the genitive case), *vindex et conditor Romanae disciplinae*.
2 A R Birley 1988, 186 and (for the date) 218.

in the line below by VSTI. The text had become *Discipu|linae | Aug|usti*, 'to the Discipline of the (one) Emperor'. This re-writing of history may now look rather crude – Caracalla, having murdered his brother, was suppressing even the slightest reference to him – but arguably it succeeded. Collingwood Bruce in 1875, although his fine drawing by David Mossman shows the ghost of GG erased, follows the first editor J D Carlisle (or Carlyle) in attributing the erasure to 'some mistake having been made'; there was little doubt, he concludes, that the emperor was Hadrian.[3]

Geta, like his brother, had spent about 3 years (AD 208–11) in Britain, and it is quite likely that the province was disturbed by the news of his sudden death next year (AD 212). This would explain the spate of inscriptions in AD 213 which protest the British army's 'duty and devotion' to Caracalla.[4] They are all much fragmented, but this phrase occurs in at least eight, betraying their common inspiration; the fullest text comes from the hill country south of the Wall:

<13.02> *Whitley Castle (?Epiacum)*

imp(eratori) Caes(ari) [divi Severi Pii Ara]-
bici Adia[benici Parth(ici) Max(imi) Brit(annici)]
Max(imi), fil(io) divi Anton(ini) Pi[i] G[erm(anici)]
Sarm(atici), nep(oti) divi Anton(ini) Pi[i p]ro[nep(oti)],
divi Hadr(iani) abnep(oti), divi Traiani
Parth(ici) et divi Nervae adnep(oti),
M(arco) Aur(elio) Sever(o) Antonino Pio
Feli(ci) Aug(usto) [P]ar[th(ico)] M[ax(imo) Bri]t(annico) M[ax(imo), pont(ifici) ma[x(imo)],
tr(ibunicia) pot(estate) X[VI], imp(eratori) I[I], co(n)suli) IIII, [p(atri) p(atriae), p]r[oco(n)s(uli)],
pro pietate ac devot[i]one
communi, curante [[G(aio)]]
Iulio Marco]] leg(ato) Aug(usti)
pr(o) pr(aetore), coh(ors) II Nervio-
rum c(ivium) R(omanorum) pos(uit)

RIB 1202+*add.* with Birley 2005, 204–5

'For the Emperor Caesar, son of the deified Severus Pius, Conqueror of Arabia and Adiabene, greatest Conqueror of Parthia, grandson of the deified Antoninus Pius, Conqueror of Germany and Sarmatia, great-grandson of the deified Antoninus Pius, great-great-grandson of the deified Trajan, Conqueror of Parthia, and of the deified Nerva, Marcus Aurelius Severus Antoninus Pius Felix Augustus, greatest Conqueror of

[3] Bruce 1875, 225, No. 445.
[4] Collected by Birley 2005, 203–6, with a full commentary.

> Parthia, greatest Conqueror of Britain, pontifex maximus, in the sixteenth year of his tribunician power, twice acclaimed Emperor, four times consul, Father of his Country, proconsul, out of their joint duty and devotion, under the charge of Gaius Julius Marcus (*erased*), propraetorian legate of the Emperor, the Second Cohort of Nervii, Roman citizens, set this up.'

Whitley Castle, unlike Castlesteads, was saved by its remote location on Alston Moor, and is now one of the best preserved Roman forts anywhere.[5] The original inscription is lost, so it must be reconstructed from two early transcripts, one made for Camden in 1599, the other at about the same time by a local schoolmaster and antiquary, Reginald Bainbrigg, who also made the replica which survives at his school in Appleby. Since Septimius Severus had claimed to be the son of Marcus Aurelius and thus heir of the Antonines, it was possible for his son to claim ultimate descent from Nerva, but it is hard to believe that the Nervii made much of this rigmarole full of abbreviations and fictive ancestry to the *n*th degree. It ran to 15 lines, 'if one can bear to count all these lines'.[6] The key phrase *pro pietate ac devotione communi* is not abbreviated, but rendered in full. It was immediately followed by the name of the governor who no doubt inspired these protestations, Gaius Julius Marcus. His name was subsequently erased, as it was in most of the inscriptions, but some preserve it and the date of AD 213. Marcus was obviously unsuccessful in convincing Caracalla of his loyalty, but his fate is unknown.

This broad hint that Caracalla suspected the loyalty of the British garrison partly explains why extra legionaries were drafted in from Germany.[7] The evidence comes from Piercebridge, where a statue was dedicated to Jupiter Dolichenus by 'detachments of the Sixth Legion Victrix and of the army of each Germany' commanded by the centurion Marcus Lollius Venator of the Second Legion Augusta (**12.82**), the date being deduced from the altar dedicated in AD 217 by one of his lieutenants, the centurion Julius Valentinus from Upper Germany (**12.83**). Tombstones also commemorate two legionaries from Upper Germany, a centurion (*ordinatus*) of the Twenty-Second Legion called Gracilis, and a junior staff officer (*beneficiarius tribuni*) whose name is now lost.[8] Piercebridge is where Dere Street crossed the river Tees, mid-way to the Wall from the base of the Sixth Legion at York, and its strategic importance was marked by a very large fort (10.8 acres/4.4 ha) of uncertain date, which however may have been built for the newcomers.[9] Its unusually large and powerful garrison was drawn from no fewer than five legions, and commanded by

---

5 Bidwell and Hodgson 2009, 128–30.

6 Gordon 1968, 129, commenting on the almost identical *RIB* 1278 from High Rochester.

7 Birley 1967.

8 *RIB* 1026 and III, 3258. Eight lead sealings stamped LVI were found at Piercebridge (Cool and Mason 2008, 291), which would imply communication with the Sixth Legion, and perhaps its presence. Its presence is implied by *RIB* 1025, *LEG VI V*, but only as builders.

9 Bidwell and Hodgson 2009, 148.

a centurion of a sixth. Lollius Venator was seconded from the legion at Caerleon in what had just become Upper Britain (see below). His cognomen is rare, and Eric Birley identifies him with Venator, a centurion in the Vigiles in AD 212 and then the Praetorian Guard.[10] In AD 217 he would have been a senior centurion, his rank in keeping with this important command.

Political calculation may have brought the legionaries to Piercebridge, but there were military implications as well. The inscriptions inspired by Julius Marcus all come from northern Britain, which would suggest that this was the limit of his authority, unless we restore his name on a London inscription, which would then celebrate Caracalla's German victory of AD 213.[11] It would also identify Marcus as the last governor of an undivided Britain, but unfortunately the stone is too fragmentary to make this certain. But there can be little doubt that he was succeeded in the north by a legate of Lower Britain:

<13.03> *High Rochester (Bremenium)*

imp(eratori) Caes(ari) M(arco) Aurelio
Severo Antonino
Pio Felici Aug(usto) Parthic(o)
Max(imo), Brit(annico) Max(imo), Germ(anico)
Max(imo), pontifici maxim(o),
trib(unicia) potest(ate) XVIIII, imp(eratori) II,
co(n)s(uli) IIII, proco(n)s(uli), p(atri) p(atriae), coh(ors) I
Fida Vardul(lorum) c(ivium) R(omanorum) eq(uitata) (milliaria) Anto-
niniana fecit sub cura [[...]]
[[............]] leg(ati) Aug(usti) pr(o) p[r(aetore)]

RIB 1279

'For the Emperor Caesar Marcus Aurelius Severus Antoninus Pius Felix Augustus, greatest Conqueror of Parthia, greatest Conqueror of Britain, greatest Conqueror of Germany, pontifex maximus, in the nineteenth year of his tribunician power, twice acclaimed Emperor, consul for the fourth time (AD 216), Father of his Country, the First Loyal Cohort of Vardulli, part-mounted, one thousand strong, Antoninus' Own, built this under the charge of (*erased*), imperial propraetorian legate.'

The governor's name at the bottom has been erased, but it can be partly restored from another building-inscription of the same year: it ended in *[...]dianus*. A third

[10] Birley 1967, 107.
[11] Birley 2005, 336.

inscription, which is undated but also dedicated to Caracalla, preserves the further names *Sempronianus Romanus*.[12] This prompted Eric Birley to identify the governor as Marcus Antonius Gordianus Sempronianus Romanus, the future emperor Gordian I (AD 238), from whose career it can be deduced that he was not yet of consular rank in AD 216, and was thus the legate of only a one-legion province. This identification is supported by a stone in York which refers to 'the *beneficiarii* of Gordianus', legionaries seconded to his staff as governor.[13] The erasure of his name from **13.03** can be explained by his subsequent rebellion against Maximinus in AD 238 as proconsul of Africa, which the British army did not accept.

From what we know of these two governors, therefore, it appears that after the fall of Julius Marcus, Caracalla divided the province of Britain into Lower Britain with its capital at York, with one legion, and Upper Britain with its capital at London, with two legions, at Caerleon and Chester. This division is explicit in some later inscriptions, such as the Bordeaux altar (**11.39**) which was dedicated in AD 237 by a decurion of York and Lincoln 'in Lower Britain'.[14] Caracalla was neutralising Britain as the potential power base of any future usurper – he had just done this for the two Pannonian provinces, by redistributing their four legions equally between them – but illogically he committed only one legion to the northern frontier, while under-employing the other two in the peaceful south. This imbalance was corrected by drafting legionaries from Germany to Piercebridge (**12.82** and **12.83**), and still more by transferring legionaries from Upper Britain to the Wall itself:

<**13.04**> *Carlisle (Luguvalium)*

I(ovi) O(ptimo) [M(aximo)]
Iunon[i Reginae]
Miner[vae Aug(ustae)]
Marti P[atri Vic]-
toriae c[eteris]
diis d{a}ea[busque]
omnibus [M(arcus) Aur(elius)]
M(arci) f(ilius) Ulp(ia tribu) Syrio [Nico]-
poli ex [p]rovi(ncia) Trh(!)[ac(ia)]
trib(unus) mil(itum) leg(ionis) XX V(aleriae) V(ictricis)
Antoninianae
[v(otum) s(olvit) l(ibens) m(erito)]

RIB III, 3460

[12] *RIB* 1049 (Chester-le-Street) and 590 (Ribchester).

[13] *RIB* III, 3193 (York). Birley 2005, 338–9.

[14] The Thorigny Marble (**10.39**) does not expressly refer to the division, unlike other non-British inscriptions such as *CIL* viii 2080 (a junior officer of the Twentieth Legion Valeria Victrix *ex provincia Britannia super(iore)*) and viii 5180 (a veteran of the Sixth Legion Victrix Pia Fidelis *provinci(a)e Br|itanni(a)e inferioris*).

> 'To Jupiter Best and Greatest, to Queen Juno, to August Minerva, to Father Mars, to Victory, to all the other gods and goddesses; Marcus Aurelius Syrio, son of Marcus, of the *Ulpia* voting-tribe, of Nicopolis from the province of Thrace, military tribune of the Twentieth Legion Valeria Victrix Antoniniana, [paid his vow, willingly, deservedly].'

This large altar was turned on its side by the Normans to make a door-head in the Castle. They cut a chamfered arch into the right-hand side which destroyed whatever corresponded to the relief-carving on the left-hand side; this shows the Phrygian youth Ganymede being carried off by the eagle of Jupiter to become his cup-bearer, and above him, a pair of clasped hands within a wreath, the symbol of concord. A later garrison of the Castle, the Border Regiment, added its own contribution by boring a hole through the word *provi(ncia)* to take an electricity duct, but the text can still be read or deduced. The dedicator came from the Trajanic *colonia* of Ulpia Nicopolis ad Istrum (Nikiup in Bulgaria), which had actually been transferred from Thrace to Lower Moesia by the date implied by the title *Antoniniana* (AD 213/22), but he ignores this, no doubt because it happened after his entry into the army. This was probably in the AD 190s, since his nomenclature includes the 'pseudo-tribe' *Ulpia*, a practice which is typical of third-century Danubian legionaries and Praetorians who turned the dynastic titles of their cities of origin into a voting-tribe, something which had been obsolete for centuries, so as to make their outlandish names look more 'Roman'.[15] Aurelius Syrio is likely to have enlisted in his nearest legion, the First Legion Italica at Novae (Svishtov) on the lower Danube, before being promoted into the new Praetorian Guard of Septimius Severus. At the completion of 16 years' service, he would have been retained as an *evocatus* and then promoted to independent command, like other officers attested in north-west Britain at this time.[16] Like other third-century 'Illyrian' officers, notably the emperors Maximinus, Aurelian, Probus and Diocletian, he was a professional soldier, not a gentleman of equestrian birth. He commanded detachments drawn from two legions, the Second Augusta and the Twentieth Valeria Victrix, whose 'concord' symbolised by those clasped hands was also expressed by the carving of two legionaries standing side by side (**12.54**).

Elagabalus (218–22)

By increasing the garrison of Lower Britain at the expense of Upper Britain, Caracalla balanced the two armies. He then turned his attention first to the German frontier (compare **9.28**), and then to the east, where the Parthian empire was being weakened

---

15 *RIB* 506 (York) is the only other British example, but compare **10.17** (Rome).

16 *RIB* 966, 988 and 1896, and compare 989. *ILS* 7713 (Viminacium) is the epitaph of Valerius Speratus, a veteran of the Seventh Legion Claudia who became prefect of coh(ors) I Aquet(anorum) (correctly read by *PME* V 38) and 'died in Britain', *(defunctus) in Britt(ania)*.

by a resurgent Persia. But all in vain. In AD 217 he was assassinated in Mesopotamia by his praetorian prefect Macrinus, whose colleague Oclatinius Adventus (**8.07**) had been procurator of Britain; Adventus' acquiescence allowed Macrinus to become Emperor, the first non-senator to achieve this, but a year later he was overthrown in a coup launched by surviving members of the Severan dynasty. Their candidate was a charismatic young Syrian, the son of Julia Domna's niece Julia Soaemias by Varius Marcellus (**8.13**) the sometime procurator of Britain, and thus a remote cousin of Caracalla, whose son he claimed to be. In token of this claim, he assumed the name *Marcus Aurelius Antoninus*, but is better known as 'Elagabalus', the name of the Syrian Sun god at Emesa (Homs) whose hereditary priest he was. With true conviction, if unwisely, he emphasised this role:

<13.05> *Chesters (Cilurnum)*

imp(erator) Caesar M(arcus) Aurel(ius) [[Antoninus P(ius) F(elix)]]
Aug(ustus) [[sacerdos ampliss(imus) dei invicti Solis]]
[[Elagabali]] p(ontifex) m(aximus), [tr]ib(unicia) p(otestate) [IIII], co(n)s(ul) [III], p(ater) p(atriae), div[i Anton(ini) f(ilius)],
divi Sever(i) nep(os) et M(arcus) [Aur]el(ius) [[Alexander nobiliss(imus)]]
Caesar imper[(i)i] [[et sacerdoti consors]]
alae II Astur(um) [[Anton(inianae)]] v[et]ustate [dilapsum restitu]-
erunt per Marium Valer[ianum leg(atum) Aug(usti) pr(o) pr(aetore)]
instante Septimio Ni[l]o prae[f(ecto) eq(uitum)]
dedicatum (ante diem) III Kal(endas) Novem(bres) Gr[a]to et Sele[uco co(n)s(ulibus)]

RIB 1465+*add.* with Birley 2005, 344

'The Emperor Caesar Marcus Aurelius Antoninus Pius Felix (*erased*) Augustus, most honourable priest of the Unconquered god Sol Elagabalus (*erased*), pontifex maximus, in the fourth year of his tribunician power, thrice consul, Father of his Country, son of the deified Antoninus, grandson of the deified Severus; and Marcus Aurelius Alexander (*erased*), most noble (*erased*) Caesar, partner in the empire and priesthood (*erased*), restored (this building) collapsed through age, for the Second Cavalry Regiment of Asturians, Antoninus' own (*erased*), through the agency of Marius Valerianus, propraetorian legate of the Emperor, with Septimius Nilus, prefect of cavalry, supervising. Dedicated on the third day before the Kalends of November, in the consulship of Gratus and Seleucus (30 October AD 221).'

The text runs to nine lines without specifying what was being rebuilt, but probably the slab was incorporated in it, which would have made this obvious. No fewer than five lines have been partly erased, hence the profusion of double square brackets.[17]

[17] The reading here follows Birley 2005, 344, in not bracketing letters of which some trace remains, which he dots instead, and in seeing Valerianus as the legate of a single *Augustus*, which (strictly speaking) he was.

The 'memory' of Elagabalus and his un-Roman priesthood, which towards the end of his brief reign (AD 218–22) he shared with his cousin Alexander (Severus), was deleted after his death with a thoroughness that extended to a much earlier dedication at Corbridge to quite another Sun god (**7.03**). But the contentious priesthood was ignored by an inscription of the previous year, which did specify what was built:

<13.06> *High Rochester (Bremenium)*

imp(eratori) Caes(ari) M(arco) Aurelio
[[Antonino]] Pio Fel(ici) Aug(usto)
trib(unicia) pot(estate) III, co(n)s(uli) III, proco(n)s(uli),
p(atri) p(atriae), ballist(arium) a sol[o] coh(ors) I F(ida)
Vardul(lorum) [[Ant(oniniana)]] [s]ub cura
Tib(eri) Cl(audi) Paul[ini le]g(ati) Aug(usti)
pr(o) pr(aetore) fe[cit, insta]nte
P(ublio) Ael[io Erasino trib(uno)]

RIB 1280+*add.*

'For the Emperor Caesar Marcus Aurelius Antoninus (*erased*) Pius Felix Augustus, in the third year of his tribunician power, consul for the third time (AD 220), proconsul, Father of his Country, the First Loyal Cohort of Vardulli, Antoninus' Own (*erased*), built this *ballistarium* from ground-level, under the charge of Tiberius Claudius Paulinus, imperial propraetorian legate, with Publius Aelius Erasinus, tribune, supervising.'

Only the left-hand portion of this slab survives, including a small conjoining piece, and it was found in 1855. The right-hand portion was found much earlier, but it was not recognised as such, and has since been lost, so we depend on a transcript by Hodgson. Like the other Severan emperors, this emperor is 'proconsul' (of Britain); but when his 'memory' was condemned two years later, his name *Antoninus* and the derived unit-title *Antoniniana* were deleted. The governor is the sometime commander of the Second Augustan Legion honoured by the Silures (**10.03**), incidentally the first governor of Britain since Agricola who is known to have previously commanded a legion in the province. The Thorigny Marble (**10.39**) fills the gap in his career by showing how he escaped the threat of prosecution in his next post as governor of Lugdunensis, and was able to reward his saviour when he was appointed to Lower Britain.

The meaning of *ballistarium* is uncertain, except that it derives from *ballista*. This was a piece of torsion artillery, a huge crossbow firing bolts or fist-sized stones which was accurate enough to be used for sniping: two recorded successes are the rebel leader at the Roman siege of Cremna in AD 276, who was shot when he looked out of a loophole, and an enemy vassal king at the Persian siege of Amida (Diyarbakır) in AD 359 who vaingloriously exposed himself, or rather his son, who was shot at his side.[18] At a crucial moment in the latter siege, the Romans rapidly concentrated five ballistas for 'machine-gun' fire against a party of Persian archers, and they could also be used in the field (one is illustrated on Trajan's Column), so it is unlikely that a special emplacement was required. Nonetheless this has been suggested at High Rochester, where much larger stone balls have been found, but these may be decorative rather than missiles, and indeed may not even be Roman. To hurl them would have required a different engine, the *scorpio* ('scorpion') or *onager* ('wild ass'), the Roman equivalent of the medieval mangonel. The much more likely meaning of *ballistarium*, therefore, is a building for the storage and maintenance of such weapons,[19] a magazine of lethal machinery which might require a specialist engineer:

<**13.07**> *Novara (Novaria), north Italy*

viv(us) fecit
D(is) Mani[b(us)]
Aelius Optatus
mil(es?) in leg(ione) XX m-
agister balista-
r(i)i ... sibi
et suis parentibus
...

CIL v 6632

'Aelius Optatus, soldier in the Twentieth Legion, master of the *balistarium*, made this in his lifetime for the Shades of the Dead, for himself and his paraents ...'

The key word *balista*|*ri* looks like BALIISIA|RI, followed by PRDVPLOI, which may conceal a reference to his receiving 'double pay' (*duplicarius*). The text concludes with a list of Optatus' household, for whom also he erected this tombstone, but reading their names is difficult.[20] Despite containing the form *D(is) Manib(us)*, the text is Hadrianic at least, since Optatus bears the imperial nomen of *Aelius*. It is strange that he omits the title of his legion, *Valeria Victrix*, which it gained in AD 61 or perhaps 83. By now it had been at Chester for many years, when a recruit

---

18 Zosimus 1.70 (Cremna). Ammianus Marcellinus xix 1.7 and xix 5.6 (Amida).

19 Donaldson 1990.

20 A variant (perhaps simplified) reading by Bruzza has been adopted here, which is quoted in the apparatus.

from Italy would have been most unusual, so it is likely that he was drafted there as an expert, to take charge of a special building like that at High Rochester.[21]

Severus Alexander (AD 222–35)

This is not the last we hear of that *ballistarium* at High Rochester:

<**13.08**> *High Rochester (Bremenium)*

imp(eratori) Cae[s(ari [[M(arco) Aur(elio) Seve-]]]
[[ro Alexandro]] P(io) F(elici) [Aug(usto) et]
[[Iuliae Aug(ustae) matr(i)]]
[[imp(eratoris) Caes(aris) et cas(trorum)]] coh(ors) I F(ida) Vard(ullorum)
[[(milliaria) S(everiana) A(lexandriana)]] ballis(tarium) a solo re[sti]t(uit)
sub c(ura) Cl(audi) Apellini le[g(ati)] Aug(ustorum duorum)
instante Aur(elio) Quinto tr(ibuno)

RIB 1281+*add.* with Birley 2005, 352)

'For the Emperor Caesar Marcus Aurelius Severus Alexander (*erased*) Pius Felix Augustus and Julia Augusta (*erased*), mother of the Emperor Caesar and of the camps (*erased*), the First Loyal Cohort of Vardulli, one thousand strong, Severus Alexander's own (*erased*), restored this *ballistarium* from ground-level, under the charge of Claudius Apellinus, legate of the (two) Emperors, with Aurelius Quintus, tribune, supervising.'

This much-fragmented slab has been accurately restored, and it can be seen that no fewer than five lines out of seven have been partly erased, resulting in another profusion of double square brackets like the dedication to Elagabalus at Chesters (**7.08**). The 'memory' of his cousin and successor Severus Alexander, and of Alexander's mother Julia Mamaea (Elagabalus' aunt), was also painstakingly deleted in due course, when they were overthrown by Maximinus in AD 235. A tiny

21 Dobson and Mann 1973, 203, n. 57.

second G has been added within the loop of the G of AVG in line 6, to imply that Apellinus was legate of *two* emperors (AVGG). Strictly speaking, this was impossible. Perhaps it was only added after Alexander had been displaced by Maximinus, who made his son Maximus his *Caesar*, thus creating two emperors.[22] But it may have been added unthinkingly, since Alexander had been briefly the junior colleague (*Caesar*) of Elagabalus, and imperial collegiality was commonplace by now; there is a similar AVGG on the altar dedicated to the *genius* of Gordian III at High Rochester (**13.19**), but the second G is incomplete, as if the mistake was recognised in time. At all events, the date is no later than AD 235. Within 15 years at most, therefore, it had proved necessary to rebuild that *ballistarium* 'from ground-level'. It can hardly have been well built.

Poor Elagabalus: an absorbing career as a religious innovator and sexual pentathlete was cut short when his extravagant behaviour not only offended conservative Romans but alarmed his own family, which tried to secure its own future by making him adopt an amenable cousin as his son and junior colleague (*Caesar*). The latter now assumed the name of *Marcus Aurelius Alexander*, but their uneasy partnership lasted only a few months until Elagabalus was assassinated in AD 222 and Alexander succeeded him as sole Emperor, adding the name *Severus* to assert continuity from Septimius Severus his great-uncle. Somewhat surprisingly, this young Syrian (he was only 13) held onto power for 13 years. Contemporary inscriptions in Britain do not reflect the political strains elsewhere, but only record the development or renewal of military installations. Progress may have been rather slow:

<13.09> *Netherby (Castra Exploratorum)*

imp(eratori) Caes(ari) M(arco) Aurelio
Severo Alexandro Pio [F]el(ici) Aug(usto)
pont(ifici) maximo, trib(unicia) pot(estate), co(n)s(uli), p(atri) p(atriae), coh(ors) I Ael(ia)
Hispanorum (milliaria) eq(uitata) devota numini
maiestatique eius baselicam(!)
equestrem exercitatoriam
iam pridem a solo coeptam
aedificavit consummavitque
sub cura Mari Valeriani leg(ati)
Aug(usti) pr(o) pr(aetore), instante M(arco) Aurelio
Salvio trib(uno) coh(ortis), imp(eratore) d(omino) n(ostro)
Severo Alexandro Pio Fel(ice)
Aug(usto) co(n)s(ule)

RIB 978

22 Birley 2005, 352.

'For the Emperor Caesar Marcus Aurelius Severus Alexander Pius Felix Augustus, with tribunician power, consul, Father of his Country, the First Aelian Cohort of Spaniards, one thousand strong, part-mounted, devoted to his divinity and majesty, built this cavalry drill-hall, long since begun from ground-level, and completed it, under the charge of Marius Valerianus, propraetorian legate of the Emperor, with Marcus Aurelius Salvius, tribune of the cohort, supervising, in the consulship of Our Lord the Emperor Severus Alexander Pius Felix Augustus (AD 222).'

The form *baselica* for *basilica* ('hall') is due to a sound-shift found in Latin by the third century.[23] This is the only Roman inscription actually to name a cavalry drill-hall, and it is uncertain whether they have been identified by excavation.[24] But according to Vegetius, the Roman army built open structures (*porticus*) for the purpose, although he adds that, even in winter, training should continue out of doors, rain and snow permitting.[25] To practise horsemanship indoors, out of the wind and rain, would have seemed a good idea in north-west Britain. This building had been begun 'long since' and was only now completed: there is a certain sense of relief. No wonder the prefect also dedicated this altar:

<13.10> *Netherby (Castra Exploratorum)*

deae sanct-
ae Fortunae
Conservatrici
Marcus Aurel(ius)
Salvius tribun-
us coh(ortis) I Ael(iae) Hi-
spanorum
(milliariae) eq(uitatae)
v(otum) s(olvit) l(ibens) m(erito)

RIB 968+*add.*

'To the holy goddess Fortune the Preserver, Marcus Aurelius Salvius, tribune of the First Aelian Cohort of Spaniards, one thousand strong, part-mounted, paid his vow willingly, deservedly.'

This title of Fortune is quite common, but there is only one other British example, an altar at Manchester.[26] Perhaps the Netherby drill-hall had not commanded universal support: on paper at least, the cavalry of a part-mounted cohort one

---

[23] Smith 1983, 902.
[24] Pitts and St Joseph 1985, 124.
[25] *Epitoma rei militaris* ii 23.
[26] *RIB* 575.

thousand strong numbered 240 as against 760 infantry.[27] It is also unusual to find cavalry doing their own building-work. At South Shields an inscription of the same governor, Marius Valerianus, celebrates a more conventional amenity which would have benefited the whole unit:

<13.11> *South Shields (?Lugudunum, later Arbeia)*

imp(erator) Caes(ar) divi Severi
nepos, divi Magni Antonini fil(ius),
M(arcus) Aurel(ius) Severus [[Alexander]]
Pius Felix Aug(ustus), pontif(ex) max(imus),
trib(unicia) pot(estate), p(ater) p(atriae), co(n)s(ul), aquam
usibus mil(itum) coh(ortis) V Gallo(rum) in-
duxit, curante Mario Valeriano
leg(ato) eius pro pr(aetore)

RIB 1060+*add.*

'The Emperor Caesar Marcus Aurelius Severus Alexander (*erased*) Pius Felix Augustus, grandson of the deified Severus, son of the deified Antoninus the Great, pontifex maximus, with tribunician power, Father of his Country, brought in this supply of water for the use of soldiers of the Fifth Cohort of Gauls, under the charge of Marius Valerianus, his propraetorian legate.'

Alexander in line 3 has been erased as usual, but the ghost of the letters can still be seen. In British building-inscriptions before the reign of Septimius Severus, emperors are hardly ever named as the agent in the nominative case, instead of being the dedicatee in the dative. The Ninth Legion's swansong (**4.16**) is a notable exception. The cohort-commander is not named, perhaps because the post was temporarily vacant, but an acting-commander (*praepositus*) might have been expected. The provision of running water at last – South Shields had been fortified for at least 60 years, ever since the AD 160s – recalls Avidius Quintianus' celebration of 'the true Waters of Health' being brought to the Libyan oasis fort of Bu Njem.[28] It was at Bu Njem in AD 222, the same year as **13.11** but some months earlier, since Elagabalus was still alive, that a successor of Quintianus celebrated in verse the rebuilding of an arched stone gate which had collapsed from age, a task his

[27] ps.Hyginus, *de munitionibus castrorum* 25–7; Davies 1989, 141–51.

[28] *IRT* 334, partly translated in the note to **2.05**.

predecessors had avoided.[29] Since we know that Bu Njem was only founded on 24 January AD 201, it sounds like the High Rochester *ballistarium* over again (**13.06** with **13.08**). The new poem, like that of Quintianus, was an acrostic, the initial letters spelling out the author's name: PORCIVS IASVCTHANVS CENT(VRIO) LEG(IONIS), Porcius Iasucthanus, the centurion of the Third Legion Augusta now in command at Bu Njem. His cognomen is Berber, but his nomen is a sentimental reminiscence of the Republican hero Marcus Porcius Cato, who killed himself in Africa rather than surrender to Julius Caesar. When his posting to Bu Njem ended, by AD 225, Iasucthanus returned to the legion's base at Lambaesis and thanked his native gods for promotion:

<**13.12**> *Lambaesis in Numidia (eastern Algeria)*

pro salute d(omini) n(ostri)
Severi Alexan-
dri P<i>i Felicis Aug(usti)
dis Mauris
M(arcus) Porcius Ia-
suctan (centurio) leg(ionis)
XX Val(eriae) V(ictricis) Severae
v(otum) s(olvit) l(ibens) a(nimo)

ILS 9293 with Rebuffat 1995, 96–7

'For the welfare of Our Lord Severus Alexander Pius Felix Augustus, to the Moorish Gods; Marcus Porcius Iasuctan, centurion of the Twentieth Legion Valeria Victrix, Severus' Own, has paid his vow willing in heart.'

This altar follows the Bu Njem posting, for Alexander has now replaced Elagabalus. Iasuct(h)an(us) has evidently been transferred to the Twentieth Legion, and is about to leave for Britain. He would be taking his memories of 'the scorching heat of the southern sun' (in the words of Avidius Quintianus again) to the more temperate north. Did the mist and rain of his new posting inspire him to write more poetry? We do not know the answer – yet – and the question is commended to future forgers of Romano-British inscriptions.

Before leaving Lambaesis, Iasucthanus might have been able to approach another officer of the legion for his own memories of Britain:

[29] *AE* 1995, 164 (Rebuffat 1995), *portam vetustate conlabsam lapidi quadrato arco curvato restituit | omnes praeteriti cuius labore vitabant.*

<13.13> *Lambaesis in Numidia (eastern Algeria)*

D(is) M(anibus) s(acrum)
P(ublio) Furio Rus-
tico praef(ecto)
coh(ortis) II Astu(rum)
prov(incia) Britt(aniae)
infer(ioris), trib(uno)
mil(itum) leg(ionis) III
Aug(ustae) p(iae) v(indicis), vix(it)
ann(os) XL, P(ublius) Furius Rusti-
cus pater
filio karissi-
mo fecit

ILS 2762

'Sacred to the Shades of the Dead, (and) to Publius Furius Rusticus, prefect of the Second Cohort of Asturians in the province of Lower Britain, military tribune of the Third Legion Augusta, Dutiful and Avenging; he lived 40 years. His father Publius Furius Rusticus did this for his dearest son.'

Unfortunately this tombstone can only be dated approximately by the reference to Lower Britain (after *c.* AD 216), and Rusticus may not have coincided with Iasucthanus at Lambaesis. But before his ill-fated promotion to the African legion, Rusticus would have commanded the Asturians at Great Chesters, as can be deduced from this slab:

<13.14> *Great Chesters (Aesica)*

imp(erator) Caes(ar) M(arcus) Aur(elius) Seve-
rus Alexander P(ius) Fel(ix)
Aug(ustus) horreum vetu-
state conlabsum(!) mil(itibus)
coh(ortis) II Asturum S(everianae) A(lexandrianae)
a solo restituerunt,
provincia(m) regente [...]
Maximo leg(ato) [Aug(usti) pr(o) pr(aetore), cur(ante)]
Val(erio) Martiale (centurione) leg(ionis) [...]
[F]us[co II et Dextro co(n)s(ulibus)]

RIB 1738 with Birley 2005, 347

'The Emperor Caesar Marcus Aurelius Severus Alexander Pius Felix Augustus for the soldiers of the Second Cohort of Asturians, Severus Alexander's Own, restored from ground-level this granary collapsed through age, while [...] Maximus the imperial propraetorian legate was governing the province, under the charge of Valerius Martialis, centurion of the [...] Legion, in the consulship of Fuscus for the second time and Dexter (AD 225).'

Northumberland's first county historian, John Wallis, who traced his interest in the Romans to being born at Whitley Castle (**13.02**), saw this slab shortly after it was dug up in 1767.[30] The last two lines, although damaged, were better preserved than they are now; there was enough to identify the consuls, but not Martialis' legion. It is the only inscription to name the third-century garrison of Great Chesters, which did not change thereafter, assuming it to be what the Notitia Dignitatum calls the *First* Cohort of Asturians. The Emperor's name is in the nominative again, as at South Shields (**13.11**), but the verb (*restituerunt*) is in the plural; as Wright notes in *RIB*, it should either have been singular (*restituit*), or the Emperor's name should have been in the dative, with MIL understood as *mil(ites)*, the soldiers who restored the granary 'for' him. But at least his name, for once, has not been erased. The governor is otherwise unknown; his nomen is lost, but must have been abbreviated to two or three (ligatured) letters; perhaps *Cl(audius)* or *Fl(avius)*, but there are other possibilities.[31] On this occasion there was no equestrian prefect like Rusticus; a legionary centurion, his legion now unknown, was the acting-commander (*praepositus*).

Gordian III (AD 238–44)

Severus Alexander was overthrown by his general Maximinus 'the Thracian' (*Thrax*), this informal title meaning that his origin and career were like those of Aurelius Syrio (**13.04**), and the Severan dynasty died with Alexander after 42 years. The next half-century (AD 235–84) is often characterised as 'the Anarchy', in which apart from many usurpers there were 'about twenty emperors who may be styled legitimate', only two of whom did not die violent deaths, Valerian as a prisoner of the Persians instead, Claudius II by plague.[32] Britain was geographically insulated from the worst effects of this crisis of Empire, which was due to a vicious combination of external pressures – the tribes across the Rhine and Danube, the resurgent Persian empire across the Euphrates – with constant civil wars as Roman armies fought each other for supremacy. Maximinus, the first 'Illyrian' emperor from the Danubian provinces, succumbed to the consequences in Italy of a revolt in Africa headed by the elderly proconsul Gordianus, the sometime legate of Lower Britain (**13.03**), which ended indirectly in the proclamation of his 13-year-old grandson as Gordian III. This Gordian was accepted in Britain, unlike his grandfather, and there is a hint of recent events in this long-winded dedication:

30 Birley 1961(b), 20.

31 Birley 2005, 347.

32 Jones 1964, 23.

<13.15> *Old Carlisle (?Maglona)*

I(ovi) O(ptimo) M(aximo)
pro salu[te] imperatoris
M(arci) Antoni Gordiani P(ii) F(elicis)
Invicti Aug(usti) et Sab[in]iae Fur-
iae Tranquil<lin>ae coniugi eius to-
taque domu divin(a) eorum a-
la Aug(usta) Gordia(na) ob virtutem
appellata posuit, cui praest
Aemilius Crispinus pr<a>ef(ectus)
eq(uitum) natus in pro(vincia) Africa de
Tusdro, sub cur(a) Nonii Ph-
ilippi leg(ati) Aug(usti) pro pr(a)e[to(re)]
[At]tico et Praetextato
co(n)s(ulibus)

RIB 897+*add*.

'To Jupiter, Best and Greatest, for the welfare of the Emperor Marcus Antonius Gordianus Pius Felix Unconquered Augustus, and of Sabinia Furia Tranquillina his wife, and of their whole Divine House, the Cavalry Regiment styled Augusta for its valour, Gordian's Own, set this up, which is commanded by the prefect of cavalry Aemilius Crispinus, who was born in the province of Africa, from Thysdrus; under the charge of Nonius Philippus, imperial propraetorian legate, in the consulship of Atticus and Praetextatus' (AD 242).

This altar with its ill-lettered, crowded text must have been concerted with the far more legible altar (**10.01**) dedicated for the 'welfare' of Gordian by the civilian inhabitants (*vikani*) of the fort. The regiment had been there since at least AD 185.[33] The prefect Crispinus advertises his origin: it can be no coincidence that Gordian's grandfather the proconsul had been proclaimed at Thysdrus by local landowners who rebelled against increased taxation. Crispinus, in expressing loyalty to the new Emperor, alludes discreetly to one of the fruits of rebellion, his own promotion, but no such overtones can be detected in these two inscriptions from Lanchester:

[33] *RIB* 903.

<**13.16**> *Lanchester (Longovicium)*

imp(erator) Caesar M(arcus) Antonius
Gordianus P(ius) F(elix) Aug(ustus)
principia et armamen-
taria conlapsa restitu-
it per Maecilium Fuscum leg(atum)
Aug(usti) pr(o) pr(aetore), curante M(arco) Aur(elio)
Quirino pr(a)ef(ecto) coh(ortis) I L(ingonum) Gor(dianae)

RIB 1092+*add.*

'The Emperor Caesar Marcus Antonius Gordianus Pius Felix Augustus restored the headquarters building and arms stores, which had collapsed, through the agency of Maecilius Fuscus, imperial propraetorian legate, with Marcus Aurelius Quirinus, prefect of the First Cohort of Lingones, Gordian's Own, taking charge.'

<**13.17**> *Lanchester (Longovicium)*

imp(erator) Caes(ar) M(arcus) Ant(onius) Gordia-
nus P(ius) F(elix) Aug(ustus) balneum cum
basilica a solo instruxit
per Egn(atium) Lucilianum leg(atum) Aug(usti)
pr(o) pr(aetore), curante M(arco) Aur(elio)
Quirino pr(a)ef(ecto) coh(ortis) I L(ingonum) Gor(dianae)

RIB 1091

'The Emperor Caesar Marcus Antonius Gordianus Pius Felix Augustus erected from ground-level this bath-building with basilica through the agency of Egnatius Lucilianus, imperial propraetorian legate, with Marcus Aurelius Quirinus, prefect of the First Cohort of Lingones, Gordian's Own, taking charge.'

So much building-work is recorded here that, until the cohort was found to have been at Lanchester already in the early AD 220s, it was thought that the fort was recommissioned under Gordian III.[34] The same prefect is responsible for both inscriptions, but which came first is not clear since the sequence of governors is

[34] Frere 1987, 170, but see now *RIB* III, 3262.

unknown. It has been loyally suggested – and indeed is reasonable – that the cohort gave priority to rebuilding essential structures before providing itself with amenities.[35] A more subtle difference has also been noticed, between the conjunctions used to refer to the headquarters building 'and' (*et*) arms stores, and the bath-building 'with' (*cum*) basilica. The implication is that the arms stores did not form part of the headquarters building itself, and in fact there is archaeological evidence elsewhere that they formed a separate building.[36] The basilica on the other hand was attached to the bath-building, and was probably a large heated room which could be used for indoor games and exercise like a gymnasium. The philosopher Seneca, that early investor in Britain whose political career ended in suicide, complains in a lighter moment of his temporary lodgings above public baths, where he was distracted from his studies by the grunts and gasps of someone working out with weights, and a ball-game player shouting the score.[37] The prefect Aurelius Quirinus, who completed these four projects within 2 or 3 years, must have been a man of unusual energy and drive, no less energetic when he relaxed, not in the baths but out on the moors:

<13.18> *Eastgate in Weardale*

deo
Silvano
Aurelius
Quirinus
pr(aefectus) f(ecit)

RIB 1042

'To the god Silvanus, Aurelius Quirinus the prefect made this.'

This altar was found in the wilderness of Weardale, and recalls the other altar there to Silvanus, in which a prefect of the *ala Sebosiana* boasts that he has been more successful in his hunting than his many predecessors (**12.39**). Gordian III is represented by other inscriptions from the frontier and its hinterland, but we may conclude his reign with this altar from the furthest north:

35 Birley 2005, 358.

36 Bishop and Coulston 2006, 263–6, although the form *balineum [et] basilicam* is used in *RIB* 605. But note *RIB* III, 3027 (Reculver), *aedem p[rinci]piorum cu[m b]asilica*, the headquarters building 'with' its basilica.

37 Seneca, *ep.* 56.1.

<**13.19**> *High Rochester (Bremenium)*

g(enio) d(omini) n(ostri) et
signorum
coh(ortis) I Vardul[l(orum)]
et n(umeri) Explora-
tor(um) Brem(eniensium) Gor(diani)
Egnat(ius) Lucili-
anus leg(atus) Aug(usti) pr(o) pr(aetore),
curante Cassio
Sabiniano trib(uno)

RIB 1262

'To the Genius of our Lord and of the Standards of the First Cohort of Vardulli and the Unit of Scouts of Bremenium, Gordian's Own, Egnatius Lucilianus imperial propraetorian legate (set this up) under the charge of Cassius Sabinianus, tribune.'

High Rochester (Bremenium) throughout the third century was the most northern fort in the Empire, and this altar is one of the inscriptions which show the outpost forts were now garrisoned by powerful part-mounted cohorts 1000-strong 'brigaded' with new units of Scouts (*numeri exploratorum*). The latter took the name of their station, like the detachments of Germans at Lanchester (**12.49**) and Housesteads (**12.50**), which had been the practice of units of *exploratores* deployed on the Upper German frontier since the later second century. These units formalised the practice of detaching élite 'scouts' like Tiberius Claudius Maximus to serve as the spearhead of an army on campaign.[38]

At High Rochester, as well as the altar dedicated to Rome by the junior officers (*duplicarii*) of its Scouts, the *exploratores Bremenienses* (**12.51**), there is ample evidence of the Vardulli.[39] At Risingham (Habitancum), where the procurator Oclatinius Adventus (**8.07**) directed the rebuilding of the defences in AD 205/8, the new garrison dedicated an enormous inscription to Caracalla: they were the First Cohort of Vangiones, the *Raeti Gaesati* ('Raetian Spearmen'), and the *exploratores Habitancenses* ('Scouts of Habitancum').[40] At Netherby and Bewcastle the evidence is less explicit, but the garrisons must have been similar. At Netherby in AD 222 only the First Cohort of Spaniards is named (**13.09**), but the presence of 'scouts' at the fort can be inferred from its Roman name, *castra exploratorum*. At Bewcastle two altars are dedicated by military tribunes who would thus have commanded a milliary cohort,

[38] Speidel 1970. Connolly 1988. Austin and Rankov 1995, 189–95.

[39] *RIB* 1263 (undated) and 1272 (Caracalla).

[40] *RIB* 1234 (Oclatinius Adventus); 1235 (to Caracalla). Two fragments (*RIB* 1243 and 1244) also refer to the *exploratores*.

and since they have both been promoted from the Praetorian Guard like Aurelius Syrio at Carlisle (**13.04**), they can be dated to the third century.[41] In the outpost forts these Scouts, closely supported by conventional forces of infantry and cavalry, can be seen as providing the Wall with 'eyes' to the north, an early-warning system which would mitigate the loss of the initiative that followed the decision to fall back on the Wall.

Later years (AD 244–84)

After Gordian's death (AD 244), the flow of inscriptions from Britain dwindles to a trickle except for milestones, which should now be regarded as expressions of loyalty to the current regime rather than evidence of building-work or renovation.[42] Most of the others are altars, which often also express loyalty, like this from the western end of the Wall:

<13.20> *Bowness-on-Solway (Maia)*

I(ovi) O(ptimo) M(aximo)
pro salute
d(ominorum) n(ostrorum) Galli
et Volusiani
Aug(ustorum) Sulpicius
Secundian-
us tribunus coh(ortis)
[p]osuit

RIB 2057

'To Jupiter Best and Greatest, for the welfare of our Lords Gallus and Volusianus, (both) Augusti, Sulpicius Secundianus, tribune of the cohort, set this up.'

The same prefect dedicated another altar, now lost, which apparently carried the same wording; the occasion would have been the successive annual parades at which 'vows' (*vota*) of loyalty were paid and renewed.[43] Trebonianus Gallus (AD 251–53) was the ephemeral successor of Decius (AD 249–51) when the latter was killed in action against the Goths, a death which was attributed to the treachery of Gallus. Like other new emperors, he then co-opted his son Volusianus to ensure continuity, but they were soon both killed by the usurper Aemilianus, who however failed to maintain himself against a general who had remained loyal to Gallus:

---

41 *RIB* 988, *ex evocato*; *RIB* 989, *ex corniculario em(inentissimorum) v(irorum)* (staff officer to the Praetorian Prefects).

42 Sauer 2014.

43 *RIB* 2058. For the annual *vota*, see 'Roman gods' before **12.58**.

<13.21> *Burgh-by-Sands (Aballava)*

[I(ovi) O(ptimo) M(aximo)]
[e]t numinib-
us Aug(ustorum trium) n(umerus)
Maur<o>rum
Aur(elianorum) Valer-
iani Gallie-
ni q(uorum) c(uram) a(git) Fl(avius)
Vibianu-
s trib(unus) coh(ortis)
[p(rae)]p(ositus) n(umeri) s(upra)s(cripti), i(n)st-
[a]nte Iul(io) R-
ufino pri-
ncipe

RIB 2042+*add.*

'To Jupiter Best and Greatest, and to the divinities of the (three) Augusti, the unit of Aurelian Moors, Valerian's Own, Gallienus' Own, commanded by Flavius Vibianus, cohort-tribune, commander of the above-written unit, (set this up) under the direction of Julius Rufinus, *princeps*.'

Valerian and his son were accepted in Britain, and throughout the Empire. But why 'three' emperors? This altar was discussed by Roy Davies in the last paper he ever wrote, in a cruelly short scholarly life (he was only 35 when he died) which nonetheless achieved 58 papers on the Roman army.[44] The mason cut the letters AVGG°G° with stops before and after the third G, which *RIB* interprets as the *g(enius)* of the *numerus* abbreviated, but such an abbreviation would be unparalleled. The mason was not consistent in his use of stops – he renders MAVRORVM as MAVR°RVM, for example – and it is easier to read AVGGG, with the 'third' *Augustus* being Gallienus' son Valerian (the younger), who was strictly speaking only *Caesar* as in **13.22** below. The *numerus* is said to be 'of Valerian, of Gallienus', but this is a misunderstanding or (to be charitable) an abbreviation of the correct dynastic titles, which in the genitive would have been *Valeriani(ani)* and *Gallieni(ani)*. The extent of Vibianus' command is also unclear: he is not only commander (*praepositus*) of the *numerus*, he is the tribune commanding a (milliary) cohort, which would either have been 'brigaded' with the *numerus* at Burgh-by-Sands like the garrisons of the outpost forts, or would have garrisoned a neighbouring fort. The latter is the easier conclusion, both because the *numerus* is recorded as the only garrison of Burgh-by-Sands by the Notitia Dignitatum, and because Rufinus as *princeps* would

[44] Davies 1989 collects ten of his papers. **13.21** is discussed in Davies 1981, 191–3, and independently by Speidel 1981, 12.

have been a senior centurion acting as its commander in the absence of the actual commander. These fine distinctions would have been more obvious at the time.

The joint-reign of Valerian and Gallienus (AD 253–60), to which this altar belongs, is also marked by the very last imperial building-inscription[45] at the legionary base of Caerleon:

<**13.22**> *Caerleon (Isca)*

imp(eratores) Valerianus et Gallienus
Aug(usti) et Valerianus nobilissimus
Caes(ar) cohorti VII centurias a so-
lo restituerunt per Desticium Iubam
v(irum) c(larissimum) legatum Aug(ustorum) pr(o) pr(aetore) et
Vitulasium Laetinianum leg(atum) leg(ionis)
II Aug(ustae), curante Domit(io) Potentino
praef(ecto) leg(ionis) eiusdem

RIB 334+*add.*

'The (two) Emperors Valerian and Gallienus Augusti, and Valerian most noble Caesar, have restored from ground-level barrack-blocks for the Seventh Cohort, through the agency of Desticius Juba, senator and imperial propraetorian legate, and of Vitulasius Laetinianus legate of the Second Legion Augusta, under the charge of Domitius Potentinus, prefect of the same legion.'

This crowded text is in sad visual contrast with Caerleon's first building-inscription, the great Trajanic panel (**4.15**), but is at least more generous with names. Desticius Juba, as Tony Birley points out, is the latest known consular governor of Upper Britain, and indeed the latest known consular governor who commanded senatorial legates and legions. Gallienus soon excluded senators from military command, and Laetinianus is the latest known legionary legate anywhere in the Empire, except for a few governors of one-legion provinces.[46] They were replaced by equestrian prefects, but Potentinus is not one; he was the camp commandant, *praefectus castrorum*.

Gallienus was abruptly isolated when his father was taken prisoner by the Persians, and he was unable to succeed him in the eastern provinces. In the further west he had failed to eliminate the separatist 'Gallic Empire' of Postumus, and was now

45 *RIB* III, 3093 was first published as an inscription of Aurelian (AD 270–75), but is part of a tombstone.
46 Birley 2005, 363.

forced to endure it for the sake of maintaining himself in Italy and the Danubian provinces. Like previous emperors, he improvised a 'field army' by concentrating detachments from the frontier armies, which included those of Britain and Germany before their legions sided with Postumus:

<**13.23**> *Sirmium (Sremska Mitrovica, near Belgrade)*

[Io]vi
Monitori [p]ro
salute adque
incolumitate d(omini) n(ostri) Gallieni Aug(usti)
et militum
vexill(ationum) leg(ionum)
[G]ermanicia[r(um)]
[e]t Britannici<a>n(arum)
[cu]m auxil(i)is [e]arum
[... V]italianus
[pro]tect(or) Aug(usti) n(ostri)
[praepos]itus
p(osuit]

ILS 546

'To Jupiter the Adviser, for the welfare and safety of Our Lord Gallienus Augustus, and of the soldiers of the detachments of the German and British legions with their auxiliaries. [...] Vitalianus, *protector* of Our Emperor, their commander, erected (this).'

The city of Sirmium in the Sava valley was the centre of communications for the middle Danube frontier, and for years it had been the campaign headquarters of Marcus Aurelius; appropriately the first chapter of Fergus Millar's great work *The Emperor in the Roman World* is entitled 'Marcus Aurelius at Sirmium', and Millar stresses how many of Marcus' successors, from Caracalla to Constantine, made Sirmium their temporary capital.[47] Its military importance finds a faint echo at Caerleon, in the pedestal dedicated in the headquarters building by a senior officer, probably the *primus pilus*, who names it as his place of origin.[48] Vitalianus' title of *protector* also has a long history, from being a term informally applied to the bodyguards of governors and senior officers to the title borne by Voteporix in sub-Roman Wales.[49] Gallienus was the first to apply it to officers like Vitalianus in his field army, to emphasise their personal bond to him, but afterwards it evolved into an important institution of the Late Empire, a 'staff college' of senior NCOs and careerists like the future historian Ammianus Marcellinus, who were attached to the imperial Court before being promoted to independent commands.

---

47 Millar 1977, 47–8.

48 *RIB* III, 3080, *[d]omo Fl(avia) [Si]rmi.*

49 Speidel 1978, 130–33; Christol 1977. Edwards 2007, 202, CM3.

The legion at Caerleon probably contributed to Gallienus' army, of which this unusual bronze disc may be a souvenir:

<13.24> *unknown provenance (now in Paris)*

(*left*) leg(io) XX V(aleria) V(ictrix)

(*right*) leg(io) secunda Augus(ta)

(*centre*) Aurelius Cervianus

(*below*) utere felix

RIB II.3, 2427.26*

'The Twentieth Legion Valeria Victrix (and) the Second Legion Augusta. Aurelius Cervianus. Use (this and be) happy.'

The disc is 117 mm in diameter, and resembles the *phalerae* worn by soldiers as military decorations, but its purpose is unknown. Eric Birley chose it for the cover of his first collected papers, *Roman Britain and the Roman Army*, and it catches a vivid moment in the evolution of the late-Roman army. The oval shields and the nomen *Aurelius* are the best indications of date, which is probably third-century; the two legions by then were the garrison of Upper Britain. A legionary eagle presides over two groups of soldiers, each bearing the banner (*vexillum*) which names the legion from which they have been detached as a *vexillatio*, the Twentieth Valeria Victrix and the Second Augusta. These are further identified by their respective emblems, a wild boar and a capricorn. The name *Aurelius Cervianus* is that of the owner, who may well have been the officer in command (*praepositus*) of these two detachments. *utere felix* is inscribed below, with a light-hearted medley of animals: a hound chasing a hare, another hound chasing a somewhat self-absorbed stag and lion; and there are two peacocks, one of which is pecking a flower.

This pairing of legionary detachments is typical of the late-Roman mobile army (*comitatenses*) in the Notitia Dignitatum, by which time they have left their old stations for good. The disc is first recorded in a north-Italian collection, so these British legionaries are on foreign service, whether it was permanent or not. That the Twentieth Legion, if not the Second as well, contributed to Gallienus' army is suggested by a stone fragment from Mainz dated AD 255, dedicated by the legion for the welfare of the civilian inhabitants, perhaps in the course of a mission.[50]

The Mainz inscription is earlier than the 'Gallic Empire' of Postumus (AD 258–67), whose name and titles appear on a milestone at Brougham (**10.06**). Two altars at Birdoswald, dedicated by the same prefect in successive years, catch the moment when his usurpation succeeded:

[50] *CIL* xiii 6780, *pro sal(ute) / canabe(nsium) ... [... ?expediti]one.*

<**13.25**> *Birdoswald (Banna)*

I(ovi) O(ptimo) M(aximo)
et n(umini) Aug(usti)
coh(ors) I Ael(ia)
Dac(orum) c(ui) p(raeest) M(arcius)
Gallicus
trib(unus)

RIB 1882

'To Jupiter Best and Greatest, and to the divinity of the Emperor, the First Aelian Cohort of Dacians commanded by Marcius Gallicus, tribune, (set this up).'

<**13.26**> *Birdoswald (Banna)*

I(ovi) O(ptimo) M(aximo)
coh(ors) I Ael(ia) Dac(orum)
Postum[iana]
c(ui) p(raeest) Marc(ius)
Gallicus
trib(unus)

RIB 1883+*add.*

'To Jupiter Best and Greatest, the First Aelian Cohort of Dacians, Postumus' Own, commanded by Marcius Gallicus, tribune, (set this up).'

Gallicus' first altar (**13.25**) refers to only one Emperor, whereas Postumus rebelled against *two*. Perhaps Gallicus was being non-committal, but his second altar (**13.26**) duly adds the title of *Postumiana*, which is repeated by one of his successors:

<**13.27**> *Birdoswald (Banna)*

I(ovi) O(ptimo) M(aximo)
coh(ors) I Ael(ia)
Dacoru[m]
Postum[i]-
ana c(ui) p(raeest)
Prob(ius) Au-
gendus
trib(unus)

RIB 1886

'To Jupiter Best and Greatest, the First Aelian Cohort of Dacians, Postumus' Own, commanded by Probius Augendus, tribune, (set this up).'

The new regime inspired more than expressions of loyalty; building-work even continued:

<**13.28**> *Lancaster*

[[...]]
[[...]] [?ob] balineum refect(um)
[et] basilicam vetustate conlabsum(!)
a solo restitutam eq(u(itibus) alae Sebussian(ae)(!)
[[Postumianae]] sub Octavio Sabino v(iro) c(larissimo)
praeside n(ostro), curante Fla(vio)Ammau-
sio praef(ecto) equ(itum), d(e)d(icata) (ante diem) XI Kal(endas) Septem(bres)
Censore II et Lepido II co(n)s(ilibus)

RIB 605+*add.*

'For the Emperor Postumus (*name and titles erased*) on account of this rebuilt bath-building and basilica collapsed from age restored from ground-level, for the troopers of the Cavalry Regiment Sebosiana, Postumus' Own (*erased*), under Octavius Sabinus of senatorial rank, our governor, and under the charge of Flavius Ammausius, prefect of cavalry; dedicated on the eleventh day before the Kalends of September (22 August) in the consulship of Censor and Lepidus, both for the second time.'

A pair of dolphins forms an attractive *pelta* to the right, no doubt balanced by another to the left, now lost. The imperial names have been erased, but there is a trace of *Postumiana* in the unit-title. The unit itself we saw long ago, as the Flavian garrison of Carlisle (**3.14**), and its prefect hunting wild boar in Weardale (**12.39**). The syntax is difficult, and Hübner was probably right to insert the preposition *ob* at the beginning to govern the two accusative nouns, *balneum* and *basilicam*, to which the neuter plural *d(e)d(icata)* then awkwardly refers. The consuls are otherwise unknown, and must be seen as appointees of Postumus who were not recognised anywhere else. The governor is likewise unknown, unless part of his name survives on a fragment from York.[51] Postumus' names were erased after Britain was recovered by the central government. This was achieved, not by Gallienus, but by the most formidable member of the junta of 'Illyrian' officers which came to dominate his field army, the Emperor Aurelian (AD 270–75). Aurelian's fellow-*juntista* and indirect successor, Probus (AD 276–82), is recognised on this crudely fashioned altar:

[51] *RIB* III, 3196.

<**13.29**> *Birdoswald (Banna)*

I(ovi) O(ptimo) M(aximo)
coh(ors) I Ael(ia)
Dacorum
Probiana
c(ui) p(raeest) Aur(elius)
Verinus
trib(unus)

RIB III, 3438

'To Jupiter Best and Greatest, (from) the First Aelian Cohort of Dacians, Probus' Own, commanded by the tribune Aurelius Verinus.'

The title *Probiana* was also assumed by the Fourth Cohort of Gauls at Vindolanda.[52] This Birdoswald altar is the last of the long series dedicated there to Jupiter by the First Cohort of Dacians, to mark their annual parades of loyalty. Birdoswald also, as will soon be seen (**14.06**), produces the Wall's last building-inscription.

52 *RIB* 1710.

14

THE FOURTH CENTURY

When does the Late Empire begin? In Oxford University until May 2005, when the Faculty of Modern History renamed itself the Faculty of History, the starting-date of the Honour School of Modern History was AD 285: Ancient History was assumed to end in AD 284, on 20 November to be exact, when the army proclaimed Diocletian emperor at Nicomedia (Izmit).[1] Next year he eliminated his last rival, a surviving son of the previous emperor, and replaced him in the west with a fellow-officer called Maximian. During his reign of more than 20 years (AD 284–305), the longest since Antoninus Pius (AD 138–61), Diocletian consolidated the improvisations of the past half-century into a system. The army and the civil administration were both enlarged but military and civil careers continued to diverge, provinces were sub-divided, fortifications were multiplied, internal disaffection and foreign enemies alike were checked as he single-mindedly mobilised the Empire's resources in a remarkable recovery.

The effects are visible in fourth-century Britain, but hardly in the epigraphic record, in which the steep decline in numbers of monumental inscriptions since the AD 240s was not reversed. Despite its large garrison, Britain seems to have lost what Ramsay MacMullen calls 'the epigraphic habit'. This may be due to a decline in the size of the garrison and its technical skills, but surely not to economic decline, since the evidence of archaeology and the abundant circulation of gold and silver in coin and plate suggest that late-Roman Britain was prosperous. Nor can a decline in literacy be easily blamed.

Persisting literacy

We have already seen the Bath tablet (**12.97**) which refers in passing to 'pagans and Christians'; here is another, likewise in the New Roman Cursive of the fourth century, and no less sophisticated:

[1] Thus '284' figures in the titles of Jones 1964 and Mitchell 2007.

<14.01> *Bath (Aquae Sulis)*

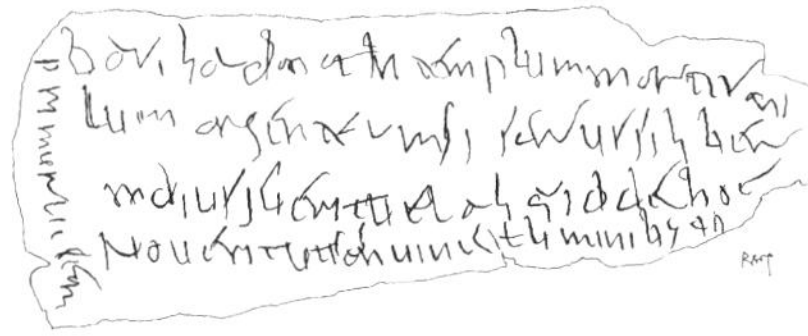

Basilia donat in templum Martis ani-
lum argenteum. si ser<v>us si liber
m<e>dius fuerit, vel aliquid de hoc
noverit, ut sanguine et liminibus(!) et

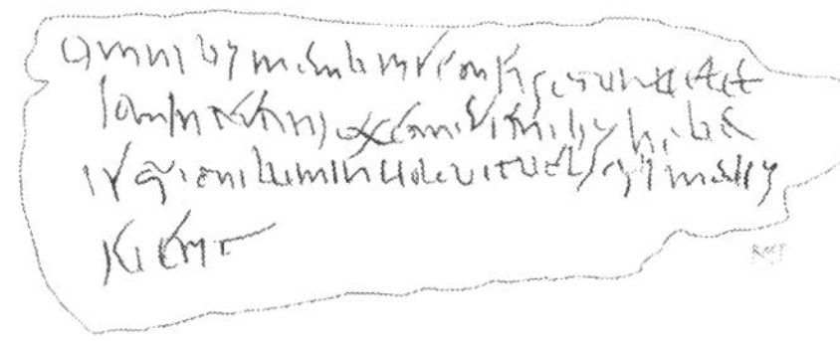

omnibus membris configatur vel et-
iam intestinis excomesis <om>nibus habe<at>
is qui anilum(!) involavit, vel qui medius
fuerit.

Tab. Sulis 97 with *Britannia* 22 (1991), 308, add. (b)

'Basilia gives into the temple of Mars her silver ring. If anyone, whether slave or free, is involved or knows anything about it, may he be cursed in his blood and eyes, or even have all his intestines quite eaten away, he who has stolen the ring or who has been involved.'

Despite the 'Vulgarisms' of *serus* for *servus* ('slave') and *anilum* for *anulum* ('ring'), and the copying-errors of *liminibus* for *luminibus* ('eyes'), *nibus* for *omnibus* ('all') and *habe* for *habeat* ('have'), the writer deploys a rich and recondite vocabulary: *medius* in the sense of 'involved' is difficult to parallel, but Virgil applies the adjective to someone who interferes unwittingly, and St Augustine to the mischief-making tongues of maidservants.[2] The verb *configatur* ('may he be cursed') is a synonym of the usual *defigatur* not found in any other curse tablet, but is not as rare as *excomesis* ('quite eaten away') in the next line. This is an intensified form of the verb *comedo* ('eat') which is not recorded by the standard Oxford Latin Dictionary since it occurs only in very late Latin, for example the sixth-century British sermoniser Gildas, who speaks of hunger for the Gospel 'eating out the bowels' of the soul.[3] The emergence of the radical theologian Pelagius from fourth-century Britain has surprised commentators ever since St Jerome, but it shows that higher education was available there, the education that St Patrick regrets having lost by being kidnapped aged about 16 by Irish pirates.[4] Bath was an urban centre, so it may not be typical, but a few late-Roman tablets were also found at the rural shrine of Uley. More striking, perhaps, is this fired-clay manuscript since it comes from a northern fort; two pieces of a brick, inscribed before firing in New Roman Cursive:

---

2 *Aeneid* i 682 and *Confessions* ix 9 (20) (*medias linguas*) respectively. *qui conscius fuerit* is the equivalent phrase in the Hamble estuary curse tablet (**12.75**).

3 *De Excidio* 85.2, *animae viscera excomedens*.

4 Patricius, *Conf.* 9–12.

<14.02> *Binchester (Vinovia)*

c(...) IIII	V	c(...) II	c(...) III
Matutini	Vincenti	Constantis	Iuvena[lis]
Cogitati	Cunovendi	Titiani	Karini{i}
Virilis	Catugnavi	Karinius	Vitalis
Florentini	Carini	(*space*)	(*space*)
Clementis	Marini		
Marini	Lucilliani		
Bellici	Seniciani{i}		
Iuventianus	Vitalia[ni]		
Cupiti	?M[...]		
[?Cu]noven[di]	[...]		
Solini			
Seni[c]iani			
[...]			

RIB II.5, 2491.78

'(4), *more than* 11 *names*; (5), *more than* 9 *names*; (2), 3 *names*; (3), 3 *names*.'

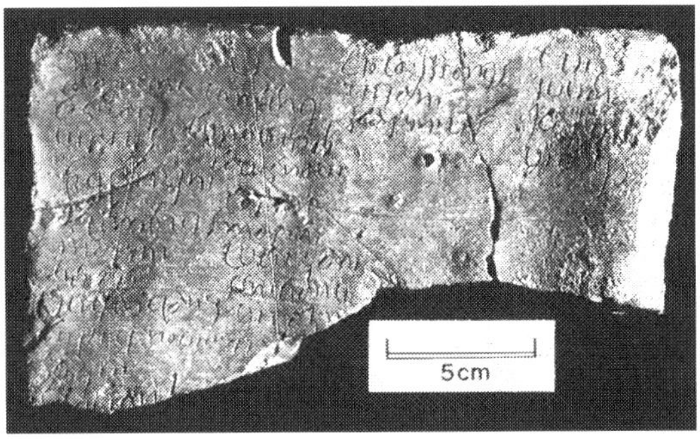

The names are all in the genitive case except for *Iuventianus* and *Karinius*, and they are grouped into four columns, each of which has a numbered heading; this is abbreviated to C, and since they were surely soldiers engaged in brick-making, it is likely to be *c(enturia)* or *c(ohors)*. This is not certain, however, since 'centuries' were not numbered but identified by the name of their centurion; whereas 'cohorts' (in a legion) were numbered, but the soldiers within them were identified by their century. Since the document is unique, we cannot be sure what the categories actually were, but the writing is fluent, and shows a military clerk using his literacy for a mundane purpose, just like the clerks who compiled military records at Vindolanda, more than two centuries earlier.

Since the names are likely to be a random sample of the late-Roman garrison of Binchester, it may be added that four like *Cunovendus* are of Celtic etymology, and 23 are Latin, including names like *Carinus/Karinus* and *Senicianus* which were popular in Britain because they 'concealed' a Celtic name-element. Only *Vincentius*, which like *Volantius* (**9.06**) and *Viventia* (**12.95**) is formed from a present participle, is typically 'late-Roman'.

Carausius and Diocletian

Diocletian in AD 285 bore the title of *Brittanicus Maximus*,[5] but he may only have taken it from his predecessor; he certainly lost control of Britain almost at once, when in AD 286 it was seized by the usurper Carausius, an admiral appointed by Maximian to a special command against German sea-raiders.[6] Diocletian and Maximian refused to recognise Carausius, despite his overtures, but his command of the sea made him invulnerable. Even after he was murdered by his lieutenant Allectus, Britain was not recovered by the central government until AD 296. But although this separatist regime lasted for a decade, only one of its stone inscriptions survives, this crude milestone:

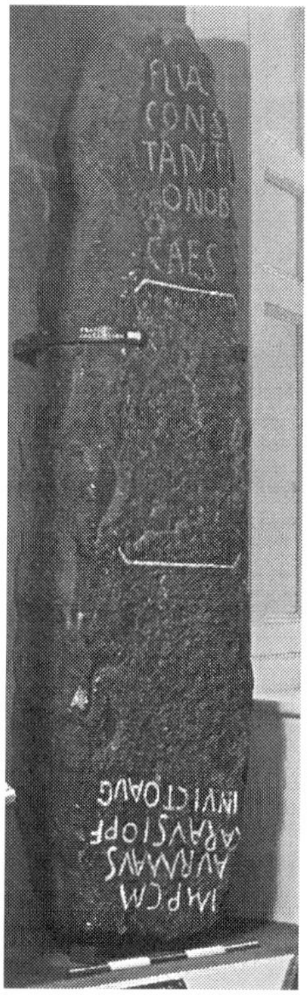

<14.03> *Gallows Hill, Carlisle (Luguvalium)*

imp(eratori) C(aesari) M(arco)
Aur(elio) Maus(aeo)
Carausio P(io) F(elici)
Invicto Aug(usto)

RIB 2291

'For the Emperor Caesar Marcus Aurelius Mausaeus Carausius, Pius Felix, Unconquered Augustus.'

The stone-cutter deleted the primary text from the middle of an earlier emperor's milestone, and cut this text instead at one end. It is ironic, as we will see (**14.09**), that Carausius' own text was superseded in its turn. MAVS here is the fullest record of his other name, which his coins abbreviate to M. The conjectural completion *Maus(aeus)* is based upon the name of a pre-Roman Gallic chieftain; it is otherwise unknown, as indeed is *Carausius* itself, except after the Roman period.[7] Carausius was a Menapian from northern Gaul, and both his names are probably of Celtic etymology.

In AD 293 Diocletian appointed two 'Caesars' junior to himself and Maximian as *Augusti*, Galerius (confusingly also called Maximianus) in the east, and Constantius in the west. Even after Constantius had reduced Carausius' continental base at Boulogne by landward attack, it took him three more years to invade Britain successfully. This was really achieved by his praetorian prefect Asclepiodotus, but the Emperor as usual took the credit. A large gold coin or 'medallion', ten times the weight of a standard *aureus*, was struck for special presentation; only one specimen has survived,

[5] *ILS* 615.
[6] Casey 1994.
[7] Nash-Williams 1950, 92, No. 101.

in the Arras Treasure which represents the savings of a Constantinian officer, and its reverse depicts the campaign.[8] Constantius in general's cloak and armour progresses on horseback, an armed galley representing his fleet crosses the Channel, and both are welcomed by a kneeling figure identified as LON, *Londinium*. Behind her is a fortified city gate which looks rather like the Porta Nigra at Trier, where this coin was struck; hence the mint legend, PTR, *(officina) p(rima) Tr(everis)*, '(Mint of) Trier, (workshop) No. 1'. Identifying the tableau is a phrase from imperial propaganda:

<14.04> *Beaurains, near Arras*

Redditor lucis aeternae

Bastien and Metzger 1977, 94, No. 218

'Restorer of eternal light.'

The glare of Constantius' victory may glimmer in the darkness of the Christian catacombs at Rome, scratched onto this stone gaming-board:

<14.05> *Rome, Catacomb of SS Mark and Marcellus*

Parthi occisi
Br[i]tto victus
ludit[e R]omani

AE 1904, 197

'Parthians killed – Briton defeated – play, Romans'

Such gaming-boards are all scratched with three pairs of six-letter words, for example *hostes victos*, 'enemies beaten', but this is the most specific, which is why it has been dated to *c.* AD 300 by the combination of 'Parthians' (loosely identified with the Persians defeated by Galerius in AD 298) and 'Britons'. After the fall of Allectus, the northern frontier was refurbished:

<14.06> *Birdoswald (Banna)*

[d(ominis)] n(ostris) Dioc[letiano] et
M[axim]iano Invictis Aug(ustis) et
Constantio et Maximiano
n(obilissimis) C(aesaribus) sub v(iro) p(erfectissimo)
Aur(elio) Arpagio pr(aeside)
praetor(ium) quod erat humo copert(um)
et in labe<m> conl(apsum) et princ(ipia) et bal(neum) rest(ituit),
curant<e> Fl(avio) Martino cent(urione) p(rae)p(osito) c[oh(ors) ...]

---

[8] Tomlin 2006(b).

RIB 1912+*add.*

'For our Lords Diocletian and Maximian, Unconquered Augusti, and for Constantius and Maximianus, most noble Caesars, under the Most Perfect Aurelius Arpagius the governor, the cohort [...] restored the commandant's house which had been covered with earth and fallen into ruin, and the headquarters building and the bath-house, under the charge of Flavius Martinus, centurion and acting-commander.'

The date is AD 296/305, the emperors being the 'Tetrarchy' (a modern term, meaning Rule of Four), which lasted until Diocletian abdicated in AD 305. Except for the corner of another 'Tetrarchic' inscription from Housesteads,[9] this is the latest imperial building inscription from the Wall. It lies unsuspected in a famous photograph of the excavators of Birdoswald in 1929, which was taken by Ian Richmond from a step-ladder on the morning of Wednesday 17 July 1929: Eric Birley (in the hat) is making an offering to Fortune at an altar in one of the barrack buildings, watched by the others who include F G Simpson in the centre and R G Collingwood on the right.[10] That afternoon Collingwood left, and next day ('A great day ... a happy day' in Richmond's diary) they began to take up the paving-stones of the barrack-room floor, and found that the altar had been standing on **8.06**. Work continued the following day, 19 July (Richmond's 'Red-letter day'), when they found that Collingwood had been standing on the adjacent **14.06**. The floor sealed a coin of Valentinian I (AD 364–75), so in spite of the lack of subsequent inscriptions, it was deduced that this was not the last refurbishment of the Wall and its forts; the evidence of other coins has since taken its occupation into the early fifth century.

This was the first Roman inscription explicitly to distinguish *principia* from *praetorium*, although the distinction had been implicit since 1831, when two altars dedicated to the *genius* of the *praetorium* were found in the ruins of the commandant's house at Vindolanda, another being found in 1998.[11] The other building restored at Birdoswald is abbreviated to BAL, raising the possibility that it was a *ballistarium* (compare **13.06** and **13.08** at High Rochester), but every fort had a bath-house (*balneum*), a large building particularly liable to accidental damage and dilapidation, and the odds are that *bal(neum)* is meant.[12] The name of the cohort responsible was crammed into the bottom right-hand corner, and is now lost. But since the Notitia Dignitatum records the First Cohort of Dacians as still the garrison, it would have been *cohors I Aelia Dacorum*, drastically abbreviated.

The cohort has only a centurion as its acting-commander (*praepositus*), perhaps because the garrison had become so reduced that the official residence of the rich equestrian tribune had become disused. The reference to its 'collapse' should be taken literally, not as an euphemism for enemy action (compare **10.35**). The governor Arpagius is not a senatorial legate but an equestrian *praeses*. His portentous title, *v(ir) p(erfectissimus)*, only means that he was a top-grade equestrian, for whom it was the equivalent of the senatorial *v(ir) c(larissimus)*. During the third century, and

---

9 *RIB* 1613.

10 Simpson's copy was made available by his daughter Grace, and is also reproduced as Wilmott 1997, Fig. 4. Richmond's diary of the Birdoswald excavation is now in the Sackler Library, Oxford.

11 **12.24**, **12.25** and *RIB* III, 3333. The Reculver fragments (*RIB* III, 3027), found in 1960, associate the *principia* with the *aedes* (shrine of the Standards) and the *basilica* (cross-hall).

12 Donaldson 1990, 209–13, argues strongly for *bal(listarium)*, but the High Rochester inscriptions are almost the only evidence of such a building; they would have been built into it, but nonetheless make this rare word explicit, as BALLIST (**13.06**) or BALLIS (**13.08**).

especially from the sole reign of Gallienus (AD 260–68), the hereditary aristocracy of the Senate was increasingly excluded from provincial governorships and the command of troops. Instead we find armies commanded by professional soldiers, and provinces governed by the procurator as 'acting governor', a process that was completed by Constantine, when military and civil careers were almost entirely separated.[13] Frontier armies were now commanded by generals called 'dukes' (*duces*), and senators governing provinces are hardly found outside Italy and Africa. This inscription apparently belongs to a transitional stage, when the governor was still responsible for the army's logistics and accommodation, but whether he also enjoyed operational command like the old *legatus Augusti pro praetore*, we do not know.

Diocletian not only refurbished the frontiers, he revived the old worship, for which the Christian tradition remembers him as a persecutor. The Birdoswald inscription finds its religious counterpart in this text from Cirencester, which was cut into the three surviving faces of a rectangular base:

<14.07> *Cirencester (Corinium Dobunnorum)*

(*front*)
I(ovi) O(ptimo) [M(aximo)]
L(ucius) Sept[imius] [...]
v(ir) p(erfectissimus) pr(aeses) B[rit(anniae) I?]
resti[tuit]
civis R[emus]

(*right*)
[...]

(*back*)
[si]gnum et
[e]rectam
[p]risca re-
[li]gione co-
[l]umnam

(*left*)
Septimius
renovat
primae
provinciae
rector

RIB 103+*add.*

'To Jupiter Best and Greatest, the Most Perfect Lucius Septimius [...], governor of Britain

13 For occasional exceptions, see Tomlin 1976.

[Prima], a citizen of Reims, restored this. [...] Septimius, the ruler of the First Province, restores this statue and its column erected by ancient piety.'

The base supported a Jupiter-column which carried a statue of the god high above his worshippers, like Nelson in Trafalgar Square, and the sad state of a monument typical of his homeland seems to have moved this governor from northern Gaul into restoring it.[14] The base is really inscribed with two inscriptions, the summary re-dedication on the front, and what was probably a three-line metrical inscription beginning on the (lost) right panel and continuing round to the other side. The two surviving lines are unClassical hexameters which must be scanned by sleight of tongue: the short *u* of *signum* is not elided before *et*, the first *e* of *religione* is improperly short, its second *i* is not scanned but treated as a semi-vowel [y], and the final *-ae* of *provinciae*, which would have been pronounced as if short *e*, must be scanned as such.

Lucius Septimius (whose cognomen is lost) is an equestrian governor like Arpagius, so he cannot be earlier than the AD 260s, but his use of a praenomen (*Lucius*) suits the third century better than the fourth. However, the reference to the 'First' Province implies Britannia Prima, one of the four provinces into which Britain was divided after its recovery in AD 296. This inscription shows that Cirencester was its capital. Although such authorities as Haverfield and Tony Birley attribute the restoration of the column to the brief pagan revival under Julian (see below), Diocletian's is more likely. The reference to 'ancient piety' (*prisca religio*) is conventional and quite in keeping with the aggressive religious conservatism of Diocletian's edict against Manichaeism which condemns this new cult, a conflation of 'dualist' ideas with Christianity, for contravening 'the piety of old' (*vetus religio*).[15] The restoration of a Jupiter-Column in particular is a compliment to Diocletian's special regard for the god whose earthly vicegerent he was. This ideology is implicit in a gold 'crossbow' brooch, now in the Los Angeles County Museum, which was found beyond Hadrian's Wall; in letters forming part of the pierced-work decoration it reads:

<**14.08**> *Erickstanebrae near Moffat*

Iovi(i) Aug(usti)
vot(is) XX

Graffito within the bow:

Fortu[nati?]

RIB II.3, 2421.43

'(Gift) of the Jovian Augustus (Diocletian) at the payment of Vows for 20 years.' '(Property) of Fortunatus.'

---

[14] Despite the risk of a circular argument, this is good reason to restore Septimius' origin as *civis R[emus]*.

[15] *FIR* II, p. 580, *neque reprehendi a nova vetus religio deberet*.

Late-Roman soldiers and officials pinned their cloaks with a 'crossbow' brooch as part of their uniform, a status-symbol which, like silver plate and gold 'medallions', might be presented to them by the Emperor. The *Vota* were the ancient ceremony of vows paid and renewed for each 5 or 10 years of power and prosperity, the celebration of an imperial anniversary like a modern Jubilee, when 'donatives' in cash, plate and jewellery, were presented to the army and officials. This brooch marks Diocletian's *vicennalia* which he celebrated in Rome on 20 November AD 303, the twentieth anniversary (by inclusive reckoning) of his accession in 284. His title *Iovius* identified Jupiter as his heavenly patron, just as Hercules was Maximian's (*Herculius*); it was a tactful expression of their relationship, which a contemporary panegyrist likens to that of 'Jupiter, ruler of the heavens, and Hercules, pacifier of the earth'.[16]

Constantine and his sons

Diocletian's health broke down a few weeks later, and after a partial recovery he abdicated in AD 305 in favour of Galerius. He forced Maximian in the west to abdicate as well, and Constantius was promoted to the vacant post of western *Augustus*. That summer, accompanied by his son Constantine – and Fortunatus – he returned to Britain after 9 years, to fight the Picts in the north. But Fortunatus' brooch was not the only casualty. In July AD 306 Constantius himself died at York, like Septimius Severus almost a century before. His army, confident that it was the western mobile reserve, did not wait for the approval of Constantius' surviving colleague, the formidable but far-distant Galerius in Sardica (Sofia), but immediately proclaimed Constantius' son *Augustus*.[17] The last imperial inscriptions from Britain are the fifteen or so milestones of Constantine, including this early one which we have just seen in another guise:

<14.09> *Gallows Hill, Carlisle (Luguvalium)*

Fl(avio) Val(erio)
Cons-
ant[i]-
no nob(ilissimo)
Caes(ari)

RIB 2292

'For Flavius Valerius Constantine, most noble Caesar.'

It is Carausius' old milestone (**14.03**), which was now reversed (thereby preserving his text) and given a new inscription on the other end. Galerius did not recognise

[16] *Pan. Lat.* x (ii), 11.6, *Ioue rectore caeli et Hercule pacatore terrarum* (trans. Nixon and Rodgers).
[17] The seventeenth centenary is celebrated by Hartley, Hawkes, Henig and Mee 2006.

Constantine as *Augustus* (and thus his equal), but he allowed him the subordinate title of *Caesar*, which Constantine dutifully accepted for the moment. But a contemporary milestone from the northern frontier emphasises his dynastic claim to be full Emperor:

<14.10> *the Stanegate one mile east of Vindolanda*

imp(eratori) Caes(ari)
Flav(io) Val(erio)
Constantino
Pio Fel(ici) nob(ilissimo)
Caesari
divi
Constanti
Pii Aug(usti)
filio

RIB 2303

'For the Emperor Caesar Flavius Valerius Constantine, Pius Felix, most noble Caesar, son of the deified Constantius, Pius Augustus.'

Constantine, like an early German king, also gave inscribed gold rings to loyal followers. At least 16 are known from the Rhine and Danube provinces, and two from Britain:

<14.11> *Caistor St Edmund (Venta Icenorum)*

Constant(ino) fides

RIB II.3, 2422.4

'Loyalty to Constantine'

The ring has only 11 facets, so the engraver crammed two pairs of letters onto two facets and curtailed *Constantino*, but it can be completed from the Continental rings inscribed *Fides Constantini* or *Fidem Constantino*. A second example was found in Kent, but is now lost.[18]

A number of milestones soon advertise Constantine as full Emperor (*Augustus*), the most complete being this long slab found in a Roman well, broken into three pieces:

[18] *RIB* II.7, 2422.7.

<**14.12**> *Caves Inn, Warwicks.*

imp(eratori) C(aesari)
Fl(avio) Val(erio)
Consta-
ntino
Pio Fel(ici)
in(victo) Aug(usto)
divi
Consta-
nti Pii
Aug(usti)
fil(io)

RIB III, 3521

'For the Emperor Caesar Flavius Valerius Constantine, Pius Felix Unconquered Augustus, son of the deified Constantius, Pius Augustus.'

Constantine, although by now a believer in the One God, nonetheless deified his father. This convention continued among his Christian successors: Gratian and Thedosius, for example, although they both repudiated the supreme religious title of *pontifex maximus* which Constantine had retained, also deified their fathers. The poet Ausonius, although he was a Christian too, congratulates Gratian for following God's advice in deifying his father Valentinian.[19]

Britain, for all its early loyalty to Constantine, receded into the background of his divinely inspired self-aggrandisement. John Casey demonstrated from the coinage that he returned in AD 312, briefly, since he invaded Italy the same summer and overthrew his western rival Maxentius, Maximian's son, at the battle of the Milvian Bridge. This British visit may have been to withdraw troops, including the garrisons of the outpost forts of Hadrian's Wall.[20] Before the battle Constantine experienced his legendary 'vision', and the ensuing victory convinced him that he was the earthly agent of the Christian God. In AD 324, after eliminating his last rival, the eastern Emperor Licinius, he wrote to his new provinces that he was come to relieve them of their burdens: 'Beginning from the British sea and the places where the sun is bound to set, I have dispersed all prevailing evils, so as to educate the human race and inspire it to the service of the Most Holy Law.'[21]

This very muscular Christian was the second founder, after Diocletian, of the Late Empire. His officials and soldiers assumed his inherited name *Flavius* to mark their status, a fashion that lasted for centuries. This may be reason to date an enigmatic tombstone from the Lake District to the fourth century:

19 Ausonius, *Grat. Act.* 10, *(Dei) auctoritati obsecutus, scilicet ut in consecrando patre.*
20 Casey 1978, 190.
21 *Letter to the Provincials* in Eusebius, *Life of Constantine* ii 28.

<14.13> *Ambleside (Galava)*

D(is) B(onis) M(anibus)
Fla(vius) Fuscinus eme(ritus)
ex ordi(nato) visi<t>(!) an<n>is LV
D(is) B(onis) M(anibus)
Fla(vius) Romanus act(arius)
vixit anni<s> XXXV
in cas(tris) ?int(er)f(ecti) ab hosti(bus)

RIB III, 3218

'To the Divine Good Shades. Flavius Fuscinus, retired centurion, lived 55 years. To the Divine Good Shades. Flavius Romanus, record-clerk, lived 35 years. Killed in the fort by enemies.'

The lettering seems 'late', and so is the usage of *ordinatus* for 'centurion'. The initial D B M is a very unusual variant of D M, and its expansion is conjectural. This is the only instance of *visit* for *vixit* from Britain, though it is quite common in Italian epitaphs; in Britain it is more usual to emphasise the [ks] sound by writing *vicsit* or *vixsit*. The extreme abbreviation of the epitaph makes it enigmatic: we cannot tell whether only the son was killed, *int(er)f(ectus)*, or whether both father and son were killed together, *int(er)f(ecti)*, which seems more likely. But were they 'murdered' by (private) enemies – think of the 'Murder House' at Housesteads, where two skeletons were found under the floor, one of them with a sword-point still between its ribs – or were they 'killed' by enemy action? The term *hostes* is more often used of external enemies, which may also be implied by the mention of the 'fort' with its tacit admission of frontier insecurity, but perhaps the tedium of barrack-room life had flared up into a murderous quarrel.

The Empire was divided again after Constantine died (AD 337), among his three sons, but the eldest was soon displaced by his youngest brother Constans as sole western emperor. Constans' visit to Britain in the winter of AD 342/3 impressed contemporary panegyrists: 'the unexpected sight of the Emperor made the British tremble'.[22] This was the last-ever imperial visit, and it was celebrated by a large bronze coin, a 'medallion' which looks like a cheap copy of his grandfather's (**14.04**). Constans as a warrior preceded by Victory bestrides another oared galley, between the two words of the caption:

---

22 Firmicus Maternus, *de errore profanarum religionum* 28.6, *insperatam faciem Britannus expavit*. Libanius, *or.* 59, 139–41.

<14.14> *minted at Rome*

Bononia Oceanen

RIC VIII Rome, p. 283, No. 338

'(From) Boulogne to the Ocean.'

We know independently[23] that Constans was in Boulogne on 25 January AD 343, but the only hint of his presence in Britain is a lead sealing found in the Thames at London. Like a coin-portrait, his head wears a laurel wreath:

<14.15> *London (Londinium)*

Constans P(ius) F(elix) Aug(ustus)

RIB II.1, 2411.23

The reason for this flying visit is not known, but the historian Ammianus Marcellinus hints at trouble beyond Hadrian's Wall.[24] In AD 350 Constans was overthrown by one of his generals, Magnentius, who is said to have been half-British by birth. After the civil war that ensued, Constantius II, the last surviving son of Constantine, appointed his cousin Julian to be *Caesar* in Gaul, but only as a figurehead.

Julian

Julian, whose first language was Greek, despite having studied philosophy at the university of Athens turned out to be surprisingly successful as an amateur general. Against the odds, his army defeated the German invaders of Gaul in AD 357; and two years later at Paris, while his senior general Lupicinus was conveniently absent in Britain, this army defied Constantius by proclaiming Julian *Augustus*. He is the first emperor known to have given one-pound silver ingots as an accession donative; and some 15 of these, though not precisely dated, have been found in Britain. They are typically of 'double-axe' shape, and here is one found in an early fifth-century silver hoard at Canterbury. It bears an abbreviated but official legend:

<14.16> *Canterbury (Durovernum Cantiacorum)*

(ex) of(ficina) Leo(nis)
Tr(everis) p(u)s(ulati)
p(ondo) I

---

23 *Cod. Theod.* xi 16.5.

24 Ammianus Marcellinus xxviii 3.8 refers to the *areani* in connection with Constans, their duty being intelligence-gathering beyond the frontier.

RIB II.1, 2402.9

'(From) the workshop of Leo at Trier, one (pound) weight of refined silver.'

Like the gold 'medallion' of Constantius (**14.04**), this ingot was produced by the mint at Trier, which was divided into 'workshops' that signed their work to allow it to be checked. This ingot would have passed: it weighs 321.5 g (the Roman pound in theory was 327.4 g), and is almost pure silver (98.6%, with a trace of gold). A solid silver bar was cheaper to make and more convenient as a store of value than 60 silver coins: think of Winston Churchill as a cavalry subaltern in British India, paid every month a string net bag full of rupees 'as big as a prize turnip'.[25]

Julian, a closet pagan, was uneasy at the example set by his charismatic uncle, but like Constantine he quickly turned his back upon Britain. In AD 361 he left Gaul to confront his cousin in the East, a campaign blandly misrepresented by this inscription now built into the walls of the citadel at Ankara:

<**14.17**> Ankara (Ancyra)

domino totius orbis
Iuliano Augusto
ex Oceano Britannico vi<i>s per
barbaras gentes
strage resistenti-
um patefactis adus-
que Tigridem una
aestate transvec-
to, Saturninius
Secundus v(ir) c(larissimus) [praef(ectus)]
praet(orio) [d(evotus)] n(umini) m(aiestati)
[q(ue)]

ILS 754

'To the Lord of the Whole World, Julian Augustus, who has travelled from the British Ocean to the Tigris in a single summer, by opening the roads through barbarian tribes and slaughtering those who resisted, (from) Saturninius Secundus, senator and praetorian prefect, devoted to his divinity and majesty.'

[25] Churchill 1930, ch. 8.

Despite the 'literary' language, the correct form *viis* ('roads') has been contracted to *vis*: the two identical vowels tended to fuse together in pronunciation, just as *Diis Manibus* is almost always *Dis Manibus*, although there is a visual hint of the second *i* in Classicianus' epitaph (**2.19**) and still more of it in Candidus' epitaph at Brecon Gaer (**3.08**). The Ancyra inscription is dedicated by Julian's praetorian prefect, but after Constantine disbanded the Praetorian Guard for supporting Maxentius, the praetorian prefect no longer had troops to command; indeed he ceased to be the virtual commander-in-chief, as Asclepiodotus had been for Constantius, but he retained great prestige as the head of the civil hierarchy. Despite his bloodthirsty text, Secundus was entirely a civilian; not only an elderly and experienced administrator, but also a pagan intellectual who became a personal friend of Julian. When he spoke of Julian crossing the Roman world from end to end, he was referring to mutiny and rebellion: after his proclamation, Julian had marched to the Rhine and across the Black Forest, then sailed down the Danube and was poised to invade Thrace when Constantius II (aged only 44) died suddenly of natural causes. The mention of the British Ocean is an unconscious echo of Constantine's letter to the eastern provinces quoted after **14.12**; Julian likewise saw himself as the instrument of the divine purpose, but with this difference: the gods wanted him to restore the old polytheism and modernise it according to Greek philosophical ideas. With the doubtful exception of the Cirencester inscription (**14.07**), the only mark he has left on the epigraphy of Roman Britain is four lead sealings, found near a villa in Kent:

<**14.18**> *Ickham, Kent*

d(ominus) n(oster) Iulianus Aug(ustus)

RIB II.1, 2411.25–28

'Our Lord Julian Augustus.'

This reading is a composite of the four sealings, which are all damaged. Their reverse shows a standing horse captioned S | RVF, which is presumably the abbreviated name of an official. Julian's 'pagan revival' ended almost at once with his fatal invasion of Persia in AD 363. He advanced down the Euphrates but was unable to reduce the Persian capital of Ctesiphon (near modern Baghdad), and was forced to make a fighting retreat up the Tigris until he was killed in a skirmish. The army offered to proclaim Saturninius Secundus (**14.17**), but he refused, and after the brief reign of Jovian, Julian was succeeded by a handsome, choleric guards officer called Valentinian (AD 364–75), a Christian like Jovian, who established himself in Gaul, first at Paris and then at the old capital of Trier. From here he overhauled the western Empire's frontier defences for the last time.

Valentinian and Count Theodosius

Valentinian's preoccupation with the Rhine was interrupted in AD 367 by an obscure episode in Britain known as the Barbarian Conspiracy, the phrase applied by Ammianus Marcellinus to a concerted attack by its external enemies which coincided with internal disaffection.[26] Order was restored by a vigorous general called Theodosius, whom modern writers call Count Theodosius, not only because he was a *comes* commanding mobile troops but to distinguish him from his son the Emperor (AD 379–95), whose accession is why Theodosius' career was lavishly commemorated after his death. Statues erected at Rome and Antioch are known only from contemporary allusions, but the base of another survives in southern Italy:

<14.19> *Canosa (Canusium)*

inclytae venerand<a>e-
que memoriae viro
Flavio Theodosio
genitori domini
nostri invictissimi
perennisque principis
Theodosi perpetui Aug(usti),
cuius virtute felicita-
te iustitia et propaga-
tus terrarum orbis et
retentus, statuam
equestrem subaura-
tam Apuli et Calabri
pro voto et devotio-
ne posuerunt,
curante ac perficien-
te Flavio Sexione
viro perfectissimo,
correctore Apuliae
et Calabriae

ILS 780

'To Flavius Theodosius, a man of glorious and admirable memory, father of Our Lord the Most Unconquered and Eternal Emperor Theodosius, Perpetual Augustus, by whose valour, success and justice the world has been extended and preserved; the Apulians and Calabrians have erected a gilded equestrian statue out of respect and loyalty, (a project) supervised and completed by the Most Perfect Flavius Sexio, Governor of Apulia and Calabria.'

[26] Tomlin 1974.

It is hardly surprising that the Apulians and Calabrians forbore to mention that Theodosius had been executed (even if unjustly) for treason, but they also provide no details of his career.[27] Their flatulent text is no worse than many fourth-century honorific inscriptions, for example an African dedication in honour of Valentinian's own father Gratianus, which likewise omits to mention that he had been a general in Britain,[28] but they compare badly with the crisp and informative career-inscriptions of the Early Empire. Theodosius was honoured with a fourth statue at Stobi, in what is now the Republic of Macedonia. Apart from a fragment from Rome which honours someone who had apparently been governor of Britain,[29] this completes the sum of career-inscriptions from the last 150 years of Roman Britain. The marble base of Theodosius' gilded statue was broken in two when it was re-used to build a church colonnade, so that two columns 0.50 m thick now cover much of the text; here is the upper half:

<14.20> *Stobi, Macedonia*

[Φλάβιον Θ]εοδόϲ-
[ιον τὸν θεῖον πατ]έρα
6 lines lost
[...] χάρμα
μέγα Βριτανῶν καὶ
Μαυριτανίηϲ μέγα δῖ-
μα, Σαξονείηϲ λυτῆ-
ρα καὶ γένουϲ Κελτῶν
ὀλετῆρα, χρυϲίον ...

Feissel 1983, 228–30, No. 273

'[Flavius Th]eodos[ius, deified father of the Emperor Theodosius...], great joy of the Britons and great terror of Mauretania, conqueror of Saxony and destroyer of the race of Celts, a golden [statue ...]'

The lower half, which is still more damaged, implies that the statue greeted visitors 'at the gates'. The text is metrical, which increases the difficulty of extracting any real information.[30] By 'Celts', the author like other late-Roman Greek writers means Germans, but he does not say whether they attacked Britain in AD 367, or figured in some unknown campaign on the lower Rhine. 'Mauretania' refers to Theodosius' last campaign, the brutal but effective suppression of a tribal uprising in what is

27 *PLRE* s.v. *Theodosius* 3.
28 *ILS* 758 (Constantina, now in Algeria). He commanded the British army with the rank of *comes* (Ammianus Marcellinus xxx 7.3).
29 *CIL* vi 1223, *[praes]es provinciae Brittanni[ae]*.
30 Well analysed by Birley 2005, 431, who also collects the literary evidence (for which see also Nixon and Rodgers 1994, 517–19).

now western Algeria. It is narrated by Ammianus Marcellinus, who previously refers to him in Britain 'rebuilding towns and forts', and 'protecting the frontiers with garrisons and outposts', but well-dated archaeological evidence is hard to find.[31] Epigraphically the best candidate is the one inscription which survives from the towers built on the headlands of the North Yorkshire coast:

<14.21> *Ravenscar, near Scarborough*

Iustinianus p(rae)p(ositus)
Vindicianus
magister turr<e>-
m castrum fecit
a so(lo)

RIB 721

'Justinianus, officer in charge; Vindicianus, Master, made (this) tower (and) fort from ground-level.'

The Ravenscar tower has not survived, but those which have been excavated are typical late-Roman *burgi* consisting of a square tower inside a walled enclosure, here correctly described as *turrem (et) castrum*. Neither this inscription nor the archaeology enables us to date them very closely, but they are likely to have been a response to the Barbarian Conspiracy. If so, this inscription is the last record on stone of the Roman army in Britain, and it is one of the worst. The syntax is better ignored, with its omission of *et* and the use of singular *fecit* with two subjects, but the letters are quite as crude as any 'centurial stone', and the stone-cutter seems to have been illiterate; certainly he misunderstood the draft in front of him, or perhaps what had been chalked on the slab, for in line 3 what he actually cut was MASBIERIVRR, gibberish due to his confusing G with S (as modern scholars sometimes do with Roman graffiti), confusing IS with B, and T (twice) with I. Justinianus' title of *praepositus* simply means that he was 'in charge' of something, a military unit or perhaps a 'sector': the post of *praepositus limitis* is attested on the late-Roman frontier in Africa. Vindicianus' title of *magister* sounds important, but he was quite a junior officer: a 'master' deputised for the centurion Iasucthanus in rebuilding the gate at Bu Njem.[32]

A distinctive group of building inscriptions from Hadrian's Wall has also been attributed to Count Theodosius, for example this pair:

---

[31] Ammianus Marcellinus xxviii 3.2 (*restituit civitates et castra*) and 7 (*urbes et praesidaria (ut diximus) castra limitesque vigiliis tuebatur et praetenturis*).

[32] *AE* 1995, 164, cited before **13.12**.

<14.22> *west of Carvoran (Magnis)*

civitas
Dum<no>ni(orum)

civitas
Dumnoni(orum)

RIB 1843 and 1844

'The canton of the Dumnonii (built this).'

They resemble 'centurial stones', but this would be a misnomer, for the Dumnonii were civilians and lived as far from the Wall as any tribe could, in what is now south Somerset, Devon and Cornwall. This group names two other southern tribes, the Catuvellauni and the Durotriges (or Durotrages), and perhaps the Brigantes in the north.[33] That they were tribal corvées levied by Theodosius to patch up the Wall was suggested by the legendary Oxford don C E Stevens, shortly before he turned his attention to fabricating 'black' propaganda for the Political Warfare Executive.[34] It remains one of his brilliant guesses, but the evidence is insufficient: Gildas may say that the Wall was built 'at public and private expense', but Gildas was writing sermonising fiction; and although the Notitia Dignitatum illustrates the *vicarius* (governor-general) of Britain uniquely with an icon of fortified towns, all the *vicarii* actually known to us are civilians. The date of this 'direction of labour', whether forced or not, is unknown; it is best discussed by David Breeze, who notes that there was a shortage of manpower in the reign of Marcus Aurelius.[35]

The last rulers of Roman Britain

In the course of rebutting Pelagius, who came from Britain, St Jerome coined a famous phrase when he said that Britain was 'a province fertile in usurpers.'[36] Classicists will be reminded of Housman dismissing a previous editor of Manilius who came from Strasbourg, 'a city still famous for its geese.' Housman's lapidary phrases are irrelevant to the epigraphy of Roman Britain, but further quotation is irresistible: 'Stoeber's mind, though that is no name to call it by, was one which turned as unswervingly to the false, the meaningless, the unmetrical, and the ungrammatical, as the needle to the pole.'[37] The quality of Gildas' research can be checked here too, for he quotes Jerome's phrase but attributes it to the 'mad dog' pagan philosopher Porphyry,

33 *RIB* 1962 (Catuvellauni); 1672, 1673 and III, 3376 (Durotriges or Durotrages); 2022 (BRICIC).
34 Stevens 1941, 359. Noted by *RIB*, and largely accepted by Frere 1987, 343.
35 Breeze 2012(c).
36 Jerome, *ep.* 133.9.19, *fertilis provincia tyrannorum*.
37 Housman 1903, *Preface*.

whom Jerome has just cited but for something else.[38] Jerome was writing in AD 415, unaware that there was no longer an actual province of Britain, but he would have been right to attribute this discontinuity not to barbarian conquest, but to a series of failed usurpations. The first is that of the absurdly named Magnus Maximus, 'Greatest Great', a Spanish kinsman of Count Theodosius, who was commanding troops in Britain when he rebelled in AD 383 against Valentinian's son Gratian. After displacing him as western emperor, he provoked a civil war with the eastern Empire by invading Italy; several milestones survive from his short-lived occupation:

<14.23> *near Brescia (Brixia)*

d(ominis) n(ostris)
Magno Ma-
ximo et F[l(avio)] Vic-
tori invic-
tis et perpetuis
Augus-
tis b(ono) r(ei) p(ublicae) n(atis)
IIIIII

ILS 788

'For Our Lords Magnus Maximus and Flavius Victor, Unconquered and Eternal Augusti, born for the good of the Commonwealth, 6 (miles).'

Victor was Maximus' son. Maximus is said to have hanged one of Gratian's generals in his own home 'by the hands of his British henchmen.'[39] Like Constantine he undoubtedly withdrew troops from Britain, even if not to the extent of the embattled Wall evoked by Kipling.[40] A generation later, in AD 407, there was still an army in Britain to proclaim a common soldier who had an auspicious name, Constantine III. By now the epigraphy of Roman Britain is dead, but here is a disturbing revenant. It is the very last inscription to name a soldier of Roman Britain, even if he was now an emperor. It is the Christian Greek epitaph of a teenaged girl from Syria:

<14.24> *Trier (Augusta Treverorum)*

ἔνθα κεῖτε Εὐϲεβία ἐν εἰρ-
ίνι, οὖϲα ἱερο<κο>μητὶ ἀπὼ κ-
ώμηϲ Ἀδδανων, ζῆϲαϲ
μικρόπροϲ έτων ιέ, ὑιπατ-
ὶᾳ Ὀνωρίου ὁ ή καὶ Κωϲτιοντί-

[38] Gildas, *De Excidio* 4.3.
[39] *Pan. Lat.* ii (xii) (Pacatus), 28.4, *manibus satellitum Britannorum*.
[40] Kipling 1906, 'The Winged Hats'.

νου τὸ ά, μηνὶ Πανήμου
ιβ, ἡμέρᾳ κιρ(ιακῃ) ἐν εἰρίνῃ

RICG I, 93

'Here lies Eusebia in peace, being ... from the village of Addana, having lived about 15 years; in the eighth consulship of Honorius (AD 409) and the first of Constantine, on the 12th of the month of Panemos (June), on the Lord's Day. In peace.'

The original was lost in 1674 when the church of St Paulinus was destroyed, but transcriptions survive from which most of the text can be recovered. Eusebia is uniquely described as ἱερομητὶ, a word of unknown meaning. Her village is not the Turkish city of Adana, but Adana (or Addana) in Syria, since the month of death is according to the Syrian calendar. But from a British point of view the interest of her epitaph lies in the consular date. AD 409 was really the joint-consulship of Honorius (for the eighth time) and his cousin Theodosius II (for the third time), but Constantine III awarded himself the consulship, without daring to displace his rival Honorius. In this he was like Carausius, who struck coins of himself 'and his brothers' (*et fratres sui*) Diocletian and Maximian. However, his consulship was recognised only in Britain and Gaul, and this epitaph is the only epigraphic evidence. Constantine himself was then in Gaul with mobile forces drawn from Britain, trying to restore Roman control after the German invasion at the end of AD 405, but in his absence the cities of Britain rebelled and expelled his officials.[41] This revolt is conventionally dated to AD 410, and its sixteenth centenary was duly celebrated in 2010. Next year, in AD 411, Constantine succumbed to Honorius' generals, but the central government never re-established its authority in Britain, so the successful rebellion of the Britons against Constantine may be taken as the formal end of Roman Britain.

St Jerome, as we have seen, did not know that Roman Britain had ended. Nor did the pagan poet Rutilius Namatianus in AD 417, when he stayed with his friend Victorinus on his estate in Tuscany; Victorinus had been governor-general (*vicarius*) of Britain, and a good one:

'True, the place is remote, the edge of the world,
But he governed it as if it were the centre.
More credit to him, for seeking approval
Of men whose disapproval hardly matters.'[42]

41 The difficult chronology is elucidated by Kulikowski 2000.

42 *De Reditu Suo* 503–6 (fully discussed by Birley 2005, 453–5), *extremum pars illa quidem discessit in orbem, | sed tamquam medio rector in orbe fuit. | plus palmae est illos inter voluisse placere, | inter quos minor est displicuisse pudor.*

BIBLIOGRAPHY AND ABBREVIATIONS

Adams, J N 2003 'The word *moritix* in a new inscription from London', *ZPE* 143, 275–6

AE L'Année Épigraphique

AJP American Journal of Philology

Alföldy, G 1986 'Latinische Bürger in Brigantium und im Imperium Romanum', *Bayerische Vorgeschichtsblätter* 51, 187–220

Alföldy, G 1988 'Ein Soldat des britannischen Heeres aus Madauros (*ILAlg* I 2203)', in A Mastino (ed.), *L'Africa romana* 6 (Sassari, Sardinia), 135–45

Alföldy, G and Halfmann, H 1973 'M. Cornelius Nigrinus Curiatius Maternus, General Domitians und Rivale Trajans', *Chiron* 3, 331–73

Allason-Jones, L and McKay, B 1985 *Coventina's Well: a shrine on Hadrian's Wall* (Gloucester)

Ammianus Marcellinus, *Res Gestae*

Augustus, *Res Gestae* (ed. Cooley 2009)

Austen, P S 1991 *Bewcastle and Old Penrith: a Roman outpost fort and a frontier vicus: excavations 1977–78* (Kendal)

Austin, N J E and Rankov, N B 1995 *Exploratio: Military and Political Intelligence in the Roman World from the Second Punic War to the Battle of Adrianople* (London)

Barrett, A A 1978 'Knowledge of the Literary Classics in Roman Britain', *Britannia* 9, 307–13

Barrett, A A 1991 'Claudius' British Victory Arch in Rome', *Britannia* 22, 1–19

Bastien, P and Metzger, C 1977 *Le trésor de Beaurains, dit d'Arras* (Arras)

Bede, *Historia Ecclesiastica*

Benson, E F 1920 *Our Family Affairs, 1867–1896* (London)

Bérard, F, Cogitore, I and Tarpin, M 1998 'Une nouvelle inscription claudienne à Lyon', in Burnand, Y, le Bohec, Y and Martin, J-P (eds), *Claude de Lyon: empereur romain* (Paris), 373–89

Bidwell, P T (ed.) 2008(a) *Understanding Hadrian's Wall: papers from a conference held at South Shields, 3rd–5th November, 2006, to mark the publication of the 14th ed. of the Handbook to the Roman Wall* (South Shields)

Bidwell, P T 2008(b) 'Did Hadrian's Wall have a Wall-walk?' in Bidwell 2008(a), 129–43

Bidwell, P 2014 'The Roman names of the fort at South Shields and an altar to the Di Conservatores', in Collins, R and McIntosh, F (eds), *Life on the Limes: Studies of the people and objects of the Roman frontiers presented to Lindsay Allason-Jones on the occasion of her birthday and retirement* (Oxford), 49–58

Bidwell, P and Hodgson, N 2009 *The Roman Army in Northern England* (Newcastle upon Tyne)

Bird, J 1974 'Godalming: Serendipity at Busbridge Park (SU 968422)', *Surrey Archaeological Collections* 70, 154

Bird, J, Hassall, M and Sheldon, H (eds) 1996 *Interpreting Roman London: Papers in memory of Hugh Chapman* (Oxford)

Birley, E 1961(a) *Roman Britain and the Roman Army: Collected Papers* (Kendal, 2nd ed.)

Birley, E 1961(b) *Research on Hadrian's Wall* (Kendal)

Birley, E 1967 'Troops from the two Germanies in Roman Britain', *Epigraphische Studien* 4 (1967), 103–7 (E Birley 1988, 251–5)
Birley, A R 1973 'Petillius Cerialis and the Conquest of Brigantia', *Britannia* 4, 179–90
Birley, A R 1979 *The People of Roman Britain* (London)
Birley, E 1983 'A Roman altar from Old Kilpatrick and interim commanders of auxiliary units', *Latomus* 42, 73–83 (E Birley 1988, 221–31)
Birley, E 1986 'The Deities of Roman Britain', in Temporini, H and Haase, W (eds), *Aufstieg und Niedergang der römischen Welt* (Berlin–New York) II, 18.2, 3–112
Birley, E 1988(a) *The Roman Army: Papers 1929–1986* (Amsterdam)
Birley, A R 1988(b) 'Names at Lepcis Magna', *Libyan Studies* 19, 1–19
Birley, A R 1988(c) *The African Emperor: Septimius Severus* (London)
Birley, A R 1997 *Hadrian. The restless emperor* (London – New York)
Birley, A R 2002 *Garrison Life at Vindolanda: a Band of Brothers* (Stroud)
Birley, A R 2003 'The commissioning of equestrian officers', in Wilkes 2003, 1–18
Birley, A R 2005 *The Roman Government of Britain* (Oxford)
Birley, A R 2007 'The inscriptions', in Birley, A and Blake, J, *Vindolanda Excavations 2005–2006* (Vindolanda Trust), 101–13
Birley, A R 2008(a) 'Some Germanic deities and their worshippers in the British frontier zone', in Börm, H, Ehrhardt, N and Wiesehöfer, J (eds), *Monumentum et instrumentum inscriptum, Beschriftete Objekte aus Kaiserzeit und Spätantike als historische Zeugnisse: Festschrift für Peter Weiß zum 65 Geburtstag* (Franz Steiner Verlag), 31–46
Birley, A R 2008(b) 'Britain: the Caesarian and Claudian invasions', in Piso, I (ed.), *Die Römischen Provinzen. Begriff und Gründung (Colloquium Cluj–Napoca, 28. September – 1. Oktober 2006)* (Cluj–Napoca), 179–205
Birley, R 2009 *Vindolanda: a Roman frontier fort on Hadrian's Wall* (Stroud)
Birley, A R 2011 '*RIB* III in its historical context', *Journal of Roman Archaeology* 24, 679–96
Birley, A R 2012 'The *cohors I Hamiorum* in Britain', *Acta Classica* 55, 1–16
Birley, A and Birley, A 2010 'A Dolichenum at Vindolanda', *Archaeologia Aeliana* 5th ser. 39, 25–51
Bishop, M C (ed.) 2002 *Roman Inveresk: Past, Present and Future* (Edinburgh)
Bivona, L 1970 *Iscrizioni latine lapidarie del Museo di Palermo* (Palermo)
BMCRE IV Mattingly, H *Coins of the Roman Empire in the British Museum*, IV, Antoninus Pius to Commodus (London 1940)
Bogaers, J E 1979 'King Cogidumnus in Chichester: Another Reading of *RIB* 91', *Britannia* 10, 243–54
Boon, G C 1977 'A Greco-Roman anchor-stock from North Wales', *Antiquaries Journal* 57, 10–30
Boon, G C 1983 'Potters, Oculists and Eye-Troubles', *Britannia* 14, 1–12
Boon, G C 1989 'A Roman Sculpture Rehabilitated: The Pagans Hill Dog', *Britannia* 20, 201–17
Bowman, A K 2006 'Outposts of empire: Vindolanda, Egypt, and the empire of Rome' *Journal of Roman Archaeology* 19, 75–93
Bowman, A K 1994 *Life and Letters on the Roman Frontier: Vindolanda and its People* (London)
Bowman, A K, and Thomas, J D 1983 *Vindolanda: the Latin Writing-Tablets* (London)
Bowman, A K, and Thomas, J D 1994 *The Vindolanda Writing-Tablets*, II (London)
Bowman, A K and Thomas, J D 2003 *The Vindolanda Writing-Tablets*, III (London)
Bowman, A K, Thomas, J D and Tomlin, R S O 2010 'The Vindolanda writing-tablets (*Tabulae Vindolandenses* IV, Part 1)', *Britannia* 41, 187–224
Bowman, A K, Thomas, J D and Tomlin, R S O 2011 'The Vindolanda writing-tablets (*Tabulae Vindolandenses* IV, Part 2)', *Britannia* 42, 113–44
Breeze, D J 1969 'The organization of the legion: the first cohort and the *equites legionis*', *Journal of Roman Studies* 59, 50–55 (Breeze and Dobson 1993, 65–70)

Breeze, D J 1974 'The organisation of the career structure of the immunes and principales of the Roman army', *Bonner Jahrbücher* 174, 245–92 (Breeze and Dobson 1993, 11–58)

Breeze, D J 1989 'The flag of legion II Augusta on the Bridgeness distance slab', *Proceedings of the Society of Antiquaries of Scotland* 119, 133–42 (Breeze and Dobson 1993, 78–87)

Breeze, D J (ed.) 2006 Bruce, J Collingwood, *Handbook to the Roman Wall* (14th ed., Newcastle)

Breeze, D J 2009 'Did Hadrian design Hadrian's Wall?' *Archaeologia Aeliana* 5th ser. 38, 87–103

Breeze, D J 2011 'Burnswark: Roman Siege or Army Training Ground?', *Archaeological Journal* 168, 166–80

Breeze, D J (ed.) 2012(a) *The First Souvenirs: Enamelled Vessels from Hadrian's Wall* (Kendal)

Breeze, D J (ed.) 2012(b) 'The end of Roman Newstead', in Hunter and Keppie 2012, 117–21

Breeze, D J 2012(c) 'The *Civitas* Stones and the Building of Hadrian's Wall', *Transactions of the Cumberland and Westmoreland Antiquarian and Archaeological Society* 3rd ser. 12, 69–80

Breeze, D J and Dobson, B 1993 *Roman Officers and Frontiers* (Stuttgart)

Breeze, D J, Dobson, B and Maxfield, V 2012 'Maenius Agrippa, a chronological conundrum', *Acta Classica* 55, 17–30

Brown, P 1971 *The World of Late Antiquity: From Marcus Aurelius to Muhammad* (London)

Bruce, J Collingwood 1863 *Handbook to the Roman Wall* (Newcastle), now in its 14th ed. (Breeze 2006)

Bruce, J Collingwood 1875 *Lapidarium Septentrionale* (London and Newcastle-upon-Tyne)

Bruun, C and Edmondson, J 2015 *The Oxford Handbook of Roman Epigraphy* (Oxford)

Burn, A R 1969 *The Romans in Britain: an anthology of inscriptions with translations and a running commentary* (2nd ed., Oxford)

Camodeca, G 2006 '*Cura secunda* della *tabula cerata* londinese con la compravendita della *puella Fortunata*', *ZPE* 157, 225–30

Campbell, J B 1984 *The Emperor and the Roman Army, 31 BC–AD 235* (Oxford)

Caruana, I 1987 'A wooden ansate panel from Carlisle', *Britannia* 18, 274–7

Casey, P J 1978 'Constantine the Great in Britain – the evidence of the coinage of the London mint, AD 312–14', in Bird, J, Chapman, H and Clark, J (eds), *Collectanea Londiniensia: Studies in London Archaeology and History Presented to Ralph Merrifield* (London), 180–93

Casey, P J 1994 *Carausius and Allectus: the British Usurpers* (London)

Casey, P J and Hoffmann, B 1998 'Rescue excavations in the *Vicus* of the fort at Greta Bridge, Co. Durham, 1972–4', *Britannia* 29, 111–83

Cheesman, C E A 1998 'Tincomarus Commi filius', *Britannia* 29, 309–15

Christol, M 1977 'La carrière de Traianus Mucianus et l'origine des *protectores*', *Chiron* 7, 393–408

Christol, M, Drew-Bear, T and Taşlialan, M 2001 'L'empereur Claude, le chevalier C Caristanius Fronto Caesianus Iullus et le culte impériale à Antioche de Pisidie', *Tyche* 16, 1–20

Churchill, W S 1930 *My Early Life: A Roving Commission* (London)

Cicero, *de oratore*

CIL Corpus Inscriptionum Latinarum (1863–)

Clark, K 1977 *The Other Half: a Self-Portrait* (London)

CMRDM Corpus monumentorum religionis dei Meni (Leiden 1971–78)

Cod. Theod. Theodosian Code

Collingwood, R G 1921 'The purpose of the Roman Wall', *The Vasculum* 8, 4–9

Collingwood, R G 1928 'Inscriptions of Roman London', Appendix II of Royal Commission on Historical Monuments, *Roman London* (London), 170–77

Connolly, P 1988 *Tiberius Claudius Maximus: the cavalryman* (Oxford)

Cooley, A E (ed.) 2009 *Res gestae divi Augusti: text, translation and commentary* (Cambridge)

Cooley, A E 2012 *The Cambridge Manual of Latin Epigraphy* (Cambridge)

Cosh, S R 2016 'The Lullingstone mosaic inscription – a parody of Martial?' *Britannia* 47, 262–6

Cotton, H, and Geiger, J 1989 *Masada* II: *the Yigael Yadin excavations 1963–1965: final reports. The Latin and Greek documents* (Jerusalem)

Cruse, A 2004 *Roman Medicine* (Stroud)

CSIR Corpus Signorum Imperii Romani

Dauzat, A and Rostaing, Ch 1978 *Dictionnaire étymologique des noms de lieu en France* (2nd ed., Paris)

Davies, R W 1967 'A note on a recently discovered inscription from Carrawburgh', *Epigraphische Studien* 4, 108–11

Davies, R W 1970 'The Roman military medical service', *Saalburg Jahrbuch* 27, 84–104 (Davies 1989, 209–36)

Davies, R W 1976 '*Singulares* and Roman Britain', *Britannia* 7, 134–44

Davies, R W 1981 'Some military commands from Roman Britain', *Epigraphische Studien* 12, 183–214

Davies, R W 1989 *Service in the Roman Army*, edited by Breeze, D and Maxfield, V (Edinburgh)

Devijver, H 1982 'Die römische Dobrudscha und das römische Britannien', *ZPE* 47, 184–92

Devijver, H 1988 'Les *militiae equestres* de P. Helvius Pertinax', *ZPE* 75, 207–14

Digesta (Justinian), *Digest*

Dio (Cassius Dio), *Roman History*

Diocletian, *Edict of Maximum Prices* (Lauffer 1971)

Diodorus Siculus, *History*

Dobson, B 1978 *Die Primipilares: Entwicklung und Bedeutung, Laufbahnen und Persönlichkeiten eines römischen Offiziersranges* (Cologne)

Dobson, B and Mann, J C 1973 'The Roman Army in Britain and Britons in the Roman Army', *Britannia* 4, 191–205 (Breeze and Dobson 1993, 511–25; Mann 1996, 39–53)

Donaldson, G H 1990 'A Reinterpretation of *RIB* 1912 from Birdoswald', *Britannia* 21, 207–14

Drexhage, H-J 1998 'Die Kontakte zwischen Britannien und Ägypten während der römischen Kaiserzeit', in Kneissl, P and Losemann, V (eds), *Imperium Romanum: Studien zu Geschichte und Rezeption, Festschrift für Karl Christ zum 75 Geburtstag* (Stuttgart), 184–201

Eck, W 2000 'Monumente der Virtus. Kaiser und Heer im Spiegel epigraphische Denkmäler', in Alföldy, G, Dobson, B and Eck, W (eds), *Kaiser, Heer und Gesellschaft in der Römischen Kaiserzeit. Gedenkschrift für Eric Birley* (Stuttgart), 483–96

Eck, W and Pangerl, A 2008 'Das erste Diplom für die Flotte von Britannien aus dem Jahr 93 n. Chr.', *ZPE* 165, 227–31

Eck, W, Pangerl, A and Holder, P 2010 'A diploma for the army of Britain in 132 and Hadrian's return to Rome from the East', *ZPE* 174, 189–200

Edwards, N 2007 *A Corpus of Early Medieval Inscribed Stones and Stone Sculpture in Wales*, II, *South-West Wales* (Cardiff)

Éspérandieu, E 1907–66 *Recueil général des bas-reliefs, statues et bustes de la Gaule romaine* (Paris)

Evetts, L C 1979 *Roman Lettering: a study of the letters of the inscription at the base of the Trajan Column, with an outline of the history of lettering in Britain* (London 1938, first paperback ed.)

Feissel, D 1983 *Recueil des inscriptions chrétiennes de Macédoine, du IIIe au VIe siècle* (Athens)

Fink, R O, Hoey, A S and Snyder, W F (eds) 1940 *The Feriale Duranum* (New Haven)

Fink, R O (ed.) 1971 *Roman Military Records on Papyrus* (American Philological Association)

FIR II *Fontes Iuris Romani Anteiustiniani* II, *Auctores* (Florence 1968)

Firmicus Maternus, *de errore profanarum religionum*

Fishwick, D 1961 'The Imperial Cult in Roman Britain', *Phoenix* 15.3, 159–73

Fishwick, D 1994 '*Numinibus Aug(ustorum)*', *Britannia* 25, 127–41

Fitzpatrick, A P 2004 'The tombstones and inscribed stones', in Cool, H E M, *The Roman Cemetery at Brougham, Cumbria: Excavations 1966–67* (London), 405–35

Forni, G 1953 *Il Reclutamento delle Legioni da Augusto a Diocleziano* (Milan)

Frankopan, P 2015 *The Silk Roads: A New History of the World* (London)

Frere, S 1987 *Britannia: A History of Roman Britain* (3rd ed., London)

Frere, S and Fulford, M 2001 'The Roman Invasion of A.D. 43', *Britannia* 32, 45–55

Fronto (Cornelius Fronto), *Letters* and *Speeches*

Funari, P P A 1996 *Dressel 20: Inscriptions from Britain and the Consumption of Spanish Olive Oil* (Oxford)

Garstang, J 1904 'Roman Brough: Anavio', *Journal of the Derbyshire Archaeological and Natural Hstory Society* 26, 177–96

Gellius, Aulus, *Noctes Atticae*

Gildas, *De Excidio et Conquestu Britanniae*

Goldsworthy, A 2003 *The Complete Roman Army* (London)

Goodburn, R and Bartholomew, P (eds) 1976 *Aspects of the Notitia Dignitatum* (Oxford)

Gordon, A E 1952 *Quintus Veranius, consul A.D. 49: A Study Based upon His Recently Identified Sepulchral Inscription* (Berkeley and Los Angeles)

Gordon, A E 1968 Review Article: *RIB* I, *Classical Philology* 63, 122–30

Gordon, A E 1983 *Illustrated Introduction to Latin Epigraphy* (Berkeley – London)

Grasby, R 1989 *Lettercutting in Stone* (Oswestry)

Grasby, R D 2013 *Processes in the Making of Roman Inscriptions: Studies* (Oxford)

Grasby, R D and Tomlin, R S O 2002 'The sepulchral monument of the procurator C. Julius Classicianus', *Britannia* 33, 43–75

Graves, R 1934 *Claudius the God* (London)

Grocock, C W (ed.) 2017, *Inscriptions of Roman Britain* (Fifth Edition, fully revised, based on Maxfield and Dobson 2006) (London Association of Classical Teachers)

Habicht, C 1969 *Die Inschriften des Asklepieions* (*Altertümer von Pergamon* viii 3) (Berlin)

Haensch, R 1997 *Capita provinciarum: Statthaltersitze und Provinzialverwaltung in der römischen Kaiserzeit* (Mainz)

Halfmann, H 1982 'Zwei syrische Verwandte des severischen Kaiserhauses', *Chiron* 12, 217–35

Halsberghe, G H 1984 'Le culte de Dea Caelestis', in *Aufstieg und Niedergang der römischen Welt 2, Principat 1* (Berlin–New York), 17.4, 2203–23

Hanson, W S 2012 'Newstead and Roman Scotland: the Flavian to Antonine periods', in Hunter and Keppie 2012, 63–75

Hanson, W S and Conolly, R 2002 'Language and literacy in Roman Britain: some archaeological considerations', in Cooley, A E (ed.), *Becoming Roman, Writing Latin? Literacy and Epigraphy in the Roman West* (Newport, R I), 151–64

Hanson, W and Maxwell, G 1983 *Rome's North West Frontier: the Antonine Wall* (Edinburgh)

Hartley, B R 1972 'The Roman occupation of Scotland: the evidence of samian ware', *Britannia* 3, 1–55

Hartley, E, Hawkes, J, Henig, M and Mee, F (eds) 2006 *Constantine the Great: York's Roman Emperor* (York)

Hassall, M W C 1973 'Roman soldiers in Roman London', in Strong, D E (ed.), *Archaeological Theory and Practice: Essays presented to Professor W F Grimes* (London), 231–7

Hassall, M W C 1978 'Rhine and the Rhine provinces: epigraphic evidence for Roman trade', in du Plat Taylor, J and Cleere, H (eds), *Roman Shipping and Trade* (London), 41–8

Hassall, M W C 1996 'London as a provincial capital', in Bird, Hassall and Sheldon 1996, 19–26

Haynes, I P 1993 'The Romanisation of religion in the *Auxilia* of the Roman Imperial Army from Augustus to Septimius Severus', *Britannia* 24, 141–57

Hayward, K M J 2006 'A geological link between the Facilis monument at Colchester and first-century army tombstones from the Rhineland Frontier', *Britannia* 37, 359–63

Henig, M 1984 *Religion in Roman Britain* (London)

Hind, J G F 1989 'The invasion of Britain in A.D. 43 – an alternative strategy for Aulus Plautius', *Britannia* 20, 1–21

Hind, J G F 2007 'A. Plautius' campaign in Britain: An alternative reading of the narrative in Cassius Dio (60.19.5–21.2)', *Britannia* 38, 93–106

Historia Augusta (Augustan History), *Vitae* (by name of Emperor)

Hodgson, J 1840 *History of Northumberland* (Newcastle upon Tyne) (II.3 is reprinted in facsimile by the Scolar Press, 1974)
Hodgson, N 1995 'Were there two Antonine occupations of Scotland?' *Britannia* 26, 29–49
Hodgson, N 2011 'The provenance of RIB 1389 and the rebuilding of Hadrian's Wall in AD 158', *Antiquaries Journal* 91, 59–71
Hoffmann, D 1969 *Das spätrömische Bewegungsheer und die Notitia Dignitatum* (Düsseldorf)
Holder, P 1980 *Studies in the Auxilia of the Roman Army from Augustus to Trajan* (Oxford)
Horsley, J 1732 *Britannia Romana: or the Roman Antiquities of Britain* (London) (reprinted in facsimile by the Scolar Press, 1974)
Housman, A E (ed.) 1903 *M. Manilii Astronomicon Liber Primus* (London)
Hunter, F and Keppie, L (eds) 2012 *A Roman Frontier Post and its People: Newstead 1911–2011* (Edinburgh)
Hunter, F, Henig, M, Sauer, E and Gooder, J 2016 'Mithras in Scotland: A Mithraeum at Inveresk (East Lothian), *Britannia* 47, 119–68
IDRE Petolescu, C C (ed.) 1996 *Inscriptiones Daciae Romanae Inscriptiones extra fines Daciae repertae* (Bucharest)
IGLS Inscriptions grecques et latines de la Syrie (1929–)
Inscriptiones Italiae IV (Regio IV), Fasc. 1, Tibur (Rome 1952)
ILS Inscriptiones Latinae Selectae (1892–1916)
Inschriften von Ephesos, Die Wankel, H, Engelmann, H and Nollé, J (eds) (Bonn 1977–)
Ireland, S 1986 *Roman Britain: A Sourcebook* (London) (3rd ed. 2008)
IRT Reynolds, J M and Ward Perkins, J B (eds), *Inscriptions of Roman Tripolitania* (Rome and London 1952)
Jackson, R H 1996 'A new Collyrium-stamp from Staines and some thoughts on eye medicine in Roman London and Britannia', in Bird, Hassall and Sheldon 1996, 177–87
Jackson, R and Burleigh, G forthcoming *Dea Senuna: Treasure, Cult and Ritual at Ashwell, Hertfordshire* (British Museum Research Publication 194)
Jarrett, M G 1994 'Non-legionary troops in Roman Britain: Part one, the units', *Britannia* 25, 35–77
Jones, A H M 1964 *The Later Roman Empire 284–602* (Oxford)
Jones, C P 2005 'Ten dedications "To the gods and goddesses" and the Antonine Plague', *Journal of Roman Archaology* 18, 293–301 (with an addendum in 19, 368–9)
JRS Journal of Roman Studies
Juvenal, *Satires*
Kennedy, D 1983 'C. Velius Rufus', *Britannia* 14, 183–96
Kent, J H (ed.) 1966 *Corinth: Results of Excavations conducted by the American School of Classical Studies at Athens*, VIII.3, The Inscriptions 1926–1950 (Princeton)
Keppie, L J F 1971 'Legio VIII Augusta and the Claudian Invasion', *Britannia* 2, 149–55
Keppie, L J F 1979 *Roman Distance Slabs from the Antonine Wall: a Brief Guide* (Glasgow)
Keppie, L J F 1984 *The Making of the Roman Army: from Republic to Empire* (London)
Keppie, L J F 1989 'The fate of the Ninth Legion: a problem for the Eastern Provinces?', in French, D H and Lightfoot, C S (eds), *The Eastern Frontier of the Roman Empire* (Oxford), 247–55 (Keppie 2000(a), 173–81)
Keppie, L 1991 *Understanding Roman Inscriptions* (London)
Keppie, L 1998 *Roman Inscribed and SculpturedSstones in the Hunterian Museum University of Glasgow* (London)
Keppie, L J F 2000(a) *Legions and Veterans: Roman Army Papers 1971–2000* (Stuttgart)
Keppie, L 2000(b) 'Legio VIII in Britain: the Beginning and the End', in Brewer, R J (ed.), *Roman Fortresses and their Legions* (London), 83–100
Keppie, L J F 2009 'The garrison of the Antonine Wall: endangered species or disappearing asset?', in Morillo, A, Hanel, N and Martín, E (eds), *Limes XX: XXth International Congress of Roman Frontier Studies* (Madrid), 1135–45

Keppie, L 2012 *The Antiquarian Rediscovery of the Antonine Wall* (Edinburgh)

Keppie, L J F 2015 (reviser and ed.) *The Antonine Wall: a Handbook to the Surviving Remains* by the late Anne S Robertson (Glasgow)

Kewley, J 1973 'Inscribed capitals on Roman altars from northern Britain', *Archaeologia Aeliana* 5th ser. 1, 129–31

Kipling, R 1906 *Puck of Pook's Hill* (London)

Kipling, R 1937 *Something of Myself: For my Friends Known and Unknown* (London)

Kolendo, J and Bozilova, V (eds) 1997 *Inscriptions grecques et latines de Novae (Mésie Inférieure)* (Paris)

Kropp, A 2008 defixiones: *Ein aktuelles Corpus lateinischer Fluchtafeln* (Speyer)

Kulikowski, M 2000 'Barbarians in Gaul, usurpers in Britain', *Britannia* 31, 325–45

Lauffer, S (ed.) 1971 *Diokletians Preisedikt* (Berlin)

Letta, C 2007 'Caduta e resurrezione di un cavaliere di Ferentino nei difficili inizi del regno di Adriano', in Solin, H (ed.), *Le Epigrafi della Valle di Comino: Atti del terzo convegno epigrafico cominese*, 43–58

Libanius, *orationes*

Liddell, H G and Scott, R (1940, New Edition, reprinted) *A Greek-English Lexicon* (Oxford)

Loriot, X 1997 'Un mythe historiographique: L'Expédition de L. Artorius Castus contre les Armoricains', *Bulletin de la Société nationale des antiquaires de France* 1997, 85–7

Lucan, *Pharsalia*

Macdonald, G 1934 *The Roman Wall in Scotland* (Oxford)

MacMullen, R 1963 *Soldier and Civilian in the Later Roman Empire* (Cambridge (Mass.))

Mann, J C 1974 'The frontiers of the Principate', in Temporini, H and Haase, W (eds), *Aufstieg und Niedergang der römischen Welt* (Berlin–New York) II.1, 508–33 (Mann 1996, 58–83)

Mann, J C 1983 'Trecenarius', *ZPE* 52, 136–40 (Mann 1996, 94–8)

Mann, J C 1984 'A Note on the "Modius Claytonensis"', *Archaeologia Aeliana* 5th ser 12, 242–3 (Mann 1996, 146–7)

Mann, J C 1990 'Hadrian's Wall West of the Irthing: The Role of VI Victrix', *Britannia* 21, 289–92 (Mann 1996, 169–72)

Mann, J C 1993 'Cavalry Promotion at Kirkby Thore', *Britannia* 24, 261–4 (Mann 1996, 54–7)

Mann, J C 1996 *Britain and the Roman Empire* (Variorum Collected Studies)

Maxfield, V A 1981 *The Military Decorations of the Roman Army* (London)

Maxfield, V A and Dobson, B 2006 *Inscriptions of Roman Britain* (LACTOR 4, 4th ed., London)

Merrifield, R 1996 'The London hunter-god and his significance in the history of Londinium', in Bird, Hassall and Sheldon 1996, 105–13

Millar, F G B 1977 *The Emperor in the Roman World (31 B.C.–A.D. 337)* (London)

Mitchell, S 2007 *A History of the Later Roman Empire AD 284–641* (Oxford)

Morton Shand, P 1964 *A Book of French Wines* (revised ed., Cyril Ray) (Harmondsworth)

Murgia, C E 1977 'The minor works of Tacitus: A study in textual criticism', *Classical Philology* 72, 323–43

Nicholson, E W B 1904 *'Vinisius to Nigra': a 4th cent. Christian letter written in south Britain and discovered at Bath* (London)

Nicolson, H 1966 *Diaries and Letters 1930–39* (London)

Nixon, C E V and Rodgers, B S 1994 *In Praise of Later Roman Emperors: the Panegyrici Latini* (Berkeley, Los Angeles, Oxford)

Notitia Dignitatum (ed. Seeck, O 1876)

Ogilvie, R M and Richmond, I A (eds) 1967 *Cornelii Taciti De Vita Agricolae* (Oxford)

Ovid, *Amores*

P. Abinnaeus Bell, H I, Martin, V, Turner, E G and van Berchem, D, *The Abinnaeus Archive: Papers of a Roman Officer in the Reign of Constantius I* (Oxford, 1962)

Painter, K S 1977 *The Water Newton Early Christian Silver* (London)

Pan. Lat. Panegyrici Latini, translated by Nixon and Rodgers 1994

Patricius, *Confessiones*

Peacock, D P S and Williams, D F 1986 *Amphorae and the Roman economy* (London)

Penney, S and Shotter, D C A 1996 'An inscribed Roman salt-pan from Shavington, Cheshire', *Britannia* 27, 360–5

Pferdehirt, B 2004 *Römische Militärdiplome und Entlassungsurkunden in der Sammlung des Römisch-Germanischen Zantralmuseums* (Mainz)

Philp, B 2012 *The Discovery and Excavation of the Roman Saxon Shore Fort at Dover, Kent* (Dover)

PIR[2] *Prosopographia Imperii Romani* (2nd ed., Berlin–New York)

Pitts, L F and St. Joseph, J K 1985 *Inchtuthil: the Roman legionary fortress, Excavations 1952–65* (London)

Pliny (the Elder), *Historia Naturalis*

Pliny (the Younger), *Epistulae*

ps.Plutarch (Aetius), *de placitis philosophorum*

PME Prosopographia Militiarum Equestrium (ed. Devijver, H)

Pointer, J 1724 *Britannia Romana, or Roman Antiquities in Britain viz. Coins, Camps and Publick Roads* (Oxford)

Ptolemy (Rivet and Smith 1979)

Purcell, N 1983 'The apparitores: a study in social mobility', *Papers of the British School at Rome* 51, 125–73

R(aine), J 1849 'A day with the pilgrims along the Roman Wall', in Abbatt, R, *A History of the Picts or Romano-British Wall* (London), 60–63

Rankov, N B 1987 'M. Oclatinius Adventus in Britain', *Britannia* 18, 243–9

Ravenna Cosmography (Rivet and Smith 1979)

Rebuffat, R 1995 'Le centurion M Porcius Iasucthan à Bu Njem', *Libya Antiqua* new series 1, 79–123

Renberg, G H 2006 'Was incubation practiced in the Latin West?', *Archiv für Religionsgeschichte* 8, 105–47

RIB Collingwood, R G and Wright, R P, *The Roman Inscriptions of Britain* I, *Inscriptions on Stone* (Oxford 1965)

RIB 000+*add. RIB* reprinted with Addenda and Corrigenda by R S O Tomlin (Stroud 1995)

RIB II Collingwood, R G and Wright, R P, *The Roman Inscriptions of Britain* II, *Instrumentum Domesticum (Personal Belongings and the like)*, in eight fascicules (II.1–II.8), Frere, S S and Tomlin, R S O (eds) (Stroud 1990–95)

RIB III Tomlin, R S O, Wright, R P and Hassall, M W C, *The Roman Inscriptions of Britain* III, *Inscriptions on Stone found or notified between 1 January 1955 and 31 December 2006* (Oxford 2009)

RICG Recueil des Inscriptions Chrétiennes de la Gaule, I (*Première Belgique* by Gauthier, N) (Paris 1975)

Richmond, I A 1950 'Excavations at the Roman fort of Newstead, 1947', *Proceedings of the Society of Antiquaries of Scotland* 84, 1–37

Rivet, A L F 1976 'Rudyard Kipling's Roman Britain: Fact and fiction' (Inaugural Lecture, University of Keele)

Rivet, A L F and Smith, C 1979 *The Place-Names of Roman Britain* (London)

RMD Roman Military Diplomas (Roxan, M M and Holder, P (eds), London)

RMR Roman Military Records on Papyrus (Fink 1971)

Robertson, A S 1975 *Birrens (Blatobulgium)* (Glasgow)

Sackville-West, V 1928 *Twelve Days: An account of a journey across the Bakhtiari Mountains of South-western Persia* (London)

Saddington, D B 2004 '*C.L.* in the Titulature of the *Coh. II Tungrorum*', *Britannia* 35, 244–8

Sandys, J E 1927 *Latin Epigraphy: an Introduction to the Study of Latin Inscriptions* (2nd ed., revised by S G Campbell) (Cambridge)

Sauer, E W 2005 'Inscriptions from Alchester: Vespasian's base of the Second Augustan Legion(?)', *Britannia* 36, 101–33

Sauer, E W 2014 'Milestones and instability (mid-third to early fourth centuries AD)', *Ancient Society* 44, 257–305

Scarth, H M 1864 *Aquae Solis, or Notices of Roman Bath* (London)

Schallmayer, E, Eibl, K, Ott, J, Preuss, G and Wittkopf, E 1990 *Der römische Weihebezirk von Osterburken I: Corpus der griechischen und lateinischen Beneficiarier-Inschriften des Römischen Reiches* (Stuttgart)

Seneca, *epistulae morales*

Seneca, *quaestiones naturales*

Sherwin-White, A N 1966 *The Letters of Pliny: a Historical and Social Commentary* (Oxford)

Sijpesteijn, P J (ed.) 1977 *The Wisconsin Papyri* II (Zutphen)

Smith, C 1983 'Vulgar Latin in Roman Britain: Epigraphic and other evidence', in Temporini, H and Haase, W (eds), *Aufstieg und Niedergang der römischen Welt* (Berlin–New York) II, 19.2, 893–948

Smith, R R R 2013 *Aphrodisias VI: The marble reliefs from the Julio-Claudian Sebasteion* (Darmstadt/Mainz)

Spaul, J 1994 *ALA² The Auxiliary Cavalry Units of the pre-Diocletianic Imperial Roman Army* (Andover)

Speidel, M P 1970 'The captor of Decebalus: a new inscription from Philippi', *Journal of Roman Studies* 60, 142–53

Speidel, M P 1978(a) *Guards of the Roman Armies: An essay on the singulares of the provinces* (Bonn)

Speidel, M P 1978(b) *The Religion of Iuppiter Dolichenus in the Roman Army* (Leiden)

Speidel, M P 1981 '*Princeps* as a Title for *ad hoc* commanders', *Britannia* 12, 7–13

Speidel, M P 1994 *Die Denkmäler der Kaiserreiter: Equites Singulares Augusti* (Cologne)

Standing, G 2003 'The Claudian invasion of Britain and the cult of Victoria Britannica', *Britannia* 34, 281–8

Stephens, G R 1984 'The metrical inscription from Carvoran, RIB 1791', *Archaeologia Aeliana* 5th ser. 12, 149–56

Stevens, C E 1941 'Gildas Sapiens', *English Historical Review* 56, 353–73

Stevens, C E 1960 *The Building of Hadrian's Wall* (Kendal)

Strobel, K 1986 'Zur Rekonstruktion der Laufbahn des C. Velius Rufus', *ZPE* 64, 265–86

Strobel, K 1988 'Optio tribunorum legionum quinque – ein Phantomposten der römischen Militärgeschichte', *ZPE* 75, 235–6

Stuart, P and Bogaers, J E 2001 *Nehalennia: Römische Steindenkmäler aus der Oosterschelde bei Colijnsplaat* (Leiden)

Suetonius, *Vitae* (by name of Emperor)

Surridge, T 1853 *Notices of Roman Inscriptions discovered at High Rochester, Risingham and Rudchester in Northumberland* (London)

Sutcliffe, R 1970 *The Eagle of the Ninth* (London)

Swan, V G 1992 'Legio VI and its men: African legionaries in Britain', *Journal of Roman Pottery Studies* 5, 1–33

Swan, V G 1999 'The Twentieth Legion and the history of the Antonine Wall reconsidered', *Proceedings of the Society of Antiquaries of Scotland* 129, 399–480

Syme, R 1958 *Tacitus* (Oxford)

Tabellae Sulis (Tomlin 1988)

Tab(ulae) Lond(inienses) Bloomberg (Tomlin 2016)

Tab(ulae) Luguval(ienses) (Tomlin 1998)

Tab(ulae) Vindol(andenses) (I) Bowman and Thomas 1983, (II) Bowman and Thomas 1994, (III) Bowman and Thomas 1994, (IV) Bowman, Thomas and Tomlin 2010 and 2011

Tacitus, *Agricola* (Ogilvie and Richmond 1967)

Tacitus, *Histories*

Tacitus, *Annals*

Tacoma, L E, Ivleva, T and Breeze, D J 2016 'Lost along the way: A centurion *Domo Britannia* in Bostra', *Britannia* 47, 31–42

Tituli Aquincenses Kovács, P and Szabó, Á (eds) (Budapest 2009–)

Tomlin, R S O 1974 'The Date of the "Barbarian Consiracy" ', *Britannia* 5, 303–9

Tomlin, R S O 1976 'Notitia dignitatum omnium, tam civilium quam militarium', in Goodburn and Bartholomew 1976, 189–209

Tomlin, R S O 1979 'Graffiti on Roman bricks and tiles found in Britain', in McWhirr, A (ed.), *Roman Brick and Tile* (Oxford), 231–51

Tomlin, R S O 1986 'Where the lightning struck: *RIB* 1426', *Antiquaries Journal* 66, 124–6

Tomlin, R S O 1988 *Tabellae Sulis: Roman Inscribed Tablets of Tin and Lead from the Sacred Spring at Bath* (Oxford) = Cunliffe, B (ed.), *The Temple of Sulis Minerva at Bath*, II, *The Finds from the Sacred Spring* (Oxford 1988), 59–269

Tomlin, R S O 1992 'The Twentieth Legion at Wroxeter and Carlisle in the first century: The epigraphic evidence', *Britannia* 23, 141–58

Tomlin, R S O 1993 'The inscribed lead tablets: an interim report', in Woodward, A and Leach, P, *The Uley Shrines: Excavation of a ritual complex on West Hill, Uley, Gloucestershire: 1977–9* (London), 113–30

Tomlin, R S O 1994 'Vinisius to Nigra: Evidence from Oxford of Christianity in Roman Britain', *ZPE* 100, 93–108

Tomlin, R S O 1996 'A five-acre wood in Roman Kent', in Bird, Hassall and Sheldon 1996, 209–15

Tomlin, R S O 1997(a) '*Sede in tuo loco*: a fourth-century uterine phylactery in Latin from Roman Britain', *ZPE* 115, 291–4

Tomlin, R S O 1997(b) 'Reading a 1st-century Roman gold signet ring from Fishbourne', *Sussex Archaeological Collections* 135, 127–30

Tomlin, R S O 1998 'Roman manuscripts from Carlisle: the ink-written tablets', *Britannia* 29, 31–84

Tomlin, R S O 2001 'A Roman will from North Wales', *Archaeologia Cambrensis*150, 143–56

Tomlin, R S O 2003 ' "The girl in question": A new text from Roman London', *Britannia* 34, 41–51

Tomlin, R S O 2006(a) 'Was Roman London ever a *colonia*? The written evidence', in Wilson, R J A (ed.), *ROMANITAS: Essays on Roman archaeology in honour of Sheppard Frere on the occasion of his ninetieth birthday* (Oxford), 49–64

Tomlin, R S O 2006(b) 'The owners of the Beaurains (Arras) treasure', in Hartley, Hawkes, Henig and Mee 2006, 59–64

Tomlin, R S O 2008(a) 'Dea Senuna: a new goddess from Britain', in Hainzmann, M and Wedenig, R (eds), *Instrumenta Inscripta Latina* II: *Akten des 2 internationalen Kolloquiums Klagenfurt, 5–8* Mai 2005 (Klagenfurt), 305–15

Tomlin, R S O 2008(b) 'Special delivery: a Graeco-Roman gold amulet for healthy childbirth, *ZPE* 167, 219–24

Tomlin, R S O 2012(a) 'The book in Roman Britain', in Gameson, R (ed.), *The Cambridge History of the Book in Britain*, I, *c* 400–1100 (Cambridge), 375–88

Tomlin, R S O 2012(b) 'Not to mention the tablets: Vindolanda's other inscriptions', *Archaeologia Aeliana* 41, 207–15

Tomlin, R S O 2016 *Roman London's first voices: Writing tablets from the Bloomberg London excavations, 2010–14* (Museum of London Archaeology Monograph 72)

Tomlin, R S O forthcoming 'The inscriptions: Ashwell, Barkway, Stony Stratford' in Jackson and Burleigh forthcoming

Toynbee, J M C 1962 *Art in Roman Britain* (London)

Toynbee, J M C 1964 *Art in Britain under the Romans* (Oxford)

Turner, E G 1968 *Greek Papyri: an Introduction* (Oxford)

Vegetius, *Epitoma rei militaris*

Versnel, H S 2005 'Prayers for justice in east and west: Recent finds and publications', in Gordon, R L and Marco Simón, F (eds), *Magical Practice in the Latin West* (Leiden), 275–354

Vipard, P 2008 *MARMOR TAVRINIACVM, Le Marbre de Thorigny (Vieux, Calvados): la carrière d'un grand notable gaulois au début du troisième siécle ap. J-C* (Paris)

Weaver, P R C 1972 *Familia Caesaris: A social study of the Emperor's freedmen and slaves* (Cambridge)

Wells, C M 1984 *The Roman Empire* (London)

West, A B (ed.) 1931 *Corinth: Results of excavations conducted by the American School of Classical Studies at Athens*, VIII 2, Latin Inscriptions 1896–1926 (Cambridge, Mass.)

White, R and Barker, P 1998 *Wroxeter: Life and death of a Roman city* (Stroud)

Wightman, E M 1970 *Roman Trier and the Treveri* (London)

Wightman, E M 1985 *Gallia Belgica* (London)

Wilkes, J J 1969 *Dalmatia* (London)

Wilkes, J J (ed.) 2003 *Documenting the Roman Army: Essays in honour of Margaret Roxan* (London)

Wilmott, T 1997 *Birdoswald: Excavations of a Roman fort on Hadrian's Wall and its successor settlements: 1987–92* (London)

Wiseman, T P 1991 *Death of an Emperor* (Exeter)

Wolff, H 1976 'Die Cohors II Tungrorum milliaria equitata c(oram)? l(audata)? und die Rechtsform des ius Latii', *Chiron* 6, 267–88

Zelazowski, J 1997 '*Honos bigae.* Le statue onorarie romane in forma di biga. Il caso dubbio di *CIL* II 1086', *Epigraphica* 59, 173–203

ZPE Zeitschrift für Papyrologie und Epigraphik

PHOTO CREDITS

I am grateful to many museums and individuals for the illustrations in this book, either for allowing the photograph to be taken or for providing one. For many years I accumulated slides to illustrate my lectures on the Roman inscriptions of Britain, in effect an early draft of this book, usually while I was recording items for the annual 'Roman Britain (Inscriptions)' survey in *Britannia*, many of which have since entered *RIB* II and III. Some two-thirds of the illustrations are photographs which I took myself, and I should add in apology that I often worked in crowded conditions and by available light, using Ektachrome film which I have now scanned into digital form. A few stones were photographed as found, for example **4.01** and **5.03**, but the present location is almost always explicit in the credits given below. However, at least two museums have since been absorbed by larger entities: Rowley's House by Shrewsbury Museum and Art Gallery, and the Museum of Antiquities, Newcastle upon Tyne, by the Great North Museum.

My particular thanks are due to the Scouloudi Foundation (Institute of Historical Research, University of London) for a grant towards the cost of illustrations. I list my other benefactors, all too briefly, but with much gratitude and my apologies for any unintended omission.

Ambleside, Armitt Museum and Library (**14.13**); Aquileia Museum (**5.05**); Paul Austen (**5.03**, **6.34**); Ben Altshuler and CSAD (**3.14**); Avenches, Musée Romain (**1.06**); Barnard Castle, Bowes Museum (**5.36**, **8.05**, **12.40**, **12.41**, **12.82**, **14.02**); Bath, Roman Baths Museum (**2.08**, **11.06**, **11.07**, **11.09**, **11.16**, **12.31**, **12.32**, **12.33**, **14.01**); Berlin Staatliche Museen, Antikensammlung (cover); Bordeaux, Musée d'Aquitaine (**11.38**, **11.39**); Bonhams (London) (**3.18**); Bristol City Museum and Art Gallery (**12.42**); Budapest, Aquincum Museum (**4.04**); Caerleon, Roman Legionary Museum (**3.07**, **4.15**, **9.27**, **9.28**, **9.29**, **9.40**, **9.41**, **9.42**, **12.70**, **13.22**); Caerwent church (**10.03**); Cambridge, Museum of Archaeology and Anthropology (**8.02**, **8.14**, **12.26**, **12.51**, **13.15**); Cardiff, National Museum of Wales (**3.08**, **3.10**); Carlisle, Tullie House Museum and Art Gallery (Intro, **3.14**, **4.08**, **5.03**, **6.34**, **7.14**, **8.06**, **9.09**, **9.57**, **10.01**, **11.23**, **12.17**, **12.37**, **12.54**, **12.91**, **12.92**, **13.10**, **13.29**, **14.03**, **14.09**); Castello della Spizzichina (**6.14**); Chester, Grosvenor Museum

(**3.13**, **4.10**, **9.21**, **9.36**, **9.49**, **11.13**, **11.14**, **11.24**, **12.20**, **12.21**, **12.56**); Chesters Museum (**5.26**, **5.35**, **5.43**, **7.08**, **9.14**, **12.24**, **12.15**, **12.29**, **12.38**, **12.50**, **14.10**); Cirencester, Corinium Museum (**2.07**, **2.20**, **9.46**, **11.08**, **12.93**, **14.07**); Manfred Clauss and EDCS (**8.13**, **10.13**); Colchester and Essex Museum (**2.01**, **2.02**); Corbridge Roman Museum (Intro, **6.03**, **6.04**, **7.03**, **8.11**, **9.34**); Dundee Musems and Art Galleries (**7.11**); Durham, Museum of Archaeology (**5.17**, **9.03**, **12.23**, **12.63**, **13.16**, **13.17**, **13.18**); Edinburgh, National Museums of Scotland (**6.07**, **6.17**, **6.18**, **6.20**, **6.33**, **6.39**, **8.16**, **9.58**, **12.80**); Ben Edwards (**10.05**); English Heritage (**10.06**, **13.04**); Glasgow, Hunterian Museum (**4.02**, **6.01**, **6.06**, **6.10**, **6.12**, **6.13**, **6.21**, **6.25**, **6.26**, **9.48**, **12.18**, **12.55**, **12.58**, **12.59**, **12.60**); Richard Grasby (**2.19**); Ortolf Harl and ubi-erat-lupa (**4.03**, **4.04**, **7.01**); Mark Hassall (**5.02**); Hexham Abbey (**4.09**); Housesteads Museum (**5.25**); Peter Johnson (**13.01**); Paul Kenyon (**14.21**); Lawrence Keppie (**1.05**); Lancaster City Museum (**4.01**); Lanchester church (**12.49**); Leeds University (**8.04**); Leiden Museum of Antiquities (**11.36**); Lincoln, the Collection (**12.44**); London, British Museum (**2.16**, **9.06**, **11.03**, **11.17**, **12.05**, **12.96**); Museum of London (**10.12**, **10.37**, **10.38**, **11.12**, **11.33**, **12.76**, **12.88**, **12.89**); MoLAS (**2.14**); Malton Museum (**11.18**); Manchester Museum (**12.11**); Maryport, Senhouse Roman Museum (**5.13**, 1**2.61**); Conchi Neira (**2.09**); Newcastle upon Tyne, Museum of Antiquities (**5.07**, **5.08**, **5.17**, **5.18**, **5.37**, **5.39**, **5.42**, **5.46**, **6.05**, **6.28**, **9.15**, **9.47**, **12.03**, **12.09**, **12.10**, **12.28**, **12.64**, **12.65**, **12.66**, **12.77**, **12.78**, **12.79**, **12.86**, **13.03**, **13.06**, **13.08**, **13.19**); New York University Excavations at Aphrodisias (G. Petruccioli) (**1.14**); Oxford, Ashmolean Latin Inscriptions project (Hannah Cornwell) (**10.30**); Oxford Museums Service (**2.03**); Silvia Orlandi and Marco Buonocoro (**6.14**); Paris, Cabinet des Medailles (**13.24**); Perth Museum and Art Gallery (**6.27**); Peter Probst (**8.13**); Margaret Robb (**5.05**); Rome, Capitoline Museums (**1.13**); Rome, Vatican Museums (**8.13**); Rugby Art Gallery and Museum (**14.12**); St Albans, Verulamium Museum (**10.10**); Saint-Lô Museum (**10.39**); Margaret Sasanow (**4.15**); Scotland, Royal Commission on Ancient and Historical Monuments (**9.16**); Shrewsbury, Rowley's House Museum (**2.12**, **3.02**, **10.04**); Grace Simpson (**14.06**); Bert Smith (**1.14**); South Shields, Arbeia Roman Fort and Museum (**9.33**, **9.35**); Sremska Mitrovica (Serbia), Museum of Srem (**4.03**); Stanhope church (**12.39**); Tredunnock church (**9.25**); Turin, Museo Archeologico (**1.05**); Scott Vanderbilt (**3.07**, **5.43**, **9.25**, **9.27**, **9.28**, **9.29**, **9.40**, **9.41**, **9.42**, **10.03**, **13.01**, **13.22**); Vindolanda Museum and the Vindolanda Trust (**5.01**, **12.16**, **12.73**, **12.84**); Whitby Museum (**14.21**); John Wilkes (**6.02**); Richard Wright (**12.82**); York, Yorkshire Museum (**3.04**, **9.02**, **9.22**, **9.44**, **12.90**); York Archaeological Trust (**11.37**).

CONCORDANCE TABLES

between previous publications and *Britannia Romana*
(1) *Roman Inscriptions of Britain* (*RIB* I, II and III)
(2) Other corpora and publications

(1) *Roman Inscriptions of Britain*

RIB I	*Britannia Romana*
3	12.76
5	10.25
12	2.19
17	9.20
19	10.29
21	10.26
66	12.74
88	12.13
91	2.15
103	14.07
105	11.08
108	2.20
109	2.07
110	9.46
121	2.05
149	11.09
151	11.07
152	12.33
155	12.32
156	11.16
159	2.08
179	10.35
200	2.01
201	2.02
213	12.43
215	12.06
250	10.16
254	2.13
255	2.04
258	3.03
274	11.17
283	6.35
288	10.04
291	2.06
292	2.11
293	3.02
294	2.12
311	10.03
365	3.07
403	3.08
481	3.16
482	3.15
491	9.21
306	12.46

316	12.70	665	4.16
323	12.57	670	9.23
356	9.27	673	3.04
330	4.15	674	10.19
334	13.22	678	9.52
358	9.39	684	12.72
359	9.40	685	9.44
360	9.25	687	9.51
363	9.41	690	9.24
369	9.28	707	10.02
373	9.42	712	11.18
430	8.03	721	14.21
445	4.10	725	10.32
448	12.20	730	8.02
450	9.08	732	12.40
451	12.21	733	12.41
460	12.27	746	8.05
468	5.32	758	9.50
507	9.26	810	12.62
526	9.36	812	9.06
544	11.24	823	5.13
558	9.49	832	12.61
560	9.54	890	9.09
582	12.52	897	13.15
583	7.04	899	10.01
594	9.31	902	0.01
605	13.28	908	9.55
612	9.32	917	7.10
620	9.37	918	12.47
627	8.14	933	10.07
643	12.15	937	9.13
644	9.02	944	12.22
647	12.19	946	7.14
649	9.10	955	12.91
658	12.90	968	13.10
662	12.07	978	13.09
663	12.08	1016	12.01

1022	12.83	1271	9.03
1041	12.39	1276	6.05
1042	13.18	1279	13.03
1054	8.20	1280	13.06
1060	13.11	1281	13.08
1064	9.35	1288	9.04
1065	9.33	1319	5.07
1074	12.49	1320	5.08
1075	12.23	1322	6.28
1077	12.63	1329	7.07
1091	13.17	1330	6.32
1092	13.16	1337	8.09
1120	12.68	1340	5/37
1125	12.53	1365	5.42
1131	12.85	1388	6.30
1137	7.03	1389	6.29
1138	3.10	1426	12.03
1142	7.06	1427	5.39
1143	8.11	1436	9.53
1147	6.03	1445	5.35
1148	6.04	1463	7.08
1166	0.02	1465	13.05
1171	9.34	1482	9.14
1172	4.09	1534	12.29
1202	13.02	1544	12.78
1208	12.09	1545	12.77
1212	9.05	1546	12.79
1124	12.10	1578	12.38
1225	10.31	1589	9.11
1227	12.26	1594	12.50
1228	9.15	1618	11.19
1234	8.07	1632	5.25
1262	13.19	1637	5.17
1266	12.64	1645	5.22
1267	12.65	1646	5.26
1268	12.66	1685	12.24
1270	12.51	1686	12.25

RIB II (fascicules 1–8)

II.1, 2404.8	3.12
II.1, 2404.34 and 35	3.11
II.1, 2404.51	11.10
II.1, 2404.62	3.18
II.1, 2409.4	5.28
II.1, 2411.23	14.15
II.1, 2411.25–28	14.18
II.1, 2411.37	10.36
II.2, 2414.1	12.95
II.2, 2414.2	12.96
II.2, 2415.39	3.06
II.2, 2415.53	5.14
II.2, 2415.56	5.43
II.3, 2421.43	14.08
II.3, 2422.4	14.11
II.3, 2423.4	4.20
II.3, 2426.1	5.10
II.3, 2427.14	5.27
II.3, 2427.26*	13.24
II.3, 2431.1	12.94
II.3, 2434.1	3.13
II.4, 2443.2	10.33
II.4, 2443.4	11.41
II.4, 2445.16	5.34
II.4, 2446.2	11.21
II.4, 2447.20	12.93
II.4, 2448.3	12.45
II.4, 2448.6	11.02
II.4, 2456.6	11.32
II.5, 2487.6	10.18
II.5, 2491.78	14.02
II.5, 2491.96	11.13
II.5, 2491.146	11.11
II.5, 2491.147	11.12
II.6, 2492.5	11.29
II.6, 2492.7	4.07
II.7, 2501.209	3.09
II.8, 2503.127	12.89
II.8, 2503.379	11.25

RIB III

III, 3001	12.88
III, 3002	10.37
III, 3005	10.12
III, 3014	11.33
III, 3049	12.31
III, 3053	12.42
III, 3099	9.29
III, 3108	9.43
III, 3113	3.10
III, 3121	2.03
III, 3123	10.10
III, 3149	12.56
III, 3180	12.44
III, 3185	4.01
III, 3195	11.37
III, 3201	10.20
III, 3202	9.22
III, 3215	8.04
III, 3218	14.13
III, 3253	12.82

III, 3290	9.45
III, 3298	5.03
III, 3332	12.16
III, 3303	5.20
III, 3316	12.28
III, 3376	10.08
III, 3407	5.21
III, 3364	5.01
III, 3438	13.29
III, 3454	5.33
III, 3459	12.54
III, 3460	13.04
III, 3480	6.34
III, 3486	6.01
III, 3503	9.58
III, 3504	9.16
III, 3507	6.13
III, 3509	6.26
III, 3512	7.11
III, 3515	6.27
III, 3521	14.12
III, 3525	10.06
III, 3526	10.05

(2) Other corpora and publications

Previous publication	*Britannia Romana*
Alföldy 1988	10.28
Année Épigraphique (*AE*)	
1904, 197	14.05
1917/18, 1	1.09
1922, 116	11.39
1925, 126	3.01
1950, 56	5.15
1951, 88	3.20
1953, 251	2.10
1956, 249	11.30
1957, 249	5.11
1960, 28	6.14
1961, 320	6.08
1963, 52	7.02
1965, 240	7.13
1973, 370	11.35
1975, 651	11.36
1980, 457	1.08
1981, 741	6.36
1982, 850	6.36
1983, 722	11.34
1985, 735	6.37
1989, 318	9.07
1989, 830	10.28
2001, 1918	1.11
2008, 909	10.39
Augustus, *Res Gestae* 32.1	1.01
Barrett 1991	1.13
Bastien and Metzger 1977, No. 218	14.04
Birley 2005, 262	7.13
Birley 2005, 347	13.14
Bivona 1970, No. 219	8.19
Breeze 2012 (Allason-Jones)	5.14
Breeze 2012 (Maheo)	5.15
Breeze 2012 (Jackson)	5.16

Britannia	
19 (1988), 496, No. 31	4.08
20 (1989), 329, No. 3	11.03
22 (1991), 299, No. 24	11.20
23 (1992), 310, No. 5	11.04
25 (1994), 296, No. 2	9.01
25 (1994), 302, No. 34	10.22
26 (1995), 387, No. 28	11.14
27 (1996), 443, No. 10	11.22
27 (1996), 455, No. 48	2.16
28 (1997), 455, No. 1	12.75
31 (2000), 440, No. 32	11.28
33 (2002), 361, No. 7	11.27
34 (2003), 362, No. 2	12.69
35 (2004), 336, No. 3	11.01
35 (2004), 344, No. 24	5.16
35 (2004), 347, No. 27	9.38
37 (2006), 481, No. 51	12.04
39 (2008), 372, No. 5	6.16
40 (2009), 315, No. 3	12.11
40 (2009), 321, No. 14	11.15
40 (2009), 337, No. 36	11.40
40 (2009), 353, No. 97	12.05
41 (2010), 444, No. 4	12.84
42 (2011), 441, No. 5	12.81
42 (2011), 443, No. 6	12.80
43 (2012), 396, No. 2	12.14
44 (2013), 390, No. 21	12.67
45 (2014), 434, No. 4	5.36
Camodeca 2006	10.38
Corpus Inscriptionum Latinarum (*CIL*)	
vi 3301	4.14
viii 21699	10.14
xi 383	10.24
xiii 2616	9.30
xiii 3162	10.39
xiii 6679	10.15
xiii 7417	8.17
xiii 14349.2	4.04
xvi 49	4.11
xvi 69	5.04
xvi 160	4.13
xvi 163	4.12
Devijver 1988	7.02
Diocletian, *Prices Edict* xix.28–9, 48	11.05
Feissel 1983, No. 273	14.20
Gordon 1952	2.10
Habicht 1969, No. 141	12.02
Hodgson 2011	6.29
Hodgson 2011, 67	6.30
Inschriften von Ephesus VII.1, 3042	1.02
Inscriptiones Italiae IV.1, 125	1.03
Inscriptiones Latinae Selectae (*ILS*)	
212	1.12
216	1.13
414	8.01
433	8.17
436	8.15
478	8.13
546	13.23

Smith 2013, 145–7, C10	1.14
Speidel 1994, No. 343	4.14
Tab. Lond. Bloomberg 44	2.14
Tab. Lond. Bloomberg 45	2.21
Tab. Lond. Bloomberg 37	10.09
Tab. Lond. Bloomberg 51	10.21
Tab. Lond. Bloomberg 12	11.42
Tab. Luguval. 44	3.14
Tab. Luguval. 18	10.27
Tab. Sulis 10	11.06
Tab. Sulis 32	12.34
Tab. Sulis 94	12.35
Tab. Sulis 97	14.01
Tab. Sulis 98	12.97
Tab. Vindol. II, 156	4.17
Tab. Vindol. II, 291	4.19
Tab. Vindol. II, 316	4.18
Tab. Vindol. III, 628	11.43
Tituli Aquincenses II, 588	4.04
Tomlin 1992	3.21
Tomlin 1993, No. 2	12.36
Tomlin 1996	10.22
Tomlin 2003	10.38
Tomlin 2008, No. 17	12.30
Tomlin forthcoming, A17	12.30
Tomlin forthcoming, SS6a	12.06
Tyche 16 (2001), 1	1.11
Vipard 2008	10.39
West 1931, No. 11	1.10
West 1931, No. 86	1.09

INSCRIPTIONS LOCATED

where each was found, with its chapter reference-number (not the page), the numeral in italics if it is *illustrated*

INDEX

1. PERSONS

listed by cognomen, unless another form is more familiar, for example 'Marcus Aurelius' and 'Septimius Severus'

2. GEOGRAPHICAL

See also INSCRIPTIONS LOCATED

3. GENERAL